THE FLETCHER JONES FOUNDATION

HUMANITIES IMPRINT

The Fletcher Jones Foundation has endowed this imprint to foster innovative and enduring scholarship in the humanities.

The publisher gratefully acknowledges the generous support of the Fletcher Jones Foundation Humanities Endowment Fund of the University of California Press Foundation, which was established by a major gift from the Fletcher Jones Foundation.

METROPOLIS BERLIN

WEIMAR AND NOW: GERMAN CULTURAL CRITICISM
Edward Dimendberg, Martin Jay, and Anton Kaes, General Editors

METROPOLIS BERLIN

1880–1940

Edited by

Iain Boyd Whyte and David Frisby

UNIVERSITY OF CALIFORNIA PRESS
Berkeley   Los Angeles   London

University of California Press, one of the most distinguished university presses in the United States, enriches lives around the world by advancing scholarship in the humanities, social sciences, and natural sciences. Its activities are supported by the UC Press Foundation and by philanthropic contributions from individuals and institutions. For more information, visit www.ucpress.edu.

University of California Press
Berkeley and Los Angeles, California

University of California Press, Ltd.
London, England

© 2012 by The Regents of the University of California

Library of Congress Cataloging-in-Publication Data

Metropolis Berlin : 1880–1940 / edited by Iain Boyd Whyte and David Frisby. — 1 [edition].
    pages. cm. — (Weimar and now : German cultural criticism ; 46)
  Includes bibliographical references and index.
  ISBN 978-0-520-27037-4 (cloth : alk. paper)
  1. Public spaces—Germany—Berlin. 2. Berlin (Germany)—History—Sources. I. Whyte, Iain Boyd, 1947–, editor of compilation. II. Frisby, David, editor of compilation.
  NA9053.S6M48 2012
  711'.40943155—dc22   2012006370

Manufactured in the United States of America

20 19 18 17 16 15 14 13 12
10 9 8 7 6 5 4 3 2 1

In keeping with a commitment to support environmentally responsible and sustainable printing practices, UC Press has printed this book on Rolland Enviro100, a 100 percent postconsumer fiber paper that is FSC certified, deinked, processed chlorine-free, and manufactured with renewable biogas energy. It is acid-free and EcoLogo certified.

CONTENTS

List of Illustrations   xiii
Preface   xv

   General Introduction   1

PART ONE. BOOMING METROPOLIS

1. The Metropolitan Panorama   9
   1. Jules Laforgue, *Berlin: The Court and the City (1887)*   13
   2. Wilhelm Loesche, *Berlin North (1890)*   16
   3. Mark Twain, *The German Chicago (1892)*   17
   4. Heinrich Schackow, *Berolina: A Metropolitan Aesthetic (1896)*   19
   5. Alfred Kerr, *Berlin and London (1896)*   25
   6. Alfred Kerr, *The Transformation of Potsdamer Strasse (1895, 1897)*   27
   7. Max Osborn, *The Destruction of Berlin (1906)*   30
   8. Werner Sombart, *Vienna (1907)*   31
   9. Robert Walser, *Good Morning, Giantess! (1907)*   33
   10. August Endell, *The Beauty of the Great City (1908)*   35
   11. Oscar Bie, *Life Story of a Street (1908)*   41
   12. Robert Walser, *Friedrichstrasse (1909)*   41
   13. Max Weber, *Speech for a Discussion (1910)*   44
   14. *Vorwärts,* [Town Hall Tower Panorama] *(1902)*   44
   15. Ernst Bloch, *Berlin, Southern City (1915–16)*   46

2. Building and Regulating the Metropolis   49
   16. Theodor Goecke, *Traffic Thoroughfares and Residential Streets (1893)*   52
   17. Rudolf Adickes, *The Need for Spacious Building Programs in City Expansions and the Legal and Technical Means to Accomplish This (1895)*   55

vi   Contents

       18. *Vorwärts*, [Deforestation around Berlin] *(1908)*   57
       19. *Die Bank*, [Speculation in Tempelhof] *(1910–11)*   57
       20. P. A. A. [Philip A. Ashworth], *Berlin (1911)*   59
       21. Walter Lewitz, *Architectural Notes on the Universal Urban Planning Exhibition, Berlin (1911)*   62
       22. Various authors, *The Greater Berlin Competition 1910: The Prize-Winning Designs with Explanatory Report (1911)*   64
       23. Cornelius Gurlitt, *Review of* Greater Berlin *and* The Greater Berlin Competition 1910 *(1911)*   69
       24. Sigmund Schott, *The Agglomeration of Cities in the German Empire: 1871–1910 (1912)*   72
       25. Patrick Abercrombie, *Berlin: Its Growth and Present State (1914)*   73

3. Production, Commerce, and Consumption   77

       26. Georg Simmel, *The Berlin Trade Exhibition (1896)*   80
       27. Albert Hoffmann, *The Wertheim Department Store in Leipziger Strasse (1898)*   84
       28. Robert Walser, *Aschinger's (1907)*   88
       29. Karl Scheffler, *The Retail Establishment (1907)*   91
       30. Leo Colze, *The Department Stores of Berlin (1908)*   94
       31. Erich Köhrer, *Berlin Department Store: A Novel from the World City (1909)*   97
       32. Karl Scheffler, *Peter Behrens (1913)*   98
       33. Karl Ernst Osthaus, *The Display Window (1913)*   101
       34. Paul Westheim, *Nordstern: The New Administration Building in Berlin-Schöneberg (1915)*   104

4. Public Transport and Infrastructure   107

       35. Anonymous, *The Concourse of the Anhalter Station (1880)*   111
       36. Alfred Kerr, *New and Beautiful!—Bülowstrasse? (1900)*   112
       37. Richard Peterson, *The Traffic Problems Inherent in Large Cities and the Means of Solving Them (1908)*   115
       38. Karl Scheffler, *The Elevated Railway and Aesthetics (1902)*   118
       39. August Endell, *The Beauty of the Great City (1908)*   122
       40. Anonymous, *The Northern Loop: A Journey on the Ring Railway (1913)*   125
       41. Peter Behrens, *The Influence of Time and Space Utilization on Modern Design (1914)*   127
       42. Karl Ernst Osthaus, *The Railway Station (1914)*   129

5. The Proletarian City   134

       43. Theodor Goecke, *The Working-Class Tenement Block in Berlin (1890)*   137
       44. Otto von Leixner, *Letter Eight: A Suburban Street in New Moabit (1891)*   143
       45. Heinrich Albrecht, *The Working-Class Tenement Buildings of the Berlin Savings and Building Society (1898)*   145
       46. Alice Salomon, *A Club for Young Working Women in Berlin (1903)*   148

47. Werner Sombart, *Domesticity (1906)*	*150*
48. Albert Südekum, *Impoverished Berlin Dwellings—Wedding (1908)*	*153*
49. Clara Viebig, *Our Daily Bread (1907)*	*157*
50. Karl Scheffler, *The Tenement Block (1911)*	*158*
51. Käthe Kollwitz, *Diary Entry, 16 April 1912*	*163*
52. Max Jacob, *From Apartment House to Mass Apartment House (1912)*	*164*
53. Victor Noack, *Housing and Morality (1912)*	*167*

6. Public Realm and Popular Culture *172*

54. Paul Lindau, *Unter den Linden (1892)*	*176*
55. Anonymous, *The New Prison for Berlin at Tegel (1900)*	*179*
56. Alfred Kerr, *In the New Reichstag (1900)*	*180*
57. Freisinnige Zeitung, *[A Military Parade] (1900)*	*181*
58. Berliner Tageblatt, *[A Sunday in Berlin] (1903)*	*182*
59. Hans Ostwald, *Berlin Coffeehouses (c. 1905)*	*183*
60. Brüstlein, *The Rudolf Virchow Hospital in Berlin (1907)*	*187*
61. Jules Huret, *Bruno Schmitz's "Rheingold" for Aschinger (1909)*	*189*
62. Anonymous, *New Buildings Planned for Museum Island, Berlin (1910)*	*190*
63. Wilhelm Bode, *Alfred Messel's Plans for the New Buildings of the Royal Museums in Berlin (1910)*	*192*
64. Paul Westheim, *Ludwig Hoffmann's School Buildings in Berlin (1911)*	*193*
65. Max Wagenführ, *The Admiral's Palace and Its Bathing Pools (1912)*	*196*
66. Fritz Stahl (pseud. Siegfried Lilienthal), *The Berlin City Hall (1912)*	*199*
67. Else Lasker-Schüler, *The Two White Benches on the Kurfürstendamm (1913)*	*200*
68. Bruno Taut, *The Problem of Building an Opera House (1914)*	*201*
69. Anonymous [Joseph Adler?], *The Opening of the Tauentzien Palace Café (1914)*	*204*

7. The Bourgeois City *206*

70. Theodor Fontane, *The Treibel Villa (1892)*	*210*
71. Alfred Kerr, *Herr Sehring Builds a Theater Dream (1895)*	*211*
72. Alfred Kerr, *Up and Down the Avenues (1898)*	*212*
73. Walther Rathenau, *The Most Beautiful City in the World (1899)*	*214*
74. Alfred Kerr, *New Luxury, Old Squalor (1900)*	*217*
75. Hermann Muthesius, *The Modern Country Home (1905)*	*218*
76. Edmund Edel, *Berlin W. (1906)*	*221*
77. Max Creutz, *Charlottenburg Town Hall (1906)*	*223*
78. Max Creutz, *The New Kempinski Building (1907)*	*225*
79. Maximilian Rapsilber, *Hotel Adlon (1907)*	*229*
80. Robert Walser, *Berlin W. (1910)*	*230*
81. Robert Walser, *The Little Berlin Girl (1909)*	*232*
82. Walter Lehwess, *The Design Competition for Rüdesheimer Platz (1912)*	*237*
83. Wilhelm Borchard, *The Picnic Season (1914)*	*239*
84. Paul Westheim, *Building Boom (1917)*	*242*

Contents

8. The Green Outdoors — 245
   85. Wilhelm Bölsche, *Beyond the Metropolis (1901)* — 248
   86. Heinrich Hart, *Statutes of the German Garden City Association (1902)* — 250
   87. Hans Kampffmeyer, *The Garden City and Its Cultural and Economic Significance (1906–7)* — 251
   88. Heinrich Pudor, *The People's Park in Greater Berlin (1910)* — 256
   89. Karl Ernst Osthaus, *Garden City and City Planning (1911)* — 258
   90. Anonymous, *Lietzensee-Park in Charlottenburg (1912)* — 260
   91. Hannes Müllerfeld, *Down with the Garden City! (1914)* — 260
   92. Max Osborn, *The Fairy-Tale Fountain in the Friedrichshain, Berlin (1914)* — 261
   93. Paul Westheim, *Workers' Housing Estate at Staaken (1915)* — 264
   94. Martin Wagner, *Urban Open-Space Policy (1915)* — 267
   95. Bruno Taut, *The Falkenberg Garden Suburb near Berlin (1919–20)* — 268

PART TWO. WORLD WAR I AND THE CITY

9. City in Crisis — 273
   96. Bruno Taut, *A Necessity (1914)* — 276
   97. *Vorwärts,* [War or Not] *(1914)* — 278
   98. General Gustav von Kessel, *Berlin in a State of War: Proclamation of the Commander-in-Chief in the Marches (1914)* — 279
   99. H. B., [War Fever in Berlin, August 1914] — 280
   100. *Berliner Tageblatt,* [Berlin Potato Shortage] *(1915)* — 281
   101. Anonymous, *Competition for Greater Berlin Architects (1916)* — 282
   102. *Berliner Tageblatt, Demonstration in Berlin (1918)* — 283
   103. Friedrich Bauermeister, *On the Great City (1918)* — 284
   104. Walter Gropius, *The New Architectural Idea (1919)* — 286
   105. Leopold Bauer, *The Economic Unsustainability of the Large City (1919)* — 288

10. Critical Responses — 291
    106. Paul Wolf, *The Basic Layout of the New City (1919)* — 293
    107. Bruno Taut, *The City Crown (1919)* — 295
    108. Otto Bartning, *Church Architecture Today (1919)* — 302
    109. Peter Behrens and Heinrich de Fries, *On Low-Cost Building (1919)* — 303
    110. Käthe Kollwitz, *Diary Entry, 11 September 1919* — 307
    111. Hermann Muthesius, *Small House and Small-Scale Housing Development (1920)* — 307

PART THREE. *WELTSTADT*—WORLD CITY

11. Planning the World City — 315
    112. Martin Mächler, *The Major Population Center and Its Global Importance (1918)* — 319

113.	Bruno Möhring, *On the Advantages of Tower Blocks and the Conditions under Which They Could Be Built in Berlin (1920)*	324
114.	Siegfried Kracauer, *On Skyscrapers (1921)*	326
115.	Martin Mächler, *On the Skyscraper Problem (1920–21)*	329
116.	Joseph Roth, *If Berlin Were to Build Skyscrapers: Proposals for Easing the Housing Shortage (1921)*	332
117.	Adolf Behne, *The Competition of the Skyscraper Society (1922–23)*	334
118.	Egon Erwin Kisch, *The Impoverishment and Enrichment of the Berlin Streets (1923)*	336
119.	Ernst Kaeber, *The Metropolis as Home (1926)*	337
120.	Karl Scheffler, *Berlin Fifty Years from Now: Perspectives on One of the World's Great Cities (1926)*	340
121.	Martin Wagner, Werner Hegemann, and Heinrich Mendelssohn, *Should Berlin Build Skyscrapers? (1928)*	344
122.	Martin Wagner and Adolf Behne, *The New Berlin–World City (1929)*	347
123.	Martin Wagner, *The Design Problem of a City Square for a Metropolis: The Competition of the "Verkehr" Company for the Remodeling of Alexanderplatz (1929)*	349
124.	Max Berg, *The Platz der Republik in Berlin (1930)*	352
125.	Werner Hegemann, *Berlin, City of Stone: The History of the Largest Tenement City in the World (1930)*	353
126.	Walter Benjamin, *A Jacobin of Our Time: On Werner Hegemann's Das steinerne Berlin (1930)*	358
127.	Hannes Küpper, *The "Provinces" and Berlin (1931)*	363
128.	Adolf Hitler, *Speech at Foundation-Stone Ceremony of the Faculty of Defense Studies, Berlin (1937)*	365

12. Berlin Montage — 367

129.	Käthe Kollwitz, *Diary Entry, 25 January 1919*	370
130.	Kurt Tucholsky, *"Berlin! Berlin!" (1919)*	371
131.	"Sling" (pseud. Paul Schlesinger), *The Telephone (1921)*	374
132.	Käthe Kollwitz, *Diary Entry, 1 May 1922*	375
133.	Friedrich Kroner, *Overstretched Nerves (1923)*	375
134.	Adolf Hitler, *My Struggle (1926)*	376
135.	Joseph Roth, *The Wandering Jew (1927)*	378
136.	Ernst Bloch, *Berlin after Two Years (1928)*	379
137.	Alfred Döblin, *Berlin (1928)*	381
138.	Franz Hessel, *I Learn: Via Neukölln to Britz (1929)*	386
139.	Carl Zuckmayer, *The Berlin Woman (1929)*	390
140.	Moritz Goldstein, *The Metropolis of the Little People (1930)*	391
141.	Karl Scheffler, *Berlin: A City Transformed (1931)*	392
142.	Siegfried Kracauer, *The New Alexanderplatz (1932)*	397
143.	Siegfried Kracauer, *Locomotive over Friedrichstrasse (1933)*	400

x   Contents

144. Jean Giraudoux, *Berlin, Not Paris!* (1931) — 402
145. Ernst Erich Noth, *The Tenement Barracks* (1931) — 404
146. Siegfried Kracauer, *A Section of Friedrichstrasse* (1932) — 404
147. Gabriele Tergit (pseud. Elise Reifenberg), *Home is the 75 (or the 78)* (1930) — 406
148. Christopher Isherwood, *A Berlin Diary (Winter 1932–33)* — 409

13. Work — 411

149. Alfred Döblin, *General Strike in Berlin* (1922) — 414
150. Ludwig Hilberseimer, *Buildings for the Metropolis* (1925) — 415
151. Franz Hessel, *On Work* (1929) — 416
152. Peter Panter (pseud. Kurt Tucholsky), *Hang on a Moment!* (1927) — 418
153. Fritz Stahl (pseud. Siegfried Lilienthal), *The Klingenberg Power Station at Berlin-Rummelsburg* (1928) — 420
154. Hermann Schmitz, *Introduction to* Siemensbauten (1928) — 424
155. Egon Erwin Kisch, *Berlin at Work* (1927) — 425
156. Anonymous, *A New High-Rise Building in Berlin: Architect Peter Behrens* (1931) — 428
157. Irmgard Keun, *Gilgi—One of Us* (1931) — 429
158. Else Lasker-Schüler, *The Spinning World Factory* (1932) — 430
159. Hans Fallada, *Little Man, What Now?* (1933) — 432
160. Herbert Rimpl and Hermann Mäckler, *A German Aircraft Factory: The Heinkel Works in Oranienburg* (1938) — 434

14. Commodities and Display — 437

161. Alfred Döblin, *Berlin Christmas* (1923) — 441
162. Alfred Gellhorn, *Advertising and the Cityscape* (1926) — 442
163. Gerta-Elisabeth Thiele, *The Shop Window* (1926) — 445
164. Peter Panter (pseud. Kurt Tucholsky), *The Loudspeaker* (1927) — 447
165. Hans Cürlis, *Night and the Modern City* (1928) — 450
166. Hugo Häring, *Illuminated Advertising and Architecture* (1928) — 452
167. Joseph Roth, *The Really Big Department Store* (1929) — 454
168. Alfred Wedemeyer, *Berlin's Latest Department Store* (1929) — 456
169. Ludwig Hilberseimer, *The Modern Commercial Street* (1929) — 458
170. Alfons Paquet, *City and Province* (1929) — 462

15. Housing — 463

171. Fritz Schumacher, *The Small Apartment* (1919) — 468
172. Kurt Tucholsky, *150 Kaiserallee* (1920) — 471
173. Bruno Taut, *The New Home: Woman as Creative Spirit* (1924) — 473
174. Martin Wagner, *Vienna—Berlin: Housing Policies Compared* (1925) — 476
175. Ludwig Hilberseimer, *On Standardizing the Tenement Block* (1926) — 480
176. Leo Adler, *Housing Estates in the Britz District of Berlin* (1927) — 482
177. Walter Gropius, *Large Housing Estates* (1930) — 484
178. Werner Hegemann, *Berlin and World Architecture: On the Berlin Building Exhibition* (1931) — 486

	179. Martin Wagner, *Administrative Reform (1931)*	491
	180. Ilse Reicke, *Women and Building (1931)*	493
	181. Siegfried Kracauer, *Building Exhibition in the East (1931)*	495
	182. Heinz-Willi Jüngst, *Housing for Contemporaries (1932)*	497
	183. Gottfried Feder, *The German Housing Development Board (1934)*	500
	184. Herbert Hoffmann, *The Residential Estate on Berlin's Große Leegestrasse (1936)*	502
	185. Anonymous, *The Construction of Communities on the Basis of the People, the Land, and the Landscape (1940)*	504
16.	Mass and Leisure	508
	186. Bruno Taut, *On New Theaters (1919)*	512
	187. Egon Erwin Kisch, *Elliptical Treadmill (1919)*	514
	188. Adolf Behne, *Großes Schauspielhaus, Scalapalast (1928)*	518
	189. Siegfried Kracauer, *Rollercoaster Ride (1921)*	520
	190. Berliner Börsen-Courier, *[Cinema] (1923)*	521
	191. Alfred Flechtheim, *Gladiators (1926)*	522
	192. Gerhard Krause, *The German Stadium and Sport Forum (1926)*	524
	193. Matheo Quinz, *The Romanische Café (1926)*	525
	194. Hans Poelzig, *The Capitol Cinema (1926)*	528
	195. J-S, *Review of Walther Ruttmann's Film* Berlin: The Symphony of a Great City *(1927)*	529
	196. Leo Hirsch, *Cinemas (1927)*	530
	197. Billy Wilder, *Berlin Rendezvous (1927)*	533
	198. Siegfried Kracauer, *Under Palm Trees (1930)*	534
	199. Curt Moreck (pseud. Konrad Haemmerling), *A Guide to "Licentious" Berlin (1931)*	537
	200. Siegfried Kracauer, *Radio Station (1931)*	540
	201. Hermann Sinsheimer, *Boxing Ring (1931)*	543
	202. Siegfried Kracauer, *Berlin as a Summer Resort (1932)*	546
	203. Werner March, *The Buildings of the National Sport Arena (1936)*	548
17.	Technology and Mobility	551
	204. Friedrich Krause and Fritz Hedde, *Swinemünder Bridge (1922)*	554
	205. Berliner Tageblatt, *[Cycling in Berlin] (1923)*	554
	206. Joseph Roth, *Declaration to the Gleisdreieck (1924)*	555
	207. Ignaz Wrobel (pseud. Kurt Tucholsky), *Berlin Traffic (1926)*	558
	208. Billy Wilder, *Nighttime Joyride over Berlin (1927)*	561
	209. Bernard von Brentano, *The Pleasure of Motoring (c. 1928)*	563
	210. Vicki Baum, *Grand Hotel (1929)*	565
	211. Siegfried Kracauer, *Proletarian Rapid Transit (1930)*	566
	212. Peter Panter (pseud. Kurt Tucholsky), *Traffic Passing over the House (1931)*	568
	213. Siegfried Kracauer, *The Cult of the Automobile (1931)*	571
	214. Siegfried Kracauer, *On Board the "Hamburg Flier": Special Press Trip, Berlin to Hamburg (1933)*	573

Contents

 215. E. Neumann, *Object—Subject (1934)*   576
 216. Anonymous, *The Intercontinental Airport at Tempelhof (1938)*   577
 217. Jakob Werlin / Albert Speer, *On the Autobahns of the Reich (1938)*   579
 218. Hans Stephan, *The Autobahn (1939)*   581

18. From Berlin to Germania   582

 219. Siegfried Kracauer, *Screams on the Street (1930)*   586
 220. Irmgard Keun, *The Artificial Silk Girl (1932)*   589
 221. Heinrich Hauser, *The Flood of Humanity at Tempelhof (1933)*   590
 222. Joseph Goebbels, *Berlin Awakes (1934)*   594
 223. Herbert Hoffmann, *The Air Ministry Building (1936)*   597
 224. Adolf Hitler, *The Buildings of the Third Reich (1937)*   599
 225. Anonymous, *The New Berlin Cityscape (1938)*   601
 226. Adolf Hitler, *Speech at the Topping-Out Ceremony for the New Reich Chancellery (1938)*   602
 227. Hans Stephan, *Berlin (1939)*   605
 228. Albert Speer, *Replanning the Capital of the Reich (1939)*   607
 229. Adolf Hitler, *Table Talk (1941)*   609

Acknowledgments   611
Photo Credits   619
Index   621

ILLUSTRATIONS

1. Berliner Schloss from the Lange Brücke, c. 1900   *21*
2. Sausage seller on the Schlossbrücke, 1906   *34*
3. Brandenburg Gate, 1910   *40*
4. Unter den Linden at the corner of Friedrichstrasse, 1908   *42*
5. Berlin Cathedral and Museum Island from the air, 1912   *45*
6. Blücherplatz and Hallesches Tor, 1907   *47*
7. Map of Berlin, 1902   *60*
8. Project for north-south railway connection through Berlin, 1910   *70*
9. Front cover of volume commemorating the Berlin Trade Exhibition, 1896   *81*
10. Interior of the Wertheim department store in Leipziger Strasse, c. 1900   *87*
11. Aschinger bar, c. 1915   *89*
12. AEG Machine Hall, Hussitenstrasse, 1912   *100*
13. Bülowstrasse Station, 1902   *113*
14. Railway bridge above the Landwehr Canal, Kreuzberg, 1905   *119*
15. Swinemünder Bridge, Berlin Gesundbrunnen, 1911.   *121*
16. Friedrichstrasse Station, 1898   *131*
17. Working-class apartment, Liegnitzer Strasse 9, Kreuzberg, 1910   *140*
18. Ackerstrasse 132–133: Meyers Hof, aerial view, 1930   *154*
19. Ackerstrasse 132–133: Meyers Hof, internal courtyards, c. 1900   *155*
20. Luckenwalder Strasse, Kreuzberg, 1912   *162*
21. Building the Reichstag, c. 1890   *181*
22. Potsdamer Platz seen from Café Josty, c. 1914   *185*

xiv   ILLUSTRATIONS

23. Rathenau House, Grunewald, 1922   *219*
24. Charlottenburg Town Hall, 1905   *224*
25. Gartenstadt Staaken, c. 1920   *265*
26. Street kitchen, Berlin, 1916   *282*
27. Bruno Taut, *Die Auflösung der Städte* (The dissolution of the cities), 1920   *309*
28. Mächler Plan for Berlin, 1919   *320*
29. Project for the rebuilding of Friedrichstadt, Berlin, 1929   *342*
30. Rebuilding of Alexanderplatz: Alexanderhaus, 1931   *350*
31. Haus Vaterland, Potsdamer Platz, 1926   *373*
32. Königstrasse (now Rathausstrasse), 1931   *385*
33. Locomotive over Friedrichstrasse, 1938   *401*
34. Control Room, Klingenberg Power Station, 1927   *421*
35. The unemployed outside the Labor Exchange on Sonnenallee, Neukölln, 1932   *433*
36. Funkhaus (broadcasting house) seen from the Funkturm (radio tower), 1930   *448*
37. "Berlin im Licht," advertising pillar from Berlin Light Week exhibition, 1928   *451*
38. Karstadt department store, Neukölln, 1929   *457*
39. Großsiedlung Britz (Horseshoe Estate) from the air, c. 1931   *483*
40. Dörchläuchtingstrasse, Großsiedlung Britz (Horseshoe Estate), 1926   *484*
41. Women's Circle, German Building Exhibition, Berlin, 1931   *494*
42. The winners of the twenty-ninth Berlin Six-Day Race, 1933   *515*
43. Kurfürstendamm, c. 1930   *535*
44. Strandbad Wannsee, c. 1930   *547*
45. Gleisdreieck Station and junction, 1927   *556*
46. Auguste-Viktoria-Platz (now Breitscheidplatz), c. 1930   *559*
47. The "Graf Zeppelin" flying above Wilhelmstrasse, Berlin, 15 August 1929   *569*
48. German Communist Party demonstration, 1 May 1929   *587*
49. Unter den Linden decorated for the state visit of Benito Mussolini, September 1937   *596*
50. Rebuilding plan for Berlin: Great Hall, 1939   *610*

PREFACE

An enormous debt of gratitude is due to the translators whose expertise and dedication have produced so many elegant texts for this anthology. David Britt, very sadly, did not live to see its completion but lives on here and elsewhere in his wonderful translations. Michael Loughridge deserves special gratitude for taking on a particularly heavy burden of texts, often of a rather technical nature, while warm thanks and congratulations on their deft and thoughtful contributions are due to Fiona Elliott and Ishbel Flett. Finally, I am most grateful to Jane Yeomans for her translation of a rogue text in this company, written originally in French.

Translation is not an inexpensive business, nor is the compilation of a large-scale anthology. For direct funding for translation I am most grateful for their substantial support both to the Graham Foundation for Advanced Studies in the Fine Arts and to the University of Edinburgh. A Senior Scholar grant awarded by the Getty Foundation to the editors of this volume for a different research project freed us from the obligations of university teaching and gave us the unstructured time essential for the collaborative gestation of this enterprise.

Two scholars of the German city were particularly helpful in recommending texts and in critiquing the overall shape of our selection. Edward Dimenberg was unstinting in his support of the project at every stage of its protracted development and played a decisive role in framing its final contours. Similarly, Francesca Rogier kindly shared with us her extensive knowledge of the planning debates in Berlin in the early years of the twentieth century. Expert advice on specific topics was generously given by Andrew Barker, Günter Berghaus, Helen Chambers, Jens Daehner, Hartmut Frank, Anton Kaes, Tim Kirk, Winfried Nerdinger, Bernd Nicolai, Anson Rabinbach, Wolfgang Sonne, and Volker Welter.

Librarians and archivists have played a central role in constructing this anthology, and I am particularly grateful to Eva-Maria Barkhofen, Head of the Architecture Archive at the Akademie der Künste, Berlin; Mary Daniels, Special Collections Librarian, Frances Loeb Library, Graduate School of Design, Harvard University; Wim de Wit, Head of Department of Architecture & Contemporary Art, Getty Research Institute; and Mary Woolever, Art and Architecture Archivist, Ryerson & Burnham Libraries, The Art Institute of Chicago.

During the years spent assembling this book, David Frisby enjoyed profitable sojourns at the Whitney Humanities Centre, Yale University, and at the Davis Center for Historical Studies, Princeton University: similarly, a two-year secondment to the Getty Foundation gave me access both to stimulating colleagues and to the magnificent collections held in the Library of the Getty Research Institute.

As the volume took its final shape, Max Whyte generated English-language lists of contents and illustrations from the German originals, and Keith Milne worked skillfully on the illustrations. Most important, Hannah Abdullah undertook the enormous task of securing translation and reproduction rights for the texts and illustrations—a daunting challenge that she pursued with enormous vigor and dedication. Finally, Alice Crossland produced a splendidly detailed and accurate index. My sincere thanks are due to all of them.

The satisfaction derived from completing this book is tempered by a profound sadness that David Frisby, my coeditor, cannot share it. David was a wonderful colleague and friend, who left life in November 2010 as he had lived it: quietly, uncomplainingly, and with great dignity. This book is dedicated to his memory.

Iain Boyd Whyte
Edinburgh, August 2011

GENERAL INTRODUCTION

From imperial Rome to Renaissance Florence and nineteenth-century Paris and London, the great cities defined the social and political realities of the moment and gave them built form and pattern. The twenty-first century will see half the world's population living in urban areas, with older global cities such as London, New York, and Tokyo joined by new megacities emerging from the dramatic economic expansion of countries like China, India, and Brazil. Such radical changes force us to call into question and investigate the nature of urbanization and the concept of the big city. Over a century ago in Europe, the acceleration in urbanization, the rapid emergence of new cities, and the expansion of others into large urban conurbations stimulated similar debates on the nature of the modern city. Although earlier in the nineteenth century the expansion of London and the transformation of Paris under Haussmann had generated discussions on the nature of the modern city, by the late nineteenth century there was one European city in particular whose astonishing growth in only a few decades came to embody and symbolize the most modern city: Berlin.

Only after the victorious Franco-Prussian War of 1870 and the unification of Germany under Prussian leadership in 1871 did Berlin emerge as a European capital city to rival London, Vienna, or Paris. At a stroke, Berlin was transformed from the residence of the King of Prussia into the capital of the German Empire and the seat of the imperial government. In keeping with its new status as the undisputed center of German communications, transportation, business, and learning, and of the emerging electrical and chemical industries, Berlin expanded at a dizzying rate in response to an insatiable demand for talent, energy, and muscle. In the period from 1850 to 1890, the population of London almost doubled, that of Paris more than doubled, but that of Berlin more than quadrupled. This expansion accelerated after German unification, with Berlin's population growing from 826,000 in 1871 to 1.9 million in 1900 and 2.1 million by 1914: among the cities of the world, only Chicago came close over these years in its rate of expansion. By 1910, the staid but reliable Baedeker Guide declared imperial Berlin to be not only the most modern city in Europe but also greatest manufacturing center in continental Europe. Its industrial development was not to be found in the heart of the city, but was concentrated in the northern and eastern suburbs, in districts such as Moabit and Wedding, where major firms such as Borsig, AEG, and Siemens were located.

Berlin's dramatic expansion generated extensive theoretical discussion on what constitutes a city. At the same time, city building (*Städtebau*) and the enlargement of existing cities (*Stadterweiterung*) generated new fields of knowledge devoted to urban design and city planning, which addressed such issues as the wider parameters of urban expansion and growth, the regulation of this growth, and its infrastructural requirements. The very concept of the city itself was not without its ambiguities. The German word for "town" or "city"—*Stadt*—did not distinguish between the two. This raised, in turn, the question as to what made a large town (*eine große Stadt*) into a big city (*eine Großstadt*). Further, could the concept of a metropolis be subsumed under that of the city, or did it require another concept such as that of the world city (*Weltstadt*)? Such issues could not be resolved merely by a quantitative approach, despite the expansion of statistical data on cities and their characteristics in this period. Nonetheless, a social-statistics conference in 1887 did define a city as possessing a population of one hundred thousand inhabitants. By 1910 Germany possessed forty-nine cities so defined. The more difficult issue of the metropolis or world city was resolved by declaring that the world city possessed a minimum population of 1 million (*Millionenstadt*). According to this definition, Germany had only one world city—Berlin—with Hamburg in second place with a population of over nine hundred thousand. The largest urban conurbation at this time was the Rhine–Ruhr area, where conglomerations of cities did not achieve a unified city status. In contrast, the expansion of Berlin into Greater Berlin proceeded in part through the incorporation of those surrounding and independent cities with populations of over one hundred thousand, such as Charlottenburg—the wealthiest city in Germany—Rixdorf, Schöneberg, Wilmersdorf, and Lichtenberg. This process of incorporation created a Greater Berlin in 1920 with a total population of 4 million.

While the suburban edges of the city, near the lakes and forests, were developed as opulent green suburbs, with street upon street of grand villas, the great majority of the population was housed in large tenement blocks that entirely justified the descriptive title of *Mietskasernen* (rental barracks). This housing type, composed of large blocks set around internal courtyards, was not unique to Berlin and could be found in other German and Central European cities at this time, such as Leipzig, Prague, and Vienna. The Berlin variant, however, was overwhelming in its volume and in the appalling housing conditions that it generated. Symptomatically, the average life-expectancy of Berliners in 1871 was 36.5 years for men and 38 for women. Although all urban housing development depends upon landownership, credit supply, and building contracts, the Berlin condition was unique. In London, urban expansion was historically controlled by aristocratic landowners; in Paris it was a domain of banking capital. Berlin had neither large landowners nor banking capital interested in long-term capital deposits, with the result that the role of developer fell to the weakest link—namely, the building contractor, financed by mortgage credit secured house by house. This capricious mechanism for urban expansion and development was exacerbated by weak local government control, fragmented across the many independent townships that made up the city of Berlin in the late nineteenth century.

Germany's defeat in World War I marked the end of Berlin as an imperial capital and as the seat of monarchy. It also saw the removal of the German parliament to Weimar as a protective measure against the revolutionary uncertainties that followed the defeat in November 1918 and the abdication of the Kaiser. During the war and in its immediate aftermath, Berlin became the focus of intensely utopian and visionary expectations that found a particularly strong resonance among the architects. Although short-lived, this phase of ecstatic expectation acted as a powerful link between nineteenth-century romanticism and the quasi-religious and messianic hopes of redemption and salvation that impelled Germany toward dictatorship in the 1930s. It also promoted the consciously political dimension that marks much of the artistic production of Berlin in the 1920s.

Remarkably, given the economic constraints imposed in 1919 under the terms of the Treaty of Versailles, the spiraling economic inflation of 1920–23, a malfunctioning democracy, and the political instability that afflicted Germany throughout the decade, Berlin blossomed in the 1920s. Particularly after the introduction of the Dawes Plan in 1924, Germany enjoyed a period of "relative stabilization" that lasted until 1929. As many commentators have noted, Berlin in the postwar decade was very aware of its modernity, of its generally positive reception of Americanization, and of its radical cultural production. The city itself was both dynamo and subject of this self-conscious modernization—a reciprocal relationship that found powerful expression in films such as Walter Ruttmann's *Berlin, die Sinfonie der Großstadt* and Fritz Lang's *Metropolis,* both premiered in 1927, and in the harsh social commentaries of painters like Otto Dix and Georg Grosz. Even the factories, city streets, and gray tenement houses of Berlin found a sympathetic eye in Gustav Wunderwald, of whose painting the art critic Paul Westheim wrote: "It also has the hard, inhumane, and cool matter-of-factness of this most matter-of-fact of all the great European cities."[1] This coolness and impersonality, however, found a positive expression in the contemporary European debates on architecture and urban design, in which Berlin played a preeminent role. Under the leadership of an enlightened Social Democratic city council and the housing associations promoted by the trade unions, Berlin became a laboratory for modern living. From the micro scale of the labor-saving kitchen to the macro scale of the new city quarter or the model town of the future, Berlin's architects, planners, and politicians developed the blueprints for twentieth-century urbanism in the industrialized world. Just as it is hard to think of industrial and product design without the Bauhaus model, so it is impossible to conceive of the global downtown without the glass office towers first proposed in the early 1920s by Mies van der Rohe for sites in Berlin.

Over the sixty years addressed by this volume, political and cultural modernism was sparked into life in Berlin, flourished, and was then mortally challenged. An ambitious and recently acquired empire collapsed, to be succeeded by new forms of democracy and of tyranny. Between 1900 and 1930, Berlin was a crucible of cultural modernity; after 1933 it was the epicenter of the National Socialist regime. This extraordinary history illuminates not only the nature and essence of both modernism and totalitarianism, but also their interrelationship, and reveals that avant-gardism in the arts did not necessarily go hand in hand with political liberalism. Nor did the National Socialist tyranny demand a consistent conservatism in the realm of artistic production. For modernism and fascism can be inextricably intertwined. As the texts in this volume indicate, some of the progressive cultural thought produced in 1920s Berlin was latently authoritarian by nature. Conversely, the arbiters of National Socialist taste were happy, on occasion, to embrace radical modernism in several areas of life.

This volume addresses not only the city of Berlin, but also the very nature of the emerging metropolis, as exemplified by Berlin. There are many ways of doing this: the approach could be statistical, in terms of demography and mortality; cultural, through the novels, paintings, and poetry stimulated by the nervous energy and danger of the city; or material, by reference to the volume of building, mileage of streets, energy provision, and the like. This dynamism also manifested itself, according to Walter Benjamin, in the language of the city, in its dialect: "The Berlin dialect is a language of people who have no time, who must often make themselves understood with a very short remark, a glance, half a word ... precisely because in Berlin all these people live together as large masses in the most diverse occupations and circumstances and at a remarkable speed. The Berlin dialect is today one of the nicest and truest expression of this racing tempo of life."[2]

In selecting the texts for this volume, however, a particular ambition has been to delineate and describe the spaces of Berlin, for as Siegfried Kracauer presciently noted: "Spatial images are the dreams of society. Wherever the hieroglyphics of any spatial image are deciphered, there the basis of social reality presents itself."[3]

To capture the complexity of the city, the selected texts are drawn from a broad range of voices and expertise, embracing economic, sociological, literary, and technical analyses by architects, city planners, journalists, cultural critics, politicians, philosophers, and social theorists. A small number of fictional texts have also been included to give a sense of how it felt to live there.

Arranged in chronological sequence, the texts were all written during the years spanned by this book, and retrospective memoirs have been excluded. They have been chosen to exemplify the characteristic questions of the particular historical moment, be it structure planning in the 1890s, radical speculation on the nature of the city in the 1920s, or the replanning of the whole of Berlin as "Germania," capital of the Third Reich, in the late 1930s. As a hotbed of new ideas on urban life and planning, Berlin did not escape the radical gaze of the National Socialist ideologues, whose thoughts on the capital city are not locked away in a poison cupboard marked "post-1933" but, rather, incorporated into the mainstream debates on the city as they had evolved over the previous half century.[4]

Following the reunification of the two Germanies in the late 1980s, Berlin captures the imagination once again as one of the great cities of the world. Out of the confusion of the divided Berlin of the Cold War, a reunited and reinvigorated city has emerged, in which a radical edginess is combined with an urbanity that is firmly embedded in Berlin's history. The texts in this volume offer a record of this defining history as it unfolded between 1880 and 1940.

NOTES

1. Paul Westheim, "Das Kunstblatt" (January 1927); reprinted in *Berlin zur Weimarer Zeit*, ed. Ruth Glatzer (Berlin: Siedler, 2000), p. 317.

2. Walter Benjamin, "Berliner Dialekt," in *Gesammelte Schriften, Band VII.1, Nachträge* (Frankfurt: Suhrkamp 1989), pp. 70–71.

3. Siegfried Kracauer, "On Employment Agencies: The Construction of a Space," in *Rethinking Architecture*, ed. Neil Leach (London: Routledge, 1997), p. 60.

4. For a magisterial selection of texts on the broader German society during the years of the Weimar Republic, readers are referred to the companion volume in this series: Anton Kaes, Martin Jay, and Edward Dimendberg, eds., *The Weimar Republic Sourcebook* (Berkeley: University of California Press, 1994). A companion anthology devoted to National Socialist Germany, entitled *The Third Reich Sourcebook*, is currently in preparation.

PART ONE

BOOMING METROPOLIS

1

THE METROPOLITAN PANORAMA

In 1887, Jules Laforgue somewhat hesitantly announced the possible emergence of the flâneur in Berlin as a result of the expansion of the city and its growing beauty.[1] Yet flânerie was perhaps already more common than he thought. The novelist Theodor Fontane declared in 1889: "I like to engage in flânerie in the streets of Berlin, mostly without a goal or purpose as is required for real flânerie [*Flanieren*]." On occasion, however, that strolling takes on more of a purpose, when he declares, "I am also gripped by a desire to study and permit myself to go and inspect all the possible old and new things that lie scattered around the city." And among these things are "panoramas and zoos, parks and statues, front gardens and fountains."[2] On the flat Berlin landscape, few possibilities for natural panoramic views offered themselves. Visitors had to make do, for instance, with ascending the tower of the city hall. Nowadays, it is the cupola of the Reichstag that is the most popular, and in the recent past it was the television tower on the Alexanderplatz. In Fontane's day, and for some decades later, one of the best-known sites for viewing the city was to be found on the Friedrichstrasse. The Kaisergalerie, a substantial arcade opened in 1875, housed a panopticon that presented such novelties as the Prussian defeat of the French army at Metz during the Franco-Prussian War of 1870 or the more exotic display around 1900 of "35 Togo negroes, 23 girls, 5 men and 2 children." And within the arcade's panopticon three large diorama images of Berlin in various periods were on display in 1888.[3]

Representations and images of the city were to be found not merely in the enclosed panoramas but also in the proliferation of textual images in an expanding world of the press. The "word city" of the feuilletons in newspapers and journals opened up a multiplicity of readings of the city, from panoramic perspectives to more modest attempts to capture the exemplary fragments and sensations of urban life in Berlin.[4] The topographies and the physiognomies of the diverse cultures in the city, and hence the varied readings of the city, were all present in a proliferating newspaper culture of the late nineteenth century onward. In particular, the feuilleton section of the newspapers carried explorations of the physiognomies of the city, whether located in the central city streets such as the Friedrichstrasse or Alexanderplatz or in the suburbs, both bourgeois and industrial. The city as spectacle was served by the advertising in its major newspapers, especially the most popular ones. Urban spectators were also drawn to Berlin's advertising pillars (*Litfaßsäulen*). As Peter Fritzsche explains, "Two meters taller than anyone in the crowd, topped with a green crown of wrought iron, plastered with the striking colors of art nouveau posters, *Litfaßsäulen* caught the glances of city people again and again." But much more than their role as advertising medium, the *Litfaßsäulen* permitted smaller, handwritten notices of everyday dramas to be appended to them, so that "tacked onto 'the last romantic herald,' the paper scraps about ordinary people . . . brought human interest to the city street."[5]

At the other end of the spectrum, in newspapers and journals, another reading of the city commenced not from its fragmentary elements but rather from attempts to conceive of the city as a whole, as a more or less coherent conception of the emergent world city. And here the urban reader was often confronted with comparisons with other major cities in order to draw out what was distinctive about the Berlin metropolis. Comparisons could be made in terms of urban growth and expansion, urban topography, built environment, aesthetic form, forms and speed of circulation, and so forth. But more often than not, such comparisons became transposed into urban imaginaries that drew out largely negative features of the new metropolis within which were embedded the dystopian dimensions of a threatening urban modernity.

By 1910 Berlin was easily the largest city in Germany, with a population in excess of 2 million. Surprisingly, the second-largest city, Hamburg, with almost a million inhabitants, was not often compared with Berlin, despite its own cultural development and the architectural innovations introduced by Fritz Schumacher.[6] Within the German Empire there was, however, the third most populous city: Munich, capital of the "democratic south," alternative cultural and artistic capital, symbol of "the other Germany." Although in the process of transformation into a modern city, Munich was not yet a site of large-scale industry. Rather, around 90 percent of all commercial enterprise in 1907 comprised self-employed or small-scale (up to five employees) enterprises. The city was, however, an expanding major cultural and artistic center, which nurtured strong views on the parvenu capital in the north. In a not untypical view from Munich, penned by Marcel

Montandon in 1903, for example, Berlin was described as a place where "everything is intensive life, unlimited ambition, energy, a desire to shift mountains, uncontrolled lust to conquest. In Berlin, modern life stands at its height, automatic, splendid, and flashing like a fully loaded cannon. In addition, it contains something fever like, capricious and American."[7]

Yet other elements of a Berlin imaginary were present in the comparisons between Berlin and other metropolitan centers. Mark Twain, who stayed in Berlin in 1892, identified Berlin as "Chicago on the Spree." For Twain, Berlin was a new city even compared with Chicago, a city full of broad, straight streets set in the topography of a flat surface. Over a decade later, Werner Sombart drew a comparison with Vienna as a city of culture in contrast to Berlin as "a suburb of New York," itself "a huge cultural cemetery." Berlin, in this imaginary, manifests the quintessence of "Americanism"—a theme from the mid-nineteenth century onward. In contrast, Alfred Kerr draws a contrast of Berlin with London, then the largest world capital city. Unusually, it is not Berlin that is the dynamic city of rapid traffic movements but London, nor is it Berlin that is the large-scale site of dwelling and consumption.

The view of Berlin from the tower of the city hall reveals another Berlin, which is not that of the imaginary constructions of the city but that of an expanding industrial sector. The notion of the Berlin metropolis derives not from its built environment in the center of the city but rather, according to Walther Rathenau, from its being "the factory city that no one in the west knows and that is perhaps the greatest in the world." Far from the city hall, the workers' panoramic view of the city was gained when traveling to and from work in the ring railway that links the outer industrial and working-class districts. As one anonymous commentator declared, "Whoever wants to get to know Berlin as an industrial and a worker's city must get up early. As the last night owls are being driven home to the west, the new day begins in the northern, eastern, and southern districts of the city."[8]

It was in these years at the turn of the century, it has been argued, that "in contrast to Paris, the capital of *aesthetic* modernity in the nineteenth century, [Berlin] was perceived as a center of a *technological,* civilizing modernity."[9] This made it all the more difficult to make claims for the aesthetic attractions of the expanding new metropolis that got beyond the equation of an industrial and technological modernity with ugliness. A view of the city as a whole (its *Gesamtbild*) that sought a more differentiated and nuanced image was perhaps more difficult to find. Rathenau's critique of contemporary Berlin in his ironically entitled essay "The Most Beautiful City in the World" (1899) castigated the lack of any organic whole in the layout of streets and houses in the metropolis. It implied a yearning for the ordered urban ensemble offered by Haussmann and a monumentality of structures that anticipated some of the submissions for the Greater Berlin competition of 1910. In contrast, the architect and critic August Endell's poetic monograph on modern Berlin, *The Beauty of the Great City* (1908), extracts beauty from the technology of the modern metropolis, from the ugliness of the city. It is the observer, he argues, who creates the aesthetic surface of the city from the formless streets and the sociospatial patterns of interactions in the urban crowd.

The urban individual's strategies for survival in the accelerating and often bewildering dynamics of circulation in the modern metropolis were more fully explored in the sociologist Georg Simmel's celebrated essay "The Metropolis and Mental Life," published in 1903.[10] Born on the intersection of two of Berlin's main streets, Friedrichstrasse and Leipziger Strasse, Simmel taught at Berlin University for most of his working life, and the city had a profound impact on his intellectual endeavors. As he noted himself: "Perhaps I could have achieved something that was also valuable in another city; but this specific achievement, which I have in fact brought to fruition in these decades, is undoubtedly bound up with the Berlin milieu."[11] In his engagement with the modern city in general, and Berlin in particular, there is no apparent aesthetic strategy to confront the unmerciful objectivity of precision, exactitude, and calculability, but rather an indifference, an intellectual distance, and the cultivation of a blasé attitude that can confront the dramatic increase in "nervous life" in the modern metropolis. The complex web of metropolitan interactions that we experience as a *chaos* of crisscrossing and entangled connections in fact emerge out of the *precision* and *calculating tactics* employed in each individual interaction. The image of the whole metropolis emerges out of the complex, intersecting hierarchies of networks of interactions, transactions (crucially, monetary transactions), and communications that possess different rhythms and spatial parameters. In consequence, the total image of the city could often be accessed only through an exploration of the fragmentary experiences of urban life.

NOTES

1. Jules Laforgue, "Berlin: La cour et la ville" (1887), in *Œuvres Complètes,* vol. 6 (Paris: Mercure de France, 1930), p. 126; (published in German as *Berlin: Der Hof und die Stadt,* Frankfurt am Main: Insel, 1981), p. 70.

2. Theodor Fontane, *Wie man in Berlin so lebt,* ed. G. Erler (Berlin: Aufbau Verlag, 2002), p. 59.

3. Jonas Geist, *Die Kaisergalerie* (Munich: Prestel, 1997), p. 45.

4. See Peter Fritzsche, *Reading Berlin* (Cambridge, Mass.: Harvard University Press, 1996).

5. Fritzsche, *Reading Berlin,* pp. 149, 152.

6. See Jennifer Jenkins, *Provincial Modernity: Local Culture and Liberal Politics in Fin-de-Siècle Hamburg* (Ithaca, N.Y.: Cornell University Press, 2003).

7. Quoted in Walter Schmitz, ed., *Die Münchner Moderne* (Stuttgart: Reclam, 1990), p. 28.

8. *Berliner Illustrierte Zeitung,* no. 39 (1912), p. 897; cited in John Czaplicka, "Pictures of a City at Work," in *Berlin: Culture and Metropolis,* ed. C. W. Haxthausen and Heidrun Suhr (Minneapolis: University of Minnesota Press, 1991), p. 25.

9. See Lothar Müller, "The Beauty of the Metropolis: Towards an Aesthetic Urbanism in Turn-of-the-Century Berlin," in Haxthausen and Suhr, *Berlin*, pp. 37–38. On the relationship between technology and Berlin modernity, see Andreas Killen, *Berlin Electropolis: Shock, Nerves, and German Modernity* (Berkeley: University of California Press, 2006).

10. Georg Simmel, "The Metropolis and Mental Life," in *Simmel on Culture*, ed. David Frisby and Mike Featherstone (London: Sage 1997), pp. 174–85. For a detailed exploration of Simmel's essay, see David Frisby, *Cityscapes of Modernity* (Cambridge: Polity, 2001), chap. 3.

11. Georg Simmel, quoted in David Frisby, *Georg Simmel*, rev. ed. (London: Routledge, 2002), p. 22.

1

Jules Laforgue

BERLIN

The Court and the City

Published as "Berlin: La cour et la ville" (1887); reprinted in Laforgue, *Œuvres complètes*, vol. 6 (Paris: Mercure de France, 1930), pp. 126–33. Translated by Jane Yeomans.

Even if he's from Berlin, the German is no flâneur. Yet as the capital grows in size and beauty, and more and more distractions appear in the streets, such a personage is emerging, more or less. There's no one German word, though, and the chronicler has to write: *der flâneur von profession.*

Berlin's heraldic arms consist of a bear posing elegantly on its hind legs.

Berlin now has forty thousand houses, and had only half that number twenty years ago. Berlin has an underground railway, a sky like a spider's web, crisscrossed with telephone wires, fairly widespread electric lighting, and, for the past year, covered food halls to replace the foul-smelling markets in the middle of public places.

There are never any traffic jams in Berlin; cars never lurch forward too quickly. The omnibus is confined to the suburbs and is used only by workmen. The trams are like toys—low roofs and no upper decks. The tramway is well thought of; uniformed army officers travel on it daily. The driver always stands; instead of our pedal horn, he has a hand bell, which he abuses horribly. The trams have no regular tariff: you buy a ticket for the distance to be traveled, and they are monitored by guards. Tram stages are marked with poles—no numbers.

The walls aren't blackened with obscenities; you don't see "long live this" or "long live that."

No one reads in the street; you never see people with leather briefcases.

No interesting street names: it's always Augustastrasse, Wilhelmstrasse, Friedrichstrasse, Karl- and Charlottenstrasse, Dorotheenstrasse, Moltke-, Bismarck-Goethe-, Schillerstrasse—no picturesque names at all, except Unter den Linden.[1]

The cafés don't have pavement terraces.

Street discipline: an apprentice balancing a pyramid of hatboxes is stopped by a policeman and forced to leave the pavement.

You never see a pastry maker in the street. Never a shoeblack. No street traders, no one shouting their wares, no market dealers, no clothes merchants, no chair upholsterers, no coopers or glaziers, and so on. The one exception is the grinder, who sharpens knives or scissors on a stone wheel. This man is sinister, though: rather than calling for clients, he hits his hammer on the grindstone, which makes a very disagreeable sound. The Parisian, transfixed, recalls the faucet seller's whistle.

The postman in his military uniform, bag of letters fixed to his belt buckle and dangling in front.

The street postboxes are delightful: big, wrought-iron, blue-painted—a pleasure to the eye. I think it was for the sake of the postal service that Prussia committed her greatest follies. Minister Stephan wanted to do things with style, and now towns with a population of only twenty thousand possess veritable palaces.[2]

Delivery men stationed here and there, with red varnished caps bearing a number and the word *Express*. For just a couple of coins, they are happy to take something to the other end of town for you. And with what rectitude! A rectitude one would scarcely have thought possible outside a small town.

The beatitude of the policemen, smug in their work. When it rains, it's quickly on with the rubber raincoat; in winter, a fur collar goes around the overcoat. The policeman's helmet has a spike cushioned with a little metal ball.

The flower sellers—always lilies of the valley—have to stay in the street, up close to the pavement. These are usually rough characters—women of dubious character and gray-haired old hags. I'm thinking of the corner of Unter den Linden Avenue and Friedrichstrasse.[3]

All the dogs are muzzled. Apart from the huge ferocious hounds like Bismarck's, which wealthy students parade, you rarely see anything but sad creatures pulling carts.

Parsimonious city council: very little watering, hoses like ours unheard of. The main streets are unbearably dusty in August—you yearn for a drop of water. Then the snow falls and freezes, sledges replace the carriages and go flying by, the horses jangling their bells in the silent carved-out groove of the street; with a sledge you can travel through the woods with ease. Then the great thaw comes and feet are clad in shapeless rubber galoshes.

A strange, scarcely credible character—the chimney sweep. Dressed from head to toe in a black-stockinged garment, like a funereal clown, he shuffles along on clogs, grasping a couple of tools and wearing a top hat! One thinks of a ghost, or of something escaped from the circus. And with his blackened eyelids, you never really know if he's looking at you.

Berliners are not quite used to their chimney sweeps yet: they just about manage to give them a smile. But their respect for the fire brigade is constant. The alarm bell beats out the rhythm of a heavy gallop; then everyone makes way, and the first vehicle comes into sight: eight firemen in their helmets, side flaps down, sit face-to-face; the driver is flanked by two policemen, with two more firemen on the running board, one ringing a bell, the other gripping a flaming pitch-soaked torch and dropping bits of fire into the road behind them.

Berlin's lack of water gives a truly unpleasant impression. You never see any water—the town is utterly dry. Here and there, just a couple of pumps. And how ugly they are! A pump handle and its neck, protruding from a shapeless wooden assembly.

On the dot of eleven at night (Unter den Linden is long since deserted), the cleaning carts begin to sweep up the dust on Friedrichstrasse—at that time the only street alive in Berlin. I say "alive"; I should rather say "high-living." What a pathetic and grotesque scene life on this street presents! Five or six wretched children squat on a doorstep, clutching matches to their knees and moaning, "Matches, matches." Youths and scoundrels accost you with the same plea, crying, "Herr Baron, Herr Baron, Herr Professor." Even an adult, sagging on his crutches, tries to sell you matches. But most shocking of all at this hour is a male torso, fitted into a box on wheels, and propelling himself around with his hands: he has a full, fair beard and spectacles, and he, too, is selling matches. During the day this world is completely out of sight; it's allowed into this lively part of Berlin only after ten at night. Something else allowed here at night—and which should be permitted during the day—the itinerant orange merchants. Their carts are stationed here at this hour, trusty dogs asleep on their rags, one eye open.

And the demimonde (for it is to this level that the Berliners have seen fit to reduce M. Dumas's word) treads the pavements and doesn't turn back. In winter, this spot is appalling. At least over there is the glow of the hot sausage seller's lantern. You buy one, and eat it bending over the gutter to keep yourself clean.

The cafés stay open all night.

Friedrichstrasse emerges again into Unter den Linden next to the Emperor's Galleries, a highly pretentious, gilded construction. The Galleries form the core of this whole little area. A Viennese café, and all the rest: shops offering junk and reproductions, the whole range and clutter of cheap bad taste. And away in a corner, a man selling photographs and brochures. The brochures: *For Men Only: Guide to Berlin at Night, from Six in the Evening until Six in the Morning, Essential for the Foreigner, Useful to the City Dweller, of Interest to Everyone; Berlin's Demimonde,* and so on.

But far from the lights, somewhere over there, a government official paces slowly, saber-bayonet at his side, military cap, bunch of keys: the night watchman.

Concierges don't exist in Berlin—either that, or they keep their doors shut after ten at night. You must always keep on you the key that opens the street door. But if you forget it, for a couple of coins the night watchman will use his duplicate to let you in.

NOTES

1. In the original French text, Laforgue translates the German names into French: "... c'est toujours la rue Augusta, la rue Guillaume, la rue Frédéric, les rues Charles et Charlotte, la rue Dorothée, les rues Moltke, Bismarck, Goethe, Schiller,—aucun nom imagé, sauf *Sous les Tilleuls*."
2. Heinrich von Stephan was appointed postmaster general of the new German Reich in 1876.
3. "Je parle ici du coin de l'avenue des Tilleuls et de la rue Fréderic."

2
Wilhelm Loesche
BERLIN NORTH

First published as "Der Norden" in Loesche, *Berliner Pflaster* (1890), p. 226; republished in *Das Berliner Mietshaus, 1862–1945*, ed. Johann Friedrich Geist and Klaus Kürvers (Munich: Prestel, 1984), p. 361. Translated by David Frisby.

One can study the transition from city to countryside nowhere as well as there, outside, almost exactly at the North Pole of the city, beyond the Gesundbrunnen.
 [. . .]
Here Berlin [. . .] theoretically comes to an end. In practice, it actually begins much farther back—there where the sky is so gray. It is the sky of Berlin North, of the factory north, a cloud of smoke by day, a cloud of red-brown fire by night, except that this mass of clouds guides no one here to the promised land. Whoever follows this sign from heaven rotates eternally on the same spot, together with thousands of others at the same time, wedged in the cogwheels of the machine, squashed, rolling round and round, mangled . . . according to circumstances. In the nighttime here outside at the crossroads without houses and lights and despite the distant reddish north light of the world city it is gruesome enough. Whoever loses their way from the sidewalk, walks in danger of falling into the strange deposits of rubbish that, in the form of a huge "ring of refuse" of the glacier-cold body of the she-bear, encircle the limits of the sea of buildings and cornfields: hills of broken porcelain crockery, rusted kettles, old shoes, defective beer mugs— everything that Berlin can no longer use, the entire flotsam of the oceans of streets. In between, there is also stored here and there a strange living structure enveloped in rubbish that is also flotsam such as pots and old iron. Berlin N[orth], when one enters the network of buildings from this North Pole, is as a whole neither a sanitary nor an aesthetically satisfying district of the city, neither with

regard to its external appearance nor in respect of its population. When one approaches the city from Gesundbrunnen on the deck of the horse-drawn omnibus, there appears in the latest extension of the central artery, the Brunnenstrasse, a bleak factory chimney. This is a symbol. There is no church, no palace dome, not even a spot of green foliage—the most prosaic that exists is a chimney stack! Only at one small place are the architectural places of interest crammed together, in the small projection adjacent to the river Spree. In all other respects the dreary street fronts take over everything. Indeed, what a series of streets these are—the Müllerstrasse and the Chausseestrasse, the Brunnenstrasse, the Schönhauser Strasse, the Prenzlauer Strasse! Like shafts, they cut through all the strata of the Berlin world: through the rural ring with its nice, small white houses, its small gardens, its dark cypress burial grounds, between which is still really a white dusty alley with a green tree roof—then through the new imposing district of elegant, brightly colored houses with balconies, with gold-colored balcony ironwork and white-red venetian blinds above them—and finally nearer the center, through the actual core of the city with its green-gray, many-windowed, but totally unadorned commercial barracks of the old type, out of whose entrances the moldy atmosphere of the constrained courtyards is exuded, and in whose realm nature's seasons cease to exist, or at best the "season" still survives. Between these huge streets, a massive block such as the Stettiner Railway Station or some kind of urban extended factory can at best play a role as landscape.

3

Mark Twain

THE GERMAN CHICAGO

First published in 1892; reprinted in *The Complete Essays of Mark Twain*, ed. Charles Neider (Garden City, N.Y.: Doubleday, 1963), pp. 87–89.

I feel lost in Berlin. It has no resemblance to the city I had supposed it was. There was once a Berlin which I would have known, from descriptions in books—the Berlin of the last century and the beginning of the present one: a dingy city in a marsh, with rough streets, muddy and lantern-lighted, dividing straight rows of ugly houses all alike, compacted into blocks as square and plain and uniform and monotonous and serious as so many dry-goods boxes. But that Berlin has disappeared. It seems to have disappeared totally, and left no sign. The bulk of the Berlin of today has about it no suggestion of a former period. The site it stands on has traditions and a history, but the city itself has no traditions and no history. It is a new city; the newest I have ever seen. Chicago would seem venerable beside it; for there are many old-looking districts in Chicago, but not many in Berlin. The main mass of the city looks as if it had been built last week, the rest of it has a just perceptibly graver tone, and looks as if it might be six or even eight months old.

The next feature that strikes one is the spaciousness, the roominess of the city. There is no other city, in any country, whose streets are so generally wide. Berlin is not merely *a* city of wide streets, it is *the* city of wide streets. As a wide-street city it has never had its equal, in any age of the world. "Unter den Linden" is three streets in one; the Potsdamer Strasse is bordered on both sides by sidewalks, which are themselves wider than some of the historic thoroughfares of the old European capitals; there seem to be no lanes or alleys; there are no short cuts; here and there, where several important streets empty into a common center, that center's circumference is of a magnitude calculated to bring that word spaciousness into your mind again. The park in the middle of the city is so huge that it calls up that expression once more.

The next feature that strikes one is the straightness of the streets. The short ones haven't so much as a waver in them; the long ones stretch out to prodigious distances and then tilt a little to the right or left, then stretch out on another immense reach as straight as a ray of light. A result of this arrangement is that at night Berlin is an inspiring sight to see. Gas and the electric light are employed with a wasteful liberality, and so, wherever one goes, he has always double ranks of brilliant lights stretching far down into the night on every hand, with here and there a wide and splendid constellation of them spread out over an intervening "Platz"; and between the interminable double procession of street lamps one has the swarming and darting cab lamps, a lively and pretty addition to the fine spectacle, for they counterfeit the rush and confusion and sparkle of an invasion of fireflies.

There is one other noticeable feature—the absolutely level surface of the site of Berlin. Berlin—to recapitulate—is newer to the eye than is any other city, and also blonder of complexion and tidier; no other city has such an air of roominess, freedom from crowding; no other city has so many straight streets; and with Chicago it contests the chromo for flatness of surface and for phenomenal swiftness of growth. Berlin is the European Chicago. The two cities have about the same population—say a million and a half. Fifteen years ago Berlin and Chicago were large cities, of course, but neither of them was the giant it now is.

But now the parallels fail. Only parts of Chicago are stately and beautiful, whereas all of Berlin is stately and substantial, and it is not merely in parts but uniformly beautiful. There are buildings in Chicago that are architecturally finer than any in Berlin, I think, but what I have just said above is still true. These two flat cities would lead the world for phenomenal good health if London were out of the way. As it is, London leads by a point or two. Berlin's death rate is only nineteen in the thousand. Fourteen years ago the rate was a third higher. [. . .]

4
Heinrich Schackow
BEROLINA

A Metropolitan Aesthetic

First published as "Berolina: Eine Großstadt-Ästhetik," *Neue Deutsche Rundschau (Freie Bühne)* 7, nos. 1/2 (1896), pp. 386–90. Translated by David Britt.

Twenty-five years of the new Reich have passed. The bronze figure of Berolina gazes out contemplatively across Alexanderplatz: the personified self-reflection of a city, pausing for a moment in her onward progress to marvel at the undreamed-of wealth of life that she has accumulated, imperceptibly, from one laborious day to the next. She raises a hand in greeting; she salutes the enormous transformations of the past, the life that surges beneath her—even the future, whose forms she seeks to discern in the distant haze of the streets.

What emerges from those mists is a turmoil of constant change. The buildings along the streets pile up and grow into massive upper stories. Alexanderplatz is surrounded by a confusion of masonry: apartment houses with their endless arrays of windows, the stony deliberation of the police headquarters, the assured lightness of the ironwork of the elevated railroad station, with its shimmering, pale-blue glass roof and its bridge across the street. The expanses of plate glass in the storefronts tremble with the vibration of the traffic, mirroring the street scene like quick-change dioramas; hectic colors wink and blink. The noisy colors and lines of competing trade signs: lettering in glass, metal, and paint; signs in long, rounded, sweeping, or straight lines: a garish, noisy plethora of contrasts.

But all these thousands of formal inventions—even the most grotesque, the most inept, the most banal—are forcibly united in one vast whole as they join in the hymn of praise that rises from these city squares, day in and day out: a hymn in praise of beauty, the beauty of Necessity.

The towering chimneys of the electricity plant; the tight-packed parallel threads of the telephone network, crisscrossing over the rooftops; the mighty snorts of the locomotives as they rumble over the bridge: here, in this setting, all this is beautiful. And behind it all, above it all, the tower of the Marienkirche stands out, clear and tranquil.

Urban mists shroud the distant scene; details are lost. Architectural features stand out in bold outline. On the open square, the dark mass of the church. Its foundation stone was laid eight hundred years ago. The tower consists of three distinct levels. Thirteenth-century ashlar blocks form a sheer, blank wall; the cornices of the intermediate story are scaled-down Baroque forms; the steeple is Gothic-Baroque. *Pendent opera interrupta!*[1] Every generation has worked on this monument in its own time. At the most recent restoration, the architects in their wisdom removed much that was venerable and full of character. But what of it? The church still stands as an emblem of the simple, sober, civic spirit; it still purveys a hint of the earliest beginnings of art in the March of Brandenburg.

Memories steal in and transport us back to that quaint age, which is still present in the little cottages that lurk—poetic in their picturesque dilapidation—behind the nave of the church. Marooned and battered by the tide of modern high-speed living, this cluster of low, sooty, half-timbered dwellings will soon be swept away.

Here, a benevolent chance has placed the very newest next to the very oldest. A block of department stores, all built to a uniform design, extends from the church through the historic city center: and their design is not only uniform but free, bold, functional, and unique in its resolute conciseness. The dressings around the door and window openings are of sandstone; the walls are of brick, a mixture of buff and a dull, bluish brick red. Additional detail is supplied by the visible iron frame structure, painted matte green. Oriels emerge discreetly from a subtle, organic formal scheme, enriched with the plain, astringent decorative forms used by the old Flemings.

This is an artistic experiment in the grand style, and these buildings can boldly stand comparison with their florid and ostentatious neo-Baroque neighbors on Kaiser-Wilhelm-Strasse.

Farther on, the Kaiser-Wilhelm-Brücke spans the River Spree. The eye looks deep into the distance along the canyons of the city, where familiar monuments stand out against the sky, laden with memories.

The age of the Joachims gave us the old fortress, its Renaissance outline dark and weighty, where the waters of the Spree edge past its walls. The age of the Great Elector speaks to us in its great monument, the product of the unique genius of Schlüter.[2] The river reflects the gigantic bulk of the Schloss,[3] and the equestrian statue with its dull gleam of bronze—on which, in a succession of shifting images, it superimposes the cumbersome barges, red with the dust of Brandenburg bricks, and the light lumber rafts—pines from the sandy soil of Brandenburg, shipped here to make the scaffolding that shapes the nascent cathedral.

And Time tells its tale in many other buildings.

Time tells of the many transformations of the "palazzo" originally planned, which the growing strength of an emergent nation transformed into the weighty monumentality of a Prussian royal Schloss. Pointing across the wide square, Time tells of one great man, intoxicated with beauty, who believed that he could transplant ancient Hellas into the March of Brandenburg, and who left the traces of his errant genius here for centuries to come: Time shows us the Zeughaus,[4] that frowning citadel, that shrine of confident Prussianism—and, again, of the fame

FIGURE 1. Berliner Schloss from the Lange Brücke, c. 1900. Berlinische Galerie, Landesmuseum für Moderne Kunst, Photographie und Architektur—Photographische Sammlung, BG-FS 48/81,3.

of Andreas Schlüter—and directs the eye upward to the richly ornamented attic story, where the Prussian banner in pure white gaily flutters in the wind and salutes the Schloss, across the way, with its soaring eagle.

Men and buildings!

Next to appear, in this inexorable historical sequence, is the Great King himself. His residences near Potsdam, with their graceful ornament that smiles down upon us from walls and ceilings, are the fruit of his own idiosyncratic artistic temperament. Strange times, indeed! And so one style shaded gradually into the next; while the rococo still frolicked, the star of Palladio was slowly rising.

Already, the exterior of the Opera House reflects the subtle harmonies devised by that ingenious native of Vicenza;[5] and Gontard's magnificent domes proclaim them across the rooftops from Gendarmenmarkt.[6]

The days came and went.

As the century drew on, the Brandenburg Gate appeared, modeled on the ruined Propylaea in Athens. Its reverend air, which even a few decades ago was still an object of enthusiasm, has now faded, overborne by the rhythmic monotone of the neighboring palaces. In one, an ossifying Antique and an ossified Gothic mingle; in another, they primly separate. Between the two, the result is the most impoverished streetscape of the years that preceded 1870.

Through this gate marched the victorious troops, with a Kaiser at their head, past old Fritz's memorial, to lay up their trophies in the Zeughaus.

And then these historic haunts sprang to new life. New buildings arose; and, amid all this new growth, the countless, strange nuances of our new life have come to express themselves in inexhaustible variety. A chaos of urgent strength and hothouse warmth, in which new ideas and more considered forms gradually took shape. Great tunes resound through all of this. It is just a few steps from here to Friedrichstrasse.

This architecture has taken shape over twenty-five years of evolution and renewal. In an unconscious process of transformation, born of a powerful, instinctive longing, it has sought new harmonies. Through much that has been erected here, there runs an honest endeavor to endow structural innovations with an aesthetic of their own, based on the open manifestation of significant advances in engineering (the art of technological invention).

Granite facades with massive portals and richly ornamented balconies loom to an immense height; dome-crowned, they dwarf the neighboring houses that seem to huddle beside them. And, alongside plaster-faced and stonework walls, plain brick construction. This has brought into our streetscape—formerly so drab in color, so lukewarm and antiquated—a refreshing note of red. Again: stone and brick, harmoniously combined in a single building: facades with socle, cornices, quoins, and superstructures in a matte stone color and the intervening surfaces in the deep, warm red of brick.

And as if in deliberate antithesis to the new aesthetic values—that is, to the slow awakening of a feeling for structure—the dead, traditional style of the ornament with which these buildings are draped.

Grotesquely jutting oriels; roofs in assorted geometric shapes, piled high with dainty dormers; chimneys with ornate cowls; slender turrets and onion domes: an architectural hodgepodge, picturesque in its richness and its variety of bold lines. Columns, capitals, obelisks, arabesques: the progeny of past ages, seldom fitting in organically, and even more seldom organizing themselves into new variations.

A bewildering, turbulent sea of buildings! Bare gable ends stand out precipitously as the street line descends in receding perspective; these stony uplands rise, fall, and split into chasms like some fantastic mountain range.

All that is best in the whole street combines in a single place: the celebrated Equitable-Palace, the House of Stone and Iron.[7] Its facades are of shimmering, gray granite; its dome, crowned with a golden lantern, stands out against the sky.

The outward appearance of the building clearly reflects the arrangement of the large, uniform spaces inside; here, the horizontals of Baroque architecture and the verticals of Gothic are sensitively interpreted and powerfully combined in monumental harmony. Swags of heavy bronze foliage cling to the glistening, decorative granite limbs. This is a noble building; from the immense repertoire of bygone formal ideas it salvages the essential. It manifests the superior artistry that is elsewhere found only as the treasured end product of a coherent school and an established tradition.

> *Hier führt die gerade Straße nach Osten und nach Westen.*
> *Ein Bilderreichtum in freigebiger Fülle!*
>
> [Here the straight highway leads on to east and west.
> A wealth of images in lavish profusion!]

The history of the construction of these stately edifices represents a curious aspect of an age in which the rapidly growing imperial city, in the full flood of its development, built on with youthful impetuosity: street after street lined with parade-ground ranks of four- and five-story giants.

[. . .]

There has, of course, been a deal of indiscriminate pilfering of crumbs from the tables of the old masters. Ideas from the Palazzo Pesaro, the Palazzo Pitti, the Château de Versailles, and heaven knows where else have been crudely, nastily copied, often with a nonsensically misplaced precision of detail.

True enough, in architectural terms these modern buildings are a farrago of lies. But they have brought detail and color into what had become an almost unendurable monotony.

And that is an achievement of sorts, after twenty-five years.

When dusk falls over these streets, and a thousand artificial lights appear—light, colored light everywhere, as far as the eye can see; light from the white moons of electric lamps; broad rivers of light, flickering, ebbing, and flowing, fading to a violet twilight in those remote depths where street lines converge—when garish brilliance floods the nearby scene, and multiple shadows crisscross on the dully reflective surface of the asphalt, leaving other objects to stand out in clear shade against a horizon veiled by flickering reflections and shimmering twilight; when architectural forms rise to unknown heights through the heavy indigo air, and from below only the details of angular cornices, fantastic caryatids, and graceful festoons stand out sharply: then it is that form becomes color. It flashes in multicolored brilliance and fades, shimmering, into a soft haze. In color, inert form comes to life.

Again: in this well-nigh inextricable chaos, this mêlée of colors and lines—an unintentional beauty, conditioned by advances in mechanical and structural engineering beneath the magic spell of artificial light—the true aesthetic of the metropolis slowly comes to fruition.

Detectable only by the sharpest intuition, an awakening is beginning to stir within modern architecture. This will become visible and convincing to all, but not until this tentative impulse finds its way to clear and conscious expression. This will be when, with the inexorable gradualness of all natural growth, the architecture of our time—so long sought after—has transmuted the character of our cityscapes.

NOTES

1. "Work hung suspended." Virgil, *Aeneid*, iv, 88:

non coeptae adsurgunt turres, non arma iuventus
exercet portusque aut propugnacula bello
tuta parant: pendent opera interrupta minaeque
murorum ingentes aequataque caelo.

Aeneid, IV. 86–89

Meanwhile the partly built towers had ceased to rise. No more did young soldiers practice arms. The construction of harbors and impregnable battlements came to a stop. Work hung suspended on gigantic, menacing walls, and the sky-high cranes were still.

Translation: W. F. Jackson Knight, from Virgil, *The Aeneid* (Harmondsworth: Penguin, 1956) p. 99

2. Andreas Schlüter (1664?–1714) was called to Berlin in 1694, where he worked both as court architect and as court sculptor. Friedrich Wilhelm I, known as the Great Elector, came to power in 1640 and was responsible for the rebuilding of Prussia and its dependencies after the ravages of the Thirty Years' War. Schlüter's equestrian sculpture of the Great Elector, completed in 1703, now stands in the forecourt of Schloss Charlottenburg, Berlin.

3. Berliner Schloss: royal palace in the center of Berlin.

4. Zeughaus: arsenal.

5. The architect Andrea Palladio, born in Padua in 1508, died in his adopted town of Vicenza in 1580.

6. The Gendarmenmarkt is a city square in central Berlin, flanked on two sides by two domed churches, the Französischer Dom (French Cathedral) and the Deutscher Dom (German Cathedral), both of which were modified in 1785 to matching designs by Carl von Gontard. A third side of the square houses Karl Friedrich Schinkel's Schauspielhaus (theater; now the Konzerthaus [concert hall]), built in 1818–21.

7. Designed by the architect Carl Schäefer, the Equitable Palace was built on the corner of Friedrichstrasse and Leipziger Strasse in 1887–98.

5
Alfred Kerr
BERLIN AND LONDON

First published as "Berlin und London" (1896); reprinted in Kerr, *Wo liegt Berlin? Briefe aus der Reichshauptstadt* (Berlin: Aufbau, 1997), pp. 191–94, 198–99. Translated by David Frisby.

[. . .] Anyone who has wandered around the whole course with the Londoner finally sees that the two cities are incommensurable. One returns to the Spree and finds that the huge community that is striven for is an idyll. An attractive city with clean streets, a pleasant zoological garden, and a somewhat less pleasing small river located at the foot of the Kreuzberg. When I explained to my landlady in London that I was from Berlin, she said in a friendly manner: "Hmm, Berlin is a nice place." In German: Berlin is a small, nice place. She is right: it is nice. It is related to the gigantic city on the Thames as an immature naive youth relates to a fully mature heroine.

To state it bluntly: London has forty to fifty versions of the Friedrichstrasse. One can travel around in a coach for an hour and still not come out of the tumult of the crowd. [. . .] Whoever first allows the streetscape of London to impact upon them feels a perceptible unease. One longs for the sight of a pause for just once in the continuous, antlike endeavors. One looks for a break in order to take in a breath of air. But it proceeds further, coldly, quietly, and machinelike, with determined indifference, without any particular haste being visible, but nonetheless with a more concentrated energy. [. . .] In contrast to this, Berlin has something lackadaisical, distracted about it—something of the comfortableness of a small town. With us, the purely expedient, the lash of the whip recedes into the background. Here one still raises one's hat in shops, one says good day, and often in a tone as if one would wish to add "dear neighbor." These are instances of provincialism.

Something similar is also true with regard to public conveyances. In Berlin they proceed at a relatively comfortable trot, and even when the pace is that of a gallop, it seems to be the result of the droll malice of the coachman. In London, the pace is that of the highest continuous speed possible. And here, too, the distinctive temperament of this people is revealed: it is speed but no haste. There is no hint of excitement in this; the cab drivers do not travel so impetuously and not with such élan as, for instance, the Viennese coachman, but they probably drive faster; and they overturn less often.

[. . .]

The omnibuses shoot along the streets, thickly packed both above and below, and although each vehicle carries thirty to forty passengers, there swarms on a single street a larger number of omnibuses than do hackney carriages in Berlin.

Whole armies of buses galloping in the same or the opposite direction, neither disturbing the other, and thousands of people are dispatched with the utmost speed. In contrast, the forward movement of the bell-ringing Berlin horse railway seems like busy idleness, a movement that pushes along the Leipziger Strasse in schematic, prescribed grooves, without being able to deviate from them, full of heavy loads, bureaucratic and miserable. [...] The cabs look wonderfully elegant, like our slender black lacquered sport carriage, and the man who drives it wears no uniform but, like the Viennese coachmen, chooses everyday attire.

For Berlin eyes, the absence of uniforms is indeed one of the most striking features of the London street scene. Neither the conductor nor the coachman on the buses is in livery. The conductor is a gentleman in private dress. [...] And even military officers here do not wear uniform on the street. It is hung up once duty has finished. "Why is that?" I asked a Londoner. He laughed. He said, " It has sometimes happened that an officer went through the streets in uniform, but now it is no longer possible. A worker would approach him and say (as has happened): 'Now, don't we dress you well, feed you well? Do you want something else? Here, I'll give you a penny!' The military are too little taken notice of here, as an unproductive stratum." This is what he said. I thought that in this respect, too, everything is fundamentally different in Berlin. [...]

Due to the maximum utilization of space, the London city railway is underground. Small, neat railway trains race around in the bowels of the earth. [...] These railway trains are less elegant to look at than the Berlin ones, but they travel twice as fast. This is again typical. Constructions of the most imposing character such as the underground railway are to be found in many places. In Berlin there is no Holborn Viaduct. This is a street built in the air, a street with thousands of wagons, houses, people, stones, shops, beneath which other streets run; a Friedrichstrasse on pillars. In Berlin, one lives merely on the ground; in London one also lives underground and in the sky.

It is hardly worth mentioning that in London the shops excel in elegance those in Berlin. Or that London is absolutely the most elegant city that I know, and not merely the foggy factory hole that we are told so much about. Whoever looks in the shop windows in Regent Street—for them the Leipziger Strasse has nothing more to offer.

As a compensation, Berlin is cleaner (towns lying on the sea always smell!), and it has better theater. For art always emanates from those who have come down in the world. These are at least two advantages. Only two.

6
Alfred Kerr
THE TRANSFORMATION OF POTSDAMER STRASSE

First published as "Die Verwandlung der Potsdamer Strasse" (1895, 1897); reprinted in Kerr, *Mein Berlin: Schauplätze einer Metropole* (Berlin: Aufbau, 1999), pp. 37–39, 43–47. Translated by David Britt.

SPRING IS HERE

These days, as you walk along Potsdamer Strasse at nine in the evening, you are surprised to note that something has changed. At other times, everyone rushes past each other in businesslike haste. Now, everything has slowed down.

Overhead, the trees are starting to bud. The air is soft. Despite the clang of the horse-drawn streetcars and the onward rush of carriages, a certain peace lies over the tree-lined streets. People go on their leisurely way, lulled by the mild air; they stop and look up—at the buds. The salesgirls from the glove shops; the little blondes who have been trimming hats until nine o'clock; the others who twine fresh flowers into bouquets and copper-beech leaves into funeral wreaths, and who often have reddened hands; those slender creatures who spend the day as living clotheshorses for the garments of elegant ladies, and who take their revenge by night on elegant gentlemen; the mischievous little dressmakers in little dark hats, with a band of black velvet around their skirt hems; the little bits of fluff who have been sitting in offices, writing out addresses and licking envelopes—they stroll along, arm in arm, in twos and threes, with a sauntering gait and a languorous swing, in blissful indolence, imbibing the soft evening air, looking up at the buds, and watching out for a mustache somewhere to left or right. One of them hums Berlin's favorite sentimental song to herself: *Es war ein Sonntag, hell und klar* [It was a Sunday, bright and clear] . . . one that never fails to stir the emotions.

Spring in Berlin is a metropolitan spring. It is a strange blend of nature and civilization. Its elements are the sky, the air, the trees, and also the special smell of the asphalt, the clothes the women wear, and the outdoor tables of the restaurants and cafés around Potsdamer Platz. The tables are out on the veranda at Friedrich's, and customers sip their Rhine wine as they nod to a passing acquaintance on Potsdamer Strasse. Farther down, at Josty's, between five and six, there is not a seat to be had; everyone sits tightly packed around the little marble open-air tables.[1] Mostly the monarchs of the west side, as elegant as they are solvent—although their silk hats and black worsted suits are outshone by the light-colored outfits of their wives, brunette or blonde, who chatter in loud voices or phlegmatically drink iced coffee through a straw. They are a sight worth watching as they sit there, talking and laughing and nibbling—or else staring into space and harboring wrong ideas and surreptitiously glancing across Potsdamer Platz, where elegant strollers dawdle past, one by one, and turn aside into aristocratic Bellevuestrasse, with its spring greenery. Even the dark pathways of the Tiergarten are livelier in the evening than at other times. There, those same little business girls stroll with amiable young men. They walk along the great cross avenues and over the narrower rides; but most of all they favor the narrow, lonely footbridges on the New Lake and by the weir—where the waters flow with a melancholy sound, and from time to time a forlorn cry drifts across from the Zoological Garden. Anyone who paces those dark, silent walks at this time will see couples standing in the middle of the paths, closely entwined, kissing; and whispers are to be heard from the benches that line the path. Spring, which brings everything to life—which creates vegetation of a kind, even in Pankow—inspires that amorous mood of mild arousal that is such a frequent feature of demure novelettes. The loving couples kiss their way down to the Charlottenburg road and wander into the Charlottenhof or the Café Gärtner. There they drink a beer. And, by the second half of April, spring, which brings everything to life, calls forth on the young man's face those little vernal spots for which Berliners have the charming name of *Pickel*. The little blonde sees them as she sits over her glass of beer at the café table, beneath the electric lights, and says with a smile: "Max, you're a perfect Piccolomini."

23 April 1895

END OF AN IDYLL

Reader, it is true: they are paving Potsdamer Strasse, because it is being widened. And no one is sadder about this than those members of the younger generation who are still in Berlin. Because this work is going on, they can barely make their way, however hard they try, along this high road to love and lust—let alone stroll there. And, most important, a new bridge is under construction: a new Potsdamer Brücke. The little, old, wooden bridge had an important place in history. Cultural history. Friendly and worm-eaten, it was a notorious trysting place for upper-class lovers. Or at least one part of it tended to be upper-class. People used to sneak out there in the evening, at eight-thirty or nine-thirty. The simplest and most obvious spot for west-side people was always this little bridge. The rickety planks and iron handrails lay shrouded in twilight. There was no overly bright light to mar the expectant mood; and the west-siders went on the prowl, purring, as a tomcat prowls the fire escapes—or, to speak with Mephistopheles, *so heimlich-kätzchenhaft-behaglich* [so secretively, snugly skittish]—in the vicinity of those same iron railings. She would appear out of the darkness. And first you both walked a little way along the bank, then up Regentenstrasse, undismayed by the Buddha, and on along the edge of the Tiergarten. Finally, you hailed a late, open cab and rode slowly, slowly, through the evening air, kissing and being kissed. Two evenings later, the trysting place was Potsdamer Brücke again. And now that modest, old-fashioned, idyllic little bridge is to become a wide, modern, showy structure with the modern convenience of glaring lights, and—as if in mockery of that lost, amorous twilight—allegorical figure groups, "illustrative of the phenomena and influence of electricity." As an eighteenth-century writer would have put it, "Sullen Cupid hides his head." A nineteenth-century columnist can only note that, in all probability, Viktoriastrasse will be the new trysting place. It is not far away, and it is as dark and mysterious as the ways of God.

25 July 1897

WITH THE LATTER-DAY SAINTS

Before long, there will be another change in the look of Potsdamer Strasse. And all the other streets will change, too. Because there will be no horses in front of the streetcars. This, too, is "illustrative of the phenomenon and influence of electricity." Those little piles that we used to see between the streetcar tracks had a homely charm. They were evocative of rural life. And in August, in particular, when the asphalt glowed with heat, many a passerby found in the deep, full-bodied smell of manure a surrogate for the vaporous country air. But this, too— *hélas, mes amis!*—this, too, must pass. We live, I should add, in a fast-moving age; there is no pause in the all-leveling advance of the Age of Electricity and so on. At all events, there will be a lot of sausages eaten in Berlin next winter. Sausages will come down in price. They will be cheap, incredibly cheap. The direct links between electricity and mass nutrition are becoming clear for the first time. Kurd Lasswitz, the philosopher, has dreamed of an artificial, universal food, which he calls Chresim; in times to come, this will be electrically manufactured to fill and satisfy the stomachs of the multitudes. This is all still a dream. But electricity has already made a down payment on the cheap mass food of the future. It is quite right, therefore, to honor the men of the age of electricity, Röntgen and Helmholtz, with statues on the new Potsdamer Brücke. And, alongside the old paganism of Buddha, the new paganism of science is free to set up its shrine in the godforsaken city of Babylon-on-Spree.

25 July 1897

NOTE

1. Favored by writers and artists, the Café Josty offered the ideal vantage point from which to view the surging urban life on Potsdamer Platz, one of the busiest traffic intersections in Europe at the time and the site of Berlin's first subway station, opened in 1907.

7

Max Osborn

THE DESTRUCTION OF BERLIN

First published as "Die Zerstörung Berlins," *Die Nation,* 5 May 1906. Translated by Iain Boyd Whyte.

And now the "opening up" of the Brandenburg Gate is on the agenda. The plan has already been known for a number of years: the two buildings on the Pariser Platz that adjoin the old, small gatehouses are to be demolished in order that the gate itself stands "free." This means that the whole thing has already been decided. It is impossible to get to know any further details; the lips of all the participants are sealed. How the whole matter will be dealt with in detail is still unclear. I have no idea whether the gatehouses, along with the guardhouse and the adjoining colonnades, are also to be demolished. In addition, a second proposal, as unthinkable as it will appear to every Berliner, is that the guardhouse on the Brandenburg Gate, a soldierlike image of Old Prussian purity, should also no longer exist. Yet, on the other hand, what's the sense of the guardhouse that now actually guards an entrance to the city when one can walk around it? What is the sense of a gateway that one can stroll around? And this is quite apart from the destruction of the most beautiful of Berlin's squares that would go hand in hand with the opening up of the square. The whole attraction of this precious, historical location would be lost, and as a substitute there would be opened up from Unter den Linden the perspective from the gate to the monumental constellation that is at present mercifully closed off. The square in front of the Brandenburg Gate is today one of the ugliest squares that is to be found in modern cities; the Pariser Platz is one of the most beautiful in the world—if this separation were to be removed then there would emerge an indescribable conglomerate, and the beauty of the one would be negated by the ugliness of the other. The whole plan seems so monstrous that one would hardly believe in it were it not for Byzantines lacking employment, who wish to make themselves loved in influential circles, by so eloquently defending and extolling it. [. . .]

It is not volcanic eruptions with steams of lava and ash rain, it is no earthquake, spring floods, and incendiary fires, it is no foreign conqueror and bloodthirsty Communards—it is we ourselves who are the destroyers of Berlin. We are in the process of destroying the remains of the beautiful city that once grew up on the banks of the Spree, with an eagerness and restlessness as if what is at issue is performing a great and good deed.

8
Werner Sombart
VIENNA

First published as "Wien," *Morgen*, no. 6 (19 July 1907), pp. 172–75; reprinted in *Début eines Jahrhunderts: Essays zur Wiener Moderne,* ed. Wolfgang Pircher (Vienna: Falter, 1986), pp. 35–39. Translated by David Frisby.

[. . .] One can actually summarize the judgment on Vienna with a single word: Vienna has culture. I don't say even "old." Just culture. Or if one wishes to add an epithet to the word, then: artistic culture. [. . .]

Old Vienna as city: in every stone a song, a melodious tune in every vine-clad courtyard, in every old palace.

And just like Vienna—the Viennese: a real human being. Not the fragment of a human being that we find so often in North Germany. Even the professional person in Vienna still has a feeling for life. Well balanced. Not awkward: not hard. Soft, flexible in the best sense. But the Viennese are called "inefficient." This is simply not true. To my knowledge, this is not the case. I know just as many Viennese men who achieve really quite as much in science, art, and public life as do North Germans. It is just that they don't make so much fuss about it as we do. (In Vienna all major avenues are still called alleys [*Gassen*], whereas in Berlin every alley is a street). And even if it were true: is it merely a matter of "efficiency," I ask myself? Do we not degenerate in "efficiency"? In the context of an efficiently performed partial achievement do we not all too often forget the whole entity, the complete human being? [. . .]

Whoever wishes to understand what Vienna means for us, for Germany, or German culture should compare it with a modern structure such as Berlin. One must first of all have experienced profoundly and painfully how terribly quickly we become impoverished if we allow ourselves to become enraptured by the nature of Berlin simply in order—I want to say—to feel a holy veneration for Vienna: as the symbol of that which we must preserve, of that which we must strive to regain.

Berlin is a suburb of New York: no more, no less. Everything of which the Berliner can be proud New York possesses ten times over: it is three times as big, it grows much more quickly, it has ten times more traffic, ten times as many theaters, its restaurants and amusement parks are ten times as large, its noise is ten times as loud, its distances are even greater.

And what is New York? A desert. A huge cultural cemetery. Is humanity to finish up there?!

What threatens our culture is the overvaluation of the voluminous, of size, of the purely quantitative. It is the overvaluation of technical means, leading us to forget ultimate and true values. It is as if "traffic" represented some kind of value and did not merely satisfy a sad necessity in the cities. The traffic of which the American (or Berliner) is so proud. It is as if "good order" in itself were in some way valuable, since really it has a meaning only if it orders things of value and not when it becomes an end in itself. It is as if it were about "achievements" of whatever kind and not about the human beings who accomplish them.

What is the use to me of the whole North German (American) culture if I see around me only fragmentary human beings—surly, loathsome fellows.

"Vienna does not progress." One should not answer to this that indeed it does. But rather: "Yes it does—unfortunately—and far too much!" If only we could recognize the profound emptiness of this god "progress," before which capitalism forces us to bow down! Rather, we should confess with all vehemence that we no longer wish to worship your "progress," which causes us to neglect our old gods. It is a destroyer of the best values. Because with a coarse hand—filled only with thoughts of utility—it strangles the great organic humanity that has grown up in us over the centuries. Vienna, too, is threatened by "progress," just as are Florence, Rome, and Paris. I spoke of Schönbrunn as a holy symbol of the highest culture: but one should view the city from there, and see how a gloomy modern proletarian district has thrust itself between them, offending every noble sentiment.

Do the Viennese really wish to invest their greatest pride in becoming "Berlin-American"?! To have traffic? A "nightlife"? To be "efficient"? They will never really be able to achieve these things. For the old cultural foundation still remains intact. And in order to give oneself up entirely to "modernity," in order to be totally impressed by the fact that a city railway train runs every two minutes: for this one would have to be completely devoid of all tradition, all culture, all qualities—just like the . . . New Yorker.

What does Vienna mean to us? We who live in the desert of modern technical culture?

Not merely the Sunday when we wish to recover from the misery of everyday life. Not only the loved one, who embodies for us all the delight of this life. More than that: Vienna is for us—to speak in a Kantian manner—the regulative cultural idea. We orient ourselves to Vienna and the Viennese manner when we wish to know what culture is. We fortify ourselves once again with Vienna when we are overcome by horror at the prospect of modern human development.

I fear, I really fear, that the disastrous current of modern pseudoculture is washing over Vienna, too, tearing down what we love, and destroying everything that we held dear. Just as it surges over Florence, over Paris, over Brussels. Then, of course, if it is a matter of which city has advanced the most, has the most industry, the busiest traffic, then Vienna will be left behind. Then it will be "backward." Yet everything that is good and valuable in us should stand up against this proletarian revaluation of all cultural values. Everything that is good and valuable in us should loudly declare again and again that culture is human creation, beauty, and harmony. Culture is the meaningful, tranquil life. Culture means Vienna.

And once this simple insight has become clear to us, those qualities that Vienna still possesses do not strike us as old-fashioned, but rather as expressions of the highest, and most admirable, ideal, which we should aspire to realize once again in the distant future. If underground railways, street cleaning, a bar for a thousand people, and good state governance were the ultimate goal of culture, it would not be worth a single shot of powder. [. . .]

9
Robert Walser
GOOD MORNING, GIANTESS!

First published as "Guten Tag, Riesin!" *Neue Rundschau* 15, no. 5 (May 1907), pp. 639–40. Translated by David Britt.

When some call of duty brings you out onto the city streets early in the morning, even before the trolley cars are running, it feels as if a giantess were shaking her locks and stretching a leg out of bed. There lie the streets, cold and white, like outstretched human arms; you walk, rub your hands together, and see people emerging from the gates and doorways of the buildings, like warm, burning saliva from the jaws of some impatient monster. You catch people's eyes as you walk along: girls' and men's eyes, troubled or bravely cheerful; legs walk along, behind and in front of you. For your own part, you leg it as best you can, and the look in your eyes is the same as that of everyone else. In every breast there lurks some sleepy secret, in every head some melancholy or inspiring thought. Splendid, splendid. On this cold, half-sunny, half-overcast morning, many, many people are still in their beds: revelers who have lived and adventured all through the night and halfway through the morning; high-born folks, for whom sleeping late is a way of life; slackers, who wake up twenty times, yawn, and start to snore again; the old and the sick, for whom getting out of bed has become either impossible or extremely laborious; women who have been making love; artists who say to themselves, "Get up? Hell, no"; the children of rich, handsome parents, fabulously groomed and protected beings who sleep on until nine, ten, or eleven in their own nurseries, with snow-white drapes on the windows, with their little mouths open, dreaming fairytale dreams. But at such an hour the maze of streets is swarming with housepainters (or maybe paperhangers); mail clerks; down-at-heel, small-time commission agents; people who want to catch an early train to Vienna, Munich, Paris, or Hamburg; little people mostly; working girls in every possible trade. In short, the gainfully employed. All this hectic activity compels the observer's admiration. As he walks along, he finds himself almost compelled to join

FIGURE 2. Sausage seller on the Schlossbrücke, 1906. Stadtmuseum Berlin, Nachlass Max Missmann, XI 22798.

in with the running, panting, and arm swinging; the haste and busyness are as infectious as a pretty smile can be. Well, not quite. There is more to the early morning than all this. Bars are still ejecting the last denizens of the night, in grubby clothes and with blotchy faces, onto the dazzling white, dusty street, where they stand for a while, cane hooked over shoulder, pestering passersby. How the night's drinking peers out of their bleary eyes! Press on. The blue-eyed miracle of early morning has no time for drunks. It holds a thousand glittering threads with which it draws you on; it nudges you from behind and lures you forward with a smile; you look upward and see a few scraps of blue in the white veil of cloud; you turn and look back at someone who interests you; you look aside at an ornate doorway, behind which some princely mansion resides in genteel lethargy. Statues beckon to you from gardens and parks; you keep walking, sparing a glance for all things whether fixed or movable: for lumbering cabs; for the first trolley cars, from which pairs of eyes stare down at you; for a policeman's dumb helmet; for a man with tattered shoes and trousers; for a man who must once have been well off but who now sweeps the streets in a fur-collared coat and a silk hat; you spare a glance for everyone, just as they momentarily look at you. The wonder of urban life is this: that individual attitudes and manners are lost among all these thousands of different variants; that sight is fleeting, judgment instantaneous, and forgetfulness automatic. Past. What was it that just went past? An Empire-style facade? Where? Back there? Can anyone bring himself to turn around, yet again, for just one more look at the architecture of the past? Oh, why bother. On, on. The chest swells; with sumptuous ease. The giantess Metropolis has now donned her shimmering, diaphanous petticoat. A giantess like this takes her time in dressing; but at every movement she fills the air with fragrance, vapor, impact. Cabs rattle and bumble past, with steamer trunks on their roofs; you are now in the park. Gray ice lingers on the still canals; the lawns strike a chill; the thin, sparse, bare trees send you on your way with a shiver. Handcarts are being pushed; a pair of lordly vehicles from the coach house of some highly placed person hurtle past, each bearing two coachmen and a footman. There is always something; and, before you can take a closer look, that something has always vanished from sight. Naturally, a multitude of thoughts occur to you in the course of this hourlong walk. Either you are a writer, and your hands can stay in the pockets of your (hopefully) respectable topcoat; or you are a painter, and on your morning walk you may well have worked out five paintings down to the last detail. In the course of the hour, you have been an aristocrat, a hero, a lion tamer, a socialist, an African explorer, a dancer, a gymnast, or a barkeeper; and for a moment you daydreamed that you had an audience with the Kaiser. He stepped down from his throne and engaged you in a half hour's confidential chat, in which Mrs. Kaiser may have joined. In your thoughts you have ridden the elevated railroad, lifted the laurel wreath from Dernburg's head,[1] married, and settled down in a Swiss village—on, on. Hello, who's that? Could it be—yes, it's your colleague Kitsch. So then you both went home together and drank chocolate.

NOTE

1. A reference to Heinrich Dernburg, an eminent professor of Roman and Prussian law, who died in 1907.

10

August Endell

THE BEAUTY OF THE GREAT CITY

First published as *Die Schönheit der großen Stadt* (Stuttgart: Strecker & Schröder, 1908), pp. 20–22, 51–53, 59–63, 82–85. Translated by David Britt.

THE GREAT CITY

As the most visible and perhaps most characteristic product of our present way of life, the most obvious single formulation of our deeds and aspirations, the great city has naturally always been the target of intemperate denunciation. It is seen as the symbol, the most forceful manifestation, of a culture that has turned away from all that is natural, simple, and naive. Here, to the horror of all right-thinking people, hedonistic license, neurotic haste, and repulsive degeneracy combine in a ghastly chaos. The city lures people to itself with fraudulent inducements, only to corrupt and enervate them, to make them feeble, selfish, and wicked. The city dweller is scorned as a person with no real home, no roots. Cities are denounced for their unspeakable ugliness, their dirt, their dismal courtyards, and their thick, foggy air. Such utterances, like so many others of the same kind, need hardly detain us—except that the city dweller himself insists on believing them; except that, for him, the very word *home* evokes dreams of some lowly farmhouse with a window glinting in the sunset, as so often seen onstage; and except that the lives of thousands are blighted by this kind of senseless talk. It is of course quite possible to look forward to the day when all cities will disappear from the face of the earth. For the time being, however, they exist. What is more, they must exist, if our whole economy is not to collapse. Hundreds of thousands have to live in cities; and instead of infecting those individuals with an unhealthy and hopeless nostalgia, it would be more sensible to teach them to take a proper look at their own city and to derive as much pleasure and as much strength as possible from their own surroundings—however little that may be in absolute terms.

We may readily admit that life in our major cities is more stressful, and more unhealthy, than in smaller localities and in the countryside. We may regret that the city dweller is becoming increasingly estranged from the soil, from plants, and from animals; and that this deprives him of many opportunities of happiness. We must also concede that the appearance of our buildings is mostly dismal, boring, lifeless, and at the same time pretentious and presumptuous; but this presents us with the task of building our cities differently, more spaciously, more decently, more artistically—and also with another task that is quicker and easier to perform: that of countering all those deficiencies by finding alternative sources of enjoyment.

For the astonishing fact of the matter is that, for anyone who has eyes to see, the city—for all its ugly buildings, its noise, its manifold shortcomings—is a miracle of beauty and poetry: a fairy tale more colorful, more prolific in formal invention, than any told by a poet; a home; a mother who every day lavishes new happiness on her children. This may sound like paradox or exaggeration. But anyone who is not blinded by prejudice, who knows how to submit to experience, whose response to the city is alert and perceptive, will soon enough perceive that its streets contain a thousand beauties, countless wonders, infinite riches, spread out before our very eyes and yet seen by so few. [. . .]

THE VEILS OF DAY

[. . .] *The fire wall.* Opposite my study window there is a lofty fire wall. From my desk, I can see nothing else. To see the sky, I have to walk right up to the window and crane my neck. The wall is not plastered; it is built of inferior bricks, some yellow, some reddish, with gray, irregular joints. But this wall is alive. Every change in the weather turns it into a different creature: gray, monotonous, and oppressive on dull days, full of life and movement on bright days. Then the red bricks shine out more brightly than normal, and all the irregularities of the brickwork stand out more clearly and lend it a grainy shimmer. Sometimes the sun comes out and lights up the higher part of the wall, which then becomes fiery and glowing above, and soft, delicate, bluish below. Between me and the wall (I live on the third floor), the tops of a few trees in the so-called garden extend their thin, glistening branches. In summer these sprout giant leaves—the tree wants to live, and it is the uppermost leaves that first absorb the energies from the sky—and their dark, saturated green stands out against the dull tones of the wall; but in the fall, when the leaves start to turn yellow, those that catch the sunlight shine out against the wall, which remains in shade; they shed a gentle radiance that makes the shadow look cool and bluish. And then, when the other leaves have reddened, there is a wonderfully delicate sight: the glowing red of the leaves against the softer red of the brick. Look out into the yard in late afternoon, when a thin mist enfolds the trees, and you seem to be in a magical land: the glowing, colored leaves hang in the darkening space against the shimmering violet of the wall, and around them, veiling and freeing them, the blue of the gathering twilight. Then winter comes, the leaves fall, and one day the topmost twig of the tallest tree, which is the only part to catch the sun, stands out as a ghostly, incomprehensible presence against the reddish and bluish shimmer of the wall, like a golden whorl.

THE VEILS OF NIGHT

Daylight casts a thousand colored veils; but night in the city casts far more. Starlight and moonlight are hardly ever seen to full effect; artificial light compensates by creating an infinity of effects of color. These begin to appear at dusk. It is a delight to watch, when, along the shimmering, bluish street, beneath a fading, roseate sky, in that subtle half-light that mutes all colors, the long lines of greenish gaslights emerge; barely visible at first, then as linked dots of color, and eventually, as darkness falls, as living sources of light. Slowly, darkness rises up the walls of the buildings, filling the street like liquid in a vessel; it is most dense at ground level. The glare against the deep blue sky helps to multiply the veils of shade below;

and in this sea of mists and shadows the perennial interplay of bright lights begins. They vary greatly, both in color and in intensity. The green and yellowish white of gas mantles, the mild blue of standard arc lamps, the red and orange of "Bremerlicht" [Bremer light] and of the newer types of arc lamp, the red and white of incandescent bulbs and of the new metal-filament lamps. Also the deep red and green of the signals. Every street has new arrangements and new contrasts to offer.

Hardenbergstrasse. Wondrously tranquil and grand: a wide street, such as Hardenbergstrasse, with just two rows of bluish arc lamps; the whole street, with its slight bend, in clear full light, unimpaired by the shrill clamor of storefront lighting. In the twilight the houses seem to fall back on either side, and the trees in the front yards take on a strange aspect that they never have in daytime; they look almost like hills of moss, with lighter green tips standing out against a deep black background. These dark green clouds lurk, ghostlike, in the nether depths of the front yards; but where the trees meet the street, and dense foliage overhangs the sidewalks, the jagged forms of the leaves catch the light from above. To the passerby beneath, they seem ringed with light; the effect is that of a luminous veil of lace, exquisitely beautiful in its dainty precision and dense, rich mobility. On the ground, fantastic networks of leaf shadows stand out in warm and delicate tones against the cool shimmer of the sidewalk.

On rainy days the picture is utterly changed. The street turns dark; the smooth, light gray of the asphalt becomes brownish, like milky coffee; its surface undulations glisten beneath the streetlights. The air fills with a fine, fresh mist, and the whole sky seems shrouded in a wondrous, bluish-violet veil.

A shopping street. The light on the narrower streets is different. The buildings close in, and the darkness seem tangible; in tree-lined streets, the upper stories are steeped in shimmering shadows that seem, to our dazzled eyes, to be bathed in a gentle light. The dry asphalt lies smooth and bright, with no reflections; only the glint of the streetcar tracks. Beneath the trees, away from the light of the lamps suspended along the middle of the street, the lower stories of the buildings, and the long rows of storefronts, emit a chaos of intense, brightly colored light, and the people on the street are turned into black shadows. The buildings that line the street seem to hang in midair; beneath them, light pours out as if from gaping jaws.

A side street. A quiet side street, on the other hand, gives an impression of darkness. On the shopping street, a corridor of light seems to run along the fronts of the buildings; here, by contrast, darkness fills the street, and the infrequent gaslights burn as if in little cages hollowed out of the air. Each casts an uncertain circle of light, but this extends barely a meter or two. From farther away they appear as bright dots. More powerful sources of light hollow out great luminous caverns in the air. And, when we enter these vaulted chambers, the light plays all around us, and it is as if we were enclosed by a transparent but clearly perceptible wall. It is particularly delightful to stand in one of these illuminated spaces and look out, as if through a veil, at the distant lights of another.

[. . .]

POTSDAMER PLATZ

Evening on Potsdamer Platz. The two tall lighting poles, with their sparkling, red arc lamps, hollow out a vast, pointed dome of light in the thick, heavy air. The openings of the side streets that run into the square are small and low; to the eye, Potsdamer Platz is almost an enclosed space. Potsdamer Strasse and Bellevuestrasse are particularly low, being lined with trees that meet to form a shallow vault. The crowns of the closest trees gleam in the harsh light, like green crags full of hollows; beyond, the giant masses of the linden trees on Leipziger Platz are dark, silent, distant mountains. The buildings around the square show delicate tones of red and violet. The sidewalk surges with humanity, and on the dry, bright asphalt, trolley cars and other vehicles surge past in a demonstration of eternal recurrence. Their tops catch the light; below, they are shrouded in darkness, which the glare seems to veil with a whitish mist. At times, the traffic becomes so dense that there is barely an inch of ground unoccupied, and those who cross the street seem to float on waves of wheels and horses' legs. And then a vehicle pulls up, with startling suddenness, right in front of the observer, and seems transformed as if by magic from a ghostly amalgam of gray and brown tones into a large, clear, palpable object. Then it is gone, and the visual field is suddenly filled by a horse's head, with nostrils flared—the beast is panting, with heaving flanks—and the profile of the head seems noble, like some bronze steed from antiquity. Then, all at once, the melee disperses, the little patch of asphalt in front of me seems to extend forever, and the dark mass of traffic gives way to a radiant brightness—which is then instantly swallowed up once more in the black tumult. In the harsh, unfamiliar light, the vehicles take on fantastic forms. A taxicab with a short wheelbase looks like a giant bumblebee. Beneath the massive, boxlike bodies of carriages, the spindly spokes of their wheels—made even thinner by their blackness—put me in mind of spiders' legs. The streetlights seem to float freely in space above the dark masses. And on the ground, beneath it all, a mad world of shadows eerily, tirelessly, flits across the pavement.

Outside the Brandenburg Gate. An evening in the fall, outside the Brandenburg Gate. The sunset has faded, and the sky has filled with the mysterious, penetrating blueness of twilight. The trees, already half denuded, form slightly reddish masses. Here, too, a pair of tall lighting poles dispense a harsh, red light, which is reflected from the lofty columns of the gate. Through the openings, Unter den Linden can be seen beyond, with its trees lit with a cool, bluish light and the shades of night

FIGURE 3. Brandenburg Gate, 1910. Stadtmuseum Berlin, Nachlass Max Missmann, IV 88/751 V.

rising above them. Only a few projecting bits of cornice on the two little gatehouses, caught in the red light that shines between the columns, stand out as anomalies against the blue background beyond the gate. The glare enshrouds the wide expanse of the square [Pariser Platz] in a reddish haze. The vehicles that converge on the gate seem to be crawling across the ocean bed. They have lost all tangible reality. They seem to consist of clouds, shadows, and light. In between, endless hordes are pouring out of the Tiergarten and crossing the square on their way home. There is no telling where the traffic ends and the people begin. Densely packed, the whole square looks like a single living thing. Not even the lumbering edifices of the trolley cars can break the spell, so powerful is the effect of light and atmosphere that enshrouds and unites everything on the square into a single vast, restless monster. A thousand cries fill the air, and yet it all seems hushed. The light muffles the noises; one is not aware of them. A monstrous presence broods over the square; it dwells on the array of marble balustrades and walls—so hideous in daylight—that line the shores of this sea of light. For on them, barely distinguishable in the light-filled mist, numberless human figures sit and stand at rest: a silent, wondering, solemn assembly. They confer on that vast arena a touch of true majesty, a sublime beauty and grandeur. This is as noble a sight as can be seen anywhere, as mighty in its address to the soul as the most powerful sensations known to us from the past.

11

Oscar Bie

LIFE STORY OF A STREET

First published as "Lebenslauf einer Strasse," *Neue Rundschau* 19, no. 3 (March 1908), p. 463. Translated by David Britt.

It starts out as Lutherstrasse, modest and middle-class, in the style of the 1880s. It is characteristic of many Berlin streets that they start modestly; in those days, nobody knew. Then it acquires a given name and continues as Martin-Luther-Strasse, in the pseudo-modern style of 1900. Ah, a splendid square, with a dominant corner building. Isn't that a fountain in front of it? No, an electric lighting post with a sandbox. Ah, a triangular intersection follows directly. This is spaciousness, the good old combination of two squares; rather South German, with curving streets ending in linked open spaces. Bravo. But who commands the rooftops? The everlasting sign of Grieneisen's, Berlin's "oldest" funeral parlor. Grieneisen I know by now. But what is that I see at the intersection? A fountain? It is a comfort station. And beyond the comfort station is the line of the great boulevard, with its central promenade. And, just where the promenade ends, on a slight rise, nestling prettily among trees, outlined against the sky, with open fields all around, we see a little old Wilmersdorf cottage with green shutters and a red roof, waiting for death.

12

Robert Walser

FRIEDRICHSTRASSE

First published as "Friedrichstrasse," *Neue Rundschau* 20, no. 8 (August 1909), pp. 1231–32. Translated by David Britt.

Above is a narrow strip of sky; the blackish ground beneath is smooth, as if polished by the friction of countless destinies. Bold, intricate, and fantastic, the buildings on either side ascend to architectural heights. The nervous air palpitates with cosmic life. Roof high, and higher, the advertisements soar and cling. Huge letters assail the eye. And there are always people walking. For as long as

FIGURE 4. Unter den Linden at the corner of Friedrichstrasse, 1908. Stadtmuseum Berlin, Nachlass Max Missmann, IV 69/472 V.

this street has existed, it has been bustling with life. Here is the heart, the breath of metropolitan life. Here life draws deep breaths, in and out, as if life itself were laboring under the pressure of its pace. Here we find the source, rivulet, stream, mighty river, and sea of movement. Here, movement and excitement never quite die down, and when life seems almost about to cease at the top end of the street, it starts up again at the bottom. Work and pleasure, vice and good intentions, effort and indolence, nobility and baseness, love and hate, fiery enthusiasm and scorn, gaudiness and simplicity, poverty and wealth—all shimmering, glittering, fooling, dreaming, hurrying, and stumbling on together in wild and helpless confusion. Here, some ultimate power restrains and soothes the passions; and here enticements without number lead directly to lustful temptations; so that the coat sleeve of abstinence brushes against the departing back of gratified lust; hot-eyed insatiability gazes into the tranquil eyes of wise self-satiation. Here, chasms yawn wide; here, indescribable anomalies hold absolute sway—not excluding an open indecency to which no reasonable person will object. Vehicles pass close to human bodies, heads, and hands; inside and on top of those vehicles, crammed tight and enslaved, people sit for whatever reason and allow themselves to be crushed and crammed and shipped along. Here, there is a good, right, intelligent, and incredibly prompt justification for any kind of stupidity whatever. Every folly here is ennobled and sanctified by the obvious difficulty of life itself. Every movement makes sense; every sound has a practical origin; every smile, gesture, or word conveys assent with an oddly appealing composure and correctness. Here, amid the pressure of the throng, the individual is under such duress that there is no denying assent to anything. No one seems to have any inclination to dissent, or any time to recoil, or any right to be upset; because here—and this is the magnificent thing—everyone feels an obligation to take things lightly and help things on their way, for neatness's sake, as it were. Every beggar, criminal, ruffian, or whatever is a fellow man; and for the time being—as everyone is so busy pushing, shoving, and pressing onward—all must be tolerated as part of the scene. This is the home of the ne'er-do-wells, the little people, not to say the very little people: those who at some stage have been dishonored. Here, tolerance reigns, for the simple reason that it takes time or trouble to be intolerant or disapproving. Here, people walk quietly in the sunshine, as if on some remote Alpine meadow; here they stroll elegantly beneath the lamplight as if through fairy-tale enchantments. It is wonderful to see how unstoppable, how perpetual is the two-way stream of humanity on the sidewalks, like a densely flowing, glinting stream of water, deep with meaning; and it is splendid to see how torments are mastered, dreams contained, inner fires damped down, joys suppressed, and desires held in check, because everyone is compelled to be considerate—lovingly, respectfully considerate—of others. Where human beings are crowded together in such close proximity, the notion of one's fellow man takes on a practical and readily understood meaning, and no one feels free to laugh too loudly, to attend too zealously to his personal causes of distress, or to be in too much of a hurry to do business—and yet how exhilarating the haste and speed, amid all the signs of pressure and preoccupation! Here, in a single hour, the sun shines on innumerable heads; the rain sprinkles and soaks ground that is, as it were, anointed with life's comedies and tragedies. And when dusk begins to fall, and the lights are lit, the curtain slowly rises on a play that is rich in all the same habits, lusts, and predicaments. Pleasure begins to sing her siren song, ecstatic and alluring; souls are torn by throbbing desires and failures of gratification; and money starts to be tossed around in a way that is beyond rational comprehension and indeed almost beyond the laborious efforts of a poet's imagination. A sensuous, breathing, bodily dream settles on the street; and all run after that prevailing dream, with faltering steps.

13

Max Weber
SPEECH FOR A DISCUSSION

First published as "Diskussionsrede" (1910); republished in Weber, *Gesammelte Aufsätze zur Soziologie und Sozialpolitik* (Tübingen: Mohr, 1988), pp. 453–54. Translated by David Frisby.

The issue as to whether modern technology [*Technik*], in the commonly understood sense of the word, stands in some relationship to formal-aesthetic values must be answered, in my opinion, in the affirmative. [. . .] Quite specific formal values in our modern artistic culture could indeed be born only due to the existence of the *modern metropolis;* the modern metropolis with its streetcars, subway, electrical and other lighting, shop windows, concert halls and restaurants, cafés, smokestacks, masses of stone, and all the wild dance of tones and impressions of color, the impressions that have their effect upon sexual fantasy, and the experiences of variations in psychic makeup—which affect the hungry rabble through all kinds of apparently inexhaustible possibilities of lifestyle and happiness. [. . .]

Quite distinctive formal values of modern painting [. . . and] their attainment would not have been possible for human beings who [had not experienced] the dynamic masses, the nighttime lights, and the reflections of the modern metropolis with its means of communication [. . .]. I believe that it is quite impossible for certain formal values of modern painting ever to have been realized without the impression, the absolutely distinctive impression made by the modern metropolis, hitherto never offered to human eyes before in the whole of history, forceful by day but totally overwhelming by night. And since what is visible—and this alone is of concern here—in each and every modern metropolis receives its specific quality *primarily* not from property relations and social constellations, but rather from modern technology, so here indeed is a point at which technology purely as such has a very far-reaching significance for artistic culture.

14

Vorwärts
[TOWN HALL TOWER PANORAMA]

First published in *Vorwärts*, 22 June 1902. Translated by Iain Boyd Whyte.

Some knowledge, which one more or less has to first laboriously seek out below and can acquire only through long observation, one can make one's own at a single viewing on the platform of the town hall [Rathaus] tower. For example, the forest of church-tower steeples and factory chimney stacks that confront us are

THE METROPOLITAN PANORAMA 45

FIGURE 5. Berlin Cathedral and Museum Island from the air, 1912. Landesarchiv Berlin, II, 13076.

immediately evident. This is an image from whose observation everyone can grasp—with their hands, as it were—that Berlin is an industrial city whose working population should be returned back into the churches. Whoever chooses to climb up the tower on a weekday will be immediately struck by something else as they view the factory chimney stacks. In the west they will notice very few of these giant smoking chimneys. The contrast between Berlin-West and Berlin-East is indeed itself striking enough. It already expresses itself so self-evidently in the differences in building density, in the mode of building, and so on that up here no one can totally fail to notice it. Even a stranger who knows nothing of the distinctive character of the individual city districts of Berlin, by walking around the pinnacle of the town hall tower would hardly be left in any doubt where the dwelling districts of the well-off and where the dwelling districts of those without means were to be found. If, however, the stranger is prepared to spare another couple of minutes penetrating with watchful eye through the thick mass of smoke that cuts off the path of the sun's rays themselves—a mass that hangs over a larger part of Berlin from the south and the southeast, above the east out to the northeast and the north—then it will be forcibly impressed upon him or her that one dwells and lives in the factory and workers' districts in a different manner than in the smart west.

A complete, unimpaired enjoyment in climbing the town hall tower is to be had only on Sundays. Then the mass of smoke that throughout the week lies above the dwelling districts of the working-class population is dispersed, allowing the eye to roam freely from all sides for miles beyond the municipal limits. Then the view extends freely and unhindered even in the east beyond the Treptower Park and the upper Spree as far as the Müggelberge.

15

Ernst Bloch

BERLIN, SOUTHERN CITY

First published as "Das südliche Berlin," *Zeit-Echo,* no. 15 (1915–16), pp. 235–38. Translated by David Britt.

It is hard to define the first appearance of the German middle classes. Retrospective efforts to discover their origins in the Peasant Wars, or in the Meistersinger, or in traditional arts and crafts probably have no bearing on ordinary life. But as soon as they begin to come to the fore, and particularly in the Biedermeier period, when the middle classes (not yet the bourgeoisie) exerted a defining influence on social and artistic life, there appears an image of such winning, feminine charm and such thoughtful enthusiasm—even in the average run of men—that we are at least entitled to wish that we could define the period in question as setting the tone of German middle-class-ness. There it was, colorful, gracious, blooming, not at all impoverished, beautifully in harmony with a still entirely agrarian countryside and with little steep-roofed cities. The inner life is still more resplendent: river rapids, quaint streets, and turquoise skies were the decor of the German soul. Not even the vilest political oppression could prevent the nation from being, in this way, a part of nature. Then came the unified Reich and the "founding years" [of the 1870s]. Bourgeois life, with its all-consuming, calculating utilitarianism—the purely mercenary existence, devoid of love, mirth, childishness, spontaneity, or any ability to appreciate the irrational as anything but a joke or an idle fancy—led to that overly practical cast of mind that turns everything into a machine and, like a machine, eventually breaks down. This, together with all those knights in shining armor, hand on sword hilt, ready to answer their nation's call, has brought about a state of affairs in which almost no nonpartisan individuals are prepared to show their faces anywhere in the world. [. . .] We need the West in order to be German. The Germany of our longings is with us, wherever we go; it is everywhere, deep down, in all intense color and in the spirit of color. Here we see Genoa and Paris, San Francisco, too; in our hearts we see those blue skies and that easy,

FIGURE 6. Blücherplatz and Hallesches Tor, 1907. Stadtmuseum Berlin, Nachlass Max Missmann, IV 64/3396 V.

colorful, melodious Mediterranean culture as if illuminated by the northern lights. Latin culture in its wider sense is itself a journey undertaken in friendship and comradeship—there are outstretched arms out there—to assist us toward our own a priori knowledge. The people know this; but only the intellectuals are aware of the Russian element within us. Russia manifests itself invisibly, at a far greater depth; although it makes an even more natural scaffolding on which to reconstruct the primal German identity.

Now, it appears that Berlin, in a very strange way, was heading toward a newly full life, discarding some of the grayness of our formal existence. Earlier, the hope had been that Munich would achieve this; earlier still, Vienna. Those are cities where the air is more southern, more in sympathy with the freedom within our souls; but the former has failed to progress beyond imported studio bric-a-brac, and the latter, for all its peasant and Balkan connections, is neither essentially nor—as it were—seriously lighthearted. Whereas in Berlin, with its fast-moving, eventful business life and its taste for circus rather than operetta, there is a streak of fantasy, which, despite the bleak and stony look of the place and the crude vitality of its excesses, nevertheless has in it something of the South: the longed-for, fertile, sentimental South, an inborn exoticism full of color and erotic visions. This city—in keeping with the ambivalent soul of the modern German entrepreneur—is a place of Columbus-like discovery. But if this trend toward freshness, color, and festivity were ever to become strong enough to arouse its slumbering counterparts in southern and western Germany—the ready friendship, the old capacity for love, the old mysterious breadth of mind, the vast speculative capacity, lightning-swift from rise to set of sun; compared with which all Latin fire is not so much as a will-o'-the-wisp—then, indeed, this remote, colonial city might become a possible capital. Not by lapsing into envy of the cultural traditions of the older, princely capitals, but by remaining a showplace, an exhibition city. Berlin can combine its inquisitive, experimental, enterprising nature with something newly vivid and colorful: a long-term change of direction. These are two phials from which one day a powerful potion might be mixed.

2

BUILDING AND REGULATING THE METROPOLIS

Addressing the "Union Parliament" in Erfurt in 1850, Otto von Bismarck railed against the big cities as cauldrons of revolution. A couple of years later in the Prussian parliament he proposed an even more extreme response to the increasing political radicalization of the cities: "Should the great cities rebel once again, the Prussian people will know how to bring them to heel, even if it means wiping them off the face of the earth." Bismarck was appointed the first chancellor of the new German state in 1871, with Berlin as its capital. This was not a propitious starting point, and Berlin singularly failed to grapple with the city planning questions that emerged both from the rapid population expansion in the last decades of the century and from the need for a greatly expanded collection of monumental public and commercial buildings that came with the city's new status. As the critic Karl Scheffler bemoaned early in the new century: "Never in the history of building had a such a vigorously ascendant nation shown itself so completely unable to cope with the task of city building."[1]

The only partially successful attempt to order the rapidly expanding city was the Hobrecht plan of 1862. James Hobrecht had been commissioned by the Prussian Ministry of the Interior to work out a plan for Berlin and its neighboring western extension, Charlottenburg, for a road system that would define the roads, the house lines, and the pattern for gas mains and sewers. His plan called for two major ring roads linked by radials. It was a structure plan rather than a building plan, and offered only the most basic outline of how the blocks should be filled in: notionally with bourgeois housing on the street front and less affluent housing in courtyards behind. The building controls were minimal, merely specifying a twenty-meter cornice height for domestic architecture, and a minimum internal courtyard size of 5.34 by 5.34 meters, so that the fire pumps could turn around. Beyond the Hobrecht plan and the pragmatic regulations on house and yard dimensions, there was no comprehensive planning strategy for the new capital of the unified German state. It is indicative that an integrated sewage system for Berlin was implemented only after 1893, in response to a series of typhus scares.

The lack of a comprehensive planning strategy for the city reflected the fragmented nature of the local government structure. In spite of attempts stretching back to the 1820s to address this problem, its resolution was not achieved until a century later, in October 1920, when the seven major townships, fifty-nine rural areas, and twenty-seven estate districts surrounding Berlin, together with the land on which the royal palaces were sited, were joined into a unitary authority named Groß-Berlin (Greater Berlin). Prior to that, the implementation of planning and traffic controls, and of building regulations, was left to these many individual town and rural councils. While this left Berlin and its environs at the mercy of the developers and speculators, in suited several vested interests. The conservative Prussian state had little interest in ceding a large part of Brandenburg to Berlin, which was turning increasingly social democratic in its politics. Similarly, the rich townships to the south and west of the city like Charlottenburg and Wilmersdorf, where social costs and rates were low, had no desire to subsidize the poor quarters in the city center or the industrial suburbs to the north and east.

When it finally appeared, the initiative for a comprehensive plan emerged not from governmental circles but from architectural interest groups, and in particular two architects' associations—the Vereinigung Berliner Architekten, and the Architekten-Verein zu Berlin—which established the Ausschuß Groß-Berlin (Committee for Greater Berlin) in 1906. This resulted in 1907 in a set of guidelines for the urban development of Greater Berlin that addressed not only the obvious issues of health and traffic, but also the monumental impression to which the city should aspire. One year later, on 15 October 1908, a "Competition for a Plan for the Development of Greater Berlin" was announced. While the competition specified that engineers should be involved in drawing up the proposals, a recurring theme in the vigorous debates launched by the competition was the need to restore pride and decorum to the capital city. As the editor of the *Architektonische Rundschau* insisted in 1908: "It is time that the artistic task of public buildings is seen as being as ambitious and serious as the dignity of a great society, a reflection of the cultural roles and obligations, and in the spirit of our forefathers."[2] The invocation of the forefathers reflected the lingering influence of the romantic and picturesque school of city design, which had originated with Camillo Sitte in Vienna. In Germany it was supported and attacked, with equal vigor, by two of the lions of urban design, Karl Henrici and Joseph Stübben: the former supporting the picturesque position, the latter arguing for rational and pragmatic planning, designed to meet the demands of the mechanized age. The passion of this debate can be judged from a review by Henrici of Stübben's canonical text *Der Städtebau* (City building), in which Henrici argues that "[in] Stübben's study, we find the following statement: 'Urban streets, like country roads, are primarily lines of communication, they are only secondarily there for the construction of houses.' This is the basic principle of modern systems of urban construction. But at the same time it is deleterious and detestable in the extreme, for it creates an antagonism between the interests of communication and commerce on one hand, and ideal interests on the other hand—that is to say, any interest in comfortable, contented living and in art."[3] The division between the urban rationalists and engineers and those more committed to visual delight in the city can also be seen in the entries to the 1910 Greater Berlin Competition, the results of which were announced in March 1910. The jury's favor generally went to those schemes that were grounded in the possible rather than the ideal, and the most dramatic scheme in terms of its visual impact, by Bruno Schmitz and colleagues, came in only fourth.[4] This was the project, however, that had the most lasting impact on future master plans for Berlin, not least that by Albert Speer, commissioned by Adolf Hitler in 1937.

While the 1910 competition stimulated a broad spectrum of proposals on how best Berlin might be planned and regulated, no built results issued from it. Less tangible but nonetheless significant, however, was the founding in January 1912 of the Zweckverband Groß-Berlin (The Greater Berlin Administrative Union), which covered Berlin itself and two of the prosperous western townships, Charlottenburg and Wilmersdorf. Although ostensibly responsible for traffic, large-scale development, and recreational areas, it had little actual power, and its principal achievement was the purchase and protection of the wooded areas to the west of the city, including the Grunewald. It was by no means representative of the whole city, however, and the vision of a Berlin city council whose authority extended across the whole metropolitan area had to wait until 1920 for its realization.

NOTES

1. Karl Scheffler, *Berlin: Ein Stadtschicksal,* 2nd ed. (Berlin: Reiss, 1910), p. 179.

2. Carl Zetzsche, "Das öffentliche Gebäude im Stadtbild," *Architektonische Rundschau* 24, no. 10 (1908), p. 75; cited (in English translation) in Wolfgang Sonne, *Representing the State: Capital Planning in the Early Twentieth Century* (Munich: Prestel, 2003), p. 109.

3. Karl Henrici, "Gedanken über das moderne Städte-Bausystem," *Deutsche Bauzeitung* 25, nos. 14, 15 (18, 21 February 1891), pp. 81–83, 86–88, 90–91; this passage, p. 86.

4. For a full account of the competition, see Sonne, *Representing the State,* pp. 104–23.

16
Theodor Goecke
TRAFFIC THOROUGHFARES AND RESIDENTIAL STREETS

First published as "Verkehrstrasse und Wohnstrasse," *Preußische Jahrbücher* 73 (1893), pp. 85–104. Translated by Fiona Elliot.

Without the goodwill of the authorities, nothing can be achieved, and this goodwill must mean first and foremost that when there is a particular need of some kind, suitable streets must be included in the development plan. Narrow streets, small houses—back to the Middle Ages! What then of the cities that have developed across the world in this modern age? Wide streets, large buildings—a clear path for the traffic, that is today's solution! It has brought undeniable benefits, but with the benefits have also come the huge, undivided, towering blocks of housing. Air and light are no more than catchwords if they only fill the streets and plazas but are denied to people in their homes; the excessive width of the blocks of housing has gradually led to ever more rear apartments, backyard apartments, and so-called garden flats; in the districts that were constructed according to the regulations that applied until 1887 it has led to generally enclosed yards, air and light shafts in the midst of built-up blocks—veritable air and light chimneys, you might say. The regulations that subsequently came into force, stipulating more generous living conditions, ensure an ample supply of air and light. But even these appear unequal and inadequate where the population is denser; the little people are exclusively relegated to the rear apartments. In addition to this, even the friendliest yard is still a yard, a place that we have a low opinion of as an abode; and the euphemistically named garden is no different. In fact, if we compare medieval town layouts with modern development schemes—the difference could scarcely be greater. However, it would be wrong to assume that the difference constitutes progress in every respect. Admittedly the former contain fewer broad streets than the latter, more so in the east of Germany than in the west; even the main traffic routes are narrow. We cannot go into the reasons for this here. But besides the few traffic thoroughfares, the plans of medieval towns also contain a high number of what are obviously residential streets that divide the town into so many small blocks that even the humblest citizen could have a house toward the front. Deep blocks were built only to accommodate trade premises or the stores behind the homes of important merchants. The relative density of many towns was alleviated by the gaps that formed lanes linking the yards. What can still be achieved by such gaps today is shown by the houses in Landgrafen-, Rauch- and Regentenstrasse. The excessive widths prescribed by the new building regulations may be held accountable for the fact that such gaps between buildings have fallen out of favor. This seems all the more regrettable in that the greater height of modern houses demands more effective ventilation of the yards. The difference between the older and the newer style of civic building thus proves, in terms of living conditions, to be regressive. Nothing is further from our intentions here than to heap praise on the nooks and crannies of our forefathers, or to suggest that they should be imitated. Nothing should be relinquished regarding the needs, as far as we can see them, of traffic and of retail establishments and so forth; but we should nevertheless take the good where we find it and seek to incorporate it into our modern achievements. Residential oases in a desert of traffic are today reserved for the top ten thousand only. [. . .] The expansion plan has to be individualized; we have to rid ourselves of a schematic approach that has left us with a wide-meshed net of uniform streets. Manufacturing areas need different buildings from those in residential areas, and large apartments need a different style from smaller ones, as do public buildings compared with private residences. The decision as to the future use of building land is generally already made by the natural lie of the land, the position of any water flows, train tracks, and country roads. The positioning of freight harbors, branch lines, canals, and storage depots will further help to point the way for any planned developments. And the workers need to be able to live near the factories, workshops, and loading bays. There should be no more talk of mixing all professions and occupations in view of the fact that large areas of workers' housing have—as it were, unnoticed—already emerged and continue to do so. In the case of such areas there should be special building restrictions, to take account of the fact that the air there is more heavily polluted than elsewhere by smoke, soot, and dust. However, the main point is to open up residential areas with residential streets; currently the majority of residents are confined to the internal and back yards; a large number of those in a position to do so are prevented from acquiring a plot of their own—this cannot be regarded as a natural situation.

Thus the following points that characterize the dominant system of civic design should be thoroughly investigated and fundamentally rethought:

1. With respect to the organization and formation of streets and plazas in towns and rural communities, the regulations regarding the preparation of perspectival and development plans (which became law on 2 July 1875) recommend the following street widths—as limits beyond which no building is allowed:
    a. Streets that, as main traffic arteries, may be expected to see lively, through-moving traffic, should not be less than thirty meters.
    b. Lateral thoroughfares of some considerable length, not less than twenty meters.
    c. All other streets should not be less than twelve meters.
   It was felt that these three rubrics would be sufficient to accommodate all the

multifarious needs of city planning. But it has been a long time since Berlin constructed any streets of twelve meters in width—that is to say, it has been trapped by the first two rubrics, which make a distinction only between main and side streets. Residential streets as such are completely lacking.

2. The hygienists locked into the same scheme have repeatedly laid down similar, even more stringent conditions with respect to minimum allowable street widths. Wide streets are expensive: they burden the adjacent plots with high costs that have to be recouped somewhere else; therefore there is a more intense exploitation of the plot and—since exploitation is more effective the bigger, and especially the deeper a block—the width of the block is also increased. But is that not the opposite of what matters of hygiene would demand? The subsequent subdivision of the block by residential streets thus becomes a necessity.

3. The local statute of the Municipality of Berlin regarding development, foundations, drainage, and lighting provision requires that all side streets should be paved throughout with so-called paving stones, third class. The price, according to the municipal ruling, is to be thirteen marks per square meter. For the underground drainage system the average charge is fifty marks per meter of building frontage. Clearly these decisions can be implemented only where the building method is relatively uniform, and they in effect hinder any more individual developments. The surfacing of residential streets should not be measured against the standards of the main traffic routes, and the drainage costs calculated for an uninterrupted housing block according to the frontage of the plot and other fixed costs should be adjusted to take account of the new dimensions of retrospectively subdivided plots.

4. Building regulations are applied to the existing circumstances; since they make no difference between the old town that evolved earlier and the constantly emerging suburbs, they, too, play into the hands of a general trend toward uniformity. They ought to be relaxed for the construction of housing in residential streets; indeed, the building regulations ought to be graded according to the purpose of the different districts, as has been attempted—albeit somewhat tentatively—in the case of the building regulations for the suburbs. For when they were laid down, the view prevailed that for the building authorities to function there had to be a certain uniformity in the regulations both internally and externally. And the administrative zeal evident in these even went so far as to declare that the merging of yards and the gaps between buildings, even though it had been entered into the property register, could not affect the implementation of building regulations because such agreements were not a matter of public law. And yet, despite this, the development of a whole district of the city—namely, the Hansa quarter behind

Schloss Bellevue—is founded on just such building regulations laid down by a civil court, thereby in practice resisting the all too pedantic interpretation of these things.

5. It is not only the need for air and light that has led to our modern streets, but also a preference for straight lines, for broad thoroughfares stretching as far as possible into the distance—with trees standing to attention in rank and file—whatever the case with a far distant *point de vue*. Barren spaces are considered tasteful, endless perspectives magnificent. The opinions of those seeking to emulate the art of antiquity are still well represented, but will have to at last step aside in light of the unstoppable changes being wrought in our view of things artistic in general.

There are ever more signs that the sole dominance of the old city-planning systems is being challenged. It will collapse due to its narrow-mindedness, like all things that are based almost exclusively on a sharp intellect. The might of the human spirit seeks to enter once again into the plans we make for our cities.

17

Rudolf Adickes

THE NEED FOR SPACIOUS BUILDING PROGRAMS IN CITY EXPANSIONS AND THE LEGAL AND TECHNICAL MEANS TO ACCOMPLISH THIS

First published as "Die Nothwendigkeit weiträumiger Bebauung bei Stadterweiterungen und die rechtlichen und technischen Mittel zu ihrer Ausführung: Leitsätze," *Deutsche Vierteljahresschrift für öffentliche Gesundheitspflege* 27 (1895), pp. 101–11. Translated by Fiona Elliot.

Reporting on their findings, Chief Burgomaster Adickes, Government Surveyor of Works Hinckeldeyn, and Inspector of Buildings Classen set out the following.

Guidelines:

1. The dense crowding of the population into rented tenements that is common in many German cities—as opposed to cities in other countries, such as England—endangers people's health, is detrimental to family life, and makes the acquisition of land and property of their own impossible.
2. Therefore, the introduction of more spacious building programs and the removal of the obstacles preventing this should be recognized as an urgent need.
3. The aforesaid *obstacles* are predominantly:
   a) The division of building land, as laid down in the development plans, into

excessively deep blocks, which in turn invite the construction of dwellings at the rear and in the yards.
  b) The approval of excessively wide streets solely intended to subdivide the interior of the block and the burden this places on the adjacent properties.
  c) The disproportionately high costs for road building and drainage systems that are calculated solely according to length of frontage, often without taking into account the number of stories and apartments.
  d) The application of building regulations (that are necessary and expedient for large buildings with several stories) to small houses with only a few stories.
  e) The inordinately high price of land in city expansion areas, due to the building regulations that allow the same level of exploitation for the land in the new districts as in the inner city.
  f) The lack of building regulations designed to protect smaller homes and gardens from the disadvantages that ensue from the construction of higher and deeper buildings next door.
4. For *the removal of these obstacles,* the following measures are recommended:
  a) In order to lessen the excessive exploitation of building land through the construction of buildings at the rear and in the yards—and insofar as building regulations (see 4.e) do not already adequately restrict such exploitation—the land set aside for residential properties should be divided into blocks of a depth that, without disproportionately sacrificing building land, can be sufficiently exploited primarily through the construction of "front houses."
  b) The streets that serve purely to subdivide the block, without having to accommodate a greater volume of traffic, should be constructed to a suitable moderate width.
  In many cases it is desirable to set the house fronts back from the street itself in order to allow for front gardens, lawns, and trees.
  c) In the streets mentioned under b) the street surfaces, the pavements, and the drainage systems should be kept as simple and inexpensive as possible. In the distribution of costs among the adjacent properties for the purchase of the land, as well as for the paving and drainage systems, the level of exploitation of the plots is, as far as practical, to be taken into account.
  d) Building regulations for smaller buildings with only a few stories should be appropriately moderated with regard to construction, stairs, and so on in comparison to those for larger buildings.
  e) Wherever land prices or the existing extent of building allows, building regulations should be drawn up as soon as possible restricting the exploitation of building land and the heights of buildings, so that this land cannot be given over to the speculative building of tenement blocks for rent, rather that the construction of houses with a small number of apartments

should be encouraged, and these should then be protected as such on a permanent basis.

18

Vorwärts
[DEFORESTATION AROUND BERLIN]

First published in *Vorwärts*, 16 August 1908. Translated by David Frisby.

Instead of planting new forests, the environs of Berlin are being deforested even further. The Hochwald, which extended from Lichtenrade to beyond Klein-Beeren and was known under the name of "Birkholzer Domforst," has disappeared. With the agreement of the government, the magnificent Hochwald was sold and destroyed by the wood merchant. Now the Hasenheide is suffering the same fate. And next in line will be the Königsheide. A start has already been made. More than a hundred acres have already been laid bare, and the Wuhlheide will also soon disappear. Large sections have already been divided up for gas and water works, and as building sites by the adjacent communities. [. . .]

Wherever one goes, it is the same picture everywhere. One section after the other has been felled in the Grunewald, which could still be reached on foot from Berlin a few years ago. At that time, one could still wander around the Halensee. And today? Charlottenburg has acquired half of the Jungfernheide, while the remainder is already earmarked for a factory and a section has already been built upon. The Zehlendorf forest is fenced in, and it is said that now the eastern banks of Krumme Lanke are to be sold off for the purposes of building. If things continue to proceed in this manner, in fifteen years' time the surrounding countryside will be spoiled, the Tempelhofer Feld will be surrendered to land speculation, the Tiergarten will become a garden without animals but with hundreds of monuments that no one takes any notice of, the Grunewald will be a meadow for birds, the Schönholzer Heide will be a barracks, the Jungfernheide will be a factory city with countless chimney stacks, the Müggelberge will be a second Westend, and so on, and so on—and only the names will still recall the past.

19

Die Bank
[SPECULATION IN TEMPELHOF]

First published in *Die Bank* 2 (1910–11). Translated by David Frisby.

Since the [Tempelhofer] Feld belongs to the village community of Tempelhof, the necessary precondition for this [development] plan was [. . .] the removal of Tempelhof from the provincial district of Teltow and its incorporation into Berlin.

But the political wisdom had a different view of this. The incorporation of Tempelhof would mean not merely the surrender of a newly emergent district [*Gemeinde*] to self-administration and weakening of the governing organs present in the provincial district, but also and above all—and this was the decisive element—the collapse of the plans directed at the fiscal cleaning up of the provincial district of Teltow.

It is an open secret that the district of Teltow, as a result of its failed speculation with the Teltow Canal, has difficulty in satisfying its financial obligations. The canal project, which proved itself so thoroughly lucrative for a very small number of private individuals, has become for the overwhelming majority of inhabitants in the provincial district an unpleasant swindle. Now influential people in the district behave like foolhardy gamblers. They double the stakes in order to make good their losses. It was their pressure that was primarily responsible for the fact that the village community of Tempelhof emerged as co-applicant for the [Tempelhofer] Feld, and as a consequence of this laid a commitment of roughly 100 million [marks] upon the shoulders of its citizens. They gambled on the fact that so much could be extracted from the Tempelhofer Feld, through taxes on turnover and taxes according to common value, that the district could again set to rights its disorderly finances. Hence the lighthearted adoption of a risk that would render every private individual in danger of being declared incapable of managing their financial affairs. The fact that this risk is not merely of a nominal nature is evident from the contract to which the community of Tempelhof has agreed with the Deutsche Bank. In accordance with this, the bank (together with its subordinate participant, the Dresdner Bank) is placing at the disposal of Tempelhof the means to purchase the field and undertake its development. In addition, the provincial district of Teltow is reimbursed for the citizens' commitment entered into, but only up to a maximum of 25 percent. A limitation that says a great deal!

The social side of this state of affairs gives the observer no less to ponder. Very recently in Greater Berlin an exhibition of dwellings took place that one hoped would have given a fruitful impetus to the debate on the nature of urban housing. The exhibition was indicative of the struggle against the rental barracks, the mass grave of the people's health, in which the military administration should have a special interest. It is well known that of the recruits in Berlin only 24 percent were found to be militarily able-bodied, compared with 54 percent from the country. This latter consideration has not prevented those in responsible positions from surrendering the Tempelhofer Feld to private speculation and thus to the rental-barracks system. Due to the high price paid, to which must be added the adjustment costs, and the profits of the big banks that stand behind Tempelhof, an alternative form of building is out of the question. Hence, on the last major land reserve in the immediate vicinity of Berlin, the promotion of the five-story housing form is given new encouragement, and at the same time the only recreational site of southern Greater Berlin, which as everyone knows is totally devoid of forest, disappears from the map.

20
P. A. A. [Philip A. Ashworth]
BERLIN
Encyclopedia Britannica, 11th ed. (Cambridge: Cambridge University Press, 1911), vol. 3, pp. 785–86.

Berlin is essentially a modern city, the quaint two-storied houses, which formerly characterized it, having given place to palatial business blocks, which somewhat dwarf the streets and squares, which once had an air of stately spaciousness. The bustle of the modern commercial city has superseded the austere dignity of the old Prussian capital. Thus the stranger entering it for the first time will find little to remind him of its past history. The oldest part of Berlin, the city and Alt-Kölln, built along the arms of the Spree, is, together with that portion of the town lying immediately west, the centre of business activity. The west end and the south-west are the residential quarters, the north-west is largely occupied by academic, scientific and military institutions, the north is the seat of machinery works, the north-east of the woollen manufactures, the east and south-east of the dyeing, furniture and metal industries, while in the south are great barracks and railway works.

[. . .]

The effect upon Berlin of the successful issue of the Franco-Prussian War of 1870–71 was electrical. The old Prussian capital girded itself at once to fulfill its new role. The concentration upon the city of a large garrison flushed with victory, and eager to emulate the vanquished foe in works of peace, and vie with them in luxury, was an incentive to Berliners to put forth all their energy. Besides the military, a tremendous immigration of civilian officials took place as the result of the new conditions, and, as accommodation was not readily available, rents rose to an enormous figure. Doubts were often expressed whether the capital would be able to bear the burden of empire, so enormous was the influx of new citizens. It is due to the magnificent services of the municipal council that the city was enabled to assimilate the hosts of newcomers, and it is to its indefatigable exertions that Berlin has in point of organization become the model city of Europe. In no other has public money been expended with such enlightened discretion, and in no other has the municipal system kept pace with such rapid growth and displayed greater resource in emergencies. In 1870 the sanitary conditions of Berlin were the worst of any city of Europe. It needed a [Rudolf] Virchow to open the

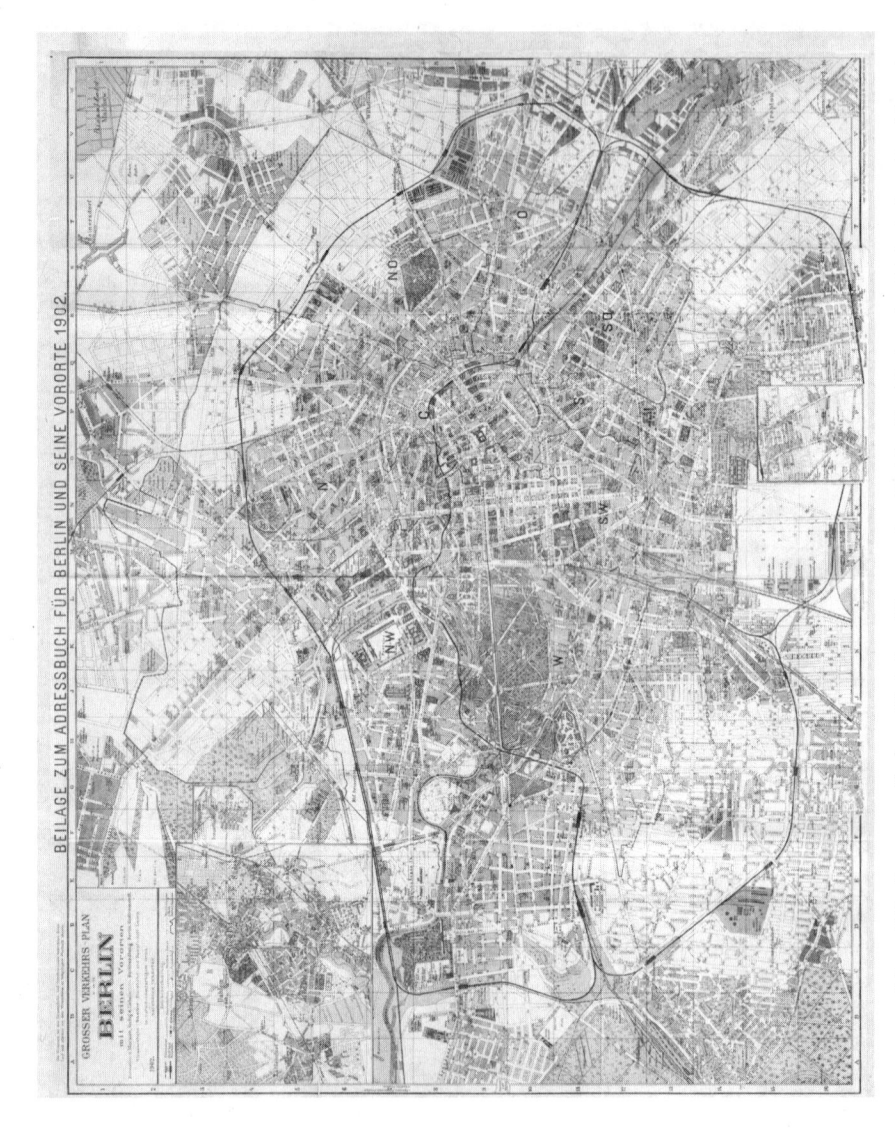

FIGURE 7. Map of Berlin, 1902. *Grosser Verkehrs-Plan von Berlin* (Berlin: Verlag der Liebelschen Buchhandlung, 1902).

eyes of the municipality to the terrible waste of life such a state of things entailed. But open sewers, public pumps, cobble-paved roads, open market-places and overcrowded subterranean dwellings are now abolished. The city is excellently drained, well-paved, well-lighted and furnished with an abundant supply of filtered water, while the cellar dwellings have given place to light and airy tenements, and Berlin justly claims to rank among the cleanest and healthiest capitals in Europe. The year 1878 marks a fresh starting-point in the development of the city. In that year Berlin was the meeting-place of the congress which bears its name. The recognition of Germany as a leading factor in the world's counsels had been given, and the people of Berlin could indulge in the task of embellishing the capital in a manner befitting its position. From this time forward, state, municipal and private enterprise have worked hand in hand to make the capital cosmopolitan. The position it has at length attained is due not alone to the enterprise of its citizens and the municipality. The brilliancy of the court and the triumph of the sense of unity in the German nation over the particularism of the smaller German states have conduced more than all else to bring about this result. It has become the chief pleasure town of Germany; and though the standard of morality, owing to the enormous influx of people bent on amusement, has become lower, yet there is so much healthy, strenuous activity in intellectual life and commercial rivalry as to entitle it, despite many moral deficiencies, to be regarded as the centre of life and learning in Germany. Dr A. Shadwell (*Industrial Efficiency*, London, 1906) describes it as representing "the most complete application of science, order and method of public life," adding "it is a marvel of civic administration, the most modern and most perfectly organized city that there is." *Streets.* The social and official life of the capital centres round Unter den Linden, which runs from the royal palace to the Brandenburger Tor. This street, one of the finest and most spacious in Europe, nearly a mile in length, its double avenue divided by a favourite promenade, planted with lime trees, presents Berlin life in all its varying aspects. Many historical events have taken place in this famous boulevard, notably the entry of the troops in 1871, and the funeral pageant of the emperor William I. South of Unter den Linden lies the Friedrichstadt, with its parallel lines of straight streets, including the Behrenstrasse—(the seat of finance)—the Wilhelmstrasse, with the palace of the imperial chancellor, the British embassy, and many government offices—the official quarter of the capital—and the busy Leipziger Strasse, running from the Potsdamer Platz to the Dönhoffplatz. This great artery and Unter den Linden are crossed at right angles by the Friedrichstrasse, 2 m. long, flanked by attractive shops and restaurants, among them the beer palaces of the great breweries. In the city proper, the Königstrasse and the Kaiser-Wilhelm-Strasse, the latter a continuation of Unter den Linden, are the chief streets; while in the fashionable south-west quarter Viktoriastrasse, Bellevuestrasse, Potsdamer Strasse and Kurfürstenstrasse and the Kurfürstendamm are the most imposing.

Among the most important public squares are the Opernplatz, around or near which stand the opera house, the royal library, the university and the armoury; the Gendarmenmarkt, with the royal theatre in its centre, the Schlossplatz; the Lustgarten, between the north side of the royal palace, the cathedral and the old and new museums; the Pariser Platz with the French embassy, at the Brandenburg Gate; the Königsplatz, with the column of Victory, the Reichstagsgebäude and the Bismarck and Moltke monuments; the Wilhelmsplatz; the circular Belle-Alliance-Platz, with a column commemorating the battle of Waterloo; and, in the western district, the spacious Lützowplatz.

21

Walter Lewitz

ARCHITECTURAL NOTES ON THE UNIVERSAL URBAN PLANNING EXHIBITION, BERLIN

First published as "Architektonisches von der allgemeinen Städtebau-Ausstellung zu Berlin," *Berliner Architekturwelt* 13 (1911), pp. 123–25. Translated by David Britt.

[. . .] *The Greater Berlin Competition.* One of the objectives, aside from the solution of traffic and housing problems, was to give the right artistic expression to the modern metropolis, the capital of the new German Reich, and thus—while opening up previously undeveloped areas of land—to make proposals for the improvement and remodeling of the inner city. Of all the work submitted, the most immediately fascinating is Bruno Schmitz's spirited rendering of the metropolis of the future.[1] In his large charcoal drawings, one does not know what to admire more: the imagination that gave rise to them, or the patient industry and artistic refinement with which they are executed down to the last detail. Here he shows us an image of the Berlin of his dreams, while basing himself firmly on the realistic foundation of a competent and highly professional traffic project. By shifting the Potsdam Station some way down the line and the Anhalt Station to one side, he gains a sizable area of ground, which he develops on a truly grand scale; so that here, in the heart of an existing city, he creates new cityscapes without the necessity of major new thoroughfares or costly clearances. (The remodeling of Leipziger Platz, which would entail considerable cost, is not an essential part of the project.) The same applies to his Forum of Art, on the site currently occupied by the Rail Finance and Revenue Office, and to his monumental public park on the site of the Moabit parade ground. His ambitious southward extension of Friedrichstrasse would probably be more difficult to execute. All of these proposals are of an architectural distinction that places them among the finest achievements in the entire Urban Planning Exhibition. The work is weighty and serious, entirely original in form, and yet not recherché. It might be objected that it is all too high-flown and too rhetorical, and that no single city could bear such a concentrated weight of monumental expression; but, after all, the artist intends this simply as a stimulus and as an eye-opener. In practice, the presence of the citizens, going about their daily business, would naturally mitigate any unduly solemn or forbidding effect.

[Bruno] Möhring's mature and sensitively conceived cityscapes are on the same high level of artistic achievement as Schmitz's powerful fantasies.[2] They are, however, conceived in an entirely different spirit. Möhring sets out to cherish and extend the historic configuration of the city. His proposal for the completion of Königsplatz seems to me to be especially successful. He creates a monumental plaza by adding governmental buildings on land that is already in public ownership, and by keeping the square itself entirely free of planting. In height and in outline, his new buildings have been sensitively and discreetly designed to set off the opulent architecture of the Reichstag building. Equally grand and unified in its effect is Möhring's plan for a new [opera house and] Opernplatz, at the intersection of Lennéstrasse and Königgrätzer Strasse, marking the termination of his proposed extension of Französische Strasse. Again, this is a project that could be carried through without financial difficulty. [...]

A tour of the other rooms in the exhibition brings many more architectural delights. Pride of place goes to Theodor Fischer's virtuoso charcoal drawings of his city hall and other buildings for Wilmersdorf, along with the many excellent things exhibited by the City of Munich and the equally fine work from Hanover (K. Siebrecht and F. Usadel) and from our own neighboring cities of Rixdorf (City Architect Kiehl) and Weißensee. In particular, the section to which the exhibition organizers have given the title "Art on the Streets" contains a number of good and attractive works of architecture: the fountains (e.g., by G. Wrba), bridges, bus or streetcar shelters, and other small street structures are of an almost uniformly high artistic standard—which deserves special notice, if only because until recently such things were simply left to city works departments. Nobody thought of attaching artistic value to them and using them to adorn the streets as well as to serve their practical functions.

The design of cemeteries, too, has undergone considerable changes of late. Grässel, in Munich, should probably be regarded as the pioneer in this respect; he was the first to combine all of the necessary structures of a cemetery to create a unified overall effect, and the first to break with the habitual and mostly inferior imitation of a feeble ecclesiastical Gothic. Since then, a distinctive style has evolved for cemetery structures, and of this the exhibition has good examples to show in the work of Karl Kohler, Fritz Schumacher, and William Müller. This is a solemn, dignified architecture that makes no attempt to be aggressively modern, but nevertheless asserts its independence from historic stylistic precedents.

[...]

I believe that the artistic outcome of the Universal Urban Planning Exhibition justifies a degree of both pride and optimism. Looking at all the suggestions for the future that are given here, and responding to the sheer profusion of ideas and the diversity of their artistic expression, one feels that things are not going downhill just yet. A nation in which so much creative power cries out for action is still on the ascendant.

There has also been a powerful impact on those wide swathes of public opinion in which there had hitherto been virtually no awareness of such a thing as urban planning. There is a feeling, surely a general one, that stylistic disputes, and quarrels over whether to imitate the Middle Ages or the Renaissance, or whether to place more or less reliance on past styles, are now beside the point; and that *the artistic battles of the future must be waged on the terrain of urban planning.*

NOTES

1. The architect Bruno Schmitz (1858–1916) trained at the Kunstakademie in Düsseldorf. After moving to Berlin in 1886, he enjoyed considerable success as the designer of office and domestic buildings in the city. Particularly gifted as a designer of monuments, he was responsible (with the sculptor Rudolf Schwarz) for the Soldiers and Sailors Monument in Indianapolis (1887), the Kyffhäuser Monument in Thuringia (1891–96), and monuments to Kaiser Wilhelm I in Porta Westfalica (1896) and Koblenz (1897). His best-known work is the Völkerschlachtdenkmal (Monument to the Battle of the Nations), outside Leipzig, completed in 1912 and inaugurated the following year.

2. Bruno Möhring (1863–1929) was one of the most important and prolific German architects of his generation. In addition to his work as a city planner and publicist—he was cofounder of *Berliner Architekturwelt* in 1899 and (with Cornelius Gurlitt and Bruno Taut) of *Stadtbaukunst* in 1920—he was particularly active in Berlin as a designer of bridges and transportation structures using iron—for example, Bülowstrasse Station (1900–1901; see figure 13) and Swinemünder Bridge (1902–5; see figure 15).

22

Various authors

THE GREATER BERLIN COMPETITION 1910

The Prize-Winning Designs with Explanatory Report

First published as *Wettbewerb Groß-Berlin 1910: Die preisgekrönten Entwürfe mit Erläuterungsbericht* (Berlin: Wasmuth, 1911). Translated by Iain Boyd Whyte.

1. HERMANN JANSEN, BERLIN, JOINT FIRST PRIZE

Foreword

Caution is needed with regard to the oft-cited munificence, so-called, behind which thoughtlessness and tastelessness are too often hidden; a conscientious and respectful approach toward all those choices that are already to hand or can be achieved without difficulty will more likely lead to artistically satisfying results, without failing to do justice in any way to the justifiable, purely technical demands of traffic, and so on.

The same is true for the principal traffic questions, for the rapid-transit railway; for without the widest expansion of this network, the financing of a future metropolis is unthinkable. From inside to out and back is the direction of all the lines. Radial and not peripheral; the latter simply to link the individual towns at the periphery with each other.

The principle focus in this competition remains an ideal pattern of settlement for the inhabitants of Greater Berlin, and appropriate, fast connections.

As the same conditions prevail for the proposals in other areas, the desire and the ability to change are consistently weighed against carefulness in this design.

Whether it is in the interest of this exceptionally difficult challenge—which is already threatened by thousands of conflicting voices, to insist blindly and pettily on the words *feasible* or *unfeasible* rather than promptly follow every good suggestion with all vigor—is a question the author leaves to the sense of fairness and the far-sightedness of competent critics.

The issue here is establishing the principle that reason and taste should be brought once again to the task of expanding further the giant organism of the future world city.

General Points

The fundamental plan for the built development of Greater Berlin as a young and ambitious world city demands an integrated, large-scale solution to the challenges of its traffic, its attractiveness, its health, and its economy. It will, at last, take the process of building and regeneration, and in particular the structure plan, to a higher level.

On the basis of this plan it should be made clear to the individual Berlin townships what prospects for development are open to them on the basis of the structure plans, which, in the main, are already in existence, and whether they find themselves connected or disconnected with the neighboring municipalities. In particular, they will see whether they have the correct relationship to the larger body of the city. Furthermore, they can judge whether the structure plan is correctly weighted, be it toward scenic beauty or in the adequate exploitation of the site, and whether possible improvements have been worked out in good time to ensure survival against the competition of neighboring townships.

The townships and municipalities should be given a basis, therefore, on which they can unite into interest groups, which should be as large as possible, in order to protect their interests and to do justice to the demands of traffic, particularly through traffic, and to acquire appropriate tracts of land preemptively, to be kept free from building in the immediate future. It is not enough, however, simply to keep this land vacant; it is more important to cultivate it, and retain or plant the trees that are needed for public squares and parks. As it takes at least thirty years of growth to reach satisfactory results, the municipalities cannot start too soon, given the current state of affairs, if they wish to remain competitive. The same is true for the development companies, which, sadly, almost alone have determined the external image of Berlin until now.

[. . .]

To prevent the recommendations of the competition, which are now to be implemented, from taking on boundless dimensions, we have concentrated for the time being on those things that that can be achieved or suitably prepared within one generation.

The determining factors here in the first instance are the problematic relationships in Greater Berlin, which, in contrast to all other major cities, is not constituted as a single political unit, and the very advanced state of implementation of the various structure plans. As many individual details have to be taken into consideration, our discussions here must talk as much about rebuilding as about new building. Greater Berlin must first be educated about the expenditure of vast sums of money on this task, similar to the sums invested by other ambitious world cities with a true understanding of their developmental potential. For this reason, it seemed advisable from the outset not to stretch the parameters too far and to remain "within the bounds of the possible"—that is, within the realm of what can actually be achieved.

As far as rapid transit is concerned, a seemingly generous system of Americanization, of the sort that has already been abandoned over there, seems inappropriate to those who have closely studied the particular conditions of Berlin and have not simply ignored those obstacles, which, if allowed to become insoluble, will put the entire outcome in question.

[. . .]

To provide modern, large-scale proposals to all, or to as many as possible, of the hundreds of municipalities and communities at the gates of Berlin appears to be the most immediate and pressing responsibility, bearing in mind, of course, their individual situations. Should the individual communities not accept them voluntarily, which is to be assumed in the majority of cases, the issue can be solved only by a special governance that sets aside all the bad structure plans that have not yet been implemented, with their unhelpful planning controls.

In the foreground, therefore, stands the regulation of housing and development. Traffic questions, however, have a very close relationship to this and should be resolved at the same time, or at least prepared, so that the communities or interest groups that will be affected by significant expenditure will not be forced to make hasty judgments.

[…]

To sum up, housing development must be taken to higher artistic and hygienic levels. As the periphery of the city, which offers virtually the only place for recreation, is pushing farther and farther out, these developments must provide significantly more open space than previously, not only for their own sakes, but also, and in particular, in conjunction with neighboring communities.

2. JOSEPH BRIX & FELIX GENZMER AND HOCHBAHNGESELLSCHAFT IN BERLIN, JOINT FIRST PRIZE

Basic Forms of the New Capital City

In our city building, the radial belt has been indissolubly linked to the city plan and, as a result, dominates the layout of the city, its expansion, its road system, and traffic technology. It seems impossible to get rid of the idea that the city is enclosed by a ring.

The authors want to attempt to break with this idea once and for all, and to arrive at a basic configuration that is appropriate to the modern metropolis. Any beltlike enclosure, call it what you will, must have a negative effect on the land-use politics and the traffic technology of the metropolis. In addition, it will have a damaging effect on the development of the structure plan and hinder the development of functionally appropriate forms of contemporary city building. With regard to the most recent proposal for enclosure—that for a woodland belt—the authors believe that this is an excellent suggestion, much to be welcomed, but one that should not determine the basic layout of the Greater Berlin plan.

For the planning of Greater Berlin, the authors demand a system of radial rather than concentric city elements, radiation rather than belt building. Above all, they propose that, rather than bands, the open spaces should adopt the form of wedges. This, at last, will make the benefit of such spaces for the population a reality, and enable the natural development and design of the entire city to follow their outlines. It is now necessary to examine whether a layout like this would be technically beneficial for Berlin, and whether it could be practically implemented. The beginnings, however, already exist in the colonization of the land beside the suburban railways.

3. HAVESTADT & CONTAG, OTTO BLUM, AND BRUNO SCHMITZ, FOURTH PRIZE

The complete reconstruction of both the Potsdamer and Anhalter stations is necessary in order to do away with the wedge of railway land that pushes right in to Potsdamer Platz, the cardinal error of the city center. The purpose of the remodeling is the construction of all the important east–west streets and of a new boulevard running south, the creation of an elegant city quarter on the land won from the railways, the removal of the disturbances that are linked to the railway operations, and an increase in the capacity of the stations despite their reduced area.

[. . .]

The reconstruction also aims to remove the second great malady of the Berlin city center—namely, the wedge of railway lines running into the Hamburger Station; to attach the city quarter of Moabit functionally to the rest of the city; and, at the same time, to bring to reality overwhelming moments of beauty and of art. Corresponding to the two great architectural axes, the so-called Lehrter freight station and the Packhof will be entirely removed, and the railway tracks pushed back into the area north of Invalidenstrasse.[1]

[. . .]

The conditions are different in the cases of the Anhalter and Stettiner stations. For a start, these stations are so far removed from many parts of the city that they can be reached only after traveling considerable distances. Given the highly important lines that leave from these stations, this represents a serious disadvantage for Berlin's long-distance connections. Moreover, both stations have already almost reached the limits of their capacities. In any case, in a few years' time their tracks will not be equal to the demands of the traffic. [. . .] The question should be debated here: whether both these stations should be transformed into more efficient through stations through the construction of a north–south urban railway, as is currently being done in other world cities—New York and Tokyo, for example—and as we have had for a long time in Berlin in the form of the Stadtbahn.[2] In this way, the trains that terminate at the Anhalter or Stettiner Station could carry on through the city, picking up and dropping off passengers in various districts of the city. The need for a new north–south city railway must, however, be thoroughly proven, for it will demand not inconsiderable investment.

[. . .]

A new north–south artery must be created for the road traffic, and all the important east–west connections must be constructed. Beauty and health demand the continuation of the large, open, green north–south penetration of Greater Berlin from the Jungfernheide to Potsdamer Platz and on to the Tempelhofer Feld.

NOTES

1. The Packhof was Berlin's customs bonded warehouse.

2. The principal east–west line of the Stadtbahn (S-Bahn), which was completed in the 1880s, runs for twelve kilometers through the center of Berlin on elevated embankments and brick-built viaducts.

23
Cornelius Gurlitt
REVIEW OF *GREATER BERLIN* AND *THE GREATER BERLIN COMPETITION 1910*

First published as "Bücherbesprechung von Cornelius Gurlitt: *Groß-Berlin. Anregungen und Erlangen eines Grundplanes für die städtebauliche Entwicklung von Groß-Berlin. Gegeben von der Vereinigung Berliner Architekten und dem Architekten Dorn zu Berlin* (Berlin: Wasmuth, n.d.); *Wettbewerb Groß-Berlin 1910. Die preisgekrönten Entwürfe mit Erläuterungsbericht* (Berlin: Wasmuth, 1911), *Berliner Architekturwelt* 14, no. 10 (October 1912), p. 418. Translated by Iain Boyd Whyte.

[...]

The stimulus provided by the "Greater Berlin Commission" established by the architects and engineers under the leadership of Otto March since 1905 proved itself to be highly valuable, in that in showed how little a one-sided engineer-driven approach to an urban-design question can lead to the desired goal, and how necessary it is to raise urban design above the realm of technology into that of art. Nevertheless, the basic principle must still be adhered to: that the art of architecture resides in creating works that respond to their purpose and give a clear expression of this purpose, and not in the imposition of decorative devices onto the functionally necessary structure. In the context of city planning, it takes an extraordinary farsightedness to define correctly future goals that are not yet clear, but will reveal themselves only at some time in the future, in a period with a way of life that we do not yet know. This vision of the future must be combined with the greatest care in the use of resources and in laying additional demands on our current and overburdened resources, in order to give tangible form to the goals. These two books show this endeavor in the context of Berlin.

The first specifies the wishes for the future favored by the architects of Berlin. Some decades ago the German architect was an "idealist"—which is to say, a splendid, elevated personage, who saw his role as the creation of beauty and who was held in the thrall of the past, in whose spirit he wanted to conquer the world. Modern architects reveal themselves as realists. They have a very clear eye for the essential and the attainable, and work toward these goals. They understand that notions of beauty are changeable, and concentrate on the question of how to reconcile the particular elements of our individual existences in the city—questions of health, of transportation, and the comfort of every inhabitant—with the realization of the large-scale vision. They realize not only that it is impossible to satisfy every wish immediately, but also that they must recognize in good time what the demands of the future might be. It is not simply a matter of trying to improve things, but above all of making sure that nothing is created that makes it difficult or even impossible to make these future improvements.

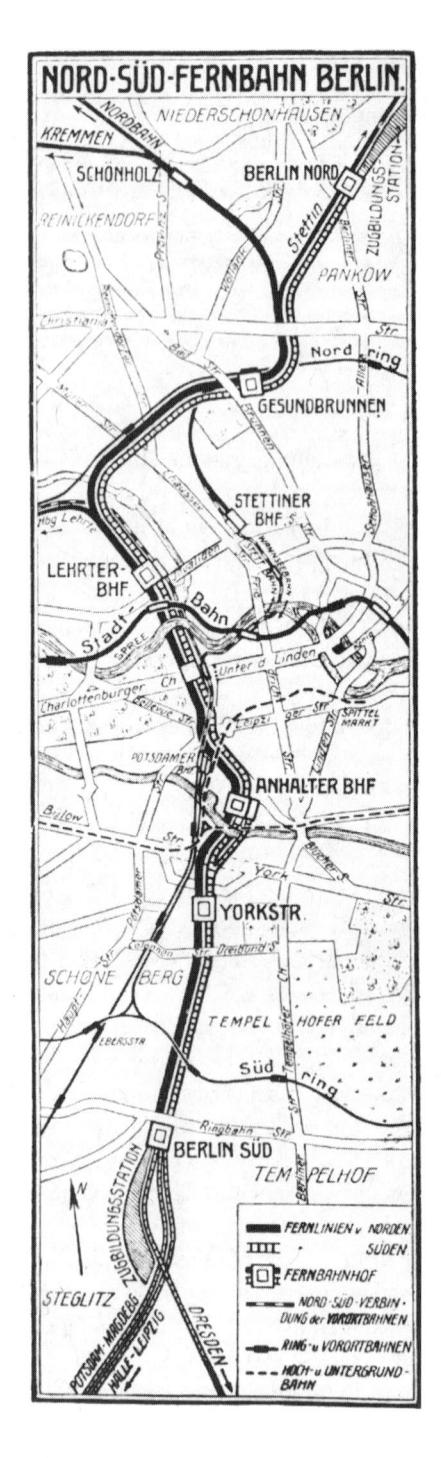

FIGURE 8. Project for north-south railway connection through Berlin (Greater Berlin Competition: Brix, Genzmer, and Hochbahn-Gesellschaft), 1910. *Town Planning Conference, London, 1910* (London: Royal Institute of British Architects), p. 322.

In the recently published volume on the competition, the four prize-winning works are presented, with a preface written by the winner of the first prize, the architect Hermann Jansen. He says of his project that it presents what might be achieved within the life span of one generation. His motto is Within the Boundaries of the Possible. A precondition for this definition of the possible, of course, is a unifying desire to embrace greater Berlin in its totality, and within this volition a strong disposition toward the artistic solution in the sense outlined above. This means: generosity in the definition of goals, care in their implementation, careful consideration of the specific circumstances, and full cognizance of how these circumstances will change over time. Above all, however, this means the never-failing recognition that structure plans are made not for today but for the centuries. They constitute one of the most permanent things in human history and one of the most all-pervading measures in the life of the city. [. . .]

The project by Brix and Genzmer prefers to concentrate on traffic and transportation. One of the singular oddities of the city administration's "practical" turn of mind is its tendency to bury its head in the sand like an ostrich in order to avoid seeing the things that are coming. If the current needs are satisfied, there appears to be no obligation to worry about the needs of the future. They can look after themselves. The individual questions addressed in the plans put forward here are principally those concerned with ameliorating existing social evils and thus with keeping further unwholesomeness at bay. In the process, it becomes clear that in planning the new city fabric, it is already necessary to consider how they will function when they are all completed. A hundred years ago, Schinkel's proposal to build the cathedral on Leipziger Platz was rejected on the grounds that the site was too far from the city center: at that point one could not anticipate the rapid expansion of Berlin. Today, however, we are used to sudden leaps in the population and must concur with those city planners who are calculating for heavy traffic in the distant outskirts of the city.

The same might be said of Möhring, Eberstadt, and Peterson, who, while paying special attention to housing, do not lose sight of the bigger question, which they address with a monumental center for Berlin that connects with the Königsplatz and the neighboring terrain along the Spree, as well as the Lehrter Station.

Havestadt & Contag, [Otto] Blum, and Bruno Schmitz make up the final part of the work. The extensive text that accompanies their scheme covers all areas of city planning and offers many extremely valuable insights into the theoretical understanding of this still very recent discipline.[1]

NOTE

1. For a detailed account of the 1910 Greater Berlin Competition, see Wolfgang Sonne, *Representing the State: Capital City Planning in the Early Twentieth Century* (Munich: Prestel, 2003), pp. 101–48.

24

Sigmund Schott

THE AGGLOMERATION OF CITIES IN THE GERMAN EMPIRE

1871–1910

First published as *Die großstädtischen Agglomorationen des Deutschen Reiches, 1871–1910* (Breslau: Korn, 1912), pp. 1-4. Translated by Fiona Elliot.

Whatever we as individuals may feel, none can ignore the fact of the uncommonly rapid growth of the number of cities in our German Empire and of their populations since 1871. No champion of calmer times who is not appalled at the monstrous dimensions of the various "hydrocephali"—no proud urban publication that does not avidly laud the "unparalleled" population increase in our communities. Be it of value or otherwise, the tangible shifts in the body of the people and its limbs incurred by this process of urbanization are captured by pen, pencil, and camera in a thousand thoughts and pictures.

But what is the extent of these changes, the x whose $f(x)$ we find has taken on so many different forms? How greatly has the number of cities increased, in absolute terms and in the context of the overall population of the empire? Modest curiosity! See the following table for the growth in the number of cities and their populations since 1871.

Year	Number of Cities	Number of Inhabitants	
		Absolute (millions)	*Percentage of the Population of the Empire*
1871	8	2.03	4.9
1880	14	3.39	7.5
1890	26	6.24	12.6
1900	33	9.12	16.2
1910	48	13.81	21.3

So, exactly six times as many cities with almost seven times as many inhabitants after four decades. But have we not bitten off more than we can chew? Statistics, like our thinking, has to define boundaries where there are none; thus statistics regards the inhabitants of the "village" of Hamborn with its population of 102,000 as city dwellers while the citizens of the Free Hanseatic Town of Lübeck, which had only 99,000 inhabitants at the last census, do not feature in our table.

Is the information in our tables dealing with actual mathematical units in the strict sense of the word? Let us look more closely and see which "units"—arranged in columns according to their size in that year—appear in which categories.

1871	1880	1890	1900	1910
Berlin	Frankfurt	Magdeburg	Charlottenburg	Rixdorf
Hamburg	Hanover	Dusseldorf	Dortmund	Duisburg
Breslau	Stuttgart	Altona	Mannheim	Schöneberg
Dresden	Bremen	Nuremberg	Essen	Gelsenkirchen
Cologne	Strasbourg	Chemnitz	Kiel	Bochum
Königsberg		Elberfeld	Kassel	Karlsruhe
Leipzig		Stettin		Plauen
		Barmen		Mülheim
		Krefeld		Erfurt
		Aachen		Mainz
		Halle		Wilmersdorf
		Braunschweig		Wiesbaden
				Saarbrücken
				Augsburg
				Hamborn

Let us start with the "figures" for the municipalities that were listed as new cities in 1910, whose excessive growth gave rise to our doubts. There we find towns, like Rixdorf, Schöneberg, and Wilmersdorf, that may, in purely formal terms, belong in our calculations, but whose exorbitant increases by fifty or sixty times are solely a consequence of their situation as suburbs of the capital of the empire. In addition to this, there are towns like Saarbrücken, Bochum, Gelsenkirchen, Duisburg, and Hamborn, each of which is a merger of previously independent boroughs and which have simply retained the name of one of its previously independent elements a postiori; meanwhile others, like Karlsruhe or Plauen, have generally simply extended their old boundaries to incorporate a number of neighboring boroughs. In short, it is the exception rather than the rule for an independent municipality to progress in its own right through our tables (from its starting point in 1871) as a discrete element in our calculations that is both factually and formally correct.

25

Patrick Abercrombie

BERLIN

Its Growth and Present State

First published in *Town Planning Review* 4, no. 4 (January 1914), pp. 309–311.

There is no doubt Haussmann and his Emperor formed an astounding combination for Paris, the like of which was not forthcoming in Berlin.[1] Added to this was the fact that so much of the work necessary to be done was outside the actual city boundary, and instead of a problem like Paris with a few minor suburbs to deal with, and a department under the control of a *préfet* which placed them in conjunction with the city, there was an important and almost rival city of Charlottenburg, provided with its own royal palace, and other populous townships inclined to resent interference from the central city. The Zweckverband, which is an attempt to unite greater Berlin for the purpose of comprehensive planning, is only a recent achievement of the last two years.[2]

Finally, in her housing conditions Berlin has developed a very remarkable method, one which to a large extent might have been expected throughout Germany as a natural result of the traditional planning and the universal provision of wide streets; but here this method has been intensified to an extraordinary extent, probably again owing to the sudden increase [in population] and to the fact that people were willing to live anywhere and anyhow so long as they could be in the capital. An ordinary city might lose its population or retard its increase if its conditions of living became objectionable—a filthy atmosphere with bad drains, insufficient housing accommodation, or prevalence of an unpleasant form of housing, might be sufficient to prevent people from going to a town and induce their children to quit it; but a rush like that of adventurers to a mining camp is deterred by nothing, so that we find a close packing and a congestion in the population of old Berlin which would otherwise be inexplicable. Since the refilling of the old original fortifications she has been an "open city", one of the few large continental cities which might have grown as loosely as an English one, her powerful army giving her protection instead of fortifications, which were still considered necessary in Paris as late as 1840 and 1870. Again, there was no building land in the neighbourhood broken up into steep and awkward hillsides, nor yet was she confined on a peninsula like New York; it is therefore all the more difficult to understand the reason for this compression. Several causes are accountable; that is to say, the universal provision of wide streets with their expensive road works for purely residential purposes, has led to the building of lofty tenements; to this must be added inelastic by-laws which were made to apply for high buildings, and therefore enforce maximum dimensions and requirements which entail unnecessary expenses on smaller buildings. But probably the most important cause of all was the land speculation and the formation of a ring of landowners forcing up the price of land to the amazing figure of £10,000 to £15,000 an acre, these manipulations being facilitated by a system of conveyancing and mortgaging, and public land registration making it easy to sell land and houses at enhanced prices.

The principal Act under which most of this work has been carried out is the Prussian Building Land Act of 1875. This is not a Town Planning Act in a general sense, like ours [the British Act], but merely a Street Planning Act, backed by the inherited powers of general town regulation. A most elaborate and scientific practice of street plotting resulted from the adoption of this Act, but was to a large extent not related to housing requirements, and not only have the streets been made wider than necessary, but the building plots have often been too big, resulting in a series of enclosed courtyards, in which there is no proper access of air and light. This Act also practically discouraged the provision of front gardens, being intended to produce a uniform character of urban construction.

So we find in modern parts of Berlin, Charlottenburg, Friedenau and other outlying districts, great stretches of magnificent streets lined with imposing buildings. One can hardly notice the difference between the mansions in the Kurfürstendamm and the workmen's dwellings on the Müllerstrasse.[3] The same scale is preserved throughout. There appear to be no narrow dingy back streets, no slums, no pawnshops, and no dealers in old clothes and decayed furniture. There is indeed a monotony of respectability and external prosperity: one longs occasionally for a shabby quarter or a narrow street; and as a compensation for this external splendour there is a population of rich and poor living to almost equal extent in the tenements; but, whereas this method of living may be quite healthy for the rich with their opportunities for obtaining fresh air outside the house, their frequent visits abroad, and their heavy feeding, the poor people suffer to the full from the injurious drawbacks of tenement dwellings. The figures quoted by Professor Eberstadt of fitness for military service in the year 1910 will illustrate the result of this extreme method of housing in Berlin: whereas the percentage for the whole German Empire is 53, and for the medium-size town about 50, for Berlin it is 27.6.

It is impossible to describe in any detail the growth which took place from 1870 to 1900. Typical of the layout favoured at the beginning of this period is Friedenau, connected to the Kurfürstendamm by the magnificent Kaiserallée. In the later part of the period numerous "villa colonies," as they are called, were established, such as Zehlendorf, Grunewald, Steglitz, Schöneberg. These Garden Suburbs, as they might be called, have no effect in drawing people out from the built-up city; they are merely luxurious retreats for the wealthy. The lofty wave of the fully-developed city is seen advancing towards them in various directions.

NOTES

1. Baron Georges-Eugène Haussmann was commissioned by Emperor Napoleon III in 1853 to modernize Paris. The results were the grand boulevards connecting the main railway terminals and radiating from focal elements like the Arc de Triomphe and the Opéra.

2. The Zweckverband Groß-Berlin was established in 1912 as an interest group linking the city of Berlin with the neighboring, independent towns of Charlottenburg, Schöneberg, Wilmersdorf, Lichtenberg, and Spandau, together with the rural districts of Niederbarnim and Teltow. The focus

of the group was limited to traffic, building development, and recreational areas. It became redundant in April 1920, when the city of Berlin was joined with seven other townships, fifty-nine rural councils, and twenty-seven private estates to form the single administrative entity of Groß-Berlin—Greater Berlin.

3. Müllerstrasse is the north–south artery running through Wedding, a Berlin borough populated historically by the industrial working class.

3

PRODUCTION, COMMERCE, AND CONSUMPTION

The fourth edition of *Meyers Konversations-Lexikon,* the leading German-language encyclopedia of the day, offers a wonderfully detailed account of the state of Berlin commerce and industry in 1890. Premier place was given to the textile and clothing industry, whose annual turnover in ladies' coats alone topped 100 million marks. Major new industries were on the march, however, and Meyer reported that "mechanical engineering is also experiencing a wonderful boom, an activity in which over one hundred establishments are now working, some of which, such as Borsig and Schwarzkopf, are world famous. Hand in hand with the construction of machines in Berlin goes the building of railway, post, and other sorts of carriage, sewing machines (Frister & Rossmann), electrical telegraph apparatus (Siemens & Halske), and precision mechanics in general." The piano builders of the city, we learn, produced 1,050 grand and 3,041 upright pianos in 1884, while in the same year Berlin's fifty-five breweries consumed nearly half a million cubic meters of malt, for which they paid 2 million marks.[1] The infant electrical industry, however, was the boom sector par excellence. The key moment came in 1881, when Thomas Edison exhibited his incandescent light bulb in Paris. The rival Berlin entrepreneurs, Werner Siemens and Emil Rathenau, promptly secured the German rights to the new invention and agreed to share the national and export rights between their two companies: Siemens & Halske, and the Deutsche Edison Gesellschaft, respectively. The latter changed its name to Allgemeine Elektricitäts-Gesellschaft (AEG) in 1887 and expanded at an unprecedented rate over the following twenty years: by 1907 it employed some seventy thousand people, who made all things electrical—from tiny light switches to giant turbines.

The AEG factories were sited in and around Berlin, and, as was the convention in the late nineteenth century, the factories were shielded from public gaze behind high walls and gothicky portals decorated with mythological figures and heraldic shields. This all changed in 1907, when the artist and self-taught architect Peter Behrens was appointed as design chief of the AEG, responsible for the visual appearance of all aspects of the company. In place of medievalist citation or the willful individuality of art nouveau, Behrens substituted an abstract, artistic language derived from the industrial process itself yet related to the austerity of Schinkel and nineteenth-century Prussian classicism, which could be applied to every aspect of the AEG's work, ultimately embracing the AEG factories, the enormous range of products made in them, and the marketing material that announced the company as a leading force in a new industrial age. The results were epochal. As the critic Adolf Behne noted in 1913: "In Germany today there is no lack of respect for the magnitude and importance of industry. Apart from the fact that industry has greatly increased, so that one can no longer conceal its premises, no one would think of doing so anymore. On the contrary, industrial architecture today is almost a matter of popular interest; the public pays more attention to it than it generally does to the construction of churches or to theater architecture."[2] Located on several sites, the AEG factories rose out of the poor housing and drab rental barracks of northern Berlin like beacons of progress and hope for the new century. The enormously positive and optimistic response to these harbingers of a new, technocratic society can be sensed in another commentary from 1913: "The force of the turbine hall and the clarity of the Brunnenstrasse factories are part of an architectural proclamation to which one instinctively responds in superlatives. No matter if it seems too lofty for that superficial view that wants to and, indeed, does see all factories as nothing other than gigantic institutions for taming and guarding dead and living slaves. In the street facade of the small motor factory, whose columns reach right up to the roof and are finished in steel-blue bricks— perhaps even more than in the turbine hall—something of that will comes to life again that downtrodden peoples have shown throughout history when they raised themselves up from the depths, the same will that designed arches for our cathedrals, that created Paestum and Stonehenge. These columns... not only draw in, carry, separate, and shade as befits them: they also make a statement; they talk of overcoming the earth—which is not, as before, to deny the earth, but is to ennoble it by re-forming it. It is the spirit of industrial labor, the pride of the workshops, the forward march of all its roaring machines that here seeks expression."[3] This forward march was contained and rationalized by the edicts on "scientific management" first published in North America by Frederick Winslow Taylor in 1911 and briskly translated into German. Berlin was particularly receptive to this agenda: as Karl Scheffler had already noted in 1910, "Everything that can be achieved through organization, the division of labor, order, application, intelligence, and enterprise, is being done in Berlin."[4]

The sense of order, sequence, and clarity that were the imperatives of the industrial process also informed contemporary office building in Berlin, for which steel frames offered the prospect of shop premises with large display windows at the street level, and rationally planned office space above, with each story the same height. In these new offices, which differed from each other only in their external decoration, an ever-expanding army of office workers attended to the paperwork of the new industrial city. As the Berlin sociologist Georg Simmel remarked at the time in his celebrated essay on the philosophy of money: "In the modern metropolis there are a great number of occupations that have no objective form and display no distinct activity: certain categories of agents, commissioners, and all the indeterminate existences of the city that live on the most varied and arbitrary opportunities to earn money."[5] Just as the Taylor system was revolutionizing the factory production line, so the technology of punch cards, also imported from the United States, brought scientific data management to the office. The Deutsche Hollerith-Maschinen Gesellschaft, which manufactured punch-card equipment, was founded in Berlin in 1912.

An entirely new workforce, located between the laboring classes and the civil service, emerged to man these and similar machines in the offices of Berlin. This army of *Angestellten*—salaried, white-collar workers—drew on formerly untapped labor resources—namely, female workers, many with working-class origins. As Felix Philippi wrote in 1913, these were the vital workers in the new Berlin: "If you simply take the trouble to look at the trains arriving in the early morning from the suburbs, you'll see the legions of tastefully clad girls, hurrying to work. *Donnerwetter!* [Heavens above!] We should bow low to these little heroines. They are the reigning force with whose courage, sense of duty, and joyfulness we can create a state."[6] Not all these well-turned-out girls were office workers, however, as the other opportunity open to young and independent women was employment in a shop or, even better, a department store.

And it was in the department store that the remorseless pace, uniformity, and social control symptomatic of the metropolis was marshaled to create the illusion of freedom, individuality, and boundless choice. With a military precision that matched the rigors of the conveyor belt, the predominantly female workforce manned the enormous new department stores that democratized the business of shopping. The undisputable pacemaker here was the Wertheim store on Leipziger Platz, built to the design of Alfred Messel between 1896 and 1904. With its plate-glass windows, massive interior light well, glittering display cases, elevators, and restaurants, the Wertheim store offered undreamed-of riches, small and large, and enticed the Berliners into wondrous worlds of display and consumption. As the critic Max Osborn later noted: "Messel's creation worked like a fanfare. None of the architects who designed department stores on other sites in Berlin—or, subsequently, anywhere else in the entire country—could free themselves from the influence of this model."[7]

NOTES

1. "Berlin," *Meyers Konversations-Lexikon,* 4th ed. (Leipzig and Vienna: Verlag des Bibliographischen Instituts, 1890), vol. 2, p. 756.
2. Adolf Behne, "Romantiker, Pathetiker und Logiker im modernen Industriebau," *Preußische Jahrbücher* 154 (October–December 1913), p. 171.
3. Franz Mannheimer, "A.E.G.-Bauten," *Jahrbuch des Deutschen Werkbundes* 2 (1913), p. 40.
4. Karl Scheffler, *Berlin: Ein Stadtschicksal,* 2nd ed. (Berlin: Reiss, 1910), p. 171.
5. Georg Simmel, *Philosophie des Geldes,* 7th ed. (Berlin: Duncker & Humblot, 1977), p. 484.
6. Felix Philippi, *Alt-Berlin: Erinnerungen aus der Jugendzeit,* 4th ed. (Berlin: E. S. Mittler, 1913), p. 94; quoted in Klaus Strohmeyer, "Rhythmus der Großstadt," in *Die Metropole: Industriekultur in Berlin im 20. Jahrhundert,* ed. Jochen Boberg, Tilman Fichter, and Eckhart Gillen (Munich: Beck, 1986), p. 37.
7. Max Osborn, *Berlins Aufstieg zur Weltstadt* (Berlin: Reimar Hobbing, 1929), p. 182.

26

Georg Simmel

THE BERLIN TRADE EXHIBITION

First published as "Berliner Gewerbe-Ausstellung," *Die Zeit: Wiener Wochenschrift,* 15 July 1896, pp. 59–60. Translated by Sam Whimster.

In his *Deutsche Geschichte* Karl Lamprecht relates how certain medieval orders of knights gradually lost their practical purpose but continued as sociable gatherings. This is a type of sociological development that is similarly repeated in the most diverse fields. The double meaning of the word *society* symbolizes this twin sense. Alongside the very process of sociation there is also, as a by-product, the sociable meaning of society. The latter is always a meeting point for the most diverse formation of interest groups, thus remaining as the sole integrating force even when the original reasons for consociation have lost their effectiveness. The history of world exhibitions, which originated from annual fairs, is one of the clearest examples of this most fundamental type of human sociation. The extent to which this process can be found in the Berlin exhibition alone allows it to be placed in the category of world exhibitions. In the face of the richness and diversity of what is offered, the only unifying and colorful factor is that of amusement. The way in which the most heterogeneous industrial products are crowded together in close proximity paralyzes the senses—a veritable hypnosis where only one message gets through to one's consciousness: the idea that one is here to amuse oneself.

FIGURE 9. Front cover of volume commemorating the Berlin Trade Exhibition, 1896. *Pracht-Album der Berliner Gewerbe-Ausstellung* (Berlin: Werner, 1896).

Through frequency of repetition this impression overwhelms countless no less worthy impressions, which because of their fragmentation fail to register. The sense of amusement emerges as a common denominator due to a petty but psychologically subtle arrangement: every few steps a small entry fee is charged for each special display. One's curiosity is thus constantly aroused by each new display, and the enjoyment derived from each particular display is made to seem greater and more significant. The majority of things that must be passed creates the impression that many surprises and amusements are in store. In short, the return to the main motif, amusement, is more effectively achieved by having to make a small sacrifice, which overcomes one's inhibitions to indulge, than if a higher entry price, giving unrestricted access, were charged, thereby denying that continuous small stimulation.

Every fine and sensitive feeling, however, is violated and seems deranged by the mass effect of the merchandise offered, while on the other hand it cannot be denied that the richness and variety of fleeting impressions is well suited to the need for excitement for overstimulated and tired nerves. While increasing civilization leads to ever greater specialization and to a more frequent one-sidedness of function within an evermore limited field, in no way does this differentiation on the side of production extend to consumption. Rather the opposite: it appears as though modern man's one-sided and monotonous role in the division of labor will be compensated for by consumption and enjoyment through the growing pressure of heterogeneous impressions, and the ever faster and more colorful change of excitements. The differentiation of the active side of life is apparently complemented through the extensive diversity of its passive and receiving side. The press of contradictions, the many stimuli, and the diversity of consumption and enjoyment are the ways in which the human soul—which otherwise is an impatient flux of forces and denied a complete development by the differentiations within modern work—seeks to come alive. No part of modern life reveals this need as sharply as the large exhibition. Nowhere else is such a richness of different impressions brought together so that overall there seems to be an outward unity, whereas underneath a vigorous interaction produces mutual contrasts, intensification, and lack of relatedness.

Now, this unity of the whole creates a stronger impression and becomes more interesting when one considers the impossibility of surveying the objects produced in a single city. It is only as a floating psychological idea that this unity can be apprehended, since in its origins the styles and emerging trends receive no clear expression. It is a particular attraction of world fairs that they form a momentary center of world civilization, assembling the products of the entire world in a confined space as if in a single picture. Put the other way around, a single city has broadened into the totality of cultural production. No important product is missing, and though much of the material and samples have been brought together from the whole world, they have attained a conclusive form and become part of a single whole. Thus it becomes clear what is meant by a "world city" and that Berlin, despite everything, has become one. That is, a single city to which the whole world sends its products and where all the important styles of the present cultural world are put on display. In this sense perhaps the Berlin exhibition is unique; perhaps it has never been so apparent before how much the form of modern culture has permitted a concentration in one place, not in the mere collection of exhibits as in a world fair, but how through its own production a city can represent itself as a copy and a sample of the manufacturing forces of world culture.

It is a point of some cultural historical interest to follow how a particular style for such exhibitions has developed. The specific exhibition style is seen at its clearest in the buildings. An entirely new proportion between permanence and transience not only predominates in the hidden structure but also in the aesthetic criteria. In doing this the materials and their intrinsic properties have achieved a complete harmony in their external design, so satisfying one of the most fundamental demands of all art. The majority of the buildings—in particular, the main ones—look as if they were intended for temporary purposes; because this lack of permanence is unmistakable they are absolutely ineffective, as unsolid buildings.

And the impression of lack of solidity works only where the temporary can claim permanence and durability. In the exhibition style the imagination of the architect is freed from the stipulation of permanence, allowing grace and dignity to be combined in their own measure. It is the conscious denial of a monumental style that has produced a new and positive shape. Elsewhere it is the meaning of art to incorporate the permanence of form in transient materials, and the ideal of architecture is to strive to give expression to the permanent, whereas here the attraction of the transient forms its own style and, even more characteristically, does this from material that doesn't appear as if it was intended for temporary use. And in fact the architects of our exhibition have succeeded in making the opposition to the historical ideal of architecture not a matter of absurdity or lack of style; rather, they have taken the point last reached in architecture as their starting point, as if only this arrangement would allow its meaning to emerge fully against a differently colored background and yet be seen as part of a single tradition.

It is on the architectural side that this exhibition reaches its acme, demonstrating the aesthetic output of the exhibition principle. From another point of view its productivity is at least as high: and here I refer to what could be termed the shop-window quality of things—a characteristic that the exhibition accentuates. The production of goods under the regime of free competition and the normal predominance of supply over demand leads to goods having to show a tempting exterior as well as utility. Where competition no longer operates in matters of usefulness and intrinsic properties, the interest of the buyer has to be aroused by the external stimulus of the object, even the manner of its presentation. It is at the point where material interests have reached their highest level and the pressure of competition is at an extreme that the aesthetic ideal is employed. The striving to make the merely useful visually stimulating—something that was completely natural for the Orientals and Romans—for us comes from the struggle to render the graceless graceful for consumers. The exhibition, with its emphasis on amusement, attempts a new synthesis between the principles of external stimulus and the practical functions of objects, and thereby takes this aesthetic superadditum to its highest level. The banal attempt to put things in their best light, as in the cries of the street trader, is transformed in the interesting attempt to confer a new aesthetic significance from displaying objects together—something already happening in the relationship between advertising and poster art.

Indeed it strikes one as curious that the separate objects in an exhibition show the same relationships and modifications that are made by the individual within society. On the one side, the depreciation of an otherwise qualified neighbor, on the other, accentuation at the expense of the same; on the one side, the leveling and uniformity due to an environment of the same, on the other, the individual is even more accentuated through the summation of many impressions; on the one side, the individual is only an element of the whole, only a member of a higher unity, on the other, the claim that the same individual is a whole and a unity. Thus the objective relation between social elements is reflected in the impression of things in unison within a single frame yet composed of interactively excited forces, and of contradictions, yet also their confluence. Just as in the exhibition the contours of things in their interactive effects, their moving to and fro, undergoes an aesthetic exploitation, so in society the corresponding patterns allow an ethical use.

German—in particular, North German—exhibitions could compete only with difficulty with French ones, where the ability to accentuate by all means possible the stimulus of appearance has a much longer history and wider applicability. Nevertheless, this exhibition shows the attempt, often successful, to develop aesthetic opportunities that through display can contribute to their attractiveness. Certainly the qualities of taste are mostly lacking in the individual items of the exhibition. Aside from the practical motive of Berlin's exhibition, it is to be hoped at the least that the aesthetic impulse is encouraged beyond the exhibition itself and becomes part of the way products are presented.

27

Albert Hoffmann

THE WERTHEIM DEPARTMENT STORE IN LEIPZIGER STRASSE

First published as "Das Warenhaus A. Wertheim in der Leipziger Strasse," *Deutsche Bauzeitung* 32, no. 35 (30 April 1898), pp. 217–19; no. 37 (7 May 1898), pp. 229–32. Translated by Fiona Elliot.

The success of the stores owned by A. Wertheim in Rosenthaler Strasse and Oranienstrasse, and specifically the organizational and technical experience gained in the store designed by Professor A[lfred] Messel in the Oranienstrasse, convinced the directors of the company that they should build a new store in the grandest style in Leipziger Strasse, the most important shopping street in Berlin. They entrusted the architectural design to the architects Messel and [Martin] Altgelt, who then succeeded in constructing and fitting out the store within barely a year.

[. . .]

The choice of a suitable site for the new Berlin store involved some not inconsiderable difficulty. It was to have as imposing a facade as possible; at the same time it was to extend backward as far as possible so that it could provide the generous space needed. The site was also to be accessible from and extendable to a traffic artery other than Leipziger Strasse. After a determined search a site was found that comprised two very deep, regularly shaped plots on Leipziger Strasse, opposite the new Herrenhaus, which would yield a splendid frontage of around 64 meters in length, and which by its position could do justice to all reasonable demands. Following the successful purchase by the firm of A. Wertheim of an adjacent site in Voßstrasse, which runs virtually parallel to Leipziger Strasse, it was now possible to contemplate a through flow of customers—avoiding bottlenecks and holdups—and possibly also an extension in this direction. At present the site in Voßstrasse is occupied by a residence, of a medium age by Berlin standards, which is partly given over to the administrative needs of the store and partly still has a number of reception rooms. If an extension were to be undertaken, it would have to be demolished.

[...]

In effect this new store is thus *one* large room devoted to sales. Any information as to the purpose of the different groups of rooms within this, other than what is shown on the floor plans, is all the more redundant in view of the fact the architects were not required to design rooms particularly suited to the selling of specific items; moreover, not only during the construction period but even now there are almost daily greater or lesser alterations in the use made of different areas. Thus this building is not a department store in the narrower, specific sense of the word, but a retail store of the most general kind, with typically constructed sales areas. The flow of customers through the building, right up to just under the roof, is guided by staircases expediently situated on either side of the foremost group of rooms, by a magnificent open stairway in the light court with the expected continuations, side stairs, and elevators at the two points that can be seen on the floor plan.

[...]

Bringing to bear their engineering expertise, Messel and Altgelt allow the structure of the building to come fully into its own. Built from stone, metal, and glass, it rises upward: powerful in its sparse granite construction, solemn in its dark metal decorations, and flooded by light from its vast expanses of glass. Slim granite pillars, whose strong outlines and deep shadows make them appear more delicate than in truth they are, support the upper floors and the roof; they seek to do no more and no less than give support. The heads decorating the top end of the pillars, carved with scant detail due to the resilience of the material, seem to sigh under the weight of the roof. Between the pillars on the ground floor there are the large display windows, at the front lying flush with the outside of the building, making best use of the interior space, but also bringing the goods as close as possible to the eager customers gazing in.

[...]

The exterior of the building thus unmistakably reveals it to be a department store; nevertheless, with its dignified bearing, it is as far removed from boastful importunacy as it is from blunt commercialism. And the same may equally well be said of its engaging interior. The site, which measures 5,091 square meters in total, was built over to the extent of 3,770 square meters, with an I-shaped structure. Passages at either end of the foremost block lead through to open courtyards, approximately 14 meters wide and 32 meters long. Beyond these are yet two more courtyards, approximately 19 meters wide and 10 meters long, separated from the former on one side by the boiler house and on the other side by a stairwell and rooms containing retail items. By virtue of this relatively simple but meticulously calculated arrangement—which had to conform to the municipal building codes, but which also had to meet carefully considered motives of expediency—and by virtue, too, of the light court, such a flood of daylight is introduced into the interior that throughout the store the goods on display are guaranteed to enjoy the most generous of lighting. The customer enters the store through an open-fronted foyer, closed off at the back by immense panes of mirror glass, behind which goods are temptingly laid out for sale. The practical function of this foyer is evident in that it protects the customer from the lively through traffic on the pavement and, in inclement conditions, allows him in peace to take the measures required for the protection of his person.

[. . .]

Inside the light court is the large, three-armed staircase leading to the upper floors; in front of this stands the immense figure of Labor, modeled by Professor Manzel,[1] and obviously designed to fit the profile of the transverse section of the light court. The light court is the only part of the building whose detail, for all the grandeur of the overall scheme, does not leave the viewer with a sense of balanced harmony. This may be due to the perhaps too shallow depth of the reliefs on the pillars, the too delicate metal lighting obelisks, and insufficient detail in the design of the figure of Labor.

[. . .]

Behind the figure of Labor, the main staircase leads up to the floors above, first to the refreshments room: with a low ceiling, cozy, largely finished in wood by Gossow, glass paintings in the windows, lighting by Spinn & Sohn. A particularly festive mood greets the customer in the carpet department (a view of which may be seen in our supplement), no doubt because here the artist, while availing himself of the new style of dispersed lighting, still draws heavily on the art of past ages, particularly Italian art, thus giving a deep sense of an uncommonly joyful, festive setting. The contrast between the light court and the carpet department is too strong not to be seen as a reflection of the artistic sensibilities of its maker. The models for the fine portal with its spiral columns, and also for the other ornamental devices in this room, were made by the sculptor Giesecke. Looking in through the portal, one's gaze meets the glowing colors of the large central window by Melchior Lechter, with its depiction of the Queen of Fashion, surrounded by garlands of roses. The staircase to the floors above this is adorned by two lamp holders, each in the shape of an unclothed female snake tamer.

[. . .]

FIGURE 10. Interior of the Wertheim department store in Leipziger Strasse (1896–1906; Alfred Messel, architect), c. 1900. Bildarchiv Foto Marburg, 1.037.550.

The elevators are fitted with electric motors. They comprise: five passenger elevators with a load-bearing capacity of 800 kilograms and one passenger elevator with a capacity of 1,050 kilograms. Four of the aforesaid have an elevation of 20.8 meters, while one rises 17.2 meters. Empty, they travel at 1.5 meters per second; fully loaded, this becomes 0.8 meters per second. The store has two elevators for goods and persons, one with a capacity of 1,000 kilograms, an elevation of 24.8 meters, and a speed of 0.4 meters per second; the same figures for the other are 750 kilograms, 20.8 meters, and 0.5 meters, respectively. A platform elevator from the basement to the yard can raise 1,000 kilograms 3.5 meters at the speed of 0.3 meters per second. In addition goods are also transported in a paternoster lift, designed to take packages of purchased goods from the individual floors to the city delivery office situated in the basement. Of particular interest are the seven lever mechanisms for the display-window podiums and the display-window screens; these can be operated either by hand or by electric motor and have a load-bearing capacity of 5,000 kilograms. The whole building, including the light court and the display windows, is lit by electricity, with 486 arc lamps and 4,600 light bulbs.

[...]

Another word about the artistic importance of the building. In the short time since its completion there has not been a shortage of the most diverse opinions; but in the main these opinions, in keeping with the times, regard the building as a manifestation of the new art.

[...]

But Messel is not an innovator in the sense of those for whom art, even as it exists in the moment, is already a thing of the past. [...] By virtue of his own past history, Messel's artistic nature is without a doubt predominantly conservative, contemplative, looking to the past, and, it would seem, more taken by what was good in days gone by than by the ruthlessness of the struggle for existence expressed in new art. At the same time he does not shut his eyes to the latter, but responds to it with gratitude and seeks to reconcile it with the sensations natural to his own spirit, as far as this is possible. In this sense the department store is modern in the extreme; its newness does not derive from a determination to be new at all costs, but arises from the intrinsic demands made by the purpose of the commission. Thus a sound education in the history of art and the requirements of modern development have amalgamated and led to an interesting process. The Wertheim department store demonstrates this process in an uncommonly attractive manner, and one that is all the more immediate due to the speed of its growth and the consequent lack of opportunity to reconcile contradictory feelings or to cancel one out by the other.

NOTE

1. The sculptor Ludwig Manzel (1858–1936) had close relations both with the Hohenzollern court and with the Wertheim family. His many public commissions included figural sculpture on Berlin Cathedral and the Reichstag, the standing figure of Kaiser Wilhelm I in what is now called the Grunewaldturm in Berlin, and the grave of the film director F. W. Murnau in Stahnsdorf, south of Berlin.

28

Robert Walser

ASCHINGER'S

First published as "Aschinger," *Neue Rundschau* 18, no. 12 (December 1907), pp. 1535–36. Translated by David Britt.

A beer, please! The barman has known me for some time. I look at the filled glass for a moment, hook two fingers around the handle, and stroll with it across to one

FIGURE 11. Aschinger bar, c. 1915. Landesarchiv Berlin 357202.

of the round tables set out with forks, knives, bread rolls, vinegar, and oil. I set the glass down on the felt coaster, as instructed, to avoid wetting the table, and wonder whether or not to fetch myself something to eat. The thought of food takes me to the blue-and-white-striped Miss Cold Cuts. From her I obtain an assorted plateful of open sandwiches, and thus provided I make my unhurried way back to my table. I use neither fork nor knife, only the mustard spoon, with which I apply a brown topcoat to my sandwiches, whereupon I contentedly ingest them: a sight to bring perfect peace to the soul. Another beer, please. Eating and drinking at Aschinger's,[1] you quickly get used to a confidential tone in eating and drinking, and before long you are talking like Wassmann at the Deutsches Theater.[2] With the second or third beer in your hand, you are usually moved to make some observations. You decide to take note of the exact way in which Berliners eat. They eat standing up; but they take their time about it. It is a myth that people in Berlin are always hurrying, rushing, or trotting around. People here know perfectly well—and to a positively comic degree—how to waste time. After all, one is only human. It is a true delight to watch people fishing for sausages in rolls and for Italian salads. The cash for this is mostly extracted from vest pockets; it is almost invariably no more than ten pfennigs. By now I have rolled myself a cigarette, and I obtain a light from the gas flame, which is under green glass. How well I know this glass, and the brass chain that you pull to get a light. All the time, people with appetites are thronging in, and the well fed are thronging out. The unsatisfied soon find their satisfaction at the beer fountain and the hot-dog tower; and, once satisfied, they launch forth into the air of commerce once more, usually with briefcase under arm, letter in pocket, task in brain, plan in skull, watch in palm to tell them that it's high time. The round tower at the center of the room is the throne of a youthful queen: she who rules over the sausages and potato salad; slightly bored in her culinary setting. An elegant lady enters and picks up a caviar roll with two fingers; at once I make myself visible to her, albeit in such a way that I appear not to give a damn. Meanwhile I have found time to attach myself to another beer. The lady is slightly embarrassed at having to bite into the splendors of the caviar, and I of course instantly suppose myself wholly responsible for her momentary loss of composure. One is so prone to self-deception! Outside, on the square, there is a din that you do not really hear: a chaos of carts, carriages, people, automobiles, newspaper sellers, trolley cars, handcarts, and bicycles. Nor do you really see it. It is almost unseemly to think of wanting to hear or see it; after all, you are not fresh up from the country. The elegantly curvaceous figure, fresh from bread crunching, now leaves Aschinger's. How long do I mean to stay here? There is a lull at the bar, but not for long; soon another influx of thirsty customers is heading for the sparkling fountainhead. People who are eating watch other people who are also working their jaws. When one man has his mouth full, his eyes watch another man simultaneously filling his. And people do not even laugh; nor do I. Since I have been in Berlin, I have learned not to find common humanity ridiculous. And, in any case, at this moment I am taking delivery of a new feat of culinary magic: a plank of bread on which a sleeping sardine reclines on a bedsheet of butter. This presents such a delightful spectacle that for two pins I would knock back the whole scene in a single bite. Is that ridiculous? Not at all. Well, then, if a thing is not ridiculous when I do it, it cannot possibly be ridiculous when others do it; for we are duty bound to value others more highly than ourselves at all times: a philosophy entirely appropriate to the high seriousness with which I now apply myself to the episodic demise of my sardine bed. A number of the people around me talk while they eat. There is something attractive about the weighty seriousness with which they do so. If you are engaged in doing something, do it with dignity and do it properly. Dignity and self-assurance are comforting things, to me at least, and that is why I like to stand in one of our Aschinger houses, where people drink, eat, talk, and think, all at the same time. How many business deals have been worked out here! And the best thing is this: you can stand here for hours on end; it bothers no one. No one, of all those who come and go, finds it remarkable. Anyone with a taste for the unassuming life can manage very well here; he can live, and no one will bother him. And, just as long as he has no pressing need for heartfelt cordiality, he is quite free to have a heart; no one will mind.

NOTES

1. Aschinger was a chain of restaurants in Berlin, founded by August Aschinger (1862–1911) and his brother Karl (1855–1909). Their first establishment, a bar, opened on the Roßstrasse in 1892. Other branches followed rapidly throughout the city. So successful was the large restaurant on Alexanderplatz that it had to be extended in 1894. The firm's own bakery, located on the Sophienstrasse, produced an endless supply of bread rolls that were served without cost with each meal. These free rolls, the cheapness of the food, and the brisk service endeared Aschinger to generations of Berliners.

2. Hans Wassmann (1873–1932) was a character actor who worked in the theater with Max Reinhardt, appearing, for example, in Reinhardt's celebrated 1905 production of Shakespeare's *Sommernachtstraum* (*A Midsummer Night's Dream*). He also acted in films such as *Tragödie der Liebe* (1923, with Emil Jannings and Marlene Dietrich), *Eine Dubarry von heute* (1927, with Marlene Dietrich), and *Der Hauptmann von Köpenick* (1931).

29
Karl Scheffler
THE RETAIL ESTABLISHMENT

First published as "Das Geschäftshaus" in Scheffler, *Moderne Baukunst* (Berlin: Bard, 1907), pp. 43–48. Translated by Fiona Elliot.

In Berlin this stepwise development of the retail establishment may still be clearly traced in many transitional structures. The retail stores at Hausvogteiplatz still look very hermaphroditic, and the large blocks on Kaiser-Wilhelm-Strasse, despite the fact that here modern needs clearly prevail for the first time, still remind one in certain crucial aspects of the facades of tenement buildings, and even the much-lauded Equitable Palace in Leipziger Strasse is still sorely betwixt and between. Thoughts of residential properties were to have been banished here, but for all intents and purposes they have survived, because the talented architect could not rid himself of the idiosyncratic notion that a retail establishment in the capital must in a sense still be grand and palatial. The old building methods still held sway—that is to say, the practice of designing buildings from the outside inward: first the grand exterior, then the necessities. Thus constructions of stone, iron, and glass came into being, neatly slotted into the street frontages, but which were absurdly adorned with details otherwise found on a freestanding palace, with the result that they are neither retail establishment nor a residential property, just interim solutions that it is hard to know what to do with.

To this day we would probably not have arrived at any clear-cut conclusions if it had not been for an artist like [Alfred] Messel, who, at the right moment, took up present-day ideas on development and, supported by bold, perspicacious clients, brought them to maturity. The achievements of this man are astounding.

[...]

Messel's accomplishments confirm once again the time-honored adage that few wish to comprehend: that every work of art, whatever it may be, involuntarily demonstrates an ethical value. When architects dared not follow the demands of necessity they disguised this with platitudes about the need for "traditions," with commonplaces about "formal treasures of the past" and "eternal beauty." But what they produced was shameful imitation, small-minded and presumptuous in one. It seemed that architecture as an art was dead; there was no longer any music in the art of building, just noises, no living aesthetic, only science—at best. Every year architectural societies celebrated their "master" [Karl Friedrich] Schinkel with grandiose words and pledged that they would continue to work in his spirit. They believed they were doing so when they—oh Lord, yes, just like him!—used the forms of the ancients. But even today few understand where Schinkel's strength as a classicist actually lies, nor the ways in which his overall achievement is so extraordinarily modern. The first to seek to take on the mantle of this Berlin architect in the grand manner was Messel. In his department stores we at last can see what was necessary in order to restart an interrupted line of development. It was necessary to do the same thing that Schinkel had done in his liveliest buildings: to find an attire for broadly understood needs, without paying heed to anything other than the demands of logic, reason, and a sense of beauty nurtured by reality. Messel's Wertheim department store at last added another to our list of notable buildings. With his striving for the modern in the best sense—which can only mean: that which is alive—this artist succeeded in creating an organic structure. The cityscape has acquired, through its retail establishments, a very characteristic nuance. By virtue of the fact that the mercantile principle is unreservedly recognized and openly proclaimed in this architectural form, it is also ennobled. The great retail premises of the company of Wertheim greet us with something of the old Hanseatic spirit; one remembers the pride merchants took in their lives in centuries gone by, and modern profit making and petty trading become, through the art form, something almost monumental. It seems that this architect, with his particular feeling for art, has anticipated what the department store may perhaps mean in the future. The fact that today there is an element of contradiction between the solemn grandeur of the architecture and the actual function of the building cannot be denied. But once the department stores have developed into the important financial and social institutions that they seem destined to become, when within them, gradually and realistically, many of their social plans are realized that today sound so utopian because they are presented in a somewhat visionary manner, then this so augustly imposing architecture will no longer seem out of place. At the sight of these buildings one is involuntarily assailed by the same sensations that arise when one contemplates old merchants' houses from the Renaissance and the eighteenth century: one thinks of the notions of style that prevailed in the old guilds, and it seems that the monumental scale the merchant's business can attain once it really takes flight is embodied in these edifices. One senses a yearning to dream of a great, modern brotherhood or syndicate, an all-embracing mercantile guild spirit of the future that is alien to petty shopkeeping. This has been achieved because the architect has faithfully allowed himself to be led by the needs of the business and, by yielding thus, has all unawares himself become the leader, for he it was that had the truly poetic notion of expressing in stone the living energies of his own time. By conducting himself—in the best sense—morally in his capacity as an artist, and by dedicating himself to the truth, he and his work have reaped the benefit of all the latent ethical and monumental needs of our times that are driving forward in a thousand different ways; while he ennobled the mercantile principle with art, the latter—retrospectively—monumentalized the architectural design.

Messel's first retail establishment, the Wertheim department store in Leipziger Strasse, was all the more audacious an act in that the company's business could not in itself have spurred the architect on to such hitherto unheard-of innovation. The bazaar was originally accommodated in the four stories of a residential property; one had to scurry through a hundred different rooms in a Berlin house in order to make one's purchases. By comparison, Messel's proposal was splendidly simple. A huge light court and around it, one endless room on all the floors at once; the ceiling supported solely by pillars, the exterior walls only subdivided by columns. The sight of the facade initially overwhelmed even the boldest. But agreement was soon reached thanks to the persuasive logic that was at work here. Stone and iron were at last openly acknowledged as materials for a department store; the strict divisions between the stories were abandoned; the columns rising upward presented the whole as a single entity, offering only the necessary support for the required anchor points and otherwise giving over the plane of the facade to glass articulated by iron window bars. The first glimpse of this building reveals to the passerby what it is and what it wants to be: a retail store, where thronging customers can freely and unhindered spread throughout all parts of the building, where the goods for sale are not hidden in cupboards and boxes, but laid out for all to see. It was a sensation of a very special kind when first one looked down from the galleries into the great light court and saw the crowds pressing around the gay sales tables, when one's gaze could move freely through every floor, penetrating deep inside them, could take in whole flights of stairs and could perceive the floor plan at a glance. The effect of space—which one as yet had no experience of in modern retail establishments—was heightened almost to the point of poetry; the scene before one had a magnificence about it at the same time as seeming perfectly reasonable. This moment, when Messel created a type of architecture for the department store, was highly significant in metropolitan design: it brought with it confirmation of what had long since made its presence felt, and an idea for the development of the city, which had so often been held back by cowardly concerns, now took shape. Messel's relationship to his tasks is characteristic of the relationship of the art of building, as we understand it today, to the fundamental questions surrounding modern functional architecture. When one talks of this architect and his working methods, one involuntarily refers to the whole movement. Specifically because the essence of Messel's approach was to draw a logical conclusion from the existing premises, because the social tendency of his work was more important than any aesthetic musicality, his approach must be regarded as exemplary, as typical.

30

Leo Colze

THE DEPARTMENT STORES OF BERLIN

First published as *Berliner Warenhäuser* (Berlin and Leipzig: Ostwald, 1908); reprinted in *Die Berliner Moderne,* ed. Jürgen Schütte and Peter Sprengel (Stuttgart: Reclam, 1987), pp. 104–10. Translated by Fiona Elliot.

There are four potentates in Berlin, uncrowned emperors, whose strict regime is nonetheless recognized by all and whose directives and exhortations to the public only give rise to discussion of a suitable kind. These uncrowned lords are our department stores: Wertheim, Tietz, Jandorf, and, after only a year, the Kaufhaus des Westens. The emergence of modern retail palaces is closely connected to Berlin's becoming a major city, an international metropolis. The unbiased observer, unhampered by political trappings, cannot but agree that it has been the department stores that have set the stone of progress rolling in the business world. If we see today in the main thoroughfares of the capital of our empire retail palaces cheek by jowl, if brightly lit display windows with the finest products of the industries of civilization not only tempt us to buy but also simply appeal to our aesthetic sense, if today the little man is in a position to acquire, at a price, luxury items for which he otherwise scarcely had the adequate means, then all this is the achievement of the modern department-store.

The Berlin department store has by now come to be regarded as exemplary, not only within Germany but more generally for trade and retail in the old and the new world. Of course, our discussions here do not pertain to the "want-to-be department stores" that, as a consequence of their inferior goods, their confined space, their poor service and attempt to appear inexpensive by pricing in pfennigs, only discredit the nature of the department store; instead we are thinking here of the modern department-store organism, whose most noble representative—uniting all the advantages, all the lessons learned in America and Germany—is known to us as the Kaufhaus des Westens.

Thus I will now and then take the opportunity to return in my discussion to this most modern of all department stores as an exemplary instance, because it is the purest organism in the modern retail business today.

In my reference earlier on to the Berlin department store I had in mind the department store purely as an independent entity, without its connections to the population of Berlin and its buying power, and this distinction will here and there play a part during the course of this essay. With regard to the latter, we have to distinguish carefully between the three domains of our uncrowned potentates.

First we have the firm of A. Jandorf & Co., with its shops in the midst of a lively workers' district. The retail store for the little man.

The stores owned by the firm of Hermann Tietz meet the needs of the middle class, as do those belonging to the firm of A. Wertheim, with the exception of their branch in Leipziger Strasse, which is devoted purely to luxury goods and, situated in the new district of Berlin West together with the modern Kaufhaus des Westens, serves the most affluent residents of Berlin West.

A walk through the streets to inspect the locality will reassure us that what we have just claimed is indeed correct.

I once saw a cartoon that depicted the modern department store as a ventilator, into whose wide-open jaws big and small, old and young, male and female were disappearing, all drawn in by its power of suction. Much about that image was convincing, even with respect to the most noble stores. I do not intend here to weigh up the advantages and darker sides of the idea of the department store; I am writing neither a treatise on the national purse nor a polemic on political economy, yet I would not want to fail to state that in my view the major department stores of Berlin have played a crucial part in the development of our capital on the Spree into a city of the first rank in the world today.

Wherever retail palaces appeared, soon afterward as a natural consequence a lively coming and going ensued. Wisely recognizing this increased human traffic—and denying the old wives' tales of the innately destructive effect the department store would have on the specialist shop—specialist shops of the most diverse kinds established themselves, with facades designed in the modern style, in form and content adopting the best of the department store for their own business.

Let us take a very recent example: Tauentzien- and Kleiststrasse in Berlin West, nowadays a boulevard for flirtatious young misses, a rendezvous for the pram-pushing female population of Spreewald and for maids. Just a few years ago this was still a genteel residential street in the elegant west.

A group of houses was bought up, barely finished palatial residences fell victim to the pickax, and soon the Kaufhaus des Westens began to take shape on this very large site. The transformation of the entire district, which proceeded in leaps and bounds, can be traced back to that moment. An early summer's afternoon. It is already twilight; having arrived at the Zoologischer Garten Station, as we reach the Kaiser-Wilhelm-Gedächtniskirche we cross the Auguste-Viktoria-Platz to the promenade running up the middle of Tauentzienstrasse. Light streams toward us. To the right and to the left, one shop window after the next, laden with masculine and feminine elegance. A smartly turned-out throng of people moves along the street, laughing and flirting, enjoying life, with time to spend. Walking, idling. Farther up at Wittenbergplatz fairy-tale luminescence, precious, glittering goods, silks, gold brocades, bronzes, ostrich feathers, display windows like jewelry boxes: the new department store. Dense and unceasing the crowd streams in, the potentate calls—the people gladly respond.

I would like to call Tauentzienstrasse the new Leipziger Strasse. The Leipziger Strasse of the flâneur. Farther up still in the old west, at Potsdamer Platz, dominated by Wertheim, Tietz, and Jandorf, we have the working Leipziger Strasse. Here the crowds hurry, are in haste, interspersed by only a few idlers, here at the Kaiser-Wilhelm-Gedächtniskirche—pleasure seekers, young people, Berlin West.

Every city, depending on its character and individuality, develops at a greater or lesser speed. Berlin, the youngest metropolis in Europe, has grown so rapidly that even alert observers may have missed some symptoms and moments that are a particularly striking sign of Berlin's burgeoning prosperity. The development of Berlin West, for instance, is just such an issue. In view of the huge expansion that our metropolis on the Spree has experienced, from the center outward, no doubt there were businessmen who involuntarily shook their heads and asked themselves how this growth was to be accommodated. Few will deny that a new metropolitan center is currently emerging in the west. It will not be a mere offshoot reflecting the hustle and bustle of old Berlin to a greater or lesser extent; on the contrary, a wholly independent, elegant, fashionable, no less busy Berlin is emerging here, with the Kaiser-Wilhelm-Gedächtniskirche as its focal point, and creating for itself in the grand style—unhampered by questions of space—new possibilities for satisfying its needs. Anyone who has followed the development of Berlin over the last few years with an observant eye, who has experienced at first hand the arrival of business at the upper end of Leipziger Strasse, will be well aware that Berlin life and Berlin traffic are gravitating ever more to the west. Particularly the area and the thoroughfares that start at the "Romanische Ecke" were by their design and architecture destined to combine the city and elegance and to give Berlin West a particular cachet. Today Tauentzienstrasse is already a modern shopping street that will be in no respect inferior to Leipziger Strasse once all the plans are realized that have been made for it. Once a quiet residential street where not a few of our leading financiers, thinkers, and artistic minds built residences, now it is fast becoming the main traffic artery in the west. Scarcely finished houses fall victim to the pick hammer to make way for retail palaces. Shops are appearing, and, astutely recognizing the potential of this district, the major companies from old Berlin West are opening up branches here; its calm, palatial residences are becoming centers of business and bazaars; at a stroke the physiognomy of the whole street has been changed. Not least, the mighty edifice of the Kaufhaus des Westens at Wittenbergplatz has played its part in giving the whole district a new face.

31

Erich Köhrer

BERLIN DEPARTMENT STORE

A Novel from the World City

First published as *Warenhaus Berlin: Ein Roman aus der Weltstadt* (Berlin: Wedekind, 1909), pp. 22–23. Translated by Fiona Elliot.

Günter looked up, a little disconcerted. "What is that supposed to mean? Why call the new shop 'Berlin Department Store'?"

"Because this name means two things at once," Nielandt burst out excitedly. "In the first place, we avoid describing our business as a department store in Berlin, just one amongst many! No, we want to be *the* Berlin Department Store! We want to show by the very name that when talk of the innovation in Berlin's commercial life turns to the department store, it can only be ours that is meant. We want to relegate those around us to staffage, so to speak! It is our aim that people should no longer say, in Berlin we have this store and that, we want them simply to say, we have the Berlin Department Store! And in the second place—what should be more fitting as a symbol of Berlin life in its entirety than a department store? Both have grown in the soil of a new age, have been grafted as young shoots onto the stems of past developments, and, in the shortest possible time, because the time was right, have shot up to gigantic heights. The department store, as I like to think, is a microcosm in which all the stages of life are echoed more sharply than anywhere else, in which the life of the individual is tangibly reflected in a larger or smaller entity. And Berlin life itself always seems to me like a huge department store. Alien and cold, all the different things stand there next to each other; on all sides the most diverse items are on offer, neatly turned out and as tempting as possible; and the advertising that plays a major part in our business is also the most powerful single factor in public life.

"In our Berlin we can no longer lead a tranquil existence as once we did, when one could still satisfy one needs at one's leisure in peaceful specialist shops! Now countless streams of people surge wildly like foaming waves over and past each other, like the hurrying throngs in a large department store. Love and happiness, wealth and peace, satisfaction, a delight in nature, art, and culture: we no longer calmly select and enjoy these at our ease! Instead we rush into purchases, for carefully calculated chance has placed all the various possibilities, neatly presented, in our path! As people pass along the street, they acquire whatever suggests itself, without lengthy deliberation, intoxicated by the sensation of the fleeting moment! And this susceptibility, on the part of the public, to external impressions is what we want to turn to our advantage, so that we may rule that same public."

32

Karl Scheffler

PETER BEHRENS

First published as "Peter Behrens" in Scheffler, *Die Architektur der Großstadt* (Berlin: Cassirer, 1913), pp. 153–59. Translated by Fiona Elliot.

Any author writing about architecture a hundred years ago, even fifty years ago, would concern himself primarily with new museums, church buildings, with grandiose, monumental structures. When foreign artists passed through Berlin, they used to write home about the impression made on them by the Brandenburg Gate, the Schauspielhaus, or the Museum am Lustgarten. In those days these were the buildings that embodied the Berlin of the future.

Today the friend of modern architecture speaks above all about the newly emergent functional buildings. This first started some decades ago when [Franz Heinrich] Schwechten's Anhalter Station was deemed worthy of discussion from an aesthetic standpoint, when Schäfer's Equitable Palace aroused more general interest,[1] and the interest in monumental functional architecture finally established itself with Messel's department-store buildings. When foreign artists or shrewd art lovers now stroll through the new Berlin, they report home, almost with disdain, of the home of the Kaiser Friedrich–Museum or of the new cathedral; at the same time they talk with great respect of Messel's Wertheim building and of the factories designed by Peter Behrens for AEG.[2] It will not be long before Baedeker will be awarding stars to a category of buildings that never hitherto seemed worthy of attention.

[...]

The Prussian town became an imperial capital; the royal residence and garrison gave way to trade and industry. The art of building is now faced with new problems. Buildings constructed today solely with a representative function appear academic and fossilized. The new age demands a new understanding of function and, with that, new building forms based on purpose and need. The architect today can no longer aim for eclectic beauty, for melodious grandeur and integrity of style alone. Rather, he must seek characteristic expression and a new kind of sobriety and truth.

[. . .]

It was a bold and fortunate act when the directors of AEG invited Peter Behrens to leave Düsseldorf for Berlin. Behrens, an artist who had moved from painting to the applied arts, was director of the School of Applied Arts in Düsseldorf at the time and had been a leading figure in the reorganization of our applied arts. Initially the intention was that he should act as a consultant for the artistic aspect of AEG's new factory buildings. That is to say, AEG commissioned Behrens little by little to create new functional yet aesthetic forms for electric arc lamps, ventilators, and all the other items that are needed for electrical lighting. The company directors had recognized the absurdity of mass-produced articles, such as those made for electrical lighting, being "decorated" with senseless acanthus leaves and Renaissance ornament; they could also see that the dreary hideousness, the absolute nonform of the products of the manufacturing process alone were also unworthy, and they were not mistaken when they supposed that Behrens would be the right artist to derive—from the technical and practical givens—forms that were simply beautiful and practical. This sequence of events is all the more remarkable in that the company in question is vast and dominant in the world market; it was thus stating in no uncertain terms that the manufacturing industry also has to consider artistic issues and that it is not enough merely to produce serviceable goods and to make profits for the shareholders. The manufacturing industry must recognize its higher obligations to the greater whole. Behrens worked on all the small forms like an engineer turned artist; he never sought to avoid the essential; on the contrary, he took it as his starting point and thus created new basic forms, new types in which the essential becomes beautiful and expressive.

And this impressive activity in fact sealed the relationship between Peter Behrens and AEG; it was just the beginning. Today Behrens is in fact the chief architect of this huge company that is constantly growing, and hence building a great deal. Step by step, artist and directors, in ideal cooperation, have progressed from one task to the next, and the result today, after barely five years, is that there is already a number of factory buildings in Berlin that seem destined to make history in the art of building in Germany and that brilliantly continue what Messel so happily started with his department stores, banks, and other buildings for trade and business. The results are already such that one of the strongest impressions that Berlin has to offer is to be had from a walk through the extensive premises of AEG, taking in the harmony of finely formed functional architecture and monumental industrial production.

The workers at AEG must have, in the high, light interiors of the new factories, a very different sense of their worth and their work than those many industrial workers who spend their working lives in terrible barracks in cheap, makeshift premises. The sense of space in the turbine hall and in the factories in Brunnen-

FIGURE 12. AEG Machine Hall (Peter Behrens, architect), Hussitenstrasse, 1912. Bildarchiv Foto Marburg, 1.056.218.

strasse, for instance, is in certain respects positively monumental. It not only needed a great mind to design the architecture of this building as it is, but needed the same from the client to accept the proposal. Work itself had to be held in higher esteem; the directors of AEG had to regard their own industry as monumental, had to behave in a culturally responsible manner, and had in a sense to accept a commanding role.

[. . .]

Standing outside the AEG turbine factory in Moabit, on the corner of Huttenstrasse and Berlichingenstrasse, one is faced with one of the most remarkable sights to be seen in Berlin today. We see a huge hall made from artificial stone, steel, and glass, with its gable end to Huttenstrasse, while one side wall extends far down Berlichingenstrasse. The other side wall faces the factory yard. One's first and last impression of the building is of power and rhythm. The iron supports set a tempo that has something irresistible about it. Involuntarily one is reminded of the uncompromising effect of Gothic pillars, although without forgetting for a moment that we are dealing here with the monumentalism of modern functional architecture. This building is as new, as original and modern as it could possibly be; nevertheless, its effect is fundamentally due to something much more general. Construction and a cool head, the logic of the material itself, and engineering calculations—all these are just the necessary prerequisites: they have been raised to the level of art by a great mind. It is not just the monumentality of the quantities that has such an effect—although the sheer mass of the building has its part to play—it is the monumentality of the expressive form. There is no hint of the sinuousness, openness, and unarchitectural nature of iron structures. The stone, iron, and glass surfaces have a certain succinctness about them, with the result that the whole creates the impression of a closed cuboid. The building is compelling by virtue of its expressive relationships. It is clear from looking at this mighty hall that it is a workplace for bold enterprises. It lies with its weighty grace in a disorderly district of impoverished, balcony-laden tenement houses, which seem quite strange next to the factory's understated might; and it truly seems to dominate the area, as a symbol not only of AEG but also of modern industrial production per se. The architectural poise of this iron-and-glass structure is of a highly charged kind; its colossal dimensions are ingeniously differentiated, and its inner logic has an artistic appeal of its own. In every aspect the whole is imbued with expressivity and a sure sense of purpose.

NOTES

1. The Equitable Palace was built for the eponymous insurance company in 1887 on a key site in Berlin: the corner of Friedrichstrasse and Leipziger Strasse. The architects were Schäfer & Hartung. (See also above, text 29: Karl Scheffler, "The Retail Establishment.")

2. The AEG—Allgemeine Elektricitäts-Gesellschaft (General Electric Company)—was founded in 1883 by Emil Rathenau and based in Berlin. From 1907 to 1914, the AEG employed Peter Behrens as its consultant in all artistic matters, and extended his remit from the company's corporate identity to its products and buildings. See Tilmann Buddensieg, *Industriekultur: Peter Behrens and the AEG, 1907–1914,* trans. Iain Boyd Whyte (Cambridge, Mass.: MIT Press, 1984).

33

Karl Ernst Osthaus
THE DISPLAY WINDOW

First published as "Das Schaufenster," *Jahrbuch des Deutschen Werkbundes* 2 (1913), pp. 59–69. Translated by Fiona Elliot.

The display window today is more factual than its predecessors. Each item, instead of telling a story, is presented as itself. The display is a display, a construct; the items on show are not bound together by a "literary" thread. The gown is for sale, not simply the raiment of a waxen beauty in a state of rapt attention. This presumes a major shift in thinking. It marks the end of romantic display windows. In itself, it is only a by-product of that sea change that has seen the rejection of historical styles in building and of painted sets on the theatrical stage, and which has found its political-economic organ in the Deutscher Werkbund.[1]

However, just as soon as the lady writing a letter departed from the window and her pen became the only item on display, so, too, the problematic nature of the new system unfolded before us. To engage the intellect or to show a picture—these are two very different aims. How can one create an image in a 4-meter-wide window using only fountain pens? At a stroke it became clear that the huge size of the windowpanes was not always an advantage. It might do for suits and fabrics, it was ideal for automobiles and furniture; it was death to stamps, pocket watches, and items of jewelry. And who could stack a thousand candles in a window without turning them into his own great pyramid of Cheops? The old adage that One Cannot Do for All surfaced again. Now, in the Adlon Hotel in Berlin, we see once again windows with dainty, precious items in a small display that is exactly right for them, precisely because of its restricted size. And Muthesius has created a positively exemplary display for the print dealer de Burlet. We have realized that variety in the size of display windows is one of the most important factors for the more matter-of-fact window displays of today.

And there is another factor that is no less important. In the streets of our capital we see displays cheek by jowl like pictures in a painter's studio. They have no frames. In some cases the side walls are even clad with mirrors. We see a thousand reflected lights and colors cutting through each other. A true feast for eyes with an impressionistic tendency. But it makes a mockery of the factual approach. And it cannot be a matter of indifference to the businessman, keen to sell his goods, if the throng of people passing by is simply intoxicated by the atmosphere of reflections and light. He wants to captivate the passers-by, to tempt them, to stop them in their tracks; the items on display should have a meaning for the individual, more important than the intoxicating glitter; Everyman should feel that the item that has caught his attention is specifically there for him. So specifically that magical suggestion spins its threads and the spellbound passer-by cannot shake off the thought: you shall be mine.

But it requires concentration to achieve this mysterious marriage of customer and goods. Every means must be deployed to isolate the item. Above all the window must have a frame.

[August] Endell, the greatest magician among the display-window artistes in Berlin, understood this better than anyone. Whenever he had the opportunity to design the facades of his shops, he placed wide columns between the windows with such special surrounds around the glass that we sense something miraculous even before we approach the windowpane.

And it was Endell who found the best solution for the lighting. Others had already dispensed with the external arc lamps, which dazzle rather than illuminate. Concealed lighting that hides the source from the viewer so that the merchandise stands out all the more brightly had already transferred from the stage into window displays. But it was only in Endell's hands that light first took on its mystical magic. Sparkling glass panes in deep colors concealed the lighting boxes from the street, while the light flowed down on the goods from above. Trademarks glisten like magic signs. The whole scene creates the feeling a child has at the sight of the curtain that will for the first time reveal to him the world of dreams. What is on offer in this magical shrine has to be something precious, even if it be no more than a pair of black leather boots. For it is Endell's skill to cast them in the fascinating glow of the light of a Thousand and One Nights. They are placed on gently sloping stands, Indian shawls spread out under their soles; all around them the paneled walls are decorated with mother-of-pearl and precious woods. Anything displayed thus has the magnificence of a king with jewels glittering in his crown and surrounded by dancers offering him golden apples on shallow dishes. Here the passer-by stands spellbound; silken apparel rustles around him, and before him the lips part that he—shod in these boots—will kiss.

The secret of a good display is this: fantasy, the tradesman's most faithful handmaiden, must come to his assistance. But it is a difficult art, and insights soon become ossified rules if the ever-playful goddess denies the artist's hand her blessing. The modern department store, devised by Messel and developed by Olbrich, has provided the display window with its final architectural framework. It is located like a glass case between stone columns that rise mightily upward to the roof. These glass cases provide untold possibilities for objects of a certain size. Elisabeth von Hahn, the artist at Wertheim, established the historical foundations for their design.

The variability in displays, which can have ever-changing backgrounds in a department store, cannot be achieved in specialist shops. Here more subtle forms are needed. In many cases a flat table on casters with a low back is preferred, which allows a view of the shop inside. This has become the customary display method for many cigar shops and victualers. It is suitable in situations where the customer's gaze is to fall upon the goods from above. Merchandise with a silhouette, like figures, costumes, and furniture, requires a high background. In these cases the rear wall is closed out of expediency. But now careful thought must be given to the fact that the window should still allow light into the interior of the shop. Glass panels, even with drapes, never form an adequate background; they do not mark a clear boundary. In any case, panels have to be so placed that they are not cut through by the display. Combining them with light boxes for artificial top light, as Endell did, is one of the most pleasing solutions. Mirrors, used as a background, are equally problematic. They detract from the self-contained quality of the display. In certain isolated instances, as in the case of glass and crystal ware, which benefit from through light, they may be suitable. But in general the background should be as calm as possible. Any characterization of the display as a room or even as a landscape should be avoided. Ornaments and architectural partitions should be used only with the greatest caution. The richer the wares, the more neutral the background has to be. And vice versa: behind black boots a gay drape of bright calico will certainly be effective. It embellishes the whole and lifts the boots. In all cases there should be contrast, albeit contrast in harmony.

NOTE

1. The Deutscher Werkbund was established in 1907 on the initiative of the architect Hermann Muthesius as an interest group that brought together designers, educators, and industrialists, with the stated goal of ennobling industrial production through good design. The yearbooks published before the outbreak of World War I coupled radical polemics with images of contemporary technology—airships, cars, airplanes, ocean liners, and the like—which had a profound and lasting impact on the visual language of modernist design.

34

Paul Westheim

NORDSTERN

The New Administration Building in Berlin-Schöneberg

First published as "Nordstern: Das neue Verwaltungsgebäude in Berlin-Schöneberg," *Die Kunst: Monatshefte für freie und angewandte Kunst* 18, no. 32 (1915), pp. 265–96. Translated by Iain Boyd Whyte.

I will call it an apparatus. If we had not become accustomed to using the word *machine* only for constructions made of iron and steel, with pistons, valves, and whirring cogs, I would not hesitate to speak of this house of thinking, writing, and calculation as an enormous modern machine—an admirable, cleverly constructed machine that, like an enmeshed gearbox, is designed in all its parts and worked out in such a way as to preclude all useless and unnecessary labor, and to make the essential work processes simpler, more manageable, more lucid, and more economical with time. In this building we experience those qualities most characteristic of modern, engineered structures: the tremendous commitment to function and purpose, and the craving for efficiency in every sense. All in all, it is an enormous organism, designed for the efficient use of labor in the context both of the broader society and of the individual employee.

[. . .]

Against expectations of what would, until most recently, be considered essential, this building is not located in the center of the metropolis [*Weltstadt*], in the so-called City, where our great commercial enterprises increasingly strive to position themselves. For certain sorts of business—for banks, shops and department stores, outfitters, newspapers and the like—a site right at the center of the main traffic flows of the metropolis is priceless. An insurance company like Nordstern, however, does not have this pressure to remain in the city center. It needs a public face, but its business does not need to accommodate masses of people flowing in and out each day. For the particular nature of an insurance company means that of the countless people already insured or about to be insured, only a small fraction need to visit the offices personally. In planning the building, therefore, the administration could exploit this advantage by locating it away from the narrow confines of the city center. Quite apart from the price difference for the expansive site, the peripheral location, where the houses are not yet wedged in beside each other, offers the chance to plan the building free of the intrusions of inconvenient neighbors, and to lay it out entirely in response to functional necessities.

The location is the borough of Schöneberg, now incorporated [into Berlin], which the local authority is striving to make into an urban focus through the construction of a new city hall, by laying out a large city park, and by bringing in a new rapid transportation system: the underground railway. There was a completely empty site here, entirely open to the street on all four sides, which offered the advantage of an abundance of light and air, so that no external factors hindered the planning of the internal working spaces. This freedom alone made possible a ground plan that, as we shall see, is supremely simple, clearly arranged, and remarkably functional. It is no exaggeration to say that such a homogenous plan would hardly be conceivable in the Mauerstrasse or the Behrenstrasse.[1] Here one would always have been hemmed in and would constantly have had to take into consideration the many dark, unsuitable spaces, which would not be so useful as every inch in this freestanding structure, in which there is not a single dead corner. For the large number of employees, too, it must be very important to be freed from the need to haul themselves into the city center every day, and to have the chance to live farther out, at the periphery of the stone desert. This first step away from the city center is an exemplary decision for businesses like this insurance company, which, when all the relevant circumstances are rationally considered, cannot fail to find followers.

It should be recognized that the scale of the enterprise is much greater than that to which we are accustomed. A few numbers are appropriate, simply to illustrate the spatial demands from which this building resulted and according to which it should be understood. The number of employees runs to some nine hundred people, the entire assets of the three insurance companies are around 285 million [reichsmarks], and the annual income from premiums and interest is around 56 million marks. The site—located between Salzburger Strasse, Badensche Strasse, Wartburgstrasse, and Innsbrucker Strasse—covers 11,436 square meters, of which between 5,000 and 5,500 are already built on. One could compare these numbers with the 3,200square-meter site of the Palazzo Pitti in order to gain a rough idea of the building volume that has been completed here in around eighteen months with the help of modern technology.

[...]

From whatever viewpoint one considers this building—from practical function, artistic accomplishment, or dignity—it invariably offers a convincing solution. In terms of expense, space, quality, materials, and luxury, there is neither too much nor too little. There is no excessive pomp, but neither is expense spared on the useful and the necessary. It is a functional building, a highly rational machine, but at the same time, both in its totality and its individual parts, it is a powerful document of our contemporary German building culture.

NOTES

Nordstern was an insurance company. The Nordstern administration building was built in 1913–14 at the intersection of Schöneberger Strasse, Badensche Strasse, and Salzburger Strasse to the design of the architects Paul Mebes and Paul Emmerich.

1. Mauerstrasse, Behrenstrasse: streets in the business center of Berlin.

4

PUBLIC TRANSPORT AND INFRASTRUCTURE

The steam age reached Prussia in October 1838 with the opening of the Berlin to Potsdam railway. As in every other European country, private enterprise built railways that ran into the major cities, where each company had a terminus. The first in Berlin was the Potsdamer Station, built in 1838, followed in chronological sequence by the Anhalter Station (1841), the Stettiner Station (now the Ostbahnhof, 1842), and the Hamburger Station (1845). There was, however, neither a central station nor tracks that ran through the city from one side to the other. The first-generation stations rapidly became inadequate as passenger numbers grew and trains became longer and more frequent. The solution was to build much larger stations on the same sites, and the result was the new Potsdamer Station, completed in 1872, with a glass-covered shed that was 170 meters long and nearly 40 meters wide, and the new Anhalter Station, opened 1880, whose shed was the same length, but 60 meters across. Fifty years later, Walter Benjamin recalled the fascination that these great portals to the city exercised on his youthful imagination—in his case, the Stettiner Station, where holiday journeys to the seaside began: "I think it is a legacy of those years that even now, here in the Chausseestrasse, the dunes of the Baltic shore float miragelike before me, released by no more than the sandy yellow tints of the station building and the vision of boundless space beyond its walls, opening up a wider and wider horizon."[1]

A track linking the main termini was built in 1851, but used only for freight. Only some twenty years later, in 1872, was it followed by a ring railway (Ringbahn), which encircled the city well outside the built-up areas and connected with the radial tracks as they converged on the city center. The Ringbahn also opened up new areas for housing development and for the new industrial concentrations that were springing up, particularly to the north and west of the city. Over the following decade an elevated east–west railway (Stadtbahn) was constructed that vaulted through the heart of the city on a viaduct composed of 731 brick arches, and crossed the Ringbahn on both sides of the city before reaching farther out into the eastern and western suburbs. With housing developments already extending out to the Ringbahn by 1890, Berlin now had a steam-driven commuter system to move the workforce both into the city center and out into the new industrial areas.

The speed of the steam trains was not matched, however, by the local transport network on the city streets. Horse omnibuses were initially seen as the solution here. First introduced in 1847, the system of horse-drawn buses was consolidated in 1868 into one enterprise that operated nineteen lines with around two hundred buses. This was a very limited technology, however, since the lines were short, with a maximum length of 4 to 5 kilometers, and the buses could carry only around twenty passengers at a maximum speed of 6 kilometers per hour. A better bet was the horse tram, which ran on rails at almost twice the speed of the buses, could carry fifty people in each tram, and could run for 7 to 8 kilometers. Unsurprisingly, horse trams were licensed by the city authorities in November 1871, following the realization that the newly established capital city of Germany needed a comprehensive transport system. The first line, from Rosenthaler Tor to Gesundbrunnen, opened in July 1873, and by 1898 the horse-tram consortium could point to no less than forty-five lines crisscrossing the city and linking the innermost suburbs to the center. In step with the burgeoning of commerce and industry and the dramatic spread of the housing stock, the number of passenger trips made in and around Berlin on steam trains, horse buses, and horse trams exploded as the century reached its conclusion, rising from 12.1 million journeys in 1870 to 345 million in 1900.

By this time, however, the days of the horse were numbered. As the city council had already noted in a report submitted on 23 October 1871, horse-drawn trams were inefficient, expensive, and an option only for the relatively prosperous citizens of Berlin. The report concluded: "In our opinion, only locomotive railways are able to satisfy the demands for a regular, mass passenger transport system, and are capable of providing an inexpensive means of communication, accessible to all classes of the population, from the whole area of the city toward the center, and from the center to all parts of the periphery."[2] Steam engines were heavy, noisy, and polluting, however, and the solution to cheap, rapid urban transit first came in the 1880s, with the invention of electric traction. Werner von Siemens, based in Berlin, produced the first electric motor in 1886, and a prototype electric vehicle was exhibited at the 1879 Berliner Gewerbeausstellung (Berlin Trade Exhibition) in Moabit. The new technology rapidly gained ground in Berlin, and the first electric tramway in the world opened for business on 12 May 1881 in the southern suburb of Lichterfelde. Siemens and Halske followed this after 1895 with a network of electric trams that served the industrial centers in Pankow and Wedding, and also took visitors from the city center to the 1896 Gewerbeausstellung, housed on a custom-made site on the banks of the River Spree in Treptow. This provided the impulse for the electrification of all the old tramway tracks, which was undertaken by the principal electrical companies, Siemens & Halske and AEG, supported by the major banks.

Private finance also launched a new initiative in 1897, with the founding of the Gesellschaft für elektrische Hoch- und Untergrundbahnen, as the beginning of the network that subsequently became known as the Berlin U-Bahn, the underground railway. With extraordinary rapidity, the first stretch of this new, all-electric system was built between 1897 and 1902, running from Warschauer Brücke in the east to Zoologischer Garten in the west. This first section, 11 kilometers long, cost 1 million reichsmarks, and set high standards of design and execution. Symptomatic of this intention was the competition launched in 1897 for the design of a high-level station, which was won by the architect Bruno Möhring and built at Bülowstrasse. Other sections of the track were entrusted to a series of talented architects that included Alfred Messel, Cremer & Wolfenstein, and Alfred Grenander. As a commentator wrote in the early 1920s, looking back on these early years of the U-Bahn: "Building work on the Berlin electric high-level and underground railway began in 1897; the first group of express lines was completed by 1914. During this period German artistic life in general and architecture in particular experienced a profound development. Whereas right into the mid-1890s, building forms drawn from various historical periods were employed side by side and one after the other in quick succession, there emerged in the period that followed an ever more marked endeavor to abandon traditional manners and to create a new style appropriate to the age. Increasingly dominant became the assertion that an artistically appropriate design was to be achieved less through the application of a formal language in the old sense than through the clearest and most simple expression of function in forms derived strictly from constructional and material considerations. This trend and its basic tenets, which were given vigorous public support from a large community of artists, quite naturally found particularly fertile soil in the artistic treatment of engineering structures. [. . .] The buildings of the Berlin high-level and underground railway stand under the banner of these efforts."[3]

As in Paris with Hector Guimard, and subsequently in London with Frank Pick, both the stations and the rolling stock of the U-Bahn in Berlin were seen as laboratories for the design strategies of the future. These strategies, however, were by no means monolithic, and the cloth was cut with great sensibility to match the particular urban fabric of the site. Thus the architect Sepp Kaiser opted for extreme simplicity in his design for the new junction at Gleisdreieck, completed in 1913. As a contemporary commented: "The decoration of the interior spaces is confined to the design of the railings and the information boards hung above the stairs. The external appearance [...] refrains, appropriately, from all architectural additions and simply expresses the internal volumes."[4] In contrast, the underground station at Wittenbergplatz, completed to the design of Alfred Grenander in 1913, pointed both to the fashion for neoclassicism that was currently gripping European architecture, and nearer to home to the nineteenth-century Prussian classicism of Karl Friedrich Schinkel and his followers. With its interior of glazed tiles and majolica details, it created a worthy anteroom to the neighboring Kaufhaus des Westens, the grand department store that opened its doors in 1907.

Challenged by the new electric trams and electric railways, the monopoly bus company reacted in the best possible way by introducing a new technology of its own. On 18 November 1905 the first two motor buses in Berlin went into service, with open upper decks and the driver barely sheltered from the elements under a small canopy. With an ever-expanding network of electric trains running above and below ground, and electric trams and motor buses on the streets, Berlin by 1910 had one of most innovative and comprehensive public-transport systems in Europe. The metropolis was set in endless motion, with the result, as Egon Erwin Kisch noted in the 1920s, that "no other European capital city has a reputation equal to Berlin's as a 'City of Work.' And, indeed, the structures and machines that Berlin uses to sustain its transportation system, and its economy as a whole, are mostly magnificent, of a perfection that is probably excelled only in America."[5]

NOTES

1. Walter Benjamin, *Berliner Chronik* (Frankfurt: Suhrkamp, 1988), p. 14.

2. Berliner City Council (Magistrat), report to Prussian Ministry for Trade, Commerce, and Public Works, 23 October 1871, quoted in Dieter Radicke, "Die Entwicklung des öffentlichen Personennenverkehrs in Berlin bis zur Gründung der BVG," *Berlin und seine Bauten*, part 10, vol. B (Berlin: Ernst & Sohn, 1979), p. 3.

3. Paul Wittig, *Die Architektur der Hoch- und Untergrundbahn in Berlin* (Berlin: Zirkel, 1922), p. 1.

4. Ibid., n.p. (section 2, second text side).

5. Egon Erwin Kisch, "Berlin bei der Arbeit," *Arbeiter-Illustrierte-Zeitung* (Berlin) 6, no. 25 (25 June 1927), pp. 8ff; reprinted in Kisch, *Reportagen* (Stuttgart: Reclam, 1978), p. 89.

35

Anonymous

THE CONCOURSE OF THE ANHALTER STATION

First published as "Die Empfangshalle des Anhalter Bahnhofes" in *Wochenblatt für Architekten und Ingenieure* (1880), p. 227; reprinted in Alfred B. Gottwaldt, *Berliner Fernbahnhöfe* (Düsseldorf: Alba, 1982), pp. 35–36. Translated by Iain Boyd Whyte.

The Anhalter Station will open for traffic on 15 June. For some time, its magnificent reception hall has attracted an extraordinarily high level of public interest. Over the last decade the major railway companies have embellished the capital of the German state with a series of large-scale installations that have replaced the old stations built like shacks. Among these, the Anhalter Station is the most recent, and at the same time without doubt the most monumental. [...]

The railway company, which merits praise for its great generosity, decided in 1872 on the building, which was planned and designed from 1874 to 1875 and constructed between 1875 and 1880, with only minor modifications. Inclusive of the entire internal installations and appointments, the structure cost four and a half million marks.[1]

The location of the building on the Askanischer Platz, or rather on the Königratzer Strasse, one of the city's most distinguished traffic arteries, suggested that the weight of artistic display should be on this side. The architect has skillfully resolved this difficult challenge and, with the relatively short facade set on the pleasingly redesigned and prettily planted square, has furnished a new, attractive picture that will bring great credit to the city of Berlin. From the convenient porte cochere on the Askanischer Platz one can survey the clear sequence of high vestibule flanked on left and right by administrative offices and surmounted by the colossal hall that soars upward to an enormous height. The richly articulated and powerfully framed gable wall has cleverly thought-out lateral abutments, while a vigorous figure group crowns its proud apex.

This hall, it should emphasized, is the highest in the world and for this reason deserves our particular attention. [...] The roof has a free, unsupported span that covers an area of 10,200 square meters, so that forty thousand people could stand under it at the same time. With a height of 34.25 meters to its ridge line, the hall is, as already noted, the highest in the world. These facts allow one to measure the task of mastering a construction on this scale, and of adapting the artistic design to the enormous expanses that result from it.

The solution can undoubtedly be hailed as a success, and the hall can lay claim to preeminence not only because of its height, but also because of its beauty. The light has unhindered access from all sides and bathes the majestic space, whose endless expanses have been impressively subdivided and enlivened by the skillful articulation of the architect. The entrance opens up three enormous portal-like arches, whose powerful framing and powerful pillars succeed in lending an architectonic character to the gable end. Opposite it, on the town side, the flat planes are resolved like a gallery, with large openings whose slim supports very felicitously continue the impression of lightness that is evoked in the viewer by the audacious vault of the hall. Beside the powerfully horizontal rhythm of the long walls, the vertical divisions are particularly striking, with the supports of the parabolic frames given a rich architectural emphasis by the pillarlike protrusions, between which, above the entrances and exits of the lateral pavilions, are set arched windows of extraordinary dimensions (7 meters across, 9 meters high). The dangers that the extraordinary lightweight roof would, when seen from the interior perspective, give an unaesthetic impression of a baffling confusion of constructional elements or that the hall would be in conflict with the harmoniously formed spaces have also been avoided. This has been achieved by giving the entire underside a light tone and picking out the 3-meter-broad panels between each of the main beams in a restrained light green color, so that the tectonic articulation of the long walls is extended to the roof construction. In this way, an agreeable unified effect is achieved, which is particularly striking at night under electric lighting.

Through its striking height the light construction gains in audacity, and rather than burden the side walls with its breadth, the roof appears more like a light, floating envelope. In the perfect mastery of the immense surfaces of this hall, art and science celebrate a great triumph.

NOTE

1. The Anhalter Station was designed by the architect Franz Heinrich Schwechten (1841–1924) and officially opened by Kaiser Wilhelm I and Otto von Bismarck on 15 June 1880. At that time it was the largest train station in Europe.

36

Alfred Kerr

NEW AND BEAUTIFUL!—BÜLOWSTRASSE?

First published as "Neue Schönheit!—Bülowstrasse?" (1900); reprinted in Kerr, *Mein Berlin: Schauplätze einer Metropole* (Berlin: Aufbau, 1999), pp. 92–93. Translated by Michael Loughridge.

The yodeling faded away behind us, the crisp air above six thousand feet in the Engadine has been replaced by the dust of Potsdamer Strasse, and Venice lies somewhere or other, by a distant sea, dead, in its beauty

But Berlin lives in . . . beauty! Nature made the south to delight man's heart, but

FIGURE 13. Bülowstrasse Station (1900–1901; Bruno Möhring, architect), 1902.

it made the North German plain more for utilitarian purposes. And there certainly is progress here, work, technology, development. Bülowstrasse has fairly changed in these past six weeks. What a startling sight: the iron framework of an elevated railway, all red lacquer and gray paint, rearing up in uncouth loathsomeness between the buildings, in among the young trees. The earth has not anything to show more foul, more barbaric, godforsaken, stupid, pathetic, half-cocked, shaming, goose-pimple naked, whipped-dog wretched than this. Yet this city, since time out of mind, has led a charmed life in matters aesthetic. It has always had a beguiling prettiness, charm, simple beauty, and, somehow, the knack of getting it right in such things. Certainly, it has been known to go beyond the pale. But the way this particular part of Berlin has been treated conforms to a certain modern pattern. It is a principle that applies everywhere. For the French, beauty of appearance counts above all things—but their technology is nothing special; the technologically minded peoples, by contrast, are not good at beauty. In a mere six weeks here the trains to Wannsee have been electrified, and new tracks have been introduced on the Kurfürstenstrasse, whose iron truss work simply sprang up out of the ground.

Wherever you look you will see progress, development, work, technology, and fresh eyesores. Is there no technology without creating eyesores?

But perhaps the problem is just that we are not yet capable of appreciating beauty of this order. For one day this, too, will count as beauty. The struggle is on to create the great architectural masterpiece of the future, the one that Zola conjures up in his artist novel, wraithlike, nebulous, enigmatic.[1] Perhaps it will be the huge hall, built of steel, like this construction on the Bülowstrasse, and of glass. And the eyes of the later born will be accustomed to that and will find splendor in such things, in the same way that we today find splendor in the Florentine palaces, chunky, brutal, slab sided, unabashed as they are and as their builders planted them there half a millennium ago. After all, my friends, consider the resplendent, exultant beauty that the modern steel-frame construction can achieve, consider the fairy-tale tower that the French have put up—that purposeless crowning technological act of a technologically backward people. They have first taught us the beauty of the new approach, rather than its usefulness. Glamorous possibilities rather than actual utility. However, in the more peaceable city of Dresden there is a building that shows how attractive a result in this futurist style can be achieved by combining steel, glass, and sparklingly bright bricks—the sunny, festive, young, resplendent railway station. It has set a standard to follow. The Berliners, for their part, have also found that their newly revised concept of the beautiful has room to embrace the station buildings of the city railway [Stadtbahn] as they appear at dusk; [Hans] Baluschek, the painter, is their gifted herald. From glass and stone and steel, again, [Alfred] Messel constructed the Wertheim palace, which—along with the new Dresden Station building—will probably set the new standards. But neither Saxon elegance, nor the superhuman audacity of the French, nor yet the reposeful and welcoming qualities of Messel's style are to be found in this deplorably transformed Bülowstrasse; all we have gained here is a lamentable makeshift, an act of casual vandalism at the expense of an unspoiled part of the city, a clumsy ad hoc solution. The Parisians, when faced with the prospect of electric trams and overhead power lines, threatened revolution. They had no wish to see their beautiful streets disfigured by wires and poles. There is little prospect of the Berliners going to the barricades! But if things go on like this there is equally little prospect of Berlin becoming "the world's most beautiful city"; Wilhelm II has dropped many a remark capable of triggering debate, and this was certainly one of them.[2]

NOTES

1. Emil Zola, *L'Œuvre* (*The Masterpiece*), 1886.
2. Kaiser Wilhelm II prophesied in 1899 that Berlin would become "the world's most beautiful city." For an article on the public works that were to bring this about, see *Der Bär: Illustrierte Wochenschrift für Geschichte und modernes Leben* 25, no. 52 (1899), pp. 827ff.

37

Richard Petersen

THE TRAFFIC PROBLEMS INHERENT IN LARGE CITIES AND THE MEANS OF SOLVING THEM

First published as "Die Aufgaben des großstädtischen Personenverkehrs und die Mittel zu ihrer Lösung" in *Städtebauliche Vorträge aus dem Seminar für Städtebau an der Königlichen Technischen Hochschule zu Berlin,* ed. Joseph Brix and Felix Genzmer (Berlin: Ernst, 1908), pp. 23–24, 49–50, 60–62. Translated by Michael Loughridge.

Traffic as a whole has been growing steadily. In the year 1904, 630 million journeys were made; in the next year 690 million, in the year after that 754 million, and in 1907 the total reached 794 million—in round terms, 800 million. Within these totals, about 60 percent of journeys were made by streetcar, a good 20 percent on urban railways (i.e., the Stadtbahn networks, plus underground and elevated railways where available), and slightly under 20 percent by omnibus. What this means is perhaps more clearly appreciated if one reflects that the rate of annual increase in traffic maintained over the last few years is equal to the total for cities such as Breslau, Cologne, Frankfurt, and Munich [tables 1 and 2].

Over the last thirty years, the population of Berlin has tripled; but transport use has increased twenty-four-fold, and the number of journeys per head of population eightfold.

[. . .]

METROPOLITAN RAILWAYS: TECHNICAL REQUIREMENTS

[. . .]

For a new urban railway to be viable, the prime planning consideration is unquestionably the choice of route. Urban railways must run along the principal arteries of the city's existing traffic movement. It can be regarded as axiomatic that fast urban rail routes must run radially, connecting a densely populated suburb via the city's commercial center if possible—but at least skirting it—with another suburb, ideally on the opposite side of the city. The construction of such a railway produces an upsurge in building activity along the line; urban expansion is concentrated along the line taken by the railway, extending in particular beyond the termini. The result is usually a marked increase in traffic along the same axis, and in due course a parallel line will be needed to help cope with demand. Only at this stage does the need arise for a railway link running transverse to the original line, and it will be considerably later still before orbital lines linking suburb to suburb can be expected to run at a profit. Such, at least, is the lesson to be drawn from the evolution that has taken place in London, Berlin, and Paris; and it is a lesson that needs to be borne in mind, as urban railway project plan-

TABLE 1 Urban Streetcar Utilization, 1905

	Population	Journeys (millions)	Journeys (per head of population p.a.)	Mean Passenger Fare (in pfennigs)
Berlin (including 29 suburbs)	2,993,000	419.4[a]	140	9.5
Hamburg and Altona	971,000	145.4	150	10.4
Munich	538,000	54.6	101	9.9
Dresden	514,000	82.3[b]	160	10.8
Leipzig	503,000	80.2	159	9.2
Breslau	471,000	49.1	104	8.2
Cologne	429,000	65.2	152	9.1
Frankfurt am Main	395,000	64.2	163	9.4
Nuremburg and Fürth	355,000	22.3	63	9.1
Barmen and Elberfeld	319,000	26.5[c]	83	9.4
Düsseldorf	253,000	26.4	105	10.3
Stuttgart	250,000	24.4	98	8.9
Chemnitz	244,000	17.4	71	9.6
Magdeburg	241,000	26.1	109	8.8
Essen	231,000	17.8	77	10.8
Stettin	224,000	14.0	62	9.2
Königsberg	224,000	13.7	61	10.7
Bremen	215,000	22.5	105	9.6

[a] Streetcars only [author footnote].
[b] Including extra-urban lines [author footnote].
[c] Including the monorail suspended railway [author footnote].

ning, for example, has tended to focus initially on concepts involving orbital lines. A textbook example of how not to route an urban railway can be seen in Vienna, where the lamentable unprofitability of the urban railway can be ascribed solely to the misguided decisions about its route. For a track length of approximately 38 kilometers, its building costs amounted to 122 million marks. Annual operating costs run at roughly 5 million marks, and fares revenue comes to about 4.5 million. Moreover, on top of the net operating loss of half a million marks per annum, there are the interest charges to be paid on the investment capital. In sum, this railway requires an annual subvention of about 5.5 to 6 million marks from the public purse. [...]

SOME REMARKS ON METROPOLITAN TRANSPORT POLICY

[...]

Appropriate determination of route, maximum possible carrying capacity and operating speed. and the lowest possible fares are thus the primary considerations

TABLE 2 Urban Public Transport (rail, streetcar, and omnibus services)

	Population (approx.)	Journeys (millions)	Journeys (per head of population p.a.)
Berlin (1906)	3,000,000	754	250
Paris (1905)	3,700,000	707	190
London (1904)	6,850,000	1164	170
New York (1904)	3,840,000	1072	280

when it comes to planning new transportation systems. This is not to say, of course, that the question of creating an attractive cityscape can be disregarded, but it would be wrong also for aesthetic interests to be routinely given precedence over economic considerations. Thus, for example, some city councilors are still demanding acceptance of a general principle that new permissions should be restricted to underground railways. To this, the answer must be a decided "No." Anyone with knowledge of the technical and financial disadvantages of underground rail systems, and accepting that the first essential is to get the economics right, will be logically bound to conclude from the arguments advanced above that when it comes to constructing new rail lines it is wrong to decide first on the system to be adopted—underground or elevated, surface or suspended track—and then select a route practicable for the chosen mode. The correct approach is the converse—namely, to ascertain the best route and then to work out which rail system would give the best results on that route. In exceptional cases, that might in fact be the underground. Outside the city centers, and in many cases centrally also, it will be possible to use elevated railways, surface or suspended track railways. Underground systems will have to be confined to where they are a necessary evil—that is to say, the more historic districts of major cities. At the same time, I should not like to be misinterpreted as advocating a policy of planting elevated railways in the streets on the model of the steel structures erected in New York or Chicago under one sole constraint—that of building as cheaply as possible. Today we have left aesthetically disastrous constructions like these far behind us, as can be seen from the completed structures of the Berlin elevated railway and from the designs and pilot projects for the Berlin suspended railway. It is quite erroneous to assume that railways are inherently ugly things. While it is true that some older railway construction has been very unsightly, that resulted from the purely utilitarian nature of the projects concerned, which were designed without the involvement of architects of any sensitivity. But the trend prevailing now across the whole spectrum of the arts is to reject the practice of concealing the real nature of things behind superficial ornament, seeking rather to find the most nearly perfect form to express function; and so, too, in matters of transportation it would be wrong to cling to half-understood aesthetic preferences of earlier years and treat transport systems as something that should on principle be kept out of sight. From the architect's point of view, the task of designing such systems is all the more rewarding for involving fresh thinking, with a dearth of existing models to copy from.

These considerations raise a point of great importance for the planning of city expansions—one that has hitherto been virtually disregarded. Very careful thought needs to be given to planning and designing the principal traffic arteries of the future city. These roads must be made wide enough to permit the future addition of a railway line if need arises. They should ideally be designed with long straight stretches, with any bends in the route made into smooth curves, and with substantial widenings at intervals for future intermediate train stops; most important of all, the routes must not be obstructed by monumental public architecture, churches, monuments, and so on. There is no need for such structures to be situated on the midline of major traffic routes. In present-day cities, an appreciable number of otherwise superbly designed thoroughfares have been rendered unusable by a church that elsewhere might have presented a much more attractive spectacle.

The severest problems are apt to arise in connection with efforts to run fast transportation links through historic city centers. As a result of the continuing growth in traffic, however, the need for streetcar and urban railway routes through the central business districts of cities—indeed, for new routes of all kinds—is becoming more and more insistent. Yet at the same time steeply rising property prices are making it ever more expensive to create new routes through built-up areas. Care should accordingly be taken, in all planning for urban expansion, to ensure that any new inner-city connecting routes needed are duly opened up: road widenings and demolition of premises for through-route purposes should be planned well ahead and with all due forethought for the needs of the future.

38

Karl Scheffler

THE ELEVATED RAILWAY AND AESTHETICS

First published as "Hochbahn und Ästhetik" *in Deutsche Bauhütte* 6, no. 14 (3 April 1902), pp. 109–11. Translated by Michael Loughridge.

Recently, the structures associated with the Berlin elevated railway have provided striking examples of how to do it and how not to do it. From the aesthetic point of view, much modern thinking has indeed gone into this project, but it is also no less well endowed with archaic ideas purporting to be modern. Nowhere is the engineering concept implicit in the project fully or consistently worked out, and

FIGURE 14. Railway bridge above the Landwehr Canal, Kreuzberg, 1905. Stadtmuseum Berlin, Nachlass Max Missmann, SK 01/42 VF.

everywhere one can read the signs of repeated cutback and compromise. But then again, it is just as frequently that one senses an impatience with yesterday's aesthetics, an urge to cut free.

What has come into being in this way is simultaneously pleasing and thought provoking, a magnificent technological achievement to which the aesthetic response must be a mixture of joy and dismay.

This was perfectly predictable. The hysterical public outcry when the plans were presented and the constant reiteration of misgivings on aesthetic grounds left no possible doubt that, when the time came, compromise would be the order of the day. The public threw up its hands in horror. Heavens above! A steel framework on the very doorsteps of their stucco-fronted palaces! Down-to-earth practical utility cheek by jowl with the lofty ideal world of their overornamented mansion blocks! It would have been the lunatic asylum for anyone daring to assert that, in reality, the forlorn pomp of yesterday's facades was marring the beauty of the new bold structures in steel, and that the high ground aesthetically speaking now belonged to the engineers. The city residents naturally got their way to the extent of gaining concessions, including a promise that the unsightly steelwork would be "architecturally screened." And on this understanding construction went ahead.

Berlin's geography is unfortunate. The historic seat of our rulers has not become a metropolis in the way that London has, or New York. It differs from them in not having a central financial district dedicated to commerce, and ringed all around by suburbs where people actually live. In Berlin, people choose to live close to the city center and feel thoroughly at home in the midst of the hurly-burly with a view of a tall stone building opposite. This is why the elevated railway, a project designed to serve commerce, is such an awkward intrusion for these metropolis dwellers with their small-town way of thinking. An elevated railway's appropriate backdrop would be the silos of Hamburg harbor, station buildings, and commercial developments such as the Wertheim store. That would lend style to the cityscape—the style of our own time. Berlin is sure to develop more and more in this particular direction, and with a little imaginative effort one can well imagine city streets so unashamedly functional in style and character that our present elevated railway would look archaic beside them. But that is a distant dream.

The architects of the elevated railway have no doubt done their best to find formal expression appropriate to the nature of the project. But they themselves were laboring to a greater or lesser extent under the legacy of outdated stylistic fashions, and in addition found their work greatly inhibited by the standing commission and various habitual objectors. The practice of combining stonework and steel, essentially dictated by bourgeois aesthetics, has led to some grotesque forms, debasing what were sound structural necessities into downright caricatures. The most barbarous practices are seen at those major road junctions where ornamental facings have been installed. Hard by slender steel supports, from which one can develop a sense of relative structural loads, one is confronted by vertical sandstone of such massiveness that the eye already schooled in mass and load registers the impression of a storybook giant struggling under the weight of a walnut. However could such a misconceived sham have been expected to produce an aesthetically worthwhile result? Where steel alone is involved, the appearance will be organic in character; given that the diameter, position, and bearing strength of every element are determined by calculation from the underlying laws, the finished structure will in its own way be as natural in appearance as, say, a male nude. Were the steel supports to be replaced by stone supports of such dimensions as the laws of statics demand, the appropriate comparison—remaining in Berlin— would be with a man with a wooden leg. But what the construction actually in place suggests is a cripple with a wooden leg fully as thick as an ordinary thigh, and ornamented into the bargain.

It is far from clear how the artistic design aspects of this project were managed. There are certain points—for instance, at the Potsdamer Strasse crossing—where the design of the steel supports is of near-genius quality. These slender structures,

FIGURE 15. Swinemünder Bridge, Berlin Gesundbrunnen (1902–5; Bruno Möhring, architect; Friedrich Krause, engineer), 1911. Berlinische Galerie, Landesmuseum für Moderne Kunst, Photographie und Architektur—Photographische Sammlung, from Bruno Möhring: *Stein und Eisen* (Berlin: Wasmuth, 1903–9), © Ernst Wasmuth Verlag Tübingen-Berlin.

their function immediately apparent, derive so intimately from purpose and material in their capital-like top sections and their bases, and they show such artistry of form, in the highest modern sense of that phrase, and such compelling truth in the proportioning of their inversely tapered columns that one knows beyond doubt one is in the presence of an architectural form of the future, more fully developed than the others we have seen, but also showing the greatest potential ahead. Then one moves a few yards farther, only to find oneself looking at a different support profile—and this one is appalling. But why? Here truly there is a field ripe for an artist in structure: his task, to ensure that magnificent engineering is not left to the whim of chance, but is selected and enhanced in terms of its own logic, and that what is revealed to us by the laws of statics is developed into a systematic art.

Siemens & Halske have a name as the leading firm in their own line; if they were to join forces with such an artist as [Henry] Van de Velde, they might be able to add the kudos of inaugurating a new epoch in the history of art, with incalculable consequences. That will sound like wild exaggeration; but it is not, for all that is lacking here at present is consistency. The superb example at the Potsdamer Strasse crossing is evidently the work of an engineer; for the artist has contrived to utterly ruin these beautiful structures by adding fussy wrought-iron ornamentation. During the construction process, from a distance one could distinguish only these supports and the great sweep of curved steel resting on them, all in fiery red lead; the design had great power. But now a modern rococo-esque latticework has been added, and moreover attached to the columns with iron curlicues borrowed from some magazine; and what was monumental is now ornamental. All this nonsense was superfluous, pointless; it is simply stuck on top and is therefore unsightly. And the last straw came in the form of the awful pale gray paint.

Why did our artists fail to see this naturally occurring beauty, when healthy young eyes were taking delight in it every day? Why do they not respect the metal's dignity, when by chance it is there in front of them? And why do they bury what is solid and genuine beneath a layer of tawdry fripperies if the only audience it pleases is that of the unthinking and undiscriminating masses? Here, precisely here, would be the best point to press for a renewal of our architectural conventions. Modernism really is more than infantile squiggles, and English floral ornamentation is more than this derivative and essentially aimless wrought-iron work. The latter is a fad, one that happens to have been perpetuated in iron, and an embarrassing mistake that reveals how poorly even well-known artists understand what modernism really is. These daring girder assemblies, hunched under the load here, thrusting zestfully there, the free-flowing and elegant lines of the essential ties, the uncontrived and therefore stunning originality of the linear combinations, decorative individual details like the webs and fillets on the T-girders with their suggestion of organic growth, the vistas created as the line proudly soars high above the obstacles—all that is modern, because it is born of the plain truth. The truth, our truth—that's modern!

39

August Endell

THE BEAUTY OF THE GREAT CITY

First published as *Die Schönheit der großen Stadt* (Stuttgart: Strecker & Schröder, 1908), pp. 55–57, 58–59, 71–73. Translated by David Britt.

THE IRON BRIDGE

We experience change through the daily scene; but there are some rarely visited streets and districts that leave specific impressions, whether of charm or of grandeur, etched in the memory. Among the most powerful things I know is an iron bridge belonging to the Stettin railroad. Behind the station, a long, straight street runs alongside the railroad embankment; on the right is a row of five-story buildings without balconies, flat, charmless, formless. But in the distance looms a dark monster. For at that point the railroad veers slightly to the right and crosses the street on a bridge 70 meters long. The street dips under it, so that the bridge seems almost to touch the ground. The immensely weighty, arched side trusses of the bridge are set off from each other and form a dark, resilient mass that cuts in close to the last house in the row and seems to bear down upon it. The bridge is a black, towering, animated mountain, like a trumpet blast. Your heart stands still when you see that crude mass in all its monstrous weightiness, its passion, its grandeur. Only once have I ever seen anything like it. That was in Kiel harbor. The ships of the battle fleet were ranged, at wide intervals, far out to sea. And one of them had hung out all her signal flags to dry. That was the same passion, the same terrible thunder, intensified by the wild colors, dominated by a brilliant red; it was like a gigantic, blood-red cockscomb, blowing lazily in the wind, from deck to masthead, in monstrous contrast to the gigantic forms of the ships in their taciturn gray.

GLEISDREIECK

Similarly powerful, but more fragmented, the sweeping curves of the Gleisdreieck triangular junction on the elevated railroad, in their strange contrast to the thin, abstruse forms of the iron supports.

SCHLESISCHER STATION

Quite different, again, almost playful, and yet overpowering: the train shed of the Schlesischer Station, with its colossal roof, 207 by 54 meters, sustained by countless threadlike iron rods, so thin that they seem to slice painfully across the eye. Disgraceful as an architectural effect, but incomparable when a thin mist fills the vast space, and the iron braces look like an endless, glistening spider web.
[...]

FRIEDRICHSTRASSE STATION

A sense of grandeur is most readily conveyed in those cases where the gigantic scale of engineering structures achieves a monumental effect even in the raw—notably in the main machine shops of factories, which of course very few people ever see, and above all in the glass roofs of railroad stations. Friedrichstrasse Station is wonderful when you stand on the outdoor platform overlooking the Spree, from which you see nothing of the "architecture," only the gigantic glass-screen wall and the contrast that it makes with the petty confusion of the buildings all around. Especially beautiful when the confused and disjointed surroundings of the station merge in the evening twilight, and the numerous, tiny panes of glass catch the red light of the setting sun, so that the whole surface is alive with shimmering color above the low, dark, menacing cleft from which the broad bodies of the locomotives lunge menacingly forward. And then, how all is intensified when one enters the darkening interior, still filled with an uncertain daylight: the gigantic, gently curving form, ill defined in the gloom; a sea of gray tones, faintly tinged with color, from the lightness of the rising steam to the dense gloom of the roof and the full black of the locomotives that thunder in from the east. Above, in the dim surface of the glass wall, there glows what looks like a towering, shimmering, red mountain: it is the gable end of a building, blazing in the reflected light of sunset.

[. . .]

VEHICLES AND HORSES

And the tide of vehicles and horses. Here, as elsewhere, some wonderful individual forms: a trotter, a English saddle horse, heavy carthorses with the thick feather on their fetlocks. As for the vehicles, they seldom attain that nimble, gliding swiftness that we admire in modern sailboats, depending as this does on faultless lines, faultless materials, and faultless craftsmanship. Cabs, worthy and dull; automobiles, still uncertain in their form; trade vehicles, often oddly garish and bizarre: as functional forms, these do not bear looking at individually, but they grow attractive and even pretty as components of an image in which foreshortening and displacement create strange new shapes, and in which gaudy paintwork is softened by the veils that mask everything. This effect of juxtaposition and accumulation is particularly apparent at dusk, when forms are filled out by clouds of shadow. Horse and cab become one; to the living eye they seem a gray mass, with occasional dark shadows and glinting highlights. Perspective seems to vanish altogether; nothing appears in front of or behind anything else, and the whole looks like a mountain on the move by night, beneath the spectral, red, misty lamplight. And so all of the vehicles become weird and wonderful living creatures: the giant yellow box shapes of mail vans, the motor omnibuses like swaying, thunderous edifices, the trolley cars with their glittering, green carcasses, gliding past like glass ships, unexpectedly swinging into the curves and throwing out bright flashes in the plate-glass windows as they turn.

40
Anonymous
THE NORTHERN LOOP
A Journey on the Ring Railway

First published as "Der Nordring: Ein Fahrt auf der Ringbahn" in *Berlin für Kenner: Ein Bärenführer bei Tag und Nacht durch die deutsche Reichshauptstadt* (Berlin: Boll und Pickardt, 1913), pp. 123ff. Translated by Iain Boyd Whyte.

From the windows of the northern loop [*Nordring:* the northern section of the ring railway, opened in 1877], we look out over a different Berlin than the one that can be seen from the windows of the Café Bauer, Unter den Linden, or on the Kurfürstendamm and the Tauentzienstrasse. The glittering masquerade drops, and the deprivation becomes visible. The north is the reverse side of the coin. Anyone who wishes to see Berlin with observant eyes should also see it once. Such an observer would then better understand some of the secrets of the huge city and feel the power that the worker in Berlin signifies. The towering chimney stacks and the human masses that stream toward them speak for the development of Berlin in a no less eloquent language than do the dazzling lights in the Jägerstrasse [in the city center]. In addition, the Berlin of the worker has become extremely large; the north has become extended as far as Weißensee. Its physiognomy has remained the same: rental barracks with deep courtyards and narrow side and diagonal buildings, depressed faces on the streets, many children, shopkeepers, many bars, hospitals, and so on. The air is thicker than in the Friedrichstadt, and a veil seems to float over the whole area.

A short visit to the north will reveal to us the characteristic features of this area. [. . .] [An electric streetcar takes us to the Turmstrasse.] Turmstrasse is the main street of Moabit. It extends to Beusselstrasse, and in it we trace from the people, houses, and life the first breath of the north. Here and in the cross streets—Wiclefstrasse and Sickingenstrasse—the Moabit riots raged in 1910. The critical site was on the corner of Sickingenstrasse.

The next stop is Beusselstrasse Station. We look around and espy halfway to the right the tops of two towers. These are the chapel towers of the Plötzensee penitentiary that stretch up here. Immediately facing the Beusselstrasse Station on the railway bridge one can see a small building in which a refreshment room is to be found. It is the last station for those who bid their farewell on entering Plötzensee, and the first station for those who celebrate here for the first time their regained freedom. It is oftentimes wild here in this pavilion.

[. . .]

To the right is the endless railway yard with freight traffic. Behind it the giant Berlin lies in wait. To the left we see something very typical for the peripheral districts of Berlin: garden allotments. There are hundreds of small gardens that the common worker has rented for the summer as a place of rest in the open air. He has planted his cabbage and salad in such gardens and spends the whole of Sunday there with the whole family. In the summer house that he has constructed himself, and which very often takes on the form of a small house provided with lock and key, cooking takes place and even the night is spent there. A typical Berlin image is when the allotment colonizers celebrate their parties, harvest festival, and so on. Then the summerhouses are decorated with flags and lanterns, and from garden to garden garlands and paper chains stretch out. Music, beer, and dancing in the evenings under the colored lanterns get the partygoers into the right mood.

Putlitzstrasse Station. To the right, released from the smoke and fumes, Berlin North emerges with its rows of rental barracks. Balconies are stuck onto them in huge numbers. Warehouses, storerooms, and factories line this stretch. From below, the sound of music from a carousel and shrieking people rises up. We travel past a rubbish dump upon which people play the most primitive games. In the background the towers of the Dankeskirche in Wedding rise aloft.

Wedding Station. To the right are the back ends of the deep housing blocks, with glimpses of the people in their apartments. The outer walls of the buildings are plastered with advertisements for debt payment in installments, cheap soap, paints, bicycles, and so on. To the right, beneath a flat covered space, is the homeless asylum of the Berlin Asylum Association. The huge municipal Asylum for the Homeless is located later on, between the Prenzlauer Allee and Weißensee stations. At all events, it is not visible from the train.

At the Gesundbrunnen Station, away from the cheerlessness, there is a view of the greenery of the Humboldthain. But soon this view disappears in the rental barracks. We vanish behind the railway embankment. When we reappear it is the old picture: buildings pressed on buildings, an eternal desert of stone.

Schönhauser Allee Station. We advance through many underpasses. Male and female workers get on and off, but no "business ladies" spruced up in modern style as on the Ringbahn to the West. Instead, poorly dressed girls, recognizable at first glance as factory workers.

Prenzlauer Allee Station. To the right behind the huge gasometer there lies the Asylum for the Homeless of the city of Berlin, which accommodates three thousand homeless each day. To the left are more garden allotments, and here for a while Berlin ceases. One has an open view. To the left lies the Weißensee; to the right the Berlin colossus seems to recede behind the terrain of the railway.

At the Weißensee Station, it seems to press nearer again. In seconds, the image disappears between embankments. Yet it is soon there again with its rental barracks and the warehouses, factories, and industrial sites, which here stamp the impression of the area and the people.

The next station is Landsberger Allee and here we alight. [. . .]

41
Peter Behrens
THE INFLUENCE OF TIME AND SPACE UTILIZATION ON MODERN DESIGN

First published as "Einfluß von Zeit- und Raumausnutzung auf moderne Formentwicklung," *Jahrbuch des Deutschen Werkbundes* 3 (1914), pp. 7–10. Translated by Michael Loughridge.

The use made of time and space could be understood, on the basis of visible effects produced, as the rhythmical principle in creating form. Rhythm is in fact tempo, a measure of movement. But it appears justifiable to adopt the term for the visual arts if these are not conceived as static but as possessing organic life. We perceive the rhythm of the age we live in as different from that of any foregoing era. So it is rhythm we have in mind when we say that our own age is rushing past faster than that of our parents.

We are possessed by a sense of haste that allows us no leisure to become engrossed in detail. Dashing in our all too speedy conveyances through the streets of our great cities, we can no longer take in the details of the buildings we pass. From the express train, similarly, no cityscape can register on us as we flit past, except as a mere silhouette against the sky. Individual buildings no longer have a voice of their own. This manner of perceiving our environment—now an ingrained habit in every situation—can be catered to only by an architectural approach that wherever practicable creates uniform, reposeful surfaces, smooth and free of complication. If a particular feature is to be emphasized, however, it will need to be placed at the end toward which we are moving. It is essential to create an easily registered contrast between salient individual features and large plane surfaces, or else a uniform array of necessary details such that these combine to form a single entity.

In marked contrast to the medieval principle of unpredictably twisting streets and quaint irregular squares, modern urban and suburban design has to conform to an overall plan drawn up in advance and has to incorporate broad, straight, long roads. In aesthetic terms, the sought-after model is not the picturesque medieval idyll, and it is in fact the axial layouts of the Baroque age that bear the closest affinity to the architecture of our own day. For example, bridges intended for heavy traffic flow across a wide river will not be hemmed in by high buildings on either bank: we prefer to have both bridge ends widen out, the better to accommodate traffic moving onto and off the bridge.

And if on the one hand it can be said that architecture created on these principles offers the most impressive results in terms of cityscape, it is also the case that it suits modern buildings themselves, especially with regard to their interior layout, better than any other. For of course the great commercial premises of the major cities have their own internal traffic flow, so that here, too, the proper utilization of time and space is of concern. If the function of such a building—determined by the major criteria of maximum internal daylight, built-in flexibility in the size and shape of the rooms, unimpeded communication, and full commercial utilization of floor space—is taken as a design principle, then here, too, the rhythmic principle will ensure that the most dignified design emerges, created by the balanced proportions of the whole. And in the process, as these basic rhythmical elements are identified, an archetypical architecture will come into being. Finding the archetype is one of the high aims of all art, not least in architecture. It is not only the individual house that will take on the archetypical form, but whole districts and even cities.

The first part of a city to acquire a distinct character of its own will be the central commercial district. The premium on economical use of time and space will ensure that buildings reach the maximum feasible height. The practical value of the American city-center principle with its skyscraper buildings is known to everyone who has transacted business there and come to appreciate the advantages of urban quarters built in this way. But aesthetically, too, it is precisely these buildings that make the strongest impact of anything in the young nation. By virtue of their bold engineering they contain the germ of a new architecture. And their expansion in the vertical dimension is important beyond the individual building, because above all it creates cityscape. In urban-design terms, after all, a city should be treated as a single architectural entity. In the case of a metropolis, so vast as to stretch farther than the eye can reach, the aesthetic use of space cannot be sufficiently served by providing for open squares, worthwhile though that is. Nor can a church spire create much in the way of effect when the city's horizontal extension is too great. City design, like other designs, requires body and silhouette, and this can be achieved only by juxtaposing compact vertical masses.

If this, then, is how the business heart of the city acquires its characteristic profile, it is only natural that the outlying suburbs surrounding large cities should become a zone of country houses, their construction contrasting in their primarily horizontal character with the vertical emphasis of the central commercial district. While there is an understandable insistence in city centers on avoidance of time-consuming distances from point to point, the corresponding desire at the end of the day to escape—using steadily improving transport facilities—to open country and natural surroundings, and to make one's home and find one's recreation in this more spacious setting, is equally justified.

It is in the nature of architecture to subsume the main characteristics of all form-giving activities. All the other visible forms in which life finds expression are readily compatible with it. And this is why the rhythm inspiring a period's architecture will also influence the other forms we see around us—first and foremost among them of course everything pertaining to transport and movement.

Thus it is already natural for us to judge the beauty of a ship, a railway locomotive, or a motor car not in decorative terms but for the sleek grace of its lines.

"There is nothing more vulgar than haste." And yet we are all in a hurry. Why this should be so is not something that can be explained in factual terms. In earlier eras, too, there were great tasks to be accomplished; whether greater than ours must be left unresolved. The life span allotted to us is no shorter than that given our forebears in past centuries; so there is really no reason to rush things. Haste is imposed by the rhythm of our contemporary age, working through the human psyche. It is one of the fundamentals of our creativity, but has not yet become a cultural form or discipline in the artistic sense. Haste is an upstart among us, and we for our part have not learned to cope properly with it: the lifestyle that we are constrained to follow has not yet acquired the graces of maturity. A characteristic of our time so basic and universal as this cannot be suppressed by Romantic-inspired counsels of quietism. What is needed now is a serious and resolute approach to tackling the challenges of our time. It is idle to spend time lamenting the billboard quality of what we see around us, but it is real cultural progress to impose order and harmony on lurid colors and bizarre forms. It is Philistine to deprecate the swift ebbing of fashion, but it is wise to be mindful of the economic return inherent in the human love of change and to enjoy change, too. Modern times have blown away many of our dreamy and reposeful pleasures, but they are confronting our art with new challenges, to which a coherent and fully worthy response will emerge, provided that we can recognize the rhythmical beauty of this present age.

42

Karl Ernst Osthaus

THE RAILWAY STATION

First published as "Der Bahnhof," *Jahrbuch des Deutschen Werkbundes* 3 (1914), pp. 33–41. Translated by Michael Loughridge.

Once, in the past, there was a time when one could speak of the poetry of railway stations. In those days there was no barrier. As a boy, one would be on the platforms for hours at a time, watching the trains pull in and depart, drinking deep of the destination plates that wafted one's imagination from Paris to St. Petersburg, from Amsterdam to the towering marble of Milan. One could see people getting out who only yesterday had been strolling about those fairy-tale cities, people whose clothing still bore the dust of the boulevards, the flying spray of the English Channel or the Mediterranean. They were met, hugged close—and there were others again who tore themselves away, shouted a few more parting words across space; then handkerchiefs waved them out of sight. Life's dramatic moments seemed to have been marshaled together in this place; the train meant joy and meant grief, all in the same instant; and the dual nature of existence impressed itself deeply on the heart of the observer of this changing scene. The trains came to symbolize life itself in all its fleetingness and transience, and often, coming away, one would still be in a state of heady emotion, as if having lifted the veil of Maya[1] and glimpsed the truth of existence.

And there are other things, too, to be seen in stations—things that etch themselves deeply into the susceptible mind. The thrill of sensing one's mystical link with the huge forces about to thrust the train, that huge and gleaming snake, out into the starry night; the silent converse of the myriad signal lights; the ceaseless flickering play of light and heat reflected in the steam from the locomotives, on the rails, on the piled coal; the rhythm of rolling wheels, whistling machines, and slamming doors; ultimately the whole marvelously calculated organization governing the life of this place: all this brings such a wealth of intoxicatingly sensuous experience that even the eye of an artist might well falter.

Observe the psyche of the traveling public today, however, and you will see no flicker of all the former excitements. The keynote now is total impassivity. The scurrying streets discharge their quick succession of hackney cabs, motor cars, and pedestrians at the main entrance portals; hardly a word is spoken as tickets are bought; registering luggage is almost a mechanical process. The seasoned traveler takes a couple of cursory glances and knows which way to head; for everyone else, there is much anxious searching and questioning first. No one has time to be alone with his thoughts: the train pulls in, compartments are invaded, doors slam, and the train proceeds on its way. Who has a thought for his neighbor? Even greeting one's fellow passengers is now felt to be a quaint practice. Everyone has shutters down against the crowd. The mutual social alienation of first-, second-, third-, and fourth-class human beings extends even to the waiting rooms. Ill humor can be read on every face, and if in our day the man on the street has a good word for the railways, it will only be because the journey frees him for a few hours from the greater scourge of the telephone. The railways as a phenomenon have lost their thrill—except for children, for whom the steam locomotive is still the favorite toy.

How far the public's attitude reflects awareness of the technical achievement that the railways represent is not an issue that will be gone into here. What can be said is that, for the architect, the modern railway station is not a setting for private elation, nor for any festive spirit. We expect it to deliver meticulous conformity to the whole complicated array of specifications and requirements, we expect it to have been perfectly designed for ease of locating any of its myriad functions, and we expect sophisticated but wholly impersonal comfort and convenience. We rightly demand impeccable quality of detail as a measure of the management's dedication to good practice. Hygienic considerations require extensive use of glass,

FIGURE 16. Friedrichstrasse Station, 1898. Landesarchiv Berlin, II 6583.

ceramics, leather, and metals. Textiles, on the other hand, should be virtually banned in stations. The smoke generated by railway engines is a compelling reason for preferring smooth, nonporous surfaces and rounded outlines. All these factors contribute to the matter-of-fact, self-contained character of the modern railway station.

[. . .]

What had seemed no more than a disparity becomes an out-and-out contrast once one casts an eye over the design of the main halls of station buildings. We have come to expect that what purports in this context to be architecture turns out to be an aesthetic disaster. [Heinrich von] Stephan's misguided notion of building modern post offices in whatever style was felt to be characteristic of the particular town has been extended to station buildings.[2] Stations have been built as Gothic stations—that is, in the same style that once gave eloquent expression to Christian religious ecstasy. A few years ago, Metz came up Romanesque. The current trend favors Baroque pomp: volutes curl below factory chimneys, and the sprightly goddesses skipping across the topmost level of the facade steadily accumulate the soot from the locomotives in the folds of their high-girdled robes. Windows are decked with hanging garlands of ivy and rams' heads—the symbols of esoteric cults, decorations in ancient times for the altars of the gods; and somewhere around the back is a magnificent castle gateway, but its lantern windows, which once were polished glass, are now totally opaque, being made of stone!

Those details all relate to a single railway station—as a matter of fact, one of the best in Prussia. Shall I invite you to step inside? To admire what has been achieved there in the way of fake Empire, lumpen Louis Seize, and painted-on tapestry wallpaper? And yet, as already indicated, this station has its good points, and I shall not name the city or the architect. But do you perhaps wonder why, in this same station, no one has thought to provide a place for timetables and official information, or why freestanding display boards and vending machines litter the place in such numbers that mothers lose their children while fathers are trying to find a porter? And yet, in this hall, a substantial number of essential notices are *not* belatedly afterthoughts, but were part of the architectural composition from the outset; and it was here, perhaps for the first time in a state railway station, that efforts were made to establish a properly demarcated area for bill posting and to impose aesthetic standards on the material displayed.

But the case described is typical. It would be pointless to criticize an architect, a planning authority, or the railway authorities. And it is no less typical that all these things are as insensitively executed as they are banal in conception. It is indicative of the way building programs are carried out in Prussia that a few hundred marks cannot be made available in connection with a station project that is costing forty million, even when they are needed for completion of an artistic detail in a key position. The minister's decrees on reduction of costs have little effect on the big spending decisions, but they never fail to wreak havoc on artistic detail.

[. . .]

But that is just the point, gentlemen: you live in the belief that you can make a thousand practical points come together into a significant whole. Something essential is missing, and that is any sense of the creative genius, which is given only to a few. Whether genius comes into contact with tasks to be accomplished or not is in the hands of Providence. But your way is to condemn genius either to waste itself on trivia or to be denied and disappointed, time after time, in its fight to be given great tasks. Our nation has a right to its creative artists. And you who have the power to distribute and to withhold, you bear the responsibility for what becomes of our civilization. Give genius its chance! Florence would never have become the Florence we know if the Medicis themselves had nursed the ambition of becoming a Brunelleschi or a Michelangelo.

NOTES

1. Deriving from Sanskrit roots, and present in much Indian religion, Maya is the restricted, purely physical and mental reality of our daily lives, held to be a mere illusion and a veiling of the cosmic truth.

2. Heinrich von Stephan was appointed postmaster general of the unified German state in 1876. He is regarded as the father of the modern German postal service and introduced, among other things, the *Postblatt*—today's postcard.

5

THE PROLETARIAN CITY

In a celebrated book published in 1930, the city planner Werner Hegemann described Berlin as "die größte Mietskasernenstadt der Welt," which translates literally, if inelegantly, as "the largest rental-barracks city in the world." The barracks to which he was referring were the enormous speculative housing blocks that sprang up in Berlin after German unification in 1871 and spread out from the city center like wildfire in the following four decades of rampant housing speculation. In the absence of a centralized planning authority, the developer was king, and tenement housing was built to suit all purses. While grand apartment blocks were the order of the day in the prestigious suburbs close to the city center, the working-class housing constructed in the industrial quarters of the city was designed to generate maximum rental profit from the most modest and cramped accommodations.

Into this housing streamed the new industrial proletariat of Berlin, drawn to the city by the prospect of employment, particularly after the agricultural depression of the 1880s, and by the glamour of the big city. The population of Berlin, excluding the surrounding townships that were not incorporated until 1920, rose from 826,341 in December 1871 to 2,071,257 in December 1910, and the great majority of this newly arrived population was crammed into the *Mietskasernen*—the tenement barracks of Wedding, Moabit, Neukölln, and Kreuzberg. Writing in 1907, the city-planning theorist and economist Rudolf Eberstadt gave the following definition of the *Mietskaserne:* "The term *Mietskaserne* is a recognized *terminus technicus:* it describes, as we know, the mode of Berlin developed in Berlin, which has conquered a great part of Germany as a result of the extraordinary speculative profits that are associated with it. The appropriate term for this form of house was coined in Berlin, and the instinctive feel for language correctly reveals in this case the determining characteristic. The concept 'barracks' contains the abolition of the individual and of individual will, and their subjugation under an overriding goal. For the housing that obliterates all individual traces of its inhabitants and entirely subjugates dwelling to the purposes of speculation, no more fitting description could be found than *Mietskaserne*. The term signifies a house type that in courtyard apartments, side wings, and rear blocks encloses an undifferentiated mass of living quarters. The *Mietskaserne* is characterized by the size of the plot, which is occupied entirely by the house, and at the same time by the plan, in which the individual apartment entirely disappears."[1] The courtyard format, however, with a block facing the street and lateral or transverse blocks set toward the rear of the deep, rectangular site allowed a large variation of apartment types within the same structure and serviced by the same sets of staircases. Thus one floor level could be divided into as few as two grand apartments, or as many as twelve single-room units. This in turn allowed for a relatively broad spectrum of residents. The *Mietskaserne* at no. 99 Skalitzer Strasse in Kreuzberg, for example, generated annual rents from its twenty-nine apartments that ranged from 2,400 reichsmarks to 276. The former from a publican (*Gastwirt*) in a large apartment on the street-front parterre, the latter from a "Miss" (*Fräulein*) on the top, fourth floor of the rear house.[2] Between them, the tenants paid a total of 23,803 reichsmarks in rent, which was the equivalent of 11.7 percent of the total cost of building the house—a remarkable level of profit. There was also a wood merchant's shop in the courtyard at Skalitzer Strasse, and this was not untypical, as many of the Berlin tenement blocks also housed workshops and commercial enterprises. The *Mietskaserne* at no. 132/133 Ackerstrasse, for example, could point in 1900 to a wide range of enterprises, which included a brush maker, a printer, a furniture maker, an umbrella-stick maker, a wood turner, a factory for gas and water pipes, and no less then three celluloid-comb makers.[3]

The economics of the *Mietskaserne* were brutally simple: increased density meant increased profit. As this was the only housing type available, the working classes were forced to move into rental apartments at exploitative rents. Statistical tables produced in 1910 highlight the considerable discrepancy that the rental structure had on the various social classes. Whereas a family with an annual income of 100,000 marks paid around 5 to 8 percent in rent, families on 900 marks a year were paying 30 to 35 percent of this income on rent. These extraordinary financial constraints meant that around a third of the city's population could barely afford the rent without resorting to other methods of raising money from their apartments. This was done by subletting beds and subleasing apartments during the day to prostitutes and similar. In this way, the direct relationship between density and income held not only for the speculator and house owner, therefore, but also for the tenants, who were often forced to raise revenue by subletting rooms and beds to non–family members. A report on living conditions published in 1893 under the aegis of the Berliner Arbeiter-Sanitäts-Kommission focused on 805 apartments located in the Sorauer Strasse in Kreuzberg, which housed 3,383 people. It established that in 30 percent of the apartments, the tenants were taking in night lodgers, and that each person had access to less than twenty cubic meters of air.

The health implications of such densities were frightening, particularly with regard to typhus. In 1848, the epidemiologist Rudolf Virchow had been sent to Upper Silesia to investigate the causes of a major outbreak of typhus. His "Report on the Typhus Epidemic Prevailing in Upper Silesia" concluded: "There can no longer be any doubt that the epidemic spread of typhus is possible only under living conditions such as those caused by poverty and lack of culture as witnessed in Upper Silesia. Remove the conditions, and I am convinced that the typhus epidemic will not return."[4] In spite of this early warning, little was achieved on the public-health front until 1872, when Virchow pressed and succeeded in arguing that a comprehensive sewage system should be constructed in Berlin. These works were essentially completed by 1895.

The dawning awareness that the health of the population and the economic benefits to be derived from a healthy workforce were directly related to living conditions began to impact housing design in the 1890s. Housing associations, unburdened by the profit imperatives of the speculator, commissioned leading architects such as Alfred Messel, Albert Gessner, and Paul Mebes to design housing blocks that provided fresh air, cross ventilation, adequate sanitary installations, and access to urban greenery. The strategy here was to assemble a number of adjacent plots across which the housing could be spread more generously, without the need for the lateral blocks and rear blocks that created the dark courtyards of the traditional *Mietshaus*. The first agency to initiate these reforms was the Berliner Spar- und Bauverein (Berlin Savings and Building Society), which commissioned Messel to design workers' housing on a double site at no. 7–8 Sickingerstrasse, in the industrial suburb of Moabit. It was completed in 1894. In these apartment houses, Messel pulled the side blocks back from the main facade in order to bring air and light into the courtyard. With this design, Messel challenged the need for the dark, enclosed courtyards of the standard Berlin *Mietshaus*. Variations on this practice followed over the following decade. At the Goethepark in Charlottenburg (1902–3), the architects Andreas Voigt and Paul Geldner drove a private street through the center of a city block, accessed by gates at each end, which was lined by apartment housing that could be cross-ventilated from back and front and which was topped by roof gardens. Shortly afterward, Alfred Messel designed the reform housing block at Mommsenstrasse 6, in which the housing was wrapped around only two sides of the rectangular site. This created both variable plans for different-sized apartments and large courtyard spaces. The asymmetry of the street front made these goals explicit.

By the outbreak of World War I, the development of working-class housing in Berlin had created the design conditions that were to lead in the 1920s to the city's emergence as the leading generator of new ideas in housing. On one hand, the regimented plans, dimensions, windows, doors, and internal fittings developed by the ruthless forces of speculation had proven the advantages of standardization in lowering unit costs. On the other hand, the manifest shortcomings of the *Mietshaus* had engendered a commitment among progressive and radical architects to bring light, air, green spaces, and proper sanitation to mass housing. Brought together, these two opposing currents generated the great housing estates of 1920s Berlin. As Karl Scheffler, that very perceptive chronicler of Berlin, already sensed in 1913: "We can anticipate with some certainty [. . .] that workers' housing will be created from concrete, steel, and glass, and will no longer be reminiscent in any way of the expanded *Mietshaus*. Instead, it will speak of the spirit of modern architecture and will be developed principally by trusts, building societies, and mutual cooperatives."[5]

NOTES

1. Rudolf Eberstadt, *Abwehr der gegen die systematische Wohnungsreform gerichteten Angriffe* (1907), quoted in Johann Friedrich Geist and Klaus Kürvers, *Das Berliner Mietshaus, 1862–1945* (Munich: Prestel, 1984), p. 219.
2. Statistics from ibid., p. 271.
3. See ibid., p. 303.
4. Rudolf Virchow, "Mittheilungen über die in Oberschlesien herrschende Typhus-Epidemie," *Archiv für Pathologische Anatomie und Physiologie und für Klinische Medizin* (1848), vol. 2, pp. 143–322; published in English translation as "Notes on the Typhoid Epidemic Prevailing in Upper Silesia" in Virchow, *Collected Essays on Public Health and Epidemiology*, ed. L. J. Rather (Boston: Science History Publications, 1985), vol. 1, pp. 204–319.
5. Karl Scheffler, *Die Architektur der Großstadt* (Berlin: Cassirer, 1913), p. 48.

43

Theodor Goecke

THE WORKING-CLASS TENEMENT BLOCK IN BERLIN

First published as "Das Berliner Arbeiter-Mietshaus," *Deutsche Bauzeitung* 24 (1890), 501–2, 507–10, 522–23. Translated by Michael Loughridge.

WHERE DOES THE WORKER LIVE?

In an inner suburb, as everyone knows. Or perhaps in an outlying suburb, provided there is a direct link to the city. But never out in the country. For preference, he will not even live in those towns closest to the city—not even, indeed, when his daily job is located there. Thus, for example, many workers employed by the factories in Köpenick return to Berlin every evening. If they had any desire to live farther out, one can be certain, the property developers would cater to any sustained housing demand locally—as well or as ill as they do here. Just where these people earn their money is of no particular concern to them.

No, the fact is that the worker prefers to spend his time in the busy urban setting; he feels at home in the hustle and bustle of the streets; he knows the advantages of the much larger community when it comes to shopping for what he needs; his amusements are here. This is why, year by year, so many are forsaking rural occupations. It would consequently be a wholly mistaken policy to attempt to set up working-class housing on a significant scale at any distance from the city. It is necessity, not preference, that drives the worker to move his home farther and farther out as the city expands and rents climb higher. Now, this is certainly not intended to imply that the building cooperatives and other comparable organizations currently pursuing exactly contrary aims are on the wrong track. For sure, there will always be some workers who actually prefer a more distant, but more agreeable, place to live, who wish to grow their cabbages in peace, who just want to live between their own four fences. The endeavors of such bodies certainly deserve to be supported; but, in the end, is what they can achieve of any real significance measured against the overwhelming majority that prefers—or is obliged willy-nilly—to make do with the minimal living space that is afforded by the tenement block? It must be borne in mind that a very large proportion of the population is tied to the city by the nature of the occupation pursued. These are the workers who have to be permanently available at short notice. Such individuals have no choice about where they live: it has to be in a tenement block. And yet the worker, like any resident of a great city, has something of the carefree wanderer in his blood; this makes him feel more at ease as a tenant, free to pack up and depart if he so chooses. The phenomenon may be deprecated by some as economically wasteful, and combated through attempts to encourage a more settled habit; however, it exists and is widespread. The population living in the circumstances described is in need of help, and it is the duty of a just society to try to meet its needs.

A number of active groups have been working to this end for many years now, but the scope they have for effective action is unavoidably very limited. As a result, their efforts make almost no impact on the overwhelming majority of the needy. In a report published in the 1867 volume of the *Zeitschrift für Bauwesen* [Building gazette], the Gemeinnützige Gesellschaft [Society for the Promotion of the Common Good] and the allied Alexandra-Stiftung [Alexandra Foundation] describe their first successes. The introductory general account of conditions at the time, particularly with regard to the distribution of the working-class population over the city area as a whole, is by and large out-of-date and no longer accurate. While it is not possible to enter here into a detailed account of the changes and displacements that have accompanied the physical expansion of the city and the increase in population, it can at the very least be confidently asserted that the working classes have crowded into certain city neighborhoods, notably Rixdorf,[1] where something approaching a wholly working-class suburb has come into being. It is true that the factories are well dispersed across the city, which contributes to some extent to mixing the workers through the rest of the population; however, as anyone can see, the older factory premises are being steadily pulled down, one after another, in order to create new expensive building land and at the same time displace the workers from their accustomed surroundings. Thus there can no longer be any real doubt as to the direction in which we are drifting. In future, as we walk to the city center—certain elegant districts excepted—we will encounter a mixed population, but conversely, as we walk outward toward the periphery, we will find the mass of the workers. They have already taken possession of a ring-shaped area of the city stretching round from the northwest to the east and on to the southwest.

IN WHAT CIRCUMSTANCES DOES THE WORKER LIVE?

This can be briefly put: in a place to sleep beside his wife. It is rare for the apartment to offer more than this, as besides the couple and their children it also has to accommodate young lodgers of both sexes. Any better-situated or childless working-class couples let one room furnished and live in the kitchen themselves; for the overwhelming majority of these apartments consist of only two rooms. This does not mean that they were all designed in that form, though this is more likely in apartments that face onto an internal courtyard. In other cases, apartments of sufficient size may be simply divided in two, and small cast-iron kitchen stoves installed in ordinary rooms. The entrepreneur planning street-front apartments with several rooms will have subsequent development potential in mind and will calculate the size of the rooms so as to allow him the most profitable use of the site.

This is how it comes about that in some districts whole terraces may be occupied entirely by workers, while elsewhere workers may be living only in the blocks built at the rear and on the sides of the internal courtyards, with the street fronts occupied by clerks and craftsmen—all categories living in extremely cramped conditions. The ground-floor level of the street facade is almost invariably taken up by shops and bars. Lavatories are still often installed only in the yards, and if provided on the landings have to serve the occupants of several apartments.

It is not surprising, therefore, that a worker will change his abode relatively frequently; after all, it has little to offer him beyond a cooking facility, four bare walls, and with luck a water supply. Many "flittings" are the consequence of a job being relocated. Workplaces are often a considerable distance away, so that even with the use of omnibus or tram, or of a rented *Kremser* [covered motor coach]

FIGURE 17. Working-class apartment, Liegnitzer Strasse 9, Kreuzberg, 1910; Ullstein Bild, 282252.

shared by a group of workers, a good part of the day is spent on travel. The evenings are devoted to recreation, to club activities, or—at times of lively public debate—to political meetings. Sundays are spent out at the Hasenheide or at the "Berlin Prater."[2] All this combines to limit the value of the domicile in people's lives. But in any case, even if the head of the household goes to the pub for a drink only once or twice a week, or not at all in the case of the lowest paid, the wretchedness of the living conditions is such as to prevent any sense of enjoyment of domesticity. The worker in the metropolis has in fact long forgotten what it is to be "at home" in the proper sense of the term.

[. . .]

WHAT DOES THE WORKER NEED?

The whole question of whether improvements can be made in the workers' living conditions therefore comes down ultimately to a technical and financial problem:

is it possible to finance the construction of tenement buildings with apartments available at the rents cited above? The writer believes this to be possible, and proposes to deliver the proofs in a continuation of the present essay. It is true that it will not be possible to make the apartments significantly larger than those now available, but they would be better aired and more comfortable; and the lower rents to be charged would mean that families could afford to rent for sole use. The family would thus be just a family once more, liberated from all the outsiders with whom circumstances at present force it to share its accommodation.

[. . .]

WHAT MUST THE WORKING-CLASS TENEMENT BUILDING CONTAIN?

The two-room apartment, consisting of living room and kitchen, can readily be identified as the metropolitan worker's prime need—a fact long known to the property entrepreneur. If one takes it as the basic element to start from when sketching the ground plan, it will be clear with the first drawing that one-room and three-room apartments will fit naturally into the same scheme. The author therefore proposes, as a norm, that the standard local staircase type be used, with each landing giving access to two apartments, the dividing wall between them being located on the center line of the stairwell. The rooms immediately adjoining the stairwell should ideally be 15 square meters in area and would provide a frugal generation with appropriately adapted contemporary equivalents of the traditional German *Diele*, or family all-purpose room. This room would be the setting for the family's everyday life. The cooking would be done here, likewise the smaller washes; and from this room one enters the rather larger front room, about 20 square meters in area, which has the beds and the regal family sofa. In the corner opposite the door a kitchen stove is installed, of the type proposed by Born in Magdeburg, in order to warm the *Diele* and to ensure plentiful air circulation in both rooms. For it is not the official standard from the code of hygiene, calling for so many cubic meters of air space per occupant, that determines the size of the rooms, but the prospect that even at current high property prices cheap family apartments might be created that will be healthier to live in than what the great majority have at present. [. . .]

It is of the greatest importance that each home should if at all possible have its own private and easily reached lavatory. The author proposes locating this in the outer corner of the protruding stairwell. [. . .]

For the residents' main washdays, particularly bearing in mind that some will be taking in washing for the sake of supplementary income, it will be necessary to provide several laundry rooms. While the most convenient location would be at attic level adjoining the drying lofts, the obvious risk of flooding speaks against this option, and having the laundering facilities in the basement would enable them to be linked to a modest bathhouse. The latter could alternatively be accommodated in an extension, depending on local circumstances. The author is prompted to make this proposal of a bathhouse because the records of users of public baths demonstrate clearly that it is only men who use them often enough to draw significant benefit from them, no matter how low the admission charge. The women of the common people, and their children, will bathe only if it costs them virtually nothing. In a big building, it should be possible to offer this. Shower baths, such as are now being introduced, and brick-built bathtubs are not expensive to install, and in order to use them the tenants would merely need to bring their own fuel for heating the water. Laundry rooms with boilers and sinks, and a bathhouse, would need to be provided in the basement. [...]

HOW SHOULD THE WORKING-CLASS TENEMENT BUILDING BE CONSTRUCTED?

Simply but solidly, with restrained ornamentation. All walls, with the exception of a very few partitions that can be of plaster over a wire-netting base, should be brick built, and the front facades should be finished outside with a lime wash, which can be left in its natural color; the openings should be outlined in ordinary clinker or simple, shaped brick, and the ground-level plinth and some intermediate cornices as well as the main cornice should be built of the same material. The balcony balustrades can be covered in the usual way with sheet metal, which working-class housewives love to scour till it shines. [...]

WHAT ARE THE COSTS OF THE WORKING-CLASS TENEMENT BUILDING?

[...]

There can no longer be serious doubt as to the feasibility in principle of constructing working-class tenements that provide healthy living conditions yet can be offered at individual rental levels one-third below the current norm. Even were one forced to build farther out, the average rental level as calculated above would fall, and what was saved in rent could be put toward transport costs. The bottom line accordingly is the same here as elsewhere: the construction of working-class tenement buildings—subject, of course, to the limitations described above, imposed by local conditions here—is a capital investment with amortization at 4.5 percent. What would really be a boon, however, would be for a financially strong development company to erect buildings of this type both centrally and in the suburbs, with a view to using the yield from rentals paid in outlying areas to recoup the extra costs of providing low-rent accommodation in the center. For this reciprocal balance to be maintained, the buildings concerned would of course need to remain under the same ownership.

NOTES

1. Rixdorf was a historical settlement on the eastern side of Berlin that had grown by the end of the nineteenth century into Prussia's largest village. It was renamed Neukölln in 1912 and incorporated into Greater Berlin in 1920.

2. The Hasenheide was the site of the first public gymnastics ground, established by Friedrich Ludwig "Turnvater" Jahn in 1811. Laid out as a landscape park by Peter Joseph Lenné in 1838, the Hasenheide developed after 1870 into a destination for pleasure trips out of the city, with several beer gardens and coffeehouses. The Berlin Prater, named after its Viennese cousin, was founded in the mid-1850s in Kastanienallee, Prenzlauer Berg, and rapidly evolved into a tavern, pleasure garden, variety theater, and ballroom.

44

Otto von Leixner

LETTER EIGHT: A SUBURBAN STREET IN NEW MOABIT

First published as "Achter Brief: Eine Vorstadtstrasse im neuen Moabit" in Otto von Leixner, *Soziale Briefe aus Berlin* (Berlin: Pfeilstucker, 1891), pp. 76–80. Translated by David Frisby.

[. . .]

A street in the suburbs. But not one of the old city districts. It was constructed in the last four or five years, and some houses are still listed in the address book for 1890 as uninhabited, despite the fact that in the last two months of the first half of the year they have been filled up to the very roof with tenants. Others have not yet been inhabited. The street lies in the northwest in that section that has been formed from Old Moabit outward in the direction of Plötzensee. Although roughly ten years ago still mostly a small sandbox, it is now one of the largest suburbs and, at the same time, one of the healthiest in the whole of Berlin. On most of the streets, trees were planted immediately as the streets were laid out. The trees have been carefully looked after and, despite the damaging influences of the gas connections, have matured very well. Though predominantly lime trees, maple trees and birch trees can also be found. In combination with the small front gardens, this gives some streets a very friendly impression.

In the buildings themselves, architecture has not exactly celebrated a victory, at least as far as the development of the facade is concerned. One would be pleased if the builder had been satisfied with simply building up his four- or five-floor-high boxes and avoided any further ornamentation, aside from unadorned, protruding alcoves and simple balconies. But in those places where he has been allowed to indulge his power of imagination, dreadful works of art have emerged. The first and second floors up to the frail pilaster are totally flat; in the third story a heavy balcony intended for two tenants suddenly protrudes outward, supported by audaciously balanced volutes, which, God knows how, have grown out of the plasterwork. On the balcony four columns are developed that are overlain with all manner of ornamental flourishes that are transposed into small-breasted atlases that in turn have to bear heavy pillars. Upon the latter there stand four of the mass-produced canephores,[1] with hands extended imploringly against the roof that bears down upon them. In addition, on the fourth floor, three balconies are squashed between the columns that look just like pulpits. There is only enough space upon them for a single person and a bunch of roses. The longer one spends observing this building, one is overcome by a touch of fever and begins to talk nonsense. The madness is quite contagious.

A kind of cheap luxury is to found almost everywhere in the dwellings of the lower stories of the frontage houses. In fact, everything is wholesale and constructed from poor material while seeking to imitate real wealth. The doors are embellished with ornamental moldings made from pressed wood, with the leaf branches and egg molding gilded over. The awnings reveal material purchased by the meter and secured with a screwdriver. Badly drawn angels and animals from fables, the former with deep red cheeks and large forget-me-not eyes, float around above in the strangest positions. What does it matter then, when a long plug into which the gas pipe flows for a chandelier hangs out of the stomach of some heavenly dweller? Most of the stories contain two apartments with three to four rooms, a kitchen, and now almost always a bathroom. The term *room* should be used cautiously, since there is no place in it for anything other than the bathtub; except the occasional, very slimly built child. Nonetheless, this is already a major step forward for which we have to thank recent developments.

The prices of these dwellings range between six and eight hundred marks. On the fourth and fifth floors, the same space is often extended to three apartments. In relation to the "smarter" districts, in this city district one can live between 20 to 50 percent more cheaply. This price difference is least for the very small apartments, which are mostly located in the back premises facing the courtyard. The street itself is one of the quiet ones. It does not connect any traffic-laden arteries; there is no railway station in the immediate vicinity; and equally there are no large factories nearby. Even the tramway only crosses the end of the street. In so doing, the rumbling and clanking are suppressed.

The inhabitants are composed of diverse strata; only the highest and the lowest are missing. The better apartments are inhabited by middle-ranking and lower officials from the post office, tax office, or the city; alongside them are several pensioned officers; small commercial people who are active the whole day in the city; modest retirees; and here and there a write or a painter. Tradespeople of all kinds are very well represented, whose dwellings are on the ground floor next to the shops. The greatest proportion of the inhabitants, however, are better-placed workers of all trades, such as foremen, fitters, molders, and so on. Here, social democracy is already very strong; yet it is much stronger in neighboring Wedding.

The shops on the street provide for almost all of the daily necessities. There are fruit vendors; bakers in large numbers, in several places next door to one another; butchers; dairy shops—grandly known as the "milk bureau"—alongside cigar sellers and barbers. Especially noticeable are the number of small alehouses, almost all of which display the bust of the Emperor Wilhelm II in their windows, even in those frequented almost entirely by social democratic workers. Unfortunately, gin shops predominate—this curse of Berlin—and female servers are also to be found in these spirit shops.

From a housing stock comprising thirty-two dwellings that has its greater side in the street being described here, I counted no less than twenty-three gin shops, including seven in which only distilled spirits were sold. In several locations, they are to be found adjacent to one another—in one case, two in the same building, to the right and the left of the main gateway.

[. . .]

NOTE

1. A canephore is a caryatid carrying a basket on her head.

45

Heinrich Albrecht

THE WORKING-CLASS TENEMENT BUILDINGS OF THE BERLIN SAVINGS AND BUILDING SOCIETY

First published as "Die Arbeiterhäuser des Berliner Spar- und Bauvereins," *Zeitschrift für Architektur und Ingenieurwesen, Wochen-Ausgabe* 44, no. 2 (14 January 1898), 17–18, 21–23, 35–36, 41–42; reprinted in *Kunsttheorie und Kunstgeschichte des 19. Jahrhunderts in Deutschland,* ed. Harold Hammer-Schenk, vol. 2 (Stuttgart: Reclam, 1985), 223–30. Translated by Michael Loughridge.

In recent years, building for the common good, especially as represented by the work of the cooperatives, has shown a welcome increase, particularly in Germany. Great efforts are now being made in all quarters to get a firm grip on the crisis situation that undoubtedly exists.

This makes it all the more singular that the wake-up call issuing from the leading figures in the welfare movement should have found so little response among architects, of all people. The search for the most appropriate design for workers' housing, it must be said, has received notably little support from this quarter. This comment is less valid with regard to detached houses suitable for a rural setting, and the associated ground-plan types. The "colony" developments established by certain big industrialists for their workforces—for instance, the Krupp firm, the Höchster Farbwerke [Höchst Dye Work], the Döhrener Wollwäscherei und -Kämmerei [Döhren Woolen Mills], and the railway-building and military-supply companies—show clear signs that the architects in charge of these projects had fully taken the measure of the problems involved. Nonetheless, even in this context, when reading the architects' own collected publications one encounters a startling proneness to schematic thinking and poor judgment. Things look immeasurably worse when it comes to the issue of ground-plan design for the working-class tenement block in the big cities. In the nature of things, the problems that confront the architect charged with creating small accommodation units are quite different from those that arise in connection with so-called superior-class apartments.

In many cases, no consideration has been given to what it may take to make an apartment a good one for working-class people to use; instead, designs have been uncritically modeled on whatever happened to be the standard, local ground plan, and thus not surprisingly failed to meet their purpose satisfactorily [. . .].

Let us now consider the position in Berlin in particular, where circumstances still to be described below have rendered the difficulties greater than elsewhere. Back in the early nineties, the Vereinigung Berliner Architekten [Association of Berlin Architects] made a serious attempt to work toward a solution of the problems. [. . .] All these endeavors were flawed in the same way: they lacked the courage to break away from Berlin's usual schematic thinking, and in particular clung to the principle that such residential building can be financially viable only on the basis of utilization of land to the legally permissible absolute maximum.

The first architect to break with this principle, in theory and practice, was [Alfred] Messel. [. . .] Discharging an obligation taken on in an honorary capacity, he was engaged [. . .] to design small-unit housing for the first urban site acquired by the Berliner Spar- und Bauverein (founded in 1892), on principles that the cooperative could approve. Transferring the principles underlying the already mentioned design to the new project was problematic in many ways, because the new site had already been selected at the point when Messel was entrusted with the planning and the responsibility of supervising the construction. The site consisted of two plots that were hemmed in between other buildings, each having the typical Berlin dimensions—highly unsuitable for small-unit housing—of 18 meters frontage and 80 meters average depth [. . .].

Right from the start, work from these drawings proceeded on the basis that there would be no attempt to utilize the plot up to the maximum that building regulations allowed. Of the double plot, measuring 2,800 square meters in all, only 1,200 square meters—that is, well under half—were built over. The appropriate conjoining of the plots yielded a very spacious courtyard, which completely lost the depressing, barrackslike air of most Berlin tenement courtyards once it had been given some elements of a garden and some simple but effective articulation of the interior facades, facing the courtyard. Between the transverse back block and the site limit at the railway line, a generous-sized children's playground was provided. The transverse block is completely freestanding. The original intention had been to have the street-front building likewise completely separate from the side wings, so that even in the re-entrant angles between the street-front building and side wings it would be possible to avoid the so-called Berliner Zimmer [Berlin room],[1] which wastes space and always makes apartments more expensive. This plan was not adhered to, however, in the face of opposition from influential members of the cooperative's managing committee, who were not yet prepared to abandon long-standing practice completely. In due course it was the architect's judgment that was confirmed, for after completion, the apartments with the disproportionately large "Berliner Zimmer" remained obstinately difficult to rent out.

As regards the layout of the apartments themselves, most have two principal rooms and a kitchen. In the side wings, all apartments are of this type. In the back block, the asymmetrical positioning of the stairwells has made it possible to divide the ground plan into four in such a way as to create a number of very small apartments consisting of living room and kitchen only; these have low enough rents to be attractive to the lowest-paid workers and thus meet what in Berlin is, regrettably, a very real need. The upper stories of the street-front building, similarly, taking advantage of the space on each floor directly above the entrance lobby, all feature a small, one-room-and-kitchen apartment fitted in between the two larger apartments. On the first floor, two three-roomed apartments have been provided, one on each side. Each individual apartment has its own front door and hall, a private lavatory, and a larder. Attention may be called here to one feature that has proved notably successful—namely, that in every apartment in the side wings and in the back block, the kitchen range and the heating stove are on the same wall; the stoves here are all so designed that the combustion gases from the kitchen range are used to heat the living room. In summer the connecting flue to the heating stove is closed with a baffle, diverting the combustion gases to the chimney. The laundry rooms, each shared by a number of families, were installed in the attics—another arrangement that has worked admirably. Having laundry room and drying loft adjacent to each other dispenses with the need to carry heavy baskets of clean laundry all the way upstairs to the top floor. At the top of the building there are also a number of bathrooms—a facility so direly needed here, in a workers' apartment block of all places, that its installation in similar buildings can hardly be too warmly recommended. Finally, each apartment has its own space in the cellar and its own slatted storage compartment in the attic.

NOTE

1. The "Berliner Zimmer" is the generously dimensioned room that forms the link between the front block and the side wing in the L-shaped apartments that were commonly built in Berlin in the late nineteenth century. With a window in one corner, it serves both as a living room and as a link to rooms in the side wing.

46

Alice Salomon

A CLUB FOR YOUNG WORKING WOMEN IN BERLIN

First published as "Ein Arbeiterinnen-Klub in Berlin," *Soziale Praxis* 12, no. 87 (June 1903), pp. 994–96. Translated by David Frisby.

The lure of the metropolis annually induces thousands of young girls to leave their homes and to seek employment in factories. This offers a degree of independence of movement and free disposal over their spare time. The dangers facing such young working girls—who, isolated and without family support, seek accommodation in industrial centers—have resulted in diverse philanthropic institutional responses. The brutalization of the female part of the young workforce is as much grounds for concern as is the intemperance of young men. Girls who at a young age leave their homes and take up employment in a factory usually do not earn enough to be able to secure a congenial dwelling place, and healthy and sufficient nourishment. The unsatisfactory nature of their sleeping quarters forces them to spend time in the evenings on the street or in low bars. If their sleeping quarters do not give the right to the use of a living room in the free evening hours and on weekends, they do not find a pleasant home in their lodgings that encourages their intellectual interests and the provision of their economic needs.

Nonetheless, the attempt to erect single homes for unmarried young working women has hitherto met with minimal success. For different reasons, such institutions have had to close due to insufficient occupancy. On the one hand, the prices that a hygienically organized home must charge are too high—more than a female worker with average factory employment can afford. And so such homes often have to be reorganized for better-paid strata of working women: for commercial secretarial and female telegraph workers and so on. On the other hand, however, the appeal of such homes to young working women has suffered from the fact that the girls do not wish to submit to the constraints and controls of an institution. For instance, by Berlin standards, it is a quite justified desire for young women occasionally to seek out pleasures that make a return to the home before 10 P.M. impossible. Yet a means of replacing this much-disputed house regulation by freer rules has not yet been found by most female institutional directors. It should also be recognized that such reforms would in fact have to overcome great difficulties. If the necessary nighttime quiet is to be secured for the girls in communal sleeping quarters, obligations like these must be maintained.

Five years ago, rejection of accommodation in such institutions by young working women led to an attempt—unique for Berlin—to found a *club for young working girls* that was thereby determined to overcome the deficient sleeping quarters, but at the same time the attempt was made to reduce their hardness in such a way that young working women were offered a city district, a sociable focal point, a pleasant place to stay in their free time. The first *residence for young female workers* was erected at 8 Brückenstrasse, in the middle of one of Berlin's busiest factory districts. Its purpose was primarily to secure for young working women—regardless of their political or religious beliefs—stimulation, education, and enjoyment in the evenings. The friendly rooms that were made freely available for a small circle of socially interested women, under the leadership of Frau Else Strauss, were indeed well occupied. And after a short period, the wish of the working girls was granted to extend *opening times to midday* and to provide a midday meal.

[...]

In the evening hours in the club, events are regularly organized by members of the committee and several assistants: courses in dressmaking and needlework, gymnastics, singing; popular lectures on hygiene, legal and economic questions, and other similar topics.

Each month the female workers themselves organize a social evening, to which they invite fellow members and friends. On such occasions, they put on small theatrical pieces, musical comedies and the like, the preparation for which always occupies the interest of all members of the home for a long time. How much the girls' taste is formed by such pleasurable occasions was highlighted recently when the working girls themselves expressed the wish to stage Goethe's play *Die Geschwister*.[1] [...] Another noteworthy result is the strong development of *a sense of solidarity* that is evident among the members of the home. The girls get to know one another, find the opportunity for friendly interaction, and offer support to one another in periods of illness or unemployment in a quite remarkable manner.

The home also exercises an important influence upon the economic circumstances of the female workers. First of all, the meals that are taken in the home are more substantial and better than those in cheap restaurants. Great emphasis is placed, when arranging the menu, on ensuring that the different nutritional elements are available in the necessary amounts, and that the female workers become accustomed to the healthiest diet possible. To this end, fruit, milk, and egg dishes are on offer at the lowest possible prices.

[...]

The considerable attendance at the club one year later made necessary the removal to larger rooms that were found in the front part of the house on the same piece of land. Unfortunately, the additional costs thereby incurred prevented the committee from proceeding with the foundation of further homes until more interested parties and friends were able to support this venture. It is hoped that with time it will be possible to secure support from a series of factory owners, whose contributions would make it possible to establish such a home in each city district.

[...]

Even though the home does not secure direct economic advantages for young working women, and even though it cannot—in contrast to *a protective law or occupational organizations*—have an influence upon the labor contract, on working hours, and on wage rates, nonetheless an indirect effect upon the improvement of the economic situation is certainly aimed for. For the interaction between female visitors in the home creates intellectual advancement, encouraging the education of a section of the population. While these ambitions should not be overestimated, one should not forget that ultimately all the efforts to achieve shorter working hours and higher wages that certainly must stand in the foreground of all efforts to improve the welfare of female workers are ultimately only a means to the end of assisting female workers to achieve a *better standard of life and a higher culture.*

Such a goal can be achieved to its fullest extent only when working women who, by entering wage labor too early in life and being deficient in domestic education, bluntly go against their own interests can be guided to a correct evaluation of their free time, to an enrichment of life and ennobling its contents. They, too, will then be able to take part in the advancement of culture. Working women must learn not to give away a part of their wages for material enjoyments of the crudest kind, but rather to develop the need for objects that make life pleasant and comfortable: to place alongside the value of material goods the new belief in ideal values. The young working women's club must strive toward this goal.

NOTE

1. Johann Wolfgang von Goethe's *Die Geschwister* (1776) is a one-act play on the theme of love between brother and sister.

47

Werner Sombart

DOMESTICITY

First published in Sombart, *Das Proletariat* (Frankfurt am Main: Rütten & Loening, 1906), pp. 20–28. Translated by Michael Loughridge.

With sure instinct, the German language uses the word *Häuslichkeit* ["domesticity," but with clear echoes of "house" and "home"] to refer to the distinctive environment that forges a family's unity. *Häuslichkeit,* domesticity, implies that the civilizing values of family life cannot evolve and flower except within an appropriate physical setting—that of the house. Domesticity is the medium through which the family influences its individual members. Without domesticity there can be no true family life. The prerequisites for domesticity, in theory at least, are a house with garden and yard, cellar and loft, stairs and cubbyholes, and an appreciable number of individual rooms. In recent times our aspirations have become rather more modest. We no longer demand a whole house as the physical foundation for our domesticity: in the big cities, one makes do with an apartment in a tenement block. But the apartment must provide a certain minimum of space, anything less being totally unacceptable if the most basic requirements of "domesticity" are to be met. [Hans] Kurella, in *Wohnungsnot und Wohnungsjammer* [Housing crisis and domestic misery], puts the point admirably. "It is evident," he says, "that if domesticity is to be the focus for a development process and for a shared life (as is implicit in the very concept of the family), it must become established in a home that, first, can be relatively permanent; second, is closed off against the intrusion of elements alien to it and against observation from outside; and, third, has enough rooms to accommodate such household belongings as afford a reasonable measure of orderliness and comfort, to allow communal family life, and to allow the individual family member space for his personal interests and the chance sometimes to be alone."[1] [. . .]

By that reckoning, if an apartment is to be regarded as truly fit for humans to live in, with adequate space for a full family life, then for the average family of father, mother, and three or four children it would need to have at least the following: a kitchen, three rooms for daytime use, and two bedrooms; a total volume of at least 250 cubic meters; and a floor area of at least 68 square meters.

But in that case it can be confidently asserted that the vast majority of the working population (at least in continental Europe and with respect to large towns and industrial centers) are currently living in conditions that make civilized family life impossible. [. . .]

Who could believe that in our day and age a considerable number of people are living in so-called dwellings in which not a single room can be heated? Yet the population statistics tell us that Berlin has over fifteen thousand such places, Barmen over eight thousand, and so on.[2] These are the exception, certainly, and the great majority of them will have only a single occupier. Yet those figures are small measured against the overall number of people living in one-room apartments, which is alarmingly large. In most German cities, indeed, as I remarked earlier, half or nearly half of the entire population are living in flats with only one room: in Barmen the figure is 490 in every thousand, in Berlin 430, in Breslau 409, in Chemnitz 551, in Dresden 374, in Görlitz 462, in Halle an der Saale 429, in Königsberg (Prussia) 505, in Magdeburg 454, in Plauen (Vogtland) 641. It can be safely assumed that only a minute percentage of the working population occupy more than two rooms.

The term *overcrowded* is used in the official census returns when an apartment has six or more people occupying one room, or eleven or more occupying two rooms. And such conditions are not at all uncommon. Even by this criterion, Berlin has almost thirty thousand "overcrowded" apartments, Breslau seven thousand, Chemnitz five thousand, Plauen three thousand, and so on. Just imagine! Six and more people in one room, eleven and more living in two rooms!

What truly completes the domestic misery of the poorer among us, at least in the cities, is that even in the cramped slum conditions, unworthy of the name "home," in which they have to live, they may not even be able to live privately as a family, but have to accept strangers lodging in their midst. These deplorable circumstances obtain, for example, in 391 out of every thousand one-room apartments in Berlin and in 370 of thousand one- and two-room apartments in Breslau, 596 in Plauen, 572 in Munich, and so on. [. . .]

And that, then, is the homely abode of the poor man, where peace has its dwelling place! We may remember how Faust stumbles his way in the dark up the four flights of courtyard stairs to the attic where his Gretchen lives, walks into her bedroom, and says:

> How this whole place breathes deep content
> and order and tranquillity!
> What riches in this poverty,
> what happiness in this imprisonment.
> [. . .]
> What order, what completeness I am made
> to sense in these surroundings! It is yours,
> dear girl, your native spirit that ensures
> maternal daily care, the table neatly laid,
> the crisp white sand strewn on the floors![3]

And then we may try to imagine this "holy place" [*Heiligtum*] located somewhere in a large tenement block, with six to eight families on every floor huddled together "in the lovely twilight" [*im süßen Dämmerscheine*], with many hundreds of tenants streaming in and out of the same entrance doorway—Faust and Mephisto among them!

NOTES

1. Hans Kurella, *Wohnungsnot und Wohnungsjammer, ihr Einfluß auf die Sittlichkeit, ihr Ursprung aus dem Bodenwucher und ihre Bekämpfung durch demokratische Städteverwaltung* (Frankfurt am Main: Hülsen, 1900).

2. At the time of writing, Barmen was an industrial town in the Prussian Rhine province. Its population rose from 116,144 in 1890 to 156,148 in 1905. In 1929 it was incorporated into Wuppertal.

3. Sombart is quoting *Faust*, part 1, lines 2691–94 and 2702–06:

> Wie atmet rings Gefühl der Stille,
> Der Ordnung, der Zufriedenheit.
> In dieser Armut, welche Fülle!
> In diesem Kerker, welche Seligkeit!
> . . .

Ich fühl', o Mädchen, deinen Geist
Der Füll' und Ordnung um mich säuseln,
Der mütterlich dich täglich unterweist,
Den Teppich auf dem Tisch dich reinlich breiten heißt,
Sogar den Sand zu Deinen Füßen kräuseln.

> English translation from Johann Wolfgang von Goethe, *Faust*, part 1, trans. David Luke (Oxford: Oxford University Press, 1987). Sombart's later two isolated borrowings come from lines 2687 and 2688.

48

Albert Südekum

IMPOVERISHED BERLIN DWELLINGS—WEDDING

First published in Südekum, *Großstädtisches Wohnungselend*, Großstadt Dokumente, no. 45 (Berlin and Leipzig: Hermann Seeman Nachfolger, 1908), pp. 31ff. Translated by David Frisby.

I have viewed, visited, and investigated many working-class dwellings. I have described them as I found them. But I have never hunted out the very worst and hence the less demonstrable instances. You have to take this into account—for there are certainly many much worse examples.

I still remember very vividly my first research journey into the bleak territory of Berlin's impoverished dwellings. It took place in the mid-1890s of the last century. A friend who was active at that time as a doctor in the deep north of the city had agreed to act as my guide.

A hot and humid August afternoon.

We arrived at one of the cross streets that extends from the Müllerstrasse to the Reinickendorfer Strasse in a very crowded mass rental bock, one of those in which real poverty had made its base. It was here, on the third floor of the traverse building, that the doctor had to visit a sick woman. As we stepped through the courtyard gateway we were overrun by a noisy crowd of children: young boys and girls of different ages, destitute starts in life, who could barely stand on their own two legs. Children of tender years and those already matured for school romped noisily among one another with that tinny banging that often distinguishes the tender plants of the big city so disadvantageously and harshly from the quieter and joyous mirth of the happy youth of the village and the small town. A couple of children with careworn, grave-before-their-years faces tore themselves away for a moment from the melee at play and called out to him unceremoniously, "Good luck, Herr Doktor!" while they penetratingly inspected me as the stranger.

The stagnating air of the narrow courtyard lay as heavy as lead upon the dirty paved floor; the walls of the building gave off a grueling heat after the sun had mercilessly sent down its arrows of blazing sun for day after day upon the stone-

FIGURE 18. Ackerstrasse 132–133: Meyers Hof, aerial view, 1930. Landesarchiv Berlin, 282252.

and-asphalt desert of the dusty city. A sense of oppression lay upon my chest as we stepped through the narrow door to the stairwell and climbed the staircase. Almost every stair creaked and groaned loudly under our steps, and although we both wore light footwear, we could not complete our ascent without making a considerable noise. Those who live "elegantly" have no conception at all of how much it crashes and quakes when a tired, heavy man stamps up the stairs of such a building in his heavy, hobnailed boots.

At every stair landing three doors lead off, on most of which were hung several door plates or cards. In this transverse building, there were almost only two-room dwellings, comprising a single room and a kitchen. Many renters still shared their rooms with night lodgers or rooming girls.

Because of the dreadful heat, my friend's patient—the wife of a casual laborer— had left open both the door of the kitchen in which she lay and the door to the stairway. She rested upon a wretched bed, which consisted only of a pile of ripped material upon a squeaking, lumpy mattress. I waited in the corridor for a moment until the doctor explained in a few words who I was and why I had come there. She invited me in with the movement of a hand. The atmosphere in the room was

FIGURE 19. Ackerstrasse 132–133: Meyers Hof, internal courtyards, c. 1900, bpk / Kunstbibliothek, SMB, Phototek Willy Römer / Willy Römer.

appalling, since because of the noise of the children playing, the sick woman was unable to open the window the whole day long. She was suffering from a painful strained foot and a pulled ligament that she had acquired through a fall on the steps while taking out the newspaper. Looked at medically, the "case" was not a cause for concern. What did come across so vividly here was what a calamity could be brought about from even a small accident, or a minor ailment in the home, so-called, of the poor.

There were only a few miserable domestic utensils to be found in the cheerless room. On the small iron cooking apparatus stood a couple of pots that had still not been cleaned since their last use. The only table was covered with a couple of plates and glasses, pages from a newspaper, a comb, a brush and soap dish, a box containing rubbing ointment, a plate with food remains, and other objects. The small collection of clothing for the family hung on the walls; a pair of half-faded family pictures and an unframed woodcut from an illustrated newspaper formed the only decoration. Aside from the wife and her husband, three children—of which the eldest was a fourteen-year-old girl, and two boys around seven and four years old—also lived in this kitchen. The bed of the sick woman, the only visible means of sleeping, was pushed slightly to one side so that she could get out of it without fully raising herself onto her feet when reaching for the tap water; a commode stood behind the bed; in the corner a wicker lounging chair, but otherwise only two wooden stools without backs.

While I was making these observations and writing up my findings, the doctor investigated the injured foot and spoke to the woman with some reassuring words. He knew from earlier visits that in her helplessness she was close to losing the last remains of her courage to face life. Her husband was a bottle washer at a brewer's agency. The work was badly paid, but was supposed to be "permanent," which meant that it continued over the coming winter, which is why the man did not risk seeking better-paid jobs elsewhere—in the building trade, for instance.

When she was willing to talk a little in response to our questions, she explained that she and her husband came from a village near Belgard in Pomerania. They came to Berlin with a child about ten years previously—and came for "political reasons," as she added, because her husband had come into conflict with the landowner. "He is a 'socialist,' but otherwise a very good man," she said by way of explanation, and at the same time apologetically.

I asked the woman about the ups and downs of her dwelling experiences in the city. At first they found accommodation in Lichterfelde, then still a relatively unremarkable village, but where a brother of her husband's already resided. Then they moved to Pankow, where her husband had two good years of work building streets. Finally they came into the city. The sick woman could not remember all the streets on which they had lived, and actually was not even able to recall which house the last two children had been born in. She could only guess approximately that on average they changed their residence every six months, and even at that time had already lived in fifteen different dwellings. Mostly they had been able to rent only a single room ever since coming to live in Berlin. For roughly two years in total, they had able to live in better-equipped, two-room apartments as a result of her husband securing better wages and more regular work. Each time when it seemed that things would get permanently better they were thrown back again as the result of illness or because of a, sometimes premature, childbirth—in total the woman had had six premature births—or because of a death. They had not yet taken up poor support, and on one occasion the sick woman had been helped out by a young girlfriend, the wife of a former bricklayer's foreman, who had suddenly come into wealth. They had already resided over six months in the present dwelling; the so-called apartment room was sublet; in addition, the kitchen cost them a further eight to nine marks per month in rent.

How did the family sleep? Husband and wife in the only bed. The children were placed on laid-out pieces of clothing and could sneak into bed only when their father and mother—usually around five o'clock in the morning—got up. The smallest of the children slept occasionally in a basket but sometimes, too, when the woman had to leave the room for some purpose, slept in a half-open drawer in the commode.

As the woman explained all this to us, the whole burden of this calamity confronted her once more. For several days now her husband appeared in the dwelling only for a short time; in the hot August nights he preferred to sleep somewhere on the grass outside instead of wandering restlessly around in the deplorable heat of the kitchen. The whole of the housework had to be undertaken by the fourteen-year-old daughter, who was employed on an hourly basis as an errand girl. The woman pleaded with the doctor to get her into a hospital and to admit the children into the asylum for orphans. When he made clear the impossibility of fulfilling these wishes and when he also reminded her that they did not accord with her other statements as to the fear of the hospital, she explained to him that she could hardly bear to stay in this dreadful mass rental block: the dreadful noise, the heat, the continuous pushing and scrimmaging of people, the loud noise and arguments above her, adjacent to her, and below her, and indeed once again in the last few days the feeling of total loneliness in this caravansary had become so overwhelming in her that she feared she was loosing her mind and thought of throwing herself out of the window. [. . .]

49

Clara Viebig

OUR DAILY BREAD

First published as Viebig, *Das tägliche Brot* (Berlin: Fleischel, 1907); published in English as *Our Daily Bread*, trans. Margaret L. Clarke (London: John Lane, The Bodley Head, 1909), pp. 96–97.

They stood in the street quite dumbfounded. Now the sun appeared. Across from the Botanical Gardens, came sweet scents and the rustling of green trees.[1] Children, dressed in white, skipped along on the hand of their parents, smartly dressed girls strolled past with their lovers. The open trams dashed by with a friendly ting-ting, the Sunday clothes of the passengers making the cars look as if flagged with gay streamers; the roll of the wheels sounded more melodious, they seemed to run more smoothly in the joy of Sunday. Everywhere Sunday faces, eyes which sparkled in expectation of Sunday joys. The people hurried along, happy to have thrown off the trammels of the week-day. Sunday air, a Sunday sky. Innumerable atoms of gold danced in the air, the asphalt looked as if sprinkled with gold.

No money! With a deep sigh they gazed at one another. "What can we do?" whispered Mina.

He rummaged in his pocket, and after a long search brought out something and held it out to her in the palm of his hand. "There, twopence-halfpenny! Twopence-halfpenny in cash. That's just enough for two beers, and a halfpenny for the waiter. *I* don't care. Come, let's go to the park at Wilmersdorf, it isn't far, we needn't take the tram."

Her face lighted up; he went out with her, although she had no money! She nodded blissfully, and trudged along by his side, her heavy woollen dress raising a cloud of dust.

Now they were out of the town, and had left the last house in the Grunewald Strasse behind them.

An immeasurable plain lay before them; no meadow, no wood. To the right and left uncultivated fields, already marked out as building sites. A light breeze played with the stunted sand-oats. No flowers. But boys were flying a kite and shouted with joy when the warm, summer wind, which yet gave warning of autumn, bore along their paper ship.

Mothers pushed squeaking perambulators in front of them, and fathers carried tired children. Young men and girls, their eyes sparkling with the thought of dancing, despised the roadway and balanced themselves on the heaps of stones and hillocks of sand on both sides of the way.

From the far distance, where an avenue of great trees rises from the edge of the plain, the wind brought the sound of music.

And over everything the sun poured its brightest beams.

With a face wonderfully beautified by happiness Mina gazed before her. They had never been so far out of the town before. She sniffed the country air with inflated nostrils. It was a long time since she had breathed anything like this! It was always the steam of the kitchen, the smoke of the coals, the greasy reek of the sink.

Her heart trembled with great joy; she imagined herself at home on the green Golmütz Common, at home, and—with him. She could have rejoiced aloud. But she was ashamed; so she only hopped over a little sandheap and said with a deep sigh of satisfaction, "It's beautiful here! We can see the sky!"

NOTE

1. The Botanical Gardens in Berlin, located in the southwestern suburb of Lichterfelde, first opened in their entirety to visitors in 1904.

50

Karl Scheffler

THE TENEMENT BLOCK

First published as "Das Etagenwohnhaus," *Neue Rundschau*, 1911; reprinted in Scheffler, *Die Architektur der Großstadt* (Berlin: Cassirer, 1913), 28–35. Translated by Michael Loughridge.

For the typical apartment block four to six stories in height, German city dwellers coined the term *Mietskaserne* [tenement barracks]. The mocking nickname reflects the feeling that to live in such a building is indeed like living in a military barracks and is, in some degree, a humiliation; also, the mockery in the term seems to suggest an element of yearning for a house of one's own.

[...]

It is the rootlessness of the modern city dweller that has made the tenement apartment block what it is today, and that also ensures that it remains the preferred accommodation type of the petty bourgeoisie, the working class, the middle class, and even of the well-to-do. And because this is the way it is, with the tenement block sure to continue for a long time yet to hold its dominant position in the outer suburbs of the cities—which means some major architectural issues of our day involve facing the problem of the tenement block—it would be wrong to be too hasty or superficial in one's consideration of this compromise design, this extemporized solution. The multistory tenement block—unfortunately, there is no equally accurate but less inelegant term for the object in question—must in fact be regarded as one of the most important realities of the current few decades, and we have a duty to work as earnestly at improving it as if it were henceforward to be a permanent feature of the modern city.

The history of this particular architectural form seems to embody in concentrated form all the wrongheadedness of the economic and aesthetic course taken by German building in recent years. Certainly, the tenement block as we know it is the result of an exceptional surge of entrepreneurial effort, but equally it is the product of unthinking and irresponsible speculative instincts. In essence it is a thing foisted on city dwellers—people already cut off from natural surroundings—by land speculation and the system of subdivision into plots that was devised to support it. The fact is that our city councils in the past failed to grasp the opportunity when it was there, roughly from 1850 to 1870 or even earlier, to assume ownership of the city's land—which would have led to a truly massive communal profit, considering that sites outside the Berlin city gates, for example, worth about fifty thousand marks in 1830, now have a proven value of approximately 50 million. Likewise, they have failed to introduce legislative measures that would have channeled private property speculation into approved paths. In consequence, a title of ownership to land within the metropolitan area has gradually become an immense prerogative, enabling landowners to become in practice the arbiters of present-day urban development. So as to push land values up as high as possible, the speculators have used all the capitalist means at their disposal to promote a close-packed, crowded pattern of building. In due course, this trend has acquired legitimacy from the way the building regulations are enforced—that is to say, with the focus entirely on public-health aspects and the bureaucratic process, and with a total lack of imagination. One regulation, for example, requires a given relationship between road width and building height. The plot owner has used this regulation in a systematic policy of building streets as wide as possible, regardless of actual need, in order to be able to build high. The high costs incurred in building these broad, paved streets, and through the consequent waste of building land, have of course to be recouped by way of the tenement block. Calculations showed that this can be most effectively achieved if the buildings are erected on deep sites with relatively narrow street frontage, notwithstanding the fact that the addition of subsidiary rear buildings and lateral wings of whatever kind necessitates various interior courtyards and light wells and is thus responsible for further profligacy in the use of space. The builder nominated by the site owner or land agent—that is to say, the individual who converts the site's theoretical value into real value by building on it—will have calculated the absolute maximum rental yield that can be extracted from this narrow, deep plot, every last square meter of it. Thanks to his rudimentary grounding in the building trades, he can attempt to dress up the street facade to look like a palace in order to give the salable object additional prestige; and his ingenuity is quite equal to cramming together two very different accommodation types that will coexist behind the impressive facade: the street-front building as housing for those of rank, and the rear blocks housing for the proletariat. In the tenement blocks that come into being in this way, two-thirds of the occupants, when not at the workplace, live out their lives around the dark courtyards. The privacy without which there cannot be a sense of "home" is denied them: they are forced to live in disgracefully unsanitary conditions, in accommodation so cramped that man and wife simply cannot allow themselves a family of any size (in other words, the population is set to decline because housing policy is capitalist in nature), and which in many further respects is morally degrading in its effects. These poky, airless, crowded mass habitations—in some districts resembling a battery of breeding cells, pasted together and layered above and below—are indeed all solicitously fitted out with running water, sewerage, and gas supply. But this is done only because without these conveniences, so loudly vaunted as trappings of advanced civilization, the accommodation provided would be simply uninhabitable. The 1905 census recorded a figure in Berlin of over 77 occupants on average for every tenement. Some, however, have well over 150 people living in them.[1] And this overcrowding occurs not only in the central districts of cities, where most of the housing is old-fashioned, but also and in fact more markedly in the tenement-dominated districts of the periphery; indeed, it is a feature even of tenement blocks built out in the suburbs on green field sites. These last blocks offer a particularly grotesque illustration of the current building trends. All around such a tenement building is nothing but open country, the potato fields practically abut the rear part of the house, and there is space in abundance for miles around; but inside that solitary tenement block standing there, about a hundred human beings will be living in the most crowded conditions. The value of the building land—hard by the building it is still cheap farmland—is artificially forced up to quite unnatural levels; and as soon as it is built over, that land will represent the capital sum, and the interest will be the rents to be charged, income prepared for with great subtlety. The ground lies unused until it is "ripe for development"; then it is divided into parcels, and the entrepreneur realizes its artificial value by dint of building artificially. That is modern town planning for you. The city dweller has no choice: he simply has to become a tenant in one of these mass habitations, and he has to pay an unnaturally high rent—in relation to his means—for what he gets. That he has to pay so much is natural enough, though, for it is his function to generate the return on the added value, the appreciating value, of the land—in effect an excessive tax that he has to pay. In most cases he will pay a fifth or a quarter or even more of his income in rent, and always proportionately more the lower his income is. In this connection there are some extraordinarily instructive statistical tables from which it can be seen that families with an annual income of one hundred thousand marks pay around 5 to 8 percent of their income to live in a tenement block—but families with nine hundred marks in income pay 30 to 35 percent. Because the ordinary worker cannot possibly afford to pay this level of rental from his income alone, he is forced to engage in practices like taking in lodgers, or allowing his home to be used by prostitutes and so forth. That is to say: the high level of rents forces people to live in unnaturally cramped conditions and thereby destroys the health, the moral integrity, and the happiness of at least a third of all those living in cities. Because human beings are prone to overrate things for which they are overcharged, however, it is not difficult for the city's professional illusionists to think of their barrackslike tenement buildings, "furnished with all modern conveniences," as actually representing a triumph of modern housing provision.

[...]

A different aspect of this unperceived drive toward uniformity becomes apparent if one takes a look at city street fronts containing a line of newly built tenement blocks at the skeleton stage, before the finishing work begins. For all that the individual buildings were put up by different entrepreneurs, one finds that, strangely enough, in essential points they are all alike. One notes that they are all of the same height, all have the same arrangement of windows and doors, and at least very similar designs for bay windows and balconies. The reason for this is that the unfinished facades are invariably products of one and the same calculation—the one that reaches its bottom line by way of the street width, then the maximum permissible building height, the standard ground-plan layout, the uniform standard width of the building plots, and, finally, the fully rationalized working practices that are common to the whole construction industry. Facades never acquire individual character until the plasterer and the stucco specialist come along with their cornices and ornamentation evoking the taste of some bygone style or other, until dormers and turrets are sprinkled along the top—in short,

FIGURE 20. Luckenwalder Strasse, Kreuzberg, 1912. Landesarchiv Berlin, 345118.

until the whole familiar repertoire of newly proletarianized facade ornamentation has been put on show. And it is just here that the speculative approach to building shows itself to be inconsistent, denying uniform treatment to a product that is by its nature fundamentally uniform, building the tenement block as if it were a detached private dwelling. Standing in a whole row of other similar buildings, the tenement block is part of an imagined whole; it is a component of something larger. Yet this part, this component, is treated as if it were an independent entity. The land it stands on will as a rule be part and parcel of a large property with a single owner; yet what does the owner do but behave as if the land in question were made up of many smaller properties? He splits up his land, creates a multitude of building plots, and sees to it that every one of them is duly built upon. To act thus is another case of casting aside the formal principle of letting things develop according to their own inherent nature. Exactly the same observation can be made with regard to planning the city as a whole, for there, too, the ideal solution is contained implicitly in the circumstances given at the outset, and so does not need to be consciously devised.

Achieving the ideal form for the city apartment block will be possible only if there is a strong communal spirit seeking consciously what at present is being done by blind instinct—and, it seems, almost in spite of itself. Effective reforms are inconceivable until we have legislation, drafted for the long term, to curb building activity; until we have comprehensive reform of property law; until we have established as a matter of principle that different residential accommodation types should be kept separate, have grouped dwellings of similar type into coherent complexes, and have introduced new, centrally regulated building-development plans that take cognizance of where the real public needs lie and will become the means of implementing these needs.

NOTE

1. Author's note in text: It was established recently that 45 percent of all Greater Berlin tenements are *"Hinterhäuser"*—buildings located in back courtyards; that in the capital of the German Reich more than four hundred thousand apartments have only a single room that can be heated, and about a further three hundred thousand have only two that can be heated; that about one and a half million people are living in these cramped quarters with only one heatable room; that there are one hundred thousand apartments, occupied by six hundred thousand people, in which there are more than four people to every heatable room; and also that it is by no means uncommon for ten and even twelve persons to be living and sleeping in a one-room apartment. (See Werner Hegemann, *Der Städtebau nach den Ergebnissen der Allgemeinen Städtebau-Ausstellung in Berlin* [Berlin: Wasmuth, 1911–13].)

51

Käthe Kollwitz

DIARY ENTRY, 16 APRIL 1912

First published in *Ich sah die Welt mit liebevollen Blicken. Käthe Kollwitz. Ein Leben in Selbstzeugnissen*, ed. Hans Kollwitz (Wiesbaden: Fourier, 1971), p. 180. Translated by Iain Boyd Whyte.

The working man Soost earns twenty-eight marks each week. Six of them go on rent. He gives his wife twenty-one. This pays for beds and bedding, leaving fourteen to fifteen marks for living costs. The family consists of Soost, his wife, and *six* children. The smallest is one month old, very healthy and strong. Because she is undernourished, the wife does not have milk for the child and already has to put it on the bottle. The remaining children are all strong and healthy except for Lotte, who was underfed by her mother and developed rickets. One of the older children is weak in the head. The woman is thirty-five years old and has had nine children, three of whom are dead. All of them, as she says, were born as strong as this youngest. They first became ill and died when she could not breast-feed them, and she lost her milk because her work was too heavy and she could not take care of herself.

52

Max Jacob

FROM APARTMENT HOUSE TO MASS APARTMENT HOUSE

First published as "Vom Miethaus zum Massenmiethaus," *Deutsche Bauhütte* 14, no. 16 (4 April 1912). Translated by Iain Boyd Whyte.

"It is the German disposition, that everyone who desires to build something new would also like it in the latest style." Dürer spoke these ironic words, perfectly describing the way in which the citizen [*Bürger*] wanted his house in the age of a powerful middle class.

Even when several households found accommodation in it, the house was built solely for its owner, and clearly and unmistakably characterized its true purpose through its individual expression, in the special use of new forms, and in the differences between itself and its neighbor. Closely packed together, the houses coexisted in peace on the streets of the towns, each one telling us a poem about the comfort-loving, embarrassing, elegant, or dissipated character of its owner.

With the massive emigration of the population from the provinces, the apartment house made its entry into the city. In accord with its function, however, it was not now built for comfortable living, but rather served as a rental block for the purposes of commerce. In the process, it was given a form aimed at gaining a rich return for the least possible effort.

Now, one might think that a new and functional form would be found for the new purpose of the house. But the moment for the solution of such tasks had not arrived at this time, which was still suffering from a poverty of artistic design. Quite reasonably, the apartment house adopted forms from the owner-occupied house, and was quite happy to stand on the street in serried ranks, as if it had no real sense of joy in its existence. Yes, on the street! The street is the sign of the times and has won the upper hand over the house. It was thought that with a checkerboard system of identical streets one could impose an adequate order on the network of streets that had been created around the old city core.

Only later, as the city appeared to grow to immeasurable dimensions, were the two functions of the street recognized—as residential street and as vehicular street. At about the same time, the revival of the expressive house front set in. Commercial buildings with generous horizontal and vertical divisions filled the main streets, and domesticity moved into the calm side streets. Love of one's own home went hand in hand with a love for color. Brightly painted shutters, bay windows, balconies, floral decoration, and climbing plants appeared. To a certain extent, this balance of architecture and nature satisfied man's eternal yearning for nature, and allowed an existence among the stony masses of the city streets to seem more or less bearable. The high roof, often pulled down over the top story of the house, gave the house a sense of natural shelter from the weather. Together with the generous horizontal articulation of the facade, the house took on a friendly appearance and awoke in men an unconscious sense of being sheltered.

One can often see, however, that to the dismay and despair of the architect who has found good solutions for an individual apartment house, some unworthy spirit dumps his botched job right beside it. How much work and effort is invested in a good design for one building without gaining any credit for it. The street line swallows up the good works, and people hurry by without so much as a look.

In today's street line, the individual house is also not well suited to being looked at with delight; for it lacks a worthy context—like the frame for a painting. Furthermore, the design of these high buildings, flanked by neighboring houses, means that they are viewed by looking up at an acute angle from the generally unfavorable position on the street. This makes demands that very few architects, if any, are aware of. In contrast to the relationships that have been well thought through on paper, the perspectival view from the street brings about changes to the planar and volumetric dimensions that are accorded little attention. In addition, the design of the house must assert itself against its neighbor, whose expressive language is derived from quite different principles. This is not the place to go into this problem in more detail; perhaps on another occasion.

And from where, after all, would one summon the courage to praise the individual houses in the mass of streets that aspire to aesthetic quality? The dominant role in the metropolis is no longer played by the house, but the street line of the buildings, which takes over its role in the development of the city.

In consequence, it is no longer the individual builder but the increasingly important cooperative building associations that are called upon to assume leadership in the apartment-house debate. With far more capital strength and a fresh entrepreneurial spirit, they are better able to assert themselves than the individual developer—the more so as they attract ever more supporters for the good cause and receive encouragement and preferential treatment of their interests from the national and local government. To expect the owner of a single building plot to achieve a more generous street layout is a doomed enterprise, since every builder is led by special interests and is convinced of his ability to find the correct form for his particular house. A new epoch has begun for our apartment housing, and reveals itself most visibly on the peripheries of the cities of Berlin, Hamburg, Leipzig, Hanover, and so forth. Because there is little prospect of reducing the high costs of land, material, and labor, the move is toward the building of mass housing blocks, built under one initiative and exploiting all the economic advantages that are inaccessible to the individual builder. I am thinking here in particular of the Berlin apartment houses of Albert Gessner, the housing built for public servants by Paul Mebes—those wonderful houses with communal kitchens.[1] The driving force will always be the reduction of the high rents and more comfortable living conditions. In the process, certain simplifications can be allowed in the building, particularly in savings to be gained from mass fabrication, and also certain aesthetic concessions made in the interior fittings, which would otherwise have to be omitted. The block dimensions that result from high-intensity occupation permit generous spacing, leading to optimal large-scale courtyards and internal gardens. The enormous gable-end walls also disappear, the product of the will of a particular moment, regardless of the comfort and welfare of all those people who were compelled to eke out their existences behind—one might say—these prison walls.

A more or less practical treatment of the brief leads to the external, functional form of the mass apartment house. For in contrast to earlier practice with single apartment houses, the architect does not lose himself in the detail, but is necessarily compelled to order the principal masses in such a way that that they sit organically in the streetscape and break the long street lines into large elements, just as in earlier times the individual house articulated the ancient, curved streets. Special spaces like shops, restaurants, cafés, entrances, the axes of the main building masses, or any other individual elements worthy of attention demand a modified form of expression, clearly differentiated from the regular rows of windows and wall elements. Should you not wish to admit the functional, if long, rows of windows as the true and attractive expression of mass housing, and should you not sense here the volition that creates something that is new, coherent, and previously unknown, you will suffer the impulses of sentimentality. This will lead you to hanker after the romantic corners and streetscapes of a lost, medieval age. Our epoch, however, wishes to speak its own language, and to be just as true and honest as previous cultural epochs have been.

NOTE

1. The architects Gessner and Mebes designed the so-called *Einküchenhäuser*, which were built at 17–19 Wilhelmshöher Strasse, Berlin-Friedenau, in 1909–12 and housed some sixty rental apartments serviced by communal kitchens.

53
Victor Noack
HOUSING AND MORALITY
1912

First published as "Wohnungen und Sittlichkeit," *Die Aktion* 2, nos. 19/20 (1912), 584–86, 618–20. Translated by David Britt.

I

Housing and morality are closely interdependent—not morality in terms of sexual conduct alone, but morality in the general sense of individual and social ethics.

The dwelling—the immediate framework of individual life. Domesticity—the sphere of social life that is the most free from outside control. To think that one is at home is to cast off social (societal) constraints. At home, the individual shows his or her true face. (This statement is, of course, subject to a number of qualifications.) Civilized constraint is crippling, and the culture of the human mind must prevail.

Admittedly, a person's ethical education is not causally dependent on outward social circumstances: its roots lie deeper, at a level hitherto accessible only to metaphysical explanation. And yet, undeniably, this deeper level rarely proves so fertile as to bear a harvest that years of social hardship cannot vitiate. Undeniably, that harvest is blessed by mental culture, which thrives only where there is material prosperity (or freedom from, or at least an endurable level of, social hardship).

It follows that any ethical shortcomings on the part of the "poor," the proletariat, should be regarded not as an unprincipled abuse of moral values—squandered in immoral pleasures—but as a predictably meager harvest from a barren field.

The harmful moral effect of bad social conditions becomes all the stronger the more intimately such conditions impinge on the individual's personal life. Bad housing conditions are therefore the prime social factors in the process of anti-ethical learning or ethical unlearning.

In what follows, I confine myself to the description of just one of many untoward consequences of our present housing conditions. It is an evil that afflicts not only the proletariat but—perhaps even more acutely—the lower middle class, and even the supposedly "better off" middle class. I refer to the practice of subletting, and the scandal of "night lodging" and "furnished rooms."

In Berlin alone, according to the land-ownership and housing statistics for Berlin and twenty-nine suburban districts published by the Berlin City Office of Statistics in February 1910, the census of December 1, 1905, recorded a total of 41,738 households that included "roomers," and 63,425 in which there were "night lodgers." In 2,532 of these households, both categories of subtenants shared living accommodation with the householder (and family, if any). Of the 102,631 households concerned, 63,291 included children younger than fifteen.

"Roomers" in Berlin comprised 52,035 men and 12,767 women, with 206 male and 161 female children under fifteen. "Night lodgers" comprised 81,106 men and 22,424 women, with 286 male and 265 female children. This army of "roomers" is distributed across a total domestic resident population of 940,445 male and 1,031,518 female individuals.

To perceive social, and in particular sociosexual, issues of this kind in their true light, the student of economics and social policy must be equipped with the perspicacity and intuition of an artist. The genius of Emile Zola vividly summed up this whole issue when he coined the phrase "the belly of Paris." The statistics reveal the thousands who, fascinated by the glowing eyes of the monster that is Berlin, fascinated by the glittering splendor of its scaly carapace, have walked into its gaping maw: the thousands who have been lured by the seething darkness within, enticed into its mysterious depths in the hope of finding treasures in the abyss—and who expected to find perilous adventures and emerge on the radiant heights of a world of riches. In the statistical record we see those thousands on their journey toward the distant goal of their hopes: their pilgrimage through "the belly of Berlin." It shows the poor and the disappointed, shoving and elbowing, trampling each other underfoot, grappling with each other in the struggle for their daily bread, sliding ever lower in the tightly packed mass of sweating bodies, choked and smothered, hemmed in ever more tightly by the atmosphere of moral disintegration; and yet nevertheless multiplying like the bacilli and worms in a giant, moribund organism. The same mirage that first guided these unfortunates on their erratic way revives their hopes after every disappointment. The "Pursuit of Happiness"—I am thinking of the celebrated painting by Spangenberg—grows ever wilder. Desperation soon turns to brutality. Every man strikes down the man in front, without compunction. Hospitals, reform schools, workhouses, jails, and penitentiaries are the staging points of a mass migration. How many sink, exhausted, into the morass of crime and prostitution!

In Berlin, as the figures from the City Office of Statistics show, there are fifteen hundred dwellings, consisting of a single habitable room, in which "night lodgers" are "discovered" to be residing together with householders and their families if any. Isolated cases appear in the statistics in which the occupiers of a single-room dwelling were found to be housing both "night lodgers" and "roomers." In the case referred to, this almost inconceivable utilization of a single room was made possible as follows. Householder: one single man. In addition to him, the one room was in use by one daughter (under fifteen), one "housekeeper" (as a person "paying rental for sleeping accommodation"), and one "roomer."

In the statistics, this is an isolated case. But this does not mean that there are not many similar situations in Berlin that the census takers were unable to "discover." Life's losers do not readily confide in strangers. They know that the state in which they live is socially unsanitary; and those who come by with long official questionnaires tend to find them mistrustful and nervously uncommunicative. The lives that are lived in deepest shadow are those that remain inaccessible to official investigation. For this reason, if for no other, the statistical numbers that embody these extremes of misery are not to be regarded as a complete record.

II

For renters and "subtenants" alike, the closer and the more intimate communal living becomes, the greater the moral dangers. In one-room dwellings, the moral corruption of both parties is inevitable. At the December 1905 census, 555 male and 1,159 female "night lodgers" and 41 male and 81 female "roomers" were found to be sleeping in the same rooms as their "renters": 140 married couples, 1,241 single women, and 224 single men, plus children where applicable. Even supposing that these people enjoyed a higher level of ethical and aesthetic education than they do, this rooming together would inevitably degenerate into a repugnant state of concubinage: repugnant because based not on any personal inclination, but solely or principally on economic factors and on the nature of the accommodation. This is a purely bestial promiscuity—with this difference: that animals blindly submit to the sexual impulse, whereas, in the last resort, these human beings are moved by economic necessity alone. To rent a room in a one-room apartment is to deprive the occupier of his rights within his own four walls. The renter and his family are now beholden to the subtenant for the roof over their heads; they live in their own home only on sufferance. Such a situation tends to arise only when the host family is in the direst financial straits, and it is therefore likely that the subtenant will be allowed the most egregious liberties. Necessity knows no law. The moral resistance of desperate people is unlikely to be very strong when the rewards of virtue are hunger and perhaps homelessness, and when wrongdoing is the only modus vivendi. The householder (the renter, the husband) becomes a drinking companion. Neither his wife nor his children (daughters) will be safe from the attentions of his subtenant.

From the lowest social strata to the "better off" bourgeoisie, this "subtenancy system" introduces alien elements into the intimacy of family life: individuals of whose moral and physical character the householder and head of the family is entirely ignorant. And yet this stranger, this alien subtenant, lives communally with the renter's family, sharing—in the poorest cases—the same bedroom, the same washing and other utensils, perhaps even the same towel, the same soap, the same drinking vessels, and so forth. That this form of communal living, barely short of cohabitation, is by no means an exceptional consequence of "subtenancy" is demonstrated by the figures from the City Office of Statistics.

Those "non-family members" who intrude into the home as "night lodgers" and "roomers" are for the most part "single individuals"; and as such they have been shown to be—as a natural consequence of their unmarried state—exceptionally liable to dermatological and related ailments. They lack the protective support that family and conjugal life afford in this respect. Additionally, as a rule, the single man lacks the benefit of regular meals. He eats lunch cheaply in a succession of restaurants, frequently shifting from one to the other without thereby getting anything better to eat. Eating out entails a certain consumption of alcohol and conduces to alcoholic and sexual excesses. The instability of his life, poor nutrition, the company of his peers, and so on weaken not only his physical resistance to infection but his moral resistance to the "dangerous opportunities," the "erotic situations," that present themselves to any "subtenant" who lives in such close proximity to the householder's family. He enjoys liberties that are properly due only to a member of the family, and with none of the natural restraints of consanguinity. Indeed, he is all too aware of his economic importance to the householder, and this inclines him to make the most of any opportunity that comes his way.

The "situation" favors adultery, seduction, and violation; and the "night lodger" or "roomer" is predisposed to take advantage of it.

Marriage—scant though my own respect for conventional marriage as an ideal may be, and fatal though it often proves to all erotic hopes—marriage nevertheless consolidates, stabilizes, grounds our purely animal existence. It promotes health and inculcates some degree of sensitivity to the demands of social reputation.

The unmarried lack the benefit of this discipline. Of course, not all roomers and night lodgers are to be regarded as domestic pests, parasites on decent family life, wolves in the sheepfold who make away with the innocence of the renter's daughters and the honor of his wife; *not every* unmarried "roomer" is infected with some dangerous disease; nor does every sick "roomer" immediately infect the renter's family. Nevertheless, *every outsider* who intrudes upon family life brings the *threat* of all these things; every family must reckon with the *possibility* of such risks.

In the year 1904, of 5,384 individuals convicted of violent sexual offenses against children and so on—the most serious forms of indecency—1,364 were single, widowed, or divorced individuals between the ages of twenty-one and forty; only 990 were married. If we take these figures for single, widowed, or divorced—as against married—offenders, and extrapolate them to the total numbers of single (and so forth) and married individuals in the same age group as a whole, it is revealed beyond doubt that, as one would naturally expect, marriage "acts to prevent the commission of the most serious indecent assaults." There can be no question that single (widowed or divorced) individuals constitute the majority of "lodgers" (subtenants).

In those apartments with only one to two rooms, covered by the 1905 Berlin census, in which, in addition to the householder's family, "night lodgers" or "roomers" (or both) were also living, the census takers recorded the presence of 12,925 boys and 13,783 girls— that is to say 27,708 children in all—under the age of fifteen. This figure does not include the children of cotenants, relatives, and so forth, or foster children.

The danger posed to children by "subtenants" constitutes a chapter of criminological history in itself.

Very few of the crimes committed against children under the mantle of family discretion ever reach the courts. Shame, a horror of scandal and of publicly revealing the unhealthy conditions in which the family lives, deters those most closely concerned from turning in the violators of their children. Nevertheless, the press almost daily reports that some "night lodger" has been sentenced for an offense against the child of his "landlord."

The daily press ought never to let such an occasion pass without pointing to the essential connection between the crime itself and the unsanitary housing conditions from which it springs. The overcrowding of apartments, and the presence of roomers who share accommodation with family members without respect to sex or age, favors and indeed conduces to sexual delinquency and crime: adultery, seduction, violation of minors, incest, pimping, and so on.

6

PUBLIC REALM AND POPULAR CULTURE

In 1871 Berlin, previously the capital city of Prussia, became the capital of the new German state. Appropriate to its new status and in response to the massive increase in its population, the city was transformed. Two great building booms, the first running from unification in 1871 to the late 1880s, and the second from 1896 to 1913, saw housing and industry pushed out of the city center in favor of government, business, education, and culture. While speculative housing marched unstoppably outward, devouring the villages, fields, and woods that surrounded Berlin, the city center was remodeled to accommodate the large-footprint buildings appropriate to a world capital.

Writing of the British cities in the Victorian period, the historian Asa Briggs notes: "They were never mere collections of individuals, some weak, some strong. They had a large number of voluntary organizations covering a far wider range of specialized interests than was possible either in the village or the small town. They were more free of aristocratic 'influence.' They allowed room for middle-class initiative and for greater independence and greater organization of the 'lower ranks of society' than did smaller places."[1] In other words, the cities were not as bad as the impoverished countryside, whence the newly arrived population had come. This generous reading of the late-nineteenth-century city has rarely, however, been accorded to Berlin. Instead, the communal life of the city, typified by the eclectic historicism of its public architecture, has generally been dismissed as menacingly inauthentic.

If acknowledged at all in the histories, the churches, theaters, museums, department stores, and grand apartment houses of turn-of-the-century Berlin were summoned simply to act as the negative pole to the positive energy of early modernism.

The simplicity and clarity of high, 1920s modernism, as represented by the Bauhaus in Dessau or the new social housing in Frankfurt and Berlin, was contrasted favorably with the massive volumes, historical manners, and heavy decoration that characterized Berlin architecture around 1900. The cultural critic Karl Scheffler set the tone in 1910: "Without a hint of true reverence they have wrought havoc on the treasures of earlier building cultures and violently transformed their noble forms to serve the ignoble purposes of the metropolis. The inhabitants of the capital city have had their pseudo-palaces built with brick, stucco, and plaster and have invented facades on which the architectural forms, ornaments, and characters of all periods and all nations writhe together in a hideous confusion." And those responsible for these excesses, said Scheffler, were not only the speculators, developers, and architects, but even the Kaiser himself: "This Kaiser has sanctioned the degenerate form of urbanite eclecticism and made it socially acceptable. He has used the forms of the modern building industry for state representation. As a result, this style has, so to speak, become a symbol of the empire."[2] Scheffler's critique became the default position of the promodernist histories that were written in the 1920s and '30s. To give one example, here is Max Osborn, writing in 1929: "Using fundamentally false means, the buildings and facilities of the state sought to achieve a monumentality, which became stranded in empty externalities. The highpoint of this misguided ambition was marked by the unspeakable Siegesallee, the 'Romanesque' enclave around the Gedächtniskirche, and the fractured building volumes of Julius Raschdorff's new cathedral in the Lustgarten, which, peppered with spires, turrets, domes, and ornaments, and completely inappropriate in its scale, barged without respect between the noble, historical buildings at the eastern end of Berlin's principal boulevard."[3] This singularly hostile account of the public architecture of the Kaiser's Berlin still holds sway to this day, and to eyes trained to admire the smooth, anonymous white planes of *Neue Sachlichkeit* (new objectivity), the architecture of Wilhelmine Berlin appears hopelessly vulgar and parvenu.

This rather puritanical position, however, is neither interesting nor illuminating. For the new public buildings—the churches, museums, theaters, hotels, hospitals, and even prisons—served many functions beyond that of merely stating a stylistic preference. While they clearly did not cohere into a larger pattern of urban design, they were able, in their rich external detail and stylistic plurality, to carry meaning. The neo-Romanesque architecture of the Gedächtniskirche, for example, was expressly designed by its architect, Franz Schwechten, to symbolize the continuity between the newly united German state and the *Staufferreich,* the Hohenstaufen dynasty that ruled the Holy Roman Empire in the twelfth and thirteenth centuries. Similarly, Raschdorff's cathedral made explicit reference to St. Peter's in Rome. In the process, these and similar buildings made specific propositions about the new German state, which created a public sphere of debate, discussion, and evaluation. Reported and detailed in the press, they also addressed the pressing need for cultural integration experienced by the recently unified state and by a population undergoing rapid urbanization. To the recent arrival, the new Berlin was a world of novelty, excess, and superlatives.

As a counterexample to the negative critiques quoted above, one might look at the post office (Reichspostamt) built in the Leipziger Strasse in the "free Italian Renaissance style" to the design of Hake and Ahrends, and completed in 1896. It featured large in an enthusiastic article on the new Berlin architecture published in a commemorative volume marking the Berliner Gewerbeausstellung, the large international exposition staged that same year in the Berlin suburb of Treptow. The author of the account, Peter Wallé, expressly singled out the decorative flamboyance of the building as the very quality that lifted it above the merely functional: "In comparison with its old predecessor next door, one look at the successfully designed facade, with its generous decoration of figures, reliefs, and ornamental devices, shows the progress of the postal service from a mechanical means of dispatch into the most important circulation system in our national life. The magnificent corner building housing the Post Museum is accentuated on its side facade by open galleries, and the parapet carries the coat of arms of the German state, topped by the symbolic embodiment of world communication. Putti and guardian spirits are set into the spandrels of the two arcades, between which portraits of the three German Kaisers shine out from a golden background."[4] This highly figurative building, designed to proclaim the wonders of the modern German postal service, was undoubtedly read as such by the passing populace. The educational reforms introduced in after 1872 under the leadership of the Prussian minister of education, Adalbert Falk, had a powerful impact, and by 1880 illiteracy had been eradicated in Prussia. Symptomatic of the public appetite for both text and image was the success of the *Berliner Illustrirte Zeitung* magazine, founded by the Ullstein Verlag in 1891, which very rapidly built up a readership of forty thousand. There are many other indices of an articulate public: the Freie Volksbühne, a theater aimed specifically at the broader masses, had been established in Berlin in 1890, while a session at the 1896 Social Democratic Party conference in Gotha was devoted to a discussion of naturalism in the arts.

It is not necessarily the case, of course, that education will invariably support radicalism or modernism. Indeed, the ability to read and to learn about history makes clear the difference between the modern age and all previous periods. It also makes it possible to sympathize with earlier epochs, which had previously been only vaguely understood. The aesthetic principle of *Verstehen,* proposed in Germany by Wilhelm Dilthey in the 1890s, suggested that modern man could actually share in the sentiments of historical figures from the past. Theodor Lipps's theory of *Einfühlung,* as detailed in his two-volume *Ästhetik* (1903, 1906), further accentuated this possibility. It is possible, therefore, to suggest that the richly eclectic and historicist public architecture of imperial Berlin was not simply the marketing of pretentious and ultimately banal architectural references to a gullible clientele, but also an invitation to an informed populace to engage actively, through association and empathy, with admired epochs of the past. The history itself may have been constructed to reflect the interests of court, state, church, and other interest groups, but the engagement was undeniably real.

In a letter from 1905, Alfred Messel—the most talented of all the architects working at this time in Berlin—insisted: "The originality of independent spirits will not be hindered by the study of tradition."[5] This freedom allowed him to create a truly metropolitan architecture that appeared in various guises, each appropriate to the task. The core feature of his Wertheim store, for example, was an enormous, glazed light well, which illuminated the goods for sale inside and was enclosed by a gothicizing skin that stressed on the outside the interior qualities of verticality, openness, and light. For banks, in contrast, Messel favored more Italianate models; for offices, the German Renaissance; and for the Pergamon Museum, which was uncompleted at his death in 1909, Doric classicism. The museum project was completed by a second great figure in the contemporary architectural firmament, Ludwig Hoffmann, who combined impressively rational, additive plans with a rich vocabulary of historical references. Explicitly rejecting a standard solution, Hoffmann designed splendid schools for Berlin in a variety of styles: classicist, Gothic, Baroque, and German Renaissance. A similar diversity marks the several public baths that he designed for Berlin, while for the Stadthaus—a very complex planning challenge—he favored an exuberant neo-Baroque, topped by a powerful dome. Hoffmann's many school buildings were particularly successful in distancing themselves from the wilder extravagances of the speculative housing. As the architect Fritz Stahl noted in the *Berliner Tageblatt*, the schools designed by Hoffmann were "islands of good taste in the wild sea of Berlin housing."[6] Hoffmann himself explained in the context of his schools that "[e]ven if the building program was in some cases the same, the varying forms of the sites and, in particular, consideration of the neighboring buildings led to different solutions, with the result that among the many school buildings that I drew up over the years, hardly any two are alike. In this extremely unpleasant, self-important, and megalomanic period, this seemed appropriate to me. Well-lit, friendly rooms with a few modest yet charming details, together with a calm and carefully chosen architecture on the exterior, differentiated the schools from the neighboring houses, loaded as they were with gables, turrets, balconies, loggia, and worthless stucco decoration."[7] No lesser critic than Karl Scheffler explicitly praised this diversity: "All in all, Hoffmann is one of most free and most experienced public architects that we at present have. To the officials he counts as modern, among the modernists as official. In this respect he represents in no bad way the spirit of the new Berlin."[8]

All was not good taste and charm, however, and it was a short step from the measured eclecticism and historical reference of a Messel or a Hoffmann to the wonderful world of excess, brashness, and vulgarity. To Scheffler, writing in 1910, all this easy glamour was to be condemned: "Gone are the old beer pubs and the good, *bürgerliche* wine houses. In their place we find French restaurants, Dutch liquor bars and teashops, Viennese cafés, American bars, Bavarian and Bohemian beer halls, Italian and Russian restaurants. Year after year new beer palaces and wine cathedrals spring up. Massive buildings, pompously decorated, high-vaulted marble halls, glittering with gilding and mirror glass."[9] As the texts in this section confirm, the cafés, restaurants, and bathing establishments of Berlin could offer a dazzling array of temptations, ranging from Roman Epicureanism in the bathhouse to Byzantine decoration in the coffeehouse and vistas of Rhineland castles in the wine restaurant. In evolving into a world city, Berlin adopted other models, manners, and cuisines with characteristically excessive vigor. As one baffled commentator asked, looking across the Rheingold restaurant to the giant statues of Friedrich Barbarossa and Wilhelm I that guarded the entrance: "Where am I? In which old German knight's castle, in which giant monastery am I? In which Buddhist tombs, in which Valhalla?"[10]

NOTES

1. Asa Briggs, *Victorian Cities* (Berkeley: University of California Press, 1993), p. 24.
2. Karl Scheffler, *Berlin: Ein Stadtschicksal*, 2nd ed. (Berlin: Erich Reiss, 1910), pp. 190, 192.
3. Max Osborn, *Berlins Aufstieg zur Weltstadt* (Berlin: Reimar Hobbing, 1929), pp. 159–60.
4. Peter Wallé, "Ein Gang durch das neueste Berlin," in *Groß-Berlin: Bilder von der Ausstellungsstadt*, ed. Albert Kühnemann (Berlin: W. Pauli's Nachfolger, 1896–97), p. 108.
5. Alfred Messel, letter to Herwarth Walden, 12 October 1905, quoted in *Berlin um 1900*, exhibition catalogue (Berlin: Berlinische Galerie, 1984), p. 239.
6. Fritz Stahl, quoted in *Ludwig Hoffmann: Lebenserinnerungen eines Architekten*, ed. Wolfgang Schäche (Berlin: Gebr. Mann, 1983), p. 166.
7. Hoffmann, ibid., p. 166.
8. Karl Scheffler, *Die Architektur der Großstadt* (Berlin: Cassirer, 1913), p. 149; quoted in Karl-Heinz Hüter, *Architektur in Berlin, 1900–1933* (Stuttgart: Kohlhammer, 1988), p. 44.
9. Scheffler, *Berlin: Ein Stadtschicksal*, pp. 224–25.
10. Jules Huret, *En Allemagne* (Berlin and Paris: Bibliothèque-Charpentier, 1909), pp. 64–65.

54

Paul Lindau

UNTER DEN LINDEN

In Richard Harding Davis and others, *The Great Streets of the World* (London: Osgood, McIlvaine, 1892), pp. 201–5.

Between three and four o'clock in the afternoon a decided movement toward the west is apparent, both upon the sidewalks and in the carriages. The Bourse has closed, and since the greater bankers and financiers, almost without exception, live in the western quarter of Berlin, particularly the Tiergarten, there is a natural current from the Burgstrasse, through the Linden, toward the Brandenburg Gate. As the day advances, the Linden grows more animated, although under ordinary conditions it never affords anything comparable to the variegated picture made by the street life of southern cities. The greater part of the Linden, from the entrance to the Kaisergalerie—which runs through to the next parallel street to the south, Behrenstrasse, and is filled with attractive shops, a café, and various places of amusement—from the Kaisergalerie to the Brandenburg Gate, and upon the opposite side as well, and also on the east from Charlottenstrasse to the castle on both sides, is perfectly deserted in the later hours of the evening. But it grows all the noisier and livelier at the crossing of the Friedrichstrasse, especially upon Kranzler's corner. Here, during the late evening and night, Berlin has in fact a thoroughly cosmopolitan character, and its evening holiday is longer than that of the other great European centres, Paris, London, and Vienna.

At this famous corner there is something going on until four or five o'clock in the morning. It never ceases, really, and the gay ending of the night's frolic, and the gay beginning of the day's touch hands. Staunch, conservative old Kranzler, who would have the best situated establishment in the city for the entertainment of nocturnal rovers from the so-called higher classes, stands fast by the respectable principles of the olden time, and shuts up his place punctually at twelve o'clock. It is otherwise with the resort across the way, the Café Bauer, whose architectural design and artistic decorations are of a magnificent character, and which has attained a fame that reaches far beyond the precincts of the city.

The "café" is an importation from Vienna which established itself among us some twenty years ago, and which has completely driven out the old Berlin Conditorei. [. . .] The old Conditoreien, even the most noted of them, such as the famous ones—now no more—kept by Stehely and Spargnapani, had, besides the shop with its tempting big pastry-table, only the most modest little quarters—two or three rooms of ordinary size—for the accommodation of their coffee drinkers. They kept on file most of the Berlin papers, the more important provincial, and a couple of foreign ones. They had their regular circles of patrons, who gathered unfailingly at the appointed hour, chatted about the events of the day, read the newspapers, and played dominoes. Some of these circles were actually famous. The greatest masters in art and science formed there a sort of club, of their choice and with no regulations. It was very sociable and very simple.

But now, early in the seventies, on the most crowded corner of the capital, opposite Kranzler's a huge café was opened, able to accommodate on its first floor alone as many guests as could all the Conditoreien of Berlin together. It was built of the choicest materials, and by artist hands. The walls were decorated with original paintings by the director of our Academy, Anton von Werner. Instead of the surly, leisurely service to which the patrons of the Conditorei had accustomed themselves, were the nimble Vienna waiters, with their excessive, sometimes even intrusive, promptness. Overseers and directors marched gravely through the rooms to see that the waiters did their duty, and that guests were shown comfortable seats when they came in. Behind the tall counter sat attractive young women, simply but tastefully dressed, who delivered to the waiters whatever the guests ordered to eat and drink, and who carefully entered every particular in the big registers. In the upper story was the very best equipment for billiards, convenient card-tables, and a reading-room of such ample variety as had never been dreamed of. In fact, all the daily, weekly, and monthly periodicals of the old and new worlds were brought together there. The Café Bauer, in which one was better housed than was possible in any Conditorei, was better served, and could satisfy every desire more easily and at no greater expense, came at once into fashion. [. . .]

The Café Bauer, therefore, is really always well filled, and in the afternoon, evening, and far into the night, it is even crowded. For a while there were permanent circles formed here also, particularly of authors and artists, who desired, no doubt, to perpetuate the dear old customs of the moribund Conditorei; but the noisy surroundings, the constant coming and going and moving about, the rattling of cups and sugar-bowls, the ceaseless striking of the call-bell upon the buffet—in a word the clamorous activity of the place—was hostile to their design. It was not suited for having your talk out leisurely. The Café Bauer has throughout an air of restlessness; it is a halting-place for passers-by, not a spot in which to settle down comfortably. It is only the latest night patrons who make an exception to this. They remain glued to the same chair, it is true, hour after hour.

The guests of the Café Bauer are from all classes of society, so far as their outward appearance does not give offence to sensitive people; that is to say, they must be respectably dressed. More than this it would be scarcely reasonable to demand of them. The uniformed Cerberus at the door, or else the black-coated purists who preside over the interior, sternly refuse entrance to people of the lower classes who are carelessly dressed, or whose clothes are perhaps worn out in honorable toil, to noisy persons who in consequence of drink are in altogether too high spirits, and to women who wish to enter the place without escort. In addition to the numerous strangers, one finds representatives of the best Berlin society casually dropping in there. For a while our most fashionable women, in returning from the theatre or from a party, used to frisk into the Café Bauer and take a final "nightcap." But that did not last long and nowadays it is exceptional. Nevertheless the most cautious, punctilious society-man can enter the café without fear at any hour of the day or evening. He may be entirely sure of finding his equals there—the higher officials, officers, well-known scientists and artists, leading merchants, and others of that class.

Toward midnight the younger generation is in the predominance. Students, young academicians, youthful civil servants, and clerks are sitting there at the round tables. But if one ever visits the café in company with an experienced criminal officer, his attention will be called to this or that gentleman, quietly and even elegantly dressed, who figures as confidence-man, cheat, swindler, and worse, in the rogues' album. The strict regulation that ladies shall be admitted to the café only under masculine escort, does not, of course, prevent the fact that at night the majority of the feminine visitors—as a tolerably experienced eye can detect at a glance—belong to exactly the class which it is the intention of the regulation to exclude. But they are unobtrusive in behaviour, and are lost in the crowd. By far the greater part of the visitors to the Café Bauer are perfectly harmless. They are just the sort of people who pass the day with a cup of coffee, the evening with a Vienna beer, and the night around the punch-bowl; who smoke, chat, and end their day as late as possible. For this café, it should be said, is open all the year round, and while the latest lingering guests are paying their reckoning at dawn, and the earliest ones are already taking their seats for morning coffee, then, at the hour when the café is least patronized, come the scrubbing and dusting women, who sprinkle the floor, sweep out, brush away the dust, wipe off the tables, and remove the untidy traces of yesterday that they may set the establishment in order for a new day.

55

Anonymous

THE NEW PRISON FOR BERLIN AT TEGEL

First published as "Das neue Strafgefängnis für Berlin bei Tegel," *Zentralblatt der Bauverwaltung* 20, no. 5 (20 September 1900), p. 29. Translated by David Britt.

To receive the convicts who have hitherto served their sentences in the Stadtvoigtei and Perleberger Strasse jails in Berlin, and also to accommodate the inmates of Rummelsburg emergency prison, a new penitentiary has been erected in Sector 56 of Tegel Forest. The site, some 7.33 hectares in extent, lies on the western side of the highway from Berlin to Tegel.

The facility comprises three cell blocks: the central block for long-term and the other two for short-term inmates, together with a reserve block, an infirmary, a kitchen and bakery, a laundry and bathhouse, lumber and storage sheds, operational workshops, storage sheds for employers of prison labor, a gatehouse, and eight dwelling houses for officials.

The central cell block contains 456 individual cells of approximately 22 cubic meters capacity and 42 sleeping cells of about 12 cubic meters, together with the requisite guard rooms, sluice and punishment cells, the visiting room, a shower bath with ten showers, some workrooms, administrative offices, a schoolroom with seating for thirty, and a chapel for four hundred prisoners. The south cell block comprises 456 individual cells of approximately 15 cubic meters capacity, 44 sleeping cells of about 12 cubic meters, guard rooms, sluice and punishment cells, a shower bath, and workrooms; a single-story annex contains three administrative offices, the visiting room, and toilets for prison staff. The north cell block (II) contains 410 individual cells of approximately 18 cubic meters capacity, 90 sleeping cells of about 12 cubic meters, and the same ancillary rooms as cell block I. The reserve block holds some 160 prisoners, so that in all 1,500 prisoners can be accommodated in single cells and 160 in group confinement. [...]

All of the buildings mentioned thus far are enclosed within a wall 4 meters high and two tiers in thickness, with a plain tile coping. The only entrance is through the gatehouse, with a weighing machine beneath the archway, a gatekeeper's lodge, and a reception suite for new inmates. Two annexes contain dwellings for two craft supervisors. [...]

Construction began on April 1, 1896, and the first inmates were moved in on October 1, 1898; on February 15, 1899, its capacity was already exceeded.

56

Alfred Kerr

IN THE NEW REICHSTAG

First published as "Im neuen Reichstag" (1900); reprinted in Kerr, *Mein Berlin: Schauplätze einer Metropole* (Berlin: Aufbau, 1999), p. 30. Translated by David Britt.

THE ACME OF TASTE

As I walked into the Reichstag, I had the disturbing realization that access to this popular institution can in certain circumstances be rendered more difficult. An attendant was peddling entrance tickets. I gave him my fifty pfennigs and was annoyed. The Reichstag is [...] the major sensation of the past few weeks. [...] The galleries teem with ladies and gentlemen carrying travel bags, in the same way as the dress worn at the Wintergarten shows all the familiar signs of provincial tailoring. I myself was having to act as cicerone to a friend from dear old Breslau. Once we were inside the Reichstag, he agreed with me that these splendid corridors, this majestic debating chamber, this whole edifice—though unduly dynastic in its symbols—was nevertheless the acme of good taste. When we entered the gallery, Deputy Marquardsen was speaking. By the time this elderly,

FIGURE 21. Building the Reichstag, c. 1890 (Paul Wallot, architect), Berlinische Galerie, Landesmuseum für Moderne Kunst, Photographie und Architektur—Photographische Sammlung, BG-FS 32/82,3.

professorially gauche and monotonous gentleman had talked for a couple of minutes, I noticed that something had happened to my friend. "His eyes have fallen shut, he has sunk into deep sleep"—I quoted from *Lohengrin*.[1] [. . .]

NOTE

1. *Lohengrin,* act 1, scene 2: Elsa recounts crying out to God in deep anguish and then, as the echo reverberated in the distance, closing her eyes and sinking into a deep sleep.

57

Freisinnige Zeitung

[A MILITARY PARADE]

First published in *Freisinnige Zeitung,* 18 December 1900. Translated by Iain Boyd Whyte.

Despite the poor weather, many thousands turned out to welcome the returning troops as well as for the official greeting.[1] State and city buildings had hung out all kinds of flag decorations. The city commander of Berlin, Major-General von

Ende, together with a number of officers were present for the welcoming at the Lehrter Railway Station, where the train with the marine troops was due to arrive at half past one. [. . .]

Behind the band, two flag bearers marched with the "Boxer flag"—the bright yellow-white-red-blue Chinese flag, taken at the capture of the Taku fortress—and the imperial military flag carried during the storming of the fortress. Behind the columns of sailors and marines, the captured Chinese heavy artillery was paraded, drawn by the second brigade of the field artillery. The route led over the Moltkebrücke, the Königsplatz, and the Siegesallee to the Brandenburg Gate, and everywhere the troops returning from China were greeted on Berlin soil with rousing calls of hurrah and the waving of handkerchiefs. [. . .]

Around three o'clock there followed the march past of the naval troops before the Kaiser. After they had taken up position, with the captured artillery on the left wing, the Kaiser ordered the two flags to be paraded before him. He then marched along the front of the companies and allowed the naval companies to parade past into the courtyard, where they marched past in squares, with the two flags in front of the figure of Borussia [Prussia] . [. . .]

Here, the Kaiser addressed the troops in which, according to the *Berliner Tageblatt*, he stated broadly the following: [. . .] "No one among you can know with what great happiness the news of your victory was received, in which both the army and the navy participated [. . .] the eyes of the great emperor and king, whose monument you have today marched past, will today look down on you. And with God's help, that has so far been with us, will also remain with us in the future." As reported, the Kaiser closed his address with the words "Wherever I set down my blue young men, on that place may no one else be set down."

The Kaiser remained with the troops until after four o'clock in the Zeughaus. There then followed a parade of the combatants from the China war.

NOTE

1. The parade was held to mark the return to Berlin of the German troops that had been had been part of the international expeditionary force sent to China in July 1900 to put down the Boxer Rebellion.

58

Berliner Tageblatt

[A SUNDAY IN BERLIN]

First published in *Berliner Tageblatt*, 4 May 1903. Translated by Iain Boyd Whyte.

The first Sunday in May. It was a real spring festival that Berliners celebrated yesterday. [. . .] Many traveled to the gardens at Potsdam, now in full bloom, where just now the lilac begins to release its fragrant splendor, while others remained in the Grunewald. Here, alongside the Schlachtensee, the newly opened station at the Nikolassee enjoys a lively circle of visitors. What an attractive contrast between the peaceful, dreamy Nikolassee—the last of the Grunewald lakes to be discovered—and, only a few minutes away, the imposing Wannsee, upon whose water surface on this blessed Sunday morning there float countless sailing, rowing, and motor boats. Occasionally between them a Potsdam steamship with black columns of smoke—like a raven among the swans. On the banks of the Wannsee, on the steep rocks behind Beelitzhof, a real seaside life unfolds. In the forest above, beneath imposing old fir trees, groups of people are resting, breathing in with boundless pleasure air that is laden with the smell of water and the scent of fir-tree needles, an air rich in ozone. Farther into the forest one notices with pleasure how increasingly wider sections of the population have a happy understanding of how best to treat nature. Almost no wastepaper lies scattered about, and even the orange peel finds its way into people's pockets. [. . .]

Things were much less naturalistic on the Schlachtensee. There one came across vigorously scrubbed children, whose uneducated mother warned them to leave the "dirty" fir cones lying where they were, because if the beautiful dress became dirty then they would be really punished. Oh, poor children, what undeserved torment: a country outing in order that you learn how to keep your dress clean ! [. . .] The parents sit patiently in the garden café with a refreshing drink or a glass of beer, and are happy when a leaf floats down into their cup.

59

Hans Ostwald

BERLIN COFFEEHOUSES

First published as "Überblick" in Ostwald, *Berliner Kaffeehäuser*, Großstadt-Dokumente, no. 7 (Berlin: Seemann Nachfolger, n.d. [c. 1905]), pp. 4–8. Translated by Fiona Elliot.

Life in the coffeehouses of Berlin, which used to be rather meager and a little restricted, has become noticeably richer over the last ten to fifteen years. Not only that the coffeehouses have multiplied as fast as the population of Berlin, maybe even faster, but at the same time the Berliners themselves have become increasingly accustomed to the coffeehouse. And so a whole range of different types of such establishments have emerged. Indeed—almost each of these cafés retained or acquired some particular feature. It would be too much to describe each single one here. Only the most important, most colorful establishments will contribute some interesting scenes to this book. [. . .]

The Berlin coffeehouse is not simply a descendant of the Viennese coffeehouse. Certainly, many coffeehouses were founded in conscious imitation of those in the

Austrian capital. At least their business and their service was Viennese. But the Berlin café remains fundamentally different from those in Vienna. In Vienna the typical café is relatively small, can be taken in at a glance, the ceiling is not too high, and the air is somewhat stifling, laden with the aroma of coffee and cigarette smoke. The Viennese café has more intimate corners, cozier tables. By contrast, in Berlin, vast halls with stucco pillars, colossal mirrors, and murals were built to accommodate the Viennese [type of] cafés. The Viennese coffeehouse patron who is so fond of leaning up against something, of sitting next to a wall, has to seek out a pillar to sit by in Berlin, so as not to feel too lost in the expansive mass of people. Cafés of this kind include the Café Bauer, Kaiserhof, Monopol, Austria, Kaiserkaffee, Friedrichshof, Westminster, and so forth.

But Berlin also has its own special kind of café. Originally patisseries, they are still combined with these today. For the Berliners have always had a predilection for a slice of cake with their coffee or tea. Indeed, often enough they will go into a café merely to enjoy a piece of cake.

This is entirely foreign to the Viennese, for whom all kinds of sweet dishes are prepared at home. The many little patisseries in Berlin—from the Biedermeier era and from the time before the great wars—developed into coffeehouses, like Kranzler, Josty, Gumpert, and others. And countless other new patisseries were established specifically as café-patisseries. Typical of these are the ladies' patisseries: Buchholz in Friedrichstrasse, and Edelweiß in Mohrenstrasse. There you will find respectable middle-class ladies with their daughters, sitting leafing through weeklies, indulging in cake. Sometimes courting couples meet there for a rendezvous. And the ladies' eyes open wider and wider. [. . .]

But—the favorite venues for these trysts are the patisseries and the cafés. And once again there are different kinds. They meet at Josty's, for instance, with its half-mixed, half-respectable clientele and its quiet memories of the elegance of late Empire style, when Berlin West was still the home of our privy councilors, and in the patisserie at Potsdamer Platz with its out-of-the-ordinary rooms, which was especially frequented by typical Prussian civil servants, with their friends and their families—Josty is the rendezvous for small, cleverly conducted affairs. Steidl, in the fashion district, is the place where the imperious ladies' dressers from smart ladies' clothing shops meet gentlemen who clearly know about fabrics, trimmings, and linings. In the Monopol and the Westminster actors and actresses congregate. And in numerous other cafés the demimonde meets its friends and acquaintances. The most extraordinary of these is possibly the Café Lang, which was also originally a patisserie but is now turning increasingly into a café.

One can observe a particular kind of tryst in the many coffeehouses that entertain their clientele with gypsy music in the evenings. The first café that attracted evening patrons in this way was the Café Friedrichshof. It must be nearly ten years ago now that the swarthy fellows from Hungary first struck up their

FIGURE 22. Potsdamer Platz seen from Café Josty, c. 1914. Landesarchiv Berlin, 72473.

fiddles and sounded their cimbaloms. Now gypsies can be found making music in the Münzhof, Café Roland, in the smart cafés on Potsdamer Strasse, even in Café Schiller at the Gendarmenmarkt—the Berliners are astonished and delighted whenever these slim, swarthy men fiddle their way through Wagner's "Ride of the Valkyries" as though they were throwing off a *csárdás*. Whole families crowd around the podium. But many tables are also taken by the elegant young man-about-town and his lady friend dressed in the very latest style, the little salesgirl, the female clerk, the typist, the governess. [. . .]

Not all the coffeehouses have adopted the fashion of music in the evenings. They do not yet have such need of it as Café Schiller, which was once the meeting place for leading Berlin journalists but now bears few traces of its former glory. Café Bauer, Café Kaiserhof, and most of the coffeehouses in Friedrichstrasse have as yet no need for it. [. . .] Café Bauer is still frequented by respectable families, particularly by wealthier strangers—and of course in the late evening hours by society people—who also appear singly in all cafés at any time.

In the Kaiserhof, which was for a time the most interesting literary café—the haunt of leading modern writers like [Karl] Bleibtreu, [Felix] Hollaender, and others—one still finds the odd journalist, and respectable elderly gentlemen, some of whom restore their spirits with a game of chess. In the forenoons young lawyers can be seen there eating their hangman's breakfasts—taking a break from the examinations they have to endure in the nearby Ministry of Justice. Later at night, too, there is a trusty crew to be found here—actors, dramatists, painters, and stage designers—waiting amid jokes and laughter for the early-morning editions: have the critics given the premiere a good review?

Other nighttime coffeehouses offer all kinds of piquant images of the city. Take for instance the demimonde cafés in Friedrichstrasse, at Moritzplatz, at the Oranienburger Tor—to name but a few. And then there is the Kaiserkaffee. All night, until the gray dawn breaks, the more venturesome elements of Friedrichstrasse parade by the café—and in. Here, late at night, the strangest fellows will be found sitting together. Over there a man with gleaming, enraptured eyes in a sunken face, with glowing color spreading patchily across his yellow parchment skin. In front of him on the table stands a highly polished, small wooden box. A moment ago—his eyes dull and extinguished—he took the small box with him up the stairs to the privy—the waiter knows him well, and knows that every night the aristocratic gentleman comes at this time and administers a morphine injection to himself. [. . .]

At another table sits a group of well-nourished fellows, dressed in an almost rustic manner, their faces glowing with wine—it is the end of the Agrarians' Week.

A large gathering of artists is engaged in noisy dispute. Others just sit silently, suffering from *Weltschmerz* [world-weariness], sobbing alcoholic tears. An older writer, a well-known Berlin novelist, turns as red as a turkey cock when a younger writer calls him a piece of dead wood. It does not take much more—and glasses are flying. [. . .]

The politicians have no particular café of their own. This one or that one may be seen at Josty's—or in the Kaiserhof—or late at night on Friedrichstrasse . . .

Bohemian life, in so far as it exists at all in Berlin, collects almost exclusively in the Café des Westens—where a number of famous artists and writers used to have their own regular table until recently; now they are a few doors away, but they still come back sporadically. [. . .]

Another rather interesting café is the Monopol, where there are large numbers of typical Russians with their pale, thoughtful—or revolutionary—faces, and where, on certain evenings—particularly when there are special lecture evenings in the hospital areas on the other side of the Spree—crowds of doctors pour in, although other well-known neurological physicians and medical men are often seen here at other times, too.

Farther out, in Berlin West, the Nollendorfcafé is one of the more interesting coffeehouses. There the usual Berlin West clientele is interspersed with sharply etched, pensive heads—scholars, musicians, great journalists—and the many others who give the coffeehouses of Berlin their particular air, their charm, and their uniqueness.

60
Brüstlein
THE RUDOLF VIRCHOW HOSPITAL IN BERLIN

First published as "Das Rudolf-Virchow-Krankenhaus in Berlin," *Zentralblatt der Bauverwaltung* 27, no. 97 (30 November 1907), p. 626; no. 101 (14 December 1907), pp. 658–61. Translated by David Frisby.

For a wide variety of reasons, the new Virchow Hospital on the Augustenburger Platz has generated an unusual amount of attention. Whereas everywhere people have marveled at its size and numerical scale, upon which the daily press has reported, the inhabitants of Berlin have greeted with satisfaction this marvelous instance of metropolitan provision for the city's less-well-off citizens. Doctors and hygienists assess the institution according to innovations in the total structure and in individual design. Architects are accustomed to observing each creation of the city planners of Berlin as an artistic achievement. But among the administrative experts, everyone is looking anxiously as to whether this largest hospital in the world, when it is in operation, will prove to be manageable as a whole and economical. In other words, whether the predominant efforts in the direction of more extensive comprehensiveness will also succeed in the sphere of care for the sick, or whether the limit of an appropriate size has already been exceeded. [. . .]

What has been achieved for the sick in this huge layout? In total, 1,260 patients are housed in pavilions, comprising 500 in the medical department and 564 in the surgery department, 18 in the section for the restless, and 178 in the group for the infectious-diseases building. A further 740 beds stand in multistory corridor buildings. Of these, 374 are reserved for men with skin and sexually transmitted diseases and 146 for females with the same illnesses, as well as 220 beds for the department of gynecology and obstetrics. These 2,000 patients are treated by a personnel of around 700 staff. Since the average period of medical care in Berlin usually extends for twenty-six days, the institution can annually care for around 28,000 patients.

Around two-thirds of the sick are accommodated in wards of between twenty and thirty beds, with the remainder in rooms with mostly one to four beds. Although this does not strictly conform to the present-day demands by doctors for the individual treatment and health care for the suffering, it is no less unfavorable than in many well-known institutions. Each patient has well-provided air space (on average around 40 cubic meters) and has available more than the regulation

floor space (of 7.5 square meters in the hallways). Even if one compares the total surface area of the land (257,194 square meters) with the number of patients, the result is a very favorable one of around 120 square meters per head. [...] The window space allotted to each patient—a measure of the guarantee of air and light—is on average considerable. For example, in the pavilion halls it amounts to 1.86 square meters. In contrast, the window's direction to the sky is not always advantageous, especially in the buildings for sexually transmitted diseases.
[...]

The architectural design of the whole structure has been outstandingly realized. [...] Even from a distance, the visitor has the impression of magnificent academic stateliness. Despite its imposing height, the horseshoe shape of the main building is broadly located as a result of the dwellings connected to it and the lower building sections on the square. The total impression is welcoming but only with very bright weather, since the identical dull gray of the many ornamental surfaces and the individualized sandstone sections has a very serious effect even with somewhat overcast lighting. This cold impression is not much transformed either by the russet-colored tiled roofs and the white woodwork of the windows, especially since the discreet architectural forms of and, relatively speaking, the quite small surfaces of the windows produce the same effect. As one approaches the front facades of the wing of the main building they thrust themselves powerfully upward, and the middle tract sinks by comparison. The uniformity of the ornamental surface of the surrounding wall is broken in sections in front of the directors' dwellings by slender high iron railings and displays attractive details around the entrances. Stepping through the by no means exaggerated main entrance, one enjoys a surprising, beautiful view into the memorial courtyard. At this point, there emerges the powerful main staircase well, and below there, in the framework of the internal driveway, there appears the imposing four-rowed main alleyway. This welcoming, extensive garden courtyard surrounded by quiet, beautifully arranged built structures is satisfying to the artist, makes the sick feel at home, and gives to those who belong here the conviction that that nothing is spared in caring for the welfare of its inhabitants. [...]

Pointed objections have been raised in relation to the new building of the Virchow Hospital. It is argued that the architect has abused the doctor and created excessive expenditures. This objection can be stated differently in terms of the following two questions. Have important medical or administrative requirements been rendered subservient solely to the artistic viewpoints of the architect? And have inappropriate means been utilized for purely external effects? Perhaps one cannot reply [...] to the first question totally in the negative. But one cannot justly accuse the artist of the second objection. In comparison with the total expenditure, the ornamentation tastefully introduced at a few points is responsible for such a small outlay that one in no way needs to have an excuse for it, but rather one should claim it as necessary. On the contrary. If the powerful built structures and the broad wards were to confront those arriving without such small elements of friendliness, then—even for the completed beauty of their circumstances—they would breathe such an oppressive seriousness, breathe such dreariness and joylessness, that the mood of the sick would have to suffer from it. And that would be the more serious objection to the builder.

61

Jules Huret

BRUNO SCHMITZ'S "RHEINGOLD" FOR ASCHINGER

First published in Jules Huret, *En Allemagne* (Berlin and Paris: Bibliothèque-Charpentier, 1909), pp. 64–65. Translated by David Frisby.

You really have to see this: the facade in medieval cathedral style, walls like pagan tombs, a ground floor taken from the Thousand and One Nights, genuine Indian castles built on rocks, the salons—like the purest throne rooms of the Gothic kings, with a row of huge rooms in onyx, marble, expensive types of wood, and untreated stone blocks—where four thousand people can take a meal.[1]

This building has cost almost 15 million marks. Where will the megalomania of German architects end?

The building consists of a basement, a ground floor, and a first floor. I have counted a total of eleven salons the size of cathedral naves.

One enters into the temple through gates of beaten copper, between marble and mosaic walls. A very low basement with a vaulted ceiling that is constructed like walls made from shellwork and pebble flint; a meager light falls now and then through brightly colored orbs upon efflorescent, shoddy statuettes that create the impression that they have survived five thousand years of all the inclemency of storms and bad weather. On the ground floor is to be found the onyx salon, the ebony and mahogany salons, richly carved and decorated. Each of these rooms can accommodate three to four hundred people. The imperial salon on the first floor can hold twelve hundred people. [. . .] Two giant copper statues of Friedrich Barbarossa and Wilhelm I, whose hands rest upon the pommel of a huge, naked sword, guard the entrance. [. . .]

Where am I? In which old German knight's castle, in which giant monastery am I? In which Buddhist tombs, in which Valhalla?

I am in a restaurant , whose cooking is poor and where I can get a meal at a reduced price. What is unbelievable about this is that this boundless but imposing history has been built, and that this fantastic ornamentation has been contrived with Nibelungen, gods, giants, and midgets, in order to enable people, who hardly give it all a glance, to be served up a dish for eighty pfennigs.

NOTE

1. Bruno Schmitz (1858–1916) was an eminent architect in Germany at the turn of the century, celebrated for such large-scale works as the Monument to the Battle of the Nations (Völkerschlachtdenkmal), completed near Leipzig in 1913; the Kyffhäuser Monument in Thuringia (1890–96); and the Kaiser Wilhelm Monument at Porta Westfalica (1892–96). He designed the palatial "Rheingold" restaurant for the Aschinger company, which opened in 1907 and could serve up to four thousand guests at the same time.

62

Anonymous
NEW BUILDINGS PLANNED FOR MUSEUM ISLAND, BERLIN

First published as "Die geplanten Neubauten der Museumsinsel zu Berlin," *Deutsche Bauzeitung* 44, no. 30 (13 April 1910), pp. 217–18. Translated by David Britt.

[...] In the Kaiser-Friedrich-Museum there has always been a shortage of space for the collections of German art. [Wilhelm von] Bode rightly says that it is the duty of the capital city of the Reich to enlarge these holdings considerably, and he therefore wishes to have a separate building for them. To this is added the need to house the finds from Mesopotamia, Asia Minor, Priene, Miletus, Didyma, and elsewhere. However, a serious obstacle to any hopes for expansion and new development has been that, with the building of the Kaiser-Friedrich-Museum at the [north] end of Museum Island [1897–1904], the remaining land presented almost insuperable obstacles to large-scale development. "With its inconvenient shape, with its haphazard building pattern, and above all with the elevated railroad running across the middle of it," the island seemed, as Bode accurately puts it, "to offer precious little hope of accommodating the necessary large new buildings at all, let alone of creating an impressive composition that would coordinate with existing buildings on the site." Nevertheless, [Alfred] Messel's present design does justice to all these requirements. Not only are the buildings so sited that a grand and coherent whole appears, with a great court, backed by the majestic Pergamon Museum, to provide a central focus for all the buildings on Museum Island; he has also, as Bode says, skillfully "adapted himself to the highly disparate earlier buildings by [Karl Friedrich] Schinkel, [Friedrich August] Stüler, [Heinrich] Strack, and [Ernst von] Ihne, while still creating something entirely individual and grand that both elevates and links the neighboring buildings."[1]

The starting point for the design was the idea that the Pergamon Altar, "as one of the most important monuments of Greek art, and as the most imposing work of art that our museums have ever possessed or will ever possess," must form the centerpiece of Museum Island as a whole. [...] But two obstacles stood in the way of the complete maturation of this idea: one was the fateful railroad, and the other was the absence of street access to the central axis of the new development. Given energy and determination, we do not regard either obstacle as insuperable.

The plan is that access to the new development will be from the [Kupfergraben] Canal. A wide bridge leads to a great court (Forum), beyond which is the Pergamon Museum, flanked by a pair of large halls to house Greek architectural remains. The wings to left and right of the Forum will accommodate German art and discoveries from Asia Minor, respectively. No attempt has been made to reflect the character of the contents in the outward appearance of these buildings. This is inspired by classical antiquity, since classical items predominate within the collection as a whole, both in quantity and importance, "not, however, in the Greek Revival manner of his predecessors on Museum Island but by reference to the classical buildings of eighteenth-century Berlin. [. . .] [Karl Gotthard] Langhans's Brandenburg Gate appears as Messel's prototype, not only for the relationship between the central block and the smaller flanking structures but even for the dimensions of the columns in the different parts of the edifice, and for the attic over the portal. This applies, of course, only to the most general features of outward appearance; for it is in the way in which he has suited and modified this to the radically different function of his buildings that the artist's true individuality and greatness show themselves; and here, despite his neoclassical style, he shows himself to be entirely modern."

In this assessment of Messel's approach we may entirely concur with Bode. The facades of the three blocks display a strong and intentional contrast: the side wings rise straight out of the water on a massive stylobate, and are articulated by solemn and extremely massive Doric half-columns. The central block, housing the Pergamon Altar itself, offers a vast expanse of plain masonry crowned with quadrigae, which promises to be highly effective; it is fronted by a tall Ionic pronaos, with the delicate detailing proper to Ionic art. The lateral blocks are articulated by fluted pilasters between tall, round-headed windows with a slight suggestion of the Baroque. In its choice of scale and in its simplicity of line, the whole promises a truly impressive effect. [. . .]

NOTE

1. Museum Island in Berlin was developed in five stages. The Altes Museum, built in 1823–30 to the design of Karl Friedrich Schinkel, was the first element to be completed. It was followed by the Neues Museum (1843–59, designed by Schinkel's student August Stüler), the Alte Nationalgalerie (1866–76, designed by August Stüler and Heinrich Strack), the Bodemuseum (1897–1904, designed by Ernst von Ihne), and the Pergamon Museum, started by Alfred Messel in 1909—the subject of this article—and completed in 1930 by Ludwig Hoffmann.

63

Wilhelm Bode

ALFRED MESSEL'S PLANS FOR THE NEW BUILDINGS OF THE ROYAL MUSEUMS IN BERLIN

First published as Bode, *Alfred Messels Pläne für die Neubauten der königlichen Museen zu Berlin* (Berlin: Grote'sche Verlagsbuchhandlung, 1910), pp. 4–5. Translated by Iain Boyd Whyte.

Messel not only has succeeded in accommodating all the buildings in their full extent on the Museum Island, but also has understood how to site and link them with the existing buildings in such a way that a single, coherent entity has been created. In the process, a spacious courtyard forms the impressive center of the Museum Island, with the mighty Pergamon Museum as its closure. In an unforeseen way, he has risen to the demands of the individual collections, and on the external elevations has responded to the considerable diversity of the older buildings by Schinkel, Stüler, Strack, and Ihne. Yet he has made something splendid and unique that at the same time ennobles and links the neighboring buildings.

Messel started from the idea that the Pergamon Altar, as one of the most important monuments of Greek art and as the most important work that our museum has ever possessed and, indeed, will ever posses, must form the dominant centerpiece not only of the new museum, but of the whole complex of museum buildings. Accordingly, he specified the form and location of the Pergamon Museum and arranged the remaining new buildings around it. Two considerable hindrances certainly mitigate against the large-scale impact of these buildings: the lack of an access street and the city railway [*Stadtbahn*], which cuts across the island at this point and runs on high arches over the canal and the canal street, the so-called Kupfergraben. In the interest of the art collections it is absolutely essential that the railway should be either removed or converted to electric power. This should be done not only because the smoke and hot steam eat away at the stonework of the buildings (as is most sadly demonstrated by Cologne Cathedral, which is twenty times farther away from the railway embankment), but also because the artworks suffer under the all-permeating influence of hot, acidic vapors and also from the powerful vibration that results from the ever-heavier locomotives of the seven hundred or so trains that dash past each day at full steam. Messel, however, could not depend on such distant hopes. His design has accomplished in a hitherto undreamed of way everything that could be achieved under the current conditions.

64
Paul Westheim
LUDWIG HOFFMANN'S SCHOOL BUILDINGS IN BERLIN

First published as "Ludwig Hoffmanns Berliner Schulbauten," *Die Bauwelt* 2, no. 21 (18 February 1911), pp. 17–19. Translated by David Frisby.

School buildings are utility buildings. Barracks, too, are utility buildings—but one can build the most pompous facade in front of the most solid of barracks without, in so doing, creating a utilizable educational institution.

For the new construction of the school building we are *lacking* in *tradition*. That is not quite true. For school buildings have been erected everywhere and spring up every year. We do indeed have a tradition—but it is a *deplorable* one. The unfortunate thing about this is precisely this failed tradition, which constrains the development of newer and more genuine solutions, and which sacrifices the well-thought-out solution in favor of the merely routine.

But again it should not be inferred that in the case of school buildings there is a tendency toward insufficient consideration. Commissions, municipal authorities, city councilors, and state officials have all deliberated on this matter. They deliberate to and fro, travel around the country, and view school after school. And when they are finished with discussions and deliberations they summon up their whole power in order that nothing else and nothing better might be considered— *by the architects* themselves. The architect is, of course, the creator, but the commission naturally is his superior and equally naturally does his thinking for him. And not merely in those questions of utility that are within the jurisdiction of the commission, but also in questions of architectural form. And should the architect at some point actually offer a new suggestion and push through an improvement, it is seized on by a lay commission that lays claim to such beneficial ideas like the hen in the fable that pecks the eyes out of the duck because it has the impudence to able to swim.

At the very outset, both personal momentum and the compelling power of a purposeful task are needed to puncture this ironically unhelpful constellation like a soap bubble in the air. The Berlin city planner, *Ludwig Hoffmann,* is capable of doing this. He possesses the carte blanche of unconditional trust. For what he does is good, is solid in its workmanship, is useful, and is admirable.

When one studies the ground plan of one of the schools that Hoffmann has built for the city of Berlin, one immediately knows quite precisely the forms of their organization. Everything is contained in this concentration of the greatest experience and the most practical layout.

For these really almost identical tasks, Hoffmann has developed a *typical solution*. Of course, each individual instance requires its particular variation. Depending on the site of the building, there are roughly five basic plan types for the articulation of the plot:

1. The school building extends in its whole length along the street, while the director's house is incorporated in the same street line.
2. The school building has the same location: the courtyard, partly enclosed by the two side wings, extends up to the parallel street, on which there stand the gymnasium and the director's house with a second entrance (Pappellallee-Lychener Strasse).
3. The building stands at a street crossing. The school stands on one of the streets, while the director's house stands on the other street along which a side wing extends (Pasteurstrasse-Esmarchstrasse).
4. Together with the gymnasium, the director's house forms a distinctive building complex in behind the school courtyard (Christburger Strasse).
5. The expensive land on the street front is partly built up with private dwellings. The school lies at the rear of this site. The director's house is inserted between the nonschool housing on the street and is provided with a large gateway as the entrance to the school (Dunckerstrasse).

In general, connected to the main wing on the left and the right are two side wings in part bordering the school courtyard. They contain the majority of classrooms, while the official director's room, the meeting room and teaching-materials room, the main hall, and physics laboratories are distributed in the main wing. The Berlin community schools are in large part double schools for boys and girls. Both institutions—apart the possibility of a shared main entrance—usually have a separate access. Since the spaces by and large are the same for each, an almost symmetrical structure is created for the whole complex.

The facade possesses the character of this architectural seriousness. It is unpretentious and carried out with loving care. Its style expresses a thoroughly convincing tastefulness. And the best of what can be said about it is that it never appears to be simply a facade—it forms a conclusion to a school from the outside, and it shows to the public what great and peaceful work for the future can be achieved behind such walls. Hoffmann is well known for the discretion with which he understands how to adapt his buildings to their surroundings. He never obtrudes displeasingly out of the broader street front. And the districts in which he has had to construct his community schools do not exactly belong to the best areas of the world city. These schools stand outside on the periphery, between the working-class quarters. It is not necessary to say at the outset how little pomp and circumstance have been brought here. Busy people live here who have no sense for decorative displays, who perhaps unconsciously feel the quiet pressure of power. Between the repetitive and generally unappealing house, the school is the public building that can serve as the dominant element in a whole district. However fine and tastefully his schools insert themselves in the already given image of the street, he always recognizes how to emphasize their worth and significance for everyone in such a way that they actually appear as the focal point in the area from which between two and three thousand children stream toward them.

However much he is personally invested in each of his works, his style is not one-sided enough to be nailed down by one of the usual everyday concepts. He is confidant with the good architecture that has emerged in Europe in the last five centuries. With the fine, loving care of the artist—in the spirit of the art historian Wölfflin—he is engrossed in each of life's essential circumstances and its architectural expression in order to gather experiences. In his creations there is embedded above all something of that core that releases the sense of their certainty and sterling quality. Hence Hoffmann was also, like no other, capable of creating bridges where tradition had prevented them. Sometimes in Berlin he draws upon the unadorned mode of building that was common here at the time of Schinkel. Elsewhere, as appropriate, he allows the old March sandstone Gothic to echo in his designs. The difficulty in building schools resides in using the fenestration to articulate the facade. For the architect, the window rips a hole in the surface of the wall. So Hoffmann has attempted to resolve the contrast between the light wall surface and the darker insets of the windows. He uses small, high windows, assembles four or five together that are separated only by small wall sections, and forms groups from them that are interesting as a group and order the facade in an appealing way. [. . .] Sometimes this grouping is given an even sharper emphasis by means of a couple of simple pilaster strips. The rhythm of this treatment of the facade is often so strong that Hoffmann can abandon any relief ornamentation.

Quite often, the main entrance is treated with special care and attention. The separation between the boisterousness of the street and the ordered and constrained nature of the school is emphasized here with a wealth of means. The porch—in keeping with the building itself—is genuine masterly craftwork made out of a beautiful wood or wrought iron. The whole is crowned mostly with relief ornamentation, for whose design Hoffmann has been able to select the most excellent Berlin sculptors (Vogel, Rauch, Taschner, Lessing, Reger, and so on).

The rooms of the school attendant and the director are usually located on the ground floor, immediately reached from the main entrance. Attached to these are the meeting room and perhaps two further classrooms for the youngest schoolchildren. [. . .] The school halls are not particularly large in the Berlin community schools due to lack of space. An appropriate wooden cladding, a lighter frieze, and fresh colored paint give them character. They are especially important due to their use as well-lit rooms for drawing that can be used both by the boys' and the girls' school. [. . .] In the cellar, as well as the heating and ventilation rooms there is often a school baths. [. . .]

65

Max Wagenführ

THE ADMIRAL'S PALACE AND ITS BATHING POOLS

First published as "Der Admiralspalast und seine Bäder," *Moderne Bauformen* 11, no. 3 (March 1912), pp. 136–38. Translated by Fiona Elliot.

Berlin has three artificial ice rinks. The first was built in the new Berlin West. At first there were dissenting voices taking a skeptical view of this newfangled enterprise. But when it vastly exceeded hopes for its success, competitors immediately set about outdoing it. The southwest, near the old botanic gardens, saw the emergence of the gigantic arena of the Sports Palace, which, owing to its situation and exaggerated dimensions, has seen its capacious halls full only on exceptional occasions.

When the Admiral's Garden Bathing Club reformed its financial arrangements, it was faced with the task of making the best use of its property, conveniently situated in the heart of the city at the point where the center leads into the Latin quarter; at the same time it had to maintain the reputation it had hitherto enjoyed for its Admiral's Garden Pool. Even an exceptional swimming pool would not suffice, since the boroughs of Greater Berlin had already made adequate provision for the needs of the population. The decision was therefore taken to concentrate on Russian-Roman baths, which would be fitted out in the most sophisticatedly luxurious style, while the remaining area would be used for up-to-date sanctuaries for physical fitness and recuperation: an ice-skating rink, in that favorable position in the flow of the nightlife of the metropolis, would be certain of a stream of visitors and despite the presence of similar enterprises could reckon on sure success; a cinema theater in the best style is also still a considerable attraction, and with the addition of a café, bar, bowling alleys, and club rooms, every last square meter of the site would certainly reap a profit. The success of the enterprise once it was completed proved the accuracy of these calculations.

One cannot but admire how skillfully the many different parts of the site are accommodated, without interfering with each other—indeed, comfortably combining on this unusually disposed terrain. The foremost rectangle, with a facade to Friedrichstrasse of 32.48 meters in length and going back to a depth of around 50 meters, has a café looking out onto the street on the two lower floors. Above this is the cinema, with its own entrance on the right of the building, separate from the main entrance and throughway. Right on top are the club rooms. The narrow side wing contains the utility rooms and provides access to the pools. The back section of this and the imposing crosswise building that together surround the central courtyard contain the entrances and extra facilities for the rink and the pools. These occupy a somewhat wedgelike area, with a frontage of 76 meters—

on average 45 meters deep—to the Prinz-Louis-Ferdinand-Strasse and service yards on either side. This part of the building is of particular interest, less for its ice rink constructed according to the newest principles than for the position of the baths *above* the ceiling, which is itself stylishly supported by powerful haunches. The design required the latticework roof to be of an unusual height, but made it possible to provide top light for the baths, thereby making clever use of the available floor space. The approximately 58-by-45-meter space above the rink could thus be used for: a relatively large gentlemen's bathing hall (with three separate pools), a large quiet room, buffet, barber's room, orthopedic room, electric baths, showers, massage room, plunge and hot-air baths, drying room, steam baths, and other side rooms. In addition there is the ladies' bathing hall, with quiet rooms, luxury baths, hot- and warm-air, steam, and electric baths with an orthopedics and massage room as well as a hairdresser's room and other auxiliary rooms, large rooms for laundering and ironing, and the necessary stairwells.

[. . .]

The architect has been reproached by certain critics for his use of typical features from Roman bathhouses.[1] There were those who would have wanted specially designed, modern-day forms for a modern institution. And aside from his use of these stylistic features there was also criticism of the way these were incorporated into the construction, which was itself in part dictated by its function and by modern technology. In view of this it is worth clarifying certain issues. The confined nature of the city-center plot, already hemmed in by tall buildings on either side, and the need to exploit every square meter make it harder, if not impossible, to reflect the internal function in the external design. The architect is generally prevented from availing himself of the eloquent language of solid forms and planes grouped to reflect the contents. When it came to the outward characterization of the function of the building, the architect had at his disposal only the facade, which is relatively little compared to the ground plan as a whole. While the facade on Prinz-Louis-Ferdinand-Strasse provided an opportunity for the architect to specifically reflect the structural concept of the ice rink with the bathing halls above, on the Friedrichstrasse side there was no architectural design that could characterize the building's division into café, cinema, and club rooms. In such cases something not unrelated to *poster design* occurs. The overall contents and main purposes of the site are to be clearly indicated, using architectural means, on one plane. And in the specific case we are examining here, this task has all the more in common with poster design since the facade on Friedrichstrasse was also to *advertise* the establishment. Similarly, on the rear facade, *specific* sections of the building could not receive particular emphasis; there could be no more than a general indication of sport and leisure activities in the city center. Since the limitations of architecture itself, without the help of sculpture and painting, mean that it is impossible to convey more than a generalized mood, the architect has no choice other than to draw on the intellectual content of broadly understood *motifs*—that is to say, if he wishes to indicate more than just a general mood. It is as in music; there, too, motifs convey sequences of thoughts that seem to take us beyond the bounds of art, albeit remaining part of that art since they are generated by artistic means and serve the overarching higher purpose of the work. The motif is, in itself, meaningless; it is endowed with a function only from without, through being positioned in a particular place or through memories of its function in another place—even in another, earlier work of art. Thus, in the case we are examining here, given that the architect wanted to allude to the time-honored tradition of the Admiral's Garden Pool and to indicate the new contents of the modern bathing halls on the front facade, then—as long as he wanted to avoid overly literary and prolix explanations by sculptor and monumental painter—he had no choice but to turn to motifs from classical precursors known the world over. The stylistic peak of Roman Epicureanism was the perfect vehicle with which to establish the parallel between the sybaritic life of antiquity and the modern longing for luxury.

Whether every detail successfully reflects this maxim is not for us to decide here. The fact that these Roman motifs are used throughout the building serves to unify the whole. Maybe in some places the modern is juxtaposed just a little too bluntly with echoes of ancient traditions—a classical radiator casing, a statue of Victory in the ice rink are easily ridiculed as anachronisms—but perhaps there is a subtle humor here that is certainly not out of place in these surroundings devoted to pleasure and delight. Finally, mention should be made of the fact that—as the pictures show—the Latinate features are in no sense overpowering or dominant; they are merely decorative, accompanying figures that here and there, especially in the actual bathing areas, stand out more clearly; elsewhere they simply add to and complement the modern building.

The particular quality of the Admiral's Palace is due—aside from its inspired program—to the skillfully construed ground plan and the successful exploitation of the entire site. The technical expertise in the use of the excess steam from the ice-making machinery for the bathing pools, the circulation of the water, the cellars under the yards—partly to house the bowling alleys—the accommodation of the building's many domestic needs in kitchens, cloakrooms, and equipment, apparatus, storage, and machine rooms are all deserving of our admiration. The high number of necessarily ensuing planning dispensations is an indication of the size of the task fulfilled here.

The facade on Friedrichstrasse is to be raised at some future date, when the demolition of the old Pépinière opposite it makes this possible.[2] The planned upward extension will provide the club rooms with a more suitable architectural setting. At present the necessary columns amusingly adorn the neighboring gable end. Perhaps the facade in its future form will silence its current critics; we find no fault with it in its present form. The generous forms and daring design (in part determined by the 6-meter-wide entrance prescribed in the building codes) perfectly fulfill their purpose—namely, to attract visitors to a modern pleasure dome—both tastefully and in a manner calculated to lift our spirits. The Admiral's Palace contrasts advantageously with its neighbors, since in a setting where one is seeking to outdo the other, only a degree of dignified restraint—albeit underlining the building's uniqueness—will make a lasting impression.

NOTES

1. There were in fact two architects of the Admiral's Palace: Heinrich Schweitzer and Alexander Diepenbrock.
2. The Pépinière was a school for military medicine, established in Berlin in 1795. A new building for the institution, by then renamed the Kaiser-Wilhelm-Akademie für das militärärztliche Bildungswesen, was opened in 1910, replacing the old Pépinière, which was demolished.

66

Fritz Stahl (pseud. Siegfried Lilienthal)

THE BERLIN CITY HALL

First published as "Das Berliner Stadthaus: Architekt Ludwig Hoffmann," *Berliner Architekturwelt* 14, no. 9 (September 1912), pp. 337–41. Translated by Iain Boyd Whyte.

The new city hall [Stadthaus], the most important building that Ludwig Hoffmann has created for Berlin, represents an impressive performance, both in the power of its overall composition and in the delicacy and carefulness of the execution, right down to the most inconspicuous detail.

City hall has a double function, although this is not the place to pass judgment on this fundamental issue. On one hand it is intended primarily as an office building, to accommodate the currently homeless departments in the administration. But at the same time it also has to represent the city to the outside world in a manner appropriate to the present status and wealth of Berlin—in other words, forcefully and magnificently. Hoffmann had no objections to this brief. He accepted both intentions and stressed both the sobriety of the internal office building and the monumental splendor of the external elevations. Yet he has managed the internal transitions from the public rooms in such a way that the styles never directly clash.

The colossal mass of the building is mastered as a unified block and developed in an organic way, with beautiful rhythms that are developed out of the ground plan. The planning was made more complex by the form of the available city site, which was a very irregular rectangle, preventing a truly axial disposition. The fact that the building actually has four fronts each of considerably different lengths would hardly be noticed by the casual observer. This is principally thanks to the consistent application of the same compositional system, which is then appropriately modified according to the scale and importance of the individual elevation. This system, basically, is nothing more than one used in Berlin since the Baroque period, in which the principal stories are articulated by pilasters and columns. Harmony is then achieved by giving the columns of the central element a greater or lesser prominence according to the importance of the particular front. Those on the main facade are particularly rounded and powerful, and the porticus is crowned by a large pediment, out of which rises the high, domed tower. The fact that the compositional system used in the building is continued on the tower contributes greatly to the unified effect of the whole. Here the window surrounds are made of rusticated blocks, set between smooth columns and pilasters. This quotation on the windows of the tower of the rusticated ground level below is surely new. [. . .] The problem of the irregular site is optically very well resolved with respect to the different corners that result. Where a corner results in an obtuse angle, the entire protruding block at the other end of the facade is also set at an obtuse angle to maintain the symmetry. And the tower is not really rectangular, precisely because it has to give the impression of being rectangular. In the interior, too, provision has been made in this respect. The main hall does not lie on the axis of the entrance. A subtle displacement of the spaces leading to it, however, helps obscure the kink in the path that leads from the main entrance to the central door of the hall. The architectural language is more severe than we are used to from Hoffmann. The public interior space for which our expectations are most stimulated by the facade, and which, indeed, is the only one that fulfils these expectations, is the great city chamber, which is also intended for public ceremonies. With its gray limestone interior, red marble floor, and large bronze candelabra, it makes a courtly impression, and the simple white ceiling reinforces this character, which is a conscious attempt to avoid the character of a municipal hall. [. . .] The vestibules and waiting rooms on the various levels, executed in good materials and with fine detailing, continue the representative tone through the building. They cannot, of course, conceal the character of the office building, which is energetically determined by kilometers of plain white corridors and staircases. With its pure lines and its handsome decorative forms, this structure, taken as a totality, is exemplary.

67

Else Lasker-Schüler

THE TWO WHITE BENCHES ON THE KURFÜRSTENDAMM

First published as "Die beiden weißen Bänke vom Kurfürstendamm" in Lasker-Schüler, *Gesichte: Essays und andere Geschichten* (Leipzig: Wolff, 1913), pp. 43–44. Translated by Iain Boyd Whyte.

One morning she was suddenly standing on the Kurfürstendamm like someone who had fallen from the heavens like a crescent moon. One of the white benches waved genially at the people coming out of the Friedrich-Wilhelm-Gedächtnis-kirche [Friedrich Wilhelm memorial church], the other white bench invited a blond beauty in ash-green velvet. Since then I've often walked past the white benches; yesterday I sat down for the first time, and then, farther up the street, on the other. If I looked straight ahead, a chaotic view was on offer. Lots of people are hurrying by with opera glasses in their hands going wherever—to the elevated railway. The theater performances begin in half an hour. Others come out of the city, make a turn into the Joachimsthaler Strasse, and make their regular stop at the Café des Westens. Two poor little girls approach; between them their own living, rosy-cheeked jumping jack, who is also able to speak. "He's two years old," they tell me, and then argue over who is looking after him—in other words, which of them will show me his tricks. "We aren't sisters," the two would-be mothers tell me, already letting their chins fall in a ponderous way and looking attentively after their little Punchinello. "We are both on our own." By that they meant that they aren't even related. Little Lisa is adopted; her foster father is a night watchman. Sometimes out of sheer exhaustion he lies down in bed when he gets home in the morning, still holding his bundle of keys and his lantern. The other Lisa—they both have the same name—says that her father helps a magician. "His father is a black Negro!" Someone calls me from the streetcar stop: a poet wearing a wide-brimmed straw hat, who wants to go out to the suburbs. "Go on your own, Torquato Tasso. I want to stay here sitting on the matching white bench." I look across to this other bench, which sparkles much more bridelike than the one I'm getting up from; and I hesitate to sit down on its myrtle whiteness. But the two lovers there don't even notice. The first Sunday souls are already coming out of the church; the narrow rays of the sun play the organ around the building. I hide my face in the shadow of the great clock tower—seeing, hearing, and thinking nothing, and yet, lost in thought, one finds oneself back on the white benches.

68

Bruno Taut

THE PROBLEM OF BUILDING AN OPERA HOUSE

First published as "Das Problem des Opernbaus," *Sozialistische Monatshefte* 20, no. 1 (1914), pp. 355–57. Translated by Fiona Elliot.

For any architect an undertaking of this kind has a colossal appeal: with the shared enjoyment of the arts by a throng of people in festive mood as the basis for a magnificent demonstration of courtly splendor. To create a suitable architectural organism for this would strike anyone as a task to be relished. So why is it that the Berlin Opera House project has become such an embarrassment, so disheartening to all: a feeling not confined to those directly involved in its construction but that has also transferred to the architects, expectantly observing events? The competition, run three times, with its sacrifice of energy and fantasy (particularly that of the general public, without a prize being awarded), the countless resolutions and declarations for and against, boundless enthusiasm and spirited altercations—all these seem to have done nothing to clarify the situation. The general confusion today concerning a solution to the Opera House question could not be greater.

We have no architects who can provide us with the solution: or so we hear and read. That will always be the case as long as the majority of people have no particular leaning to one solution or another. And how might such a solution arise—a solution that will stand as a pure and faithful reflection of its own time? And what are the particular conditions that our own time lays down with regard to this task? A modern empire, a caste system, and the ordinary populace: all three are to be embodied in one whole. This would be possible if the zeitgeist were not against these three notions being depicted as distinct entities. The fear is that this might lead to certain harsh divisions. Untroubled enjoyment of the arts is supposed to be on offer here, and yet the fellow in the third balcony should not be using the same foyer as the fellow in the first balcony. The imperial box should be placed in the heart of the auditorium, just as the salon connected to it should lie at the center of the stairwell so that the emperor can, from his vantage point, make contact with the public. Only not with the patrons from the upper balconies. Despite this, the opera house should also fulfill its function as a venue for mass events with twenty-five hundred seats. This is not to say that it is impossible to create a major opera house to be enjoyed by princes and ordinary people alike. Just as it was possible in the past (in Paris, Vienna, Dresden, old Berlin), so it should be today—if only the lack of clarity that prevails in our life and times did not prevent the formation of such a thing.

There *can be* no architect who will provide us with a solution; perhaps that is how it should be put. But what if an architect were to have the courage to leave behind the pettiness of current attitudes and were to give significant form to the things that really matter—would then a time such as ours actually understand its own child? Even after the third open competition for a design for an opera house, apparently no design appeared that could redeem the situation. And yet there was one, of which scarcely any notice was taken, that stood out from all the others. This was the work of the architect Hans Poelzig (Breslau[1]), which alone was untrammeled by decorative columns and truly struck a note of its own. Externally it had an unforgettable structure, which demonstrated a clear understanding of the heights that modern theatrical stage design can reach; internally it had a distinctive ground plan that was, however, disquieting to our overly sensitive current attitudes, in that people from all the different balconies would use one foyer, and the emperor would be visible to all in the main hall, appearing as a prince among the people. The public at large did not respond to this design as one ought to a precious gift. Thus it is fair to say that it is not the architectural production of our time that is weak, but the time itself.[2]

The contradictions in our own times are clearly reflected in our struggle for a new style of architecture. In the same way that we see at all levels in our civilization the productive, forward-striving element in the realization of social ideals, in the subordination of the individual to the greater commonality, which should lead to a new heightening of individual consciousness (Walt Whitman), so, too, in architecture we find an analogous tendency to strive for organic structures in our buildings. In all of this the aim is: to construct the building as a living organism, to recognize first and foremost its functional and structural premises and from this—in a necessarily logical manner and subordinating one's own individuality—to allow the appropriate form to emerge that will, as it were, breathe and live. This is the only viable path, which, leaving behind the aesthetics of the past—be these the aesthetics of space or of the plastic, architectural form—can guide us toward an artistic solution to the many problems of our times. This path, which is where we find Poelzig's design, contradicts conventional notions of architecture that like to rely on Palladio and that were particularly clearly embodied in his style. Palladio expressly demanded that the viewer should allow only those parts of a house to affect him that he, as architect, specifically drew attention to; hence his practice of emphasizing certain parts by special columns while the rest is left quite plain. Since it is not possible to arbitrarily become a historic or a modern person, designs are produced that are neither one thing nor the other, as we have seen most recently in the case of the opera house. The immutable law of our existence demands that our designs should be organic, yet one cannot escape the traditional in the above-mentioned form: and so it is that columnar designs and grand facades are combined with organic intentions, and degraded such that they may be seen adorning the sides and backs of buildings, the stage house and repositories—in all sorts of situations where there is nothing grand to be said.

Thus we inevitably lose all the grace that old buildings achieved with the same exterior forms: simply because this kind of grace is not innate to us. And we are left with the dryness and emptiness that we know from countless recent creations, which, as a result of the non sequiturs in their own logic, are unable to make sense of the issues affecting architectural form in our own times. The desire to disguise the fact that the building contains a stage is symptomatic of this in many opera-house projects. Involuntarily the practical bent of modern man comes to the fore as he calculates the extra costs involved in favoring the height of the stage house over that of the auditorium and, arriving at the figure of one and a half million, asks himself what social improvements could have been made with the money lost in this nonorganic architecture.

Every era presents its own typical challenges for the architect and builder, which derive from the zeitgeist and ultimately lead to innovation in architecture.

The typical idea of our own times, the idea that everyone shares today, must be the notion of social improvement. And it is not courtly opera that will give us our new architecture, but the peoples' theaters, the new garden cities, and all those buildings that are rooted in that same social idealism.

NOTES

1. Now Wroclaw, Poland.
2. In 1919 Hans Poelzig was commissioned by the impresario Max Reinhardt to convert the old Zirkus Schumann building in central Berlin into the Großes Schauspielhaus, complete with revolving stage, cyclorama, and seating for thirty-five hundred.

69

Anonymous [Joseph Adler?]

THE OPENING OF THE TAUENTZIEN PALACE CAFÉ

First published as "Eröffnung des Tauentzien-Palast-Cafes," *Die Aktion* 4 (17 January 1914), pp. 48–50. Translated by Fiona Elliot.

"On the invitation of Herr Heinrich Braun, the proprietor of the renowned Café Piccadilly at Potsdamer Platz, yesterday afternoon a throng of guests gathered in Mr. Braun's new café in the Tauentzien Palace in Berlin, at no. 19 Tauentzienstrasse, near the Wittenbergerplatz underground station. The guests had come for a preview, in more intimate circumstances, of the splendid architecture of the new refreshment rooms and rendezvous in Berlin West. Immediately upon entering the rooms one is flooded by a sea of light from on high, so extravagantly bright that one is initially quite dazzled."

Unfortunately the sea of light only floods from on high. If only it had also washed everything away. But: "Gradually one becomes accustomed to the sunny illumination and now perceives with astonishment how the architect has brought back to life in Greater Berlin the magnificence of ancient Byzantium."

No mean feat. But Greater Berlin can accommodate and tolerate everything. With astonishment one sees how duplicitously everything is re-created. And: "The gleam of mother-of-pearl, gold-bronze, marble, and mirrors combine to create an overall impression that, with its nobility and finely structured architecture, is shown off *at its most resplendent* by the magnificent lighting. The light red coffered ceiling and the dark red furniture introduce a warm tone to the gleaming, real splendor of this café that might be compared with that of any banqueting hall, its upper levels extending upward through two stories, and presenting the visitor at the entrance with a picturesque, very beautiful sight. Outstanding proof of the diligence of German artist-craftsmen is evident on all sides, pleasing in its *well-considered* forms, skilled execution, and *finish*."

This snob is remarkable for his evident courage. Nothing will prevent him persisting with this intellectual diarrhea. For this is no average snob. He cuts through language be it thick or thin. He will hold his own. He has already found the path that leads through dark night to the sea of lights. What? you say. Prevent him going any further? Run him through with a sword? Unfortunately impossible. And yet: "Quite miraculous the tiles with their dazzling mother-of-pearl gleam on the upper-level parapets, quite excellent the artistry of the lighting fixtures. And of course all the other details meet the same degree of luxury of the 'Cafésaal' and, as in the Café Piccadilly, in the Grand Café Tauentzien Herr Braun offers his guests, besides first-quality refreshments, the aural delectation of an artistically trained orchestra. On the opening days this newest monumental attraction in Greater Berlin was decked with luxuriant flora, a greening, blossoming symbolization of our wishes for the success of this newest enterprise in the safe hands of Herr Braun."

I could weep at the dazzling mother-of-pearl gleam on the upper-level parapets for Byzantium brought back to life, and I would dearly love to castrate the greening, blossoming *symbolization* of our wishes for the success of this virginal enterprise—as truly as there is a God who did not have these flowers grow for the benefit of fawning, mercenary, self-seeking snobs and frock coats.

7

THE BOURGEOIS CITY

In comparison to Britain, France, or the United States, the bourgeoisie in Germany, although comparably large in number, was a remarkably embattled class. Fritz Stern has noted: "In no other state did feudal and proletarian forces confront each other so directly, for in no other country did the bourgeoisie play so insignificant a political role."[1] Berlin—the seat of the court and the largest industrial city in Germany—was the key site of this confrontation, with the bourgeoisie caught in the crossfire. As the bourgeois constituency was in large part Jewish, the uncertainties of its position were aggravated by the anti-Semitism that was a constant factor of public life in the new German state. One of the great commentators of Berlin at this time, Karl Scheffler, noted: "In fact the bourgeois patriciate, in so far as it exists at all, has come mainly from Jewry. Nowhere have they become so much the representatives of bourgeois family culture as in Berlin."[2] Kept at a distance from the court and the old aristocracy, the Berlin bourgeoisie constructed its own realm, consolidating its own interests—intellectual, cultural, and social—and its footprint within the city.

From the early 1860s, when the architect Friedrich Hitzig created the Albrechtshof villa colony there, the Tiergarten was a favored site for the prosperous Berlin citizens who could afford to move out of the polluted air of the city. The prevailing style here was a modest Prussian classicism, with two- and three-story houses set in generous gardens. Urban expansion engulfed this idyll, however, in the 1880s, when the Tiergarten became a sought-after location for the palacelike villas of the new commercial rich, for embassies, and for the prestige offices of national institutions, trusts, and foundations. The landed nobility, army officers, and courtiers who had lived in the Tiergarten in the midcentury were now replaced by bankers, industrialists, and assorted entrepreneurs. They were joined by the academic elite and by the cream of the new generation of artists.

At least half of this new bourgeoisie was composed of Jewish families. In earlier decades, this group had attempted to adapt to and adopt the feudal manners of the court and military caste, but this strategy became increasingly fraught with the rising tide of anti-Semitism in the 1870s. Forty years later, in 1911, the eminent Jewish businessman and writer Walther Rathenau had long abandoned any illusions of full assimilation into German high society, recalling: "In the adolescent years of every German Jew occurs that painful moment that he remembers all his life: the first time when he becomes fully conscious that he has entered the world as a second-class citizen and that no achievement and no service can liberate him from this condition."[3] As an alternative, and much more interesting, strategy, the Jewish *haute-bourgeoisie* of Berlin evolved as the stronghold of an educated left liberalism, which was much more open than the court elite to current international developments in the visual arts, theater, and music. Indeed, the important collection of French Impressionist paintings, bought for the Berlin National Gallery specifically against the will of the Kaiser, was substantially paid for by the Jewish *haute-bourgeoisie:* by the coal baron Eduard Arnhold, and by such private bankers as Robert and Ernst von Mendelssohn, Julius Bleichröder, and Fritz Friedländer-Fuld.[4] Instead of pursuing the doomed path of feudalization, the new Berlin bourgeoisie, which although dominated by Jews was not exclusively Jewish, opted for liberal intellectualism and cosmopolitanism.

The great charm of the Tiergarten was its close proximity both to the traditional industrial quarters in Moabit, just north of the Spree, and to the city center, which was easily reached by horse tram. Increased traffic pressure on the city approaches, including the Tiergarten, in the 1890s, coupled with the introduction of suburban trams and railways, persuaded the middle-class money to move farther out, into the fresh air of the fields and the woods. The path westward had already been marked in the 1860s, with the establishment of the Villenkolonie Westend. Set at the highest point of Charlottenburg, before the road runs down to the Havel lake and to Spandau, Westend held a particular attraction for successful publishers, writers, and artists. Residents included the Ullstein family, the sociologist Georg Simmel, academics and writers like Ulrich von Wilamowitz-Moellendorf and Robert Walser, and the composer Richard Strauss, who lived at Reichskanzlerplatz (now Theodor-Heuss-Platz) from 1913 to 1917. Other villa suburbs sprang up at Lichterfelde, Nikolassee, and Zehlendorf to the south, and in Frohnau in the north, where it was called a garden city, in imitation of the British model. The big money, however, favored Grunewald, the most expensive and exclusive suburb of Berlin, located at the edge of the Grunewald forest.

Writing in 1873, no lesser figure than Bismarck urged that the Kurfürstendamm be widened into a grand boulevard giving access to the Grunewald, which would, he urged, become the Bois de Boulogne of Berlin. Grand apartment houses were built along the new street, which was 33 meters broad, and the first steam trams ran up this magnificent new boulevard in 1887. Two years later, 234 hectares of forest were enclosed as the site of the Grunewald villa colony, and four artificial lakes were constructed between the natural lakes of the Halensee in the north and Hundekehlesee to the south, heightening the picturesque qualities of the site. Such attentive landscape planning was rare among contemporary villa developments and gave the Grunewald site a certain painterly quality as a carefully composed coulisse for the good life. Very soon, the new wealth of the city was streaming westward along the Kurfürstendamm and settling in grand villas, each rivaling the other in scale and pretension.

Carl Fürstenberg's progress was typical of many. Complementing his house in the Tiergarten, the banker Fürstenberg commissioned the court architect Ernst von Ihne to design for him an enormous villa on the Königsallee in Grunewald, the main thoroughfare of the new development. The result was a palatial residence whose ground floor extended over 300 square meters, with the main public rooms arranged around a large central hall designed to host receptions. Gardens and parklands led down from the house past the tennis court to the Dianasee, one of the artificial lakes. The Grunewald colony was the Beverley Hills of its day, and attracted an instant and envious response. Writing in 1901, Paul Voigt—by no means a supporter of much of the new suburban development in Berlin—heaped praise on the new colony in the woods: "The Grunewald, which is increasingly becoming the lungs of Berlin, has gained a magnificent approach road in the Kurfürstendamm, which will assuredly attain the full significance in the life of Berlin traffic that Prince Bismarck has already prophesied for it. A luxurious township has sprung up in the Villenkolonie Grunewald, which looks in vain for its equal in Europe, and which makes possible—albeit only for the upper classes—the most perfect satisfaction of all housing requirements. At the same time, it has become one of the sights of the capital city of the Reich, where scenic beauty and architectural elegance fuse together to create a most attractive and painterly picture, which attracts many thousands of visitors on bright summer days. The many and splendid country houses in a rich multitude of styles have given a new impulse to Berlin architecture and exercise an influence on the refinement of artistic taste that is not to be underestimated, and which is already reflected in the Berlin apartment houses on the streets in the west of the city."[5]

This reciprocity, between the extravagant villas in the suburbs and the grand apartments in the new west of Berlin, also found a resonance in the city itself in the crop of new clubs and grand hotels that sprang up in two waves around the turn of the century. There were very few neutrally social areas where members of the court and aristocratic elite could meet with the new money derived from commerce. Two did emerge, however, as a combination of new technologies and royal patronage—namely, the Kaiserlicher Automobil-Club and the Kaiserlicher Aero-Club. At a lower level of exclusivity, but nevertheless in the realm where old and new money met, were the new generation of grand hotels. The first wave included the Kaiserhof and the Central Hotel, opened in 1875 and 1880, respectively. They were built in response to increased overnight-visitor numbers in Berlin, which doubled between 1896 and 1913 to reach 1.4 million. A second wave of hotel building followed in 1906–12, in response to the challenge both of the leading European hotels, like the Ritz in Paris and the Savoy Hotel in London, and of the Plaza Hotel in New York City, which opened in 1907. In responding to this challenge, the Adlon and the Esplanade created important intersections in the life of Berlin. They attracted the cream of the local elites: aristocratic, political, commercial, and intellectual. They also catered for a growing international clientele, which expected the mechanized, push-button conveniences of the leading American establishments. In terms of taste, style, and glamour, they also formed an urban pendant to the grand suburban villas by attempting to outshine even the most spectacular private houses.

There was, of course, no single taste shared by all residents of the Grunewald villas. Judging from contemporary accounts and photographs, the bankers and the industrialists appeared to favor historical modes in their interior decorations, be it heavy German Renaissance, neoclassical, or florid rococo. For his house on Koenigsallee, Walter Rathenau, who was both an industrialist as the son of the founder of the AEG and also a intellectual and politician, favored the simplicity of Prussian classicism, as it had evolved around 1800. The pretentiousness and lack of restraint that became synonymous with the Grunewald villas became a chief target of the attacks of the reformers, and in particular Hermann Muthesius, who argued for a more British approach to bourgeois life that was grounded on need, comfort, and function rather than on mindless display. This world of excess, however, also accommodated some of the great brains and artistic talents of early-twentieth-century Berlin. In addition to Walter Rathenau, the city's intellectual and academic elite was represented by the likes of Max Planck, Adolf von Harnack, Werner Sombart, and Hans Delbrück. Leading figures in belles lettres and the arts also featured prominently, and a list of the great and good would include writers like Alfred Kerr, Maximilian Harden, Gerhart Hauptmann, Vicki Baum, und Lion Feuchtwanger; the theater director Max Reinhardt; the dancer Isadora Duncan; and Friedrich Murnau, pioneer filmmaker and creator of *Nosferatu*.

Looking back on his childhood in the Grunewald, Nikolaus Sombart concluded: "Without excessive exaggeration, one could say that this so lavishly laid out reservation for the bourgeois lifestyle was essentially Jewish territory. Every second or third of the large villas was in Jewish ownership. Here the Jewish patriciate lived—which included not only the *haute finance juive*, but also a family like that of Walter Benjamin—in palaces. . . . With the 'Third Reich' this world perished."[6] The memories, however, remained. Alfred Kerr, who had lived on the same street as Friedrich Murnau—Douglasstrasse—looked back from his exile in Amsterdam and offered an ironic summing-up of bourgeois life in Berlin, as practiced in the grandest villa suburb of all: "When I look back today on the vanity of the afternoons and evenings in these villas, I have to allow myself a decorous laugh (this, I believe, is deemed one's duty in apocalyptic times, when 'a world is in its death throes'), but I know, nevertheless, that despite all of that, there was often beauty, beauty, beauty."[7]

NOTES

1. Fritz Stern, *The Politics of Cultural Despair: A Study in the Rise of a Germanic Ideology* (Berkeley: University of California Press, 1961), p. xxviii.
2. Karl Scheffler, quoted in Reinhard Rürup, "'Parvenue Polis' and 'Human Workshop': Reflections on the History of the City of Berlin," *German History* 6, no. 3 (1988), p. 235.
3. Walter Rathenau, *Gesammelte Schriften*, vol. 1 (Berlin: Fischer, 1925), pp. 188–89.
4. Race, of course, was not the only variable. See Robin Lenman, *Artists and Society in Germany, 1850–1914* (Manchester, UK: Manchester University Press, 1997), especially pp. 172ff. Interestingly, Lenman speculates that "the vogue for Impressionism/Secessionism, like the contemporary migration to the suburbs, was linked to the strains of urbanisation" (p. 175).
5. Paul Voigt, *Grundrente und Wohnungsfrage in Berlin und Vororten* (Jena: Fischer, 1901); quoted in Helga Gläser, Karl-Heinz Metzger, and others, *100 Jahre Villenkolonie Grunewald, 1889–1989* (Berlin: Bezirksamt Wilmersdorf, 1988), p. 10.
6. Nicolaus Sombart, *Jugend in Berlin, 1933–1943: Ein Bericht*, rev. ed. (Frankfurt am Main: Fischer Taschenbuch, 1991), p. 16.
7. Alfred Kerr, *Walther Rathenau: Erinnerungen eines Freundes* (Amsterdam: Querido, 1935), p. 38; quoted in Jan Andreas May, "Die Villa als Wohnkultur und Lebensform: Der Grunewald vor dem ersten Weltkrieg," in *Berliner Villenleben*, ed. Heinz Reif (Berlin: Gebr. Mann, 2008), p. 305.

70

Theodor Fontane

THE TREIBEL VILLA

From *Frau Jenny Treibel* (1892); English translation by Ulf Zimmermann in Fontane, *Short Novels and Other Writings* (New York: Continuum, 1982), p. 146.

The Treibel villa was situated on a large property that extended spaciously from the Köpenicker Strasse to the Spree. Here in the immediate vicinity of the river there had once been only factory buildings in which every year uncounted tons of potassium ferrocyanide, and later, as the factory expanded, not much smaller quantities of Berlin blue dye had been produced.[1] But after the war of 1870, as billions poured into the country and the newly founded empire began to dominate the views of even the soberest heads, Kommerzienrat Treibel found his house in the Alte Jakobstrasse no longer suited to his times nor his rank—though it was supposed to have been the work of Gontard,[2] and according to some, even that of Knobelsdorff.[3] He therefore built himself a fashionable villa with a small front yard and a parklike back yard on his factory property. The house was built with an elevated first floor, yet because of its low windows it gave the impression of a mezzanine rather than a *bel étage*. Here Treibel had lived for sixteen years and still couldn't understand how he had been able to endure it for such a long time in the Alte Jakobstrasse, unfashionable and without any fresh air, just for the sake of a presumptive Frederickan architect. These were feelings more than shared by his wife. Although the closeness of the factory, when the wind was unfavorable, could bring a good deal of unpleasantness with it, the north wind, which drove the smoke fumes over, was notoriously rare, and one didn't after all have to give parties during a norther. Besides, Treibel had the factory chimneys built up higher every year and thereby removed the initial nuisance more and more.

NOTES

1. Created in 1704 by the Berlin chemist Heinrich Diesbach, Prussian blue or Berlin blue was one of the first mineral dyes.

2. Carl von Gontard (1731–91), architect, was active in Berlin and Potsdam during the reign of Frederick II of Prussia.

3. Georg Wenzeslaus von Knobelsdorff (1699–1753), painter and architect, designed Rheinsberg Castle, the State Opera in Berlin, and the Palace of Sanssouci in Potsdam.

71

Alfred Kerr

HERR SEHRING BUILDS A THEATER DREAM

First published as "Herr Sehring baut einen Theater-Traum" (1895); reprinted in Kerr, *Mein Berlin: Schauplätze einer Metropole* (Berlin: Aufbau, 1999), pp. 80–81. Translated by Fiona Elliot.

Another matter that is increasingly making its presence felt is the Theater des Westens, which is slowly—if we may be so bold—reaching up toward the heavens. Slowly—for our building authorities and their ever-so-thorough codes ensure that there can be no excess of speed. All the same: the new undertaking will be finished at the appointed time, and, to judge by what one can already see, it will be one of the most interesting buildings in Berlin. I mean: structurally. What it will achieve in artistic terms is known only to the Lord and Mr. Witte-Wild.[1] [. . .] At first he will not, in my view, have to make any so very great efforts; the theater itself will be such an attraction that half Berlin will make the journey to Charlottenburg in order to see the building; this will guarantee the takings in the early days. The whole thing is a huge undertaking on a huge terrain, with a park and a special restaurant and works of art by leading masters and with more than the usual level of comfort in this modern age: in addition there are the fantasies from a decorative and worldly mind of one such as Mr. Sehring.[2] No corners have been cut, and by the beginning of the first performance a full 6 million marks will have been spent. The theater itself will have particularly attractive features. And there would have to be some strange demons at work if the westerners were not to applaud a theater that has—according to the Paris fashion—a reception salon on the stage, a *foyer des artistes,* where one can express one's rapt admiration to a gentleman member of the theater—perhaps even to a lady member?—for the performance they have just given. And, as Mr. Sehring recently told me, there will also be a new kind of theatrical box: the Gigerl box.[3] These will be directly by the stage, visible to the whole auditorium, and extraordinarily delicate. Of course these will be expensive, while the price for the remaining seats will be readily affordable to the bourgeois audience. And the principle of keeping prices low is wise; for that is how Mr. Barnay at the Berliner Theater made his million.[4] Perhaps, however, I should reiterate that I am not talking here of the artistic qualities of the theater.

NOTES

1. Fritz Witte-Wild was a theater director and actor.
2. The architect Bernhard Sehring (1855–1941) established his own office in Berlin in 1890 and enjoyed a very successful career in the city. His first major work was the Künstlerhaus St. Lukas in Fasanenstrasse (1889–90), which was joined shortly after by the neighboring Theater des Westens on Kantstrasse (1895–96). The success of this project led to several other theater commissions: the temporary "Alt-Berlin" theater at the 1896 Berlin Trades Exhibition (Berliner Gewerbeausstellung); Stadttheater Bielefeld (1902–4); Schauspielhaus Düsseldorf (1904–5); Stadttheater Halberstadt (1904–5); Stadttheater Cottbus (1907–8). In 1927–28 he designed the Delphi-Palast cinema on Kantstrasse, Berlin, on a site directly beside the Theater des Westens.
3. "Gigerl" was a contemporary term, particularly favored in Vienna, for a dandy.
4. Ludwig Barnay (1842–1924) was an actor and director of the Berlin Theater, Berlin, from 1887 to 1894.

72

Alfred Kerr

UP AND DOWN THE AVENUES

First published as "Die Alleen auf und ab" (10 April 1898); reprinted in Kerr, *Mein Berlin: Schauplätze einer Metropole* (Berlin: Aufbau, 1999), pp. 55–56. Translated by David Britt.

"Oh how little there is to the town!" they cry in Berlin, echoing Goethe. For sometimes gentle breezes blow, when the hail happens to leave off; and sometimes we receive an invitation to dinner at the Café Grunewald. This café is not a café at all, but a place of refined gluttony in the general and, in a sense, universal sense of the word. A modest tavern, in the "Forest," where a three-hour snack does a man good; the "wayfarer" refreshes himself with a few spoonfuls of caviar, a modest brook trout, a bit of tongue winking coquettishly from beneath piles of champignons; some white-breasted poularde; and the thirsty throat is refreshed by a delicious draught of Pommèry Grèno. When Goethe satirized the "Muses and Graces" of the March of Brandenburg, he made his youthful swain exclaim: "Let us creep into the village, with the pointed steeple here—what a matchless tavern without equal, all stale bread and sour beer!" [*Zu dem Dörfchen lass uns schleichen, mit dem spitzen Turme hier,—Welch ein Wirtshaus sondergleichen, trocknes Brot und saures Bier!*] Times have changed. Grunewald's leading families occasionally eat their midday repast in this tavern. Others drive out from Berlin, together with their guests, on rubber tires; and it is very agreeable to sit in an open carriage, at three o'clock or so, a little drowsy from the spring air, and ride down Kurfürstendamm, quietly chatting. Very agreeable. When the repast is over, one climbs back into the carriage, and, as the cool evening air wafts past cheeks heated by champagne, that, too, is very agreeable. Indeed, one might say that it is particularly agreeable.

In general, carriage rides in the March of Brandenburg have their advantages. There are, of course, rides and rides. Among the latter category I include those that we sometimes take at night on the country estates of friends. There we are, driving through the forest at one in the morning; and sometimes, dear me, we are on the very conveyance that takes the metal milk churns to the nearest railroad station. It is pitch-dark, and the horses dart like ghosts along the narrow rides, through the wondrous gloom of the conifer forest. The coachman does no more than sit there, making no attempt to steer them: the horses can see the way as they gallop, *hurre, hurre, hopp-hopp-hopp.* We wonder why the milk does not turn into buttermilk; and we arrive, shaken but in a curiously blissful state, at half past two. We pat our bones, and all are present and correct. Much less adventurous and more comfortable are those postprandial rides on rubber tires, when the golden evening sun, full of eternal poetry, shines upon the still-uncompleted villa of the younger Bleichröder. He is having this built in order to have somewhere to lay his head besides his downtown apartment in Berlin and his villa in Charlottenburg. It stands close to the carriage road; and, as its battlements catch the last rays of the sun, the passengers in the rubber-tired carriages devoutly sing: "Golden evening sun, how art thou so fair, / How without delight can I see thee there." [*Gold'ne Abendsonne, wie bist du so schön, wie Kanone Wonne deinen Glahanz ich sehn.*] We dash up and down the rides, and it is truly wonderful how the soft air caresses our cheeks. It is charming when carriages meet and part, and we wonder in which ride we shall meet again. All the while, a young woman talks about her life in Boston. She regards conditions in Berlin as somewhat primitive. Over there, one had fourteen servants in the house, all with their own bathrooms. Whereas, here—well! . . . We listen, with profound interest, and from time to time a recollection of the champagne and champignons rises to the surface.

73

Walther Rathenau

THE MOST BEAUTIFUL CITY IN THE WORLD

First published as "Die schönste Stadt der Welt" in *Die Zukunft*, ed. Maximilian Harden (Berlin: Verlag der Zukunft,1899), pp. 36–48; also published in *Impressionen* (Leipzig: Hirzel, 1899), pp. 158–62; extract taken from *Die Berliner Moderne*, ed. Jürgen Schutte and Peter Sprengel (Stuttgart: Philipp Reclam, 1987), pp. 100–104. Translated by David Britt.

[. . .] Berlin is the parvenu among cities and the city of parvenus: and that is nothing to be ashamed of. After all, a *parvenu,* in plain German, is a *self-made man.* Of course, we have no *corso,* no dinner hour, no fashionable suburbs, and no business district. Enter the business district of London or New York on a Sunday afternoon, and it feels like a ghost town. Not a soul to be seen, and cats crossing the street. In Berlin, an individual lives on Jerusalemer Strasse and does business on Kurfürstendamm. Carriages roll, share prices permitting, and the most venerable palaces go back no further than the 1870s. Strictly speaking, Berlin the metropolis does not exist. Our only claim to fame lies in Berlin the industrial city, which no one on the west side knows, and which may well be the largest in the world. The workers' city extends its black tentacles to the north, south, and east; it binds the puny west side with sinews of iron, and who knows what may one day—no, I shall not go into all that today.

As for the Berliners themselves, I am not really sure: do they exist no longer, or do they not yet exist at all? It is not exactly the fertility of the soil that has made the population grow by a factor of ten in the course of three generations. I believe that most Berliners are from Posen and the rest from Breslau. None of this means that the city is unappreciated, however. The Englishman likes our wide, welcoming streets, with their neatly whitewashed buildings; the Frenchman likes the colorful strings of streetcars and the mounted policemen; the Russian loves our knack of converting all public squares into charming little vegetable patches. One man from Chicago took home a sample paving stone and declared Berlin to be a charming summer resort. And a great American inventor said: "I didn't stop at Cologne, for I don't care for old things," and added that we shall soon be overtaking Philadelphia.

We are human, and thus not unsusceptible to praise. Our hearts swell, and our voices join in the refrain that drifts down to us from the sphere of the noblest of the arts:

*Berlin wird doch noch einmal
Die schönste Stadt der Welt.*

[Someday Berlin will be
The loveliest town in the world.]

In our mind's eye, we see Paris deserted and London fallen on hard times; we see the world's millions pouring into Berlin's waiting lap. To the piping strains of world peace, the nabobs and the silver barons march past on Unter den Linden, and the Sun of This World shines down on Parvenupolis. [. . .]

Berlin did not grow; it metamorphosed. Schinkel and Wertheim, Schlüter and Begas just do not go together.[1] The royal, Prussian Berlin finds no place in the imperial, all-German Berlin. Athens-on-Spree is dead, and Chicago-on-Spree is on the way. [. . .]

To find oneself hastening along one of the great main streets of the west side is a delirious experience. Yonder stands an Assyrian temple; next door is a Nuremberg patrician's mansion; a little way along is a fragment of Versailles, followed by reminiscences of Broadway, of Italy, of Egypt—the monstrous, inchoate offspring of a polytechnician's beer-addled brain. A thousand misconceived forms spring from the walls of these lower-middle-class dwellings. Plaster, stucco, cast stone, and cement throb and coagulate in noodles, crinkles, braids, and ringlets of borrowed finery. And what lies behind the art-historical Babel of these facades, with their oriels, towers, colonnades, balconies, gables, and pediments? Is this a world's fair à la Nizhni-Novgorod, assembling legendary tribes and farfetched aspirations from all over the globe? Dear me, no; far from it. Here dwell a few hundred officials, store owners, and brokers; and each and every one of them has exactly the same personal habits, aspirations, and income as all the others—and, of course, an identical home as well. Eleven-foot ceilings, Berlin parlor and two anterooms, majolica stoves and gold wallpaper, thin doors with flimsy locks, and parquet floors with gappy joints. The fairytale facade is meant to make up for all of this. It's all "for show." [. . .]

If I were mayor of Berlin with unlimited powers—and if I were not writing articles for *Die Zukunft*,[2] I think I would like to be mayor—I would bring in a new regime that would have delighted the Emperor Nero. I would convene my senate at once. "Assembled senators," I would tell them, "beware of political partisanship. I know full well that ill-intentioned citizens wish to reduce your august assembly to a party battleground, a surrogate parliament for also-rans. Nor has it escaped my notice that there are some ambitious businessmen who would like nothing better than to have their sons and sons-in-law, or such of them as cannot get themselves elected to the Prussian Diet, find their way onto your hallowed benches in order to stir up division and discontent—or, as they call it, introduce new 'viewpoints.' For my own part, however, I remain convinced that you will not permit nonmembers or malcontents to distract you from carrying out the solemn duties of your office. You will transform the great city into a metropolis; you will transform the new city of the rich world into the world city of the new Reich. To which end, assembled senators, let me have a credit of one billion, plus the power of ruthless expropriation, and you may depend on it that your money will be better invested than in mortgage bonds or consols.[3] For all the nations of the Orient and the Occident will present themselves here to be your guests, and will lay down piles of gold and precious stones at your feet; and your descendents will bless your memory with as much fervor as if you had bequeathed them ten thousand soup kitchens."

The work of planned destruction starts at once. Gendarmenmarkt is extended in one direction to Leipziger Strasse and in the other, across Unter den Linden and through the site of the Art Academy—which is demolished—as far as the River Spree. This new and colossal *Via Triumphalis* absorbs the traffic currently carried by Friedrichstrasse, since a wide street continues it as far as the Oranienburg Gate. Its central portion, on either side of Unter den Linden, will be the site of the imperial monuments of the future. At the Spree end, its conclusion is marked by the facade of the great new opera house. Leipziger Platz is united with Potsdamer Platz. The elevation of Josty Corner [Bellevuestrasse and Potsdamer Strasse][4] is shaped into a monumental cascade, on the lines of the Trevi Fountain. On the ground currently occupied by Potsdam Station, a southern boulevard runs south to Feldherrnring, and beyond to the new central station. Land currently belonging to the railroad—which the treasury will hand over with a charming smile—will become the most elegant residential quarter in Berlin.

A western boulevard, wider than Unter den Linden, leads dead straight from Potsdamer Brücke to the Gedächtniskirche. From there, a four-lane park avenue runs slap through the Zoological Garden to the Großer Stern. And so, incorporating Charlottenburger Chaussee and Siegesallee, which is also extended southward to Potsdamer Brücke, we have a circuit of magnificent promenades unequaled in any other world metropolis.

Königsplatz is opened up; the Victory Column, with a lengthened shaft and a simplified base structure, is shifted north to the center of Alsenplatz. The Kroll site is occupied by a new academy building. In the center of the square, which now extends south as far as Charlottenburger Chaussee, stands the monument to the heroes of the new Reich. Its [southern] termination consists of a pair of vast, curved colonnades, joined together by a triumphal arch at the entrance to the Siegesallee—

Forgive me, gentle reader; I was only joking. I had no intention of submitting "practical propositions" to any competition for the beautification of Berlin. We were discussing ways and means of turning Berlin into a world metropolis, and I meant only to point out that this cannot be done by widening sidewalks and setting up Urania pillars.

Never fear, I have no desire to be mayor. And, as is well known, our municipal authorities do not by any means have unlimited powers; indeed, these are limited in the extreme. Nor do corporations take orders from anyone; and billions are more readily applied for than granted. No, there are not going to be any cascades or triumphal ways. And out there, past the Brandenburg Gate, nothing will change, any more than it has in the past twenty-five years. I do believe that the blind hurdy-gurdy man is still there, in whose tin box I as a child was permitted to deposit many a three-pfennig piece whenever my grandmother took me through the Brandenburg Gate to watch the old Kaiser drive out. In those days he used to play *'s gibt nur a Kaiserstadt, 's gibt nur a Wien* [There's only one imperial city, only one Vienna]; now, if he has moved with the times, he probably has a new and more joyous refrain on his cylinder:

> Someday Berlin will be
> The loveliest town in the world.

NOTES

1. While the architects Schinkel and Schlüter stand for the old Berlin as constructed in the eighteenth and early nineteenth century, the department store Wertheim and the neo-Baroque sculpture of Reinhold Begas stand for the new, imperial Berlin as it had burgeoned after 1871.
2. The weekly journal *Die Zukunft* (The future) was founded by Maximilian Harden (1861–1927) in 1892, and became one of the most influential polemical voices in the Germany of Kaiser Wilhelm II. Starting as a monarchist and as a vigorous supporter of Bismarck, Harden and his journal evolved into sharp critics of the politics of the Kaiser. *Die Zukunft* was at its most influential in the years leading up to the outbreak of World War I in August 1914. A failed attempt to assassinate Harden in July 1922 brought an end to the journal.
3. "Consol" is an abbreviation for "consolidated annuities."
4. The corner site occupied by the Café Josty, one of Berlin's most famous literary and artistic cafés.

74

Alfred Kerr

NEW LUXURY, OLD SQUALOR

First published as "Neuer Luxus, alte Not" (1900); reprinted in Kerr, *Mein Berlin: Schauplätze einer Metropole* (Berlin: Aufbau, 1999), pp. 72–73. Translated by David Britt.

This week the housing shortage continued. All the experts assure us that it will still be with us next week. We on the west side are barely aware of it. We may get repossessed, but we are not homeless. On the north and east sides, things are bad. As so often, it is the little people who suffer. On the west side, half of Kurfürstendamm is still unoccupied. The buildings may be tasteless from the outside, but they are wonderful inside, and extremely comfortable. We have an agreeable feeling that Berlin is a new city; everything is an "achievement." A delight to live in! There are some new arrivals who take a while to acclimatize themselves to this state of bliss. "What are you doing with yourself these days? We never see you," says a man to his front-row neighbor, during the intermission, with an eloquent gesture and a solicitous expression. "What am I doing?" says the other; "what am I to do? I'm settling." He is settling.

These vacant west-side apartments are the acme of perfection, at least by Continental standards. Paris, which normally sets the standard in Europe for all that is good and expensive, is far behind Berlin in this respect. Elevator, central heating, electric light, and ingenious bathing equipment are the basic prerequisites of any better-quality vacant apartment on the west side of Berlin. In Paris, even the rich frequently live just as people lived fifty years ago. Next to the door hangs a colored cord that you pull, and it operates a little bell; that is the doorbell. The doorbell becomes symbolic of the whole. There is another symbol: a small room of which the chronicler cannot write without a blush. Dissembling Gaul! This is all too typical of your preoccupation with outward show—and of your inadequate provision for the more intimate human needs. Dissembling Gaul! I say no more. In Berlin, however, such facilities, although they offer no scope for public ostentation, are invariably "achievements." Whatever technology can offer, they have. Whatever hygiene requires, they have. It is a delight to live in them.

Now, these apartments are all vacant. Over on the north side, the housing shortage persists. But even there, the occupied dwellings are more comfortable than those in any other European capital, with the single exception of London: there the workers live on cheap land, far out of town, in tiny houses, each with a narrow, two-bay frontage and no space to either side, in endless, unbroken rows. [. . .] On the north side of Berlin there is a shortage not so much of good housing as of any housing. If the shortage continues, the municipality will have to make up its mind to rent out the vacant "achievement" homes on Kurfürstendamm and fill them with poor people. That would really be something.

October 28, 1900

75

Hermann Muthesius

THE MODERN COUNTRY HOME

First published as *Das moderne Landhaus* (Munich: Bruckmann, 1905), pp. xx–xxi. Translated by Iain Boyd Whyte.

[. . .] This pretence, under which today's culture groans, also expresses itself, sadly, only too clearly in the average German villa or country home. This becomes obvious when, for example, it is compared with the English country home. Moved

FIGURE 23. Rathenau House, Grunewald (1910; Gabriel Siedl, architect), 1922. Landesarchiv Berlin, 83 900.

back from the street, the English house is designed in the most simple manner, without the least attempt to make architecture or to create a picturesque grouping. Restful walls and roof planes embrace the house, which has been conceived entirely from the inside out and has no aspirations beyond being a house for living in. If one compares these examples with the pretentious faces made by the houses in our villa suburbs, the difference in sensibility and thought between the English and German occupants becomes immediately clear. The villas are lined up along the street and outbid each other in architectural motifs and labored compositions. They make a show for the public on the street. The single aim that the designer had in mind appears to have been to suit the general public. And in this respect, the sensibilities of many villa owners are entirely in accord with those of the architect who wishes to parade his art. These owners are not content simply to build a house, but want, above all, to show that they can afford to do it.

This, in part, is one of the disagreeable transfers from the condition in the city. In the city, the small part of the house that is visible is the street front. Many considerations suggest that this front should be designed to be as expressive as possible, not least those of commercial competition. For competition is ever present in the tenement house, which tries to attract the constantly changing tenants by means of its external appearance. This conception of the street front has now been transferred to the freestanding detached house in rural surroundings. And it is not the only false position derived from city housing that has been applied here, for many of the unwholesome features of the city apartment have been dragged routinely into the country house. The kitchen that is much too small and too narrow, which we find in the German country house, the stunted storage rooms and pantries, the mindlessly rectangular rooms, the dark corridors, the fanlights—all of them have their origins in the apartment, which, in the sense of manufactured dwellings, is a factory product. What is more, it is a product with an investment in impressing people.

Complementing these external features in the city apartments are the often excessively large and high living rooms—which is to say, the rooms in which the tenants themselves live, and, above all, in which they receive guests and serve the monster meals that are now customary. This generous scale in the front rooms is achieved, however, by stealing space from the utility rooms, anterooms, and bedrooms. For if these rooms were to be matched in scale to the mode of life of the front rooms, the apartment would be twice as big and, as a result, twice as expensive.

The fact that the views of the city apartment-block owner can be dispensed with in the country house is something that has by no means found a clear expression yet in the design of German villas. It has not been recognized that the villa is a free and unrestrained entity, which can be sited and designed however one will; that the particular wishes of the inhabitants can be taken into account to the most far-reaching extent; that each room can be formed individually; that the kitchen can be large and the anterooms and storage rooms generously proportioned. Not only that: the villa residents themselves have not yet freed themselves from the bad habits that had been cultivated in them by their sojourn in city apartments. Even though they have now moved to the country, they will not forgo the showy rooms. Even in the small family house they want the same five-meter-high spaces and the enormous dining room that they had in the apartment. The pleasure of living in the countryside and the spiritual influence of the rural surroundings have not yet exerted a strong enough influence to wean them from the ostentatiousness of the metropolis, which in many cases exceeds the means available, when they attempt to replicate it in their own house.

But all in all, the worst impact on the country house does not come from the big city apartment. Rather, it is articulated by the fact that in Germany there is not even the most inarticulate consensus over the functional ordering of the ground plan. The average architect who is planning a country house on his drawing board is guided by any number of determining factors, but not that of functionality. He thinks initially about the external appearance: the house should look pretty from the street. In drawing up the ground plan, greater importance is laid on the adjacency of the principal living rooms for social purposes. How many people can be seated in the dining room, where the society retires to on leaving the table, how they circulate . . . these are the main considerations in the design. The first question that an architect in Germany submits to his client is: how many people does he want to seat at table—a question that makes one think that the conversation is about a tavern rather than a private house. After that, a country house must, above all, have a pompous hall, ideally extending through two stories. Many of the clients even want a skylight here (a makeshift solution for a city house jammed into a tight site!). There is a request for a "cozy bar" in the cellar. With that, the wishes of the client for his house and the exertions of the architect are, in the most cases, exhausted. The kitchen, pantry, and storage rooms are automatically relegated to the cellar; the bedrooms are situated any old how on the first floor. The location of the house on the site is predetermined by the fact that the house lies on the street, set back by the distance prescribed in the building regulations for front gardens, with the living rooms, of course, set on the street front. When the street front faces north, one lives facing north; if it faces west, one lives facing west. No consideration whatsoever is given in the entire planning of the house to its orientation.

The process of transferring the characteristics of the city apartment to the country house displays, incidentally, a mechanism that can be observed in all the artifacts designed by man—namely, that new conditions do not immediately find appropriate forms of expression. One has only to think of the first railway carriages, which looked like mail coaches; the first gaslights, which disguised themselves in the form of candles; or the first automobiles, which resembled hackney cabs without shafts. In contrast to the customary city house, the modern country house is also a creation determined by new conditions, for which a new and appropriate form has not yet been found. The development of this form should be the task of the present day.

76

Edmund Edel

BERLIN W.

First published as Edel, *Berlin W.: Ein paar Kapitel von der Oberfläche* (Berlin: Boll & Pickardt, 1906), pp. 3, 6–8. Translated by David Frisby.

Twenty-five years ago, this Berlin W[est] still didn't exist. Twenty-five years ago one still lived in the Oranienburger Strasse, or in the Krausnickstrasse [an adjoining street], or one had a house in the Friedrichstrasse. In the "great" Friedrichstrasse, as one then called the section from the Schiffbauerdamm up to the Oranienburger Tor. [. . .]

Berlin W. had not yet been discovered.

Yet one day it was there. There it was like a soap bubble. [. . .]

Berlin W. Out there, where the overbearing moneyed strata border onto the Kurfürstendamm, where the "Jugendstil" architectures of the "Bavarian Quarter" descend into countless aberrations of taste, out there where money circulates, the housemaids wears white caps, and the "head" porters maintain noble order, and where Berlin is really Charlottenburg, Schöneberg, or Wilmersdorf—out there lies Berlin W.

"One" lives out there. One has from eight to twelve rooms. One has an elevator and an official certificate stating that one may use it, for which one pays five reichsmarks, and has the uncertain feeling that from time to time one can get stuck in it. One has warm and cold water at one's disposal, a vacuum-cleaner motor built into the house, and the servants no longer need to polish the lamps as they did earlier, or to tap the incandescent mantle, or to heat the oven. In order to perform the absolutely necessary bodily functions, one has two or three quiet but decoratively furnished rooms. One has an "entrance hall" that is furnished according to one's taste and reflects the inhabitants' summer vacation in an Oriental, Friesian, or "Markiewicz" style. If one has among one's family members someone with a higher flight of fantasy, then this entrance hall is stained white in Biedermeier style, with Darmstadt basket furniture. For the rest, the dwelling is tastefully furnished. If one has married prior to the foundation of the absolutely latest artistic tendency, then the forms of the furniture oscillate between "Jugend" and "Pfaff." If, however, one has entered into the holy state of marriage in the last five years, then the dining rooms and the libraries, the drawing-room arrangements and the marriage beds tend toward being in the spirited waving lines of Van de Velde or the artist workshops of Dresden and Munich.[1] In the gentleman's quarters one has a club easy chair for one's own comfort and because there must be somewhere where one can sit down; and on the many floors and small tables there stand French bronzes, Copenhagen porcelain, and genuine Meissen, all of which have a stamp of authenticity on their reverse side and are usually not wedding presents. In the drawing room there hang genuine oil paintings in imposing gold frames, which one has acquired by auction at Lepke's, at Cassirer's, or in Italy on a tour, or that are painted by the dear wife herself before her marriage; and in the children's room English or Dutch lithographs hang in white blocks. On the writing desk lie books and journals, as if fortuitously forgotten, with dutifully cut pages, revealing the literary inclinations of the inhabitant: *Neue Rundschau*, Maeterlinck, Scandinavians, Oscar Wilde, and somewhat coarse German eroticism with a French cover. And the telephone stands in an ornate, black small box with a nickel hearing apparatus alongside the electrical cigar lighter, alongside the electric standard lamp with red and green glasses, and alongside the writing album with the English silver clasp.

NOTES

Berlin W.: Berlin West, a general term for the prosperous western suburbs of Berlin—Charlottenburg, Wilmersdorf, Zehlendorf—which were developed in the last decade of the nineteenth century and the early years of the twentieth.

1. The Belgian artist and architect Henry van de Velde (1863–1957) was one of the leading art nouveau designers working in Germany in the early years of the twentieth century. The Münchner Werkstätten für Wohnungseinrichtung (Munich Workshops for House Furnishing) joined forces with the joinery company of Karl Schmidt in 1907 to form the Deutsche Werkstätten für Handwerkskunst (German Workshops for Arts and Crafts), based in Hellerau, a model garden estate located in the suburbs of Dresden. The goal was the production of modern, well-designed furniture that combined the economic advantages of machine production with the delight of hand craftsmanship.

77

Max Creutz
CHARLOTTENBURG TOWN HALL

First published as "Das Charlottenburger Rathaus," *Berliner Architekturwelt* 8 (1906), pp. 239–40. Translated by David Britt.

For a municipality such as Charlottenburg—with its rapid development, its dangerously fortunate location, which threatens to absorb all the vital power of Berlin, and its entirely progressive mentality—the building of a new town hall was an issue that made supreme demands on the intelligence and ability of the creative individuals involved. The task at hand was to concentrate in one place the complex and diverse network of a modern urban organism; to establish, as it were, the new and unified expression of civic evolution and civic will. Inevitably, the central idea was that of a monumental statement, an expression of all-around capability. For the city is a conjunction of the most disparate energies, united by the common purpose of enhancing vital power; and a building that unites within itself all of the city's manifold concerns becomes the living and speaking image of its mental and physical resolve.

In keeping with time-honored civic tradition, Charlottenburg Town Hall strongly emphasizes material capability. The exterior of this well-planned, gable-fronted edifice, dominated by its tall central tower, is a triumphant assertion of the qualities of its material. A massive complex of large Wünschelburg sandstone ashlar blocks, its detailing has a grandeur of proportion and a firmness of handling that has few parallels anywhere in the north of Germany. This strong emphasis on material marks a significant advance in an age in which architects have preferred to display their art, or artifice, through elements of form while mostly ignoring the effects specific to each material.

As is only natural, however, this building, too, exemplifies the modern talent for the ingenious, artistic working of materials in partial isolation from the archi-

FIGURE 24. Charlottenburg Town Hall, (1899–1905; Heinrich Reinhardt und Georg Süssenguth, architects), 1905. Landesarchiv Berlin, II 4 660.

tectural organism itself, through work that is added on later as something extraneous to the fabric. This is the case with the numerous figures along the facade; their small-scale outlines make no real effect when set against the restless, painterly texture of the sandstone itself. But in our age, when people are not content—or rather are not yet able—to appreciate the pure, ideal effect of architectural form, such a building as this is expected to tell a story. All kinds of figurative work are displayed, though it has no real effect on any but naive minds. This does not mean that we should give up figurative elements altogether; however, their justification must be more than merely superficial: it must emerge directly and logically from the architectural organism.

One stroke of genius is the structure of the tower, at least in the compact outline of its apex, in the subtle balance between its individual parts, and not least in the figures at the very top, which evoke in our minds the idea of a wide and distant view, far beyond the crowded city streets.

The staircase affords internal vistas of overwhelming grandeur. The dominant principle in the interior design is that of a sustained, massive solidity, especially in the woodwork. The ornament speaks the same language. The right historical conclusions have here been drawn: this building will stand witness to the destinies of generations of Charlottenburg residents yet unborn. And yet, in dealing with so permanent—not to say eternal—a monument, have the architects, Reinhardt & Süssenguth, managed to transcend the narrow, fickle, historically limited perceptions of our age and attune their individuality to the pursuit of universal and enduring significance? The answer is all too evident; for work done in collaboration is not the coherent expression of personal intuition. In each specific instance, the responsibility for doing more or doing less rests on not one but two pairs of shoulders. The outcome is collective art rather than the art of a single personality. The principal credit for the result is due to the supreme technical and manual skill that nowadays executes the most difficult tasks with seemingly effortless perfection. [. . .]

Perhaps it can be said that that the nervous energy of metropolitan life makes the pulse beat faster, creating a state that is not entirely favorable to artistic creation: a state best described as "fragmented." Evolutionary aesthetics supplies analogies for this. In those ages in which great events inevitably aroused great excitement, there has always been a kindred tendency toward the Baroque and the picturesque. This conspicuous phenomenon of our own age seems in some indefinable way to spring from the sheer intensity of modern life.

78

Max Creutz

THE NEW KEMPINSKI BUILDING

First published as "Der Neubau Kempinski," *Berliner Architekturwelt* 9 (1907), pp. 283–88. Translated by Fiona Elliot.

As society develops in modern Berlin we are beginning to see a completely new type of wine parlor in the grand style. The romantic cellar vaults of the older generation are now really there only for those in the know. For the rather different demands of the new social classes emerging in modern life, a number of wine saloons of a completely new kind have sprung up, although in some cases creating rather doubtful mixtures—not only in an artistic sense. The Trarbach Wine House (designed by Walter) was the first to show that modern elegance can be very well combined with artistic aspirations. The interior (by Riemerschmid) caters to the whole spectrum of temperaments, from thoughtful contemplation and cozy togetherness to festive celebration and abandoned gaiety—although it has to be said that these rooms have a distinctly southern German or Rhenish character.[1] Berlin itself has no tradition in this area as yet. But for architecture of this kind it is important to bring out the local character. Even if it is initially only an indefinable something and hard to grasp, it is nevertheless present in all the things that distinguish Berlin from every other major city. Whether one is well-disposed or otherwise toward the city, it is still a factor that one must take into account architecturally. The architectural physiognomy of Berlin has hitherto won only a few friends; more was demanded of it in a short space of time than it was able to manage. That will change, and has indeed has already changed. Berlin has unusually malleable qualities that will shortly give it a completely new appearance. It is important that the aspects that are characteristic of the city of Berlin should not fall by the wayside, but that they should be revived with the change in its appearance.

This impression is particularly strong at the sight of a new building that has just been completed in the hustle and bustle of Leipziger Strasse. Kempinski, a company that is particularly dear to the hearts of Berliners, has taken a number of disparate architectural elements and created from these one unified wine house.

The premises of the wine merchants M. Kempinski & Co. were increased by the purchase of a plot of land in Krausenstrasse and underwent complete reconstruction, carried out by the firm of Joseph Fraenkel under the guidance of the architect Alfred J. Balcke. The front building at no. 25 Leipziger Strasse is now exclusively occupied by the company and its owners.

On the ground floor there are sales of bottled wines and the revolving door leading to the restaurant; on the first floor there are the owners' accounts offices and administrative bureau; the apartment on the second and third floors is occupied by the senior executive of the company; on the fourth floor the promissory notes are handled.

For the architect (Balcke) the task was a particularly complex one and in certain respects not very gratifying because not only were older architectural features to be included intact in the new building, but business had to continue throughout the refurbishments as usual.

The special difficulty concerning the facade was to combine artistic motifs with judicious advertising.

A department store such as Wertheim makes an impact without advertising of any kind—merely by its very existence. In the case of Kempinski's wine house it was much harder to fulfill the same task in a busy street. Above all passersby should register Kempinski's location. This the architects have achieved with admirable success by means of a facade that, in marked contrast to the rest of the street, rises well above the other residential houses around it.

The two lower floors are finished in red-brown, polished Swedish granite, which effectively mutes the sound of the busy traffic outside the facade and the main entrance. The windows on the mezzanine floor, which were previously large display windows, have been subdivided and thus reduced in size: a first attempt to return unconscionably large panes to a reasonable size. In addition, there are also ornamental ceramic inlays by Mutz, large star-shaped forms, plaques and rosettes, some of them extremely skilled workings and revisions of Haeckel's natural forms.[2] The same material is used for the consoles and the frieze between these below the granite stringcourse, as well as for the parapet fillings under the second-floor windows.

[...]

This innovative combination of figuration and abstract, ornamental shapes is not without artistic risk. Modern art today is an odd mixture of ornamental, abstract forms and naturalistic, illustrative motifs. The latter are in fact the less artistic, but sadly for the widespread lack of taste, these are what are wanted. It is in fact a nonsense to suddenly transform powerfully stylized forms into crass naturalism. Such design, which is prevalent today, completely negates any innately organic quality a piece may otherwise have. Generally such art is found in wine parlors, where the atmosphere invites contemplative imagery and pithy sayings. At its most obvious in the Rhineland, this genre seems also to be a permanent encumbrance in Berlin. And it may well be that some tipplers take delight in these masks and dancing maenads, in the putti and panthers, more or less replete with wine.

At Kempinski's these and other motifs—let there be no doubt—are most tastefully executed and fortuitously distributed.

Entering from Leipziger Strasse the visitor passes through the padauk-wood inlaid revolving door into the vestibule: walls and floor in Napoleon marble, mosaics by Odorico, information desk in padauk wood by J. Jarotzki. The gray marble and the finely drawn ceiling form the perfect transition to the more intimate rooms beyond. Of particular beauty here are the mosaics in a powerful combination of green, red, and gold.

The entrance doors to this area and to the ground floor café are genuine bronze, made by the firm of Ferd. P. Krüger; the hollow-ground glazing is by E. Schmidt, whose company also executed all the other decorative glazing according to designs by the architect.

From the *vestibule* the visitor comes to the *cloakroom,* with an inlaid mahogany panel with mirrors on one side. The barrel-like curved ceiling is richly painted, with a lunette and figurative depictions at either end. Made by Lommatzsch & Schroeder (wood) and Mayer & Weber (painting). Marble floor: Saalburger Marble Works. Lighting: Leander.

A short flight of steps leads out of the cloakroom and into an oval hallway with genuine mosaics covering the walls; a bronze embossed door leads to the writing and telephone booths in the basement, a second opens onto the *main stairwell.*

Here, a magnificent staircase in Skyros marble gives access—as does a passenger elevator—to the "new rooms" on the floor above.

The walls of the *stairwell* are clad in Greek Cipollino marble. A wall fountain with a relief depicting the young Dionysus and faun masks by the sculptor Hans Latt adorn one of the long walls. The fillings in the balustrade are in *stucco,* as are those on the window wall. A large, three-section window with rich glass painting after cartoons by the painter Fr. W. Mayer shows a bacchanalian procession, dancing maenads, panthers, and so on. From the richly gilded ceiling hangs a bronze embossed light fixture decorated with ruby glass droplets. Indeed all the light fixtures here are made according to designs by the architect.

Everything here bubbles with life, in white, green, and gold. The splendor of the picturesque impression of color reaches heights hitherto unseen in Berlin. Once again the green mosaics are particularly beautiful, in a squamiform design with hanging droplets of shimmering mother-of-pearl around the edges. The allure of the materials is utterly overpowering. One would have to compare these with Byzantine glories, if one were searching for something similar in nature. It does indeed seem remarkable that our own time has rediscovered a strong interest in these Rhomaic and Romanesque styles—a fact that is not unrelated to the modern impressionistic approach.

Halfway up the stairs is the luxuriously appointed ladies' powder room and restroom. The staircase itself is decorated with perfectly formed stuccowork based on Haeckel's natural forms, all the more pleasing in view of the fact that these models have generally spawned rather more unfortunate progeny. The height of the stairwell is cleverly disguised by a glorious light fixture.

The glass windows recall the colorful glow of medieval windows. The lively, linear motion of the dancing maenads depicted here is especially pleasing, and yet further enhanced by the scatter motifs.

Indeed one is very pleasantly entertained on this staircase. The top landing then leads to the Gray Salon.

First, however, it is worth taking a turn through the older rooms on the ground floor in order to appreciate the innovative nature of the artistic impression.

The Gray Salon is finished in gray-stained Swedish birch wood and smooth and grained maple wood. Plaques, moldings, and decorative listels are worked in silvered *carton-pierre;* the columns clad with silvered metal rods are echoed in the light fixtures. A continuous Napoleon-marble base forms the lower termination of the paneling. From the oval domes of the ceiling hang the light fixtures, also silvered and decorated with amber lozenges. On the back wall, above the rounded niches, are reliefs showing vines growing, the grape press, and dancers. The columns are topped with unusual masks. Two large windows with red silk appliquéd drapes illuminate the salon.

The chairs are made in the bentwood style and upholstered in green leather (made by the Kohn brothers).

The walls are painted in a restrained pale shade with antique silvering.

All the sculptural works are by the sculptor Robert Schirmer, who also carried out the ceiling of the cloakroom and the stairwell. The paintwork is by Mayer & Weber, the wood and *carton-pierre* by the Röhlich brothers, the metalwork by Carl Legel.

This salon is by far the most pleasing and dignified.

From the Gray Salon one passes through a short passage finished in red-stained oak into the Castle Salon! In a tall, greenish panel of stone oak on one wall there are four depictions of castles by Wywiorski. These are: Burg Rheinstein, the Wartburg, Burg Eltz, and Schloss Heidelberg. The window wall has a simple artistic glaze; the ceiling is by Sellge & Voderberg in an unusual design of yellow and blue. Comfortable sofas with appliquéd embroidery give the room a welcoming feel. High candelabralike light fixtures supplement the ceiling lighting.

It is remarkable that Kempinski failed to grasp the opportunity to have the murals executed by leading artists. In strictly business terms, genuine works of art would provide the best advertising and ambiance, as well as being of lasting significance.

NOTES

1. In tune with the spirit of Jugendstil (the German variant of art nouveau), Richard Riemerschmid (1886–1957) was an architect who also designed interiors and furniture. His lasting fame rests on the workshops for the Deutsche Werkstätten für Handwerkskunst (German Workshops for Arts and Crafts), which he designed for the pioneering garden suburb of Hellerau, outside Dresden (1909–11).

2. Ernst Haeckel was a biologist, zoologist, and philosopher who coined the phrase "ontogeny recapitulates phylogeny." He reached a wide audience with his often fanciful illustrations of natural organisms, published between 1889 and 1904 under the title *Kunstformen der Natur* (Art forms of nature). These prints had a profound influence on contemporary artists and architects. See Olaf Breidbach, *Visions of Nature: The Art and Science of Ernst Haeckel* (Munich: Prestel, 2006).

79

Maximilian Rapsilber

HOTEL ADLON

First published in Rapsilber, *Hotel Adlon*, 1907; reprinted in *Berliner Leben, 1900–1914*, ed. Dieter Glatzer and Ruth Glatzer (Berlin: Ruetten & Loening, 1983), pp. 166–67. Translated by David Frisby.

In the mighty competition between the four world cities, Berlin has achieved a new victory. The Hotel Adlon, which has just been completed in these sunny October days, will be joyfully welcomed by every German who has eyes to see as evidence of the German enterprising spirit and as a monument of national art. The conflict that flared up two years ago concerning the classical Schinkel corner

[Schinkel's Palais Redern on the southeast corner of the Pariser Platz] has found a peaceful resolution. Tempers ran high in opposition to the demolition of the Palais Redern because it was to be feared that a modern building and, in particular, a hotel would destroy the enclosed nature of the most beautiful of Berlin's squares. Here two different world views confronted one another: on the one hand, reverential veneration, and on the other, the drive for new deeds. Certainly it was risky to challenge the spirit of Schinkel. Yet insofar as the gigantic march of modern times has now successfully asserted itself, it has simultaneously developed a creative force that understands how to replace a classical work with one of an equal rank. . . . The Kaiser, who in this instance asserted the facade rights of the crown, personally promoted the successful outcome of the enterprise through the recommendation of certain individual details and through the monumental accentuation of the main doorway. It is also characteristic that the Kaiser insisted that hygienic factors be viewed as equally important as artistic ones. And all this in order that the Adlon Hotel might exemplify German expertise and German taste to the elite of all nations. . . .

With our very first steps into the new building, our eyes marvel at a long perspective of intoxicating beauty. A magnificence of marble, bronze, and fresco in the broad entrance hall, marble and bronze again in the winter garden, and further on, lovingly surrounded by architectural splendor, an extended, gardenlike inner courtyard, flanked on left and right by dazzling public rooms, and terminating in the white wooden paneling with gold inlay and the magnificent painted vaulting of the banqueting hall of—and let us say it quite openly—this marvel of Greater Berlin.

80

Robert Walser
BERLIN W.

First published as "Berlin W.," *Neue Rundschau* 21, no. 10 (October 1910), pp. 1479–80. Translated by David Britt.

Everyone here seems to know what is socially correct, and to some degree this casts a chill. It further seems that everyone here is entirely self-sufficient: hence the insouciance that so disconcerts the newcomer. Poverty seems to be dismissed either outward, into those districts that border on open country, or inward, into the gloom and darkness of the back annexes that hide behind the massive bulk of genteel street frontages. Here, or so it seems, humanity has ceased to sigh and has begun to enjoy life, once and for all. But appearances are deceptive, and all this splendor and elegance are only a dream. And, then, perhaps even the squalor is no more than an illusion. As for the elegance of the west side of Berlin, it seems to be marked by great vivacity, and at the same time just a little spoiled by the fact that it is impossible to deploy it at leisure. Here, everything is constantly unfolding and changing. The men are as modest as they are unchivalrous; and this is entirely a matter for rejoicing, since chivalry is invariably three-quarters inappropriate. There is something extraordinarily silly and presumptuous about gallantry. Consequently, there are few scenes of elevated sentiment; and where some delicate affair of the heart runs its course no one notices; which is of course very well-bred. Today's masculine world is a world of business, and a man who has a living to earn has little or no time to behave with conspicuous elegance. Hence a certain businesslike brusqueness of tone. In general, there is plenty of amusement to be had on the west side; life's absurdities live on, as delectable as anyone could wish. There is the parvenue: a forceful lady, and as naive as a baby. For my part, I have a lot of time for her; she is so sumptuous and, at the same time, so droll. And there is the Kurfürstendamm girl. She is like a chamois, and there is much good in her. Then there is the elderly man-about-town. There are not many specimens of this type left strolling about the well-bred world. They are a dying breed, and to my mind this is a great shame. I saw one of them recently, and he looked like an apparition from the past. And then we have something quite different: the man up from the country, with new money. He has yet to cure himself of the habit of raising his eyebrows, as if in amazement at himself and at his good fortune. His manners are far too good, as if he were nervous of revealing his true origins. Then we have the august and venerable lady of Bismarck's time. I am an admirer of severe faces, and of good manners that have become individual second nature. I am touched by age, whether in buildings or in human faces, but I nevertheless find spontaneity, newness, and youth refreshing. This is a youthful place, and to me the west side seems healthy. Does health to some extent exclude beauty? By no means. The liveliest is also the most beautiful. Well, perhaps here I am stooping to flattery, just a little—as, for example, by writing the following sentence: the women here are lovely and charming. The gardens are neat; the architecture may be a little crude, but what of it? Everyone is convinced by now that we are fumblers when it comes to the grand, the stylish, and the monumental—probably because we harbor too strong a wish to own, or to create, grandeur, style, and monumentality. Wishes are tricky things. This age of ours is undoubtedly an age of sensibility and principle, and I must say this is pretty nice of us. We have welfare institutions, hospitals, and baby homes; and I am quite prepared to regard this as an achievement on our part. Why expect to have everything? Think of the horrors of Fritz's old wars—and then think of his Sanssouci.[1] We have few contradictions; which proves that we aspire to a clean conscience. But I digress. It that allowed? There is a so-called old west side, a newer west side (around the Memorial Church), and an entirely new west side. Of these, perhaps the nicest is the one in between. The acme of elegance is surely to be found on Tauentzienstrasse.

Kurfürstendamm, with its trees and its open carriages, is charming. I find, much to my regret, that I am coming to the end of my space, with a troubled sense of having left unsaid a great deal that I imperatively wanted to say.

NOTE

1. Fritz: Frederick II ("the Great"; 1712–86), king of Prussia, 1740–86. In 1745–47, Frederick the Great built a small rococo palace named Sanssouci on a site overlooking the River Havel near Potsdam, to the west of Berlin. It was designed by the architect Georg Wenzeslaus von Knobelsdorff, following the king's own sketches and plans.

81

Robert Walser

THE LITTLE BERLIN GIRL

First published as "Die kleine Berlinerin," *Neue Rundschau*, September 1909; reprinted in Walser, *Das Gesamtwerk*, ed. Jochen Greven (Geneva: Kossodo, 1966), vol. 1, pp. 310–19. Translated by David Britt.

Papa boxed my ear today—in the most fatherly, affectionate way, of course. I used the phrase "Father, you're cracked." This was a little careless of me. "Ladies must use refined language," says our German teacher. She is horrid. But Papa won't have it that I regard her as a joke; and maybe he's right. After all, one goes to school to display a certain eagerness to learn and a certain respect. It is also cheap and unworthy to find fellow human beings comic, and to laugh at them. Young ladies must accustom themselves to all that is refined and distinguished. I can see that quite well. No one expects me to do any work—nor will they ever—but I shall be expected to behave with dignity. Shall I practice any kind of profession when I grow up? Certainly not. I shall be a refined young woman, and I shall marry. It is quite possible that I shall torment my husband. But that would be terrible. Once you feel you have to despise someone, you always end by despising yourself. I am twelve years old. I must be very advanced, intellectually speaking, or such things would never occur to me. Shall I have children? And what will that be like? If my future husband turns out not to be someone I despise, then yes, I am sure I shall have a child. Then I shall bring that child up. But of course I still need bringing up myself. The stupid things that come into your mind sometimes.

Berlin is the loveliest, the most cultivated city in the world. It would be detestable of me not to be firmly convinced of the fact. Doesn't the Kaiser live here? Would he have to live here if he didn't like it best of all? The other day I saw the crown prince and princess in an open carriage. They are charming. The crown prince looks like a young and joyful god; and how beautiful the lady at his side looked to me. She was entirely swathed in fragrant furs. Blossoms seemed to rain out of the blue sky onto the imperial couple. The Tiergarten is marvelous. I take a walk there almost every day with our *Fräulein*, the governess. You can walk for hours, on straight and crooked paths under the trees. Even Father, who really has no need to be enthusiastic, is enthusiastic about the Tiergarten. Father is a cultivated person. I believe that he loves me to distraction. It would be frightful if he ever read this, but I shall tear up the paper. It is not really appropriate for anyone as silly and immature as myself to start keeping a diary. But sometimes one does get a little bored, and then one is easily tempted to do inappropriate things. The *Fräulein* is very nice. Well, generally. She is loyal, and she loves me. She also has a real respect for Papa; that is the main thing. She is thin. Our last governess was as fat as a bullfrog. She always looked about to burst. She was English. She still is, no doubt, but then she ceased to be any concern of ours when she started to take liberties. Father sent her packing.

The two of us, Papa and I, will soon be traveling. This is the time of year when well-bred people simply have to travel. In a season of greenery and blossom, isn't there something rather suspect about a person who does not travel? Papa is going to the seaside, and there of course he will lie on the sand, day after day, and roast himself dark brown in the summer sun. He always looks at his healthiest in September. The pale, washed-out look does not suit his face at all. In general, I like a man to have a suntanned face. It makes him look as if he has just come back from a war. This is all really childish and silly, isn't it? Well, I am still a child. And, as for myself, I shall go south. First to Munich for a while, then to Venice, where the person who is so unutterably close to me lives, Mama. For reasons too deep for me to understand, and therefore to judge, my parents live apart. I live with Daddy most of the time. But of course Mama has the right to have me at least some of the time. I am tremendously looking forward to the journey. I love to travel, and I believe almost everybody does. You climb on board, the train starts, and you are off into the beyond. You sit there and are carried on into the unknown distance. How lucky I am. Do I even know the meaning of want and poverty? Not at all. And I don't really see that I ever need to learn. But I am sorry for poor children. In their place I would jump out the window.

I and Papa live in the best neighborhood. Good neighborhoods are those that are quiet, spotlessly clean, and of a certain age. The new ones? I would not like to live in a totally new house. There is always something slightly wrong with new things. Poor people—workers, for instance—are hardly ever seen in our neighborhood, where the houses all stand in their own grounds. The people who live near us are factory owners, bankers, and rich people whose profession is being rich. This means that Papa must at least be pretty well off. Poor and badly off people simply cannot live around here, because real estate is far too expensive. Papa says that the class that has all the poverty lives on the north side of the city. What a city! What is the north side, exactly? I know Moscow better than I know the north side of our own city. I have had plenty of picture postcards from Moscow, St. Petersburg, Vladivostok, and Yokohama. I know the Dutch and Belgian beach resorts; I know the Engadine, with its sky-high mountains and green meadows; but my own city? Perhaps Berlin is a mystery to very many of the people who live here. Papa supports art and artists. His work is dealing. Monarchs do deals, after all; so Papa's business is entirely an aristocratic one. He buys and sells paintings. There are some very beautiful paintings hanging in our apartment. The thing about Father's business, as I see it, is this: artists mostly know nothing about business, or for some reason or other they are not allowed to know. Or, put it like this: the world is a big and heartless place. The world never gives a thought to artists and their survival. So along comes my father, who is a man of the world and has all kinds of important connections; and, discreetly and cleverly, he makes the world—which may not feel any particular need for art—aware of art and of the starving artists. Papa often despises his clients. But then he often despises the artists, too. It all depends.

No, I don't want to live permanently anywhere else but in Berlin. Do children have a better life in small towns, the kind of towns that are old and moldy? Of course, those places have a lot of things that we don't have. Romantic appeal? I think I can safely say that anything that is only half alive counts as romantic. Things that are defective, crumbling, sick—things like ancient city walls. Things that are no good for anything, but are beautiful in a mysterious sort of way: that is romantic. I like to dream of such things, and in my opinion that is just what they are good for. After all, the heart is the most romantic thing there is, and every sensitive person carries old cities, complete with city walls, inside them. Our Berlin is bursting with newness. Father says that everything of historical interest is going to disappear, so that nobody will recognize the old Berlin at all. Father knows everything, or nearly everything. And of course his daughter gets the benefit of all this. Yes, small towns out in the country may be beautiful in their way. There must be delightful nooks and crannies, places to play games, caves you can crawl into; meadows, fields, and the woods just a step away. Such places are completely surrounded by greenery. Like a garland. But Berlin has an Ice Palace, where people skate even in the hottest summer. Berlin is ahead of all other German cities in everything. It is the cleanest, most modern city in the world. Who says so? Well, Papa, of course. How good he is. Yes, I have a lot to learn from him. On our Berlin streets, dirt and bumps are a thing of the past. They are as smooth as ice rinks, and they gleam like laboriously polished floors. Nowadays you occasionally see people roller-skating. Who knows, maybe one day I'll do that, too, unless it has gone out of fashion by then. There are some fashions here that barely last long enough to catch on. Last year all the children, and quite a few adults, were playing diabolo. Now that game is right out of fashion; no one wants to play anymore. So everything changes. Berlin always sets the tone. Copying is not compulsory, and yet Mrs. Copycat is the supreme authority in this life. Everyone copies.

Papa can be charming, he is always nice really, but sometimes he goes really wild, there is no telling what about, and then he is ugly. I can see, looking at him, how a bad humor, suppressed rage, makes a person ugly. When Papa is in a bad mood, I find myself feeling like a whipped dog; and that is why Papa ought to stop inflicting his off days, his inner discontents, on those around him—or even on just one daughter. In that respect, fathers are sinners. I feel strongly about this. But then who is there with no weaknesses, no faults at all? Who is without sin? Parents who feel no need to conceal their inner storms from their children are turning those children into slaves. A father should vanquish his evil moods in silence (but how difficult that is!), or else take them and inflict them on outsiders. A daughter is a young lady, and in every civilized father there should be a gentleman. I want to be quite clear about this: I am in heaven when I am with Father, and if I do find fault with him, it is the intelligence I have inherited from him—his, not mine—that is observing him. Let Papa vent his anger, rightly, on those who depend on him in some way. There are enough such people hovering around him.

I have my own room, my own furniture, luxuries, books, and so on. God, I am pretty well off! Am I grateful to Papa for this? What a tasteless question. I am obedient to him, and after all I am his property, and he has a right to be proud of me. I give him trouble, I am his domestic concern, and he has the right to bawl me out; and when he bawls me out I see it as a kind of duty, in some peculiar way, to laugh at him. Papa does like to bawl people out. He has a sense of humor, and he is temperamental at the same time. At Christmas he gives me heaps of presents. Also my furniture is by a painter who is certainly not unfamous. Almost all the people Papa deals with are people who have a name. He deals with names. If there is a human being behind the name, so much the better. How hideous it must be to know that you are famous, and yet to feel that you do not deserve it. A lot of famous people must be like that. In such cases, is not fame like an incurable disease? What a way to put it. My furniture is white and painted with flowers and fruits by a skilled, artistic hand. These look charming, and the man who painted them is an exceptional person whom Father prizes very highly. But anyone whom Father prizes ought to feel flattered. I think that if Papa is well disposed toward someone, it means something; and those who don't feel this, and who behave as if they did not care, of course they are harming no one but themselves. They have not gotten things clear. I think my father is an exceptional individual. It is plain for all to see that he has an influence in this world.

Many of my books bore me. That just shows that they are not the right ones—such as so-called children's books, for instance. Such books are a disgrace. How can anyone have the effrontery to give children books to read that do not expand their horizons? It is wrong to talk down to children; that is childish. I may be a child myself but I hate childishness.

When shall I give up playing with toys? No, toys are sweet, and I shall go on playing with my doll for a long time yet, I know, but then I play consciously. I know it is silly, but things that are silly and useless are beautiful. That is how it seems to artistic temperaments, or at least so I think. A number of younger artists often come to dine with us—with Papa, that is. Well, they get invitations, and then they show up. The invitations are sometimes written out by me, sometimes by the *Fräulein,* and then there is a lively and amusing conversation around our dinner table, which naturally—without any deliberate ostentation—looks like the dinner table of a distinguished household.

Papa seems to like surrounding himself with young people—people younger than himself—and yet he is always the liveliest and the most youthful of them all. His is the voice that you hear, most of the time. The rest listen, or they slip in brief comments, and this is often very funny. Father is head and shoulders above all of them, in culture and in breadth of outlook, and I can see all of these people learning from him. Often I can't help laughing out loud, at dinner, and then I get a gentle or not-so-gentle reprimand. Yes, and after dinner we all turn bone idle. Papa lies down on the leather couch and starts to snore, which is actually rather bad form. But I am enamored of Papa's way of doing things. I even love his honest snoring. Does anyone want, or is anyone able, to make conversation all the time?

I am sure Father must spend a lot of money. He has incomings and outgoings; he lives, makes profits, and lets live. He looks a little like someone who squanders and overspends. He's always on the move. He's clearly one of those people who find it a pleasure, even a necessity, to be constantly taking risks. There is much talk of success and failure in our house. Anyone who eats with us, and spends time with us, has had some kind of major or minor success in the world. What is the world? Rumor, hearsay? My father is in the thick of it all—of the hearsay, I mean. Perhaps he even controls it to some extent. Papa's aim is to have power, whatever happens. He sets out to develop and to establish both himself and those in whom he is interested. His principle is this: "Anyone who does not interest me has only himself to blame." This means that Papa is always securely convinced of his own value as a human being and can assert himself firmly and confidently; and that is as it should be. A person with no idea of his own importance will have no hesitation in playing dirty tricks. What am I saying? Do I get this from Father?

Am I having a good upbringing? I see no reason to doubt it. I am being brought up as a metropolitan lady ought to be brought up: informally, but with a certain measure of strictness that permits me, and at the same time commands me, to acquire the habit of tact. The man who marries me will have to be rich, or else to have solid prospects. Poor? I just can't be poor. For me, and for those like me, pecuniary embarrassment is impossible. That is just silly. For the rest, I definitely intend to choose a simple style of life. I cannot abide ostentation. Simplicity must be its own luxury. Everything must be clean and neat, just so, and that kind of absolute neatness costs money. Life's little pleasures are expensive. How very categorical I am being. Isn't all this a little presumptuous? Shall I fall in love? What is love? What strange and marvelous things must lie in store for me, since I feel my own ignorance of things that I am still too young to know about. What will happen in my life?

82

Walter Lehwess
THE DESIGN COMPETITION FOR RÜDESHEIMER PLATZ

First published as "Der Wettbewerb für die künstlerische Ausgestaltung des Rüdesheimer Platzes," *Berliner Architekturwelt* 14 (1912), pp. 33–35. Translated by David Britt.

A new and highly contemporary assignment confronted the artists who took part in the competition for Rüdesheimer Platz in Schöneberg, held under the auspices of the Berlin Land Company and endowed with substantial prize money. The functions of this particular square are not those performed by the squares in our ancient cities. It does not serve as a marketplace; nor does it regulate and absorb vehicular traffic, as do those squares that lie at the intersections of important traffic routes. It is a quiet square, secluded from the traffic. To distinguish it from those busy squares that have trolley cars and automobiles racing through them, I would term it a residential square. It is surrounded by five-story apartment blocks, and its setting is strongly architectural in its emphasis.

It follows that, in tackling this particular task, prototypes from the past were of no use. Nor could it be treated as a tranquil village green, such as we still so often see in villages close to the capital of the Reich—for this would be incompatible with the metropolitan setting, the massive scale of the buildings, the whole Berlin W. character of the neighborhood—nor, despite the height of the surrounding facades, could older urban prototypes such as the marketplace in Verona be considered, because these owe their effect entirely to their spacious size and the proportions of the buildings.

This square is intended to form a happy, refreshing oasis of tranquillity in a desert of masonry. Here, children may play, away from the dust and free from the dangers of the traffic; here, adults whose dwellings lack a balcony or a scrap of open space may rest from the day's labors; here, the busy city dweller, as he passes on his way, may find a brief respite to rest, collect his thoughts, and calm his nerves. Additionally, it is intended to add an artistic, enlivening, decorative motif to the cityscape with its "monotonous alternation" of apartment-house facades.

These being the requirements, it is clear that a garden was the right solution for this particular square. For, whatever may be argued against greenery in urban squares, and in favor of the pure architecture and masonry of the squares of earlier ages, metropolitan residents at the present time have a deep-rooted need to see something green amid all the stonework; to see lawns, trees, and colorful flowers that remind us—however remotely—of nature, the woods, and the fields.

Additionally, the various requirements of a children's playground, an ornamental garden, and a recreational area require the layout to be subdivided in a way that is well suited to its elongated form. Such a subdivision appears in most of the designs, and it leads to the most attractive visual effects.

For the rest, the projects submitted are of widely varying quality. From improbably childlike efforts to introduce ghastly figurative sculptures—most of which seize on the name of Rüdesheimer Platz to bring in the cycle of legends associated with the Rhine—by way of dull, routine work, to mature and poetic works, creative achievements, some of which are reproduced in this issue. But among the most atmospheric of the works there are some that fall into the error of neglecting the urban nature of the square; they introduce segments of parkland, the effect of which would infallibly be ruined by the bulky apartment blocks all around. There is just one project that falls into the opposite error of giving the square a purely urban, architectural treatment and entirely overlooking its function as a haven of rest for young and old.

In delivering its verdict, the prize jury has given clear expression to its view on the way Rüdesheimer Platz ought to look. It has singled out three designs that look very similar, or are at least based on the same idea: a calm, central lawn, between a playground at one end and an ornamental plaza at the other, with trees of medium height and light garden architecture. The selection of prizewinners is an entirely acceptable one, although the entry that was awarded the third prize does not seem completely successful in uniting its components into a coherent whole; in this respect, and in overall artistic quality, it is inferior to a number of other designs that were not singled out for an award.

It is highly gratifying to find a real-estate company prepared to invest so much effort and expense in making its streets and squares more beautiful; it is also gratifying that the competition aroused such a response in the artistic community, and that submissions included such an impressive quantity of good and practicable designs. At the same time, it must not be forgotten that *the tasteful design of ornamental squares is not the central task that confronts us in the planning and development of our major cities.* The essential and truly important tasks lie elsewhere: first in *the large-scale planning of urban expansion in general,* and second in *housing.* The artist must be enlisted for the creation of the development plan itself, rather than brought in as an afterthought when a square here or there needs to be landscaped. Furthermore, we shall not have truly beautiful cities until we have truly healthy cities. So long as blocks are built with thirty or forty self-contained apartments that can never be fully aired, venting their effluvia into enclosed courtyards; so long as we have no basic reform of urban land allocation, or of the social conditions under which housing is built; for just so long, attempts to make a city habitable through schemes such as this will remain beside the point. *They serve only to pull the wool over people's eyes, and to conceal from them the true drawbacks of our system of urban development, a system in which the owners of the land have so profound a vested interest.*

83

Wilhelm Borchard

THE PICNIC SEASON

First published as "Die Zeit der Picknicks," *Elegante Welt* 3, no. 29 (22 July 1914), pp. 7–8. Translated by Michael Loughridge.

Violets in the meadow grass, violets in her eyes, and of course the hamper with the host's exquisite selection of delicacies ... A leaf floats gently down from the linden tree ... Wouldn't it be such fun? You at least would have to be there, Baroness, wouldn't you, you've always been one for a spot of self-indulgence, trifling or outrageous.

If it's a war veterans' outing, a coach trip to the country, one sees no such glamour, none of those quick dainty movements and those exuberant high spirits. Then there is no amusing storm in a teacup over someone having forgotten the eggcups. The makeshift fun of dining off real grass is out of the question. But if the picnic party is small and intimate, there is a fascination in watching a strong hand twist the sardine tin open, or the blond lass breathing ever so daintily on the tumblers prior to polishing them with one of the fine paper napkins.

Of course, to do that she has to kneel down ever so gracefully in the grass, and her light, ankle-length skirt leaves her free to scramble up easily to the sheltered spot in the lee of a huge tree—her kitchen. After all, it's quite the thing nowadays to interrupt a day's hacking for a picnic luncheon, and one always has an extra pony to carry the hamper with all the things ...

Must be pretty dull for us in Berlin at this time of year ... you think so? Oh come on, you know us better than that! July nights are for the latest pastime—camping!—sleeping out in the open air! There are a few delicious anecdotes about that, as you can imagine—I'll tell you next time. And we are up and about bright and early in the mornings, too, you know. Any sleepyheads are rudely shaken out of it at 4 A.M. by the roar of the engine, and half an hour later the motor is conveying us along the Heerstrasse, past the new Exhibition Hall (which looks as if it is going to become a positive palace!) and on out to the bathing place at the Wannsee. And here without a moment's delay we are all in the water ducking for the bracelets tossed in by our little Countess (how slim she is!). You know, I can see it coming: this afternoon you'll tell *Frau Kommerzienrat*[1] about our Olympic Games here, and next thing she'll have *your* husband in the water looking for the ruby necklace.

Then after a quarter of an hour or so it's time for our picnic. The hamper with the provisions is lugged up to the chosen spot and set down in the midst of the crickets and the wild honeybees, and of course we do all this with our own fair hands; there is no standing on ceremony, and anyway we all try to be as helpful and courteous as possible, because we want to be asked again. And simply no one says no to sugared melon, no one thinks of coming without nice female company, and there is no one whose doctor won't allow him sweet champagne. Anyway, all the migraine sufferers and people with high blood pressure and anyone who is not quite—you know—all that sort are nowhere to be seen, because they all went off to the seaside or some spa or other ages ago.

And we recline on the grass, flowers everywhere basking in the sun, but we've got a nifty bit of shade to ourselves, the lake glinting blue no distance away, and from a higher vantage point, circling incessantly, tirelessly, over our group, the attentive gaze of our Lady President, for it was she who saw to all the arrangements for our picnic. A couple of nightingales are singing their hearts out . . . that's like Julia's garden . . . The motorcar always stops like magic somehow at a perfect spot like this, and the weather always turns out as the morning promises. Things can never suddenly go wrong on us, because if it does come on to rain, all we do is simply decamp with our biscuits and our inflatable rubber cushions, our pickled herrings and our seat cushions from the motorcar, and set ourselves up in the nearest shooting box—although unfortunately the government, no less, have now banned all the forester people from providing eats and drinks themselves. So we just make do with a cozy corner in the summerhouse, because we have all we need with us—the spirit stove, aluminum platters, thermoses—they'll keep drinks hot or cold, whichever you want, for a whole twenty-four hours—small tumblers for wine and liqueurs, a butter tin, insulated containers fit to carry a whole fillet of beef in, a tin for the English mustard and O.K. Sauce, and finally of course the gourmet's operating tools, all the folding cutlery from which the very excursion itself borrows its name.[2]

And now our diminutive hostess is distributing the bounty that the chauffeur has brought from the trunk, and everything does the rounds: cardboard plates, little bowls with hors d'oeuvres, lots of salads, sprats bottled with tomato, aspic, or button mushrooms, marinated herring, olives, hard-boiled eggs in a remoulade. Then after that you have the meat course, which has been all made up beforehand in individual servings—always roast beef. There's cold capon as well. Any salad the lady of the house has made up herself is certain to taste heavenly when served in the open air. Cucumber, cress, celery, or those pale golden inner leaves of lettuce in a "green" salad—anything at all, it doesn't matter. Dessert favorites are fruit compotes, sorbets, tartlets (the fresh fruit goes in only at the moment of serving!), Roman plums, ginger, liqueur-filled chocolates, and lots of sweet things. We don't do bread and sliced cheese; instead of that we serve beef extract on toast at this stage. The really smart people bring along metal cold boxes with ice, maybe a *bombe glacée,* or maybe just lump ice for chilling the wine and lemonade. And when the same dainty hand finally sets to preparing the cups of mocha, just picture the sense of contentment as one lights one's cigarette . . . real contentment, certainly much more sheer enjoyment than [there is in] a set-piece meal with scarlet lobsters and elaborate pheasant dishes served up on a table and six hundred other guests all around of whom you know nothing. It's simply that I believe—truly, my dear Baroness—that on principle no more than six people should be involved in getting up a picnic. A big crowd just spoils the delightful away-from-it-all feeling of peace, with nothing intruding but the puttering flame of the methylated burner and the tap-tap-tap of the woodpecker.

Time to pack up. The gnawed bones and other leavings are dumped unceremoniously in a hole in the ground. A sparrow does its damnedest to angle a stray brisling. Under the fir-tree, a simple wooden stave: to the memory of our forest picnic . . . a garland of sweet peas draped over two names—two hearts . . . that beat as one.

Still a few moments in hand before the engine of the motorcar is fired up; they pass pleasantly with the latest dance number from Paris, "Le Rouli-Rouli." The gramophone always has its perch beside the chauffeur. The wind has got up and a scrumpled-up ball of parchment paper is dancing, too . . . and is gone.

And you can be quite sure, when I next invite you to join me on my motorboat on the Wannsee, I shall not forget to include a picnic on the program, out on an islet at the Pichelsberg.[3] You will have to admit that it was no empty promise when I undertook always to have a lovely surprise for you . . .

NOTES

1. *Frau Kommerzienrat:* the wife of an influential businessman.

2. The word *picnic* derives from the French *pique-nique,* something to do, perhaps, with spearing food with a fork or similar. The Oxford Dictionary, however, is happy to record that *pique-nique* is "of unknown origin."

3. Pichelsberg is at the northern end of the Havelsee, where a monumental iron bridge—the Freybrücke—links Berlin and Spandau. This bridge was built in 1908–09 to the design of Karl Bernhard, who also worked at this time on the structure of the AEG turbine hall (see above, text 32: Karl Scheffler, Peter Behrens). Pichelsberg was also chosen by the National Socialists as the site of the Faculty of Defense Studies, on which work began in 1937 (see below, text 128: Adolf Hitler, Speech at Foundation-Stone Ceremony of the Faculty of Defense Studies, Berlin).

84

Paul Westheim

BUILDING BOOM

First published as "Bauluxus," *Sozialistische Monatshefte* 23, no. 2 (1917), pp. 1103–5. Translated by David Britt.

One characteristic of Germany between 1870 and 1914 was the dispatch with which construction work was put in hand. From wish to decision, from decision to execution was now but a step. The railroad stations in Leipzig need to be centralized; and in a few years there is *the world's biggest station*. Berlin needs a central market hall; and, almost as a matter of course, it will be *the biggest hall on the Continent*. Barely has Tempelhof Feld been handed over to the speculators when, over on the east side of Berlin, at Treptower Park, a stretch of building land is designated to provide new housing for forty thousand people. And so rapidly does this project proceed that the municipality seems to have no time even to assess the pros and cons of two incompatible development plans that will decide the fate of forty thousand citizens. The era dawns with the megalomania and speculative greed of the 1870s. The subsequent crash slows things down, but only briefly. People learn to make their estimates a little more realistic, but then they press on with yet more audacious proposals. The reign of Wilhelm II ushers in an almost proverbial construction fever. Berlin is to be made into *the loveliest city in the world*. As in the days of the Roman Empire, construction proceeds without a break. Monuments, churches, museums, libraries: the old is torn down without a twinge of reverence, and the new, which replaces it, cannot be too spacious or too magnificent. From one summer to the next, whole neighborhoods appear, each with its own due quota of public buildings. Prestige seems to demand that every municipal building assume a monumental air—even one so indispensable as a fire station. The work of a city architect's department starts to become unmanageable. Ten or twenty major buildings, each of which would at one time have sufficed for a whole generation, are in hand at the same time. In the last decade, it is taken for granted that every city is going to build itself a new city hall. Public baths, reading rooms, water towers, hospitals, crematoria—all appear; and there is still time and money to spare for decorative features such as the fairy-tale fountain.

[. . .]

Looking at the Nordstern Insurance head office building in Berlin, I calculated the ratio between its size and that of the Palazzo Pitti: the Renaissance edifice covers a ground area of 3,200 square meters; the modern office building covers 11,436 square meters.[1] In the years that preceded the outbreak of war, one major development on the same scale was completed almost every week. Even the specialist had no hope of keeping track of all this.

Undoubtedly, this gigantic spate of building activity was the reflection of our economic prosperity. Money, wages, and materials were cheap, and there were plenty of solvent taxpayers and affluent customers. The population grew with startling rapidity to fill the spaces provided, which for all their size were almost overtaken by the sheer weight of the annually emerging masses.

Whatever the outcome of this war, one thing seems certain: the factors that combined to stimulate construction at such a rate and in such volume no longer apply; nor will they for a long time to come. Everything will be in short supply: cheap money, cheap labor, cheap materials, and above all mass purchasing power and tax revenue. We shall not soon see another building boom. After the war—as after 1813—less will be built. We shall reduce the demand for space to the minimum; we shall get by with the space that is there for as long as feasible; and where a new building becomes indispensable, we shall try to achieve the greatest utilitarian benefit with the least possible expenditure of resources.

The construction industry as a whole will be brought down to earth, but the mental tone of its creative sector will infallibly be raised—a far from unwelcome development. In the last two prewar decades there was much talk of down-to-earth sobriety [*Sachlichkeit*] in connection with architecture. And yet there was precious little sign of it in the buildings themselves. There was not quite so much molded plasterwork, and less ornament in general; but nothing really changed. There was no attempt to make any use—let alone any artistic use—of the most rational working methods. No one has as yet seen any advantage in the handiest and most functional construction methods offered to us by modern advances in technology. A typical example of the customary irrational approach: in Berlin, a few years ago, an office building constructed entirely from reinforced concrete was valued by the lending bank at fifty thousand marks less because it was not mantled in stone and bedizened with columns; this method of construction meant that building costs were at least fifty thousand marks lower.

Interior design does not base itself on the conditions of present-day life; it is not designed to ease our lives as we live them today. It is dominated by the attempt to create moods and atmospheres that refer to some point in the past. Nor is there a sign of anything that could be described as the ennoblement of materials through quality of workmanship. That effect has merely been simulated through a prodigal use of valuable or even precious materials. There have been virtually no cases in which the materials have been limited to those naturally available and made precious by intensive and skillful working. Instead, marble has been shipped in from Greece and Italy and precious hardwoods from Africa, Australia, and South America, and—for all their inherent refinement—these materials have been subjected to some decidedly rough treatment. Just as, in the past, a room would be hung with finely worked tapestries, now it is lined with valuable wood or marble. In the near future, it is unlikely that anyone will be able to afford such superficial display, and we shall have to use form—mental performance—instead. The actual quantity of decorative ingredients is largely irrelevant. As the so-called Puritanism of the immediate past has shown, it is quite possible to be pretentious and irrational in the extreme while using sheer facades and plain interiors. The question will be whether we can make a virtue of necessity, as Schinkel did a hundred years ago; whether we can confer meaning and grandeur by purely architectural means on those few buildings that will still have to be constructed.

Who is going to make this architecture? Will it be new architects, or will it be those who were receiving important commissions before the war? What kind of a cull will there be when this vast army of architects, previously awash with commissions, is suddenly confronted with a comparatively small range of tasks? These are questions that will be further discussed in later installments of this review.

NOTE

1. See above, text 34, Paul Westheim, Nordstern.

8

THE GREEN OUTDOORS

Like all great cities, late-nineteenth-century Berlin was dirty and noisy. It was also very unsanitary. The *Mietskasernen* (rental barracks) that made up the overwhelming majority of the city's housing stock made it particularly dangerous, even when compared with other major European cities of the period, and life expectancy was shorter than in London or Paris. The heightened risk of infection in the *Mietskasernen*, with their dark courtyards and lack of cross ventilation, can be gauged from a remarkable statistic dating to 1873, which confirms that 150 out of 153 people who suffered that year from typhus in Berlin's 61st sanitary district (*Medizinalbezirk*) were resident in the same house—namely, 31 Müllerstrasse, Wedding.[1] The desire to escape from these pestilent courtyards into the fresh air and into the greenery of the urban periphery gathered pace around the turn of the new century and became a dominant concern of urban and social reformers, city planners, and architects.

For the prosperous middle classes this flight from the city was easily achieved. As Walter Benjamin recalled in the memoir of his Berlin youth: "My parents being wealthy, we moved every year, before I went to school and perhaps later, too, notwithstanding other occasional summer trips, into summer residences not far from home."[2] Another option for the privileged bourgeoisie was to move out from the city entirely, and into one of the villa colonies at the green edges of the city. The great mass of the Berlin population, however, had fewer options and were dependent on philanthropic and public initiatives, which worked at different scales ranging from the allotment and the urban park to complete new garden estates and garden suburbs. So-called gardens for the poor (*Armengärten*) had first appeared in German cities in the 1820s. In the Berlin context these were developed on a large scale in the early years of the twentieth century, initiated by the

Gartenfeld Jungfernheide, a set of allotment gardens in the northern suburbs, administered by the Red Cross. Organized according to strict regulations, these groups of ten to twelve gardens rapidly expanded across the city, so much so that the borough of Charlottenburg alone housed over a thousand gardens in 1913, spread across six sites.

A step up from the city allotment is the communal park *(Volkspark)*. The first in Berlin was the Volkspark Friedrichshain, laid out by the City Council in 1840–48 to mark the crown jubilee of Friedrich II, king of Prussia. Others followed, predominantly located in the northern suburbs (Humboldthain, Prenzlauer Berg, Rehberge, Schönholzer Heide), where they created green lungs for the industrial working classes. In 1903, the Berlin sociologist Georg Simmel detailed the intensified nervous stimulation and rootlessness experienced by city dwellers in his essay "The Metropolis and Mental Life." At the same period, gardeners and landscape architects argued for green space as the essential antidote to the overstimulation experienced in the great city. There was a conservative tenor to many of these polemics, with authors like Paul Schultze-Naumburg and Wilhelm Bölsche arguing for a return to unspoiled nature.[3] The theme also engaged more-progressive spirits, however, and it is significant that the doctoral dissertation of Martin Wagner, who was to emerge in the 1920s as Berlin's most radical city architect, was on the sanitary advantages of green space within the city.[4]

One way to unite the excitement of the city with the healthy conditions of the countryside was to combine the two in one place. This was the theory proposed by the garden-city movement. The most influential and effective advocate of this policy was the British polemicist Ebenezer Howard, who first published his key text, *Tomorrow: A Peaceful Path to Real Reform*, in 1898.[5] He had been preempted, however, by a slim volume penned by the German writer Theodor Fritsch, under the heading *Die Stadt der Zukunft* (The city of the future), published in 1896. Although the plans of both Howard and Fritsch were structured in concentric zones allotted to differing functions, the Fritsch plan was dynamic, and the city could expand outward until an optimum size was reached. While Howard's scheme is universally known, that of Fritsch is conspicuously absent from the literature on city planning. His rabid anti-Semitism may well explain this fall from grace. Shortly before *Die Stadt der Zukunft* appeared, Fritsch had also published a racist rant entitled *Antisemiten-Katechismus* (Anti-Semite catechism), which enjoyed enormous success and reached forty-nine editions by 1944. The revisionist left in Germany, however, was also strongly attracted to the garden-city ideal, and the Deutsche Gartenstadtgesellschaft (German Garden City Association) was established in 1902. It was the progeny of several idealist-socialist communities that had been established on the edges of Berlin, such as the Friedrichshagener Dichterkreis (Friedrichshagen Poets' Circle) and the Neue Gemeinschaft (New Community) commune, located at Schlachtensee. It is a measure of the universal desire to escape from the deprivations of the *Millionenstadt* that the garden-city alternative was espoused with equal vigor by the anti-Semitic right and the anarcho-socialist left.

The subtitle of Howard's first edition, *A Peaceful Path to Real Reform*, marked the ideological terrain occupied by the pragmatists in both the British and the German garden-city movements. The revolutionary pressures created in the cities by poor housing, disease, infant mortality, and by the merciless exploitation of the workforce, were to be vented and dispersed by good design, hygienic planning, and access to light, air, and greenery. The goal was a community that expressed itself in both the physical form of the housing, which favored consolidated groups and rows of housing oriented around a central, community focus. Community, at this point, was a key argument for the social-reform movements, whose arguments were grounded on the enormously influential book, published in 1887 by the sociologist Ferdinand Tönnies, with the programmatic title *Gemeinschaft und Gesellschaft* (community and society). Whereas society for Tönnies meant a superficial association driven by individual material or commercial interests, the ties of community—based on family, kinship, neighborliness—are more cohesive, more binding, and more lasting. The physical construction of community ideals was the goal of the garden-city movement. As the British architect Raymond Unwin noted in an article published in the journal of the Deutsche Gartenstadt-gesellschaft: "The principle of community does not automatically mean that every single house will be more attractive, but rather lends to the totality of the buildings a unity that finds expression in the harmonic beauty of the overall picture, which, in turn, derives from communal life."[6]

In the Berlin context, the most significant impact of the garden-city movement was the Gartenstadt Falkenberg, built in the southeastern suburbs in 1913–14, principally to the design of Bruno Taut, who had been appointed advisory architect to the Deutsche Gartenstadtgesellschaft in 1912. In spite of its name, however, the development at Falkenberg was not a garden city (*Gartenstadt*) but rather a garden suburb, which could be translated into German as *Gartensiedlung*. *Siedlung* is a key term in the German discussion of decentralization and rural resettlement. It is also a term that is impossible to translate consistently with one English word, as in its many German uses it means everything from an overseas colony to a small development of suburban houses. Between these two extremes it is used to describe large housing schemes on the model of the British garden city, smaller rural developments, and dedicated company workers' housing. It is variously translated in these texts to catch the particular meaning in each instance.

NOTES

1. See Jörg Vögele, *Urban Mortality Change in England and Germany, 1870–1913* (Liverpool: Liverpool University Press, 1999), p. 144.

2. Walter Benjamin, *Berliner Chronik* (Frankfurt: Suhrkamp, 1988); English translation from Benjamin, *One-Way Street and Other Writings*, trans. Edmund Jephcott and Kingsley Shorter (London: NLB, 1979), p. 322.

3. See, for example, Paul Schultze-Naumburg, *Gärten* (Gardens; 1902) and *Die Entstellung unseres Landes* (The disfigurement of our countryside; 1905); and Wilhelm Bölsche, *Stirb und Werde!* (Die and become!; 1913).

4. Martin Wagner, "Das sanitäre Grün der Städte: Ein Beitrag zur Freiflächentheorie" (Sanitary green in cities: A contribution to open-space theory, doctoral dissertation, Technische Hochschule, Berlin, 1915).

5. Republished in 1902 and subsequently as *Garden Cities of Tomorrow*.

6. Raymond Unwin, "Baugenossenschaft und Städtebau" (Building cooperative and town planning), *Gartenstadt* 4, no. 1 (January 1910), p. 2.

85

Wilhelm Bölsche
BEYOND THE METROPOLIS

First published as Bölsche, *Hinter der Weltstadt: Friedrichshagener Gedanken zur ästhetischen Kultur* (Leipzig: E. Diederichs, 1901), pp. v–xi. Translated by Fiona Elliot.

This summer it will be exactly thirteen years since my friend Bruno Wille and I started to find life in the metropolis so insufferable that we were simply no longer able to tolerate it. At the time we both lived in Judenstrasse, in spiritual wedlock—in a house that had a cheese shop at the front and a leather merchant's at the back; and there was a third spot marked by a glacier in winter; when it started to thaw you knew that spring had come upon the world. The bells pealing in the Parochialkirche rang out touching melodies to us as we made our way home from the night café, like true city dwellers, at five o'clock in the morning, but in the long run even this did not make the situation bearable.[1] At the time, although we both earned more or less enough to assuage our basic hunger, suddenly we developed a completely new, burning hunger—not for a properly cooked potato but for one thriving *in natura,* an unassuageable hunger for even the scraggiest heath pine—so much prettier than the lampposts in Friedrichstrasse—and for a patch of pure blue sky without telegraph wires and chimney soot.

Now, as it happens, an hour's journey by train from Berlin, in the wooded heathlands to the east, there lived a dear friend of ours who went by the as yet wholly unremarkable name of Gerhart Hauptmann.[2] Behind his house there was forest as far as the eye could see, here and there interspersed by the smooth, white mirror of a shallow reed lake, its succulent shores the yellow of golden ducats, marsh gas rising like seltzer water from its muddy bed at each touch of the steering pole. Juniper and blueberries and arid bracken. Dragonflies and butterflies. The chuck of a woodpecker and squirrels chasing each other. Not that it was a ravishing landscape of the kind one had to see before one died. But it was a landscape.

And once we had been out there a few times, that hunger took hold of us with such force that one day we failed to go home. We just stopped one station down the track, but still in the forest: in Friedrichshagen. Friedrichshagen, as the little children learn in school, was established by old King Frederick; so it is called Friedrichshagen, has a Friedrichstrasse and a monument to the old king. The reason for establishing it was the silk trade, although that was never a success; I have no idea whose fault it was, the old king's or the silk worms'. Whatever the case, today there are still a few ancient mulberry trees on the main road, which almost give the place something strangely exotic. When I moved here, there were still a few more green moss roofs and a herd of cows that walked through the streets each day. But now the global culture that is making such headway everywhere has become the order of the day. But, to put it in a nutshell, it is still a good place with a truly wonderful blue lake; it even has a few hills on the other side, which some unjustly claim were made by diluvial moles when all the time they are in fact a sand dune between two arms of the Spree, and the perfect place to revel in a really seriously magnificent view.

In the pine scent of the endlessly lonely woods—that one can see from there, rolling on as far as the horizon like a bluish green woolen carpet—over the years I slowly washed the black grime of the city out of my mind and my body, collecting insects and philosophizing and discussing aesthetics with one or the other dear comrade on distant forest paths, in red coppices with succulent white mushrooms. And gradually the pervasive, undefined hunger turned first into peaceful satisfaction and then, as behooves all good Germans, into a theory.

Like the skins of an onion, the diverse, nervous wisdom of the metropolis and its exalted attitudes to life fell away from me and were replaced by a rougher layer of farmer's bark, which gradually induced completely different thoughts and feelings in me. Since having been thus reborn, I am not only estranged from the city but I in fact believe that it truly is a monster that sucks away our spiritual life. The higher a building rises up under the smoke-filled sky, the shallower becomes the human spirit and the wheezier its utterances as it climbs the stairs. We lose our sense of the values in nature and art—that is to say, precisely those things that sustain our development—which never just bubbles up in a spring, but only ever makes its way through the finest capillary tubes of world physics. No individual can change it on his own, and there is nothing for it but to flee: happy the one who manages to do just that. I personally have left the metropolis behind me; and now I can quite comfortably watch as its smoke intermittently reaches out like ghostly claws on the red horizon in the west—untroubled by Ulyssean longings or by the fear that this black feline will yet devour me.

[. . .]

The century that we are now embarking upon will in all probability need huge crises, terrible storms before it can raise itself up again and the philosopher, the man of ethics, the scientist, and the artist are united as one. Perhaps plagues will break out and teach us that scientific research is not yet all-powerful. Perhaps a horrific revolt by the starving masses will shatter all art into a thousand pieces, because the marble form of Venus de Milo is not bread—and only then, out of the depths of the soul of humankind, the impassioned attack on this violated art will at last appear in all its might as the search for nourishment of a higher kind. How that may come about—it is up to each individual to say what he thinks, now, before it is too late. The apocalyptic riders will ride their part, obeying the might of the laws of nature, when the hour is right. Perhaps the metropolis will really disappear then, once and for all, crushed by fate like a colossal puffball. When the smoke spreads its raven-black wings in the west over my forests, I often think I can already see the city's foul-smelling fumes rising upward. But perhaps first the last city dweller with a sense for aesthetics will have to have moved into the forest—like the patient Ulysses, who was freed from Poseidon's curse only when he found a place inland where people took the oar on his shoulder for a grain shovel.

NOTES

1. Located on Klosterstrasse in central Berlin, the Baroque Parochialkirche was built between 1695 and 1703 to the design of Johann Arnold Nering and Martin Grünberg. A tower was added by Jean de Bodt in 1713–14.

2. As the enormously prolific author of prose, dramas, and poetry, Gerhart Hauptmann (1862–1946) was celebrated at this time as the most important German naturalist writer. The award in 1909 of honorary doctorates by the universities of both Oxford and Leipzig was followed in 1912 by the Nobel Prize for Literature. His best-known play, *Die Weber* (*The Weavers*; 1982), was condemned by conservative critics as social-democratic propaganda and led Kaiser Wilhelm II to cancel his box in the Deutsches Theater, Berlin, in November 1893, following its staging of the play.

86

Heinrich Hart

STATUTES OF THE GERMAN GARDEN CITY ASSOCIATION, 1902, § 1

From Franziska Bollerey, Gerhard Fehl, and Kristiana Hartmann, eds., *Im Grünen wohnen—im Blauen planen* (Hamburg: Christians, 1990), pp 102–3. Translated by Michael Loughridge.

It is the purpose of the Garden City Association [*Gartenstadtgesellschaft*] to gain the support of large sections of the population for the idea of building garden cities on the basis of common ownership of land both urban and rural, and to promote measures likely to serve that end.

The Garden City Association advocates homeland colonization—that is to say, an economically harmonious dividing up of the countryside and creation of appropriately dispersed new cities; it works for housing reform on the basis of the organized migration of industry to open country, where spacious, hygienic, and aesthetically acceptable premises can be erected, with the needs of industry itself taken fully into account, and where cooperation and integration with local agriculture will benefit the latter not only with markets close at hand but with cheap mechanical power and good communications; the association is endeavoring to institute a large-scale housing development in the country [*Siedlung*[1]], to which end a dedicated founders' society may be set up.

NOTE

1. On the various meanings of *Siedlung,* see the introduction to this section.

87

Hans Kampffmeyer

THE GARDEN CITY AND ITS CULTURAL AND ECONOMIC SIGNIFICANCE

First published as "Die Gartenstadt in ihrer kulturellen und wirtschaftlichen Bedeutung," *Hohe Warte* 3 (1906–7), pp. 105–8. Translated by David Britt.

The last century brought us the transition from craft to machine production. This immense technological upheaval placed economic life and the structure of society on an entirely new footing, and the same was true of our people's cultural life and public health. There then emerged the vast range of problems that we summarize under the single heading of "The Social Problem"—none of which can be understood without its wider context. We therefore do well to clarify for ourselves the antecedent causes and evolution of the housing question in general, and of the garden-city problem in particular.

THE GROWTH OF MAJOR CITIES

The plight of modern housing springs from the development of our industrial centers. One hundred years ago (see [Karl] Bücher, *Die Entstehung der Volkswirtschaft* [The emergence of economics]), Berlin was the only city in Germany with more than one hundred thousand inhabitants; Hamburg was just short of this total. In 1850 there were just five cities that met this same technical definition of the term *Großstadt* [major city]; in 1905 there were forty-one. In 1850, one in every thirty-eight Germans lived in a major city; in 1905 the proportion was one in five.

This rapid expansion of the cities has faced the organs of state and above all local government with challenges to which they have failed to rise. On the contrary, "Manchesterism,"[1] with its aversion to any governmental limitation on the "free play of [market] forces," ensured that public authorities either deliberately steered clear of the housing question or, at best, remained indifferent to it. The evil consequences of this—economic, hygienic, and cultural—have turned the housing question into one of the most vital tasks of our day.

RESIDENTIAL RENT AND LAND VALUES

Let us examine for a moment the causes of poor housing in an expanding city. The growth of existing businesses, and the establishment of new ones, attracts large numbers of workers who seek accommodation in the vicinity of the factories. When demand outstrips supply, they are forced to make do with very inferior housing. It often happens that numerous families who can well afford to pay rent find nowhere to live and need to be accommodated by the police in hutments or other emergency accommodation. The deficiencies of the available housing stock, both qualitative and quantitative, arise from the difficulty of predicting future urban housing needs. Nowadays, the responsibility for satisfying the demand for housing generally falls on a builder and developer, who will invest in new construction only when he expects a quick return from rental or sale. Furthermore, it is often against the developer's interests to build small dwellings, since these are administratively more difficult and carry the risk of inadequate rates of return. Since supply falls short of demand, rents naturally soar. For a squalid dwelling, the proletarian is often obliged to pay one-quarter, even one-third of his annual earnings, the proceeds of eighty or one hundred days' hard labor. Such inflated rents translate themselves into a higher sale price every time the property changes hands. The building as such does not increase in value. Its intrinsic value decreases as a result of wear and tear. But the occupier is willing to pay a high price because the location of the building is advantageous to him. A building in a prime commercial location can often be sold for fabulous sums: for example, the lot on which the Wertheim department store in Berlin stands is worth 18 *million* marks.

Every improvement in traffic access and transportation, every new public building, every park, even every new resident, increases the value of the land. For, naturally, a lot occupied by a five-story tenement house yields better, and will fetch a higher price, than one that contains nothing but a small single-family house with a yard of its own. And since in Germany neither established custom nor building code does anything to resist the advance of the rental apartment block, in our major cities the luxury of occupying a single-family house with a yard is confined to millionaires.

In 1890, a dwelling house in Bremen had on average 7.6 occupants, in Munich 22.4, in Breslau 35.4, in Berlin 52.6. Let us have no sonorous platitudes to the effect that the tenement house is an indispensable means of housing large urban populations; instead, just compare the figures just cited with the following: in England, in 1891, a dwelling house in London had 7.6 occupants, in Liverpool 5.7, in Manchester and Birmingham 5, in Leeds and Bradford 4.7. These figures show that, in the very country where industry is most concentrated, the single-family house is the prevalent form of dwelling.

It is customary to argue the economic superiority of the mass tenement house over the family house by referring to a saving in building costs. In answer to this, City Building Inspector Fabarius (*Zeitschrift für Wohnungswesen* 5, no. 81) demonstrates that this arises mainly from wholly impractical and arbitrary building codes, whereby small single-family houses must have the same wall thickness, fireproofing, and staircase dimensions as the rental apartment buildings for which the codes were originally drawn up. In London, by contrast, construction costs per cubic foot for a municipal mass-rental block are higher than for a small cottage. What is more, even Voigt, the champion of the rental block, is compelled to admit that its construction costs are inflated by the uneconomic and irrational luxury associated with it. What is more, as mentioned, the price of land tends to rise in proportion to the number of stories that are built on it—thus canceling out any savings in the cost of construction. So much for construction costs and land prices!

CITY DWELLERS ALIENATED FROM NATURE

One of the greatest dangers of the modern major city is the increasing alienation of its inhabitants from nature. Elevating its occupants four and more stories above the surface of Mother Earth, the tenement house takes them farther and farther away from the open countryside and sets up more and more ramparts of masonry between them. Private gardens have disappeared, and those public gardens that are created and maintained at disproportionate cost are no adequate substitute. We can tramp for hours along uniform, straight rows of houses without encountering a single shade tree or a single flower. Only an arduous railroad journey can take us into the open air. For the city dweller, the dew-spangled meadow and the golden wheat field are now a spectacle to which he must gain admission by purchasing an expensive rail ticket.

OVERCROWDING

Let us take a look inside the houses. "Statistically, a dwelling is defined as overcrowded when six or more individuals inhabit one room, or eleven or more two rooms. And even under that definition there is plenty of it: in Berlin nearly 30,000, in Breslau 7,000, in Chemnitz 5,000, in Plauen im Vogtland 3,000, etc. Just think, six or more people in one room, eleven in two rooms!" (W. Sombart, *Das Proletariat,* Rütten & Loening, Frankfurt am Main.) Within the narrow compass of those four walls, the whole life of a family takes place. Here they cook, eat, sleep. Here the pieceworker's sewing machine whirs, and the washerwoman's copper boils and steams. The parents live tightly packed together with their grown and growing children, and are often compelled to take in night lodgers in order to pay the high rents on time. The moral perils attendant on this overcrowding are constantly and alarmingly evident from the court reports. As for the health dangers, the reports of sick funds and physicians paint a horrifying picture. For example: in a careful study, Marcuse, a public-health specialist, concludes that mortality rates from tuberculosis—that devastating scourge of our time—are directly proportional to population density. Physicians have determined that the horrendous cholera epidemic in Hamburg had its breeding ground in the unsanitary and overcrowded harbor districts. In a number of cities, attempts have been made to control overcrowding by means of building codes. In Dresden, for instance, the code stipulated a minimum capacity of 10 cubic meters per person. But even this requirement—which medical opinion regards as too modest—has proved unenforceable, because no healthy dwellings are available at affordable prices. The regulation has remained on paper.

But let us look on the brighter side. The minimum cubic space stipulated by the physicians has been achieved for one group of German citizens at least: the inmates of the penitentiaries. No doubt for the first time in their lives, these individuals find themselves in clean and healthful surroundings. It is a moot point whether they would ever have been there if their previous lives had been spent in dwellings truly fit for human habitation.

CULTURE AND HOUSING

It is impossible to overestimate the influence of housing on the human psyche. A thousand strands tie us to our immediate surroundings. Consciously or unconsciously, we make our own mark on them, and at the same time they constantly influence us. Now, let us just picture the sheer volume of bad taste that accumulates in the ornate, trumpery facades of apartment blocks, with their cheap, sham, dime-store furniture, and threatens by its sheer presence to block the way to something better. Then we shall see in its true light the importance of the housing question for the culture of our people.

In the interests of that culture, we would like to encourage people to take pleasure in the look of their own domestic interiors; to take pleasure in a colorful lithograph or a plain, handsome piece of furniture. But can we ever succeed in this as long as wide sections of the population are doomed to eke out their wretched lives in unsanitary and overcrowded rooms in mass apartment buildings? We enthusiasts for mass education never pause to reflect that we are recommending the reading of good books to people who all too often lack even a quiet corner into which to retreat, undisturbed, in the evenings after work. What right have we to blame them for preferring a dingy, smoke-filled bar to their own homes, and for seeking to drown their sorrows in drink?

EDUCATION AND THE HOUSING CRISIS

The desperate state of housing weighs most heavily on our young people, who are our nation's future. What do they know of those blissful rambles through woods and fields that first inspired us to embark on nature study; or of drowsing in a meadow full of spring flowers, peering through half-open eyes at passing clouds and butterflies, amid a sunlit, vernal landscape that conveys to the child his first inkling of the omnipotence and beauty of nature? What a poor thing an urban childhood is! "Father," says the child, "it's spring!" "How do you know?" "We did it in school today." One's heart misses a beat, sometimes, looking at those pale, sickly little faces. At home, they are in the way. Their playground is the gloomy, evil-smelling courtyard; or else they play on the grimy street, in constant peril of being struck by a horse's hoof or run over by an automobile. The city of Charlottenburg has set up woodland schools for children whose health is weak. This is highly commendable. But it would be even more worthwhile to create living conditions in which children's health would not suffer in the first place.

I have set out the ways in which current housing conditions negate the requirements of the economy and of public health, culture, art, morality, and education. I hardly need, I think, to demonstrate that the adverse effects of such conditions extend far beyond the proletariat; wider sections of the population, including sections of the affluent middle class, have a keen interest in a solution to the housing question. It is now my task to show how the garden-city movement hopes to improve matters.

It will be clear from what I have said that truly satisfactory housing conditions cannot possibly be created on the expensive land that exists within any major city; and that families can be accommodated in houses with front and back yards of their own only where the land is still unencumbered by high ground rents. If such favorable housing conditions are to last, it will further be necessary to prevent any arbitrary increase in ground rents and to regulate the prices of dwellings, workplaces, and real estate in the interests of the population at large. These new settlements will of course be planned in such a way as to take account of all the needs of their future inhabitants. Similarly, it will be necessary to ensure that such settlements do not, like our existing major cities, expand out of control. Such, in a nutshell, are the ideas that govern the activities of the garden-city movement, on which we shall enlarge further in what follows. [. . .]

NOTE

1. "Manchesterism" is a shorthand term for the British Free Trade Movement of the nineteenth century, advocating freedom of trade and noninterference by the state in private economic activity. Grounded on the theoretical work of Adam Smith and David Ricardo, it flourished in the 1830s and 1840s in Manchester—then the epicenter of the industrial revolution in Britain—under the advocacy of Richard Cobden and John Bright. The term "Manchesterism" has always had a negative resonance in Germany, being synonymous with *heartless* or *coldhearted*.

88

Heinrich Pudor

THE PEOPLE'S PARK IN GREATER BERLIN

First published as "Der Volkspark von Groß-Berlin," *Der Städtebau* 7, no. 2 (1910), pp. 21–22. Translated by David Frisby.

It has been calculated that in thirty years' time Berlin will have 6 million inhabitants. It has been stated, on the other hand, that the twentieth century will be the century of hygiene. If one puts these two facts together—the huge piling up of human masses within a relatively narrow space and the requirements of health doctrines—then the building plans for Greater Berlin are faced with powerful demands. Today, London already has 6 million inhabitants including its suburbs, but the dwellings of London's inhabitants are largely arranged horizontally, as a result of the predominant building pattern of one- and two-family houses, whereas the dwellings in Berlin are basically layered vertically. As a result, a city such as Berlin requires, to a much greater extent than does London, green oases as breaks in the lines of streets. Yet in reality London possesses many more green squares and gardens than does Berlin. And now imagine this vertically layered, giant city of the Greater Berlin with a future population of 6 million inhabitants, and one must admit that something quite extraordinary must occur if these human masses are not to suffocate in the labyrinthine network of buildings and rental barracks. [. . .] So much is certain—namely, that such a gigantic piling up of human masses as will be created in Greater Berlin is the most certain means of destroying the living conditions of its inhabitants. [. . .] We must not only break through the countless housing blocks here and there in order to make the network of housing as wide meshed as possible, but also create places within this tangle of houses from which elemental fresh air might rise, reinvigorating the musty, dead air of the housing quarters. These sites, as it were, would be like fountains, or mass-production sites for oxygen and woodland ozone.

[. . .]

Now in the enormous area of the Grunewald, Greater Berlin is in the fortunate position of possessing a site of oxygen production such as we desire. And it is not simply a matter of preserving this forest intact and not broken up, but also of tending it so that it constantly has the most vigorous plant growth that can be achieved, making it the most abundant source possible of ozone.

[. . .]

But the Grunewald on its own is not enough, and basically benefits only the western side of Berlin. It is understood, of course, that we are speaking of the Grunewald not as place for excursions, but as a source of ozone. And Greater Berlin must have more of these sources, in the north and south, and also, on a more modest scale, in the center.

As is well known, ozone is created by the exposure of air to sunshine, through the radiation of air by the sun. If follows, therefore, that we should create as many points of light and areas open to the sunlight, and, in general, design the housing blocks in very wide-meshed layouts, creating the largest urban squares and broadest streets that are possible on the particular site, taking front and rear gardens into consideration. In short, we must above all bring light into the modern metropolis, light and sun; for we know that light, precisely, is the best weapon against bacilli and microbes.

And these bright patches amid the confusion of housing will demand life: there must be life and new shoots in them; they must grow, flourish, and—even more— blossom! After all the gray black of the house walls and sidewalks, our eyes will devour and our souls savor not only the light, but also the green of the plants, and our heart and lungs will delight in the herb-scented air after all the soot, fumes, and dust. Beauty spots, even if easily accessible, do not suffice, for one cannot go on an excursion every day. Above all, we need pure, strong air in the apartments in which we live and sleep. For this reason, every housing block should be offset by an appropriate green space, and the more dense the housing, the more attention should be paid to verdant planting. And we should not think only of greenery and only of grass and trees, but also of flowers. Flowers not only paint colors in the dead stones; they bring joy to the eyes and senses, and also to the heart and soul. They are a picture of joy and also awaken feelings of joy. And there is no reason why this joy, this most powerful affirmation of life, should be missing in the dead stone desert of the metropolis. And for this reason, landscape gardening and flower growing have a major task to accomplish in the Berlin of the future, whose oases will radiate life and light, strength and joy.

[. . .]

We must have people's parks like these in the north and south, and, where possible, in the center. I am thinking of something like this: the largest possible lake should be created in the city center. It could be formed artificially on the already low-lying Tempelhofer Feld, or, as in the east and west of the city, by making use of the naturally occurring water and lakes. Such a lake must be given over in every respect to the health and the pleasure of the inhabitants through extensive opportunities for swimming, rowing, or skating. It should be pointed out, however, that the beneficial effects of a lake like this reside not only in the volume of water and in creating a desire to pursue sport, but also in the fact that a sheet of water acts as a source of reflected light, which cheers and brightens up the city. [...] One might mention in this context that the River Spree is not properly exploited, for its canals are all set much too low, thus losing this illuminating and cheering effect. It has been hidden, as if something to be ashamed of, instead of being raised wherever possible and drawn toward the light. We are touching here on an important aspect of the aesthetics of water and water flow, which, like the aesthetics of the woods and forests, is something that our cultural planners must consider much more carefully in future.

[...]

To sum up: we have a people's park in front of us such as we can imagine in various parts of the enormous urban area of Greater Berlin. It will be a people's park that the population will use for recreation on Sundays, that will promote delight and education, and that will provide the surrounding city quarters with fresh air, day after day and night after night. It will weave light, green, and joyful colors into the excessively uniform gray weave of the street network, and bring colorful nature into the culture of the city.

89

Karl Ernst Osthaus

GARDEN CITY AND CITY PLANNING

First published as "Gartenstadt und Städtebau" in *Bauordnung und Bebauungsplan,* ed. Deutsche Gartenstadtgesellschaft (Leipzig: Deutsche Gartenstadtgesellschaft, 1911), pp. 33–40; reprinted in *Im Grünen wohnen—im Blauen planen,* ed. Franziska Bollerey, Gerhard Fehl, and Kristiana Hartmann (Hamburg: Christians, 1990), pp. 119–23. Translated by Michael Loughridge.

But what exactly is this art of urban planning? Let us first of all remember that urban planning is one of the plastic arts—that is, an art that uses the eye as its route to convey sense impressions to the brain. Thus one could speak of the visual quality of urban planning and thereby make the point that this particular form of creativity is not concerned with questions of functional efficiency, performance of materials, and the like. The artist in urban design simply accepts all functional requirements and all constraints imposed by current technological limits as givens; it is not from these that he derives the laws of his craft, but from the constitution of the human eye and the human spirit. Where conflicts occur, he is entitled to assign to his imperatives the same priority that we accord to the spirit when any conflict arises between our higher needs and our digestive needs. Whether we are to be seen, from the perspective of the future, as a civilized nation will turn on our attitude to this balance. In an age of uninhibited material preoccupations, the point can hardly be emphasized too strongly. As for the creative art of the urban designer, I would sum it up as follows: he has to take the constituent parts allowed him by the municipality's head of finance and from them, with due attention to current technical capabilities and constraints, evolve a unified visual design that when realized will yield a cityscape supremely expressive of the life of the people.

Given this approach to planning, what shall be said of the garden city? Here, beyond question, the urban designer is facing one of his most important contemporary challenges, for seldom before in history has it been possible to see such comprehensive planning work become reality. And indeed, the unprecedented nature of the tasks facing us has caught the architectural fraternity somewhat unawares. Far too many problems have been dealt with piecemeal, as if the object were a slow-growing historic village, built one house at a time. The delightful higgledy-piggledy layout of the villages of Bavaria or Holland, and their gables, little oriel windows and turrets—all this has been re-created in a spirit of affectionate revival of a past age of woolen nightcaps and hand-embroidered slippers. But, charming and imaginative though they may be, these designs have an unfortunate resemblance to the present-day churches and town halls for which the old German vernacular style was made the model: the buildings lack spontaneity, because those responsible for them lacked the courage to tackle a modern problem in the modern way. A further mistake was made, over and over again. Garden cities were thought of as a mix of town and countryside. The means chosen to express their rural character was extravagant use of space, with unduly wide separation between buildings. In some cases, their roads were laid out as very broad thoroughfares with continuous grass strips; in others, houses were built to the smallest internal dimensions that regulations permitted, only to have long front gardens placed between them and the street, complete with rhododendron shrubbery. The result often enough was that the roads and other unbuilt spaces soon became so unkempt as to recall the unprepossessing appearance of provincial small towns with pretensions to city status. And there was yet another problem with this type of garden city: its very expansiveness cuts it off from the very contact with Nature that was its purpose in the first place.

In the face of such strong tendencies to romanticize and sentimentalize, it needs to be emphasized that, as always, there can be no aesthetically satisfying solution without the essential prerequisites of precise analysis of the problem and minutely thorough preparation of the urban design plan. We must avoid Rousseau's pointless enthusiasm for untouched Nature. There is no such thing as Nature—or we are it. The force that nurtures human culture is the same force that brought forth the fragrance of the flowers and the splendor of the butterflies. And what we like to call "Nature" has been shaped by humans since time out of mind, and has become culture. Forest, meadow, and cornfield are surveyed by trigonometry and cared for by the countryman's skill. One has to retreat to the highest snowy peaks or to the ocean shore if one is to find Nature free from any interwoven strand of human planning. All we see around us is culture: that is, Nature tamed and given new forms. There is a rural culture and an urban culture; each has its own laws and its own logic, and we will do well not to confuse the two! City and country are antithetical, and the more sharply we draw the antithesis, the greater the resulting impact on our sensibility. Thus the garden city must not become a throwback to the semiculture of small provincial towns; it has to be a more advanced development, the next stage beyond the metropolis.

90

Anonymous

LIETZENSEE-PARK IN CHARLOTTENBURG

First published as "Lietzensee-Park in Charlottenburg," *Berliner Architekturwelt* 14, no. 9 (1912), p. 376. Translated by Iain Boyd Whyte.

The city of Charlottenburg has announced and in the meantime realized its very welcome intention to purchase the remaining free land adjoining the existing Lietzensee-Park—namely. the section south of Kantstrasse—and to retain it as parkland. With this, the Lietzensee-Park will gain an extension of around 10 hectares,[1] and thus exceed considerably in size the new city parks in Schöneberg (Stadtpark), with 7.5 hectares, and Wilmersdorf (Seepark), with 5.5 hectares. It would seem in this case that the rivalry between the larger Berlin suburbs is producing gratifying fruits.

NOTE

1. 10 hectares = approximately 25 acres.

91

Hannes Müllerfeld

DOWN WITH THE GARDEN CITY!

First published as "Nieder mit der Gartenstadt," *Die Gartenstadt* 8 (1914), pp. 56–57; republished in *Im Grünen wohnen—im Blauen planen,* ed. Hartmann Fehl (Hamburg: Christians, 1990), p. 170. Translated by Michael Loughridge.

Gentlemen: it must be clear to all that the Social Democrats have a private agenda every time they agitate publicly for something new. I am in no doubt whatsoever that they have it in for property owners like ourselves—in other words, they have it in for those who uphold the state and true religion. First it was allotment gardens and wooden cabins, and now they want gardens with detached villas to sit in, and in a few years it's going to be stately homes to keep them happy, and we'll be the stable lads and the footmen. Anyone who upholds true freedom must fight this. And it mustn't be just people already in politics, like ourselves. All those nature lovers must fight it, too. What's it going to be like when there are these garden cities all over the place, gentlemen, what are they going to have in their gardens?—red roofs, red window frames, red carnations and red roses all over the front of the place, red poppies up the gable, vegetable patches full of red cabbage, and the only birds they'll allow will be robins. But thank God for men who still blush red with shame and anger at such a spectacle and who will lead the charge against this invasion of our country by rampant red.

Gentlemen: it used to be the privilege of those who had earned themselves something a cut above the average to be able to buy a nice villa. In a way of speaking, it was a sign you were an educated person with a bit of substance. And now the Universal and Equal and Secret Suffrage is to be extended, if you please, to where you live. I ask you, my friends, what pleasure is there going to be now for a man of culture living in a villa residence of his own when Tom, Dick, and Harry and their in-laws are all doing that, too? And do you know the best thing of all: we are the property owners and we pay just about all the taxes there are, and now we are going to have to pay out on top of that again, and see our houses standing empty. Why? Well, once all these jumped-up working-class types have their own villas to live in, you'll see, they're all going to want the town council to pay up out of public funds for them to have their own cars in which to drive to the factories.

NOTE

Although Müllerfeld's wrath was aimed at a 1914 plan to build a garden city in the Brunswick suburb of Riddagshausen, his reactionary response enjoyed a national resonance.

92

Max Osborn

THE FAIRY-TALE FOUNTAIN IN THE FRIEDRICHSHAIN, BERLIN

First published as Osborn, Der *Märchenbrunnen im Friedrichshain zu Berlin* (Berlin: Verlag für Kunstwissenschaft, 1914), n.p. Translated by Iain Boyd Whyte.

To create a popular art work in the grand manner—this was the aim of the Berlin City Council when it decided to endow the Friedrichshain with an ornamental feature such as none other of the parks in its charge can boast to date. In its scale and in the funds required, it exceeded almost everything that the Prussian capital had previously undertaken in the service of art. It was a scheme that called to mind similar creations, designed with festive intent, from the joyful age of the Renaissance.

A monumental adornment for the city and a gift to its populace was to be created. Out of this double purpose the basic idea and the form of this beautiful work emerged organically; here lay the stimulus but also the difficulty of its conception and implementation. The way in which the project matured and reached its successful outcome under the guiding hand of Ludwig Hoffmann will forever constitute a glorious chapter in the history of the promotion of the arts in Berlin.

The site, above all, determined the character of the whole scheme. In a heavily populated part of the city, blessed with many children, an installation was to be laid out, the sight of which would refresh and delight the gaze of thousands of people during their day-to-day lives and in their hours of leisure. It was to appear in the corner of an old park that is hemmed in by streets. The choice of a large scale was self-evident. For what has been created here as the focus of a joyful and contemplative public life could not have been achieved with a modest little fountain. For this reason a separate, formal garden was laid out at the Friedrichshain, which both makes a feature of the entrance to this extensive recreational parkland and also marks the site of the former Königstor [king's gate]. The result is an imposing triangle at the intersection of two roads, formed of various sections, surrounded by beech hedges, and lockable behind wrought-iron park gates.

Even from a distance the visitor is greeted by the view onto the main architectural feature of the installation, which reveals itself ever more broadly to the access paths. Approaching through flower beds, one gains a view of the whole ensemble, whose centerpiece is formed by a soaring structure of pale Thuringen travertine, which establishes the transition from the neighboring mass of housing to the sculptural scheme of the fountain. A curved wall punctured by nine arched openings, reminiscent of the garden architecture of the late Renaissance, offers the eye a point of rest. In its joyfulness and serenity, the wall stands out against the treetops in the park, yet the porous granularity of the material protects against a hard contrast. The open arches, flanked by pairs of freely handled ionic half columns, point toward the interior of the grove and announce to the stroller that further surprises await beyond the picturesque openings of the wall. The powerfully molded main entablature supports a balustrade, and, on plinths set above the pillars between the arches, a witty collection of animals proclaim far and wide that we find ourselves here in a realm of fairy-tale and folklore visions. Dog and donkey, boar and bear, lion and cow, ibex and lamb, wolf and lamb peer down gravely, adding a humorous tone to the rigor of the architecture. They live in splendid harmony with the four deer, who, wonderfully aware of the decorative impact of their silhouettes, lie on the transversely set plinths above the entablature that spans the arches. In the most felicitous manner these generously formed sculptures, which are the work of Josef Rauch, lead the eye down to the fairy-tale group of the basin, which now ring out the basic chord of the whole ensemble.

Here in the basin, the water gushes and flows across three shallow terraces, surrounded by monumental benches. Bubbly and frothing, the playful water springs with a merry murmuring from many small springs. Strange frogs perch among them, dominated by a goggle-eyed frog king. And around the edge appear eight charming figures, which we know well, yet appear new in the loving execution that Ignaz Taschner has brought to them, with an extraordinary sensibility for the laws of small-scale sculpture in a context such as this. We see Puss in Boots, Lucky Hans [*Hans im Glück*], Snow White, Sleeping Beauty, Little Red Riding Hood, and Cinderella, the Seven Ravens, and the little sister whose brother is turned into a deer. In the foreground, as droll harbingers of this fairy-tale parade, we see Hansel and Gretel riding toward each other on the downy backs of two ducks. And with melancholy thanks we lay a fresh laurel wreath on the early grave of the artist who devised and created this delightful gathering.

Taschner's limestone figures appear soft and innocent, in contrast to the more sturdy stones of the walls. With the water, the green of the trees, and the blue or gray of the sky that stretches above, the two notes of this accord join together into a lovely symphony of shimmering colorfulness. All around are secret whisperings from old tales of children and animals that point to the natural poetry of the Germans that is lost in the depths of time. This atmosphere is further reinforced by the half-grotesque, even slightly scary half-length figures of the giant's daughter, of Rübezahl,[1] of the Man Eater, and of Mother Holle, who suddenly peep out of the bushes along the mazy, hedge-lined paths on each side. The children and the animals form a further union at the entrance pillars and at the farthest fountain element, where the fairy tale comes to an end in the depths of the Friedrichshain. A slender jet of water rises here from a circular basin, the highest in the whole ensemble, visible through the central arch of the architectural wall. Georg Wrba, who had also modeled the fantastic giant herms, set lively groups of putti and surging animals on the edge of the basin, and allegories of childhood in the encircling shrubbery.

Then a new gateway opens, revealing the serpentine pathways of the Friedrichshain. A realm of beauty and playfulness, of dreamlike innocence and whispering secrets, which hover enticingly around our childhood fantasies, had cast a spell over us and now releases us into the silent tranquillity of the park. How distant is the city, with its worries, its bustle, and its daily hubbub. . . .

NOTE

1. Rübezahl is the mountain gnome of the Riesengebirge (Giant Mountains), the mountain range that divides Poland and the Czech Republic (Karkonosze in Polish, Krkonoše in Czech).

93

Paul Westheim

WORKERS' HOUSING ESTATE AT STAAKEN

First published as "Arbeitersiedlung Staaken," *Sozialistische Monatshefte* 21, no. 2 (1915), pp. 618–20. Translated by Michael Loughridge.

Interesting as it is from the design point of view, the housing project now taking shape at Staaken, outside Spandau, also represents a particularly notable development in social policy. The requirement for a working-class estate here originated in a severe shortage of suitable housing for the workers of the munitions factories at Spandau. It was decided to tackle this problem by creating living accommodation in sufficient quantity and of reasonable standard in a kind of workers' garden city on a site close to Staaken Station, about ten minutes' traveling time from Spandau. The bulk of the funding was to come from the Reichswohnungsfürsorgefonds [Imperial Housing Support Fund]. In this instance, however, the government did not content itself with an appropriate handout to a housing cooperative. Unprecedentedly, the Reichsamt des Innern [Ministry of the Interior], which was the prime mover in this case, chose to oversee the project itself and involve the cooperative only on completion of the first houses—an approach that, as will readily be envisaged, could open up significant new perspectives for the future of working-class housing provision.

[...]

The estate is designed to accommodate approximately one thousand families. It conforms to what now looks like becoming the standard pattern for this type of estate—namely, single-story multiple-unit housing.[1] There are only a few one-family homes, and these are intended for exceptional families with six and eight children. The standard house types are two-family and four-family houses. Internal layout is in one of five standard types. Every unit has a washhouse with bath, a pigsty, and at least 150 square meters of garden ground. The smallest type of apartment, with a kitchen–living room and one bedroom, as one unit of a four-family house, costs sixteen marks per month (including water rate). The two-bedroom type costs twenty-four marks; two bedrooms and a storeroom / third bedroom, twenty-eight marks; three bedrooms (in a two-family house), thirty marks; and the single-family house has three bedrooms and costs thirty-three marks. These extraordinarily low rentals would be unthinkable were it not for the support fund.

[...]

So much for the financial and project-management aspects. At present, at a time when the authorities in East Prussia and in Alsace are facing colossal housing problems, there is a special interest in ascertaining what the designers' re-

FIGURE 25. Gartenstadt Staaken (1914–17; Paul Schmitthenner, architect), c. 1920. Landesarchiv Berlin, 223 473.

sponse to such a state commission looks like in terms of concept and aesthetics. True, it will hardly be necessary by now to repeat at length that in this area of urban design the architect's art lies above all in a clear vision of essentials, in the coordination of all functional requirements, and in a radically functionalist approach in general. In a working-class housing estate project, it has to be borne in mind that any element of Romanticism is a potential source of trouble: Hellerau is a notorious example, and not the only one, for Gmindersdorf suffers likewise under the legacy of certain Romantic notions, as does the Margarethenhöhe development outside Essen. The constant priority is to simplify, using standardized design components, and this of course means, in essence, an improved understanding of the actual living needs of the class of people to be housed, and the sharpest possible focus on designing to these needs. It is good to be able to record that this resolutely functionalist approach was adopted at Staaken—nowhere else, indeed, has it been applied so radically—and was adhered to throughout the decision-making processes; no concessions whatever were allowed, even on allegedly aesthetic grounds.

On this crucial issue Staaken joins hands with Potsdam—more specifically, with the wholly admirable Frederician settlement of the Dutch Quarter, whose streets of gabled houses in fact were used as a model for Staaken. As is well known, the latest publications on urban design are full of enthusiasm for what the Baroque monarchy created there. The difference from today was that the autocratic will—though one might call it the public-spirited will—of the ruler precluded interference on the whim of private individuals, and took decisions for the generality on the basis of a more mature understanding than can be expected of an estate resident with no experience of architecture and design. However, there was more involved than simply the artistic instinct to create a unified design (an instinct surely not entirely lacking in this modern estate, either); no less important an inspiration was the insistence that everything should be built to the highest quality standards possible. That Friderician tradition has been picked up here in Staaken; that this, the first *Reichsarbeiterstadt* [state-sponsored workers' township], can be regarded as a paradigm for all future developments is due to the good judgment and the insight of those who designed it.

This sober functionalism would have less appeal were it not the achievement of an individual endowed with so sure an instinct for form that every decision of consequence was one that also made sense from the point of view of the general aesthetic quality of the estate, or indeed even enhanced it. The individual who could do this was found in the architect Paul Schmitthenner. A native of Alsace, Schmitthenner completed his qualifications before moving across to the eastern part of the Reich, where a private land developer in Breslau engaged him to design and build the suburban residential estate at Carlowitz [now Sremski-Karlovci, Serbia]. Then the Reich Ministry of the Interior launched the Staaken development project, and Schmitthenner, whose art offers a distinctive, curiously charming blend of functionalism and dignified homeliness, was discovered.[2]

NOTES

1. Westheim uses the word *Reihenhaus* here. Like *Siedlung* (see the introduction to this section), *Reihenhaus* takes on several meanings in German, including terrace houses sharing party walls, semidetached houses, and freestanding, two-story houses with separate apartments on each floor.

2. In 1918, the success of the Staaken housing led to the appointment of Paul Schmitthenner (1884–1972) to a chair at the Technische Hochschule in Stuttgart, one of the most influential architecture schools in the Weimar period, with a marked preference for traditional building methods.

94
Martin Wagner
URBAN OPEN-SPACE POLICY

First published as Wagner, *Städtische Freiflächenpolitik* (Berlin: Carl Heymanns Verlag, 1915), pp. 91–92. Translated by Iain Boyd Whyte.

The results of the present study can be summarized in the following propositions:

1. The significance of the "sanitary green spaces" for the metropolitan population lies less in their existence value than in their use value. The mere availability of open spaces or their total size does not yet determine their specific sanitary value. Only when the open spaces have been set out into places for playing and sport, into people's parks and city forests, into allotments and family gardens do they become absolutely necessary for the city dweller.
2. The size, the location, and the layout of open spaces must be apportioned to the diverse uses according to the diverse population strata. Each inhabitant is to be apportioned, on average, 2.4 square meters for children's playgrounds, 1.6 square meters for sports fields, 0.5 square meters for strolling, 2 square meters for parks, and 13 square meters for city forest.
3. The playgrounds should not be located farther than ten to fifteen minutes away from places of dwelling, parks not more than twenty minutes away, and sports fields and city forests not more than thirty minutes away. Only in the case of the last group should requests for means of transport at the lowest possible tariff come into question.
4. The city's open spaces must be projected in the closest cooperation with the preexisting modes of building. In accordance with dwelling density, tall buildings are to be provided with open spaces to an equal extent as low buildings.
5. The creation and initial layout of city playgrounds and parks must be legally executed at the cost of the development of land for dwellings. The city forests are to be procured from the local authority.

[. . .] *The metropolitan conditions of health press with full force upon the enlargement of the sanitary living space.* This movement to assist a natural development will be the task of urban authorities in the coming years. *The cities, which today already include more than half of the total German population, have a duty to the public to ensure the health of the body of the German people and to raise the German people's energy.* Of course, one could resolve this task irresponsibly if, as in America, one could project its fulfillment to a point in time at which it was no longer possible to resolve it in a natural manner. The erection of five city playgrounds in the form of a five-story skyscraper, as is planned for one of the most densely populated city districts, is typical of the direction of an urban open-space policy that builds upon *lost* opportunities.

NOTE

These are the concluding remarks to the published version of Martin Wagner's doctoral thesis. He was later to be chief city planner in Berlin from 1926 until his dismissal in 1933.

95

Bruno Taut

THE FALKENBERG GARDEN SUBURB NEAR BERLIN

First published as "Drei Siedlungen: Gartenstadt-Siedlung Falkenberg bei Berlin," *Wasmuths Monatshefte für Baukunst* 4, nos. 5/6 (1919–20), pp. 183–84. Translated by Michael Loughridge.

The land in question, amounting to 70 hectares in all, is situated close to the suburban station of Grünau, and the German Garden City Association took up its option to purchase during 1913. The development plan that I drew up aimed to cater to all classes of the population, providing for all needs, from the smallest living units comprising only kitchen, bedroom, and small spare room, and grouped in small, detached apartment houses, to middle-class terrace houses with five rooms. After extensive consultations with the Alt-Glienicke community, particularly on such topics as the principal roads and their resistance to wear and tear, open spaces, and the land to be reserved for the church, the school, and so on, the plan was adopted by the government and the then only recently founded Verband Groß-Berlin [Greater Berlin Group of the German Garden City Association] as an exemplary model.

The first homes were built on land surrounding the Akazienhof in 1913: one detached house by Tessenow, the others by me—thirty-four in all. There were two different types of terrace houses, and small, eight-apartment blocks. In 1914 a large new tract of land by the through road, the Gartenstadtstrasse, was developed, resulting in the addition of ninety-three further homes—these, too, in an assortment of different types ranging from the one-room flat with storeroom to accommodation with five rooms. This stage was executed to my design. Future stages of the garden suburb's development, in any case significantly affected by the merger between the local building cooperative and the Spar- und Bauverein [Building and Loan Society], will also reflect the changed national circumstances by being designed to allow considerably more garden area. Compared with an area of about 120 square meters for the smaller gardens at present—which can be extended by adding leasehold land—future houses will have much bigger gardens (500 square meters has been suggested), to the great benefit of the smaller terrace houses.

The complete development of the whole 70-hectare site, notwithstanding some part commissions to be executed by other architects, will be subject to my direction, as laid down in the contract signed for the Garden Association's Building Division in the context of the option negotiations. However, this responsibility will be understood in a team sense, without suppression of individuality, and is intended only to ensure continuity of line, consistency in roof pitch, and harmony in the combinations of colors and materials.

The various ground-plan types represented in the buildings completed so far all represent the simplest solution available. They are too diverse, however, to be reported on in detail here. What is quite clear is that the policy of intermingling the different classes of occupier has been remarkably successful. Life in the garden suburb has a vigorous pattern of both coexistence and mutual sharing, which reduces the social divisions and creates civilized values. A similar pattern characterizes its outward appearance: a cheerful variety of house size and shape is held together by the uniformity of roof line and material, and positively enlivened by vivid and sometimes intensely rich color choices. In the early days the colorful scene caused much consternation, the formerly ubiquitous conventions in color having been abandoned completely. No one took it harder than the visitor from a conventional Berlin suburb dominated by uniform gray tenement blocks, who could not find words adequate to his righteous indignation and could only keep repeating that the architect "ought to be put under arrest." But now at last the storm of protest is abating, and the realization may be slowly dawning that color, too, can be—and should be—one of the components with which we build. Acceptance has been helped to some extent by the fact that over the past six years the colors have become much more subdued. Using color as a major element in design presupposes refurbishment of the color at least every three years with a fresh coat. Maintenance work of this kind also makes sense economically, since paint is a relatively cheap way to improve the appearance of buildings compared with any kind of relief decoration. The use of color is indeed the only appropriate, or necessary, treatment for buildings standing in a natural setting: one must not think of summertime scenes alone, for it is the winter landscape above all that cries out for color glowing heartwarmingly across the snow. Unfortunately, the required care and maintenance, in the form of a fresh coat of paint, has not been carried out here, so that the buildings' present appearance, while less offensive to the complaining city dwellers than before, falls far short of what tradition requires in terms of house color, and is in definite need of attention. It was Muthesius who said we should have the same attitude to house painting that we have to laundering our clothes: colors need renewal from time to time—a practice still observed annually in Holland and in some areas in the Elbe Valley by the residents themselves, and which used to be universal. As for the Falkenberg residents, they soon became used to the multicolored scene in which they found themselves; they enjoy hearing their estate nicknamed the "Paint Box Colony"—a newspaper reporter gave currency to a local joke—and they compare the garden suburb they live in, not unkindly, to their children's cardboard villages. They realize that an estate consisting mainly of small houses needs to present an innocent and cheerful scene to the beholder, devoid of grand architectural gesture.

PART TWO

WORLD WAR I AND THE CITY

9

CITY IN CRISIS

The outbreak of World War I was greeted with a great upsurge of nationalist fervor in Germany. As Thomas Mann wrote to his brother in August 1914: "Shouldn't we be grateful for the totally unexpected chance to experience such mighty things? My chief feeling is of tremendous curiosity—and, I admit it, the deepest sympathy for this execrated, indecipherable, fateful Germany, which, if she has hitherto not unqualifiedly held 'civilization' as the highest good, is at any rate prepared to smash the most despicable police state in the world."[1] Nowhere was this enthusiasm for demolishing the British Empire and its allies more marked than on the streets of the capital city, Berlin. The celebrated Danish actress Asta Nielsen describes the mood on Unter den Linden on August 3, 1914:

> The streets of Berlin were like an agitated sea of people. Troops marched to the front in endless columns to the strains of music and with flowers on their bayonets. Women in tears clung on to the arms of the soldiers and tramped along to the death march as long as they could. *"Deutschland über alles"* resounded from every throat. One heard men's husky voices roar out: *"Gott strafe England!"* ... The city was transformed into a boiling witch's cauldron. Stones flew into the windows of the English embassy, and the splinters of glass clattered down upon the furious, screaming crowd below. Mounted police forced the masses down Unter den Linden. One screamed because the others screamed, one trampled others in order not to get trampled down oneself.[2]

The battle between an aristocratic and cultured German civilization and crass Anglo-Saxon materialism had been a recurring theme in the ultranationalist stirrings of the late nineteenth century. It was typified by Heinrich von Treitschke's famous observation that the British confused soap and civilization, and by Julius Langbehn's characterization of the noble, German spirit as the *Rembrandtdeutsche*. Langbehn's arguments were tailor-made for recycling as wartime propaganda, and it is unsurprising to find the *Rembrandtdeutsche* cited at length in the yearbook produced by the Insel publishing company in 1916, assuring its readership: "As an aristocrat ... the German already dominates Europe; as a democrat America, too. It will perhaps not take too long until the German as a man dominates the world. ... The German is destined to constitute the aristocracy of the world."[3] This struggle, between culture and civilization on one hand and materialist and capitalist greed on the other, however, had serious implications for Berlin, which was seen by many Germans as the epicenter of ruthless entrepreneurism, vulgarity, easy money, empty modishness, press sensationalism, and Jewish intellectualism—in short, all those qualities that were under attack by the prophets of the aristocratic German spirit.

In his standard work on these prophets, *The Politics of Cultural Despair*, Fritz Stern repeatedly cites the antagonism of the ideologues of the nationalist right against the city of Berlin and all it stood for. Paul de Lagarde, for example, described Berlin in 1866 as that "big and loathsome city," which he had grown to hate; Langbehn argued that "spiritually and politically, the provinces should be maneuvered and marshaled against the capital," while fellow reactionary Moeller van den Bruck damned Berlin as "essentially the ugliest city there is."[4] Doubtless with criticisms like these ringing in his ears, the great defender of Berlin, Karl Scheffler, proposed in 1910 a utopian vision of Berlin in which the city would play a key role in reconciling the inventiveness and audacity of North America with the stable, historical values of old Germany, thus uniting the realism of the Americas with the cultural conscience of Europe. More realistically, however, he concluded in reality that "as the capital city of the new-German materialism, Berlin will become even more powerful than it already is: but it can never, in the highest sense, be the spiritual capital of Germany."[5]

The commercial prosperity of Berlin was not to last, however, as the impact of the war on the German economy led to shortages of labor and raw materials in industry, and food and coal rationing for the civil population. In crass contrast to the luxurious café life enjoyed by wide sections of the Berlin population pre-1914, the Charlottenburg municipal authorities declared on 25 March 1915: "Yeast, baking powder, and similar may not be used for the preparation of cakes."[6] More seriously, in the monthly reports of the president of the Berlin Police from 1915, a potato shortage was noted in February, the lack of margarine and higher fruit prices in June, and restrictions on the supply of milk, petroleum, and coke in September. In March 1917, the police president described a demonstration by housewives at the Charlottenburg Town Hall, demanding access to the store of turnips, while the October report of same year concluded that even Field Marshall Hindenburg's birthday "had not succeeded in smoothing away or even reducing the discontent that prevails in broad sections of the population."[7]

Following the Russian Revolution of October 1917 and Lenin's Decree of Peace, organized labor in Germany became markedly more militant in its antiwar stance, culminating in industrial unrest and a national strike in Germany early in 1918. Berlin, home of the radical communist Spartacus group, was the epicenter of this unrest, and some four hundred thousand workers downed tools in the city on 28 January 1918. In the same month, President Woodrow Wilson, with his Fourteen Points, offered peace with honor to Germany. The German response was Ludendorff's ultimately unsuccessful spring offensive, which decimated the German reserves and opened the way for the decisive Allied counterattack, spearheaded by a decisive victory on 8 August when British and French infantry, supported by over four hundred tanks, overwhelmed the forward German divisions east of Amiens. German defeat was now inevitable, and the impact on the civilian population at home was predictably devastating. As one Berliner wrote in his diary: "End of August in Berlin. Virtually everything has changed. Immense impact of the reversals on the front. Those who were formerly the most vocal are now those trembling the most. Double fear of the bourgeoisie. Revolution and defeat. Everyone is speaking of the former, apart from the Social Democrats; no one dares to talk of the latter—and even the most realistic have no idea what it means. Everything terribly sad."[8]

To the terrors of defeat and revolution came the further horror of Spanish influenza, which appeared in Germany in the spring of 1918 and peaked in October and November, in tandem with the military collapse and the German Revolution. The statistics are inexact, but some 250,000 Germans are thought to have died of the pandemic flu in 1918 and 1919, with the civil population, paradoxically, hit harder than the military, and women more vulnerable than men.[9]

Together with Chicago, Berlin was one of the world's most dynamic and prosperous cities in 1900. By the end of 1918, wartime deprivation, military defeat, and the total collapse of the old order had reduced it to a city of fear and starvation, with armed insurrectionists fighting on the city streets. It is not mere coincidence that Oswald Spengler's enormously influential book *Der Untergang des Abendlandes* (*The Decline of the West*) was first published in 1918; in it he proposes a sequence of urban growth and decline that seemed, at the time, to sum up the history of Berlin: "This, then, is the conclusion of the city's history; growing from primitive barter center to culture city and at last to world city, it sacrifices first the blood and soul of its creators to the needs of its majestic evolution, and then the last flower of that growth to the spirit of civilization—and so, doomed, moves on to final self-destruction."[10]

NOTES

1. Thomas Mann to Heinrich Mann, 7 August 1914, *The Letters of Thomas Mann,* trans. Richard and Clara Winston (Harmondsworth, UK: Penguin, 1975), p. 67.
2. Asta Nielsen, *Den tiende muse* (Copenhagen: Gyldendal, 1945); published in German as *Die schweigende Muse,* trans. from the Danish by H. Georg Kemlein (Berlin: Henschelverlag, 1977); quoted in *Berliner Leben, 1914–1918: Eine Historische Reportage aus Erinnerungen und Berichten,* ed. Dieter Glatzer and Ruth Glatzer (Berlin: Rütten & Loening, 1983), p. 50.
3. Julius Langbehn, *Der Rembrandtdeutsche* (1890); quoted in *Insel Almanach auf das Jahr 1916* (Leipzig: Insel, 1916), pp. 171, 172.
4. See Fritz Stern, *The Politics of Cultural Despair* (Berkeley: University of California Press, 1974), pp. 15, 130, and 186, respectively.
5. Karl Scheffler, *Berlin: Ein Stadtschicksal* (1910; reprint, Berlin: Fannei & Walz, 1989), p. 216.
6. "Verordnung über die Einschränkung des Kuchenbackens, 25. March 1915"; quoted in *Deutschland im Ersten Weltkrieg,* ed. Ulrich Cartarius (Munich: Deutscher Taschenbuch Verlag, 1982), p. 69.
7. "Berichte des Berliner Polizeipräsidenten," 23 March 1917 and 22 October 1917; quoted in Cartarius, *Deutschland im Ersten Weltkrieg,* pp. 276, 295. On the Charlottenburg Town Hall, see above, text 77: Max Creutz, Charlottenburg Town Hall.
8. Kurt Riezler, diary entry, 13 September 1918; quoted in Cartarius, *Deutschland im Ersten Weltkrieg,* p. 314.
9. See Marc Hieronimus, *Krankheit und Tod, 1918: Zum Umgang mit der spanischen Grippe in Frankreich, England und dem Deutschen Reich* (Berlin: LIT Verlag, 2006), p. 9: "the macabre joke told at the time [November 1918] was that God had invented the new plague to even out war's imbalance between the sexes."
10. Oswald Spengler, *The Decline of the West,* trans. Charles Francis Atkinson, vol. 2 (London: George Allen & Unwin, 1928), p. 107.

96

Bruno Taut

A NECESSITY

First published as "Eine Notwendigkeit," *Der Sturm* 4, nos. 196/97 (February 1914), pp. 174–75. Translated by David Britt.

It is a joy to live in our time; and anyone who cannot feel this is beyond help. An intensity has taken hold of artists, in all the arts: a religiosity that refuses to content itself with vague impulses but aspires to create forms that are subject to laws of their own. Sculpture and painting find themselves on paths of pure synthesis and abstraction, and everywhere the talk is of the construction of images. This term rests on an architectural conception of the image: a conception that is not to be taken simply as a metaphor but corresponds to an architectural idea in the plain sense of the term. A secret architecture runs through all of these works and holds them together; very much as in the Gothic age. In the same way, the Gothic cathedral embraces all those artists who were filled with the idea of a wondrous unity and who found their resonant, universal rhythm in the architecture of the cathedral fabric.

Architecture seeks to join this new endeavor. In its best exponents architecture, too, is filled with a new and profound intensity. Architecture, too, in great works that rise above purely utilitarian requirements, seeks expression and a resonant rhythm and dynamism. And the same tendency, with the same intensity, finds expression through the simplest and most utilitarian structures, in the striving for the greatest simplicity imaginable and in the elevation of primitive form to symbolic status. Here, again, there is an affinity with the Gothic mentality, which in its major works infuses structure with passion and at the same time pursues in practical and economic terms the very simplest and most expressive solution. In this, there lies a degree of intense concern with construction that far transcends the complacent classical ideal of harmony. For the new architect, the materials of glass, steel, and concrete are the means whereby he achieves this intensity, transcending the architecture of mere material and function.

In the new art there lies a necessity, which this conjunction of architecture, painting, and sculpture must consummate. Modern architects will work creatively and—in a higher sense—traditionally only by acknowledging the necessity of this conjunction. Architecture is Cubist by its very nature, and it would be perverse to use, for instance, exclusively angular forms. For the paintings of a [Fernand] Léger combine the angular and the soft within themselves. The architect must beware of taking this conjunction superficially and thus misunderstanding it. He must absorb all possible architectural forms within his own creative scope—just as they find expression in the witty and inspired compositions of [Wassily] Kandinsky. The reason is that architecture, if its productions are to last, must face up to all possible combinations of circumstances (artistic, constructional, social, and financial). The functions of the frame are not the same as those of the painting. Furthermore, the architect must recognize that by its nature architecture already carries within itself the very quality that the new painting has achieved: freedom from perspective and from all restriction to a single viewpoint. The buildings of the great ages of architecture were devised in the absence of perspective; those that are the productions of perspective are so many set pieces.

It is a fine thing, and for us architects an exceptionally fruitful thing, to be aware of this connectedness. But something tangible must also happen: the ideal architecture that is already visible in the new art must eventually manifest itself in a visible building. And it is a necessity that this must happen.

Together let us work on building a magnificent edifice! An edifice that is not architecture alone: one in which everything—painting, sculpture, all together—forms one great architecture, and in which architecture in its turn is subsumed within the other arts. Here architecture must be both frame and content, all at once. This will be an edifice that needs no purely practical function. Architecture, too, can emancipate itself from utilitarian demands. A modern collection would furnish the pretext for creating a space for the custodianship of works of art, together with an adjacent hall that can serve any possible artistic purpose. A simple architectural organism is set up, on open land close to the metropolis, so that it can assert itself, externally as well as internally, as an artistic organism. The building must contain spaces to accommodate the characteristic phenomena of the new art: [Robert] Delaunay's compositions of light in vast stained-glass windows; on the walls the rhythms of Cubism, the painting of a Franz Marc, and the art of Kandinsky. The pillars, outside and inside, will stand in readiness for the soaring structural sculptures of [Alexander] Archipenko. The ornament will be by [Heinrich] Campendonk. This list of contributing artists is not intended to be exhaustive. All must work as independent creators—as is entirely possible within an architectural organism—so that the whole may constitute a single, all-embracing, magnificent harmony. This would be the necessary step that must be taken in order to rescue the arts from the servitude of the salons, to which current practice and aesthetics have hitherto confined them. All talk of "applied arts" in modern art would thereby cease of its own accord.

The building need not be completed all at once. No harm will be done if some of its individual parts are not complete within a generation.

All idea of social purpose must be avoided. The whole must present itself as exclusive—just as great art always starts by existing only within the artist. The people may then spontaneously use the art to educate themselves, or else they may wait upon the coming of their educators.

97

Vorwärts

[WAR OR NOT]

First published in *Vorwärts*, 26 July 1914. Translated by Iain Boyd Whyte.

The imperial capital has seldom seen such a vision as it did yesterday evening. Thousands upon thousands, especially in the center and in the Friedrichstadt, waited on the streets and squares for the latest news on the Austrian–Serbian conflict. The air was pregnant with the wildest rumors. The frightful question was planted on everyone's lips: has war already been declared? Is the die cast? The special newspaper editions were simply ripped out of the hands of their sellers, and over many a single page five, six, or more faces hung, all greedy to devour the meager text.

The more time passed, all the more did tempers run high. With feverish tension, everyone braced themselves for the coming events. Everything else paled into insignificance except this question: war or not? This question was discussed heatedly in cafés, on the street—wherever people came together. In front of the newspaper offices long lines of the anxiously curious were to be found, who stood stationary, like bronze statues, as if stuck for hours on end. Some of them looked on, pale and gloomy. "When it starts, seven members of my family will also have to go as well, and I have four small children," one declared. A somber bitterness, like that emanating from these words, gripped many thousands yesterday evening.

98
General Gustav von Kessel
BERLIN IN A STATE OF WAR: PROCLAMATION OF THE COMMANDER-IN-CHIEF IN THE MARCHES

First published as "Berlin im Kriegszustand: Bekanntmachung des Oberbefehlshabers in den Marken," *Berliner Tageblatt: Wochenausgabe für Ausland und Übersee* 3, no. 32 (6 August 1914), p. 5. Translated by Iain Boyd Whyte.

By sovereign edict, a state of war is declared for Berlin and the Province of Brandenburg.

Executive authority is thus passed to me. With regard to this, I am hereby suspending articles 5, 6, 27, 28, 29, 30, and 36 of the Constitution of 31 January 1850 for the areas declared above to be in a state of war until further notice, and decree the following:

a) The civil and local authorities retain their functions but must obey my orders and instructions.

b) House searches and arrests may be undertaken at any time by the authorized agencies and state officials.

c) All aliens who are unable to give a proper account of the purpose of their sojourn must leave the area declared to be in a state of war within twenty-four hours when ordered by the local police.

d) The sale of arms, gunpowder, and explosives to civilians is forbidden. Civilians may carry arms only when specifically permitted to do so by myself or by the local police. Whoever does this without such permission will be immediately disarmed.
[. . .]

The love of fatherland, which has always marked out the citizens of Berlin and the March of Brandenburg, and the patriotic enthusiasm that has shown itself in these earnest days, give the certain guarantee that no one will by lacking in patriotism in the serious times that we are approaching.
[. . .]

I am certain that the population of Berlin and of the Province of Brandenburg will support the civil and military authorities gladly and with all its might. In this way we can all contribute to helping the army accomplish its great national duty. Then the army will also maintain and magnify military renown, and will emerge victorious before the eyes of the Kaiser and of the German nation.

Commander in Chief Mark Brandenburg
and Governor of Berlin, General von Kessel

99
H. B.
[WAR FEVER, BERLIN, AUGUST 1914]

First published in *Berliner Tageblatt: Wochenausgabe für Ausland und Übersee* 3, no. 32 (6 August 1914), p. 5. Translated by Iain Boyd Whyte.

These days remind one of the great moments of the German Reich, of the days of great decision, when the final word on the destiny of the nation was spoken in the gray palace on the River Spree. Nothing was to be heard of the noisy turmoil, which, without justification, had particularly taken hold of Berlin's youth on the Saturday and Sunday before last.

[. . .]

At five o'clock on Friday afternoon, the proclamations and warnings about the state of war were pasted to the advertising pillars, advising Berlin's inhabitants of the German government's first step toward war. From this moment on, the gravity of the moment sunk in for thinking, sensitive souls, and silence descended on the singing, which a few days earlier had swelled up in a thousand-voiced choir at each and every opportunity.

Berlin now had it in black and white. The news was not taken home cheerfully, but with a heavy seriousness. And when evening came and the city lights flared up in their thousands, broad columns of people streamed toward the old main boulevard of Berlin [Unter den Linden], which has always been the center of activity in times of crisis. Here, where every stone tells a story of the sorrows and joys of the German Empire, enthusiastic crowds will someday witness the return of our victorious troops, and tearful women and children walk alongside their breadwinners and protectors as they set out for the uncertain destiny of the battlefield.

There may have been two hundred thousand people outside the palace that evening. The estimation of such a mass is almost impossible, even for the expert. The dark wall of people stood in the Lustgarten in rows some 150 deep, and nearly 120 of these rows were jammed beside each other. Songs swelled up and soared into the darkness that lay over the palace. People waved their hats in the air, and rousing cheers were sent up at rhythmic intervals to the windows behind which they assumed the Kaiser was to be found. The Kaiser, however, exactly in these tumultuous hours between seven and nine, had gone to the Bellevue Palace to attend the marriage of his son. But then, when he had returned from the solemn ceremony, a feeling of confident strength and happy, nervous excitement broke through, and the cheers and supportive shouts went on and on.

The hours passed quickly, and the darkness fell. But the people still formed a solid wall in front of the palace, and a three-part stream of humanity surged up and down Unter den Linden. Motorcars and countless wagons roared among the crowd. The farther the stream rolled toward Friedrichstrasse, the louder it got as it increased in strength and agitation. At this intersection, saturated in the light from the many roofs and gable ends, the crowd divided. Thousands turned for home, to make room for the thousands who had arrived later.

[. . .]

Berlin is in a state of war! These words weigh more heavily than many now seem to think. Of course, they carry confidence, strength, and the knowledge of a just cause. But the war that is now pounding so loudly at the gates will be difficult, and its path accompanied by sorrow. And for this reason in Berlin, too, the passionate hope is rising that the disaster for our country might be avoided in the final hours.

100

Berliner Tageblatt

[BERLIN POTATO SHORTAGE]

First published in *Berliner Tageblatt,* 17 February 1915. Translated by Iain Boyd Whyte.

For many weeks now there have been no potatoes in the individual suburban districts, neither in grocery stores nor in the markets. And some housewives—especially since the imposition of the law on the limitation in the use of bread—looked with concern at the small store in their cellar as it diminished from day to day. What would happen when it was finally exhausted? For this reason, therefore, the large red poster on which the Schöneberg City Council announced for yesterday and subsequent days the opening of a city sale of potatoes was greeted like a salvation. It priced the potatoes at 3.90 marks per metric hundredweight and declared that, given the current situation, each person should receive only half that amount.

[. . .]

The Schöneberg population—men, women, children of all ages with wagons and carts of all descriptions—stood in the thousands in front of the long wooden planks that surrounded the city's store yard in the Rubensstrasse. After waiting

FIGURE 26. Street kitchen, Berlin, 1916. Landesarchiv Berlin, II 7 187.

for many hours, the small wooden gateway was finally opened, and the excited crowd stormed inside in wild disarray. But wait! The first disappointment already approached. It was necessary to bring one's last tax receipt in order to prove that one was also really a Schöneberg citizen. Many were wise enough and had brought the small, vital receipt, but many, many others had to return home disappointed and complaining. And so there emerged around two o'clock in the afternoon in the neighboring streets a flood of angry people surging incessantly back and forth.

101

Anonymous

COMPETITION FOR GREATER BERLIN ARCHITECTS

First published as "Wettbewerb für Groß-Berlins Architekten," *Der Städtebau* 1 (1916); reprinted in *Berliner Leben, 1914–1918: Eine historische Reportage aus Erinnerungen und Berichten,* ed. Dieter Glatzer and Ruth Glatzer (Berlin: Rütten & Loening, 1983), pp. 201–2. Translated by David Frisby.

A section of the Volkspark in the Wuhlheide is to be transformed into a heroes' grove, and in it a square of roughly five hectares is to be created as an assembly place for celebratory meetings . . . Plans should be drawn up for cable masts on the overhead wires of electric streetcars, lamps for street lighting, for clock mountings, street fountains, telephone boxes, stalls to sell milk and newspapers, for a public lavatory, for waiting rooms at a busy streetcar intersection, and for a refreshment booth in a park. The prizes made available amount to ten thousand marks together. Submission date is 15 March 1916.

102

Berliner Tageblatt
DEMONSTRATION IN BERLIN, NOVEMBER 1918

First published in *Berliner Tageblatt*, 9 November 1918. Translated by Iain Boyd Whyte.

With reference to the precipitous events, the reports are here reproduced in the order they were received:

Ten o'clock: Workers in all factories of the Allgemeine-Elektricitätsgesellschaft [AEG] have downed tools. The commercial offices have been closed by the administration. On the Brunnenstrasse, a procession of several thousand workers formed who, beneath unfurled flags, demonstrated for an immediate declaration of peace.

Ten thirty: In Moabit, striking workers have persuaded the streetcar drivers to leave their wagons standing still. Where the drivers have not complied with this request, the streetcar wagons have been turned over and the electric supply wires cut through. At the same time a procession of around fifteen thousand workers advanced from the north of the city to the center. Soldiers carried large posters upon which was written: "Freedom! Peace! Bread! Brothers, don't shoot—come and join us!"

Eleven thirty: The streetcar wagons suddenly stop and form long queues. We soon learn that the strikers had been partially successful in disrupting the electrical current . . . Only on isolated lines are the streetcars still working. At the present time, the streetcar controllers are considering measures to bring the whole streetcar traffic to a standstill.

Twelve o'clock: Up to now, reports on worker stoppages have come in from the following factories: Daimlerwerke Marienfelde, Geschossfabrik von Otto Jochmann Borsigwalde, Silexwerke, almost all factories in Weißensee, Knorr-Bremse AG, Stock & Co. in Mariendorf, Fritz Werner Aktiengesellschaft Mariendorf, Siemens & Halske, Argus-Motorenfabrik in Reinickendorf.

At the close of our edition, we also learn that work has stopped at the following factories: Borsig, Akkumulatorenfabrik-Oberschöneweide, Mix & Genest, G.u.C. Krausser & Co. Neukölln.

The Berlin Town Hall [Rathaus] is occupied by armed security people. Since yesterday afternoon the main chamber of the town hall has been occupied by the police. The huge courtyard of the town hall is like a war depot. Here the mounted

Berlin Police has assembled in large numbers. On the tower of the town hall several defense posts have been erected; they wave with red cloths to the huge crowd assembled on the Königstrasse. The crowd returns the greetings with enthusiasm. The office workers in the town hall continue to go quietly about their business.

Twelve thirty: Since around ten o'clock in the morning, troops of striking workers have been on the move from the southern suburbs, some toward the edge of the city, and others, who have also been joined by soldiers, assembled into larger formations and moved toward the inner city. On the Invalidenstrasse, by the barracks of the Gardefusiliers, large demonstrations took place. It is reported that shots were fired and that some of the streetcars were damaged.

A huge crowd moved up and down Unter den Linden. Large groups formed themselves around soldiers who identified themselves as members of the Workers' and Soldiers' Councils and delivered speeches. Patrols of soldiers very politely seek to disperse the crowd. The main telegraph office on the Französische Strasse and the main post office on the Spandauer Strasse are protected by the military. The streetcar lines that are still operating carry a veritable storm of passengers out of the city.

Quarter to one: the whole area around the Schloss is closed off. The entrances to the Schloss are occupied by the military, who permit no access to pedestrians.

The Reichsmarineamt [Imperial Naval Ministry] is particularly heavily guarded. All the surrounding bridges that lead over the canal, the exits to the Bendlerstrasse, the Hohenzollernstrasse, the Friedrich-Wihelm-Strasse, and suchlike are fortified with machine-gun posts and troops. The people who live on these streets study the battle plan drawn up for the defense of the Reichsmarineamt with very mixed feelings.

103

Friedrich Bauermeister

ON THE GREAT CITY

First published as "Von der Großstadt" in *Tätiger Geist!: Zweites der Ziel-Jahrbücher*, ed. Kurt Hiller (Munich and Berlin: Müller, 1918), pp. 294–300. Translated by Michael Loughridge.

Never until now, at the end of a year living elsewhere, have I perceived the great city as being in essence absurd. It is true that I always had dim intimations of that kind, but I lacked the opposing perspective that would give a basis for judgment. Now at last I have looked ahead to the future. To declare that I feel unhappy would be to exaggerate. But my will is directed, with daily greater intensity, to a great future city that will be meaningful. I still love the great city. In the great city that was my home I grew up, never leaving it for long. For two decades, my life took its course on weekdays between stone walls, in the noise from city traffic, and on

Sundays under trees, on the fields and riverbanks, out where the sounds of the city are barely heard. If I had the poetic gift, I could give form to all the beauty that those living outside cannot imagine because it is purely of the city—and I could shape it from my own resources, for I have been absorbing that beauty into myself for years. I know myself to be dead when I am not able to live in the city. I can understand those who abhor the great city, because they belong to the petit-bourgeois milieu of small provincial towns—but I cannot love such people. For me they do not count; they are not my brothers. And I know that they for their part do not even understand me.

[. . .]

I need not trouble to repeat the shallow stuff with which schools have kept bombarding us ad nauseam, debasing the words of great thinkers—to the effect that prosperity is the prerequisite of culture. No, I say, and even were the great cities poor, were they wretched, starving huddles of slums, harboring stench and pestilence, it is still here, here alone and par excellence, that the Spirit could glow white-hot, their suffering would be the fuel for its flame to leap high, burning away all the dross and all the torment and clearing the space for paradise. We must demand paradise, build it step-by-step, perfect it; only the unresting Spirit can take us to that place where physical and metaphysical agony are no more—only that Spirit that in its ecstasy sees the goal ahead; that, seeing the goal, storms forward; that is unceasingly on the move; that insists on the tempo that only great cities know.

[. . .]

It would be possible to imagine a great city that had no tenement blocks, only separate houses. And it is not inconceivable either that one day, whether as a result of planned demolition and reconstruction or as a result of a propaganda-induced general flight from the tenements, such a garden province might be born. But there is a snag: even with the modern garden-city practice of joining houses in terraces, the amount of land taken up by individual houses is always going to exceed that needed for the compromised, denser settlements based on apartment blocks. The corollary: highly developed transport facilities, carrying us speedily and cheaply from the metropolis to the outlying townships and from these townships back into the heart of the metropolis. That would enable the city worker living in the township to grow closer once more to nature to become familiar with fields and woods through daily contact. I do not imagine that every individual would become a cultivator of farmland or garden land—though I would have no fault to find with any that did. I would not want the comforts of civilization, drainage, community cooperation, and the like to be abolished. But a number of benefits currently derived from economic division of labor and from heavy consumption would certainly disappear. The city's public amenities would be less utilized and consequently less economic to run. On the other hand, we could well dispense with a few other benefits of civilization forced upon us by the big city. Who would shed a tear for asphalt roadways if they were to vanish from all but the principal thoroughfares? Who would mourn for the elevator, or for the marble-clad stairwell? In sum, we will in no way become rural peasants: we will remain inhabitants of the metropolis, or rather, it may even be said, we would truly become metropolitans only if we could one day find that difficult path that leads between wasteland on the one side and superficiality on the other. That would break the dominance of the democratic argument. Industrialism and the labor mentality will have no place in the true and ideal metropolis. That means that decentralizing the metropolis must also involve separating it from the working city: sending industry out to the countryside; transplanting whole enterprises with their workforces; creating new settlements; bringing industry and agriculture economically closer to one another; integrating the world of work.

Yet on the other hand we also need a differentiation; this economic and spatial decentralization needs to be balanced by a more intense concentration of our intellectual and spiritual life. Historically, the cities were above all the seats of the clerical and political power from which commerce and—very hesitantly—industry sought protection and patronage. We do not seek to turn back the clock. We do not lament over the good attributes of former times and the present decadence. But we do deplore the fact that in our day it is no longer mind and spirit that dominate, but industry, and we seek a metropolis whose intellectual leadership will make itself more felt than has ever happened in history before. Here the artist, the scholar, the statesman will reside. Young people, their preparatory phase of unharried isolation behind them, awakened now to the active life, will here fight their battles, will make their impact on the life around them, drive it on, knock it forward. All the hot blood coursing in a nation's veins will meet centrally in the metropolis. Whereas in our day the community—guardian and continuing source of all stable and healthy life—is still obliged to sequester itself away from the bustle of the metropolis, to quit its true home, in that future time it will have no alternative but to remain in the metropolis and there develop and flower to its full potential. In that day, the metropolis of the future will have become the dwelling place of the Spirit, the altar at which we serve God.

104

Walter Gropius

THE NEW ARCHITECTURAL IDEA

First published as "Der neue Baugedanke," *Das hohe Ufer* 1, no. 4 (April 1919), pp. 87–88. Translated by David Britt.

What is architecture? Surely, the crystalline expression of human beings' noblest thoughts, their fervor, their humanity, their faith, their religion! It once was all these things. But who, of all those living in our accursed age of expediency, still comprehends its all-encompassing, beatific nature? We walk down our streets and through our cities, and do we not weep for shame at such deserts of ugliness! Let us be clear about one thing. The gray, hollow, mindless shams in which we live and work will reveal to posterity the mental hell into which our generation descended when it forgot the one great and only art: building. Let us not imagine, in our European arrogance, that the pitiful architectural exploits of our own day can in any way palliate the bleak desolation of the overall picture. All our works are but fragments. Forms that satisfy function and necessity cannot still the longing for a world of beauty, new-built from the very foundations, and for the rebirth of the spiritual unity that accomplished the miracle of the Gothic cathedrals. We shall not experience that unity again. One consolation remains to us; and that is the *idea*. To construct an architectural idea—bold, incandescent, far in advance of its time—that will surely find fulfillment in a happier age to come. Artists, let us cast down the walls that our delusive scholastic wisdom has erected to separate the "Arts," and *let us all once more be builders!* Let us work *together* to decide, devise, and create the new architectural idea. Painters and sculptors, break through the barriers that separate you from architecture, and turn fellow builders, comrades-in-arms, for art's ultimate cause: the creative conception of the Cathedral of the Future, which will once more be everything in a single form: architecture *and* sculpture *and* painting.

But ideas die when they turn into compromises. Clear watersheds, therefore, between dream and reality, between celestial longings and everyday work. Architects, sculptors, painters—we must all go back to craftsmanship! For there *is* no such thing as "professional art." Artists are artisans, manual workers in the true sense of the term. Only in rare moments of grace and illumination, beyond the control of the individual will, can the work of their hands blossom, all unawares, into art. Painters and sculptors, become artisans, too: smash the salon frames around your images; go into buildings, give them the benediction of fairy tales in color, carve ideas into the bare walls, and *build* in your imagination, undismayed by technical difficulties. Imagination is more important than technique, which always submits to the human creative will. As yet, there *is* no such thing as an architect; we are all merely *harbingers,* preparing the way of the one who will one day earn the name of architect. For this word in itself means Lord of Art: he who will turn deserts into gardens and will build wondrous, heaven-ascending towers.

105

Leopold Bauer

THE ECONOMIC UNSUSTAINABILITY OF THE LARGE CITY

First published as "Die Unwirtschaftlichkeit der Großstadt," *Der Bauinteressent* 26, no. 32 (9 May 1919), pp. 251–52; no. 33 (16 May 1919), pp. 259–60. Translated by Iain Boyd Whyte.

Because it cannot adjust to the demands of the age, the organism of the great city is becoming progressively an extraordinarily costly and uneconomic element in our national economy. The nonspecialist generally has only a limited understanding of the monstrous amounts of energy and materials that have to be wasted in order to make the life of the large city possible. For this reason, the large cities have become the instigators and flashpoints of the social revolution that we are currently experiencing; for all the defects of the social structure are intensified and greatly magnified in the context of the large city.

The new order of human society that is now beginning to unfold must, therefore, assert a profound influence on city building if it really wants to banish from the world one of the main evils of the old order—namely, the planning and design of the large cities, which was as unpractical as it was unhealthy. Basically, we have simply extended and adapted the old urban patterns as they have been handed down to us from the Middle Ages and from the Age of Absolutism, ignoring the fact that the impact of technology on all forms of work must also have a decisive impact on the housing problem.

In addition to the right to a living wage, everyone also has the right to live in a healthy and natural manner. In rural conditions these demands are easily met. Even the most modest artisan has his own little house or an apartment with a garden. A large percentage of all the workers engaged on the land have access to a garden plot, however modest, or even a small field. And however meager the house, its inhabitants will be incomparably more content that the residents of a rental barracks in the city, as nature has not entirely disappeared from his life, and its myriad wonders are still able to affect his soul. It is not easy for someone to live in constant discord with himself and the world around when the fruit trees are blooming in his garden and when he can enjoy each day the growth of the vegetables that he has planted on his own scrap of ground. For this reason, people who live on the land are well known to be more conservative, as the politicians put it—or, as I would rather say, more content. To attempt with all the means at our disposal to regain the great joy of contentment is one of the most important tasks facing the leaders of the nation. Never before has greed and covetousness reached such a high level as at present; never before was the culture of millennia under such constant threat of destruction through discontent and hatred. The foundation of a happy and comfortable existence for each individual is given by the ownership of a healthy place to live for himself and his family. Only in this way can we hope that, in time, our stock will develop to be a healthy and cheerful species once again.

How should modern city planning achieve this foundation? Although we know the goal, it is now necessary to search honestly and thoroughly for the paths that will lead us to it.

One of the principal evils of the large city, as we now experience it, lies in the fact that colossal sums of money are necessary for its infrastructural and running costs, which, for various reasons, cannot be utilized in such a way that the inhabitants of the city can derive real benefits from it that are commensurate with the expense. This represents, of course, a monstrous waste. In the following, I will select only a few points from this area to show how this waste might be controlled.

[. . .]

The workplace—the factory—should, as already noted, always be integrated with housing areas to create, so to speak, an interdependent totality. Structures for food provision (cold-storage depots, glass houses for growing vegetables, and so on), as well as welfare institutions like baths, should be linked to factories, from which they would draw the necessary energy.

In the workers' state that we want to create in some form or other, the factory is the most characteristic building and, for that reason, justifiably lays claim to be regarded as the center of the surrounding urban area. The factory means the same for the modern metropolis as the temple precinct did for antiquity and the cathedral for the medieval cityscape. And as the working class has won such a dominant political position, this significance should be reflected in the building of their workplaces. Over the last decade, the artistic problems related to factory building became known to us. For a long time we have been searching for the new building style appropriate to the age, and are surprised that we do not find it easy to achieve with domestic buildings, churches, castles, and palaces. For the origins of all these building types are not rooted in the present, and their external appearance is associated in our imagination with fixed, traditional notions of form. The factory, in contrast, is a child of the present, which rests on no specific tradition. For that reason, we do not particularly miss the reference to a previous building form in the context of the factory. The factory alone is in a position to help us develop the new building style that we are hankering after, the style that is at least characteristic of our own epoch.

I have no misgivings, therefore, on either practical or artistic grounds, about proposing that in the design of new city quarters, a factory or similar industrial plant should be placed at the center of the planned housing area, with the housing for public servants and workers grouped around it. This sort of development must not in any way have the character of our present suburban streets. Rather, each person living there would have the right to own a small parcel of land on which to make the garden of his choice. As a result, the monumental factory building would be surrounded by a sort of garden city—the absolute opposite of the desolate workers' quarters that we are used to today.

10

CRITICAL RESPONSES

As Georg Simmel noted at the very start of the twentieth century: "With each crossing of the street, with the tempo and multiplicity of economic, occupational, and social life, the city sets up a deep contrast with small-town and rural life with reference to the sensory foundations of psychic life."[1] When, for reasons of war, or famine, or pestilence—or all three—the city becomes a site of fear and danger, the instinctive reaction is to flee, either intellectually or physically, into the safe environment of the land, the countryside, and the small town. This is precisely the condition that prevailed in Berlin during the war years 1914–18.

In the decade leading up to the war, the calls for a return to the land became ever stronger, and were institutionalized with the establishment of the German Garden City Association (Deutsche Gartenstadtgesellschaft) in 1902. The romantic pull of the land and of the soil was brutally reinforced by the food shortages that were already becoming apparent in Berlin and in the other German cities by the early months of 1915. As hunger became a dominant factor in urban life, the calls to the city dweller to grow as much food as possible wherever it was possible became louder. Indeed, growing fruit and vegetables on small city plots was hailed by the authorities as important war work in a proclamation of February 1917, which urged: "You, who work in small gardens! In the two years of war you have proven and shown that you can and will play your part. It is now vital that you persevere: do not sleep or rest or idle, but rather be a shining example for all those who are not yet part of our enterprise. . . . So heed the good advice and work in this spirit! *Exploit to the full every tiny plot of soil!*"[2] This move, on a small scale, from the patterns of urban production and consumption to those of the countryside, was reflected at the level of the city in the calls for decentralization that first emerged during the war and that were reinforced by the poverty and desperation of the immediate postwar years. While architects like Peter Behrens and Hermann Muthesius had argued around 1910 for standardization and industrialization in the realms of architecture and industrial design, they now supported inexpensive housing in rural settings as the only means of regenerating German society.

The return to the soil, however, was accompanied by an insistence that the intellectual and spiritual life of the nation be nurtured in parallel with its physical well-being. Both arguments are to be found in the writings and designs of the Expressionist avant-garde. In his text *Die Stadtkrone* (The city crown), for example, the Berlin-based architect Bruno Taut proposed a radically new form of city—one that could serve both the material and spiritual demands of the community. To achieve this he argued for a clear delineation between the profane and the sacred dimensions of human existence. The housing in the ideal city, therefore, would be modeled on the simple cottage structures that Taut had built before the war at Falkenberg, in the Berlin suburbs, for the German Garden City Association. The monumental buildings in the city center, however, would support both the intellect—opera house, theater, library, meeting rooms—and the spirit, in a radiant glass structure that would encapsulate man's desire for brotherhood, social harmony, and innocent beauty. The modern equivalent of the Gothic cathedral, the glass temple would reflect its beneficent rays over the entire city, as a counterargument to the speculative housing and dark courtyards of Wilhelmine Berlin.

This heady mixture of urban design and utopian socialism was developed in a further publication by Taut with the self-explanatory title *Die Auflösung der Städte* (The dissolution of the cities), published in 1920. Once again, the target was the Berlin of 1900, with its pestilent housing and high mortality among the working classes. Urging the abandonment of the city, the first of Taut's annotated drawings contrasts small, petal-like settlements spread evenly across the land with the dense city fabric of Berlin, which he dubs "built vileness" (*gebaute Gemeinheiten*), adding that "houses of stone make hearts of stone."[3] (See figure 27.) Although Taut was located on the political left, very similar arguments appeared on the extreme right, often aimed at precisely the utopian tendencies in art and politics represented by Taut and his kind. Very typical is the complaint of Ludwig Finckh, a doctor, poet, and novelist, based in the Hegau in southern Germany, which was published in January 1919 at the height of the Spartacus uprising in Berlin: "A small minority in Berlin keeps the German people in suspense. What do they want? At bottom, nothing other than what the pacifists and cosmopolitans want: the worldwide brotherhood of peoples. . . . As peasants in their villages do not look beyond their district, become selfish, and pursue parish pump politics, so the Berliner is trapped within his four walls, dictating, setting the tone, believing that his and the German horizon are one. *But Berlin is not Germany.* Berlin is not even Prussia. . . . To the spirit of Berlin another must be opposed, *the spirit of Germany!*"[4]

The utopian building schemes of the Berlin-based, Expressionist avant-garde were conceived, however, as polemical gestures rather than as blueprints for construction. Although unbuilt and unbuildable in the early 1920s, they did have a lasting impact in Berlin when the powerful notions of community and of the socially regenerative power of architecture and city planning that had been nurtured in the Expressionist phantasies were given tangible form in the great estates built by the trade-union housing associations and the socialist city council toward the end of the decade. It is not mere coincidence that saw the dreamers of 1919 and 1920—Bruno and Max Taut, the brothers Hans and Wassili Luckhardt, and Hans Scharoun—emerge as Berlin's most inventive and productive house builders during the years of the Weimar Republic.

NOTES

1. Georg Simmel, "The Metropolis and Mental Life" (1903); republished in *Classic Essays on the Culture of Cities,* ed. Richard Sennett (Englewood Cliffs, N.J.: Prentice-Hall, 1969), p. 48.
2. "Der Kleingärtner als kriegswichtiger Faktor" (February 1917); quoted in *Deutschland im Ersten Weltkrieg,* ed. Ulrich Cartarius (Munich: Deutscher Taschenbuch Verlag, 1982), p. 73.
3. Bruno Taut, *Die Auflösung der Städte* (Hagen: Folkwang, 1920), pl. 1.
4. Ludwig Finckh, "Der Geist von Berlin," *Schwäbischer Merkur,* 10 January 1919.

106
Paul Wolf
THE BASIC LAYOUT OF THE NEW CITY

First published as "Die Grundform der neuen Stadt" in Wolf, *Städtebau: Das Formproblem der Stadt in Vergangenheit und Zukunft* (Leipzig: Klinkhardt & Biermann , 1919), pp. 85–93. Translated by Michael Loughridge.

The war has brought home to us, unforgettably, how important it is for a nation to be self-sufficient in foodstuffs. Back in the 1870s, Germany had a ratio of three self-sufficient individuals in the population to every one consumer. Now, however, for every single self-provider there are 3.8 consumers. That means there is a question that must now be faced. Is it possible—making use of all the advantages and nutrient value of artificial fertilizers, improving the quality of barren land, and so on—to increase output in livestock rearing and agriculture to a point where, even at unprecedented population levels, Germany will be able to provide for its own needs? Is this possible, and how is it to be done? It seems entirely conceivable that a forward-planning policy of this nature may be adopted in the not-too-distant future that would not only impose revolutionary changes on agriculture, but mean completely rethinking the whole question of housing provision and settlement. Agricultural experts consider that, given the maximum possible increase in output and the settlement policies essential to underpin it, Germany has the potential to provide animal-based and crop-based foodstuffs for a population of 90 to 100 million inhabitants. It would be necessary for the cities to greatly extend the scope of their present policy of incorporation, especially where the neighboring communities concerned are rural and agriculture based. In order to save manpower, it would be desirable in the early stages to develop the system of allotment land to the very fullest extent possible.

As a result of wartime food shortages, the magnetic attraction that the cities exerted on the masses over the last half century, like that of light for the moth, has been steadily waning in favor of a different preference, and it is a fairly safe prediction that the coming period of economic depression will make this change more and more emphatic. Given the present grossly excessive construction and installation costs involved in urban building, road making, and drainage provision, with no likelihood that such costs will come down significantly in the foreseeable future, there is little prospect that the housing shortage affecting all German cities can be resolved over the next few years using the hitherto customary methods. With wage levels as high as they are, there must be serious doubt as to whether German industry in the major cities can remain competitive in world markets in future. Yet there is no chance of wage reductions being imposed unless and until industrial workers experience a significant corresponding reduction in living costs, or alternatively are given access to a second job to bring in additional income. For either of these to be practicable, industrial workers will need to be accommodated in rural settlements, and every working family will need to be able to manage its own modest smallholding on at least 1,200 square meters of land. The eight-hour working day means that it will be easily possible for a working family to manage a plot of this size. The costs involved in providing and running a worker's house in a rural area will be lower than in the cities, as land is cheap and the provision of roads and sewerage also cheaper; consequently it will be possible to reduce the outlay involved in renting accommodation, which in the years before the war would absorb a quarter of the average big-city worker's income. Most important of all, food costs will be substantially reduced by having families provide for themselves.

It can be assumed that the overcrowding factor for urban housing is at present about 5 to 10 percent—that is, that for every one hundred thousand population there is a need for new accommodation provision for five to ten thousand people, or alternatively for the same number to be resettled. It seems to me that there are four routes by which this problem might be comprehensively solved:

1. By migration to the country or to country towns. In this case the main concern would be that those migrating from the cities should seek new sources of income, mainly in agricultural pursuits. In essence this would amount to a process of reverse migration involving the masses who made the journey

from the country to the cities in the same numbers during the second half of the last century.
2. By the migration of industrial workers from city to country and resettlement on the land with a role like that of the old *Ackerbürger* [smallholders of urban origin]; the parcels of land involved would be roughly 1 to 2 hectares in area and created by subdivision of big estates into many small properties, as was intended by the Reich government.
3. By the creation of rural settlements in the vicinity of cities; and
4. By creation of garden cities farther out in the countryside, on the model of Letchworth Garden City in England.[1]

[...]

All four of these routes seem practicable. Which will be taken must depend primarily on the future development of our industrial sector. The development of industry in Germany, the transformation from an agrarian to an industrial economy, has been stunted since the earliest days by our country's inability to produce its own industrial raw materials, which has meant in effect that the foundations of the whole structure are transplanted abroad. However, if a large proportion of industrial workers transfer to agriculture, and if industry is gradually adapted to work for the most part on home-produced raw materials, it seems distinctly possible that in the remote future, over the course of a number of generations, a degree of integration between city and country might come about and that Germany might be able to subsist largely independently of imports and exports.

NOTE

1. The world's first garden city was founded by Ebenezer Howard in Letchworth, Hertfordshire, in 1903.

107

Bruno Taut

THE CITY CROWN

First published as Taut, *Die Stadtkrone* (Jena: Diederichs, 1919), pp. 58–69. Translated by Iain Boyd Whyte.

RAISE A FLAG!

Today, as in the historic townscape, the highest, crowning ideals must be embodied in the religious building. The house of God will for all times be the building toward which we are always striving, which can carry our deepest sentiments about mankind and the world.

Why then in recent times, roughly since the high point of the Jesuit faith, has no great cathedral been built, or at least seriously planned? [Karl Friedrich] Schinkel's romantic character led him to a project for a great cathedral on Templower Berg near Berlin, driven by the urge finally to create something that would focus men's longings and hopes for community. Yet the suggestion found no resonance.[1]

[. . .]

The religious creed, it would seem, no longer has its old strength. No confessors, no fighters speak out on its behalf. That which once inspired great movements appears today, stripped of its dogma, to have retreated into individual experience and to be in the process of a complete transformation.

But faith still exists. It is unthinkable that millions of people, entirely enslaved to materialism, live from day to day without knowing the purpose of their existence. In every human breast there must live that quality that elevates the individual above temporal concerns and enables him to feel a communion with his contemporaries, his nation, with all mankind and with the entire world. Where is it? Is it melting away, too, or is there something—something new that is flowing into all mankind and waiting for its resurrection, its radiant transfiguration and crystallization in magnificent works of building? Without religion there is no true culture, no art. And should we, divided into isolated currents, simply vegetate, without creating for ourselves the true beauty of life?

"Religion's steps are large, but ponderous. One pace takes millennia. Its foot—already raised in the direction of progress—is hovering in the air, slowly descending. When will it set itself down again?" (Gustav Theodor Fechner, in *Tagesansicht*).[2]

There is a phrase that pursues both rich and poor, which echoes everywhere and which, as it were, promises Christianity in a new form: social commitment. A feeling exists, or at least slumbers in all of us, that somehow we should help to improve the lot of mankind, that somehow one should struggle to achieve spiritual salvation for oneself and thus for others, that one should feel a sense of solidarity with all men. Socialism in the nonpolitical, suprapolitical sense is the simple, straightforward relationship between men, far removed from any form of domination. It straddles the divide between the warring classes and nations, and binds mankind together. If today anything can crown the city, it is—above all— the expression of this idea.

The architect will wish to form this, if he does not want to make himself redundant and if he wants to know for what he is living. What, after all, is the point of prettifying this or that house or building when we know nothing of that great element that feeds all the little streams? The low esteem in which architecture is held, as already described above, springs quite justifiably from this lack of knowledge. The architects are implicated in this. When they do not know their ultimate goal, when they cannot—at least in hope and longing—imagine the highest aspiration, their existence has no value. Their talent is then dissipated in the commercial struggle and frittered away in aestheticizing minutiae and the overestimation of trivia. They are so exhausted by glorifying the past, by eclecticism and such conceptual speculations as "Heimatkunst" [vernacular art], function, material, proportion, space, plane, line, and so on, that they end up entirely unable to make anything beautiful, since they are entirely cut off from the last, inexhaustibly sparkling fountain of beauty. The study of old building styles offers them no help, for they remain fixated on individual forms, as their eyes are blind to the light that radiates through all these magnificent structures. The architect must ponder his noble, priestly, magnificent, divine calling and seek to raise the treasure that lies in the depths of man's soul. With total abandon he should immerse himself in the soul of the people [*Volk*] and discover both himself and his noble calling by striving to give material expression to that which slumbers in every soul. An ideal given built form, bringing joy and happiness, should arise again and lead all men to the awareness that they are elements of a great architecture, just as it was in former times.

Then color will at last flourish again, the colored architecture that today is longed for only by the few. The spectrum of color, pure and simple, will once again flow over our houses and rescue them from their dead, gray-on-gray existences. The love of splendor will awake, and the architect will no longer shun plain naked, polished forms. He will now know how to make use of it and, from his new vantage point, far removed from the old prejudices, turn each and every thing to new effect.

If it really is now social commitment that is striving upward toward the light and lies buried under the top layer, is it even possible to give force to something latent? The answer is: the cathedrals, the giant temples, also came into being. They were not always there, but at a certain point the ideas for them were born, always in the mind of an individual architect. That which today stands as resplendent as it is self-evident was at one point conceived for the first time as an idea, and planned when the desire for it was still unclear and locked up in the indeterminate vision of the spirit of the people [*Volkseele*]. Yet we would say that these were small beginnings and modest attempts, out of which the great cathedral gradually grew, as the result of a tradition that created the same thing over and over again, resulting after long practice in the great, audacious climax. Already in the smallest beginnings, I believe, the idea or the direction was there, as this is, after all, the work of man. Admittedly, the final result was inexplicable, so that today in the popular stories of the Indians the building of the wondrous temples is ascribed to the gods, even though the name of the architect (Divakara) of such an enormous structure as Angkor Wat has been handed down. Should not we, perhaps, have beginnings like this? Nothing grows out of nothing. And architecture comes into being only when it is supported by action. It is impossible to transform a mere thought into architecture without positive action and engagement, which is why all attempts to build modern monuments are doomed to fruitlessness. They cause nothing to happen and are intentionally based on the surface imitation of misunderstood works from the past. The religious ritual in the temple, the sacrifice, the mass, and the like were essential to the creation of the majestic buildings.

[...]

We have the idea for a new city, yet it is a city without a crown. Now, however, we know the form that its head, its crown, must take.

THE CITY CROWN

The design [...] is an attempt to show how the crowning feature, the highest ideal, might be striven for in the new city. Given the examples illustrated and cited here,[3] it may seem more than audacious, even presumptuous, to venture something in the same direction. But at some point the attempt has to be made, at the risk of being chided for immodesty or utopianism. Quite simply, the design should illustrate in concrete terms the heights to which we aspire. It should not be regarded as an end in itself, but rather as a stimulus for the realization of that which we already know, and for bringing nearer the envisioning of our future goals.

First, that which is to be crowned—the city—should be described in detail. [...] The whole site covers a circle with a diameter of around 7 kilometers, at whose center the "City Crown" is located. The crown is a rectangular area of 800 by 500 meters that is reached by the main traffic arteries. For circulatory and aesthetic reasons, these arteries do not climb up to the center of the crown, but touch it tangentially and radiate out from the center in broad arcs. The railway access, similarly, is planned to follow a similar arc on the eastern side of the city, so that commercial life can develop between the station and the city center. For reasons of practicality, the administration center, town hall, and similar buildings will be located at particular points within this quarter of the city. Stretching along the railway line to the periphery of the city and beyond, the factories are located to the east side so that the city is spared the industrial fumes.

From the west side, the direction of the prevailing wind, a large park that is divided into sectors penetrates into the inner core of the city, bringing sweet air from the woods and fields. It links the heart of the city with the open countryside like a major artery, and should function like a true people's park, with playgrounds, playing fields, water basins, a botanical garden, flower beds, rose gardens, and an expansive grove and wood that stretches right out into the open country. Axially to the city center, three churches are set in the housing areas, through which the schools are distributed, with a teaching center (university) in the park. Farther out again are the hospitals. Two main roads lead diagonally to the station, to shorten the connections.

The streets in the living quarters essentially run from north to south, in order to give the house front on both sides east and west sun, and shelter from the wind for the streets and gardens. Their design is conceived entirely in the manner of the garden city, with rows of low-rise, single-family houses and deep gardens for each house [...] so that the housing area itself has the character of a nursery garden, making additional allotment gardens unnecessary. The agricultural zone begins beyond the belt of parks at the periphery of the city. The total area of the city comprises 38.5 square kilometers, the living area around 20 square kilometers, with a population of 300,000 in the garden city layout, which gives a density of 150 per hectare. As necessary, the population could be expanded to 500,000. Interspersed between the housing areas are public gardens, playing fields, and green-belt parks, to separate the living and the industrial areas. Other individual features are not shown in detail. The distance from the periphery to the city center is not much more than 3 kilometers, which equals a half hour by foot. Within the living area itself, the streets are kept as narrow as possible (5 to 8 meters) to save wasting funds unnecessarily. The main roads are designed to accommodate trams and heavy traffic.

Following the program of the garden city, the height of the houses in the living areas is kept as low as possible. The commercial and administrative buildings are allowed to exceed the height of the houses by one story at most, so that the City Crown reigns supreme, mighty and unattainable.

The centerpiece, the City Crown itself, reveals a grouping of all those buildings that are the focus of the previously mentioned social tendencies, and which a city of this size needs for its entertainment and cultural life.

Four large buildings, forming a cross rigorously oriented toward the sun, and made up of an opera house, theater, and people's meeting hall or large and small auditoria, form the crown of the design. Their exit routes point in the four different directions, to facilitate the rapid dispersal of the crowds. On each side they have open space, in case of mass panic. At the center of the group there is a courtyard with wings for the storage of stage scenery, for stores, refreshment rooms, and so on. They are linked and embraced by a colonnade, which at its corners to the left and right of the Hall of the People [*Volkshaus*] form reception rooms with terrace gardens for smaller, more intimate occasions (weddings and the like), and on the other side an aquarium and a plant house, again with a similar garden. This colonnade allows the most intimate use of the entire complex; one can spend the afternoon in the terrace garden and the evening at a concert, at the theater, or in a meeting.

Whereas the exits from the theater and the small auditorium building lead via broad external staircases [...] to tree-lined squares, to the left and right of the two main halls are aligned a sequence of courtyards, arcades, and buildings, varied according to site and function. From the opera house—whose companions are the aquarium and the plant house, with the silent beauty of the fish, flowers, and exquisite plants and birds—a covered loggia with several flights of steps leads across a water courtyard, again surrounded by arcades, and from there finally to the stopping place for vehicles: a worthy finale after the aesthetic delights within, or an equally worthy overture to the delights in store. The museum and central library adjoin the external courtyard—serious buildings with two upper stories, but not too massive. For in the new city, hopefully, we will not undertake the mass storage of everything that is merely old, or of every possible questionable novelty, in the excessive manner favored by museums today.

The living arts do not in any way need to be stacked up; in the new city they should no longer eke out their miserable existences in the museum, but should play a vital role as an integral part of the whole project.

[. . .]

The crowning climax is formed by the massive complex made up of the four large buildings, which, in their cruciform plan, can be seen as a symbolic expression of fulfillment. On this plane, the socially oriented aspirations of the people find their realization, where theater and musical drama give the united citizens the spiritual impulse that they long for in their daily lives. In joining together in the Halls of the People, they sense what they have to offer each other, and in the process ennoble the primeval force for community: the herd instinct.

[. . .]

The cruciform group formed by the four large buildings is the summit of the entire building group. Yet this monumental group itself is not itself the crown. It is a base for a transcendental building, which, entirely freed from function, reigns over the entire complex. It is the Crystal House, constructed of glass—the building material that, in its shimmering, transparent, and reflective essence, is much more than a commonplace material. A steel construction lifts it above the plinth formed by the four major buildings and forms its framework, within which the whole rich spectrum of glass architecture is displayed, in prismatic glass infills and glass panels. The Crystal House contains nothing apart from an incredibly beautiful room, reached by steps and walkways to the right and left of the theater and the small meeting hall. But how can one describe something that can only be built? Every intimate, every major sensation will be awakened here, when the full sunlight cascades over the high room and breaks into countless delicate reflections, or when the evening sun fills the upper dome and intensifies the rich polychromy of the glass panels and sculptures with its red glow. Architecture will renew here its beautiful union with sculpture and painting. Everything will join in a single work, to which the architect will contribute the overall conception; the painter, glass paintings of enraptured, all-embracing fantasy; and the sculptor, pieces that are inseparable from and thus integrated into the totality. Everything forms but a part of the great architecture, one element in the great compulsion to give form, which at the same time inspires all the artists and compels them to find their ultimate expressive powers. Cosmic, spiritual thoughts find reflection in the colors of the painters—the celestial spheres [*Weltgegenden*]—and a new richness of sculptural form decorates all the architectural elements—the recesses, connections, supports, consoles, and so on—showing that sculpture can once again be something more than chiseling figures out of stone and the like. Sculpture will awake again and reveal all those riches of which it has so long and so unfairly been deprived. Totally freed from the prescriptions of realism, the world of form that lives in waves, clouds, and mountains, and which transports every element and organism of the soul of the artist far beyond the constraints of the figurative and naturalistic, will arise again. It will sparkle and shimmer in all the colors and materials—in metal, precious stone, and glass—in all those points in space where the play of light and shadow demands it. This space will not be composed of plain walls, but of the harmony of rich and highly articulated elements. From its galleries great music rings out acoustically pure—a music that, just as far removed as the visual arts from its everyday equivalent, serves only the highest purpose.

Suffused by the light of the sun, the Crystal House reigns like a diamond over everything, sparkling in the sunlight as a symbol of the greatest joy and of the purest spiritual peace. Within its interior a solitary wanderer discovers the pure joy of building, and, ascending the internal stairs to the upper platform, he sees the city at his feet, and behind it the rising and setting sun, toward which the city and its heart are so strongly oriented. [. . .] The glowing light of purity and transcendence shimmers over the carnival of unrefracted, radiant colors. The city spreads out like a sea of color, as proof of the happiness in the new life.

NOTES

1. The Templower Berg was a small hill eminence on the southern edge of Berlin, one of the few hills in the city. Karl Friedrich Schinkel's monument to the Napoleonic War, called the War of Liberation in Prussian history, was built there between 1818 and 1821, and the hill was renamed the Kreuzberg in response to the cruciform motif that tops the monument. The poet Heinrich Heine, however, used the old name in his poem "Verkehrte Welt" from the verse cycle *Zeitgedichte* (1844):

Swim not, brothers, against the stream,
That's only a useless thing!
Let us climb up on to Templow Hill
And cry: God save the king!

[Laßt uns nicht schwimmen gegen den Strom,
Ihr Brüder! Es hilft uns wenig!
Laßt uns besteigen den Templower Berg
Und rufen: Es lebe der König!]

2. Gustav Theodor Fechner (1801–87) was a physicist who dedicated himself to psychophysics and experimental aesthetics. Taut's reference is to Fechner's book *Die Tagesansicht gegenüber der Nachtansicht* (The view by day contrasted to the view by night; 1879).

3. In *Die Stadtkrone,* Taut illustrates the great temples and cathedrals of the Asian and European faiths.

108
Otto Bartning
CHURCH ARCHITECTURE TODAY

First published as Bartning, *Vom neuen Kirchbau* (Berin: Cassirer, 1919), pp. 121–23. Translated by Michael Loughridge.

The recent spiritualization of the church and of church architecture indicates a spiritualization of human society and its blossoming out into a true community, and thus in some sense is to be identified with a spiritual ordering of political and social life, with a hierarchy of values replacing that of inheritance or that of material wealth. It stands for a religion of the spirit that is broadly based and thoroughly comprehensive in form. Even an attempt to sketch the general outlines of these impossible possibilities—and, I believe, unrecognized imperatives—facing Christendom would quite disproportionately overshadow our foregoing observations, like a vast cloud hanging over them, and could not itself be other than nebulous and highly speculative in character. Accordingly, I confine myself at this concluding stage to asserting that the question proposed and deliberated upon in the foregoing pages—the prospects for a new religious architecture—must, from the standpoint of the Protestant Church, be answered negatively for the present; whereas from a standpoint of maximum confessional and political breadth and maximum rigor in religious observance it must be answered positively for the future—albeit perhaps only for the furthest future horizon of the European peoples.

And if the architect's attention turns back now from the speculative receding perspectives of the future to focus on the empirical present, if he applies himself to the problems it poses, condensing them into forms that will serve practical uses, it can nonetheless be predicted that these forms will have derived from the conscious or unconscious memory of that distant vision, and that they will weave the fabric of tomorrow even as they multiply in our today.

But what is being demanded of him in our day by the Protestant Church? The architectural problem that gave rise to the present reflections—one that returned to weigh heavily once more upon our hearts following the material and spiritual destruction, the acts of neglect, and the wholesale changes wrought by the war—can now be seen and understood clearly. Two branches of the program hitherto entangled in each other and causing conflict now have separate identities: building requirements for pastoral care and for teaching and preaching, on the one hand, are distinct from those for worship and sacrament on the other.

The curing of souls is the pastor's noblest charge in his capacity as an individual human; its architectural expression is the church house. To make it not merely a combined home and office in the usual sense but a true workshop of pastoral care (such as the modest example that I endeavored to describe in my opening chapter) should be the common purpose of the commissioning authority and the architect, a purpose that might be termed their "immanent building program."

But the pastor's care for his flock is only the vocational exercise, by the individual specially called to it, of a faculty that ultimately bonds every human being with his neighbor, his family, his friends, and those under his protection, and that accordingly makes of every man's house not just a place to find rest, but a workshop for his soul. And this is why the "immanent building program" for church houses could well exert a clarifying and ordering influence on the secular house-building program, which is technically and aesthetically overloaded.

[...]

Practical Christian charity and community find their appropriate architectural expression in what are called "community resources"—such as schools, hospitals, reading rooms, one-room apartments, residential estates, and civic amenities—and should constitute the "immanent building program" of all such facilities. Only this program for building, driven as it is by active Christian charity, not by speculation, propaganda, competition or vanity, can determine the general attitude of mind in which client and creative architect, working together, create what is needed today and will be needed tomorrow. The Church's building obligations in this precise area comprise meeting rooms and teaching accommodation where the minister can discharge his obligations to teach and instruct, offices for administration of parish affairs, and living quarters for church officials and helpers. These premises come, together with the vicarage, essentially to serve a single purpose, and therefore need to be conceived as an architectural entity, whether all in a single building or in a cluster of buildings, which may be appropriately designated the parish house [Gemeindehaus]. If the "immanent building program" for the individual parts is to be successfully fulfilled, it is important that the aesthetic impact of the whole should reflect their equal value relative to each other.

109

Peter Behrens and Heinrich de Fries
ON LOW-COST BUILDING

First published as Behrens and de Fries, *Vom sparsamen Bauen: Ein Beitrag zur Siedlungsfrage* (Berlin: Bauwelt, 1919), pp. 15–16, 71–73, 78–79. Translated by Iain Boyd Whyte.

THE NEED TO CARE FOR THOSE WITH LOWER INCOMES

Some real-life figures may serve to support our view. In one of the newer, rightly admired housing estates in a Berlin suburb, which was blessed with a favorable financial situation, the smallest kind of terraced house costs a family 37 marks per month in rent. This amounts to an annual expenditure on rent of 444 marks; added to this there are the travel expenses for the working members of the family, so that the family has to reckon with an average minimum of 500 marks a year to cover rent and travel. However, Dr. Kurzynsky, director of the Office of Statistics in Schöneberg, has calculated that the average annual income for the working classes, before the war, was 1,200 marks. If the aforesaid 500 marks are subtracted from this sum, the average family of five is left with 700 marks, or 140 marks per head per year for food, clothing, doctor's bills, education, and so on—that is to say, not quite 40 pfennigs per day. These are only averages, but these calculations also apply to those on even lower incomes. The almost brutal crassness of the contrast between the weight of the facts and the little that has so far been achieved in the attempt to solve the small-dwellings problem clearly casts the work still to be done in the harshest light: *there is a vital need to solve the small-dwellings question for the great masses with lower incomes.*

THE NEED FOR EXTREME COST REDUCTION

It seems necessary to bear in mind the acute nature of these calculations in order to be absolutely clear about what must happen, in order to devote our energies exclusively to the urgent work we must do in future, free from all sentimental considerations and with one goal in our sights: to create a form of small dwelling in housing estates and apartment blocks that fully meets all the necessary modern social, hygienic, and cultural standards, but that is also affordable for the great mass of those with a *low income*. This aim makes the greatest imaginable thrift the overriding principle in all the various aspects of the future low-cost housing developments. *The task of taking care of the housing needs of the masses will be fulfilled only by an extreme reduction of the costs of the housing fabric.*

But even following this path will not entirely alleviate the misery of our housing situation. The increasing incidence of nomadic life in our major cities—in Berlin, around half of the population move to different accommodation in any one year—points to a terrifying sense of homelessness. These are the consequences of building methods and designs that are no longer of real value to the majority of people, so that there seems to be nothing to be said for holding on to what they have. The message here is clear enough. It is the most compelling proof of the qualitative inadequacy of the small dwellings we have at present.

THE NEED FOR THE BEST POSSIBLE QUALITY

The fact is that these small dwellings are still too greatly influenced by their origins in bourgeois domestic life. For what may be justified in the construction of a roomy bourgeois apartment is an evil if applied to the small dwelling that is intended to be as economical as possible. Let there be no mistake: the lifestyle of the worker is very different from that of the civil servant or the comfortably-off citizen; his views, his customs, his demands, and his rights are quite distinct, and they give his circles their particular character, just as they leave their mark on where he lives. It is pointless to present him with model homes that he is then supposed to become accustomed to but that he will always register as alien, imposed on him from outside, and not in keeping with his own nature. He will never love a dwelling of that kind; he will never feel at ease in it.

Thus the form of the small dwelling must also be thought out from the point of view of the worker. We demanded that the problem of mass small dwellings be solved by extreme thrift in their construction. A really inexpensive dwelling is, however, worthwhile only if it is also really good, if it fulfills as far as possible the tenant's justified demand for quality within the context of reduced costs. *The fundamental need for an extreme reduction in costs must always also take account of the need for the best possible quality.*

[...]

One of the major challenges facing us today is to respond to architectural forms in their own right so deeply and so immediately, reacting as we would to an artistic experience, that it will in the end be possible to express the whole spectrum of human emotions directly through architectural form, without the aid of literary, lyrical, or sentimental ornament. There can be no doubt that the desired pleasure can be much more powerfully and readily generated by the artistic expression of a small housing estate than by enlisting nonarchitectural means, and where this seems not to be the case, the error lies not with the inadequate expressive capacity of the architectural form but with that of the architect.

These basic principles of artistic creation will have considerable influence on the planning of the small housing estate. Architecture in its purest and least falsified form is primarily about forming a body, whether this stands wholly independently or relates to its surroundings, whether it involves a mass of houses or the square in the midst of them. And a cubic notion of the artistic structure of a housing estate is most likely to produce results that leave a powerful impression and have a beauty all their own, as long as the architectural bodies conform to the above-mentioned principles of silhouette, rhythm, and living energy.

[...]

A housing estate should therefore be regarded as a single organism, the individual components of which not only should be artistically construed within themselves but should always relate to the overall body, setting up connections that in turn become the main factors in the artistic appearance of an estate. Such connections should be created by means of the suggested stepped construction method in conjunction with the other larger buildings that serve the needs of the community.

One of the architect's most important tasks is to generate and to regulate the multiple relationships between these bodies in such a way that, within the organism of the estate, the individual components come together as one, with the connections between them defining the particular artistic expression of the whole area—just as the composition of a fine relief on an even background seeks to hold together differently modeled layers as one, bringing the various elements together by means of well-chosen high points and carefully balanced accents, creating one unified, compelling effect. So, too, not only would the architectural result be an impression of the most powerful vitality and artistically expressive beauty, but the bodies would themselves be so designed that the disappearance of some apparently inconsequential element—just one house—would necessarily destroy the overall artistic impression.

[. . .]

The design of the buildings themselves is, therefore, primarily an artistic problem, with engineering and economic considerations of necessity coming second, despite their undeniable importance. Contrary to the ever more prevalent view that the construction of small housing estates is not so much an artistic task as a matter of diligent economics and careful engineering, it seems entirely possible to strive for purely artistic aims by employing a design that makes decisive and conscious use of the given space, and by applying a clearly defined, spiritual notion of form at the same time as taking account of reasonable economic considerations in order to construct an estate that will express the lively and memorable beauty of a new age and that will reflect a new spirit in creative forming.

[. . .]

It must be the task of the immediate future to pursue more actively that particular direction in the area of construction engineering that has as its goal the broad replacement of human resources with machinery. Moreover, in view of the particular conditions that apply in the construction of small dwellings, more attention should be paid than hitherto to the creation of equally effective new building materials.

Aside from these practical considerations, however, the significance of the demands made on the human spirit should not be underestimated. In light of this, the question of artistic design is far from secondary; it must be treated as seriously as the material requirements. Without doubt, what is at issue here is to come closer to a solution for one of the most significant national economic problems of the future—namely, to find a way to take the idea of the small housing estate, which occupies so many of our citizens, and—drawing on all our resources and all the means available to us—to turn this into reality. But realizing this idea will be worthwhile in the deepest sense only if it not merely fulfills actual demands but in addition enriches the form and content of the lives of the working classes in this nation. Thus the great and serious challenge in the construction of small estates is—by striving for values that are in fact within our capacity—to relieve the spiritual pressure weighing our people down after the long years of war. A deep understanding of the special significance of the campaign for small estates is demonstrated by none other than Field-Marshal-General von Hindenburg in a remark made in March 1918: "My dearest wish would be to see every worker in his own small house and garden, so that when his work was done, life could also be a source of joy to him."

110

Käthe Kollwitz
DIARY ENTRY, 11 SEPTEMBER 1919

First published in *Ich sah die Welt mit liebevollen Blicken: Käthe Kollwitz: Ein Leben in Selbstzeugnissen*, ed. Hans Kollwitz (Wiesbaden: Fourier, 1971), pp. 195–96. Translated by Iain Boyd Whyte.

Walked around our district of the city, sat down at Wörther Platz. Having returned from the country, the Berlin children have never before seemed so emaciated to me. No, there's no other way: the big cities must be abolished. It is above all a question of healthy children.

111

Hermann Muthesius
SMALL HOUSE AND SMALL-SCALE HOUSING DEVELOPMENT

First published as Muthesius, *Kleinhaus und Kleinsiedlung*, rev. 2nd ed. (Munich: Bruckmann, 1920), pp. 28–30, 34–36. Translated by Iain Boyd Whyte.

One thing is certain: in housing, too, we shall have to contract massively. The cheapest means to reduce costs, and the one that almost alone promises success, is the spatial contraction of the house. Building costs depend principally on the volume of the building. For this reason, we can save most effectively when, for example, we occupy 500 cubic meters rather than 1,000. Extreme simplicity must also determine the construction and furnishing. We are still facing hard times in every sphere. Nevertheless, the difficulties that are piling up today might indicate only a transitional period, to be succeeded after it has run its course by a return to normal conditions. For dwelling houses have to be built, come what may, just as people must be provided with clothing. But when the way is free again for building, when commercial undertakings are able once more to produce housing, there will be a deluge of building tasks that will take all our energies to master.

The scale of the task that the future provision of housing sets for our time brings with it the responsibility to engage in a serious questioning of whether the paths we have previously followed were the correct ones, and, if not, which new ones we should pursue. No one believes any longer the advocates of the five-story rental barracks [*Mietskaserne*], who claim that this building type offers the best that can be achieved to those looking for homes. The weaknesses of this way of building are known. We now know that it is not absolutely necessary to build five stories high across the entire city, and that side wings, courtyards, and transverse blocks can be avoided. We also realize that it is precisely the excessive height of these houses that necessitates broad and expensive streets, for only in this way can the lower stories of high buildings gain light. We no longer have any doubt that this sacrifice of land to the streets led retroactively to deep sites and thus to the side wings and lateral blocks that loom upward in the narrow and dank courtyards, in which millions of people eke out their existences. We can also specify the ways and means by which the entire basis of building might be changed. For if the height is limited to three stories, the streets do not need to be so wide. In the process, the expenditure on costly land and roadwork will be reduced to such an extent that money will be freed to limit the depth of the building plots, making side wings and transverse blocks redundant. The degree to which the building plans of the large cities, currently grounded on false principles, are able to change, and the extent to which our current financial difficulties can be overcome by sensible legal measures—these are the fundamental questions affecting postwar housing improvement in the large cities.

It cannot, of course, be the goal of housing reform to do away with the cities entirely. The idea of taking industry from the city and relocating it on the land also has its limits in the current conditions. Experience shows that manufacturing firms needing a high-quality workforce can function only in cities; for only here can one find a workforce both large and diverse enough to cover the changing demands. The large cities will continue as before. But we can develop the new city districts in ways other than with multistory apartment houses. A loosening of the built fabric can be introduced here, which is the goal of the new urban theory. And we can also establish completely rural suburbs if we ensure that they have good transportation links to the city.

A circumstance directly related to the war has had a particular impact on raising interest in the small housing estate. The demand arose soon after the outbreak of war that the war injured should be offered housing under favorable conditions in the countryside after their return, in recompense for their sacrifices for the fatherland. The Veterans' Housing Movement [*Kriegerheimstättenbewegung*] deserves the credit for overcoming the indifference that formerly hung over the housing question. As so often happens, the particular question promoted the more general issue and brought it into general circulation.

In other respects, too, the war made very manifest the advantages of country

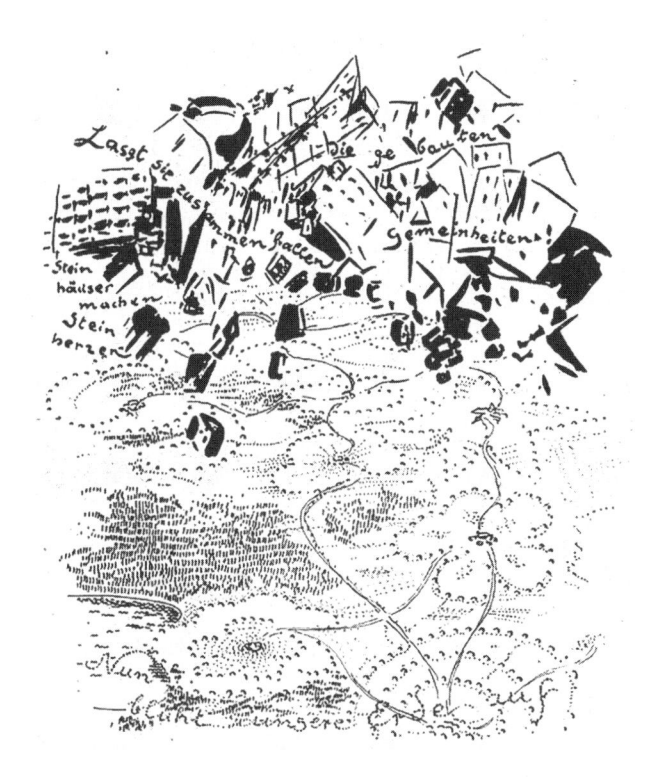

FIGURE 27. Bruno Taut, *Die Auflösung der Städte* (The dissolution of the cities) (Hagen: Folkwang, 1920)

living. In the big cities food shortages reached acute levels. Whoever lives on the land, in contrast, or in a small town surrounded by agriculture, or whoever even owns a garden or a parcel of land, has priceless means of self-help. Today, many city dwellers are vigorously engaged with the idea of moving toward the natural condition of man, toward living on the land. Also the urban working-class family, which experienced the shortages most intensely, wants to return to the land, as does the richer class, whose ambition is directed toward the acquisition of rural property. The settlement of the land will also be necessary to house and feed those workers who are no longer needed by industry. The question of peripheral housing estates, therefore, has turned sharply in the direction of internal colonization; of releasing agricultural land for housing.

[...]

In addition to the sense of ownership of the house and all the sensations that go with this, rural housing brings the joy and delight of the garden. Just how strong the urge is among city dwellers to work a plot of land is still shown today by the success of the movement promoting the urban allotment garden [*Schrebergarten*]. Wherever land is put aside for this purpose, it is immediately taken, and, in the summer, the working man uses every hour after work and Sundays, too, to hurry there and be active in the allotment. Here is proof that the inner relationship between man and the soil on which he lives is neither dead nor rooted out. In her greatness, Nature exercises her fascination even on the most hardened urbanite. People who have no garden at least go outdoors on Sundays, and the long summer vacation, previously a privilege of the better situated, is slowly becoming a necessity for the broad population of the large cities. How clearly this indicates that life on the land should not be made an exceptional condition, but should be raised into a permanent state. The small house in a rural settlement puts the means to do this within reach.

In studies of the advantages of country life it has become customary to elevate the purely physical influences to first position. The statistics for healthy recruits from the countryside, which were much higher than those from the city in the period preceding the war, are commonly cited as the most powerful evidence. Now, it is true that the physical condition of the rural population in general is much more optimal than that of the urban dwellers. But the mental influences that derive from a rural existence should be valued just as highly. The child who grows up in the countryside is reared on natural foundations and thus is better equipped for the life of the intellect than the city child. His imagination is enriched through the daily observation of natural processes, which creates a secure and solid base for his subsequent intellectual life. It is a known fact that the majority of important figures—those who advance the human condition—come from rural stock or from small towns. According to Goethe, the countryside is the great reservoir from which the strength of the nation is progressively renewed. Only through this flow can a nation gain the strength to keep itself undisputedly at the highest level and to remain defiant in the competition with other nations. The development of the people confirms the necessity for this. The highest levels will be achieved not with physical but with mental strength. Our weapons are changing from the physical to the intellectual. The nation that will be ultimately victorious in the peacetime as well as in the wartime competition will be the one that displays the highest level of intellect. This superiority is all the more firmly grounded when the intellectual and mental strength is to be found not only in the leaders, but in all classes of the people. A victorious commercial life is conceivable only when not only the great business leaders but also the workforce are lively and energetic. Similarly, a specialist industry whose products would be recognized throughout the world as the best cannot be maintained without an intelligent and highly trained workforce. Even wars are won more through spiritual strength than strength of muscle. The collapse of Germany resulted from the ultimate failure of this internal strength, which, although it had so remarkably and for so long resisted the enemy, was not strong enough to achieve the final goal. The false direction that the development of housing had taken in Germany is one ground for the dissatisfaction of the masses, the mutual alienation of the various social classes, the distrust the lower classes have for the upper classes, and the political immaturity that dominates broad circles of society. The collapse of the state has simply caused the long internalized unrest to erupt violently. The issue now is to find remedies. One way of doing this, perhaps the most important, is to ensure that in future the people are properly housed.

If Germany wishes to recover again and to assert itself in the world, there remains no other alternative than to strengthen itself spiritually and intellectually. Its geographical location also points strongly in the direction of spirit and intellect. The international situation will become more acute in the future, since this war will have a stimulating effect on all the nations. If we must accept economic restraints of unimagined severity, this can only be a stimulus to pay even more attention to the realm of the intellect. May this also lead the German people, above all, to overcome that tendency toward superficiality, which was such an unpleasant trait in the opulent years before the war.

Every means of popular instruction must be employed to reach this goal: general education, promotion of political maturity, encouragement of family life, selection of the most able, intensification of the sense of home and of fatherland, an increased engagement of the general population in science, technology, and art. All these means can be effective, however, only when the foundation of our physical and mental life—our living conditions—have been improved, so that not only has everything detrimental to our physical development been eliminated, but also no serious impediments impinge on our inner life. The more the idea that the housing question is one of the key questions for the positive development of a nation becomes consolidated, the more widespread will be the conviction that its solution must form the basis for the future rebuilding of Germany.

PART THREE

WELTSTADT—WORLD CITY

11

PLANNING THE WORLD CITY

The Greater Berlin Competition of 1910 rewarded schemes driven by considerations of traffic and circulation rather than the desire to give Berlin the monumental cityscape appropriate to the capital city of the German Empire. Indeed, the entry that most successfully expressed monumental ambitions—by Havestadt & Contag, Otto Blum, and Bruno Schmitz—was awarded only fourth prize. The idea did not disappear, however, and was taken up by the city planner Martin Mächler in a plan developed between 1917 and 1919. Rejecting contemporary calls for decentralization or for the total rejection of the industrial city, Mächler rejoiced in the city center as a site of concentrated energy and power. The physical expression of this power was a new axis, to be driven through the city from the Spreebogen in the north, past the existing Reichstag, and southward through the Tiergarten and the marshaling yards of the Potsdamer Station. Two major railway stations anchor the axis at each end—the Central Station at the north, the Potsdamer Station at the south—linked by underground tracks set below the axis. A group of buildings housing the Foreign Ministry, Ministry of the Interior, State Council, and other principal departments are grouped around the Reichstag at the northern end of the axis to form the governmental quarter on a monumental scale. Other ministries are located farther down the axis, with a second major cluster set on a roundel at the southern edge of the Tiergarten. With exhibition grounds located north of the Spree in Moabit, and generous provision of hotels, restaurants, and cultural facilities, Mächler's vision focused the energies of the metropolis to create a political and economic dynamo for new, republican state. Although it was dismissed by the city council on economic grounds, the Mächler plan nevertheless exerted a powerful presence in the Berlin planning debates of the 1920s: it was published in *Der Städtebau* in 1920 and subsequently exhibited at the 1927 Great Berlin Art Exhibition.

With hyperinflation accelerating toward its macabre climax in November 1923, when one American dollar was worth 14 billion marks, the struggle for daily existence was a more pressing matter in Berlin than large-scale rebuilding. The architects, however, did not abandon their visions. As an anonymous writer (perhaps the architect Martin Wagner) observed in April 1922: "The nation gasps under its everyday burdens, but the architects—they dream! They are building high towers. The idea of high-rise tower houses has taken hold of them. Just as they used to design and build towering monuments to Bismarck, so today commercial and business houses in the form of towers are reaching up toward heaven, albeit a paper heaven."[1] Two principal components of this paper heaven were the polemics for a city crown, which had driven the expressionist rhetoric, and a growing fascination with the North American skyscraper. In architecture, as in many other areas of life, America was regarded in 1920s Germany as the rightful leader of the industrial world, superseding the tired and embittered European powers France and Britain. America stood for advanced building technologies, steel frames, skyscrapers, and a skyline that did not have to respect the royal palace and the cathedral: precisely the new condition in Berlin.

On the basis of a report commissioned from the architect Bruno Möhring, and published in 1920 under the pointed title "On the Advantages of Tower Blocks and the Preconditions under Which They Could Be Built in Berlin," a competition was announced in November 1920 for the design of a tower beside Friedrichstrasse Station. The lack of real building opportunity prompted, unsurprisingly, considerable interest and 144 projects, some from such leading designers as Hugo Häring, the Luckhardt brothers, Ludwig Mies van der Rohe, Hans Poelzig, and Hans Scharoun. While the Luckhardts won second prize, the conservatively inclined jury favored a dumpy, fifteen-story block, clad in brick. The ultimate winner was Mies van der Rohe, whose soaring crystalline block was summarily dismissed by the jury, but which created the undisputed prototype for the twentieth-century glass-and-steel office block.

While the Friedrichstrasse competition was driven by the desire for a new and symbolic focus for Berlin—for a city crown—the debates that it prompted devolved in many cases into passionate support or denunciation of the American way of life. The combination of ruralized impoverishment at home and an aggressively successful economy on the other side of the Atlantic promoted a very ambivalent relationship with all things American, which oscillated over the Weimar years between loathing and envy. While cultural critics applauded the shimmy, the Charleston, and the Tiller Girl, they harbored deep uncertainties about the capitalist society that produced them. This ambivalence also drove the debate on the Berlin skyscraper. Writing in favor of the tower, the eccentric and visionary architect Otto Kohtz insisted: "In spite of the difficult economic and political conditions, the idea of the tower block is attracting lively interest at present, both from the public authorities and from private capital interests. This is entirely justified, since the current shortage of sites means that only through the construction of multistory buildings can extra office spaces be created to match the current level of demand. This will, in the process, also help alleviate the housing shortage. In Berlin's endless sea of housing, which is both boring and turbulent, well-sited and harmoniously designed towers will create architectonic focuses, offering visual direction and goals. The construction of buildings of this sort, therefore, would simultaneously serve economic, practical, and urban-aesthetic demands."[2] In complete contradiction, however, the celebrated architect Max Berg saw in the skyscraper "ruthless and brutal egoism as the expression of capitalistic America, an indictment in stone against the despotism of capital."[3]

The despotism, however, was not limited to the realms of capitalism, and several extreme schemes for the remodeling of the center of Berlin emerged from the radical avant-garde. The best known are Cornelis van Eesteren's proposal for Unter den Linden of 1925 and Ludwig Hilberseimer's project for the redevelopment of Berlin Mitte from 1928. Van Eesteren distinguished between the historic, eastern section of Unter den Linden, which he left more or less to its own devices, and the western end, which was to be completely remodeled with high towers at each end—at Pariser Platz and Friedrichstrasse—four lower towers on the south side of the street, and one vast block running the entire length of the north side. Hilberseimer's scheme was even more radical, with nine enormous slab blocks running north–south on both sides of Friedrichstrasse. In this scheme, the individual becomes part of the collectivity, the single housing cell the module for the metropolis. As Hilberseimer explained: "The architecture of the metropolis depends essentially on the solution of both the elementary cell and the urban organism as a whole. The single room as the constituent element of the habitation will determine the form of the habitation, and since the habitations in turn form blocks, the room will become the decisive factor of urban configuration."[4] In reality, however, it was not the cell but circulation that determined the new forms taken by central Berlin in the 1920s.

Circulation is the dynamo of all cities: the circulation of money, of traffic, and of ideas. The key to transforming Berlin from a *Residenzstadt,* oriented around the palace and the cathedral, into a *Weltstadt,* a world city or metropolis, was movement and circulation. As the city architect at the time, Martin Wagner, wrote at the end of the decade: "The traffic engineer must calculate the traffic capacity of a major metropolitan plaza and adjust this capacity to match the increase in traffic over the next twenty-five years.... Out of these demands such a plaza develops into a very specialized and technical building project, whose costs must be defrayed either in full or in part from the surrounding buildings. The through traffic on the plaza must be set against the 'stationary traffic' that holds the purchasing power of the human masses that cross the square (shops, bars, department stores, offices, and so on) . . . A metropolitan plaza is simultaneously a stopping point and a sluice gate: arresting the consumer power while allowing the through traffic to pour through."[5] Wagner's key argument, however, was that even with the most technically advanced traffic system, integrating both the underground railways and the surface traffic, no planner could anticipate what demands the metropolis would be making in twenty-five years' time. For this reason, urban design and building projects in the city center should be planned on a short-term cycle, with the old fabric giving way to the new every twenty-five years or so.

In contrast to Mächler's major north–south axis, however, Wagner proposed that the east–west direction should be developed as the humming, modern axis of Berlin. To quote Wagner once again: "The westward migration of Berlin—a typical development of the European metropolis—will have its termination at Witzleben: from Witzleben to the city—that is the axis along which Berlin's business and entertainment life will vibrate."[6] To anchor this new axis at each end, Wagner and the city building authority initiated two competitions in 1928; one for the reconfiguration of Alexanderplatz in the city center, and a second for a large exhibition site (*Messegelände*) at Reichskanzlerplatz (now Theodor-Heuss-Platz) in the western suburbs. As the neon lights on the new buildings at Reichskanzlerplatz announced in 1930, "We are building here the new center of Berlin."[7]

Back in 1920, Mächler's vision of a new governmental feature at the northern end of his north–south axis, in the bend of the River Spree, spurred Otto Kohtz to propose an enormous fifty-story, cruciform block, stepped back in the manner of a ziggurat, as a ministry building. It was to flank the Reichstag on the south side of the Platz der Republik and provide office accommodation for the government and the ministries. Although unbuilt, this project heralded a series of competitions and proposals that sought to establish a new governmental quarter on this site, to replace the improvised and rather domestic sequence of ministry buildings that ran along the Wilhelmstrasse. A feeble competition of 1927 was followed two years later by a grander affair that invited submissions from several of the leading designers of the day, particularly those with a sympathy for the monumental: Peter Behrens, Hans Poelzig, Paul Schmitthenner, German Bestelmeyer, and Wilhelm Kreis. Poelzig's scheme was favored by Martin Wagner, but the impending world economic crash prevented the realization of any major initiatives at this time. By the end of the Weimar Republic in 1933, neither the short-life, high-energy axis running east–west, nor the more monumental north–south axis, had moved beyond the drawing board and on-site. Under the architectural leadership of Albert Speer, however, the National Socialist regime adopted the cross-axial scheme in its plan to remodel Berlin as Germania, capital of the Third Reich.

NOTES

1. Anonymous [Martin Wagner?], "Hochhäuser," *Soziale Bauwirtschaft* 2 (1922), p. 93; quoted in Karl-Heinz Hüter, *Architektur in Berlin, 1900–1933* (Stuttgart: Kohlhammer, 1988), p. 298.
2. Otto Kohtz, *Büroturmhäuser in Berlin* (Berlin: Kohtz, 1921), n.p.
3. Max Berg, "Hochhäuser im Stadtbild," *Wasmuths Monatshefte für Baukunst* 4/5 (1921–22), p. 102.
4. Ludwig Hilberseimer, *Großstadtarchitektur* (Stuttgart: Julius Hoffmann, 1927), p. 98.
5. Martin Wagner, "Städtebauliche Probleme der Großstadt," lecture delivered on 18 March 1929; republished in *Martin Wagner, 1885–1957*, exhibition catalogue, ed. Klaus Homann, Martin Kieren, and Ludovica Scarpa (Berlin: Akademie der Künste, 1986), pp. 105–6.
6. Martin Wagner and Hans Poelzig, description of the Ausstellungsgelände, Witzleben, Berlin; quoted in Ilse Barg, "Der Sozialismus ist ein Kind der Weltstadt," in *Die Zukunft der Metropolen: Paris, London, New York, Berlin*, exhibition catalogue, TU-Berlin, ed. Karl Schwarz (Berlin: Reimer Verlag, 1984), vol. 1, p. 360.
7. Paradoxically, in the context of a scheme designed in the boom years of the late 1920s to combine a short life with a high economic return, the most visible results of Wagner's initiative—two office blocks by Peter Behrens on Alexanderplatz and the Amerikahaus at Theodor-Heuss-Platz by Heinrich Straumer—survived National Socialism, wartime bombing, and street fighting and are to be seen in Berlin to this day.

112

Martin Mächler

THE MAJOR POPULATION CENTER AND ITS GLOBAL IMPORTANCE

First published as Mächler, *Die Großsiedlung und ihre weltpolitische Bedeutung* (Berlin: Ring-Verlag, 1918); reprinted in *Martin Mächler—Weltstadt Berlin*, ed. Ilse Balg (Berlin: Galerie Wannsee Verlag, 1986), pp. 73–74. Translated by Michael Loughridge.

The first phenomenon of this nature to be placed in German hands is the court and forum of the all-conquering businessman: it is the world metropolis Berlin.

Greater Berlin at present has a population of very nearly 4 million souls. Ninety per cent of them are crowded together within an area measuring about 615 square kilometers.

If we compare the space actually available to this mass population with that which the public-health expert regards as a minimum requirement for every individual—the space each individual needs merely to sustain his basic physical existence—it is found that the space that these advisers regard as meeting the vital needs of a population mass of this order is several times larger than the space within which this population is actually forced to live. Even so, our view is that the requirements incorporated in current projects are not nearly demanding enough, given that our aim is not merely to provide for the basic animal existence of every individual, but to give him the opportunity to develop his higher faculties

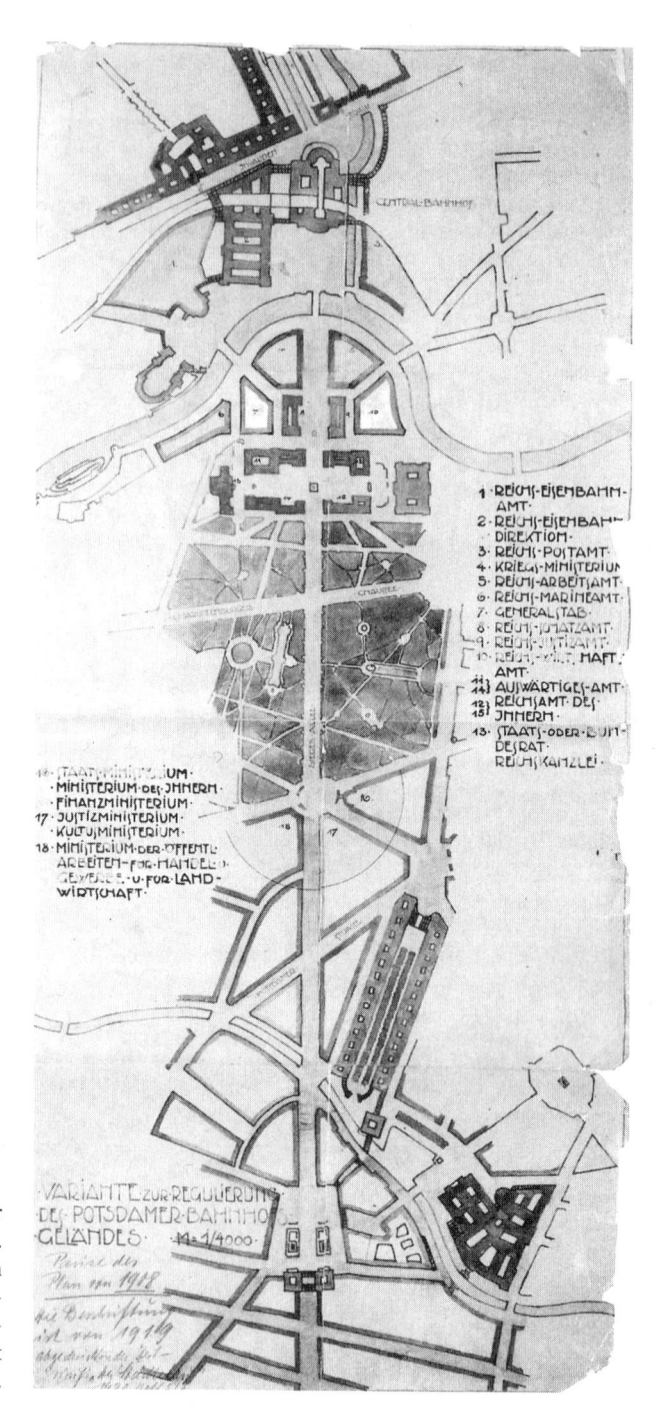

FIGURE 28. Mächler Plan for Berlin, 1919. Nachlass Martin Mächler, Architekturmuseum der Technischen Universität Berlin.

and physical powers in a harmonious way. The individual at work and at rest must have such space available as he needs in order to shape his life, in the sense that we have so often described.

But fulfillment of these requirements with regard to individuals is still not the complete solution of the problem of Greater Berlin. As we have already indicated, Berlin does not exist for itself alone: it has a more important role than that of merely providing, in the fullest sense of the term, for the vital needs of every one of its inhabitants. It has the task of serving the vital interests of a whole nation within the great mechanism of the world at large. It has to function as a world metropolis—and this is the ultimate criterion on which the calculation of the necessary building area must be based.

In the sum of the two sets of needs, the individual and the collective, the measure is given for the demands that Greater Berlin must meet if it is to fulfill its national and global roles.

As yet it is not within our powers to determine with mathematical precision what area will be needed to accommodate Greater Berlin's land requirements as it expands. However, given the palpable nature of these needs, and using such calculations as are possible on the basis of the scanty statistical information available, it is possible to form an approximate idea of the amount of land required.

In our opinion, the best estimate is that Greater Berlin will need to occupy a roughly circular area of average radius 50 kilometers measured from the tower of the Berlin Town Hall [Rathaus]. That corresponds to a total of approximately 7,800 square kilometers.

Within this area, there now needs to be a basic restructuring of the present building pattern, with elements regrouped to meet not only present demands but those of the future.

National and municipal buildings for representative and administrative purposes, trading floors and industrial-shop floors, educational and research institutions, domestic housing, playing fields and other recreational areas, and—last but not least—hotel and other accommodation for the city's visitors: all these must find the place ideally suited to their respective needs. The enormous obligations imposed by the metropolis to maintain food supplies and ensure public health have to be duly planned for, and, as one of the absolute priorities, appropriately located accommodation has to be found for the forces of law and order in such measure as is necessary.

What we must set out to achieve is whole-scale reorganization based on the principle of a living germ cell around which the whole cellular tissue develops and grows as it does in natural organisms. The vital nucleus of the world metropolis is trade. Accordingly we assign a central circular area of 5 kilometers radius around the Berlin Town Hall to be devoted to trade and commerce.

This central circle is enclosed in a ring of radius 10 kilometers that functions as a reserved area for commercial expansion, anticipating future development of the city center and consequent restructuring.

These two areas—the inner circle and the surrounding ring—will be the site of the immense work of reconstruction that has become a matter of urgency now that our metropolis is a focal point for the world economy. The very large outer ring, bordered on its inner edge by the commercial expansion area described above, and with its perimeter marked by the 50-kilometer radius from the center, will be given over to industrial sites grouped by sector, to housing, to sewage treatment and market gardens, and to assembly points and training grounds for police and military forces.

In the western part of the city, a sixty-degree wedge sector will cut into the central trading zone and the inner expansion ring, its radius equal to their combined radii and its northern boundary running along the east–west axis. This area will accommodate the following, reading from the center outwards: administration, public and ceremonial buildings, visitor accommodation, and institutions dedicated to the arts, research, and education.

The trading zone must be the central point and supreme regulator of German economic life. It must respond as sensitively as a manometer to the slightest external pressure. At the same time it acts for us is as the central clearinghouse of worldwide German trade and commerce.

Construction methods will need to be far more advanced than the most modern current practice, with the most intensive use possible made of available space. By employing the most exacting standards of precision in design and construction, it will be possible to erect the mighty trade centers and financial institutions almost literally without intervening spaces—indeed, to pile them one upon another—while inside there will be well-planned coherent working areas for countless people and countless institutions, all of them with ample space for their needs, yet working in close proximity to facilitate easy and excellent communication with each other. The exterior of the buildings will have a modern monumentality appropriate to the commercial and financial greatness of the nation.

The wedge sector running west and southwest from the center will be architecturally of a different character from the two zones just described, to reflect the different nature of its functions. Whereas the commercial zones will be dominated by the monumental character peculiar to modern Gothic revivalism,[1] the architecture here will have a more classically inspired monumentality, deriving from the unsung industry of civil-service workers; from the ceremonial and dignity of public occasions, the cloistered inwardness of research and scholarship, and the lofty calling of art; and finally from the welcoming openness of the hotels to visitors from outside the city.

To ensure that the design of this sector is appropriate to its specific character, it will have its focal point and origin at the city's official central building, the town hall; will be laid out to embrace Unter den Linden and the Tiergarten; and from there will reach out westward on diverging lines, pushing out toward and finding the open countryside beyond.

In the area covered by the great outer ring, our land-use planning will be exclusively determined by the existing natural waterways.

Both toward the southeast, on the Spree-Dahme water system, with its centre at Königswusterhausen, and along the Havel and the heavy-vessel waterway in the northwest, centered on Oranienburg, we will find the areas needed for industrial development.

The southeastern quadrant not only has its large network of waterways with their potential for further development, but at its back—that is, southeast again—it has the priceless asset of immediate access to the extensive lignite deposits that form a great semicircle stretching from Sonnewalde to well beyond Frankfurt an der Oder and represent an incalculably vast wealth of energy reserves to support future economic growth.

The northwestern quadrant has an advantage of its own in the form of the deep-water channel, which allows direct access by seagoing vessels.

These industrial areas have been planned to include space for workers' housing estates. Industry and the workforce belong together. Industry has a duty to establish itself in areas that permit its workforce to be housed in civilized conditions. The notably extensive sites that we have earmarked for these developments represent the definitive solution to the problems of finding suitable locations for industry and for workers' housing.

The two main residential areas, serving people whose employment is in central Berlin as well as the infirm, the retired, and the like, will be located to the southwest and northeast, along the rivers, and set between the industrial areas just described.

One of these residential areas is reached along the River Havel in the direction of the Grunewald, and has its center at Potsdam. The other, in the northeast, will follow a line through Frohnau, Wandlitz, Lanke, via the chain of lakes leading to the Werbellinsee, and leading on to Eberswalde, Freienwalde, the Märkische Schweiz, Straußberg, Kalkberge, Erkner, and Friedrichshagen.

The considerable land area needed for sewage treatment and for food production will be located in the south, between the industrial districts to the southeast and the residential districts to the southwest. In the northeast, the residential area whose curving axis we have outlined above will fold around the second of our two planned market-garden and sewage-disposal areas. There can be further food-production areas in the east, between the industrial and residential areas on that side of the city, and again in the west, at the wide horn-of-plenty mouth of the proposed wedge-shaped sector defined earlier. On the outer perimeter of the food-growing areas, at all four points of the compass, the assembly points and training grounds of the law-and-order forces will be located.

Precise and detailed structural planning depends for its success on the comprehensiveness and integrity of the transport network. This is not the place to go into detail. We will confine ourselves to declaring that a first priority must be to do away with all terminus stations in central Berlin. A system permitting through trains is absolutely essential.

This, then, is the overall structural-planning vision that we believe should result from the forward-looking eye of not only the architect, but also the technical expert and the economist, when they assess the problem of Greater Berlin and its world role from the vantage point of the world economy.

It makes no sense to talk of Utopianism and of unrealizable projects. Wherever such tasks exist and are recognized, wherever necessity commands, wherever the achievement of new goals would relieve human want—in all such circumstances, only lethargy and indifference will hide behind talk of impossibilities. All that is required to start with is insight and the will to action. Intellectual and practical skills have to be applied. Then the right way forward will always present itself.

Those who believe are sure to find their Holy Grail in the end. It remains out of reach only for those who allow themselves to be deterred by the prejudices and inhibitions of fossilized tradition handed down from earlier centuries.

NOTE

1. The preeminent model for the "modern Gothic revivalism" favored by Mächler was undoubtedly Alfred Messel's Wertheim store on Leipziger Strasse. See above, text 27: Albert Hoffmann, The Wertheim Department Store in Leipziger Strasse.

113

Bruno Möhring

ON THE ADVANTAGES OF TOWER BLOCKS AND THE CONDITIONS UNDER WHICH THEY COULD BE BUILT IN BERLIN

First published as Möhring, *Über die Vorzüge der Turmhäuser und die Voraussetzungen unter denen sie in Berlin gebaut werden können: Vortrag in der Preußischen Akademie des Bauwesens am 22. Dezember 1920* (Berlin: Zirkel Architekturverlag, 1921), pp. 1–2, 8, 18–19. Translated by Iain Boyd Whyte.

I am no utopian. As a result of my thorough investigation of the question that you have asked of me, I have come to the firm conclusion that here in Germany, too, tower buildings will rise up in the near future, unless dark forces drive us into a ruinous civil war that will destroy everything. The spirit that currently supports the tower block in Germany is the spirit of order and concentration, of improvement. It is the spirit that opposes shallow debate and despair, the spirit that strives with creative longing for great results and calls for work and for action, the spirit that should rouse even the most apathetic. A nation that does not build dies. Building brings life, courage, and trust.

With the idea of building high, above the human scale, and higher than simple need dictated, prehistoric man performed a phenomenal act. He entered the realm of art. The will to create something that surpassed the habitual and the commonplace led to the sublime. It makes no difference, therefore, if the first taller building was a defensive structure, erected for the defense of the community, or a sacred monument. What a progression: from the cave, the tent, the hut, to the temple! What experience, what knowledge had to be assembled to make possible the construction of the sacred stone building in which dwells the all-powerful god to whom the simple folk would pay honor and tribute. What exertions, spiritual and physical, were needed to build a Pyramid of Cheops, a Parthenon, a domed church like Hagia Sophia, or one of the great Gothic cathedrals. What faith, what passion, what idealism is needed to produce something like this! The age of the cathedrals is past, although churches and towers are still being built. But even in the land of vast dimensions and enormous wealth in the distant west, no great cathedrals are appearing. The high buildings that spring up there are of a different kind. In the frantic pursuit of novelty and new sources of wealth, they serve not transcendental ideals, but profane goals.

Our city lacks a *Stadtkrone* [city crown]. If we were to construct multistory buildings at only one location, the cityscape would certainly become more exciting, but would not necessarily gain the look of a modern city. However much it seems that Berlin is going downhill, we find to our amazement that we have not yet been excluded from the list of global cities. From all sides there is pressure from companies who want to have their subsidiaries, offices, or headquarters in Berlin. There are few spaces to accommodate these commercial demands, and the prices for them are high. Foreigners who buy sites in the best locations do so not out of foolish infatuation, but from the firm conviction that they will do good business; that Berlin will not decline into provinciality, but will gain new impetus. These foreigners have a lively interest in the revival of Berlin, and will make their contribution to this. [. . .] It is important to show the world that Berlin will remain a global city and is not on the decline or going to ruin.

The best way to do this is by developing a "city" [English in original], a section of the city with high commercial buildings that proclaim far and wide that Germany is not a dying nation, that we are still working, and that we understand new ways to build and regenerate. Nothing is more convincing than building. That was already the wisdom of Fritz [Frederick the Great].

[...]

Allotment colonies are a source of renewal and joy for the poorer population, but they are inconvenient and exhausting to get to. Would not a multistory apartment house in the middle of such an allotment colony offer a better way of living than the meager housing estates that are so much praised at present? Children's playgrounds, stables, gardens—all so close that one could reach them in a couple of minutes.[1]

What a joyful picture of the city such a mixture of high-rise and low-rise building would present!

NOTE

1. In this text, Möhring cites statistics collected in Vienna detailing the incidence of typhus and diphtheria on different levels of the apartment house, which indicate that the higher one is in the building, the lower the chance of contracting diseases like typhus and diphtheria. A high-rise, multi-story building, therefore, offers healthier housing.

Floor	Typhus	Diphtheria
4th	23	16
3rd	139	147
2nd	192	218
1st	280	289

114

Siegfried Kracauer

ON SKYSCRAPERS

First published as "Über Turmhäuser," *Frankfurter Zeitung,* 2 March 1921. Translated by Michael Loughridge.

The enforced inactivity endured by German architects for years now has failed to still their hunger for grand projects. Artists such as Poelzig, prevented from building in real life, have been driven to create Expressionist cinema architecture, while dreamers like Taut conjure up glass palaces of delight or utopian Alpine Architecture from the Utopian Alps.[1] But in the long run, pasteboard fantasy creations—however brilliant—and literary production can never be satisfying fodder for the architect; he has an inner urge to conceive and erect buildings in which real people come and go, creations that will last, that belong not to the world of theatrical backdrops but to that in which real people live. It seems that the concept of the *skyscraper,* the focus at present of so much discussion in the daily press, in magazines, and in professional journals, may be destined to confront our creative architects with a challenge that is not only worthy of their mettle, but also appropriate to the age in which we live.

What is it that one seeks to achieve in putting up a "skyscraper" or tower building? A report published in the P.P.N. a few weeks ago was responsible for a widespread assumption that such buildings were exceptionally lofty apartment blocks, and that it was hoped that building them would represent an effective measure for coping with the housing crisis. (See the morning edition of the *Frankfurter Zeitung* of 7 February.) This view, however, is erroneous. For one thing, the erection of such buildings is unlikely in practice to achieve the result expected; for another, it would constitute a very considerable backward step with respect to our whole current house-building and residential-development policy—one to be opposed tooth and nail. At those places in Germany where skyscrapers are being planned, they are intended as *office blocks,* to be built primarily to serve the needs of trade and industry. Here the advantages of such tower buildings are clear. In the first place, it is hoped that they will reduce the pressure on the *housing market,* as it is now often the case in large cities that a multitude of offices are taking up space in former apartment blocks and villas, space that the construction of tower blocks could make available again for its original purpose. It is also of great importance that the erection of tower buildings leads to *local concentration of business activity,* which in turn is likely to be beneficial to our economic development. Accommodating the maximum possible number of offices within a single building, or in a small group of such tower blocks, considerably reduces the time expended in the conducting of business and hence contributes to greater economy in the use of valuable labor resources. Finally, it should be borne in mind that tower buildings make possible a radically different *level of utilization* of expensive land in relation to previous practice, and that—subject of course to favorable economic conditions—it seems that mortgage financing of the capital sums required for construction would be feasible even at present prices.

For all the above reasons, moves are afoot in a number of major German cities to promote the erection of office tower blocks, generally with a fair wind from the local and regional authorities. As the projects mooted are rightly causing considerable concern in the public mind—though very few are likely to have progressed beyond the preparatory stage and taken on tangible form—it may be appropriate to give brief details of a few of them here.

[. . .]

In *Berlin,* as is natural, the need for skyscrapers is felt particularly strongly. The Prussian Academy of Architecture commissioned the noted architect Prof. Bruno Möhring to report on where, and in what circumstances, tower buildings might be built in Berlin. His recent academy lecture on this subject, published in the journal *Stadtbaukunst* (Architekturverlag "Der Zirkel," Berlin), makes it clear that, following intensive study of North American conditions, Prof. Möhring strongly advocates the erection of tower buildings in Berlin. One of his proposals, for instance, is for an office tower on the prestige site lying to the north of the Friedrichstrasse railway station. The project that he has developed for this location—illustrated together with some further tower block projects in issue no. 7 of the current year's *Berliner Illustrierte*—makes a promising impression.

[. . .]

The practical and aesthetic objections to tower buildings are numerous, but only a few of them really stand up to closer scrutiny. Reservations on such grounds as fire risk in skyscrapers, or the alleged danger that the steel framework will rust, have been comprehensively and repeatedly refuted. Other drawbacks, however—for instance, the concentration of traffic around the towers at certain times of day, the effects of excessive load on the subsoil, and the exclusion of light and air—cannot be dismissed. It was the recognition of such problems, we learn from Prof. Möhring's study cited earlier, that led in New York in 1916 to the introduction of a building-height ordinance (the Zoning Resolution), which among other things regulates the height of skyscrapers in the so-called Height District in proportion to the width of the street, permitting a breach of the height limitation only for aesthetic reasons and only in very precise, legally defined circumstances.[2] In most American cities, the current maximum permitted height is 61 meters. When the time comes for the erection of tower buildings here, we shall have a lot to learn, not least in construction technology, from the practical experience accumulated in America.

The remaining reservations with regard to tower buildings tend to be of an aesthetic or emotional nature, and are much less serious. Where they do not simply proceed from the philistine mentality that refuses under any circumstances to budge from what is known and familiar, they often reflect the misconception that we in Germany will copy American models wholesale and uncritically, or they may be based on the hazy notion that skyscrapers embody the very spirit of materialism and capitalist rapacity that it is felt we should be combating with every means at our disposal. The ugliness of the New York financial district is familiar to everyone. Monstrous towers, born of predatory private enterprise and its unbridled will to power, stand there in profligate confusion, clad in some cases, inside and out, with an pretentious pseudo-architecture that is at violent odds with the utterly secular nature of their business. Building development of that nature is not appropriate for Germany and will not happen here: for that, we can rely on the sound aesthetic training that most of our architects have undergone. Nonetheless, if the problem of integrating tower buildings into the major German cities is to be satisfactorily solved, a whole range of relevant factors will have to receive the most scrupulous attention. Along with economic considerations, pride of place must go to proper urban planning; artists and technical experts, business leaders and local politicians must cooperate in bringing about an end result that ultimately will be neither more nor less than an exact reflection of the spirit that has moved those involved in producing it. In an essay entitled "Zum Problem des Wolkenkratzers" [On the skyscraper problem], which appeared in the two most recent issues of the excellent journal *Wasmuths Monatshefte für Baukunst,* Wilhelm Mächter[3] hails the tower building of the future as the *economic focal point of a quite specific and naturally articulated living and working* community.[4] It will not be the creative genius of our architects alone—it will also be the social conscience, the community spirit, of our entire nation—that determines whether this lofty vision of the tower building will soon be realized.

NOTES

1. In 1919, Hans Poelzig remodeled the former Zirkus Schumann in central Berlin into the Großes Schauspielhaus. The front of the old building was reskinned—prompting Kracauer's reference to pasteboard—and a large-scale theater installed for the director Max Reinhardt, combining a normal stage with a revolving stage and a cyclorama. In the same year, Bruno Taut published a folio of drawings of utopian glass architecture under the title *Alpine Architektur* (Hagen: Folkwang, 1919).
2. In response to the enormous shadow cast by the forty-two-story Equitable Building, built in 1915 on lower Broadway, the New York city authorities drew up the 1916 Zoning Resolution, which established height and setback controls for skyscrapers.
3. Mysteriously, Kracauer renames Martin Mächler "Wilhelm Mächter" in this text.
4. See below, text 115: Martin Mächler, On the Skyscraper Problem.

115

Martin Mächler

ON THE SKYSCRAPER PROBLEM

First published as "Zum Problem des Wolkenkratzers," *Wasmuths Monatshefte für Baukunst* 5 (1920–21), pp. 191–205, 260–73. Translated by Michael Loughridge.

The current housing crisis has prompted all manner of attempts to remedy this sad state of affairs. Every available and remotely usable space that could be found in the tenement blocks was made habitable. In addition, relatively large-scale financing was made available for provision of acceptable residential developments and temporary housing; and yet, in spite of all this, the crisis is growing from day to day.

Recently, there has been serious consideration even of the skyscraper model as a way of escaping the predicament of acute housing shortage. The idea is that the construction of office skyscrapers would create the office space essential for trade, industry, and government. This would permit the release of living space currently being used as office accommodation, restoring it to its original function.

The present submission will not discuss the financial or engineering aspects of this proposal, but it will demonstrate that the proposal, in the form currently under discussion in several cities, will merely aggravate the housing shortage.

[...]

Here in Germany, when the aim is to create something new for the benefit of the people as a whole, let us not be seduced into choosing as a means to this end an object that during its own history has not served the same end, and was never intended to serve it.

What end is to be served by future German skyscrapers? The logical purpose of transferring administrative and commercial offices to tower buildings means that these towers need to be located in the central urban areas where the relevant activities are carried on. The prime requirement arising from that is a strict separation of the business area from the residential area. Stacking government and commercial premises vertically is acceptable, provided that enough air space is available for the area immediately surrounding the tower buildings; indeed, in some situations it may even be necessary. *But to jumble together tall commercial and administrative buildings and low-rise residential property, with narrow streets, excessive traffic, and insufficient light and air, is unacceptable; nor is it justifiable on grounds of immediate need.* In the first place, it would be an error to assume that the immediate need can be dealt with in this way. On the contrary: it would be aggravated. If we are to understand why this is so, it is essential to confront exactly what the American skyscraper means as building type and symbol. The American skyscraper is not an expression of a planned, rational housing policy evolved in the interests of a collective mass of people that has come together as a metropolitan community; it is, rather, the expression in stone of the ruthlessness of the pure capitalist entrepreneur, solely concerned with extracting huge profit from material goods.

[. . .]

It is our task to awaken the German creative genius, that genius that can alone be Germany's salvation. The present reflections aim to set out before it the problem of the tower building and to show that this problem, too, can stimulate our national genius to prove its creativity and produce a solution that others will want to emulate. If the German genius succeeds in grasping the true essence of the tower building and expressing this through form, it will thereby achieve a necessary and inestimably useful deed for the rapid, inevitable development of the metropolis by the industrial nations of the world. It will then be called to the completion and perfecting of an achievement that in its material aspects has indeed been developed, across the ocean, to a certain degree of perfection, but whose spiritual aspect has hitherto gone unrecognized by its material creators. The tower building must be understood in its deepest essence as equivalent to what church and town hall represent for the single community, and public administration buildings for province and state. Just as the church is the religious center, the town hall the focus of the community, and the ministry building the focus of the state, so the tower building should act as the economic focal point of a quite specific and naturally articulated living and working community: only in such terms can the meaning of such centrally located buildings be defined—albeit with the difference that the significance of the tower building is not political but purely economic, not circumscribed by national borders but commensurate with economic growth worldwide.

The tower building is the material expression of the current trend of civilization toward mass agglomeration. This being so, we must regard it as the first of the cultural problems we will have to tackle in the course of economic, social, town-planning, and architectural development over the coming years. The problem has as yet not found a practical and appropriate solution, which is why we seek here to commend it to the creative genius of the German architect. Unable though we thus are to adduce a practical example in support of our arguments, we are by contrast abundantly provided with negative counterexamples testifying to the inadequacies of solutions tried hitherto. Although an example is wanting, a counterexample is to hand. Let us take one of the latter, a peculiarly characteristic counterexample; let us identify in it what has been wrong with all attempts thus far to solve the skyscraper problem, and let us endeavor, by navigating our way through what is untruthful, to penetrate to the true essence of a cultural problem that it will be our task to solve.

As a prime counterexample in the above sense, we think immediately of the tower that holds the American record for height, the Woolworth Building. The largest and most recent product of skyscraper development, it furnishes us with a telling picture of the spiritual and material values that inform American creativity.

[A detailed, statistical account of the Woolworth Building follows.]

This technical overview demonstrates the pragmatic nature of American economic life and American civilization. Materials are exploited to the limit; not a brick too many, not a provision too few. It is the Taylor system become steel and stone,[1] the record of an achievement in which speed dictates quality; and quantity is the overriding impression conveyed by the result as a whole.

Yet from the outer skin of the building right through to the elevator doors, the architectural achievement contradicts the utilitarian nature of the structure. One has the impression of a nouveau riche festooned in trinkets. Even the general disposition of the building is misconceived and highly unnatural. Doubtless it is perfectly correct in terms of static load calculation, but in organic terms it looks like something completely without roots.

In its external detailing, the Woolworth Building resembles Strasbourg Cathedral. But what is Strasbourg Cathedral if not the Gothic genius become stone, a work for eternity? And what is one not to say when faced with a utilitarian building—its components exploited to the limit, a building good for all purposes—that has been draped in the sacerdotal vestments of the Gothic style? What is one to say when the latest and most sophisticated product of pragmatic economic development comes dressed up in a fairy-tale sugar icing of vertical ornamentation, or when—to cite one last detail—the creation of the utterly worldly American entrepreneurial spirit has been crowned with a European church spire, that pointer to Heaven?

[. . .]

Concealed behind this papier-mâché facade, we sense the mammoth production facilities—the Armour slaughterhouses,[2] the Ford car plants—with the appalling monotony of their mass production, compelling the worker endlessly to perform the same hand actions year in, year out, reducing him gradually to a stultified, animal state; and in this type of mass production we sense America's nemesis.

[. . .]

The American trend toward mass agglomeration will slowly and inevitably create a nation of slaves. Let us, here, look to how we can foster the German genius and its creativity, for then the Germans, too, without having weapons in their hands, and despite the whole encircling ring of oppressors, will grow into a nation of freemen, a nation to which the world, for the sake of its future, will need to look for leadership on the paths of creativity and of freedom. And yet: we must recognize that the German genius, so apt to lose itself from sight on the otherworldly heights of Gothic imagination, needs to equip itself with the down-to-earth pragmatism indispensable for the realization of its ideas in practice.

The prime challenge for the German Gothic genius in relation to tower buildings will be to equip itself with and accept this pragmatic, down-to-earth footing, which, bound to the high-flying imagination, will produce the masterpiece of the future.

NOTES

1. The American engineer Frederick Winslow Taylor introduced the time-and-motion study to industrial production with the publication in 1911 of his book *The Principles of Scientific Management*. It was translated into German in 1913 under the title *Die Grundsätze wissenschaftlicher Betriebsführung*.

2. Founded in Chicago in 1867 by the Armour brothers, Armour and Company developed by 1880 into the largest slaughterhouse and meatpacking company in America.

116

Joseph Roth

IF BERLIN WERE TO BUILD SKYSCRAPERS: PROPOSALS FOR EASING THE HOUSING SHORTAGE

First published as "Wenn Berlin Wolkenkratzer bekäme ... Vorschläge zur Behebung der Wohnungsnot," *Neue Berliner Zeitung—12-Uhr-Blatt*, 18 February 1921; reprinted in Joseph Roth, *Berliner Saisonbericht: Unbekannte Reportagen und journalistische Arbeiten, 1920–39*, ed. Klaus Westermann (Cologne: Kiepenheuer & Witsch, 1984). Translated by Michael Loughridge.

For some time now, there has been talk of building *skyscrapers in Berlin*. The reasons advanced are the huge *shortage of housing* and the number of private residences currently occupied by civil-service departments, official bodies, and the like. The only reason not to build skyscrapers is that building them would be extremely expensive. Of those who purport to be in the know, some claim that the skyscraper's moment has passed, at least for the present. Skyscrapers, they assert, would make sense only if it were a case of saving outlay on expensive building land. Today, with building costs as high as they are, the land price is argued to be so low in comparison that there would be no problem with putting ordinary houses up, if only the materials were available cheaply.

However, apart from their most obvious role of saving space, skyscrapers seem to have other, no less important roles and advantages. Putting them up would indeed be expensive, but *rentals* for offices, business premises, shops, and department stores would rise correspondingly. The internal layout of skyscrapers offers real convenience—simple, relatively inexpensive convenience—while the *prestige value* gained by a business simply by locating in a skyscraper is not inconsiderable.

On top of that, it really is high time for *homeless renters* to be given their flats back and for permanent commissions and officialdom to be housed in accommodation built for the purpose. It is an appalling *waste of space* for offices to take up residence in people's homes, with bathrooms, kitchens, servants' quarters being converted from their proper function. In the majority of offices one can observe a solitary typist sitting at her machine by the window, while the rest of the room is so dark that it is no use for working in and serves at best as a corridor. Officialdom and commerce need accommodation that has been designed expressly for their activities. The *housing problem* would be *solved* by the erection of skyscrapers.

And so the authorities, having apparently first taken the time to recover their energies, are now seriously considering erecting at least an experimental skyscraper in Berlin. It could be ready for use within *nine months* from now. Costs are at present still uncertain. The number of stories is immaterial. You can build five stories or sixteen—it makes very little difference in price. However, if the building is to call itself a "skyscraper," it has must have *at least ten* stories.

[. . .]

Skyscrapers are in fact *the* representative form of our century. Their steel frames are alive with the belt-and-pulley rhythms of the modern age. They are the answer to the Babel problem. For behold: we build towers that reach up to heaven, there shall come earthquakes, but the towers of Babel do not fall. Why shouldn't Berlin build skyscrapers?

117
Adolf Behne
THE COMPETITION OF THE SKYSCRAPER SOCIETY

First published as "Der Wettbewerb der Turmhaus-Gesellschaft," *Wasmuths Monatshefte für Baukunst* 7 (1922–23), pp. 58–67. Translated by Michael Loughridge.

It would be deceiving oneself to imagine that in America the aesthetic problem of the skyscraper has now been solved. And yet: on comparing the visionary projects that have appeared in Germany since the end of the war with the American buildings, one might well ask whether the latter, for all that their decoration recalls Baroque palaces, are not in fact preferable to the German designs.

[. . .]

The competition organized by the Skyscraper Society was the first opportunity for the German architectural fraternity—or at least members of the professional body B.D.A. [Bund Deutscher Architekten][1]—to tackle an immediate, specific skyscraper project. There has been justified criticism of the organizers' failure to open up such a groundbreaking project for consideration by *every* creative architect in Germany. There were other criticisms, too: the time allowed (six weeks) was much too short; the prizes offered were distinctly modest; and the jury was too heavily academic. The idea of linking any prize to an actual commission was ruled out from the start. The site in question is a triangle formed by the Friedrichstrasse Station, the Friedrichstrasse itself, and the River Spree (at the Reichstagufer). The American solution would have been extremely simple: build as high as possible on all three sides, and install the battery of offices, capacity being an easy calculation of area times height. And then, beside that, the next office battery. But it will not be for us, here, to follow the Americans. The difference between our approach and theirs is not so much in the formal aspects as over the relation of the tower to its setting. For us, the high building is bound to be an urban-planning issue, with "urban planning" understood not as an aesthetic but as an ethical issue. It is likely enough that the American approach, being unhampered by any social considerations, will eventually produce a new urban beauty of overpowering impact, far beyond any aesthetic effect we can achieve, given our sense of social obligation. Certain overall architectonic effects have to be sacrificed even though we know full well what vitality they would bring! For the American planner, it is immaterial whether virtually everyone in the building and nearby is working by artificial light. Thus he can build his towers close together, and this in turn generates the most striking aesthetic quality of his skyscraper groups: profiles soaring vertically in close parallel, the ensemble so overwhelming in its effect that a sprinkling of mock classical columns and architraves can really do very little harm.

We, by contrast, feel it is wrong to allow one building to steal the light from another. Consequently, should a time ever come when skyscrapers are built here in appreciable numbers, they will virtually never be grouped close together, and so the special effect of sheer parallel lines will not be seen. Generally speaking, every German skyscraper will stand alone, and the aesthetic considerations for the planners will accordingly be quite different from those obtaining in New York. These are not formal differences; they are real, practical differences, and they are plain for everyone to see. It is therefore only a pseudorealism—in fact, under the anti-Romantic veneer, it is pure Romanticism—that would plant a massive American-style block on the site by the Spree, as several voices have proposed.

The extreme opposite of such proposals is represented by the prize-winning project designed by Hans Scharoun of Insterburg: while Romantic in appearance, it is in reality a thoroughly practical concept, apart from a few, easily changed external details. It is probably more closely tailored to the character of the site than any of the other projects. The height differences in Scharoun's design are not arbitrary or whimsical, not "art": they derive logically from the circumstance that the three sides of this particular triangle have differing urban qualities. Friedrichstrasse is narrow, which rules out anything very high on that side, while the riverfront permits a truly soaring backdrop to the Reichstagufer. Scharoun's skyscraper is not ashamed to be a skyscraper. Yet he does not simply categorize the whole block schematically as "a skyscraper," which would be to disregard the realities of its siting, but confines that style to where it is genuinely appropriate. The notable sophistication of his design is apparent also in the complete absence of pretensions to "monumental" character. This is in no sense a building erected to represent something special. To treat it as symbolic, investing it with a heavily serious, dignified, lofty character, would be quite inappropriate. It is, rather, a building created for office work and commerce, a collection of shops, café, restaurant, cinema, arcade, elevators, stairs, and offices—none of which warrants any architectural rhetoric. So while others end up with a ponderous colossus, its dead weight compressing the multifarious trivialities of everyday needs behind the rigidity of a tragic mask, Scharoun's deliberately matter-of-fact approach yields for him a flowing, responsive building that makes no pretense of being anything other than what it in fact is: a sensational feature for the metropolis. By this means—and virtually alone among all the entrants—he enables himself to draw on all the resources of advertising. Standing as it does alone, free of neighboring and competing structures, and visible from a considerable distance on the bridge side in particular, this building with its expressive, swooping silhouette is an enhancement of its surroundings—which, indeed, it also is in practical terms—and not an intrusion.

NOTE

1. The Bund Deutscher Architekten is the professional body for German architects, equivalent to the AIA in the United States or the RIBA in Great Britain.

118

Egon Erwin Kisch

THE IMPOVERISHMENT AND ENRICHMENT OF THE BERLIN STREETS

First published as "Verarmung und Bereicherung der Berliner Strassen," *Lidové noviny* (Brno), 22 February 1923. Translated by Iain Boyd Whyte.

The Urania-system electric clocks that hang, illuminated, at underground stations and street corners are in keeping, if anything, with the tempo and character of prewar Berlin: *Carpe horam!*[1] Now they are being taken down; the coal shortage, electricity consumption, and the cost of their upkeep are the reasons for this. What a shame!

The "*Rotunden*" [pissoirs], too, are being gradually closed down. These are the little structures promoted by a foundation, the impulse for which was given in Paris a hundred and seventy years ago—to general annoyance and amusement—by the original and fearless journalist, Sebastien Mercier, with his blazing essay in the *Tableaux de Paris*.[2] But what for Paris was a necessary evil was for prewar Berlin an institution that had been incorporated into the hourly rhythm of the day. The Berliner, who left no time for eating and had no instinct for love, the coffee house, the pastry shop, indeed for any pleasure, also had no time and no taste for anything apart from business. And by business he understood only that which brought him money. For any other business he availed himself of the nearest *Rotunde* on his way back from lunch to the workplace. Thus every *Rotunde* had its regulars. Not even the most modest living, however, can be made from regulars with no interest in pleasure.

Among the many other curtailments of street life has been the ringing of the last bell for the dogs. They have eaten too much and now are being eaten themselves. These are wretched times—not fit for a dog. Building activity, which, at least as far as putting one story on another is concerned, was reasonably active, has been completely suspended. And yet the Berlin street life can register one enrichment, and something that is still being built. At the end of every street and at every corner "dollar stalls" [*Dollarhäuschen*] are springing up. Glass houses, set right on the street, where foreign currency can be exchanged. Most vigorously, for example, at the corner of Leipziger Strasse and Friedrichstrasse. At the corner of Nürnberger Strasse and Kleiststrasse, they stand in the middle of the road. Even on the holy avenue of Unter den Linden, where the electric tram is only allowed to cross under the street, a similar dollar stall has been pitched at the so-called Kranzler-Corner in front of the Café Bauer, the site before the war of the most expensive building site in the world.[3] These exchange stalls are also located in the most distant suburbs. They are constantly full of people, and as there is little room inside, there is a throng of people outside. They are a surrogate for the "*Rotunden*," the most modern public convenience, for whose construction there was no need for the summons of a Sebastien Mercier. They are also a substitute for the disappearing electric public clocks. For here you get the modern version of the exact time, which is regulated direct from the modern observatory—the Stock Exchange, which continuously transmits the exchange rates. [...] lei,[4] pesetas, pounds, Czech and Viennese crowns, Polish marks, dollars, and yen are exchanged here; this is the temple where Nietzsche's "revaluation of all values" reaches its consummation. Beside it stands a "*Rotunde*," doomed to extinction. The For Gentlemen door is closed, the For Ladies door is closed, and not even a dog raises its leg to its walls. There are no dogs anymore, and if there were any, they would run to the dollar stall.

NOTES

1. *Carpe horam!*: Use the hour! (Latin).
2. Louis-Sébastien Mercier, *Tableau de Paris*, 1782.
3. See above, text 54: Paul Lindau, Unter den Linden.
4. The leu (pl., lei) is the currency of Romania.

119

Ernst Kaeber

THE METROPOLIS AS HOME

First published as "Die Weltstadt als Heimat" in *Probleme der neuen Stadt Berlin: Darstellungen der Zukunftsaufgaben einer Millionenstadt,* ed. Hans Brennert and Erwin Stein (Berlin: Deutscher Kommunal-Verlag, 1926), pp. 194, 205–8. Translated by Iain Boyd Whyte.

It is one of the peculiarities of the metropolis that those things that should be self-evident become questions. The natural processes that are self-regulating in the countryside and in the small town become in the metropolis the product of regulating willpower and rational thought. The way in which its residents feed and clothe themselves, how they live, work, and find pleasure, how they feel and think—all this is determined by the governing spirit that forms every modern metropolis.

Even the most primeval sensibility that binds man to the soil, even the love of home becomes a problem. Indeed, the problem has become so acute that to critical minds the notions of metropolis and home [*Heimat*] seem to be contradictory. For sure; the big city dweller's sense of home can never be as straightforward or harmonious as that of the farmer on his native soil or of the house-owning citizen of a small town. There are too many class differences among city dwellers of origin, social status, and material and intellectual demands. Even for the great cities, there is no formula that consistently covers all options. [...] The problem looks different if we think of London, Paris, and Rome, and different again when we consider Vienna, Berlin, St. Petersburg, or the million-inhabitant cities of China and India, or the representatives of the New World: New York, Chicago, Rio, or Buenos Aires. So, without committing violence on the general framing of our theme, we may look at it in the particular context of Berlin.

[...]

The path to an organic structure and with it to the regaining of the masses was opened by the law of 27 April 1920.[1] Now the woods and meadows, the rivers and lakes no longer belong to Köpenick, Spandau, or whatever the lucky previous owners were called; they no longer belong to the state or to a bloodless interest group [Zweckverband],[2] but to each and every Berliner embraced by the expansive boundary of the metropolis. Once again the Berliner has a share in nature. The most general and liberal right to vote gives him a direct right of disposal over this valuable estate and also over the mighty economic enterprises and social institutions of the unified metropolis. Possessing equal rights and responsibilities, every inhabitant now becomes a full citizen. The overwhelming mass of problems and the almost superhuman difficulty of finding solutions to them in a time of extreme political and economic confusion awaken a passionate engagement in the work of the city of Berlin. The citizens of the old Berlin, together with those recently joined, respond to the decisions of the civic authorities either supportively or negatively. At the same time an authentic consciousness of one's native home is flowing from the peripheral boroughs and into the stony mass of Berlin, rubbing off in the process any hint of the petty or parochial. A new metropolitan sense of home [Heimat] is coming into being. It cannot be the same as that of the medieval city-state, or of the Biedermeier Berlin of the Prussian monarchy. The future generation will bring a prouder, more active, and more cosmopolitan consciousness to Berlin. This space-conquering sense of being at home in the metropolis will be first discovered by the same youth that must build the new Germany. To open the gates for them and to prepare the way is the task of the older generation.

Four roads lead into the new land. One leads the citizens of the stony urban desert, where they are deprived of light and air, to the source of all organic existence. The dark courtyard and smoky pub should no longer imprison the bodies and spirits of our young people. The greensward of the playgrounds and sports fields, spread across the city in a planned manner, calls them to life-renewing physical activity in the sun and fresh air. Shady pathways and rapid railways lead the tired and fatigued out of the city and into the peace and calm of the woods and meadows, which can no longer be destroyed by the madness of building speculation. Access to Mother Earth is no longer the privilege of those favored by destiny. The metropolis opens to all its residents access to free nature, completing the work that was begun with the lesser resources of the old, smaller city.

The second road is a spiritual one. In following it, Berlin will become directly aware that it is more than a random agglomeration of workplaces and that it is an organism, the purpose of whose existence has only now been revealed by the demolition of restraints that had become too tight. Our goal is to stimulate an awareness of local history and geography [*Heimatkunde*] in every Berliner and thus create an inner bond with this organism. The experience of the world war and of the upheavals that followed has created the psychological conditions for an intensive engagement with local history, while the creation of the metropolis has awakened questions about the process of its historical development. The Berliner is once again thinking about his history. In thinking about the reasons that made it possible for a small colony on the River Spree in the March of Brandenburg to become the preeminent city of the German empire, he positions himself as a link in the historical process. [. . .]

Less of a consolidation that a revolution of the intellectual habitus of the metropolitan dweller, however, is being brought about by the tearing down of the intellectual barriers that continue to divide the social classes. The joint elementary school and the advancement of poor but talented children into higher schools are steps toward this goal, to which adult education classes and, to a certain extent, the press are also contributing. But much more important is wireless broadcasting, which reaches hundreds of thousands regardless of age, sex, or class. The metropolis has been gifted not only the most modern but also the most powerful and effective means of public education and instruction. Only after several years will it be possible to assess its impact, which is growing day by day. But it is certain that a fundamental change, linked to a marked leveling out of the intellectual attitudes of the metropolitan dweller, will be the result. It is to be hoped that this leveling process will mean the attainment of a higher level. Accompanying the radio is the only slightly earlier invention of the wordless stage—the cinema, which works more strongly on our feelings and senses. There is no doubt that even if it is not the most elevated form of theater, it is the one best attuned to the rhythm of the metropolis as the medium of relaxation for the city dweller of every educational level. For better or worse, the cinema, like the radio, is here, and both will fulfill their mission.

And now for the final path leading into the land of the future. It is a future in which the metropolis must solve the housing problem and in the process stimulate our sense of home and place to take natural root. However heavily the consequences of the war weigh on Germany and its capital city, the preparations must already begin today. The building regulations and the general structure plan proclaim the new era, in which no courtyard dwellings, deprived of light, can still be built. We cannot at the moment foresee how the negative side of the task—the disposal of the vast number of unfit dwellings—might be achieved. It is certain, however, that they must go, and that this is the goal whose achievement will prove the right of Berlin to exist as a metropolis. The day will then have come on which the metropolis will have become home [*Heimat*] to all its children.

NOTES

1. On 27 April 1920, following a vote in the Prussian Legislative Assembly [Preußische Landesversammlung], the city of Berlin was joined with seven other townships, fifty-nine rural councils, and twenty-seven private estates to form the single administrative entity of Groß-Berlin—Greater Berlin.

2. See above, text 25: Patrick Abercrombie, Berlin: Its Growth and Present State.

120

Karl Scheffler

BERLIN FIFTY YEARS FROM NOW

Perspectives on One of the World's Great Cities

First published as "Berlin in 50 Jahren: Perspektiven einer Weltstadt," *Uhu,* June 1926; reprinted in *Uhu: Das Monatsmagazin,* ed. Christian Ferber (Berlin: Ullstein, 1979), pp. 127–30. Translated by Michael Loughridge.

Before the war, the utopians among us were trying to prove that in a few decades the population of Berlin would reach 12 million. Miles of roads—to be lined by high, many-storied buildings—had already been marked out, and indeed in some cases drainage and asphalt surfacing work had been completed. The city seemed set to go on growing just as it had ever since the foundation of the German Empire.[1] Things look quite different now, following the catastrophe of the war. Not just in Berlin, but everywhere. In all the major cities, a quite different type of development is getting under way. It may be somewhat delayed in Berlin, because the country lacks cash and also the freedom to manage its own economy; however, nothing can suppress the new trend, not even the unnatural economic constraints that have been imposed upon us. Throughout Europe, and in the United Sates as well, the problem of the great cities is essentially the same, both in its genesis and in its consequences. What has changed is that the trend is no longer toward further agglomeration, further hypertrophy at the expense of the countryside and the towns; instead, there is an unmistakable shift toward loosening the structure of the city, extending the urban feel out into the countryside, making city and country a single entity, and to some degree making the whole region into a spaced-out metropolis. Young architects are now less interested in city expansion plans than in overall population plans that envisage the zoning of whole states and provinces by region. The trend in industry to move out of the metropolis and settle its workers and administrative staff in the country, close by the factories; the recent but rapidly growing phenomenon of a population movement that, in contrast to rural depopulation, is at bottom a particular type of urban depopulation; the efforts, now taking effect, to provide the worker with enough land to support himself in the event of future unemployment; the systematic parceling up of the great estates into small farms; the democratization of the rural population, the industrialization of their working routines, the urban character of their lifestyle; and last but not least the subjugation of space and time by telephone, radio, railway, motorcar, and airplane—all of these are symptomatic of the impending dissolution of the socially and physically overconcentrated metropolis, symptomatic of its future dispersal in new guise over the country as a whole.

This is an inexorable development from which Berlin will not be exempt. Those who envisage the expansion of Berlin as meaning ever-greater concentration, with skyscrapers going up in the city center and the suburbs spreading out of sight, are in for a disappointment. Berlin will *indeed* grow much more, and will change more than those now living can imagine, but the city's character will evolve in a way not experienced in the past. The day will come when Greater Berlin includes Küstrin and Frankfurt an der Oder to the east, and in the west stretches beyond Brandenburg, so that in fact Berlin and the March of Brandenburg will broadly be one and the same. The imperial capital will be something like a city-state, a wholly urban province alongside many other German city-states. And in this metropolitan region known as Berlin, with its population of millions, the country dweller will have become an inhabitant of the metropolis, just as much as the onetime inner-city resident will breathe fresh air and become a resident of the countryside—in some cases, even a cultivator. The new city province will be served by a close-knit system of well-surfaced roads, and mass public transport will be express transport. Forty years ago, the Borsig factories were at the Oranienburger Tor; today they are ten kilometers farther out, at Tegel; a few decades on, and they are likely to have moved out fifty kilometers from the center. Much the same will apply to the AEG works and to the premises of other major industrial concerns. The settlement pattern of the city of Berlin, which to this day is still being developed in a generally unsystematic way—notwithstanding the twelve hundred new apartment homes just completed at Britz[2]—will have to take on the character of a massive colonial development. At that point the mass production of houses will lead inevitably to the industrialization of building, regardless of what those most concerned may feel about it. Houses will in future be constructed no differently from motorcars and airplanes; the craftsmanship of the future age is called Technology. The consequence will be that the building industry will adopt standardized, normalized components, and that this approach, the actual construction method, will come to determine architectural style, with individual imagination in design making way for a collective will.

The ancient heart of Berlin, the present city center, will not lose in importance

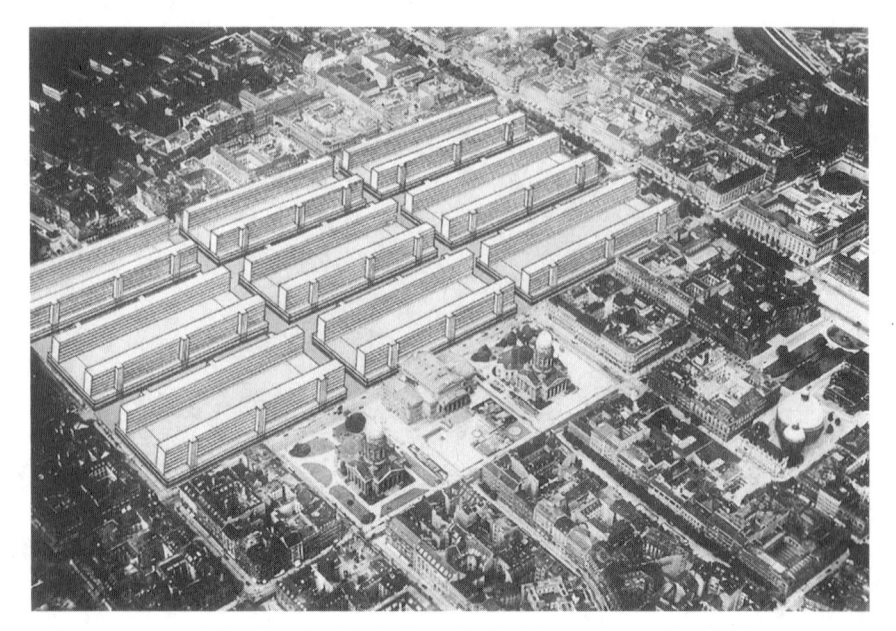

FIGURE 29. Project for the rebuilding of Friedrichstadt, Berlin (Ludwig Hilberseimer, architect), 1929, The Art Institute of Chicago, E21663-A. Photography @ The Art Institute of Chicago.

as a result of the looser urban structure. On the contrary: the center of such an extensive city will acquire all the more significance in its roles as intersection point of major routes, as general clearinghouse, as trade-exhibition location, seat of administration, seat of government. For these reasons the "city" quarter will have to be redeveloped on as grand a scale as Berlin's known physical drawbacks will admit. Inevitably, now, some of the long-planned through routes must have their path cleared, and others, still more radical, will have to follow. There has been a proposal for a central railway station, to be built underground on site of the Humboldthafen, accessed from afar with electric trains. But no matter what solution is ultimately found for this problem, whether a main station in the city center or several large termini farther out, the fact is that the present situation cannot be sustained for much longer. In particular, the wide swathes of permanent way cutting deep into the city from all points of the compass cannot in the long run be dispensed with as building land. They rip up the city plan, block the traffic, and to all intents and purpose lie there as dead space. The wide tracks serving the Anhalter and Potsdamer railway stations may be cited as particularly blatant examples, as can the extensive area bounded by the Stadtbahn, the Spree, the Packhof, and Schloss Bellevue, opposite the northern part of the Zoological

Gardens. This would have been an ideal site for museums and exhibition halls; developing it would have helped make this northern end of the zoo into a lively social rendezvous point.

The idea of a city having several focal points is absolutely correct. Besides Alexanderplatz and Friedrichstadt—the latter is by no means dead—a new center has grown up on the Kurfürstendamm, and in just the same way further focal points for the business and social life of the city will develop in due course. The same can be seen in London and Paris. The westward migration has persisted. The right bank of the Havel from Spandau to Kladow has so much potential that it has been truly said Berlin will one day lie as much on the Havel as on the Spree, and will merge physically with Potsdam. This prospect in turn points to the need to move the university, the art colleges, and other educational and cultural institutions out of the city center. All such institutions, together with their libraries and research centers, belong out in the country. A student's proper place is not a bed-sitting room in Linienstrasse[3] but an attractive "college" with gardens and playing fields, somewhere not far from lakes and forests, where sports can be pursued. Within the widely dispersed metropolis, it will be essential to create a self-contained university city.

[. . .]

But the coming decades must see a start made on changing the things in Berlin that need changing. The question is whether the approach will be piecemeal, timorous, forced through against resistance, grudging—or will be imaginative, enterprising, and bold. Berlin will become more important for Germany as a whole to the extent that political and economic unionism takes hold, and that what is described by the term "the United States of Europe" becomes a fact. To the degree, however, that Berlin grows more important, it will also grow more German. Yet its new importance will not be symbolized by skyscrapers. In Germany, very high buildings will remain rare. Berlin's importance will be proclaimed in the radical redevelopment of the city center and in the systematic loosening of the excessively dense urban structure; both these tasks will require master plans on the grandest scale. The work of preparing them should be entrusted to a study group that will include men able not only to see the future shape of things as a whole, but to set out the ways and means by which that future may be realized.

NOTES

1. The German Empire—*das deutsche Reich*—was founded in 1871.
2. A reference to the Hufeisen (horseshoe) housing estate at Britz, built in 1925–31 to the design of Martin Wagner and Bruno Taut. See below, text 176: Leo Adler, Housing Estates in the Britz District of Berlin.
3. Linienstrasse is a back street in central Berlin, running parallel to Torstrasse between Friedrichstrasse and Rosenthaler Strasse.

121

Martin Wagner, Werner Hegemann, and Heinrich Mendelssohn
SHOULD BERLIN BUILD SKYSCRAPERS?

First published as "Soll Berlin Wolkenkratzer bauen?" *Wasmuths Monatshefte für Baukunst* 12 (1928), pp. 286–89. Translated by Michael Loughridge.

Prefatory note: Since the day two years ago when Peter Behrens, lecturing in Berlin, voiced his wholehearted admiration for the chaos that prevails in the New York financial quarter, no one need be surprised that the fantastic skyscraper concepts of the gifted American draughtsman Hugo Ferriss find imitators over here, and that the Romantics of the skyscraper forests regard factually based opposition to the building of skyscrapers as old-fashioned and reactionary. These issues therefore need to be reviewed from time to time. Accordingly, we here reprint the full text of three interviews published on 27 April by the "12 Uhr Blatt" [midday edition] of the *Neue Berliner Zeitung,* which is noted for the reliability of its interview reporting. The three interviews are reproduced here in the sequence of their original publication in the daily newspaper.[1]

The following is quoted verbatim from the "12 Uhr Blatt":

DR. MARTIN WAGNER

Currently Impossible!

Unlike New York, Berlin is not compressed between the shores of an island. There is therefore no immediate reason to build upward rather than outward.

[...]

Thus the situation at present is that although there is more than a square kilometer of building land existing in the "City,"[2] it is not practically possible to satisfy the increasing demand for space. But the civic authorities must bear the responsibility for controlling unplanned multistory building, which would re-create New York's problems here. Certainly, the risk of such developments here is still low. Over here, the construction costs for a skyscraper rise so sharply once the height exceeds six or seven stories as to be uneconomic at present in relation to our land prices. Additionally, experience gained in any department store, for instance, assures us that the public greatly prefer ground-floor space to upper stories, and will visit the latter only with some reluctance. It would therefore have to be borne in mind that in Germany the higher floors would prove considerably less attractive to users.

A high-rise building imposes a greater public burden. Increased demands are made on street cleansing and transportation, and this would have to be recouped

through special tax measures. If one takes into account the increased operating costs that would result from, for instance, the need to install water-pressure pumps and an elaborate heating plant in each building, the idea of skyscrapers being suitable for our circumstances is unlikely to be pursued.
[...]

DR. WERNER HEGEMANN

Only as an exception!
[...]

A skyscraper acts like a suction pump, drawing in all life and traffic from the surrounding area. Experience in the United States has shown that the land behind it remains devalued for years and effectively cut off.

The entrepreneur who builds an office tower gains light, air, and advertising value—at the expense of a host of other individuals whose buildings have lost in value. The mass of the people can count themselves fortunate that the decentralizing inventions of the modern age, such as telephone, telex, and urban rail networks, have done away with the need to live crammed together in overcrowded, comfortless, and unhealthy proximity.

The progressive outward relocation of the best New York shopping districts demonstrates that expansion and decentralization are feasible even on an island and can be implemented even in the face of immense obstacles. In the case of quite a number of trades, concentration around a single focal point is due to nothing more than mass delusion.

The demand for high buildings is generated in areas where traffic is heaviest. But that is just where they should not be allowed, so as not to further overload the areas in question.

The high building can be designed for full aesthetic effect, but must be permitted only as the great exception to the rule—for example, as an accent occurring just once in the overall cityscape, as city hall or as a single central office block, and only at a specially selected location lying outside the principal traffic flows. Care must also be taken to ensure that profits accruing benefit the community rather than particular individuals.

In no circumstances should features of historic value, such as our showpiece boulevard, Unter den Linden, be permitted to suffer as a consequence of such high building or extensions. There must be no question of our remaining city-center green areas suffering as a result of such development; never again must one of them be made into a mere backyard as at the Europahaus.[3]

HEINRICH MENDELSSOHN

High-Rise Buildings for Specific Purposes!

[...]

The period reflected by Berlin's architecture is, approximately, the century from 1800 to 1900; the great changes since then in the city's way of life, and in the constraints under which it lives, are scarcely reflected at all in visual form.

The main reason for this is that the buildings are financially anchored in place by the huge capital sums invested in them: they are *immeubles* in the literal sense of the term: immovable. In complete contrast, buildings in the United States, including skyscrapers, are not *immeubles* in this sense, as it is well known that income suffices to pay off the loan finance within sixteen or at most twenty years, after which in the vast majority of cases the building is demolished to make way for a new and up-to-date high-rise.

The continuous process of change and the continuous financial evolution that characterize the American scene, ensuring progressive renewal of cities and their buildings, is not something that can be reproduced in German cities, Berlin in particular. The reason is the high cost of property loans.

However, there is no reason why the development of fresh construction sites in the Berlin "City" should not produce modern and efficient buildings to reflect the new face of the city's commercial life.

[...]

In the interests of introducing greater efficiency into the city's commercial activity, skyscrapers must be seen as appropriate for Berlin in relation to certain specific ends, and there is no cause for fear that a chaotic development resembling New York's would ensue. In the first place, there is no money to finance the construction of such buildings in quantity; second, there is no demand.

Of course, skyscrapers should not be allowed on relatively narrow streets where they will deprive neighboring properties of light and air. It is not just desirable but essential that where building has a strong vertical presence, this should be compensated for by reducing its horizontal footprint.

At this point in history, when industry routinely exploits new knowledge in order to stay competitive, it makes no sense to ignore the significant discovery that for a city of world rank, for certain purposes, development in the vertical plane—in other words, the skyscraper—is a vital necessity.

NOTES

1. Martin Wagner was the city architect [*Stadtbaurat*] of Berlin; Werner Hegemann was the editor of *Wasmuths Monatshefte für Baukunst* and author of the definitive 1920s critique of Berlin architecture and city planning; *Das steinerne Berlin* (Berlin: Kiepenhauer, 1930); Heinrich Mendelsohn was a property developer, responsible for a "skyscraper torso" at the Anhalter Station in Berlin.

2. "City," written in English, is used throughout the original German text to refer to the central business district of Berlin and is retained in the translation.

3. The eleven-story, steel-framed Europahaus on Stresemannstrasse was built in 1931, after considerable controversy, to the design of the architects Bielenberg and Moser. One of the first high-rise office blocks in Berlin, its large neon advertising signs and a fifteen-meter-tall illuminated tower made it a salient point in the 1930s city skyline by both day and night.

122

Martin Wagner and Adolf Behne
THE NEW BERLIN—WORLD CITY

First published as "Das neue Berlin—die Weltstadt Berlin" in *Das Neue Berlin,* ed. Martin Wagner (Berlin: Deutsche Bauzeitung, 1929), pp. 4–5. Translated by Michael Loughridge.

Our Imperial capital city owes its architectural character to the kings of Prussia. Beyond this dynasty's achievements, all that was created by the corporate spirit of the citizens, by business and private-enterprise builders in the way of squares and street vistas, from the foundation of the empire to the outbreak of the World War, is of little account in terms of civic architecture. Not until after the world war, not until Berlin received its *second* christening as imperial capital of the German Republic, and with it its new constitution as a unitary civic administration, did public interest in reshaping the city first become significant. The first major impetus toward a new civic architecture came from *residential* building. Major new housing developments such as Britz and Zehlendorf, featuring whole residential areas built to a unified design, provided the model for larger-scale urban design solutions. In parallel with this civic restructuring in the outlying parts of Berlin, restructuring also took place in the old, outdated urban area, driven by the unprecedented demand for transport facilities. Over the coming twenty years, traffic in the old city and house building in the new districts will totally change the urban design face of Berlin.

There would have been considerably less impetus behind the redevelopment and expansion of the city had not the municipal finances of the imperial capital been progressively reinforced, at an accelerating rate year after year, since the end of the war. The capital's improving economic position can be illustrated by means of some statistics that speak for themselves:

1. Between 1913 and 1928, the population of Berlin increased by about 275,000. That is almost equivalent to the establishment, during this period, of three new cities of *Großstadt* rank (100,000 inhabitants) within the Berlin city boundaries.
2. Incoming rail and canal freight tonnage rose from 12.2 million in 1913 to over 21 million in 1928. Export tonnage rose over the same period from 3.5 to over 7 million.

3. Cooperative Society annual turnover rose from 194 marks per customer in 1913 to over 355 marks in 1928. Even allowing for the devaluation of the currency, the purchasing power of the working population of Berlin has clearly risen.
4. Deposits in the Berlin Savings Bank rose from 15.64 million marks in 1913 to over 70 million in the first eight months of 1928.
5. The number of motor vehicles in Berlin rose from about nine thousand in 1913 to over eighty thousand on September 1, 1928.

These few figures should suffice as evidence that Berlin is both *working* and *saving*. A city that can show growth of this order has no option: it *must* build, must restructure, must evolve a new spirit and a new body.

The new spirit of Berlin is not the spirit of Potsdam, the spirit of court and aristocracy, taking its cue from Rome and Paris, modeling Berlin on the seats of power of foreign rulers. The new spirit is that of the *world-rank metropolis,* it is the spirit that works to draw out the people's resources in labor and recreation, civilization and culture—resources superior to those of all a nation's other cities—and to bring them to fruition in the form of *unsurpassable* achievement. This world-metropolis spirit will by definition be national in underlying character, international in style. But its most essential characteristic is *self-belief,* its awareness of its significance and of the responsibility it bears vis-à-vis other cities in other countries. The spirit of the new Berlin is a world-metropolis spirit and so must transcend the local focus of old-style civic loyalties. And this world-metropolis spirit it is that must define the content and form of the urban setting in which it will dwell.

There will be no lack of *problems* facing the new Berlin, and even the *form* chosen for the solutions must be designed to surpass the standards of ordinary, smaller cities. And the nature of these problems? Whether the issue be the planning of transport routes below, at, or above ground level, of large schools and hospitals and administrative buildings, the construction of factories, power stations, and office blocks, the provision of open-air and indoor swimming pools together with playgrounds and sports fields, the building of central market facilities and slaughterhouses, the opening up for the populace of the natural attractions surrounding the world metropolis, the establishment of new residential areas and the replacement of outdated residential areas with modern business districts, the creation of new roads to accommodate the increased traffic, the redesign of city squares to help the flow of increased traffic—all these problems, confronting the new Berlin today, will have to be worked on and solved in full consciousness of the responsibilities that go with the city's world status. Currently, in the city of Berlin, the tempo of new construction represents an investment rate of at least 600 to 700 million marks annually. These building costs are equivalent to those of a brand-new town with a population of seventy-five thousand. Expenditure of this order must be made *visible,* must find superb formal expression, must produce real civic distinction at world level.

In terms of formal expression, Berlin has not yet attained world quality. The creative brains that could produce fitting forms of expression are not lacking. What we do lack is *purposive leadership,* the coordinating brain capable of so harnessing and concerting all resources as to produce a cityscape that is a visible statement of world rank. We have not yet found the maestro who will direct the production of Berlin, world metropolis. The will that used to command and direct, the will of the ruling dynasty, has become extinct. The world metropolis of Berlin is governed today not by a single democracy, but by a whole complex of democracies, without strong or unified leadership. Whatever solution may eventually be found for this problem of coordination and leadership for the world city, it will ultimately have to be one that operates similarly to the former dynastic rule, one that paves the way for the new Berlin to be created in a new spirit and a new visible form by a world citizen enjoying the trust of the people.

123

Martin Wagner

THE DESIGN PROBLEM OF A CITY SQUARE FOR A METROPOLIS

The Competition of the "Verkehr" Company
for the Remodeling of Alexanderplatz

First published as "Das Formproblem eines Weltstadtplatzes: Wettbewerb der Verkehrs-A.G. für die Umbauung des Alexanderplatzes" in *Das Neue Berlin,* ed. Martin Wagner (Berlin: Deutsche Bauzeitung, 1929), pp. 33–41. Translated by Michael Loughridge.

[…]

A city square for a metropolis of world rank is no small-town project. The design of a central square for a small town, the design of a marketplace, can follow purely architectural considerations without coming into conflict with the traffic-flow requirements, which are occasional (market-day) rather than constant. The world-rank city, by contrast, has squares that are in near-continuous use as sluice gates for traffic, sorting points for a circulatory system of major traffic arteries. Now, one can argue that the primary and essential requirement is to funnel the traffic speedily through the sorting point, and that formal design, the specific solution chosen, is secondary. Yet for any urban-planning architect neither of these can be seen in isolation from the other, and closer inspection of the problem will lead to the conclusion that function and form, plan and elevation, ground surface and street front fuse together into an *organic unity.*

FIGURE 30. Rebuilding of Alexanderplatz: Alexanderhaus (top right; Peter Behrens, architect), 1931. Landesarchiv Berlin, 61/2006

In a metropolis of world rank, the city squares are organisms of formally distinctive visual appearance.

Organically designed squares fitting for a world metropolis remain unknown to this day in Europe, even in Paris. If one were to set up a list of requirements for designing such metropolitan squares, the following points could be made:

1. The traffic-flow expert must calculate the square's traffic capacity and adjust this figure to allow for an increase in traffic over the next twenty-five years. A square's traffic capacity is itself a function of the traffic capacity of the roads debouching on the square. There is a direct reciprocal relationship between the two figures. It is therefore primarily the task of the traffic-flow specialist to calculate the dimensions for a metropolitan square, and he must calculate and estimate accurately.
2. The reference to the limited life span of a metropolitan square implies that the buildings surrounding the square do not possess permanent economic or architectural value. No urban planner or traffic expert will be in a position to estimate traffic growth over a period of twenty-five years to come. To make a square too large because of fears about future traffic growth would amount

to a waste of public money. This means that in future all financing required in the construction of metropolitan squares will need to be repayable over a term of at most twenty-five years, so that at that point the design can be modified in the light of current needs.
3. Traffic must be enabled to cross the square with the maximum achievable dispatch, smoothness, and clarity. A metropolitan square therefore requires separation of the paths used by railed vehicles (streetcars), wheeled vehicles (motorcars), and pedestrian traffic. The ideal of a square used as a traffic intersection is a design that permits each of the three categories of traffic to pass through the intersection without same-level crossings. (Traffic circulating at different levels.)
4. Every metropolitan square to be used by traffic needs to be so designed as to permit a thoroughly effective differentiation of traffic according to speed. This differentiation of traffic speed should be sought by means of underground railways below surface level and expressways for motorcars above ground, each linking two traffic hubs.
5. The effect of these requirements is to make the metropolitan square a highly sophisticated and expensive piece of engineering, the costs of which have to be wholly or partly recouped via the buildings surrounding the square. The circulating traffic on the square has to be balanced by what may be termed "standing traffic," which taps the consumer wealth of the crowds passing through the square (shops, restaurants and cafés, department stores, business premises, and so on). This results in a concentration of buildings, the facades of which need to be aligned along the circulation paths of pedestrians—that is, of the consumers.
6. This requirement establishes the link between the traffic solution and the architectural design. Maximum clarity of form, achieving its characteristic aesthetic effect both by day and by night, is a basic essential in any metropolitan square. Light flooding *in* by day and flooding *out* at night ensures that the square's visual character is totally changed. Color, shape, and light (advertising) are the three main building components required in new metropolitan squares.
7. It must not be forgotten that metropolitan squares are treatments of *volume*, in contrast to the linear traffic flow of the straight connecting roads. Those resident in the metropolis have the natural wish to experience these volumes as such. This means that the overbuilding of certain streets from the third story upward is as far from representing a "cutting off" of these streets and their hinterland as a railway station or a sluice gate could be deemed to cut off what lies beyond it. A metropolitan square is at one and the same time a stopping place and a sluice gate: a stopping place for consumer wealth, and a sluice gate for flowing traffic.

On the basis of these requirements for city squares in the metropolis, Berlin, too, will witness new designs for its squares, designs radically different from what it has known so far.

124

Max Berg

THE PLATZ DER REPUBLIK IN BERLIN

First published as "Der Platz der Republik in Berlin," *Zentralblatt der Bauverwaltung* 50, no. 9 (5 March 1930), pp. 185–88. Translated by Iain Boyd Whyte.

Berlin's responsibility derives from its position as the capital city and representative city of the tribes that have united to form the German state. The principal substance of this task, consequently, is to portray the nature and character of the German nation and its economic and cultural position in and relationship to the world, and to act as a vehicle for the collaboration of the German people in peaceful competition with the other nations of the world.

[. . .]

As a result of this unique responsibility, the urban design of Berlin is not only the task of the inhabitants of Berlin, the city authorities, or of Prussia, but of the German people—indeed, of the German state. As the one-sided view still persists, particularly in the city administration, that the redesign of the Platz der Republik is simply a large-scale architectural task with only local implications, it is once again necessary to stress the much broader significance, extending far beyond this local context, that is due to this square since its change of name.[1]

It is necessary in the Platz der Republic and the surrounding city quarter, to give the "World City Berlin" an urbanistic expression—political, economic, and cultural—both in its content and in its formal design: the Reichstag building (dedicated to the German people) sets the political tone for the ministerial buildings (the governmental organs of the German nation), embassies, consulates, and legations (the nations of the world). A central station for all long-distance and local railways, in which the existing east–west line (Charlottenburg to the Schlesischer Station) crosses at right angles with a north–south track that still has to be built. To do this, the existing termini (Lehrter, Potsdamer, Anhalter, and Görlitzer stations) would be removed and underground links to the north–south track created via the appropriate branch lines. In this cruciform station, which should be situated not on the Platz der Republik itself, but farther north, both above and below ground in axial alignment to the Humboldthafen, global transportation and the German state will be brought together both practically and symbolically. From here both foreigners and native Germans will reach their embassies, consulates, and governmental offices.

But in the context of the commercial life of the German nation, foreigners and natives should also be able to meet at the same place. For this purpose a large exhibition park is planned following the model of the world exhibitions, on a site adjoining the central station, currently occupied mainly by warehouses and freight sheds. [. . .] As the representative focus not only of the world city but of the German nation, Berlin as the city of the German Reich would grow in its urbanistic totality as a massive showpiece of the German spirit.

Three architects—Hans Poelzig, Peter Behrens, and Hugo Häring—were commissioned by the city of Berlin to produce design proposals for the Platz der Republik, which, together with the Mächler plan,[2] were shown at the 1927 Kunstausstellung.[3]

NOTES

1. Like many of the principle streets and squares in Berlin, the Platz der Republik has had a checkered history of naming and renaming. Originally an army parade ground outside the city wall, from 1730 to 1865 it was called the Exerzierplatz vor dem Brandenburg Tor (Exercise Grounds beyond the Brandenburg Gate). Following the Prussian victory over Denmark in 1864, it was renamed Königsplatz (King's Square) on 19 January 1865. The abdication of the Kaiser in 1918 prompted further debates on the subject, and on 26 February 1926 it was renamed Platz der Republik. This designation had little appeal to the National Socialists, however, who on seizing power in 1933 reverted to the former name of Königsplatz. Finally, on 31 March 1948, the square reverted once again to another previously favored name, Platz der Republik, which has survived to this day.

2. For Mächler, see above, text 112: Martin Mächler, The Major Population Center and Its Global Importance.

3. The Berliner Kunstausstellung 1927 (Berlin Art Exhibition 1927) was held at the Landesausstellungsgebäude near the Lehrter Station. It is entirely possible that either Albert Speer or Adolf Hitler, or both, would have been aware of the works exhibited and the vigorous discussion stimulated by Berg and others on the need for a north–south axis in Berlin. These discussions predated the National Socialist dream of a great, north–south axis in Berlin, anchored at each end by railway stations that would be linked underground. On the Hitler/Speer version, see below, text 227: Hans Stephan, Berlin; and text 228: Albert Speer, Replanning the Capital of the Reich.

125

Werner Hegemann

BERLIN, CITY OF STONE

The History of the Largest Tenement City in the World (1930)

First published as Hegemann, *Das Steinerne Berlin: Geschichte der größten Mietskasernenstadt der Welt* (Berlin: Gustav Kiepenhauer, 1930), pp. 23–24, 344–45, 359–60, 469–72, 485. Translated by Iain Boyd Whyte.

Similar to German foreign policy, German city building also became infected, and with dreadful results, by the achievements of the all-knowing, overactive, but in every meaningful sense of the word irresponsible bureaucracy, whose characteristics were admired by many as "truly Prussian." And this in spite of the fact the Bismarck himself had already prophesized that "sooner or later the point will be reached when we shall be overwhelmed by the weight of subaltern bureaucracy." With a sideswipe at the old-time, military school of Frederick the Great, Bismarck complained that the native Prussian blood did not produce high-level political leadership and was unwilling to assume responsibility for its own actions.

This Prussian sterility has greatly damaged our city building, and in particular the problematic development of our capital city. What Bismarck detected in the aristocratic Prussian diplomats is equally true of the national and civic administrators of Berlin: specifically, Prussian bureaucrats "could not easily be given the polish of their European counterparts." But they succeeded in creating a German capital that, as the greatest accumulation of tenement houses in the world, can perhaps be called one of the most astonishing creations of the German spirit. This achievement can be appreciated only through comparisons. In London—the largest city in the world—eight people live, on average, in each house; in Philadelphia the figure is five, in Chicago nine, in the island and skyscraper city of New York twenty, and in the compressed and formerly fortified city of Paris thirty-eight people live in each house. In Berlin, however, which like London, Chicago, or Philadelphia can expand without restraint across the flat, surrounding land, seventy-eight people on average live in each house, and most of these barracks are without gardens.

In this unique urban creation of the bureaucratized German spirit, a dispute flared up before the war between the statistical offices of the cities of Schöneberg and Berlin over whether 600,000 or "only" 567,270 residents of greater Berlin lived in housing in which each room was occupied by more than four people. At the same time, there were no playgrounds for half a million children. Neither by the state nor by the Berlin city authorities, however, were any effective steps taken to address the desperate need for housing and for playgrounds.

[. . .]

Bismarck's criticism of the "legal excrement" of Prussian bureaucracy fits particularly well the Berlin structure plan, which together with the Berlin building swindle produced the breeding ground for the inflation of the *Gründerjahre*.[1]

Before the [Franco-Prussian] War of 1870, just as before the world war, tenement-house building had come to a stop. In contrast, a series of villa developments, which were clearly stimulated by the writings of Huber and Faucher,[2] achieved very promising successes. Already in 1886, the charming villa colony was established at Berlin-Westend, beyond the jurisdiction of the structure plan. The remains still survive today as alien elements, set between the canyonlike rows of the Berlin tenement barracks.

Someone who deserves greater attention as one of the most important city builders of Berlin is the Hamburg businessman Carstenn. Like Faucher he was a really brilliant man, but in his efforts to transfer to Berlin such concepts as generosity of scale and the elegant life, which he had acquired from historic cities like Hamburg and London, Carstenn—just like Faucher—made the fatal mistake of underestimating the superior strength of the Prussian bureaucracy.

[...]

Bringing with him the experience he had gathered in London and Hamburg, Carstenn came to Berlin and in 1865 acquired from the nobility the estates of Lichterfelde and Giesendorf in order to establish there an elegant villa colony in the English style, outside the jurisdiction of the structure plan, which had already been corrupted by the official agencies. He subsequently also bought the Wilmersdorf estate. These large estates were composed mainly of grazing land for sheep, surrounding quiet villages, whose modest agricultural produce was brought by horse and cart to Berlin or to the nearest stations; Zehlendorf or Großbeeren. In contrast to the Prussian state, which had taken the whole period between the War of Independence and 1862 to prepare a bad street plan for Berlin, Carstenn did not need decades to establish his layout. Already in 1868 he sold his first building site. On the occasion of a visit made in 1869 by Kaiser Wilhelm I to the flourishing development in Lichterfelde, arranged by his patron, von Roon, Carstenn replied to the question of the probable development of Berlin: "Your Majesty, after the achievements of 1866,[3] Berlin is destined to be the first city of the Continent, and as far as its physical expansion is concerned, Berlin and Potsdam must become *one* city, linked by the Grunewald as a park."

Viewed not only from the contemporary perspective but also from that of today, this urban vision enabled Carstenn to achieve extraordinary things. In order to get cheap building land, Carstenn went beyond the expensive "second ring," so-called, and moved into what was described as the "third" or "village ring," Already in 1869, Faucher wrote that "through his vigorous activity in street building, lighting by means of self-produced gas, tree planting and the laying out of gardens, the creation of omnibus connections with the city and with the nearest railway stations, setting up restaurants, and so on, and above all through the cheapness of the building sites, Carstenn had already sold enough plots by the second year (1869), some of which were already built on, that that price of the site and the costs of the works were already covered. The income from the remaining plots, which assuredly would be developed, was pure profit for him." The statistician Engel subsequently announced that Carstenn's net profit from Lichterfelde was estimated at several million thalers.

[...]

Strousberg continues the story: "The expansion across the borders of the distant Berlin, the withdrawal from agricultural production of countless fields miles away Berlin, the fact that we can now see young trees being planted where potatoes should be growing in order to mark the boundaries of future streets on sites that 10 million inhabitants could not occupy, sites that are owned by commercial companies and private individuals, thousands of whom have lost their fortunes—for all this we can thank Herr von Carstenn.... His successors, however, are mostly cheats and swindlers, and have not brought to the business the understanding, the means, and the honesty of Herr von Carstenn. It was he, however, who showed how to transform sandy soil miles from Berlin into building land, he who invented the market sites like this. There were more than enough sandy sites. The time was ripe, and others continued the business on a scale that has led to barely calculable damage and loss." These words of the fallen "Railway King," Strousberg, who was admired by Carstenn and promptly followed him into economic decline.[4] Even harder than Carstenn's developments in Lichterfelde, the million-dollar swindle hit the Westend speculation. Its founder, Quistorp (like the Mehring/Piscator "Kaufmann von Berlin"[5] in the recent inflation period), arrived in Berlin as a basically decent man. [...] But as the speculation fever set in after the [1870] war, he became one of the "bloodiest" of the *Gründer,* the new breed of entrepreneurs. He pronounced society to be "the experiment of a humane principal" and turned himself into a private company. The shares in this company became one of the main speculative investments of the *Gründerjahre.* Westend became the hub of the rat kingdom of fraudulent building projects and a classic example of the devastating impact that can result from land speculation under the Prussian administration, and the Prussian fiscal, bond-issuing, and planning legislation, when rising rents and land values conjure up the fantasy of unlimited possibilities. What occurred at Westend also happened at that time all around the outskirts of Berlin.

[...]

The battle fought by the housing reformers in Berlin since the beginning of the 1840s can hardly look forward to a victorious outcome in the future. On the other side, the need to return to the small, single-family house is much less pressing then it was fifty years ago, or even before the war. Low-rise and small houses are needed primarily in a country with a growing population and promising future. While childless families and even families with few children are quite happy in multistory housing within close range of the city-center entertainments, children in general need not only the sun in order to thrive, but also access to the soil and to a garden. The enforced accommodation of the population in tenement barracks and the child-unfriendly living conditions in Berlin, which the Prussian state has imposed on Berlin over the centuries, perfectly reflects the postwar crisis and the falling birthrate of the postwar period.

[...]

The overcrowding of Berlin apartments, under which half the officially registered multichild families suffer, has, however, improved since the war. [...] Nevertheless the living conditions today are worse rather than better. For as a result of the falling birth rate and the economic crisis, there are more non–family members lodging in the apartments than before the war. The structure and stability of the family, as well as the health of the children, is now at more risk than before the war as a result of the many lodgers and bedders.

In addition, living conditions have become substantially worse, as the old apartments, which since the beginning of the war have been scheduled for demolition, cannot be replaced. According to the most extensive data available, the Berlin City Architect, Martin Wagner, calculates the "objective shortfall" in Berlin at around 200,000 apartments. Already in 1928, some 32,000 certificates confirming the need for housing were issued to newly arrived families, a number which is increasing by 5,000 to 6,000 each year. "In addition, there are requests for housing from 40,000 newly married couples each year, from 11,600 households who are accommodated in barracks and makeshift lodgings, and from 36,000 families who are living in apartments that will have to be abolished over the next ten years. In order to compensate for the current shortage and the annually increasing demand, and to eliminate the Berlin housing shortage within ten years, 70,000 apartments will have to be built each year. According to the current policy, however, only 25,000 apartments are scheduled to be built each year, of which only around 20,000 are actually constructed."

Given the fact that 4.7 million marks were spent on alcoholic drinks in 1928, and given that the annual consumption of beer per head among Germans rose from thirty-eight liters in 1920 to ninety in 1929, and given the reality that Germany is compelled to limit its spending on armaments, it will perhaps not be impossible even for our war-weakened fatherland to join in the new initiatives for peace in international city planning, and succeed, at very least, in confronting the most pressing housing problems facing the nation. Perhaps then in the capital city, which has been so sorely neglected in terms of city planning, something exemplary might be achieved.

NOTES

1. The *Gründerjahre* were the boom years of rampant speculation in the 1880s and 1890s.

2. Anton Huber wrote on housing questions; Julius Faucher (1820–78) was a journalist and political economist.

3. A reference to Prussia's victory over Austria at the Battle of Königgrätz, fought on 3 July 1866.

4. After growing up with relations in England, Bethel Henry Strousberg (1823–84) moved to Berlin in 1855, where he acted initially as an agent for British firms, and subsequently as an independent entrepreneur. In spite of the vast fortune he made from building railways in Prussia, Russia, Hungary, and Romania, he was declared bankrupt in 1875.

5. Hegemann is referring here to a play by Walter Mehring, *Der Kaufmann von Berlin* (The Merchant of Berlin), which premiered at the Piscator-Bühne in Nollendorfplatz on 6 September 1929.

It tells the tale of an Eastern European Jew named Kaftan, who arrives in Berlin early in 1923 with one hundred dollars to his name and within a few months becomes one of the great financiers of the city, thanks to the economic madness of the inflation, which peaked later that year. Politically naive, he is persuaded by a corrupt lawyer and racketeer to finance a right-wing putsch. The play provoked a political scandal, with SA troops marching outside the theater and Joseph Goebbels, the future Nazi minister of propaganda, penning an inflammatory pamphlet entitled "An die Galgen!" (To the gallows!).

126

Walter Benjamin

A JACOBIN OF OUR TIME

On Werner Hegemann's *Das steinerne Berlin*

First published as "Ein Jakobiner von heute: Zu Werner Hegemanns 'Das steinerne Berlin'" (1930); republished in Benjamin, *Gesamelte Schriften*, vol. 3 (Frankfurt am Main: Suhrkamp, 1980), pp. 260–65. Translated by Iain Boyd Whyte.

For two hundred years Berlin, in common with other cities, has had its extensive special literature, in which its local history is chronicled and handed down. It is a body of writing, however, that stays strictly within the realm of Berlin-ness, in which the city is concerned more with presenting rather than understanding itself. Even the proverbial appetite of its inhabitants to criticize everything came to a touching stop at the appearance of the hometown. You can satirize particular aspects of the city and make quips made about the monuments, but do not abuse the tenement housing [*Mietskasernen*]. The critique of the city is now getting stronger, however, as the love of the Berliners for their city becomes looser and loses its provincial sentimentality. Writing about the metropolis is striving to take on a more open, European character. This development has been the result of the quiet and tireless work of Werner Hegemann, the editor of *Wasmuths Monatshefte für Baukunst und Städtebau*.[1] Hegemann, who now steps up with a monumental building history of Berlin, is one of the very few key thinkers, who has not only spread his immense specialist knowledge outward in ever broader circles, but also developed it internally through an ever more intense concentration. As he now presents himself as a someone of the most pronounced civic culture, a man who understands intimately the mutual play of culture and politics in any situation with which he is confronted, a man who approaches the planning of public facilities in American cities and the historical studies of the Prussian kings with the same exactness and imagination.

It is, admittedly, an extraordinary fantasy that has consistently driven his work within the sphere of a strong rationalism—namely, a rebellious fantasy. As Chesterton noted: "Fantasy has is highest purpose in retrospective realization. The trumpets of fantasy, like the trumpets of resurrection, call the dead from their graves. Fantasy views Delphi with the eyes of a Greek, Jerusalem with the eyes of a crusader." It is wonderful how well this interesting, if questionable, definition fits the historian Hegemann. He does, indeed, see events with the eyes of the contemporaries of the period in question, and one who is fundamentally dissatisfied. For he has studied the sources with such unrivalled thoroughness, and his knowledge is so secure in all its details, that he gets to the bottom of the myriad weaknesses and shortcomings of those people who formerly stood and still stand at the peak of civilization. He writes an eternally topical history—in other words, the history of scandal. He would insist, however, that this word be understood in its full sense, from the Latin *scandalum,* as vexation. Read in this way, the role of enlightener takes on a hint of the theological. And one spontaneously looks for him and misses him in our morality plays in which a role is still waiting for him— that of the troublemaker at the Last Judgment.

Now he is accusing the city of Berlin in front of this court. Heaven knows, we as the violated taxpayers have the right to accuse in every court possible this city, which staggers from one humiliation to another. In spite of this, however, we should consider how far we would wish to accuse it on Judgment Day. Hegemann calls Berlin "the biggest rental-barracks city in the world." Who is not terrified at the realization of what this name means. And who is not seized with anger and disgust when the evidence for the defense is summoned. Treitschke, for example, who found these unforgettable words: "No one is so wretched that he cannot hear the voice of his God in the cramped little room," and Hobrecht, who brought out all the slumbering poetics of a Courths-Mahler[2] when he wrote in 1868: "In the rental barracks the children from the cellar apartments go to the poor school through the same hallway as those of the councilor or the businessman on the way to the grammar school. Wilhelm the cobbler from the attic story and the old, bedridden Frau Schulz in the rear house . . . are known to those who live in the large apartments on the first floor. Here is a bowl of soup to build up strength in illness, there a piece of clothing, over there some effective help in obtaining free tuition or similar, and all of this the result of the cordial relationships between people of both similar and very different social station. It is a succor that also exercises an ennobling influence on those who offer it." Whose breath is not taken away when following the negotiations that involved everyone from the Hohenzollern kings, who spread the barrack style of housing across the civil population, laying the basis for the Berlin land profiteering with senselessly high buildings? And what of the supercunning police assessors, who first had the idea of sparing the city the costs of expropriating land for street building by granting the land owners unlimited power to exploit their remaining tracts of land with building laws that permitted the three internal courts of the average rental block to extend to just over five square meters each. Or the "million builders," whose land— inflated in value by speculation—encircled the city well into the 1880s with a belt of iron. Who could escape from the disturbing power of the *corpora delicti*,[3] which are to be found fully recorded in the files: "the Spittelkolonnaden[4] as the site for advertising columns" or number 62b, Schönhauser Allee, whose imposing and cheerful facade betrayed the stinking bleakness of three courtyards lined up one behind the other, contrasting the Große Stern in Schinkel's noble plan with its bestial implementation in the Wilhelmine period.[5] Here, where the author has departed from the dialogic form of his "Fredericus," his "Napoleon" and "Christus," he has penetrated to the absolutely highest dialogical, indeed forensic level of eagerness. The profit that the reader gains from this broad-ranging but never diffuse exposition is a benchmark for his knowledge in public and political matters.

Hegemann dedicated this monumental work to the memory of Hugo Preuss. In the words of Wermuth,[6] it was he who "gave form to the Berlin idea for the construction of the new metropolis." The same is true, of course, of the idea for the construction of the new state: Preuss is one of the creators of the Weimar constitution. It is hardly a daring conclusion, therefore, that Hegemann is also a democratic spirit. But anyone who sees radical left tendencies in today's sense lurking behind his fanatical negativism is very mistaken. This fact—and you can respond to it as you like—is uncontestable. Indeed, it is the key to the highly intriguing, incomparable presence of the man. For sure, there has been democratic fanaticism in the past—the Jacobinism of 1792. Today, however, the democratic credo is understood not for nothing as standing for law and moderation. Toughness and ferocity can serve a dominant cause, fanaticism never. Hegemann presents us with this anachronism: the fanatical democrat, the Jacobin of our time. The eternally alert suspiciousness of Robespierre, his incorruptible nose for corruption, his unworldly purity—all this has been resurrected in Hegemann. It reflects the methodological location of his work. It is political in the Enlightenment sense, and aims to be critical through and through. But in no sense is it concerned with exposure. Whatever Hegemann discovers—and his work is full of discoveries—happens fortuitously. They are annoying, improper, scandalous deviations from the norm or from the rational; but never the results of the particular, concrete, hidden constellations of the historical moment. In essence his account is a singularly imposing and doubtless unchallengeable correction of pragmatically conceived history, but never the revolutionary rejection of it toward which historical materialism is striving, when it detects in the productive relations of the epoch those concrete and changing forces that determine, unconsciously, the conduct of both the rulers and of the masses. Wherever he encounters the laziness and corruption of the ruling classes, Hegemann declares it. But even the most incorruptible spirit remains in the realm of the pragmatic. The inner workings of history are protected from the dialectical gaze. The result is the problematical, at times downright contrary nature of the work. Or must the complete democrat of our days necessarily be muddleheaded?

Hegemann's book is undoubtedly a standard work. It is hard to put down, without asking what the reason might be that it fails to make the short step that separates it from ultimate perfection, which would allow the book to exist independently of its subject and render it instead the destiny of its subject. If anything is needed at the Last Judgment, it is ventilation. Both in the practical and metaphorical sense. The site of negotiation is not ventilated, and the questions are not comprehensive. Of course, we live in these rental barracks. *Nostra res agitur.*[7] But the discourse here is not on what is happening now, but in the past. And it is right that from time to time the cooling wind of time past should blow gently through the overheated actuality of debates. Even on the Day of Judgment the fact that everything is located in the distant past must count as an extenuating circumstance. For the passage of time has a moral dimension. This does not, however, lie in its progression from today to tomorrow but in the reversion of today into yesterday. Chronos holds in his hands a Leporello picture book,[8] in which the days fall peel off backward, one out of the other, and in the process reveal their hidden reverse side and the life unconsciously lived. This is what the historian works with. And from here comes Goethe's: "Be it as it may, it was so wonderful."[9] History is reconciliatory.

Certainly, life as lived in these Berlin rooms for centuries by hundreds of thousands of people is unhealthy and unworthy. Of course, the diabolical nature of the rental barracks impacts today as in earlier times on married and family life, in the sufferings of women and children, in the narrow-mindedness of the social relations, in the ugliness of daily life. But it is equally certain that this city has been created by the soil, the landscape, the climate, and above all the people—and not only the Hohenzollern rulers and the police chiefs—all of which have left their imprint in the barrackslike tenements. Even the unplanned rawness of the housing developments, in which existence is a struggle to the finish, has its own beauty, not only for the snobbish flâneur, but for the Zille-Berliners themselves.[10] It is a beauty that is most intimately linked to their language and their customs. Hegemann, admittedly, would not be a Jacobin if he were to allow himself to be guided by the genius of history, revealing to him the mercifully physiognomic existence. This enlightener with his sharply chiseled features has no sense of historical physiognomy. His genealogical tree has its roots in the most gnarled and original, but also most unseeing subjects, which populated North Germany in the second half of the eighteenth century. It never occurs to him that these barrackslike tenements, however dreadful as housing, have created streets whose windows reflect not only suffering and crime, but also the morning and evening sun with a desolate nobility found nowhere else. He finds it incomprehensible that the constant substance for the childhood of generations of city children has been drawn from stairwells and asphalt, just as it has for country children from stables and fields. But a historical account has to embrace all this; not only for reasons of truth but also for the sake of its impact. That which we wish to destroy cannot be presented simply as an abstract negative or as a counterexample. For seen like this, it reveals itself only for a brief moment under the illuminating flash of hate. What you want to annihilate, you must not merely know; to complete the job you must have felt it. Or, as dialectical materialism has it: it is good to identify thesis and antithesis. But one can intervene in the process by recognizing the point at which one reverts to the other, the positive coinciding with the negative, the negative with the positive. The enlightener thinks in opposites. To expect dialects of him is perhaps unreasonable. Is it unreasonable, however, to expect of the historian an insight into things that sees beauty even it is deepest disfigurement? A negating understanding of history is nonsense. Nothing testifies more for the power, the passion, and the talent of the author, that he has succeeded at the epicenter of the impossible to create a work of this richness and solidity. Nothing attests more conclusively to his standing.

NOTES

1. Literally, "Wasmuth's monthly journal for architecture and city building."
2. Hedwig Courths-Mahler (1867–1950) was one of the most successful novelists of her era. Born in Nebra/Unstrut, she lived in Berlin from 1905 to 1935. Brought up in a children's home and with little formal education, she nevertheless published over two hundred romantic novels, which enjoyed worldwide sales of 30 million copies. The secret relationship between aristocrat and commoner, invariably ending happily, was a favored theme.
3. *Corpora delicti:* the substantial and fundamental fact or the material substance of a crime; in murder, for example, death by foul means or the body of the victim.
4. Spittelkolonnaden, Leipziger Strasse, built to the design of Carl von Gontard in 1776.
5. Dating originally from the reign of Friedrich I, the Große Stern was the point of intersection in the Tiergarten of eight avenues. It was greatly expanded in scale in 1937 by Albert Speer to house the Siegessäule (victory column), relocated from its original site in front of the Reichstag.
6. Adolph Wermuth was appointed mayor of Berlin on September 1, 1912, and continued as the first mayor of Greater Berlin from its formal inception on 1 October 1920 until 27 November 1920, when he resigned under pressure from both Communist and conservative factions in the council.
7. *Nostra res agitur:* "It is our concern, our business."
8. Leporello books are of indeterminate length, made in one strip and folded like a concertina. The term was first used by German music publishers to describe a folded, single sheet, and was probably derived from the ever-expanding notebook in which Don Giovanni's servant, Leporello, recorded his master's countless amatory conquests.
9. Ihr glücklichen Augen,
    Was je ihr gesehn,
    Es sei wie es wolle,
    Es war doch so schön!
    Johann Wolfgang von
    Goethe, *Faust* II, 11300
10. The artist and photographer Heinrich Zille (1858–1929) devoted his working life to recording the life of the poor and underprivileged in the Berlin slums, the so-called Berliner Milieu (pronounced "Milljöh" in Berlin dialect). His images combined sentimentalism with a sharp critical view.

127

Hannes Küpper

THE "PROVINCES" AND BERLIN

First published as "'Provinz' und Berlin," *Der Querschnitt* 5 (1931), pp. 307ff; reprinted in *Berlin im "Querschnitt,"* ed. Rolf-Peter Baacke (Berlin: Fannei & Walz, 1990), pp. 179–81. Translated by Michael Loughridge.

The terms *Provinz, provinziell* and *Provinzler*—provinces, provincial, a provincial—have their origin in, and refer to, Berlin and its suburbs.

Geographically, the provinces begin abruptly at the city boundary of Greater Berlin. Anyone living twenty kilometers out is just as much in the sticks as he would be eight hundred kilometers away.

The word *Provinz* as used in Berlin connotes something second-rate, inferior, just as the word *Berlin* has a special sense when used out in the provinces.

In the provinces, *Berlin* means petrol fumes, morphine, assaults, fraud, asphalt culture, immorality, kitschy nature, superficiality, hysteria.

For Berlin, *Provinz* signifies mothball fumes, lily-of-the-valley, flannel petticoats, Cäsar Flaischlen,[1] cultural philistines, "thick as two short planks," "asleep on their feet," "don't know the meaning of work," "clodhoppers."

This kind of attitude to Berlin and the provinces, so frequently encountered in what one hears and reads, is trivial and pointless, because it misses the real differences; it is just chat, a topic for beer drinkers, for ladies at coffee parties, for the golf club and bridge evening. To the objective observer, provincialism in the generally accepted sense of the term is there to be found in Berlin, just as Berlin attitudes are also encountered in the provinces. The nudging and whispering set off in Münster when Lieschen Neumeier, three months married, gives birth to a bouncing baby boy is awful, typically provincial; when the same predicament befalls Miss Traude Krüger, resident in the capital and daughter of a high-ranking civil-service family, there may be no smutty gossip, but other people's inquisitiveness will be given its satisfaction in the pamphlet format of certain evening newspapers, which will lose no time in informing their readers that the honeymoon preceded the wedding; which is no less typically provincial.

Seen at this level, Berlin is the provincial capital of the German Reich.

As for the antithesis between *Berlin* and *the provinces,* its origins are manifold. Ideas possessing general validity—communicable ideas—are not taken up; instead, one finds again and again that what the provinces do take up are Berlin ways; naturally they get some of them wrong—and fail to realize it. The result is the same confusion and disappointment that were felt some time ago when Germany set about adopting all things American, without the slightest insight or feeling for what is truly American. The verdict on this American invasion of Germany was formulated some time ago by an American tycoon: "We can give you American currency, no problem—but it's your job to convert it to German!"

Berlin suffers from a tendency to underrate the provinces, casting itself in the role of an exporter; but its way of fulfilling this role is reminiscent of, say, a furrier with an obsession about selling his goods on the equator. The Berliner confines his study of the provinces to studying the provincials he encounters in Berlin, where they behave quite differently from at home. He thus gets a quite false impression. The alien surroundings in Berlin oppress and intimidate the visiting provincial, making him monosyllabic in company, and this in turn only feeds the Berliner's notorious garrulity. He carries on a conversation with himself. But our provincial visitor is quite capable of drawing his own conclusions. He is not lacking in intelligence or perceptiveness; he is trained to be observant of detail, and so he is quick to spot the Achilles' heel. After a while, when he comes to draw his conclusions, based on what he has seen of the pace of life in Berlin, the unending stream of telephone calls about pure trivia, the many committee meetings held only, it seems, to hold things up, the bureaucratic obstacle course that must be followed before any project can be realized, all the fiddles and private understandings—and above all, when he sees to his wonderment that a thesis is not inferred from empirical results but is constructed a priori and then propounded: then he finds himself baffled in the face of the result achieved; for he cannot help feeling that such nugatory results could well have been come by with a good deal less pother.

This is the strength of the man from the provinces, and this is what encourages him to get a foothold in Berlin. And it is a law of nature that Berlin undergoes periodic renewal as a result of provincial invasion. The Silesian invasion of Berlin, which began fifty years ago and has now reached the optimum stage for study, confirms the view of scientists that the Berlin population type is the historical product of mixed blood, and not that of German tribes alone, for hosts of Dutchmen, Frenchmen, Swiss, Bohemians, Slavs constituted the original colonist prototype. Berlin has never renewed itself from its own resources; it is (so to speak) anemic, in need of an occasional boost from the provinces.

That the word *province* cannot be used with reference to economic life or the related politics is significant. These two aspects of human activity cannot exist in isolation, and the more one reflects on the issue of Berlin and the provinces, the more one will find oneself reinforced in one's conviction that, when all is said and done, the differences are very superficial: indeed, that they obtrude only in that stratum of society referred to summarily as the intelligentsia. In economic circles everyone talks the same language, and everyone knows exactly where mutual understanding begins and ends. It is nothing to the waiter at the Kempinski, after all, if the provincial guest orders plain *Reibekuchen* rather than calling it *Kartoffelpuffer*; what matters is that he does order something, and pays.[2]

And if the intellectuals could only see their way to acquiring the attitudes and the working methods of the business sector, the world would indeed have to make do without the terms *Provinz, Provinzler, provinziell;* in the process, their activity would at long last gain a new and vital energy.

NOTES

1. Cäsar Flaischlen (1864–1920) was a poet with a proclivity for the Swabian dialect and an unshakeable optimism. His best known poem, "Hab Sonne im Herzen" (Have sun in your heart), insists with dull sentimentality that sunshine in the heart and a song on the lips will bring courage and help, even on the darkest days.

2. Berthold Kempinksi (1843–1910) opened a restaurant in the Leipziger Strasse in 1889 with several dining rooms, the biggest restaurant in Berlin at the time. The hotel business bearing the same name evolved from this restaurant in 1897. A *Kartoffelpuffer* is a potato cake.

128

Adolf Hitler

SPEECH AT FOUNDATION-STONE CEREMONY OF THE FACULTY OF DEFENSE STUDIES [*WEHRTECHNISCHE FAKULTÄT*], BERLIN, 27 NOVEMBER 1937

Published in *Hitler: Reden und Proklamation, 1932–1945,* ed. Max Domarus (Neustadt an der Aisch: Schmidt, 1962), vol. 1, pp. 765–66. Translated by Iain Boyd Whyte.

Today begins in Berlin a period of structural remodeling, which will change most profoundly the image and—I am convinced—the character of this city. The former capital city of the Hohenzollern princes, kings, and Kaisers will from now on become the eternal capital city of the first German Empire of the People [*Volksreich*]. This new capital will redress that deficiency that led a great historian to the very perceptive conclusion that it has always been the misfortune of the Germans to have possessed capital towns, but never a true capital city. For every insight and historical experience tells us that a truly lasting state structure of the community of the *Volk* is conceivable only when the leadership of such a community possesses an indisputable governmental center. [. . .] The scale of this project and its constructions should not be measured by the needs of the years 1937, 1938, 1939, or 1940, but should be determined by the recognition that it is our task to build for a millennial nation, with a thousand-year heritage of history and culture, a worthy, thousand-year city for the distant future that lies before it. We intentionally withhold, therefore, for the next twenty years any criticism of the work that must be performed for this purpose in Berlin, and submit it for the judgment of those generations that will follow us in days to come. However this judgment should turn out, one vindication will not be denied us. In this project we have not thought of ourselves but of those that follow us. In this sacred conviction, I lay the foundation stone for the Faculty of Defense Technology of the Technische Hochschule in Berlin, as the first structure to be built in the execution of these plans. It should be a monument to German culture, German learning, and German strength.

12

BERLIN MONTAGE

"'A metropolis?' said my friend Lisa on returning from Paris. 'A metropolis?' On Potsdamer Platz, my dears, you can hear the chickens clucking."[1] Lisa was not alone in finding Berlin provincial, even during the supposedly "golden" twenties. One of the most damning critiques of the city was penned in 1932 by Wilhelm Hausenstein, a South German art historian and journalist who published in the Frankfurt and Munich press: "There exists the strong temptation to declare that Berlin . . . appears to be no more than a mechanism; a phenomenon of addition; a mechanically assembled volume, a bare quantum; the categories of this city and its inhabitants are mechanical ones." And the mechanism, says Hausenstein, is mistaken for the essence: "The jostling throng is taken as 'life.' The nervous congestion of the cars, the confusion and the rhythm of the pedestrians—everything that can be called circulation—is counted as the essence of vitality." In contrast, "Paris . . . is a flower of nature; it is a landscape, a fairy-tale picture, where tropical vegetation is hidden in the boulevards. . . . Brussels blossoms, Antwerp grows rampant. Berlin is constructed; it has fabricated itself rather than been born. . . . This is the tragedy of an anticathedral city: it cannot reach its goal since, in reality, it has never properly begun."[2] Unlike London or Paris, which had evolved over centuries around the court and the cathedral, Berlin in the 1920s was an entirely different urban phenomenon, which had sprouted out of the sandy soil of Brandenburg with extraordinary haste and vigor over the preceding forty or fifty years. Not only were the rate and volume of expansion unprecedented in Europe; it came about with very little centralized planning. Greater Berlin, as already noted, was stitched together in 1920 from seven adjacent townships and fifty-nine rural communities that surrounded the urban conglomeration. Rather than a city in the conventional sense, stretching concentrically from a single core, Berlin was a polycentric conurbation.

Not only was Berlin physically disparate; it also lacked by the 1920s those major social and communal forces around which the traditional capital city is structured, and which Berlin itself had shared in its brief moment of imperial glory between 1871 and 1918. Following the defeat of 1918, the army, which had previously been the mainstay of Prussian society, had been decimated and marginalized. The Kaiser himself had abdicated, and the court and aristocracy were stripped of their influence. The church, which had never played a dominant role in the city, slipped into obscurity. The pillars of society—famously satirized in Georg Grosz's eponymous painting of 1926—had collapsed, and the way was open for Berlin to fashion itself as a modern city, untrammeled by the dominant narratives of the past.

Parvenu and provincial by comparison with the more established European capitals, yet Americanized and radically modern by comparison with the German provinces, Berlin could not help but arouse powerful emotions, both for and against. In its favor, it had a cultural life that was unparalleled in contemporary Germany in its breadth, diversity, and quality. There was radical theater of Max Reinhardt and Erwin Piscator; both the progressive musical compositions of Kurt Weill and Arnold Schönberg and the grand tradition of musical performance that flourished under the batons of Wilhelm Furtwängler, Bruno Walter, and Otto Klemperer. The pens of Carl von Ossietsky, Leopold Schwarz, and Kurt Tucholsky produced acerbic political journalism, while that of Alfred Döblin wrote the definitive novel about the city—*Berlin Alexanderplatz*. This flood of words and opinions fed the great publishing empires of Mosse, Ullstein, and Samuel Fischer. In the visual arts, Berlin provided the essential context for the works of artists such as Max Beckmann, Georg Grosz, and Hannah Höch, while the radical architects and planners of the city—Walter Gropius, Erich Mendelsohn, Ludwig Mies van der Rohe, Bruno Taut, Martin Wagner—created visions of a modern city that not only reshaped Berlin in the later 1920s and early 1930s, but ultimately served as models for the great cities of the industrial world. This energy and vitality acted as a magnet for talent and ambition, which was drawn irresistibly to the capital city.

The Berlin of the Weimar Republic, however, was defined less by its high or radical culture than by its anonymous vastness and its unhistorical presentness. Even though central Berlin could boast parade boulevards, art museums, opera houses, and even an unoccupied royal palace, the defining elements of its cityscape were to be found elsewhere, in its many suburbs—all of which were different but shared a common anonymity and an indifference to the heroic symbols of the traditional German city. Neither the grand modernist villas built around the

Havelsee by architects like Mendelsohn and the brothers Luckhardt, nor the massive new housing estates built around the city perimeter, referred in any way to traditional modes of urban life.

The sense of beginning afresh, cut off from historical patterns and expectations, was powerfully underlined by the hyperinflation that marked the start of the decade, which destroyed the prewar social hierarchies and the power of inherited wealth. The city as the site of stability, wealth, and reassurance became one of endless restlessness and motion, of rebirth and redefinition, of uncertainty and fear. Siegfried Kracauer found all these characteristics in an underpass that ran below the railway tracks:

> Close by Charlottenburg Station, beneath the tracks, is a dead-straight street that I often take in order to reach the station entrance on the far side of the embankment. I confess that I never pass through that underpass without a twinge of horror.... My horror probably arises from the contrast between the solid, unshakable construction system and the fleeting chaos of humanity. On the one hand, the underpass: a premeditated, stable unit, in which every rivet and every brick is in its place and helps the whole. On the other, the human beings: scattered parts and particles, incoherent fragments of a nonexistent whole. They are able to create a combination of brick walls, girders, and supports, but they are quite incapable of organizing themselves into a society. Brutally and horribly, the perfect, systematic arrangement of the inanimate materials shows up the imperfection of the living chaos. The baker stands idle and useless, while the iron supports around him serve a purpose; and, by contrast with the walls, which are allowed to bear a weight, the beggars are mere ballast. What is inhuman is, however, not only the unplanned drifting of the human beings but the planned design of the underpass. How could it be otherwise, seeing that it is built by human hands? These supports look like enemies, these walls remind us of convicts, and these girders combine into a nightmare. A system as impervious and as desolate as the anarchic mixture of passersby and beggars.[3]

The majority of the passersby, of course, were hurrying to or from their workplaces, and ceaseless and often joyless work was a dominant theme in the Berlin narratives of the 1920s.

From manual laborers to bank directors, via the ever-increasing army of white-collar workers, the Berliner was hectically preoccupied with work. Indeed, as Alfred Polgar noted in 1922, even unemployed Berliners were totally absorbed by their own activity: "Not one bench in the Tiergarten is occupied by a real do-nothing. He is either reading or doing sums in the sand. What appears in Berlin to be a standstill is, viewed more closely, marching, if only temporarily, on the same spot."[4] Reflecting the social transition of the postwar years, a significant section of the workforce was female, and the 1920s witnessed the emergence of a new breed of working woman, who was single, socially emancipated, financially independent, and sporty. With bob-cut hair and dressed in the latest creations of the booming Berlin fashion industry, the new working woman looked more to America than to earlier German eras for her models and inspiration. Even the most critical observer could not but be struck by the energy of the city and the seductive charms of its dazzling surfaces. Here, once again, is Wilhelm Hausenstein, writing of Friedrichstadt: "The illuminated perspective leads the eye into an illusory infinity, but even a false infinity fills us with enthusiasm; we have no scruples.... The vista is flanked by the impassive faces of girls: beautiful faces, perfectly made up—their eyes have an infinite depth born of blue eye shadow and atropine, but then they *are* infinitely deep. Gaze raptly enough, and the illusion will be taken for reality."[5]

NOTES

1. Kurt Tucholsky (1928), quoted in *Berlin ist das Allerletzte,* ed. Detlef Bluhm and Rainer Nitsche (Berlin: Transit, 2001), p. 30.

2. Wilhelm Hausenstein, "Berlin," in *Europäische Hauptstädte* (Erlenbach: 1932); reprinted as *Eine Stadt, auf nichts gebaut* (Berlin: Archibook, 1984), pp. 13, 17, 20, 31.

3. Siegfried Kracauer, "Die Unterführung," *Frankfurter Zeitung,* 11 March 1932. On Kracauer and Berlin, see David Frisby, *Fragments of Modernity* (Cambridge: Polity, 1985), pp. 137–47.

4. Alfred Polgar, "Mit ihrer Beschäftigung beschäftigt" (1922); quoted in Bluhm and Nitsche, *Berlin ist das Allerletzte,* p. 62.

5. Hausenstein, "Berlin," p. 9.

129

Käthe Kollwitz

DIARY ENTRY, 25 JANUARY 1919

First published in *Ich sah die Welt mit liebevollen Blicken: Käthe Kollwitz: Ein Leben in Selbstzeugnissen,* ed. Hans Kollwitz (Wiesbaden: Fourier, 1971), pp. 193–94. Translated by Iain Boyd Whyte.

Today Karl Liebknecht was buried,[1] and with him thirty-eight others who had been shot. I was allowed to make a drawing of him and went early to the mortuary. He was lying in state beside the other coffins. Red flowers had been laid around his wounded forehead, the face was proud, the mouth a little open and distorted by pain. A slightly startled look on the face. Hands crossed in the lap, a couple of red flowers on the white shirt. There were other people there who I didn't know. Karl, Hans, Stan had come with me. Stan also drew. I then went home with the drawing and tried to make a better, more complete version.

Lise was in the city to follow the cortège. The entire city center was blocked off. The enormous procession of demonstrators was diverted—white guards everywhere—via Moabit to Bülowplatz. From there it was to go on to Friedrichshain.

Lisa did not go any farther with it. From Friedrichshain the procession followed behind the coffins.

How petty and wrong all these precautions seem. If Berlin—a majority in Berlin—wishes to bury its fallen, that is not a revolutionary matter. Even between the street fights there were periods of calm for the burial of the dead. It is unworthy and provocative to harass Liebknecht's supporters to his graveside in this military manner. And it is a sign of the weakness of the government that it has to tolerate this.

NOTE

1. Karl Liebknecht (1871–1919) came from a political family: his father, Wilhelm Liebknecht, was a leading socialist politician and member of the Socialist Democratic Party (SPD). A convinced antimilitarist, Karl Liebknecht was imprisoned in 1907 for publishing a pamphlet entitled "Militarismus und Antimilitarismus." While still in prison, he won a seat in the Prussian Landtag, and in 1912 he entered the Reichstag, the German Parliament. In 1914, he was the only parliamentarian to vote against war credits and was conscripted as a noncombatant on the Russian front. Returned to Berlin in October 1915 in a state of physical collapse, he returned to political activism and founded, together with Rosa Luxemburg, the revolutionary Spartakusbund (Spartacus league), a subversive group that in 1918 evolved into the German Communist Party (KPD) with the support of the Bolshevik Central Committee in Russia. The KPD was heavily involved in the short-lived German Revolution that began on 29 October 1918, precipitating the collapse of the German war effort and the abdication of the Kaiser. On 5 January 1919 a confused alliance of left-wing revolutionaries launched the so-called Spartacus uprising, advocating government by council on the Soviet model. The rebellion was short-lived, however, and by 13 January the uprising had been crushed and its leaders captured. Following violent interrogation, both Rosa Luxemburg and Karl Liebknecht were executed without trial on 15 January.

130

Kurt Tucholsky

BERLIN! BERLIN!

First published as "Berlin! Berlin!" (1919); reprinted in Tucholsky, *Gesammelte Werke*, vol. 2 (Reinbek bei Hamburg: Rowohlt, 1975), pp. 129–31. Translated by Iain Boyd Whyte.

> *Quamquam ridentum dicere verum*
> *Quid vetat?*
>
> [*What prevents me from speaking the truth with a smile?*]
> HORACE, *SATIRES*, BOOK 1

There is no sky above this city. Whether the sun shines at all is questionable; you see it only as it blinds you when you want to cross the street. Everyone curses the weather in Berlin, but there is no weather in Berlin.

The Berliner has no time. The Berliner generally hails from Posen or Breslau and has no time. He always has something to do: he telephones and makes appointments, arrives breathless and slightly too late for meetings—and has an awful lot to do.

People don't work in this city—they slave. (Even pleasure is work here; something from which you hope to gain, prepared for by first spitting on the hands.) The Berliner is not industrious; he is wound up like a clock. He has entirely forgotten, unfortunately, the reason for his existence. Even in heaven—assuming that Berliners get to heaven—he'll have "something on" at four o'clock.

Sometimes you see Berlin women sitting on their balconies, which are glued to the stone boxes that people here call houses. There the Berlin women sit and take a breath. Just at that moment they are between two telephone conversations, are waiting to meet someone, or—and this is very rare—are too early for something and are sitting and waiting. Then they shoot very suddenly, like an arrow from the bowstring, to the telephone . . . and on to the next engagement.

This city drags its carts with a furrowed brow—*sit venia verbo!*[1]—along the eternally same track and doesn't realize that it is marching around in circles, going nowhere.

The Berliner can't make conversation. From time to time you see two people talking, but they aren't conversing, merely sharing their monologues. Neither can the Berliners listen. They simply wait anxiously until the other one has finished, and then cut in. This is the way many Berlin conversations are conducted.

The Berlin woman is practical and straightforward: even in the realm of love. She has no secrets. She is a sweet and worthy girl, enthusiastically celebrated by the gallant local songsmiths.

The Berliner doesn't have much of a life, always assuming that he has earned some money. He doesn't cultivate sociability, because that is too much trouble. He meets up with his acquaintances, chats a bit, and is sleepy by ten o'clock.

The Berliner is a slave of his mechanisms. He is a passenger, theatergoer, guest in a restaurant, and a salaried employee rather than a human being. The mechanisms pluck and pull at his nerve ends, and he yields without restraint. He does everything that the city demands of him—but living . . . sadly, not much of that.

The Berliner grinds his way through the day, and when it is finished, it has been all work and effort. Nothing else. You can live for seventy years in this city without the least benefit for your immortal soul.

At one point Berlin was a well-functioning machine, a brilliantly manufactured wax doll, which could move its arms and legs when you put ten pfennigs in the head. Nowadays, you can throw in a whole lot of ten-pfennig pieces and the doll hardly moves. The machine is rusty and works only sluggishly and slowly.

There are also a lot of strikes in Berlin. Why? I don't know exactly. Some people are against it, and some people are for it. Why? I don't know exactly.

The Berliners avoid contact like poison. If they have not already been formerly introduced somewhere, they snarl at each other on the street and in the train, for

FIGURE 31. Haus Vaterland (1911–12; Franz Schwechten, architect), Potsdamer Platz, 1926. Stadtmuseum Berlin, Nachlass Max Missmann, IV 68/181 Vb.

they don't have very much in common. They have no interest in each other; everyone lives for himself.

Berlin unites the disadvantages of an American metropolis with those of a German provincial town. Its advantages are to be found in Baedeker.

In the summer holidays, the Berliner discovers each year that one can also live on the land. He tries it for four weeks, but doesn't succeed—for he hasn't learned how to do it, and has no idea what that thing called living is. When he lands back happily again at the Anhalter Station, his eyes sparkle at the site of his streetcar line, and he is overjoyed to be back in Berlin. He has forgotten how to live.

The days rattle past, the daily routine rolls by—and even if we lived to be a hundred, we in Berlin, what then? Would we have achieved anything, had any effect, gained something for our life—for our true, inner, real life? Would we have grown up, developed, blossomed; would we have lived?

Berlin! Berlin!

NOTE

1. "Excuse the word," Pliny, *Letters,* V, 6, 46.

131

"Sling" (pseud. Paul Schlesinger)
THE TELEPHONE

First published as "Der Fernsprecher," *Vossische Zeitung*, 14 November 1921, evening ed.; reprinted in *Berliner zur Weimarer Zeit: Panorama eine Metropole, 1919–1933*, ed. Ruth Glatzer (Berlin: Siedler Verlag, 2000), pp. 89–90. Translated by Iain Boyd Whyte.

A month ago the telephone was still very expensive, and on 30 September we all made our emotional farewells to it. Since then, all the other prices have increased insanely. Panic has set in, one could call it *Delirium emens*.[1] One person is buying suit material, the other coffee, rice, chocolate, yet another bedsheets. When out shopping for nappies, cautious fathers buy a complete whole trousseau. One never knows . . . it might be a girl. Someone told me that in one shop a lady had bought stockings for her two feet to the value of thirty-eight thousand marks. The boss of the firm, however, canceled the sale and gave instructions that no single shopper could buy stockings for more than eight thousand marks.

At the same time the prices go up from hour to hour into dizzying heights.

I would also like to squirrel things away, but while I'm thinking about it, the things become more expensive. A tailor, who fourteen days ago still was offering suits for sale at 550 marks, presents them today at 800. What can you do? If I invest my wealth in underpants, coffee goes up. When I throw myself at jam, ties go through the roof. Even thinking about it has cost me ten times the fortune that I actually possess. My thoroughgoing consideration, however, has at least led to one conclusion: just about the only thing that has not gone up in price over the last six weeks is the telephone.

My tip: now is the time to telephone.

Don't come for tea, my dear friends. The cakes are too expensive. We also don't want to meet in a café or tea shop, for the prices are going up by the hour.

Let's sit at home of an evening by the telephone. It costs only twenty-five pfennigs. For two marks fifty we can converse splendidly with ten different families. Now is the moment, for prices rises are already in the offing. In four weeks we will, perhaps, have to pay twice as much. But at present telephoning is the cheapest thing in Germany. Take advantage of the opportunity with all your vigor: do nothing but telephone!

NOTE

1. A word play on *Delirium tremens* (a severe form of alcohol withdrawal): Latin *emere* = "to take, buy"; *emercor*, "to buy up." Thus *Delirium emens*—purchasing fever.

132
Käthe Kollwitz
DIARY ENTRY, 1 MAY 1922

First published in *Ich sah die Welt mit liebevollen Blicken: Käthe Kollwitz: Ein Leben in Selbstzeugnissen,* ed. Hans Kollwitz (Wiesbaden: Fourier, 1971), p. 201. Translated by Iain Boyd Whyte.

Cold, windy, rainy.

In spite of all this, a demonstration in the Lustgarten, the like of which we haven't seen before. The Social Democrats, the Independents, and the Communists all demonstrating as one. Endless columns merged and flowed together. The red flags were blowing in the wind, bands played the "International" and the "Marseillaise," children decorated with garlands marched in the procession. There were also open wagons for the children, decorated with red flowers and ribbons, and the red flags with the Soviet star fluttered beside those of the SPD. A wonderful picture of joyful and festive resolve for the fight. Although 1 May is as much or even more a day of struggle than of celebration, it is still festive. The universal festive day!

On the way home, Karl had the idea that we should go to the Café Dalles. It was fantastic. You wouldn't find a better bunch of racketeers and criminals in the Caveau des Innocents.[1] Girls—half children—totally debauched. A young chap sat at the back of the saloon playing the piano, and people sung along. We couldn't keep up with this, it was too obvious, and too uncomfortable for us. The most frightening thing was the barman, a character from Zille, with a blocklike neck, as strong as a horse, and unspeakably villainous and brutal in appearance.

NOTE
1. The Caveau des Innocents was a bar and cabaret near Les Halles in Paris.

133
Friedrich Kroner
OVERSTRETCHED NERVES

First published as "Überreizte Nerven" (1923); reprinted in Hans Ostwald, *Sittengeschichte der Inflation* (Berlin: Neufeld & Henius, 1931), p. 74. Translated by Iain Boyd Whyte.

There's nothing you can do. It beats on the nerves every day: the money madness, the uncertain future, the today and tomorrow that once again were thrown overnight into doubt. An epidemic of anguish, of the most naked necessity. Once again, the food queues that we haven't seen for a long time are snaking around the shops, first in front of one, then in front of all of them. No illness is so infectious as this. The queue has something suggestive about it: the look of the women, with their kitchen clothes thrown on and their careworn, patient faces. Time and time again, the queues act as a beacon: once again the shoppers are stripping the city— the great stone city—bare. Rice, which sold yesterday for 80,000 a pound, costs 160,000 today, perhaps double that tomorrow, and the day after the man behind the counter will shrug his shoulders and say: "Rice is sold out!" Noodles then! "Noodles are sold out!" What about barley, semolina, beans, lentils, just buy, buy, buy! The bit of paper, brand spanking new banknote paper, still damp from the printer and paid out early this morning as a week's wages, shrinks in value on the hurried way to the grocer's shop. The zeros, the mounting zeros! "A nought's just a nix!" As the dollar climbs, so does the hatred, the despair, and the hardship. The emotions of the day go with the day's exchange rate. With the dollar they collapse in cynicism and laughter: "Butter cheaper! Instead of one million six hundred thousand marks, only one million four hundred thousand marks." This is not a joke, but the truth, written in all seriousness with a lead pencil, hung in the window, and read with all earnestness. As the dollar increases, so does the urgency to turn the piece of paper into something that can be eaten and fills you up. The weekly markets are jammed. The police regulate the traffic. The queues pick the stalls clean.

134

Adolf Hitler

MY STRUGGLE

First published as Hitler, *Mein Kampf* (Munich: Franz Eher, 1926), pp. 288ff.; English translation by Ralph Manheim (London: Hutchinson, 1969), pp. 240–42.

What recent times have added to the cultural content of our big cities is totally inadequate. All our cities are living on the fame and treasures of the past. For instance, take from present-day Munich everything that was created under Ludwig I,[1] and you will note with horror how poor the addition of significant artistic creations has been since that time. The same is true of Berlin and most other big cities.

The essential point, however, is the following: our big cities of today possess no monuments dominating the city picture, which might somehow be regarded as the symbols of the whole epoch. This was true in the cities of antiquity, since nearly every one possessed a special monument in which it took pride. The characteristic aspect of the ancient city did not lie in private buildings, but in the community monuments which seemed made, not for the moment, but for eternity, because they were intended to reflect, not the wealth of the individual owner, but the greatness and wealth of the community.

[. . .]

Even the Germanic Middle Ages upheld the same guiding principle, although amid totally different conceptions of art. What in antiquity found its expression in the Acropolis or the Pantheon now cloaked itself in the forms of the Gothic Cathedral. Like giants, these monumental structures towered over the swarming frame, wooden, and brick buildings of the medieval city, and thus became symbols which even today, with the tenements climbing higher and higher beside them, determine the character and picture of these towns. Cathedrals, town halls, grain markets, and battlements are the visible signs of a conception which in the last analysis was the same as that of antiquity.

Yet how truly deplorable the relation of state buildings and private buildings has become today! If the fate of Rome should strike Berlin, future generations would some day admire the department stores of a few Jews as the mightiest works of our era and the hotels of a few corporations as the characteristic expression of the culture of our times. Just compare the miserable discrepancy prevailing in a city like even Berlin between the structures of the Reich and those of finance and commerce.

Even the sum of money spent on state buildings is usually laughable and inadequate. Works are not built for eternity, but at most for the need of the moment. And in them there is no dominant higher ideal. At the time of its construction, the Berlin *Schloss* [palace] was a work of different stature than the new library, for instance, in the setting of the present time. While a single battleship represented a value of approximately sixty millions, hardly half this sum was approved for the first magnificent building of the Reich, intended to stand for eternity, the Reichstag Building.[2] Indeed, when the question of interior furnishings came up for decision, the exalted house voted against the use of stone and ordered the walls trimmed with plaster; this time, I must admit, the parliamentarians did right for a change: stone walls are no place for plaster heads.

Thus, our cities of the present lack the outstanding symbol of national community which, we must therefore not be surprised to find, sees no symbol of itself in the cities. The inevitable result is a desolation whose practical effect is the total indifference of the big-city dweller to the destiny of his city.

NOTES

1. Ludwig I, King of Bavaria, 1825–48.
2. The Reichstag was built in 1884–94 to the design of Paul Wallot. (See above, text 56: Alfred Kerr, In the New Reichstag.)

135

Joseph Roth

THE WANDERING JEW

First published as Roth, *Juden auf Wanderschaft* (Berlin: Die Schmeide, 1927), rev. ed. 1937; translated into English by Michael Hofmann as *The Wandering Jews* (London: Granta Books, 2001), pp. 68–72.

No Eastern Jew goes to Berlin voluntarily. Who in all the world goes to Berlin voluntarily?

Berlin is a point of transit, where, given compelling reasons, one may end up staying longer. Berlin has no ghetto. It has a Jewish district. This is where emigrants come who want to get to America via Hamburg or Amsterdam. This is where they often get stuck. They haven't enough money. Or their papers are not in order.

[...]

The struggle for papers, the struggle against papers, is something an Eastern Jew gets free of only if he uses criminal methods to take on society. The Eastern Jewish criminal was generally a criminal in his past life. He gets to Germany on false papers, or with none at all. He doesn't register with the police.

Only the honest Eastern Jew—honest and timorous—registers with the police. It's much more difficult in Prussia than in Austria. The Berlin police like to undertake house-to-house searches. They check papers on the streets as well. They did a lot of that during the Inflation.

The trade is secondhand clothes is not prohibited, but it's not sanctioned either. No one without a hawker's licence is allowed to buy my old trousers. Or sell them for that matter.

But buy them he does. And sells them too. He stands on the Joachimstaler Strasse, or on the corner of Joachimstaler and the Kurfürstendamm, pretending to mind his own business. He has to be able to tell from the look of a passerby, first, whether he has old clothes to sell, and second, if he needs money.

[...]

Anyone who is good at selling old clothes will soon graduate to selling new clothes. He will go from a shop to a fashion store. Someday, he will have his own department store.

It is possible for a hawker to make a career in Berlin. He will assimilate faster there than his equivalent would in Vienna. Berlin levels out differences and kills off particularities. Hence the lack of a Jewish ghetto there.

There are just a couple of small Jewish streets around the Warschauer Brücke and in the Scheunenviertel. The most Jewish street in Berlin is the melancholy Hirtenstrasse.

The Hirtenstrasse is the saddest street in the world. It doesn't even have the unreflective joy of real dirt.

The Hirtenstrasse is a Berlin street softened perhaps by its Eastern Jewish inhabitants, but fundamentally unchanged. It has no streetcar line, no buses, only rarely an automobile; mostly just trucks, carts, the most functional and plebeian of conveyances. There are little hole-in-the-wall bars. You climb a few steps to reach them. Narrow, filthy, worn-out steps. The step equivalent of down-at-heel shoes. Rubbish is piled up in the doorways of houses. Sometimes this rubbish is collectible, even marketable. Rubbish as stock-in-trade. Old newspapers. Torn stockings. Widowed soles. Shoelaces. Apron strings. The Hirtenstrasse is drab like a slum. It lacks the character of a street in a shtetl. It has a new, cheap, already-used-up, bargain-basement quality. A street out of a department store. A cheap department store. It has one or two dirty window displays. Jewish bakeries, poppyseed cakes, rolls, rye loaves. An oil canister, sweating flypaper.

In addition, it has Jewish Talmud schools and prayer-houses. You see Hebrew writing. It looks out of place on these walls. You see the spines of books behind sullied windows.

You see Jews walking, with their tallith under their arms. Emerging from the prayerhouse, going about their business. You see sick children and old women.

There are repeated attempts to transform this boring Berlinish semisanitized street into a ghetto. But Berlin is always stronger. The residents fight an unavailing fight. They want to spread out? Berlin repeatedly presses them back.

136

Ernst Bloch

BERLIN AFTER TWO YEARS

First published as "Berlin nach zwei Jahren," *Die Weltbühne* 24 (1928), pp. 32–33. Translated by David Britt.

An entirely different place. Or so one heard on the journey here. Resplendent, elegant, wild, unrecognizable.

I recognized it, all right. The change is not so great as all that. All the same, I could see what was truly new. As always, the same endless rebirth—a rebirth that never actually comes to a birth.

First, however, the old and the familiar. On which the city, in its fearless elegance, is said to have turned its back as never before. This is just not so. Even the food is its same old self. The bouillon potatoes, the haste, the queasy feeling inside. (At lunchtime, anyway; in the evenings, the light does mellow somewhat.) Same old faces, same old rudeness, same old purposeless haste. These people have nothing to lose but time and money. Everything stinks of industriousness—slavish, drab keenness—even among the grandees, for they, too, are nothing but coolies. Of course, it is the same everywhere—that is the curse of capitalism—but nowhere has resistance been so slight as it has here. Nowhere is there so little sign of what else might remain when capitalism turns sour. In Berlin, socialism was always merely the reverse of the same coin.

And those neat, chilly streets! Walk them with an open mind, and they appear quite unchanged. As for the Berlin housing shortage, time has not moved on. It is still 1920. Strange that the shops are all full again, and there is peace and quiet everywhere—but not in domestic life, where it most urgently belongs. Without a room to go to, you roam the streets, through long, rain-soaked neighborhoods, observing the rising prosperity, the New Objectivity, the overly lavish lighting of which you have heard so much, the new cafés, the theaters, Berlin as the leading edge. So what? A few electric cars that look like those in Paris ten years back? A subway that is no more than a piecemeal beginning, by comparison with Paris—a few lines at random but not a network? Theaters that no longer play Sudermann but Toller, and a bourgeoisie that nowadays believes in both?[1] But the New Woman—people will say—so girlish and graceful along the streets of Berlin! Thusnelda without Brünne, and not even Thusnelda any longer![2] Well, you see a woman like any other; fashion makes them all look alike. At home, the German housewife may be a little less obvious than before, but she has certainly not disappeared. The only difference is in the bob. The new, strangely "ladylike" or feminine look that is seen on the streets, or in interior design, is so provoking and inept that its falsity is immediately evident. Elegance has been twisted into sickly sweetness; the old monumentalism has acquired a wedding-cake and cookie-jar overlay. In Berlin now, the powder puff and the plate of cold cuts coexist, but the cold cuts remain the stronger force. The window displays may be more elegant, and often they are rich and striking; but you do not believe in them. Isolated in a lastingly Berlinerish giant village, they are ultimately no more than Balkan ostentation. Deep down, the only thing solid and genuine is still Steglitz.[3] On the surface, Berlin is the Balkans of Germany, intent on copying New York and Paris. It is characteristic of the Levantine that on occasion he outdoes the person he imitates; he has always been the most elegant character in any operetta.

The bad requires to be spoken of. The good speaks for itself. The good, in the case of Berlin, is its well-known dynamism, its constant journey to unknown climes. The bourgeois tends to mistake a treadmill—if it revolves fast enough—for an airship. Of those other climes nothing is to be seen, though heaven knows they ought to have been visible by now. Berlin is a potato of a city, all hard work and rationalism, with more hinterland than facade; all the rest is froth and movies. In the war, Berlin was the world capital of vulgarity and fraud. Are the military communiqués any different under democracy? I wish that it were night, or that the Russians would come. Then there would be more to say—perhaps about the new, the unrecognizably altered Berlin.

NOTES

1. Alongside Gerhart Hauptmann, Hermann Sudermann (1857–1928) was regarded during the 1890s as one of the leading playwrights of German Naturalism. Ernst Toller (1893–1939), in contrast, was a socialist playwright and poet who wrote his most important early plays while in prison for high treason.

2. Thusnelda was the daughter of a noble Germanic family, who, together with her son Thumelicus, was taken as a trophy to Rome by Germanicus and probably died as a sacrifice to Jupiter. In the twentieth century, however, the noble associations linked to Thusnelda were inverted when Thusnelda became "Tussi"—a slang and exclusively negative tag attached to a vain, fashion-obsessed, and difficult young woman. Brünne, in contrast, is Richard Wagner's erring but noble Brünnhilde.

3. Steglitz was one of the surrounding townships that were incorporated into Greater Berlin in 1920. Located on the southwest side of the city, it now forms part of the borough of Steglitz-Zehlendorf.

137
Alfred Döblin
BERLIN

First published as the foreword to Mario von Bucovich, *Berlin* (Berlin: Albertus, 1928), pp. vii–xii. Translated by David Britt.

You cannot speak of Berlin in the same style and tone that might be used to describe, say, Paris. This sort of thing: "The advertising lights are like a punch in the face, the loudspeakers bellow constantly, and goods are piled high in the store windows that were once so tasteful and restrained. Giant buses from the remotest continents roar through these strange streets, which blaze with a bogus international luxury, and meanwhile in the suburbs . . ."—or, as in Balzac's description of Paris: "All is steam, smoke, glitter; everything roars, flames, vaporizes, vanishes, rekindles itself, sparkles, glimmers, and is gone . . ." Berlin is an unpoetic and deeply uncolorful, but also a very truthful, city. Whenever the big buses laden with out-of-town visitors set off from Zoologischer Garten, from Potsdamer Platz, from Unter den Linden, you can be certain that the driver and the guide are operating in the grip of a false and poetic illusion. I can tell, even at this distance, that the pair of them are going to take their buses the wrong way: they are not going to travel around Berlin at all, but around Paris. They will pass through the Tiergarten, point out the Siegessäule [Victory Column], then the imperishable Siegesallee; there will be the Brandenburg Gate, then Unter den Linden, the royal palaces, the Zeughaus, the museums, and whatnot. Visitors will contemplate the Rathaus and the Stadthaus, travel across Potsdamer Platz and along Lützowufer to the Gedächtniskirche [Kaiser Wilhelm I Memorial Church], and continue as far out as Sanssouci; and they will see this and that department store. The out-of-town visitor looks at all of this; and, if he is smart, suppresses the thought that

Paris or London does all of these things better. The visitor will also find a handful of places of entertainment; but in these, if he has any knowledge of the world, he will yawn or shed tears of homesickness. In the end, the visitor will conclude that there is not much going on here. He will observe (without realizing that he has been on the wrong tour) that this is a large, boring, and unrestful city. It has no color. At some stage, a number of prominent individuals with an interest in building must have passed this way and left something behind them: one the Schloss, another a museum, a third Sanssouci: the kings, maybe. And now, there it all stands—all those unwanted gifts that no one knows what to do with—and people go about their business just as they do in other cities. The out-of-town visitor and the stupid native complain, in unison, that Berlin was never systematically laid out.

This is perfectly true. Berlin consists, first, of the leavings of a number of deceased individuals, and second, of whatever the present-day individuals do.

Part One is readily accessible to all, in the form of a cemetery visit (sightseeing tour), and the castoffs and properties of the dead may readily be photographed. The greater part of Part Two, on the other hand, either cannot be photographed or is not worth photographing. Berlin, in other words, is largely invisible. A curious thing: this is not the case with Frankfurt am Main, or Munich—or is it? Might not all modern cities be invisible—with nothing in them visible but dead men's castoffs? That really would be something. But it would be a good symbol of the mental life of the present day, because that is the way our notions and thoughts are: they mostly belong to yesterday and the day before. Today finds its way into our thoughts with incredible slowness. Cities reconstruct themselves no less slowly; perhaps, in fifty or a hundred years' time, Berlin will be visible: today's Berlin, of course.

I am to give some account of the almost invisible present-day city of Berlin, which lies geographically in the March of Brandenburg, at latitude 52° 31′ N and longitude 13° 25′ E, thirty-six meters above sea level, bordering on the rural districts of Teltow, Zauch-Belzig, and Beeskow-Storkow to the south, Osthavelland to the west, and Niederbarnim to the east and north. Tracks enter and leave the city in all directions, and the Reich Railroad Region of Berlin contains 20 main-line stations, 121 suburban stations, 27 belt line stations, 14 elevated stations, seven switchyards, and seven workshops.

The people of the city are carried on the way to work, to shop, or to be entertained by the elevated railroad and subway, by streetcars, and by the bus company. In 1925, almost 13 million people left the city through the main-line railroad stations.

The capital was a city of ninety thousand inhabitants as recently as 1871. It took twenty years to reach a total of 2 million. Over the past thirty years, this figure has doubled.

It will be said that, this being so, it will be all the easier to photograph today's city. Plainly, these last 2 million people are not living in the old buildings. They must have done some construction work on their own account. Indeed they have; and I shall speak of their homes and workplaces. Their homes are called tenement blocks; their workplaces are factories, offices, and stores. To know what this new city looks like, you need only pass along one eastern, northern, or southern street. What is more, you need only photograph one street, since Berlin has made things easy for the photographer; 95 percent of all streets look exactly like this one. One building looks just like the next: along those immensely long streets, one utilitarian building or one tenement follows another, all equally faceless. And yet: the whole is not faceless!

Look at a honeycomb: each individual cell has its own hexagon, but this hexagon does not exist in its own right: we understand its configuration, its form, in terms of the layout of the whole honeycomb, the needs and the ethos of the whole bee community. You may incline to despair, therefore, as you walk the endless uniform streets of Berlin, past an endless succession of blank facades. Here I refer to the abodes of the living. The buildings of the dead have plenty of character; they are, as it were, artistic, and are therefore what are called tourist sights. But just ride into this ocean of stone from the south or west, in an express train—say, in the late evening—and open your heart to the astonishing spectacle of this city. You will become aware that this is truly a modern city, a magnificent city, and a contemporary human community. The streets are dimly lit; you fly from one station to the next; you have long been inside the city limits, but still nothing falls into shape. Only one street after another: main streets, side streets, one bright light—that must be a movie house—and sudden flurries of lights, but how ineffectual against all this darkness; on the stations, people soberly making haste; and then more streets, tenements, chimneys, bridges. All this has the monotony of true greatness. To be smart, pretty, varied, or graceful is to be small.

That mighty whole is there to be seen. It makes no sense to speak of a piece of Berlin, or to point to any single building (unless it be a tenement multiplied by one hundred thousand). Only the whole has a face, and a meaning: that of a powerful, sober, modern city, a productive community of the masses.

In the south of the city—in the Siedlung at Britz, and elsewhere—the single, big idea of the cohabitation of gigantic masses of humanity finds a clear expression. The power of uniformity is there before your very eyes. Uniformity finds expression like an article of faith. In buildings along ordinary streets, the masses were packed together, compressed—soiled, in a way—with no self-regard. Here, all is peace and composure. As elsewhere, people live separate lives; but the magnificent buildings are wiser than they themselves and express what is happening here. The effect is slowly educative, like a silent, daily sermon.

The factories are located around the edges of the city, to the south, north, and east, in Tegel and Oberschöneweide; they also intrude into the city itself. Once, when Goethe was in Berlin, in the reign of King Frederick the Great, he wrote to Frau von Stein: "If only I could tell you the whole story, after I come back; if only I might—from the motions of the puppets one can infer the motions of the wheels, and in particular the big, old cylinder inscribed *FR,* with its thousand pins that bring forth all these melodies one after the other."

There is no big, old cylinder in the music box now; but, in this city built on sand, there is one central, autocratic authority: a single, immense will to work. Everyone who enters this atmosphere—even one who comes here from the coziest depths of Vienna—is caught up in the momentum, the urgency, the earnestness, and the puritanical rigor of this determination to work. Here no true places of amusement thrive, even though the Berliner is a fun-loving creature who has lost none of his sharp wit. But his sense of humor is not of the kind that vaudeville singers and farce writers still cling to: they give us the types of yesterday and the day before, the historical types of the vanished lower middle class. The new types are sharper, harder; they thrive in industry and around the factory walls; these are types with an aura of politics and class warfare.

In the factories, large and small, the working people spend their days—those who are not reduced to lounging on street corners and claiming welfare. Main streets in every section are lined with shops. Each district has its own department stores, small, medium, and large; at the moment, the biggest are Wertheim's and Tietz's.

In Berlin there are more than three hundred thousand industrial locations, employing more than 1.5 million people, of whom six hundred thousand are women. Among Berlin's major industries is electrical engineering, with two hundred thousand employees. The garment industry is equally large.

To look after the bodily welfare of those who live in this mass human settlement is the business of over thirty thousand people, to whom we must add more than three thousand physicians.

Some idea of the social stratification in our vast community can be gained from the fact that 70 percent of male children in Berlin are in elementary schools, the rest being divided between high and junior high schools. Among female children the division is even more obvious: almost 80 percent are educated by the municipality.

To show the full truth of the growing, invincible settlement that is Berlin, I would need to transcribe page after page of the *Statistical Yearbook:* births and deaths; company creations, liquidations, and bankruptcies; medical-care plans, unemployment relief, refuges, insane asylums, hospitals for incurables, night shelters, youth welfare programs, day nurseries. I ought at the same time to allude

FIGURE 32. Königstrasse (now Rathausstrasse), 1931. Stadtmuseum Berlin, Nachlass Max Missmann, IV 65/1228 V.

to the distinctive regional structure, the internal organization of the city. Individual neighborhoods tend to specialize: at the south end of Friedrichstrasse is the motion-picture district; not far away, on Kochstrasse and Zimmerstrasse, is the newspaper district; and there is a Latin Quarter, with university clinics and institutes, to the north of Friedrichstrasse Station, between Luisenstrasse and Invalidenstrasse. All around the Gedächtniskirche and Tauentzienstrasse are the entertainment district and the chic quarter; then there is the shady, dubious area between Münzstrasse and Rosenthaler Platz.

And so, dear visitor, you must leave your bus, put your hands in your pockets, and look away from the buildings; there is nothing to be seen there. Instead, stop, listen, look around you, breathe, move: this is where things are happening. This is a modern, young, forward-looking, gigantic community! Suddenly you, too, will no longer be troubled by the monotony of their buildings; you will become aware of the energy, liveliness, and courage of this human breed, the sheer multiplicity of its types. You see: here they live, here they work and build; here, quite at ease on its bed of sand, is the vast and serious collective entity that is Berlin.

138
Franz Hessel
I LEARN; VIA NEUKÖLLN TO BRITZ

First published as "Ich lerne" and "Über Neukölln nach Britz," in Hessel, *Ein Flaneur in Berlin* (1929); reprinted as Hessel, *Spazieren in Berlin* (Berlin: Arsenal, 1984), pp. 12–15, 192–93. Translated by David Britt.

I LEARN

Yes, he's quite right, I need to improve my mind. Just strolling around won't do it. I must take up local history; I must delve into the past and future of this city—this city that is always on the move, always on the point of turning into something different. No doubt this is what makes it so hard to locate, especially for one whose hometown it is.—To begin with the future.

The architect takes me into his spacious, light-filled studio. He leads the way from one table to the next, showing me plans and three-dimensional models for site landscaping; workshops and office block; laboratories for an accumulator factory; he shows me designs for an aircraft exhibition hangar, and drawings for one of the new, light, and airy housing projects that will rescue hundreds and thousands from housing shortages and squalid tenements. He goes on to tell me of all that Berlin's architects are now planning and—in part—about to execute. Not only are the city and suburbs to be remodeled by systematic redevelopment and resettlement; the old fabric of downtown Berlin is to be remodeled. High-rise buildings, twelve stories tall, will surround the Potsdamer Platz of the future. The Scheunenviertel will vanish. Around Bülowplatz and Alexanderplatz, a new world will arise in massive blocks. Project after project is worked out to resolve the problems involved in reconciling real-estate interests with the needs of traffic. In future, the speculator and the master mason will no longer be allowed to build piecemeal and ruin the stylistic unity of the city. Our building code will not permit it.

The architect goes on to speak of the ideas of his colleagues. The city will gradually expand along one bank of the River Havel as far as Potsdam, and one architect produces a plan for railroads and other communications, within which he incorporates the beautiful woods and lakes along the way, so that the Havel between Pichelsdorf and Potsdam will eventually turn into a kind of outer Alster.[1] Another proposes to lay out a vast square between the Brandenburg Gate and the Tiergarten, so that the Siegesallee [Victory Avenue] will mark the park boundary. On the Showground, an Exhibition City will assume the shape of a gigantic egg, with inner and outer rings of exhibition halls, a new Sports Forum, and a canal leading to a waterside restaurant flanked by garden terraces. The Potsdam and Anhalt stations are to be moved down the line to the switchyard of the innermost suburban station, making way for a broad avenue lined by department stores, hotels, and big garages. Completion of the Mittellandkanal will bring changes to Berlin's waterway network; the remodeling of towpaths, bridges, and other structures, and the construction of new ones, will present important tasks for the future. And then there are the new building materials: glass and concrete, with glass taking the place of brick and marble. Buildings already exist with floors and stairs of black glass and walls of opaque glass or alabaster. Then there are steel buildings with ceramic siding, gleaming bronze framing, and so on.

The architect notices my confusion and smiles. Time for an object lesson. Down to the street and into his waiting car. We roar along Kurfürstendamm, past old architectural horrors and new "solutions" and salvations. We stop in front of the Revue Theater and Picture Palace, which together form such an impressive unity, subtly differentiated but both soaring and circling in space, tracing their bold lines with captivating simplicity: one horizontal in emphasis, the other vertical. The master at my elbow expounds the work of another master. In order to elaborate from within the building, he takes me along a broad, dimly glowing, dark red passageway into one of the auditoria and shows me how the whole theater is developed out of the arc of a circle, and how the light-colored walls are articulated by two-dimensional patterns that eliminate all detached and distracting ornaments.

Then we turn along a side street, through a petit-bourgeois area of Charlottenburg and past the shores of the Lietzensee, to the Funkturm [radio tower] and Exhibition Halls, which he expands, in a few words, into the greater Showground of the future. By the time he is through with this, we have reached Reichskanzlerplatz [now Theodor-Heuss-Platz], and he tells me about the entertainment district that will one day arise here: the two blocks of movie theaters, restaurants, dance halls, a grand hotel, and the Light Tower that will loom above it all. We enter a street that runs parallel to Kaiserdamm and pull up in front of a vast construction site. Here my guide is himself the developer. Foremen come forward and report to him. Meanwhile, I look out across an expanse of chaos from which emerge the two entrance pylons, their basic structures already complete. Then I walk beside the master across rubble and scree to the edge of the central abyss. The outline of the building, hitherto readable only on the drawing board—the score of this "frozen music"[2]—now lies spread out before me. There will be the two great sheds, overnight accommodation for the rolling stock. Railroad tracks will run the full length of these. Around the edges will be gardens, in which—beneath the windows of the many light and airy apartments—the children of officials, engineers, and conductors will play. We drive along the street that runs along one side of the great quadrilateral. At one point the street is still under construction, and we have to walk some of the way over rankly overgrown paths. All around us, a whole city takes shape from the architect's words.

After conjuring up this vision of a work in progress, he turns to a work that he can show me in completed form. Crossing the Spree by the bridge alongside the palace of Schloss Charlottenburg, our car races along the canal bank to the wide expanses of the Westhafen. A view of the gloomy prison walls of Plötzensee. We drive down the endless length of Seestrasse, past cemetery walls and tenements, as far as Müllerstrasse. The vast colony of railroad cars and people appears. A wide entrance affords a view of three iron-pillared sheds. We walk through the gate; from inside, we can see the flanking, three-story residential wings, the four stories of the front elevation, and the massive pylons at the corners. We enter everywhere in turn. First, the glass-and steel shed where the cars are kept: we look up at the canopy and down into the strange world of the gangways beneath the tracks. Then into the administrative offices and the repair workshops; finally, we climb an inviting stairway to one of the pretty residential apartments.

Walking around the complex, I understand (though I cannot say it in technical language) how, by such devices as repeating specific motifs, emphasizing specific lines, emphasizing sharp edges on rising surfaces, the artist has conferred an unforgettably coherent overall character on this colossal mass of brickwork, designed to serve simultaneously as a railroad depot, an office, and a human habitation.

[. . .]

VIA NEUKÖLLN TO BRITZ

To visit Neukölln for its own sake is not recommended. Perhaps, behind the giant scaffolding that currently towers above Hermannplatz—the square at or near which the district approximately begins—some beautiful new architecture is taking shape. But Neukölln in itself is just one of those Berlin suburbs that had barely ten thousand inhabitants apiece in the 1870s and now have two or three hundred thousand. On Hohenzollernplatz, naturally, a bronze Kaiser Wilhelm I rides horseback. There are wide streets with plenty of department stores, movie theaters, bars, hot dogs, radio hobby shops, and majestic facades that conceal the squalor of the apartments in back. There is one area, between Hermannstrasse and Bergstrasse, where poverty becomes more visible; this is the so-called Bullenviertel, where every night weary folk climb out of overloaded streetcars, and countless frail-looking children hang around on the streets. A cheerless place. When it still bore the name of Rixdorf, and people used to make excursions there, no doubt it was more interesting. There is no "music" in Neukölln now, as there once was (according to the song) in Rixdorf. Otherwise, I know little of the suburb in question. Its more recent monuments, a Reuter fountain and a statue of King Friedrich Wilhelm I (erected in honor of his establishment of a colony of devout Bohemians); I have never brought myself to pay it a visit. I have never done more than speed through Neukölln by streetcar on the way to somewhere else. Usually Britz. After rounding the bend into the center of this little suburb, past a few endearingly low-roofed summer cottages of great antiquity and the gasoline station with its Olex and Shell advertisements, you pass along a winding street to a wooded slope. Walking a little way alongside a "withered fence," you see first a tree and a pond—a welcome sight—and then the community: the *Siedlung* [housing estate].[3] Its colors are bright yellow, white, and red, punctuated by the blue of the door and window frames and of the balconies. We enter the round complex by one of the converging streets that lead out of the open side of a quadrilateral, the other sides of which are lined with narrow houses around a large landscaped garden. No back annexes are to be found; there are curved recesses in the staircases. Everyone has his own yard, as in the summerhouse colonies—only far more neatly kept, and in a more communal setting. We enter the central ring and finally set eyes on the pond, the rising banks of which form a horseshoe lined with houses. With pleasing regularity, the houses present a row of dormers, windows large and small, and colorful, recessed balconies. On the narrow side of the horseshoe, this happy little township has its own marketplace, lined with the shop windows of coops that cater for the residents in—we are assured—a socially responsible way. We enter one of the houses. It is colorful inside as well as out, but there is no superfluous ornament; everything is unadorned, and yet good-looking. This is one of the many housing developments that are now making impressive inroads into the chaotic transitional area between town and country. Here—as at Lichtenberg, at Zehlendorf, and at other extremities of the city—the housing shortage, the longing for beauty, the contemporary move toward communal living, and the zeal of the younger generation of architects have combined to create dwellings fit for human beings to live in: work in progress, and probably the most important thing now happening to Berlin. This new, emergent Berlin is something that I cannot as yet describe, only praise.

NOTES

1. The Alster is a tributary of the River Elbe and forms two artificial lakes in the center of Hamburg.

2. The idea that architecture is "frozen music" was first offered by Friedrich Schlegel in the course of a lecture series entitled "Über deutsche Literatur" (On German literature), delivered in Paris in 1802–3.

3. The Horseshoe Estate [Hufeisensiedlung] in Britz was designed by architects Martin Wagner and Bruno Taut. (See below, text 176: Leo Adler, Housing Estates in the Britz District of Berlin.)

139

Carl Zuckmayer

THE BERLIN WOMAN

First published as "Die Berlinerin" in *Hier schreibt Berlin,* ed. Herbert Günther (1929; reprint, Berlin: Ullstein, 1998), pp. 101–2. Translated by Iain Boyd Whyte.

This is how I first saw her: queuing up outside shops, waiting at night by the station barrier, trudging along the wet asphalt, swinging her handbag back and forth, waiting, lurking, freezing, hungry, bickering, silent—then in long columns entering through the gates of the big factories, standing in the third-class carriage of the Stadtbahn on the way home, dead beat, with a briefcase under the arm, at the wooden desks of badly heated offices, in the clouds of steam in the overcrowded canteen,—

and in the delivery room of the Charité,[1] groaning, bawling, silent, cracking jokes, nagging, holding still,—

and once I saw one swimming in a canal, and another said: "She's got it right!" and carried on by,—

and marching time and again like soldiers, in their thousands and hundred thousands into work, into battle, into the daily Armageddon,—

and I know her in the sport schools, in the Lunapark,[2] in the cinema and the open-air pool, in the modest pleasures of the excursion and in meetings, moving house, at shooting incidents, in graveyards,—

and this, if you really want to know, is the real "Berlin Woman"—(for the elegant, beautiful, captivating, ravishing woman is timeless and international).

This is the Berlin woman who works, copes, marches, presses forward: quiet, courageous, tenacious, full of strength, full of the future.

NOTES

1. Founded in 1710, the Charité in Berlin is one of the oldest and largest hospitals in Germany.
2. The Lunapark was a large amusement park located beside the Halensee at the western end of the Kurfürstendamm. It opened in 1914 and closed in 1933.

140
Moritz Goldstein
THE METROPOLIS OF THE LITTLE PEOPLE

First published as "Die Großstadt der kleinen Leute," *Vossische Zeitung*, 21 September 1930; reprinted in Goldstein, *Berliner Jahre: Erinnerungen, 1880–1933* (Munich: Verlag Dokumentation, 1977), pp. 249–50. Translated by Iain Boyd Whyte.

A juvenile defendant in a law court said that she was seventeen years old, was born and grew up in Neukölln,[1] and had never been to the Berlin city center.

The world is wide. Precisely for this reason we have invented the age of travel. We travel by train right across Asia to Vladivostok on the Pacific Ocean. We roll along by car from Cape Horn to Cairo, and float in a luxury hotel to New York. We fly to Paris in less than six hours, around the whole earth in a couple of days. If the world wasn't wide, what would we do with our railways, cars, ships, and planes?

Who is it that travels, rolls, floats, flies. The people? The people till their own field, cling to their native soil, put down roots in the empire of their own home, go no farther than from one village to another. At one point the war scattered them across Europe: the Pomeranian country boy to Turkey, the Rhineland wine grower to the Baltic, the Russian peasant [*Muschik*] to Laon. That's all ages ago. For a long time now they have been striding along once again behind their plows.

Here's Berlin. First a fishing village, then two communities on the banks of the River Spree that grew together. Later, when it was had already swollen into a city of millions, it was still surrounded by a garland of suburbs embedded in meadows, fields, and heathland. Today Berlin is a stony incomprehensibility. Imagine yourself on the Kreuzberg and look around: you can no longer see any countryside; only houses and the occasional cluster of trapped trees.

The old town and the surrounding villages have become districts of the city. All you businessmen, lawyers, doctors, or whatever else your Berlin existence is grounded on, you don't differentiate between these quarters. You don't say and never think, "It's too far to go for me since I don't know my way around there." You have your car, or you flag down a cab, or you climb on a bus, or trust yourself to the subway. From apartment to office, from office to courthouse, to the customer, to the patients, mornings in the city center, afternoons in Wedding, evenings somewhere around the Gedächtniskirche, in all directions, right through the middle or around the outside. It all belongs to you; you're at home everywhere. You are always moving along in the bustling throng, and when you open your eyes, you see the people running, riding along, cycling, and you think that they are all doing what you're doing, and are happy roaming around the vast terrain of Greater Berlin.

But you're wrong. You know nothing of the life of the zoological species *Homo sapiens*. You have no idea that you are the exception, and that the others live under quite different conditions and with utterly different habits.

When you go on your summer holidays, the express train carries you past the farmers working in their fields. All they have to do is climb on board, you think to yourself, assuming that you have any thoughts at all on the way to summer holidays. But they don't climb on board. Some of them have never boarded a train and never will. The express travels outside their lives.

And it is no different when you take the tram across Berlin. They simply have to climb on board; but how many never do. Someone is born—let's say in Neukölln. He goes to school in Neukölln and serves his apprenticeship in Neukölln. He finds a girl from Neukölln for himself and takes her to the movies or to a café in Neukölln. He gets married, in Neukölln. He sets up as something like a plumber in Neukölln. He has no clientele outside Neukölln. At a pinch he visits the neighboring districts, and goes to Britz, to Tempelhof, to Mariendorf.

You have to picture it clearly: this is how people live in Steglitz, in Siemensstadt, in Reinickendorf, in Adlershof. One or two will drift back and forth over the years for occupational reasons. They also travel once in a while along Unter den Linden or Kurfürstendamm, in much the same way as people like us, when we're lucky, go to Paris or Constantinople. But in general they don't get very much out of living in a city of 4 million inhabitants, either in their working lives or leisure time.

You probably have no idea how a life can pass with so little social life, friendship, and love. Nor can you imagine the tiny radius within which some lives are played out. If you can't change it, at least look at it as you speed past.

NOTE

1. Neukölln is a working-class suburb to the south of the Berlin city center.

141

Karl Scheffler

BERLIN

A City Transformed

First published as Scheffler, *Berlin: Wandlungen einer Stadt* (Berlin: Cassirer, 1931), pp. 169–72, 178–80, 185–87. Translated by Iain Boyd Whyte.

Can one speak of a new Berlin? Of a Berlin that is different or will become different from what it was before the war, of new city districts and a new urban spirit?

Yes, we can. With the hindsight that is constantly growing longer, it is becoming ever more clear that the war was no chance event or merely the external expression of a passing phase. Rather, it is powerfully related to our whole existence and destiny, and also with the development of our thoughts on the metropolis. The Great War is the grave of an entire epoch and the cradle of a new one. Whether it is better or worse is of no consequence; these terms have no currency in history, since nobody can achieve a position from which such a judgment might be reached. It will be a new life; and all of us who live it will be forcibly made to recognize this fact and to form it according to our own abilities. In the final analysis, it is we ourselves and not the higher authorities who determine how our lives are and what they will be in the future.

The new realities with which Berlin must come to terms and with which, considering the conditions, it is doing extraordinarily well are those that in the same way affect all major cities—throughout Germany, and indeed throughout Europe. They are grounded on profound economic and social realignments. The political sphere, however important it seems at the particular moment, is nothing more than a reflexive response to these changes in the economic and social realm. This signifies no less than a complete recasting or transformation of the capitalist economic system; sometimes violently, sometimes slowly, sometimes revolutionary, sometimes evolutionary. It signifies a concomitant destruction of societal structures for the sake of an incipient socialization of our complete existence—initially taking various transitional forms—and for the sake of the dissolution of the entrepreneurial forces of the bourgeoisie. We are witnessing an epoch-making development of the greatest significance.

That being the case, it is self-evident that the metropolis, whose appearance and essence are due almost entirely to the bourgeois entrepreneurial spirit, is first to become the subject of this immense transformation. The bold and pioneering thoughts on city planning that were proposed by vanguard spirits before the war must now be realized or at least activated. For the need for somewhere to live comes directly after the demand for food and the chance to work. It is becoming clear that almost all the demands for the reform of the metropolis that were raised some twenty or thirty years ago have, in practical terms, been accepted. Many of them, of course, cannot be implemented because old, long-term, and inadequate city plans stand in their way, and because there are not adequate resources simply to get rid of that which is ugly and harmful. On the other hand, the real world has gone far beyond the theoretical postulates, and reality has shown itself to be much more visionary than all the programs. In those days, when closely cognate initiatives began to play with the image of a new, better metropolis, no one could know that a war—and such a war—would be necessary to clear out of the way all the obstacles that had piled up over the years. The war was predictable, but neither the form it took nor its scale, nor its outcome, nor its apparently historical inevitability, nor—in spite of everything—its dynamic and rejuvenating power. There was no way of anticipating the strange phenomenon that appeared simultaneously throughout Europe, and which we call the housing shortage, nor the general clamor that it provoked for decent housing conditions. There was no way of foreseeing this unparalleled declaration of the will of the masses. One can understand why the dignity and value of human life cannot be valued highly enough, given the fact that it took no less than a million murders to produce this progress. That this was the case, and that it will not recur that often, is beyond doubt.

Before the war, the urban renewal programs proposed a metropolis with a business core [*Geschäftscity*], commercial zoning, industrial areas, suburban housing, garden cities, high-speed rail links, radial arterial roads, and so on. Now the building activity is predicated on nothing less than large-scale regional planning, with the expansion of the metropolitan spirit across an immense number of housing settlements spread through the entire land: a conquest over the pernicious antithesis of city and country. Before the war, the campaign against the urban tenement block, which was waged on aesthetic grounds and as a social reformist attack on the criminal living misery in high-density quarters, proposed the unification of the individual facades into large-scale, architecturally unified housing blocks with garden courts. In this case, too, postwar reality has gone far beyond the prewar demands, with large-scale housing developments creating massive, coherently designed housing blocks with central facilities. These are to be found on the periphery of almost all the major cities in Europe and give these cities a completely new dimension.

[. . .]

Today's architects are so preoccupied with the naked necessities of living, with costs, materials, and ground plans, that they do not have the internal calm to engage with issues of pure, representative form. For this, they will need calmer times, established building conventions, and a surplus of both external wealth and inner resource. There is little to bring the aesthetician to the new Berlin, as everything is still a matter of trial and experiment, and nothing has yet matured. In spite of its steel frame and ferroconcrete construction, this entire architecture may well be destined to disappear after thirty or fifty years to make way for something more conclusive. It is all just a trial run. But this is not to say that it does not have a mission—a mission both social and assuredly artistic. This is proven by its surprising and impressive homogeneity. The new architects disappear as personalities behind their work. Uniformity is also promoted by the building technology, by a building industry that favors rational structures, and by the comprehensive standardization and typification of building components. The decisive fact is that the housing needs of the metropolitan masses have also in a certain way become standardized. Out of this has come a pragmatic style [*Sachlichkeit*] with broad common goals. At present this style is still only the framework, tending more to exclude than promote individuality, but which still possesses the qualities of a taut and compelling rhythm; of good, harmonic proportions; and of monumental massing. The basis, in other words, of a new artistic language. We should not, however, push this artistic dimension; we must content ourselves with all those innovative elements that are imminent in the essential form, with everything they contain that appears to be organically linked to the demands of the age. Significantly, it is not uncommon to find new Berlin housing estates by architects of modest abilities, in which the grouping of the building is no less impressive than in similar developments by much more talented colleagues. The building tasks demand a uniformly positive attitude from all the architects, and dictate the same basic dispositions. In the building of a housing estate, hundreds of small housing units have to be brought under one roof. The edges of this collective structure are to be surrounded by large garden courts; the large site is to be subdivided by roads; a central communal laundry and a district heating scheme are essential; kindergartens for the children of working mothers are desirable; sports grounds and swimming pools turn out to be essential. All these needs demand the development of standard solutions and the exchange of ideas and experience among the architects, out of which spontaneously emerge formal and design similarities. It is not uncommon for several architects to work together on the large estates; yet it is hard to work out the particular contribution of each one. In this way something emerges that we perceive as a style. On close inspection there is much that is disturbing, even repellent. Sometimes a certain proletarian, prisonlike uniformity has not been overcome. The effect of cheap materials heightens this effect. But time and again, if the building groups are viewed from a distance, when you see their generous volumes shimmering white behind the trees, you get a vision of the metropolis of the future. Then the meaning of the sentence "Quantity can become quality" becomes transparently clear. Quantity compels uniformity, which it turn demands a standardized formal language—one that is not only rationally arrived at but that gives symbolic form to the shared goals of the people and to the fundamental significance of building. In this sense, the flat roof, to take one controversial example , is more than the result of savings in loft space and more than merely a fad. For the people perceive the flat roof as a characteristic form. They live in forms derived from necessity that have taken on symbolic meaning.

[...]

In the inner city, life rotates around natural hubs. The oldest center lies between Alexanderplatz and Spittelmarkt, the second oldest between Spittelmarkt and Potsdamer Platz, the third and most recent between Tauentzienstrasse and Kurfürstendamm. One can speak of Alexanderplatz as a center of production and commerce, and visualize it, together with its radial streets (Landsberger Strasse, Dircksenstrasse, Münzstrasse, Königstrasse) and their cross streets (Molkenmarkt, Mühlendamm), only in the cool light of a bustling working day. Many bureaus and offices, masses of small shops, crowds of shoppers and shopgirls, small-business people, groups of unemployed, and figures from the Berlin underworld gathered from the streets to the east all belong to this center. In this working hub is located the Central Market Hall, which each day turns a whole section of the city into a big, multicolored market. The police headquarters are also there, together with the County Court [*Landgericht*] and Lower Court [*Amtsgericht*] forming a small bureaucratic state. On one of Berlin's oldest commercial streets are set the main post office and the city hall, while almost the entire volume of traffic that is trying to go from the eastern side of the city to the center and the west squeezes tightly through this district. The main time for this city center is the morning hours. The afternoon belongs essentially to the area between Spittelmarkt and Potsdamer Platz, which is accessed by Friedrichstrasse and which has the Leipziger Strasse as its main axis. In contrast to the working center in the east, this a focal point for business and transportation. North of Leipziger Strasse one finds the most important bank buildings, and the press is concentrated in the area to the south, abutted by the governmental buildings on Wilhelmstrasse. Department stores and large hotels dominate this part of the city, while the entire Berlin art trade is concentrated in the streets around Potsdamer Platz. which is the busiest traffic junction in the whole city. Postdamer Platz itself is the crossroads of everything that the metropolis can offer in terms of the wit and spirit that keep the economic wheels turning, and the favorite base for visitors, who visit the German capital city for business or pleasure. An architectural reframing of Alexanderplatz is currently under way; a fundamental reordering of the hopelessly messed-up Potsdamer Platz is always being proposed.

The western center between Wittenbergplatz, Kaiser-Wilhelm-Gedächtniskirche [Kaiser William Memorial Church], and the Kurfürstendamm is essentially the leisure and entertainment quarter. Accordingly, its real character reveals itself best in the artificial light of the evening. Then we see the long rows of brightly lit, broad-fronted luxury shops—the flagship shops of the big firms. We see a large department store, which seems to contain a hundred small shops, and the major cinemas bathed in sparkling light, which every night welcome many thousand visitors and then release them at set times. Closely packed together are also restaurants, confectioners, and cafés, with their outside tables shielded in the summer by awnings, plus nightclubs and cabarets. This whole section of the city glows at night with bright, multicolored, neon lighting, and the mainly ugly houses disappear in the twilight or light up in a mysterious and romantic way in the harsh strip lighting. Here, as if on a *corso*, gather the well dressed, the theatrically made up, the actors and actresses who voluntarily act out their parts in the review that is metropolitan life. At certain times in the evening, the traffic builds up so much that jams result. The private cars park in long rows, and even the broad boulevard of Kurfürstendamm proves itself too small to handle the volume of traffic. In this part of the city the metropolitan life seems to be at its most concentrated and its most European, comparable to life on the boulevards of Paris or around Piccadilly Circus in London. Here it assumes the extraordinary fantasy of the great city, which is both kitschy and fabulous in one, and which is impressive and overwhelming in the manner of a cheap fairground. This is the setting for the triumph of the masses, of quantity. Yet the light spiritualizes and transfigures the material reality, and creates a sense of visual festivity unprecedented in history, such as was unknown even in the creations of princes. It is a festival of life that the reignites anew every evening, whose essential shallowness is compensated for by the vast amount of energy that it contains. This is the leisure-time apotheosis of the metropolis; it is the triumphal march that the new Berlin sings over and over again about its new self.

142

Siegfried Kracauer

THE NEW ALEXANDERPLATZ

First published as "Der neue Alexanderplatz," *Frankfurter Zeitung,* 18 November 1932. Translated by David Britt.

While Alexanderplatz was under construction, it was a formless, open space, through which the winds whistled from every direction; now it has become a model of organization. The wind, of course, still whistles. On the downtown side, the square is now closed off by two gigantic high-rise office buildings, which look like a defensive wall. Even with the most modern weaponry, no one could ever take that wall by storm. It is therefore fortunate that the wall parts to admit the end of Königstrasse. The walls interrupt their course, allow Königstrasse to pass though, and simultaneously afford a wonderful prospect of the elevated railroad. Across the tracks, which form a kind of horizontal connection between the two skyscrapers, the trains roll in constant, colorful procession; the iron structure of the railroad station also peeps through the gap.

But this urban transit operation bears no relevance to the activity on the square proper; with an autocratic gesture, the office buildings relegate it all to the background. The buildings clear the way for Alexanderplatz—and one of them even runs alongside it for a little way, to enable it to unfold that much more freely. The area of the square is immense, like a lake whose shores are partly lost to view. Were it not divided by a circular garden plot that fills the center, people and vehicles would probably lose their bearings and begin to collide. Entering the square from all sides, they are set on leaving it in as many directions. However, the circle, which they are not permitted to cross, compels them by its very presence to describe an elegant arc around it. Automobiles, buses, trucks, pedestrians: all circumnavigate this green expanse of turf, which lies there like a no-man's-land, demarcated at regular intervals by streetcar poles and traffic policemen. It emanates an ineffable peace that even the yellow streetcars cannot destroy. On the contrary, as they hurtle nonstop across the circle, they only accentuate the impression that it is a protected nature reserve.

Below ground, too, Alexanderplatz is impeccably organized. Three superimposed subway stations are connected by a labyrinth of passageways, landings, and stairways. Perhaps this hygienic splendor affords some compensation to the members of the local proletarian population for the squalor of their own living rooms—places where such hygiene would be more to the point. The stations are tiled in different colors and also, for clarity's sake, marked with letters. Although the colors and letters are repeated in every possible location to put the seeker on the right path, it remains extraordinarily difficult to get to the place you are looking for. The system is of an artificial perfection that mocks any impromptu attempt to grapple with it; it can be understood only by long and painful study. A fanatical concern with tidiness—understandable in itself—has caused a number of the tracks and exits to be so well concealed as to be simply impossible to find. You want to get to A and you get to D, from which you have to find your way back via B or C. By way of compensation, you have the pleasure of using an extensive array of escalators. One of these so far defies the norm as to travel downward instead of upward. Why it is that most of those who use the escalators—presumably in order to save effort—dash so madly up or down them is a matter that remains to be investigated.

In the immediate vicinity of Alexanderplatz, and visible from it, is the boxlike office block built by a department-store company. It is separated from the two office blocks that front the elevated railroad not just by the square itself but by half the world. The block in question is a gloomy citadel of private enterprise, with a colossal facade entirely composed of pilaster strips that inspire an involuntary shiver. Cut off flat at the top, they succeed each other in incalculable profusion, repeating without a pause right across the front of the central tower—for all the world as if someone were setting up a Vertical Trust to corner the pilaster market. Every one of them is a perpendicular atrocity. In the narrow spaces between them the windows fit as if in grooves: undernourished, timorous windows that remind us of office clerks. Their operations are fully rationalized, their salaries in accordance with a standard rate. They will soon be dispensed with. Then the business will carry on without them, and the pilaster strips will stalk still more brutally across the windowless facade. On the other hand, the business itself might well one day have to close down . . . In comparison with this corporate edifice, which is all menace, the two office buildings on Alexanderplatz itself have a more welcoming appearance. Instead of succumbing to megalomania, they somehow contrive to adapt to their surroundings. And instead of flaunting a bombastic array of piers that lash the windows into submission, they pair off their windows and house them inside little boxes. These buildings are at least built for human beings rather than for the glorification of anonymous capitalist power. For the time being, they are largely vacant. One of them houses a well-known restaurant that occupies two stories and is fitted out with choice hardwoods and modern lighting fixtures. Customers enjoy the interior design as a free bonus with their beer and frankfurters.

Closed off on the side facing the railroad, Alexanderplatz remains wide open in the opposite direction. Whole neighborhoods crowd into the square from the east, each with its own street alignment, which the eye can follow from a vantage point on the square. These streets recede and ultimately vanish into a gray squalor. At the point from which they diverge, a fragment of the past has survived: a small-town idyll. It is made up of a few low, ancient houses, huddled around a bright red brick church. As you approach this knot of buildings the metropolis progressively disappears from view—until in the end you find yourself on a secluded little square where no sound from the outside world penetrates. In the midst of the Alexanderplatz district, you are miles away from it, somewhere out in Brandenburg. One cottage has a Biedermeier gable, and the church—no expense spared on bricks—is undoubtedly the pride of the parish. It towers above the rooftops, so that from the little square it is visible only thigh high. Its choirs are generously rounded; its bricks assemble themselves into ingenious ornaments. Here, between the church walls and the cottages, would be the place for a picturesque duck pond and some willows. On returning to real life—a process that takes a minute at most—you immediately forget that tranquil enclave. The subway roars through your consciousness, and the thousand noises of Alexanderplatz are far too insistent to allow memories to surface. Were it not that the church can still be seen in the distance, you would take that cozy corner for a dream.

The throng passes along the construction hoardings that still curve across the surface of the square. These are plastered with handwritten bills advertising cheap lunch counters and bargain offers. In front of the bills stand street traders of unsurpassable eloquence. One of them holds a little snake made of spirals of wire, which you have only to stroke the right way in order to make it coil and writhe on its little paper plate. Tickle its tail, and it acts mad and angrily rears its green head. The vendor accompanies its maneuvers with remarks that are by no means lacking in ambiguity. He talks the onlookers into breathing imaginary life into his inanimate coil of wire, and makes no secret of his low opinion of all those who balk at paying ten pfennigs for so amusing and entertaining an object. Thus pressured, many buy the packets containing the paper tray with the snake on it. They will soon be the richer by a disappointment. But how eagerly this street audience of workers, unemployed people, and petit bourgeois clutches at any illusion that represents some escape from the daily round. Wherever a chink appears, they take refuge. Against the hoarding, which generates one diversion after another, a woman painter leans with a sketchpad in her hand. She already has Police Headquarters down on paper and accurately shaded; the tall office blocks will soon follow. Girls, men, and women crowd around the artist, follow the direction of her gaze when she gauges heights and widths, and delight in the precise reproduction of a reality that they know all too well. They survey their own surroundings in an unaccustomed way; for a second, they escape their own desperate existence by immersing themselves in its reproduction.

143

Siegfried Kracauer

LOCOMOTIVE OVER FRIEDRICHSTRASSE

First published as "Lokomotive über der Friedrichstrasse," *Frankfurter Zeitung*, 28 January 1933. Translated by David Britt.

Crossing Friedrichstrasse toward the railroad station, one often sees a giant express locomotive halted above. It stands directly over the center of the street and belongs to some long-distance train that is arriving from the west or departing for the east. Does it engage the attention of the crowd? Nobody gives it a glance. Cafés, display windows, women, automats, headlines, luminous advertisements, cops, buses, vaudeville photographs, beggars—all these ground-level impressions preoccupy the passerby far too deeply for him to grasp the apparition on the skyline. Even the upper floors along this street are lost in a blur; the caryatids on the facades have no interlocutors, the dormers might as well be cardboard, and the roofs vanish into a void. The locomotive suffers the same fate. With its long body, its gleaming rods, and its array of red wheels, it is a wondrous sight to see, but it lingers, neglected, above the throng of vehicles and people that surges through the underpass. It is an alien visitant, arriving and gliding away amid the nocturnal vapors, as unnoticed as if it were always there—or never there at all.

But what a spectacle Friedrichstrasse itself presents to the man on the locomotive! Imagine that he may have been driving his machine through the darkness for hours on end. The open iron road still rings in his ears: tracks hurtling toward him, signals, line keepers' cabins, forests, plowed fields, and pastures. He has passed through little depots and has brought his train to a halt for a few minutes at a time beneath the vast gloom of a station roof. Freight trains, local trains, lamp-lit parlors, church towers, voices calling. But, time and again, all this life has been swallowed up by the earth and lost in the sky. Towns? Brief interruptions. Villages? Scattered clusters in the countryside. Nothing has endured but embankments and telegraph poles, field patterns, endless spaces. Sometimes the fields have dropped away beneath the blaze of the fire hole, to be replaced by the surface of a river. Carts and wagons have waited at level crossings, smokestacks have

FIGURE 33. Locomotive over Friedrichstrasse, 1938. Landesarchiv Berlin, 310143.

sliced across the landscape, childish hands have waved from below. And, always, looming masses of blackness, rapidly growing and instantly disappearing.

The man on the locomotive has just left all that behind him. After a journey on which everything but earth and sky has fled from him, he suddenly comes to a halt above Friedrichstrasse, which obliterates both sky and earth. To him it must seem like the axis of the world, stretching away to either side, dead-straight and immeasurable. For its brightness obliterates his memories, its din drowns out that of the railroad, and its activity is sufficient unto itself. This is no mere halt along the way, but a sojourn at the very center of life. Himself an alien visitant, the man above peers down at the street as if through a chink. His eyes, accustomed as they are to darkness, may fail to distinguish details, but he nevertheless perceives the turmoil that explodes out of this narrow canyon of buildings; he registers the glare that is redder than the wheels of his own machine. In his perception the glare and the turmoil mingle in an eruption of festivity that has—like the string of arc lights—no beginning and no end. It looms out of the distance, enfolding rich and poor, harlots and escorts, and lines the facades with a roof-high, tumultuous blaze of words and signs. The man feels as if he were invisible, with the street of streets surging over and past him. A chain that never breaks. A human ribbon that ceaselessly unrolls, through the flickering air, between one plowed field and the next.

When he moves on, the night seems darker than ever. Everywhere he looks, behind and before, he sees a glowing line. It haunts him, and soon it can no longer be reduced to time and space: it becomes and emblem of redly glowing life. On Friedrichstrasse no one has noticed the locomotive.

144

Jean Giraudoux

BERLIN, NOT PARIS!

First published as "Berlin, nicht Paris!" *Der Querschnitt* 5 (1931), pp. 295ff. Translated by David Britt.

Berlin is not a garden city: Berlin is a garden. The average Frenchman, let alone a French architect or a building contractor, disfigures the natural beauty of the landscape; although it can—and has proved that it can—be made even more perfect by human hand. In Germany man's presence, his house, beautifies a landscape that is charmless by nature. In France there is not one modern invention—train station, streetcar, garage, generating plant—whose very name does not evoke the notion of filthy and eternally prostituted urban areas. In Germany, on the other hand, the words *gas, steam, electricity* possess the same associations that we attach to parks and gardens. There is, in Berlin, not a single train station, warehouse, or newspaper printing office that you could not photograph with flowers or trees in the foreground. No city in the world has so many streetcars as Berlin, but they run among trees and across grassy lawns. Every journey out of or into Paris strikes a chill to the heart. It is impossible to enter or leave the so-called City of Luxury without passing through the most appalling slums; it is impossible to enter or leave the so-called City of Art without sustaining a visual injury from the bad taste, vile design, and inferior execution perpetrated by an irresponsible municipality; it is impossible to traverse the City of Liberty, from the wheat fields of Brie to the Louvre, without constantly being confronted with manifestations of the most atrocious and degrading utilitarianism: manifestations that could have sprung only from a false view of the nature of modern life.

In German, the word for suburb, *Vorort,* is full of promise and arouses a sense of eager anticipation; the French equivalent [*banlieue*] is the grisliest item in the whole vocabulary of ugliness and grief. Berlin was vanquished, crushed, with no history of urban planning, in the midst of alluvial plain and marshland. Paris was rich and victorious; every one of the city plans decreed by its kings and emperors might have been extended into environs ringed with châteaux and parks. In Berlin, a black river and a canal; in Paris, a great and beautiful river, adorned with islands, bends, and slopes. The advance toward pure water—which is the law of all civilization, for the individual as well as for the state—was almost complete, for Parisians, by the time of Flaubert or Maupassant.

What remains of the lead that Paris once enjoyed? An overcrowded "no-man's-land" in which all the civic monuments of the future—schools, libraries, and hospitals—are nothing but sheds. A river with bare banks, without a glint, without eyelashes, its waters mere mud, its islands like garbage heaps. It is the prerogative of the city fathers to lavish their care on the fuchsias of the Jardin du Luxembourg and the begonias of the Tuileries, to extirpate every tree or plant for miles around, and to fill every cubic meter of pure air—the protection of which should surely take precedence over that of any historic monument—with reinforced concrete.

Berlin, on the other hand, eats its way with platinum dentures into a plain that is as flat as a tabletop and can attract no luster except from the reflected glory of the seasons. The last rye and potato fields of Brandenburg directly adjoin the most exemplary, audacious, and elegant residential developments, with gardens of rhododendrons and geraniums. The ramparts of Berlin are colorful citadels, in which the plainest workers' dwellings have bathtubs and telephones. And, in years to come, those outlying citadels will be joined by processions of new developments and villas that will trap within them none but encircled poplars, pines, and lakes.

A defeated generation is in no position to build up the fatherland; instead, it has built a home of its own. All the architectural flourishes and urban improvements that in former times no one but a victorious king dared undertake have arisen here because a defeated country has pulled itself together and devoted itself to its democratic institutions and to its collective life, in which it now sees its own future. A general staff of dedicated architects—Peter Behrens, Erich Mendelsohn, Hans Poelzig, and Max Taut—have found in the heart of Berlin what our architects have found only in Morocco, in the sands, and on the savanna: space, line, and freedom.

Wide streets, on which one is never held up by traffic congestion, and to which is appended an automobile highway to the Wannsee, lead into an open, airy city whose gigantic public buildings, even where still unfinished, seem to be inspired by an exemplary architecture of the future, not of the past.

The army is a matter of barracks, said a German general who had made his men's living quarters into a model home, complete with library and indoor swimming pool, and had turned his units into a model corps. The nation, says the German statesman today, is a matter of urbanism. In this respect, Berlin deserves the leading role that Germany has assigned to it. A people made up of individuals who enjoy freedom of movement will sooner or later develop its civilization to the full.

This new Berlin, between Lichterfelde and Grunewald, is a spa without medicinal springs, a seaside resort without the sea; but here the idea of the vacation, which for the French citizen is lost somewhere between July heat and September rains, is present on every day and at every hour. Rest breaks, three times a day, afford the pleasures of wealth, of idleness, and—this being the year 1931—a victory that is unknown to us.

145

Ernst Erich Noth

THE TENEMENT BARRACKS

First published as Noth, *Die Mietskaserne* (1931; reprint, Frankfurt am Main: Ullstein, 1984), pp. 104–5. Translated by Iain Boyd Whyte.

This dreadful house has a hold on people, has a hold on the parents, on Walter, on everyone who lives here. When it is not the racket of the tenants that you hear, then it is the gramophone of the Paschkes, who live on the floor below, rasping late into the night. There's a lot going on down there since Herr Paschke was hospitalized after his hand was torn off by a machine. The adolescent children pay no attention to the remonstrations of their mother and have fun just as they please. Or you hear Lehmann beating his wife, whose shrieks pierce through the floor and the walls. You can't escape anything in this house. All day you can hear every word of the gossip on the landing, the nagging tones of the women, who yesterday were good friends but today scream the most foul-mouthed curses at each other, regardless of who else might hear. And the others, they listen in—initially from compulsion, then for amusement, and then by getting involved themselves. Each month brings a particularly serious confrontation; every month the warring parties and groups realign themselves anew. Children are dragged in: "You heard what she said about me!" Learning from bitter experience, Frau Krause had forbidden her son ever to have heard anything. As a result, he did better than Walter, who was cited when Paschke accused Lehmann of defamation. He spoke up for Frau Paschke and on the same evening was beaten up for his trouble by Herr Lehmann. Now there is a new battle, a new version of the old one—Bahm versus Lehmann—because Frau Paschke is supposed to have said, on hearing of Karl Lehmann's insidious attack, that he was ripe to be taken into care. Harrowing glimpses every day into strange, tension-laden human relations gave Albert grounds enough for serious thoughts. Every day brought new experiences, which made the massive tenement block hateful to him. It seemed to be like a sinister giant, a tormenting nightmare from which there is no escape.

146

Siegfried Kracauer

A SECTION OF FRIEDRICHSTRASSE

First published as "Ein Stück Friedrichstrasse" (1932); republished in Kracauer, *Schriften*, ed. Inka Mülder-Bach, vol. 5, fasc. 3 (Frankfurt am Main: Suhrkamp, 1990), pp. 15–17. Translated by David Britt.

Shortly before noon, on the southern section of Friedrichstrasse. The street runs dead straight from Belle-Alliance-Platz, with its sooty, undersized mythological groups, to Friedrichstrasse Station; but in this part of it we are not particularly aware of its geometric rigor. It is rather run-down and full of small, poverty-stricken stores that have a very temporary look about them. This is undoubtedly because the owners of many buildings have let their store premises on a short-term basis to avoid leaving them empty. Between the short-term businesses and the established ones there is, however, no very great difference. Today, nothing is there for keeps, and many of the sales bespeak a final shutdown.

A transient bustle, containing many signs of poverty that only gradually impinge on the passerby. Presumably the large number of photographic stores has some connection with the fact that this part of town is the chosen home of the motion-picture business. Not that the photographic stores have the field to themselves; they constantly find themselves cheek by jowl with little radio stores. The presence of the latter may possibly be explained by the close relationship between eye and ear. The popularity that radio has already achieved is illustrated by the abstruse technical specifications that appear alongside the little black or brown boxes in the shop windows. Young lads peruse the texts with an expert eye that they evidently do not apply to the study of political events. If only they did, politics in this country would be different, and less dominated by loudspeakers. Nearby are a number of little stores that seem to have crept, by some unerring instinct, out of an arcade somewhere. They are narrow and deep, and they conceal themselves behind a fluttering curtain of scenic picture-postcard strips, which serves only to draw attention to their nakedness. For, amid the "Berlin Street Scenes," even their storefront displays contain images that concern the Art of Love; and a sign politely invites amateurs of "works of sexology" to step inside. Wherever the mind turns to thoughts of love, hairdressers' shops are generally not far away. As befits the location, those wax dummies that are such a feature of these establishments do not look remotely as refined as their sisters on Kurfürstendamm, though they wear elaborate coiffures in the last fashion but one. Fortunately, the popular songs of the moment remain the same, whatever the district in which they are warbled. The one from the Charell movie *Congress Dances* seems to have caught on particularly strongly: "*Das gibt's nur einmal—das kommt nie wieder*" [Only once, never again.] A cigar store uses it to advertise a cut-price cigar, and it is as if we could hear Harvey himself singing the touching refrain. In the picture, unfortunately, the line comes back again and again. The cigar in question no doubt tastes good in one of the numerous cafés hereabouts. One place, which seems to have come a long way down in the world, has assumed the appellation of "Bourgeois Café"—not intended as an aspersion, I hope. Others make reference to the availability of booths, thus evoking sexological associations that are presumably good for business. Other inducements offered to patrons include the Hungarian Iron King. To judge from the photographs, he bends iron bars in a trice and is altogether one of those strong men that people in this country so long for.

It is noon, the stores are a confused mass, and the din of the automobiles and omnibuses is unrelenting. Suddenly, music strikes up on the street. In among the postcards, the cigars, and the coiffures, songs are heard that would be in place out in the woods, or in distant back courtyards, but not here in this commercial district. Sung to the accompaniment of guitars and fiddles, they sound as carefree as if no one else were present at all. The performers might be students; at all events, they are neatly dressed, and their faces are not work worn; however, their rosy complexions are more likely to be the effect of cold than of a healthy diet. Like exiles from a foreign land, they stand on the southern section of Friedrichstrasse and make music about true love, home, and faith—all folk melodies, full of yearning, that ought to be accompanied by the rustle of village linden trees, not by trucks and taxis. Passersby dawdle nearby: workers, women with baskets, bargemen's children, and men who defy definition. They do not stir; they listen as if rooted to the spot, and stare fixedly at the players and singers. It is as if they felt themselves transported into a Sunday outing in the country, hiking and lying on the grass, and meeting with the same young people who are singing to them now. They forget the stores and their own cares. Nature, with her *Wandervögel*, her happy hikers, has appeared in the center of the city . . .

The singing breaks off, and a silence follows; even the roar of the traffic dwindles. No one moves from the spot; the pavement is as fragrant as grass. In the midst of the silence, one of the group detaches himself and goes around with a hat. This instantly breaks the spell. The buses move on, the wax dummies resurface, the postcards spring to life. Mutely, and without giving any money, the passersby move on. Their brief dream is dispelled.

147

Gabriele Tergit (pseud. Elise Reifenberg)
HOME IS THE 75 (OR THE 78)

First published as "Heimat 75 resp. 78," *Berliner Tageblatt*, 19 February 1930; reprinted in Tergit, *Atem einer anderen Welt: Berliner Reportagen* (Frankfurt: Suhrkamp, 1994), pp. 24–27. Translated by David Britt.

Home is not the fountain, or the linden tree, or the walk out from the city gates, or the path around the ramparts—as it is, even today, if you live in Zerbst or in Schweinfurt. Home is my 75. It used to be called the S or the O. When we were young girls, and used to go see the classics directed by Reinhardt—what bliss—do you remember, Harry Walden played Don Carlos, Moissi was Posa, and Bassermann King Philip; and *Turandot*, and the *Henry*s, and Theodor Loos as Oswald Alving. That was the S and the O. The S and the O, however, used to cross the Hitzigbrücke and go along the Lichtensteinallee, which is now totally quiet. Later,

I used to ride the S and the O to the university. It was lovely, wasn't it, going through the Tiergarten? Always the same stores on Dorotheenstrasse: poultry man, Schrop's Maps, academic beer halls. Always the same faces around nine in the morning, rather raffish, with notebooks bound in waxed cloth.

Now I am back, living on the same route from Tiergarten via Dorotheenstrasse. When you move into a new apartment, you wonder what "home" is going to mean from now on: not the walk along the new street, not the name of the nearest butcher, or the vegetable store, or the caryatid on the building next door, or the new shortcut, but the name of the beast that gets you to and from work every day. The 75. Good old 75, noble and obliging 75. Long-lost home of my youth. No longer hopeful green, you have turned yellow, 75 (or 78).

Yet I confess that you both pale into insignificance by comparison with the 76 (or 176). This starts way out in Grunewald. Comes in along Kurfürstendamm, traverses the world of new stores, exquisite sweaters, smoke consumers, and bridge parties, runs along Lützowstrasse, Potsdamer Strasse, and Leipziger Strasse to Spittelmarkt, that great entrepôt for human merchandise from the West and from the East. Home is the 176: Molkenmarkt, Stralauer Strasse, Lange Strasse, Ostbahnhof. In the thick of all the soap dealers and the fruit-and-vegetable stores, and the little bars, the joiners and locksmiths are in back; then, far beyond, carrying weary people to Frankfurter Allee Station and on to Lichtenberg, out beyond Lake Rummelsburg.

Or home is the subway. From October through April, in the morning twilight; from April through October, in the morning light: that dear, familiar conveyance, the yellow nonsmoking car in the center of the train. Cheerful green tiles at Potsdamer Platz, with primroses, tulips, roses, carnations, dahlias, asters above: "Summer, Winter, Spring and Fall, is that any life at all?" Black tiles at Kaiserhof, a refined, Prussian kind of station. Red at Friedrichstadt, red tiles for love. Yellow at Gelbstern, Hausvogteiplatz. Wise builder of the subway, honored Symbolist of 1910.

And the old west side? Luxury travel, 1 and 2? Fashion show and pimping, too, 1 and 2. Pioneer intruders and bringers of noise into those quiet streets: Königin Augusta- and Lützowufer, Hohenzollern- and Dörnberg-, Bendler-, and Genthiner Strasse. Transportation for those who have no automobile but who once used to run a carriage. Transportation for the carless wives of gentlemen with cars. When she moved away from the 1 and the 2, I asked her, "What will you do?"

"I'll have the 25," she said. "My 25," she calls it now.

And the ABOAG buses![1] The Number 12, at 11 or 11:30 A.M., full of newspaper people, on the way to the press district. And the Number 10 at 8:30, full of folks from Moabit: attorneys, personal-injury claimants, bankrupts, people who have been humiliated and swindled, the hysterical lady from the defamation case in Court 272, judges and public attorneys. Oh, the 9, the University bus, the Tech

Institute bus, the Business School bus: blond girl, pale youth, "my old lady," "the laws of spiritual communication."

But the ABOAG is not home to anyone. It furiously rings its bell, roars away, leaves you standing. It finds its way along no predetermined tracks. Ruthlessly, at five before nine, it makes you late for work, the brute.

There are some poor wretches who live on Kantstrasse, with nothing but streetcars 93 and 72 since time immemorial; then the 53 came along, not that that improves matters. And there are children who grow up on Kurfürstendamm knowing nothing but the 1, with no idea that there is such a beast living as the 23; not knowing that there are faithful old mutts by the name of 47 that go to Britz; not knowing that the only way to get to Tegel is the 25. What a dear old friend that is! Coming from the deepest south, from the Teltow Canal, amid a welter of summerhouses, old gardens, new houses, factories, and the canal; Tempelhof, that's good, new land for young households and little children; Belle-Alliance-Strasse, old streets, the old, dignified, privy councillors' Berlin; Großbeerenstrasse. All at once into the pandemonium of hotels and train stations, the din of the new and the unfamiliar. Königgrätzer Strasse, Friedrich-Ebert-Strasse, and then it's the north. AEG, student quarter, clinics, medical bookstores, theaters, barracks, Karlstrasse, Friedrichstrasse, Institute of Agriculture, Invalidenstrasse; world of learning, world of research, world of teaching. Wedding. Factories, courtyards, squalor. And there it ends up, hard by the Humboldt brothers' park, close to Tegel Forest. Such streetcar lines there are, lines that traverse many neighborhoods. Every five blocks, the city takes on a new face. The people on the 1 at noon are very different from the people on the 25 at 7 A.M.

But none of them feels so good as our speedy, warm, eternal elevated. You know it, do you? Through a cutting in Halensee, above Savignyplatz, day after day past the wreckage, the dead city, the iron frames rusting in the water, the hundreds of thousands who languish in the morass: quagmire, decay, and death. Zoo Station, Tiergarten, daily vexation at the banks of the Spree, occupied by nothing but dead machinery instead of living people, warehouse sheds instead of riverside boulevards. Lehrter Station, and then—amid all the bustle of Kunze & Fröhlich, Wholesale Tubing—an eighteenth-century pavilion, a graceful temple of love, left behind in the steel depot next to Friedrichstrasse Station.

How well we know this street, Dircksenstrasse, just before Alexanderplatz! Slipper Manufactory, all the way across the facade, Wholesale Fruit, Butchers' Equipment, Milk Pans, Hoppers, Cutters, Meat Grinders, Sausage Ends, Eisenhuth Cheese; and Alexanderplatz from an unfamiliar angle. Past Jannowitzbrücke there is a little old house with Custom Tailoring on the ground floor; upstairs is the Thanatos Funeral Parlor. But far beyond, at Rummelsburg train depot, Alexanderplatz itself lies piled up in high, white, soft mountains of sand.

The ground on which the first private tailoring and cutting academy once stood has now turned into a sand so fine that you could bake cakes with it.

In the summer of 1917, amid the gunfire of the Chemin des Dames, two young men argued and wagered ten bottles of champagne—a real prewar bet—as to whether the R and the P run along Hardenbergstrasse or not. They were thinking of home, and all their love of this city concentrated itself on a dispute over those amiable beasts the R and the P, which they rode every day to the Institute of Technology.

Home to us is not the fountain, or the linden tree, or the walk out from the city gates, or the path around the ramparts—as it is, even today, if you live in Zerbst or in Schweinfurt. Home is our own streetcar line; home is our 1, our 25, our 47. It is bounding up and down the stairs, ninety-seven steps from the subway to Friedrichstrasse Station.

NOTE

1. ABOAG (Allgemeine Berliner Omnibus AG) was a Berlin bus company that joined in 1928 with the Gesellschaft für Elektrische Hoch- und Untergrundbahnen (underground railways) and the Berliner Strassenbahn-Betriebs-GmbH (streetcars) to form a consolidated transport corporation, the Berliner Verkehrs-Aktiengesellschaft.

148

Christopher Isherwood

A BERLIN DIARY (WINTER 1932–33)

In Isherwood, *The Berlin Stories* (New York: New Directions, 1963), pp. 186–87.

Tonight, for the first this winter, it is very cold. The dead cold grips the town in utter silence, like the silence of intense midday summer heat. In the cold the town seems actually to contract, to dwindle to a small black dot, scarcely larger than hundreds of other dots, isolated and hard to find, on the enormous European map. Outside, in the night, beyond the last new-built blocks of concrete flats, where the streets end in frozen allotment gardens, are the Prussian plains. You can feel them all round you, to-night, creeping in upon the city, like an immense waste of unhomely ocean—sprinkled with leafless copses and ice-lakes, and tiny villages which are remembered only as the outlandish names of battlefields in half-forgotten wars. Berlin is a skeleton which aches in the cold: it is my own skeleton aching. I feel in my bones the sharp ache of the frost in the girders of the overhead railway, in the ironwork of the balconies, in bridges, tramlines, lamp-standards, latrines. The iron throbs and shrinks, and stone and bricks ache dully, the plaster is numb.

Berlin is a city with two centres—the cluster of expensive hotels, bars, cinemas, shops round the Memorial Church, a sparkling nucleus of light, like a sham diamond, in the shabby twilight of the town; and the self-conscious civic centre of buildings round Unter den Linden, carefully arranged. In grand international styles, copies of copies, they assert our dignity as a capital city—a parliament, a couple of museums, a State bank, a cathedral, an opera, a dozen embassies, a triumphal arch; nothing has been forgotten. And they are all so pompous, so very correct—all except the cathedral, which betrays, in its architecture, a flash of that hysteria which flickers always behind every grave, grey Prussian facade. Extinguished by its absurd dome, it is, at first sight, so startlingly funny that one searches for a name suitably preposterous—the Church of the Immaculate Consumption.

But the real heart of Berlin is a small damp black wood—the Tiergarten. At this time of year, the cold begins to drive the peasant boys out of their tiny unprotected villages into the city, to look for food, and work. But the city, which glowed so brightly and invitingly in the night sky above the plains, is cold and cruel and dead. Its warmth is an illusion, a mirage of the winter desert. It will not receive these boys. It has nothing to give. The cold drives them off the streets, into the wood which is its cruel heart. And there they cower on benches, to starve and freeze, and dream of their far-away cottages.

13

WORK

While the industrial and commercial infrastructure of Berlin—its factories, workshops, shops, and offices—emerged in 1918 from the war unscathed, the financial landscape was quite different from that of 1914. The foreign capital investments of the large industrial firms like Siemens and AEG had been lost, and traditional sources of raw materials both in Silesia and in the French-occupied Ruhr region were no longer under German control. Following massive expansion during the war years, the mechanical-engineering sector had particular difficulties in adapting to the postwar economy. Electronics, in contrast, boomed in 1920s Berlin. New firms like Osram were established in 1919 through the cooperation of Siemens, AEG, and Auer, to produce light bulbs, which found a ready market on its doorstep in a city of 4 million inhabitants. Telegraph and telephone technology also burgeoned, symbolized in 1922 by Arthur Korn's first wireless transatlantic telegraph message. Radio technology developed in parallel, and by 1923 regular light entertainment programs were being broadcast from the Vox building on Potsdamer Platz. Yet for all the native inventiveness, it was clear to the victorious Axis powers that German industry could not revive itself without external help, and under the terms of the 1924 Dawes Plan, foreign investment flowed vigorously in the German economy. In 1925, for example, the British tobacco firm Adbulla opened a Berlin factory in rented premises, and rapidly went on to build a new factory at Johannisthal in the southwest of the city. In the same year, the Swiss firm Maggi, which made gravy sauce and similar products, opened a large distribution center in Schöneberg. In the new atmosphere of optimism, new conglomerates in banking, publishing, brewing, and electronics were established and centered in Berlin. Quite remarkably, real incomes, production, and export volumes already equaled prewar levels by 1926. The industrial consolidation generated an architectural boom, which favored the standardizing rationality, simplicity, and economy of *Neues Bauen*—the new architecture of modernism. As the critic Max Osborn observed in 1929: "The ideas of the new architecture were victorious across the whole front.... The city today is surrounded by an enormous sweep of industrial buildings, which result from the functional way of thinking, the sense of space, and the new monumentality of modern architecture. Nowhere has the new beauty of the technological era found freer expression than in this unmissable development of machine halls, fortresses of production, storehouses, and pounding workshops, which with their administration buildings, internal circulation systems, fantastic steel structures, chimneys, mobile cranes, and soaring landmark towers spread in all directions far and wide across the formerly calm lands of the March of Brandenburg."[1] Enjoying favorable rates of both communal and commercial taxes, these new businesses attracted large-scale immigration to the city, with eighty to one hundred thousand arriving in the city each year in the mid-1920s. As the mayor of Cologne, Konrad Adenauer, complained: "Berlin has immense incomes from commercial taxes for the simple reason, unfortunately, that everything has concentrated itself in Berlin."[2]

Two mighty new building projects are representative of the industrial boom enjoyed by Berlin in the later 1920s. The first is the printing house for the Ullstein publishing empire, designed by Eugen Schmohl and built on the banks of the Teltow Canal in Tempelhof in 1925-26. Through a process of fusions and takeovers, Ullstein had become the biggest publisher in Germany, producing not only popular newspapers like the *Berliner Morgenpost,* but also books and magazines. Outgrowing its original offices on Kochstrasse, the traditional newspaper street of Berlin, all the technical, printing, and distribution functions of the firm were moved to the new printing house, claimed at the time to be the most advanced in the world. A second mighty industrial fortress was the Siemens administration building, located in Siemensstadt—the firm's own suburb of Berlin—and built in 1928-30. Designed by the architect Hans Hertlein, this enormous structure was composed of a series of interlocking blocks assembled around a large internal courtyard and topped by a 57-meter-high tower. The steel structural frames of the blocks were clad with smooth, brick facades, decorated only by steel-framed windows arranged in a variety of vertical and horizontal formats, depending on the interior function.

The proximity in Siemensstadt of an army of factory workers tending the conveyor belts, of blank-faced administration blocks manned by thousands of white-collar workers, and of standardized row housing built by Berlin's leading modern architects to accommodate the workforce suggests an easy alliance between rationalist production methods and rationalization in housing design. The reality, inevitably, was more complicated, and the workforce looked for their aesthetic cheer not in the white walls of the contemporary housing, but in the easy coziness of the bar and the cinema. As Siegfried Kracauer noted at the time, as soon as one went beyond the *Neue Sachlichkeit* facade of the Haus Vaterland dance hall, "one was in the depths of the most voluptuous sentimentality."[3]

The glory years of the 1920s were short-lived, however, and the dependence of the Berlin economy on foreign capital made it particularly vulnerable following the global economic collapse that began in 1929. The results were drastic cuts in pay, massive unemployment, and, ultimately, the collapse of long-established and venerable companies. The Borsig engineering company, for example, which had been founded in 1837 and by the 1870s was one of the leading locomotive makers in the world, closed in 1931 with the loss of two thousand jobs in the Tegel factory alone. While Kracauer had explored the world of the Berlin working classes in the mid-1920s, he was now reduced to reporting on a workforce that was no longer in work. In an essay on the employment exchange, he recorded in 1930 that in the textile trade, only ten out of two thousand job applications were successful. The result, as he wrote: "In the employment agency, the unemployed occupy themselves with waiting. Since in relation to their number that of positions vacant may at the moment be negligible, the activity of waiting becomes almost an end in itself. I have observed that, when the situations vacant are read out, many hardly still listen. They are already too indifferent to be capable of believing in being selected."[4]

Only with the accession to power of the National Socialists in the early months of 1933 did the Berlin economy revive, but then under the particular conditions of the dictatorship, which saw both the trade unions and the employers' associations forced together under party control into the "Deutsche Arbeitsfront," the national labor front. The mass employment and propaganda successes created by the autobahn building program and by other works on the national transport infrastructure were reinforced, particularly after 1936, by a massive expansion of the armaments industry. The former Borsig factory in Tegel, for example, was turned over to the production of antiaircraft guns. "Once again," in the words of a commentary from the 1980s, "Berlin became a leading arms manufacturer. The tried and tested factories produced dependable guns, ammunition, mortars, and the whole spectrum of traditional weapons."[5] This conventional armory was reinforced by new instruments of war, recently developed in such high-technology industrial sectors as optics, telecommunications, the nascent telex and television technologies, and the aeronautical industry. In all these areas, Berlin industry played a leading role.

NOTES

1. Max Osborn, *Berlins Aufstieg zur Weltstadt* (Berlin: Reimar Hobbing, 1929), pp. 193–94.
2. Konrad Adenauer, quoted in Henning Köhler, "Berlin in der Weimarer Republik," in *Geschichte Berlins*, ed. Wolfgang Ribbe, vol. 2 (Munich: Beck, 1987), p. 852.

3. Siegfried Kracauer, *Die Angestellten: Aus dem neuesten Deutschland* (Frankfurt am Main: Suhrkamp, 1971), p. 96. See also Iain Boyd Whyte, "Berlin 1870–1945: An Introduction Framed by Architecture," in *The Divided Heritage: Themes and Problems in German Modernism*, ed. Irit Rogoff (Cambridge: Cambridge University Press, 1991), pp. 223–52, and particularly pp. 238–42.

4. Siegfried Kracauer, "On Employment Agencies: The Construction of a Space" (1930); reprinted in *Rethinking Architecture: A Reader in Cultural Theory*, ed. Neil Leach (London: Routledge, 1997), p. 62.

5. Werner Hildebrandt, Peter Lemburg, and Jörg Wewel-Blake, *Historische Bauwerke der Berliner Industrie* (Berlin: Senator für Stadtentwicklung und Umweltschutz Berlin, 1988), p. 25.

149
Alfred Döblin
GENERAL STRIKE IN BERLIN

First published as "Großstreik in Berlin," *Prager Tagblatt*, 14 November 1922. Translated by Iain Boyd Whyte.

I write as if before the deluge. Two candles stand in front of me, slowly flickering out; a strange, not unpleasant light. By this light I'm allowed this Sunday evening to make marks on my dear, empty sheet of paper. For twenty hours strike in Berlin. The railway men have already been on strike for two days. A deeply moving image awaits you if you go to entrances of the local Stadtbahn stations or to the main-line stations: the broad station forecourts are empty: no cabs, no cars; the doors closed; the whole mechanism, stretching for mile after mile, of tracks, locomotives, trackside buildings, signals, coal depots—the racing, whizzing express train, the smoke, the whistles, the shunting: silent, all gone. The hand of man rests on the mechanism. At this moment, with the whole gigantic apparatus lying still, we realize its enormous, anonymous power, and at the same time how this power can be subdued, paralyzed, and disrupted by human control . . . ; no foreign newspapers for three days, no long-distance mail, food supplies interrupted; the government has already requisitioned the coal supplies in the possession of private merchants.

Yesterday evening the phenomenon hit closer home. I went into the city, through the city, and around the city with the electric trams, the overhead railway, and the underground. Around ten or eleven o'clock the trams returned to the depot; tramway officials approached the drivers and conductors at the main city squares; a couple of words between them; and then: "Everybody off the tram; we're going back!" At midnight the last cars drove into the depots. No rebellion; the toys were taken away from under our noses. Thousands of people in their best clothes and in costumes were under way to fancy-dress balls; I've no idea how they got back. This nocturnal dash for the overhead railway: rushing, crushing, superstressing, running, pushing, noise, shouting, bawling, forming queues. Furious pilgrims on icy, snow-blown streets. Sunday. Chattering, loud conversation in the courtyards. Trotting on the *trottoir;* you try the electric light; switching on and off doesn't help; the gas on the stove flickers weakly; an hour later it breathes its last. The water taps are open: no water; no water for washing, for drinking, for cooking, for the water closet; misery. The hand of man rests upon events.

150

Ludwig Hilberseimer

BUILDINGS FOR THE METROPOLIS

First published as Hilberseimer, *Großstadtbauten* (Hannover: Appos, 1925). Translated by David Britt.

Historicism brought important new insights for mankind. These were in large part rendered worthless by being applied, inappropriately, to the arts. The extreme case was architecture. The vast store of architectural forms from past ages, wide open to study and readily adaptable, gave rise to a succession of epigonic generations who took it upon themselves to Classicize, Gothicize, Renaissancize, and Baroquefy the entire world. Architecture became more and more exclusively mere decoration. In parallel with its progressively more academic character, it became ever more estranged from its raison d'être in real life. The quickening touch of present-day needs was studiously avoided. The problem of architecture was misunderstood at a basic level and treated as a purely formal one; ornament and stylization were used to mask artistic sterility. The prevailing aesthetic held that architecture is a matter of visual form only. Yet its real nature lies deeper, and it is by no means adequately represented by visual impressions alone. Architecture cannot be considered in isolation. It always relates to the surrounding matrix of contemporary social, economic, and psychological conditions and indeed is the means by which these are articulated in art. [. . .]

What distinguishes present-day architecture from that of the past is primarily the very different character of the social conditions giving rise to it. New functional requirements give rise to distinctive formal characteristics, which in turn define contemporary architecture. These characteristics are the life-giving infusion of the new, and once they are integrated into a design they represent our own era's legitimate artistic impulse. Today it is not cathedrals, temples, and palaces that we need, but housing, office blocks, and factories—which need, however, to be built as cathedrals, temples, and palaces once were. To design the appropriate forms for the home, the office block, and the factory is one of the most important tasks facing modern architecture. Pure paradigms for these building types have not yet evolved: they have still to be created. Given the similarity of function, there is no obstacle to thoroughgoing standardization and thus to the industrialization of construction work in all its forms—an essential task, but one on which not even a beginning has been made. To date, architecture has sought to evade the process of standardization fundamental throughout modern industry. It still rests on foundations of individualism and craftsman tradition, in an age when everything else operates on a mass industrial basis. [...]

    The future architect will have to forgo the practice of embellishing buildings with external detail or imposing on them a would-be monumental mask. He will have to rid his mind of all the stylistic lumber of the past, deposited there by his years of academic training. It is not the ornamental tradition of some past style that should be paradigmatic for him, but the functional design of an express train coach or of an ocean liner. When tackling the new problems he must seek the solution that emerges naturally from the function, the structure, and the material used. Above all, he will have to focus on the problem of structure, for nothing new can evolve without secure foundations in terms of structure and function. The structural concept must be imbued with the creative spirit of architecture. The distinctiveness of design that tends to result from the engineer's input must not be smoothed over by formal preconceptions. The constraints of the division of labor, along with his own ignorance, have left the architect with no control over the engineering dimension. Only when he regains that competence, and can exploit it creatively, will he be able to at last transcend the barren years of imitation and move ahead to truly original achievement.

151

Franz Hessel

ON WORK

First published as "Etwas von der Arbeit" (1929); reprinted in Hessel, *Ein Flaneur in Berlin* (Berlin: Arsenal, 1984), pp. 21–24. Translated by David Britt.

Other cities, no doubt, are more noted for the enjoyment of life, for pleasure, and for distraction. There, perhaps, people have the knack of amusing themselves with greater spontaneity as well as greater sophistication. Their pleasures are more visible, and more beautiful. All the same, Berlin has its own special and visible beauty; and this is to be found only when and where the city is at work. Berlin must be visited in its temples of the Machine, its churches of Precision. There is no building more beautiful than the monumental hall of glass and reinforced concrete created by Peter Behrens for the turbine factory on Huttenstrasse. And no cathedral gallery affords a more impressive view than the gallery that surrounds that hall, at the very eye level of the man whose aerial perch moves in unison with the cranes that grip and move heavy loads of steel. Even before we see how the metal monsters below are acting to prepare other monsters of similar and dissimilar kinds, we are moved by the simple sight of them: castings and housings, unfinished blanks for geared drums and gear shafts, half-completed pumps and generators, drilling machines and gear mechanisms ready for installation, giant and dwarf machinery on the test bed, components of turbine generators in their concrete pit.

In the turbine hall, we admire more than we understand; in the smaller workshops, there is much that is more accessible. We see nickel steel in bar form being milled and ground on the blade; sheet-metal teeth being inserted in the grooves of the inductor shaft; exciter coils fitted in between gearwheels. We visit the forge, where workmen hold red-hot steel parts beneath the steam hammer that notches and planes them.

We stand on the waterside, outside the transformer works, and see a trolley hoist transferring coal from a Spree barge to a hammer mill that pounds it, without human intervention, into coal dust. We enter a hall, in which we are alone, and see the combustion in a glowing hot cavern. From the great machine shops, we move on to visit rooms where women workers wind extra-thin wires and mill kraft paper, which they press into layers of light, hard, smooth rolls; rooms where the narrow stamping tool is passed from hand to hand, heated, oiled, cut.

In the meter works, one operation of the machine turns the flat, circular metal blank into a dish with a raised rim; a second perforates it. Amid a shower of sparks, it is riveted and welded. Magnets are fitted. This whole building is a chain of operations that runs uninterrupted along the workbenches from one story to the next and is inserted into shafts to continue its journey. As the meter takes shape, all the bits and pieces that the women have at hand are inserted, mounted, screwed, and tested; finally, the completed meter is packed. Crates are secured with steel bands, moved on rollers to the elevator, and there lifted not by human hand but with a lever. All waste of strength and all exhausting effort is avoided; increasingly, the worker is reduced to supervising and starting the machine. Along with the machine parts, the conveyor belt carries cups and mugs into which the girls have put their tea, coffee, and cocoa; these will make the round trip via the kitchen and return brewed and ready to drink. Each worker, as she sits, has only a small area of tabletop to call her own, adjoining the conveyor belt; and yet there is room for a few brightly colored cups, plates, and spoons, contributed by the neighbors of the one who has a birthday: objects that sit touchingly amid the unceasing movement of the production line.

There is no need to understand all of this; just keep your eyes open and observe how something is always moving and changing. In one of these shrines of pious zeal there is a metal that has, you are told, a particularly high melting point and is very hard to vaporize. It can't be melted down in a furnace; the furnace would disintegrate. And so the powdered metal derived from the ore has to be pressed, sintered, hammered, and then annealed before it can be forged into a solid rod and then drawn into a wire. And now you can see how the wire passes through forging machines and wiredrawing dies, is pointed at the ends, and heated and drawn out until it eventually becomes the hair-thin filament that is used in an incandescent electric lamp. All this is done by machines; only the machines insert, remove, and move on. And while thousands of these ever-thinner wires are made, in other shops a thousand glass bulbs are fashioned. At circular machine benches that revolve beneath their hands, the patient workers sit, reach out for the handles, and pull them down, and obediently the machine clamps the base of the bulb, deploys holders, tensions the frame, melts, evacuates, attaches screw bases, solders, etches, stamps, and packs. And even this is only a part of the work. The product still has to be tested, metered, sorted, frosted, and/or tinted.

All of this goes on unceasingly in Siemensstadt, Charlottenburg, Moabit, and Gesundbrunnen, beyond Warschauer Brücke, and along the Upper Spree.

In the machine shop, from the stairs, from the gallery, it is magnificent to watch the humming, spinning machinery; equally, it is moving to see the bowed necks and the hands of those who work there, and to catch their eyes as they look up. As a result of these people's work, light comes into your little room, passes along house fronts, illuminates, praises, advertises, and remodels. Brightly lit moldings in the ceiling of a giant room form a festive, tented pavilion of light. Lighting picks out the contours of the facade of a building; floodlights are the lifeblood of shop windows. Blue daylight lamps blaze in the silk showroom, and the color of the fabric displayed by the salesman is the same color that appears in daylight. Outdoors, illuminated letters move across banners, or form themselves into words and disappear; images appear and change; colored wheels silently revolve.

Now whole buildings are designed with a view to the structuring of the fabric by light. One imagines the department store of the future: its walls and ceilings are all glass, and all uniformly bright; the sun shines in everywhere by day, and by night the light is the light made by men and machines.

152

Peter Panter (pseud. Kurt Tucholsky)

"HANG ON A MOMENT!"

First published as "'n Augenblick mal!" *Vossische Zeitung*, 1 January 1927. Translated by Iain Boyd Whyte.

It is well known that Berliners, no matter where they find themselves, sit quietly staring at the floor and then suddenly, as if bitten by a tarantula, jump up shouting: "Where can one make a telephone call here?" If there were no Berliners, the telephone would have invented them. It reigns over them, and they are its creatures.

Imagine an audacious young man who wants to disturb a serious businessman during important negotiations. It is simply not possible: halberdiers block the way; private secretaries hurl themselves across the threshold. The only way through is over their gentle bodies, and every attack by the young man is doomed to failure. Unless he phones up.

If he telephones, he can interrupt the president as he governs, the editor-in-chief as he chases after typos, or the actress in rehearsal. The telephone for the Berliner is not merely a mechanical apparatus: it's an obsession.

When the masses hammer menacingly on the door, the Berliner feels no urge to open it. But when a little machine rings he waves away even the noblest visitor, mumbling with the kind of obsequious look that one normally finds only in religious sects—"Hang on a moment!"—and hurls himself with wild interest into the black funnel. Business, midwives, stock exchange and composition proceedings go out the window. "Hello? Yes? This is—who is that—?"

To talk with a Berliner for fifteen minutes without being disturbed by a telephone call is an impossibility. How many points are blown away! How much collective energy drifts like smoke out of the window! All in vain the cunning negotiation, the malice, and the magnificently contrived perfidiousness! The telephone is not the invention of Messrs. Bell and Reis: the devil put this insidiousness object into the box. It rings only when you don't want it to.

How often have I experienced it . . . the powerful argument of a visitor who convinces the entire room; he's almost reached the summit, victory is near, only one more step . . . then the phone rings and that's the end of it. The fat man at the writing desk, who had just been three-quarters hypnotized, letting his double chin sink onto his necktie and happily extending his lower lip, now pulls a frozen mask over his face. With a nervous hand on the telephone receiver, he forgets his partner, his business, and himself. "Dinkelsbühler here—who's that?" Zealously swirling around in the strange waters, held completely captive by the other voice, he is disloyal to his interlocutor of a minute ago, and given up totally to deceit and betrayal.

The other man in the room is the fool. He sits there hollow and empty; the emotional words he uttered just a few moments ago hang senselessly out of his mouth like an old banner in the arsenal. The flag of a troop that is long dead. He sits humiliated, weak, and exposed, and with his unfulfilled wishes boiling glumly inside. What now—?

Now the fat man at the desk is conversing for as long as Berliners talk on the phone, and there is only one who talks longer—namely, the person at the other end. He must be pouring it out like a medium-size waterfall. The eyes of the fat man at the desk peer pensively at the blotting paper, wander across the inkwell, look confusedly and vacantly at the bald head of the duped partner, and then he starts to doodle matchstick men and rectangles. As the membrane whiningly makes clear, the person at the other end is pouring whole dictionaries into the telephone.

Soon the guest starts to shift impatiently on his chair, as the first hints of a conclusion of the endless conversation start to appear. "So then . . . !"—"Let's agree that . . ." The guest starts to cheer up, just as the spirits of the concertgoer start to move toward the cloakroom when the flapping gestures of the conductor throw ever more brass into the deafening racket . . . but it has not quite got that far. The telephoners remain in the same state for quite a while longer. Even though they keep making farewell noises, the end doesn't come. Slowly the desire grows in the waiting party to bang the other man on the head with the commercial law code . . . Finally, he says : "So—cheerio then!" and hangs up the receiver.

And this is the worst moment of all. In the eyes of the man at the writing desk the lighting has changed; you can actually hear it crack when he readjusts himself and turns blinking, with a rather feeble expression on his face, back to the old, betrayed partner once again. "So—where had we got to . . . ?"

Now you start all over from the beginning again. You gather up once more the broken pieces of your speech from the floor, take a deep breath, and try to get back on track . . . good night. The energy is gone, the humor has been lost, the will is no longer there. The conversation limps to a conclusion. You've achieved nothing. That's what the Lorelei did with their singing.[1]

At this point the reader quietly and happily puts the book down and ponders for a moment. The he springs up like a hunted deer, the *Mona Lisa* falls smiling to the floor . . . and he runs to the telephone.

NOTE

1. The Lorelei is a high rock on the eastern bank of the Rhine near St. Goarshausen, above a very narrow and dangerous stretch of the river. It is also the name of a water spirit whose captivating singing lured boatmen to their doom on the rocks.

153

Fritz Stahl (pseud. Siegfried Lilienthal)

THE KLINGENBERG POWER STATION AT BERLIN-RUMMELSBURG

First published as Stahl, *Das Großkraftwerk Klingenberg* (Berlin: Wasmuth, 1928), pp. 5–12. Translated by Michael Loughridge.

On completing one's exploration of this immense industrial complex, one realizes with some bemusement just how much "architecture" and how much Romanticism still lingers on in (or has found its way back into) the buildings of those very architects who, from their unshakable belief in their matchless modernity, repudi-

FIGURE 34. Control Room, Klingenberg Power Station (1925–27; Walter Klingenberg und Werner Issel, architects), 1927. Landesarchiv Berlin, II 873.

ate and mock both these things. For it is in a place like this that one finds, at every turn, the ultimate *Sachlichkeit,* the ultimate and in fact *true* "objectivity," the objectivity that simply excludes not only any element of whim or randomness, but all undue emphasis.
 [. . .]
 The modernism [of the early AEG buildings[1]], with form growing out of function, has failed to satisfy a group of creative architects now coming to the fore. Once again keeping step with painting and sculpture—and responsive, like those arts, to a zeitgeist favoring extremes—they seek to reproduce the shock effect of the advertising poster or even the caricature. But *Sachlichkeit* is not a style that lends itself to extremism. Those back-to-basics cubes, those unnecessary (and impractical) all-glass walls, those assaults on our structural intuitions—are at bottom a return to "architecture,"—a familiar equation but with all the signs reversed. They represent designer intention exactly as did yesterday's facades. And the effect is Romantic through and through. It is an effect totally in harmony with the literary notion of technology—but not with the actual handling of actual technology. It has more than a whiff of Fritz Lang's *Metropolis* about it.[2]
 [. . .]

What first strikes one about this major generating station is the invisible nature of the work being done to create its unimaginably vast output of power. Were there no guide present to correct one's impressions, it would be easy to imagine not that the plant is out of commission—noise, and the heat in the boiler house, preclude that—but that production has been temporarily suspended, with staff away and only a few watchmen on duty. Over long stretches of the walking tour of the premises, one encounters not a soul.

Here is the technology of the future, effectively demolishing all the thinking built up on the basis of the technologies of the past. All work done here—starting with the discharge of coal—is mechanized. There are no coal porters, no boiler men—as already indicated—and none of the things that have proved a stimulus to certain artists over the last few decades in particular.

These observations are directly linked to another one: extreme cleanliness. The only visible trace of the operation in progress is the coal dust on the steps of the crushing plant, and that "shouldn't be there," as the guide pointed out. Walls here are white—for the most part simply whitewashed brick. These materials were chosen purely for the sake of economy, yet contribute significantly to the place's overall appearance: in striking contrast, window frames and the metal banisters on the stairs are finished in brilliant red, and the doors, for practical reasons, in blue black. There is a consistent policy of using colors as far as possible to mark off one section of the operation from another and identify the various areas for the benefit of the workforce. Thus, for example, at ground-floor level in the crushing plant the powerhouse is painted yellow, the crushing shed green, the control room blue, and at other levels we find a red area, a white area, and so on—all absolutely clear and simple, with color never used whimsically.

And so nothing remains but the plain enclosed space with its machinery, various appliances, and piping, all finished in black or colored paint and standing out with the utmost clarity against the uniform background as three-dimensional shapes. The effect lies entirely in how they interrelate.

One finds oneself here in the domain of strict necessity—an area in which no human will has legitimacy unless it serves the plant's operation. The exponent of this will is the chief design engineer: he has the first and last word on all aspects, from the disposition of process stages to the volumetric planning, and necessarily combines exceptional breadth of focus with the capacity for minute calculation.

[. . .]

The outside observer is in no position to discern where the AEG engineers' share leaves off and that of the architects begins. There could be no better proof of the closeness and the success of their collaboration, enormous though the problems can be assumed to have been. Now, on completion, it can be seen that everything done to serve operational requirements has become finished form: the credit for this belongs to the architects entrusted by the AEG with the architectural design of the power station, Klingenberg and Issel. They were able to rely on the effect bound to result from the extreme concision of design of this huge plant, and accordingly shunned dramatic overemphasis completely. All elements are reduced to their simplest form, to complete clarity of form. This approach, which to the observer's perception reflects the interior treatment—and, one might even say, the power-generation process itself—confers coherence and grandeur on the whole site, while at the detailed level it results in a wealth of purely architectural interest.

Given the vast dimensions of the plant, it is natural that the buildings should together constitute a strong horizontal mass. That is there already. It will be all the more so when the plant's size has been doubled, as already planned. It is no mere aesthetic fancy, but a psychological need, long acknowledged and catered to, that an extended horizontal should be balanced by verticals. (Even landscape artists know this.) Here, the vertical is provided by the tower building, for which the justification in practical terms is that the cistern at the top provides the water pressure essential for the needs of the whole complex. The tower building itself is enhanced in return by the presence of the horizontal mass. The tower is, so to speak, the station's public face. On the far side of the road, the vertical note is picked up by the six stairwell projections rising like square-sectioned towers at regular intervals up the walls of the thirty-thousand-volt transformer building. (An indication of where the natural affinities of such buildings lie is to be found in the unsought similarity of appearance between this building and the Aurelian Wall in Rome.) One further point is that the configuration of the tower building facade, with its continuous narrow verticals, is continued in the wall of the ancillary building flanking the turbine hall, which itself is built along the road. Though the repetition of the pattern might seem to threaten monotony, this is dispelled by the broad entrance and the linking building.

[. . .]

The turbine hall and boiler house relate to the more monumental elements, with which they share the same method of construction, with steel framework, and infill walls clad with the same panels. And yet they are clearly different; the form they have taken reflects different laws—laws prescribed by the interior. It is primarily the need for light that has dictated the nature of these laws. More light is needed, and it has to be light that comes in through vast areas of surface. Accordingly, the windows here are spaced out around the whole length of the walls. The boiler house additionally has top lighting. The link with the first buildings to be described is provided here by the boiler house's stairwell towers. The turbine hall is framed between the boiler house and the tower building, and forms a natural caesura.

[. . .]

To comment on individual architectural effects is much more difficult. That is natural enough, as they are not planned effects—simply the consequence of well-designed parts coming together and being seen as an ensemble. To that extent, certainly, they could be called coincidental; but good design is not chance. Arising in a modern industrial complex, such effects obviously will be of a different character from what one sees in a historic town—and yet, at a fundamental level, they are the same types of effect, unexpectedly catching the eye from different vantage points: views through gaps, felicities of line, intersecting planes. Some of these have been captured by the photographer. Others still await the visitor's casual glance into such places as the underworld of basements and subterranean conduits—places that play an important role in the plant's operation. Rational, clear in structure, its every detail a proof and an exemplar of efficient operation: there, in a few words, is the Klingenberg Power Station.

The realm of the fantastic is invisible, or at least no longer visible. It lies in the work done, of which site photographs and drawings during construction give some idea. And it lies also in the power that is generated here and fed to the world outside. There is no way to make it visible. Any attempt to convey it symbolically could only invite ridicule. Yet—everywhere here, the fantastic is somehow present. And this background feeling is part of the effect.

NOTES

1. See above, text 32: Karl Scheffler, Peter Behrens.
2. Fritz Lang's film *Metropolis* (1927), one of the masterpieces of the German silent cinema, offered poetic images of the city of the future, created by the set designers Otto Hunte, Erich Kettelhut, and Karl Vollbrecht.

154

Hermann Schmitz

INTRODUCTION TO *SIEMENSBAUTEN*

First published in Hans Hertlein, *Siemensbauten* (Berlin: Wasmuth, 1928), pp. 5–7. Translated by Iain Boyd Whyte.

No other area of architecture stands more central to our present life than industrial architecture, with everything that belongs to it. Nothing else can point to such definitive and conspicuous success in the context of our modern life. Industrial architecture has understood more than any other branch of building how to implement successfully the demands that have asserted themselves over the last thirty years—that architectural design should derive from the function of the building and the materials. Indeed, one could honestly say that the strongest impulses for the architectural creation of our generation have come the pragmatic tasks of the industrial architects. As the most important tasks of the present, these have assumed the leading role in shaping current architectural style, just as the church did in the Middle Ages, for example, and the aristocracy in the Baroque period. The creations of industry, among which the infrastructure for transportation in all its dimensions is also included, have become the most outstanding symbols of our epoch.

[. . .]

Absolute practicality is demanded as the fundamental condition of industrial and commercial building, the creation of form directly from the function and the abandonment of all extraneous elements and overlays. While this is a self-evident truth, it is one that must be articulated by our generation, as it was forgotten by our predecessors, who forced the forms of historical and even romantic architecture onto the buildings of industry and transportation. Yet the strictly functional satisfaction of the demands of production, hygiene, illumination, and friction-free circulation within the building do not make it a work of architecture [*Baukunst;* literally, "building art"] in the true sense of the word. That is first achieved through the work of the creative architect [*Baumeister;* literally, "building master"], who understands how to give architectural expression to the purely functional building. His artistic ability reveals itself precisely in the fact that he can imbue the building with tectonic powers that are derived exclusively from the given practical task, without deviating in the slightest way from the realization of the functional program.

[. . .]

The diverse range of buildings created by Hertlein on the commission of the Siemens concern achieve at the highest level the reconciliation of total functionality and practicality with a healthy and forceful architectonic sensibility, which in certain instances achieves a stark monumentality. Free of contradictions and entirely at the service of the enormous global enterprise of German labor established by Werner von Siemens, the designs of Hertlein belong in the first rank among the best examples of the modern industrial architecture of our fatherland.

155

Egon Erwin Kisch

BERLIN AT WORK

First published as "Berlin bei der Arbeit," *Arbeiter-Illustrierte-Zeitung* (Berlin) 6, no. 25 (25 June 1927), pp. 8ff. Translated by David Britt.

No other European capital city has a reputation equal to Berlin's as a "city of work." And, indeed, the structures and machines that Berlin uses to sustain its transportation system, and its economy as a whole, are mostly magnificent, of a perfection that is probably excelled only in America. Masterpieces of technology, beyond comparison with the pitiful installations of those industrial fragments that fell into the hands of the Russian workers after the collapse of the Czar's and Kerensky's Russia (not without first having been reduced to ruins by the White Guards during the civil war).

In the Socialist state, however, reconstruction has been carried out upward from below. There, industrial enterprises have been reconstructed with passionate enthusiasm, and the work has been a collective undertaking, performed collectively, voluntarily, and hopefully by the organized masses (rather as political and labor-union work is done here). In the capitalist world, work has long since lost any pleasurable quality, and for the proletarian it is no more than an expedient for the avoidance of starvation. But there, the establishment and the development of a new factory are matters for the whole people. In Leningrad, Moscow, Yerevan, Tiflis, and other cities, on the tenth anniversary of the founding of the Workers' Republic—which the capitalist states sought to subvert by plotting assassinations and waging war—gigantic new power plants were handed over to the public, with a meaning and a significance and a rejoicing very different from those with which churches or memorials to the Battle of Leipzig are dedicated in Western countries . . . Here, even the opening of so important an enterprise as the Rummelsburg electric power plant arouses very different feelings in the workers. In itself, the criminal haste with which, for financial reasons, the work was conducted caused a number of severe and even fatal accidents; and its completion did nothing to create new employment, and thus to reduce the enormous number of unemployed, since mechanized operation made human strength almost entirely dispensable (and hence wage demands and all forms of resistance to injustice and so on, impossible), without the very least benefit to the working population.

It is by now an established tradition that modernized machinery and factory buildings bring neither tolerable wage rates and conditions nor any restructuring of employee protection and labor welfare. By reducing wages, Germany has always contrived to cut its export prices in such a way as to imperil world trade, thus causing incessant conflicts and affording the international armaments industry, Germany's included, free scope for its warmongering activities.

In a metropolis such as Berlin, working hours are substantially increased by the enormous distances that must be covered between home and workplace. The morning journey in an overcrowded streetcar is an effort in itself, and the journey home drains the exhausted worker of whatever bodily and mental strength he may have left. What is more, there are tens of thousands of workers who get no rest at night; for transportation to work must never be held up, and so the streetcar tracks are welded under tents in the middle of the streets, faulty lengths of subway track are replaced, and laborers with pick and shovel smooth out the road surfaces so that the gentleman's automobile will not rattle on the way into town from his villa... A contrast? There are plenty of those. On the landing field, mechanics stand ready to repair the motors of the transoceanic pilot's aircraft; and on the Landwehr Canal a fruit barge floats exactly as it might have done a hundred years ago. On the AVUS track,[1] racing cars lap each other, and their drivers are killed for the sake of a little publicity for the owners; while the mailman must climb three, four, five stories, day in, day out. At Gleisdreieck Junction, the mainline, elevated, and suburban railroads intersect in midair; and not far away the baker's man delivers bread to his customers on a dog cart. At the Nordhafen, cranes lift hundreds of tons at the press of a button; but no machine helps the poor female day laborer to heft bricks out of the Spree barge onto the bank. Even in the age of electricity, the women's wages are still cheaper than the press of a button! Contrasts? There are plenty more! Behind every luxury, there is the hard labor of those who will never know what luxury means; behind every theatrical spectacle, behind every lavish motion picture, stands the army of those who are hounded, day and night, in return for a pittance; whose names are unknown even to the man who drives them, let alone to the public that admiringly repeats the names of its favorites, the "great," splendidly paid directors and the "great" actors and actresses. And those places of entertainment that welcome the metropolitan public with costly paneling, gilt ornaments, velvet borders, and crystal chandeliers, the places that make money out of champagne and Charleston and cheating: they have no thought of being modern when it comes to paying anything over forty pfennigs to the woman who labors in the early morning to get the floors clean before the first customers arrive. Berlin never stops. When enjoyment retires for the night, labor must spring into the breach; when the morning paper is on the streets, the worker must ready the rotary press for the midday edition; when the restaurant locks up, meat and vegetables have to be bought from the market for the next day; when the houses go to sleep, the sewers have to be cleaned. Berlin, the metropolis, is active day and night, its contrasts plain to see; but thousands never perceive that those who do the work have no share in the enjoyment.

NOTE

1. For a description of the AVUS track, see below, text 209: Bernard von Brentano, The Pleasure of Motoring.

156

Anonymous

A NEW HIGH-RISE BUILDING IN BERLIN

Architect Peter Behrens

Originally published as "Ein neues Hochhaus in Berlin: Architekt Peter Behrens," *Wasmuths Monatshefte für Baukunst* 15, no. 7 (1931), pp. 289–92. Translated by Michael Loughridge.

In preparation for the redesign of Alexanderplatz necessitated by the new traffic-flow pattern and the construction of the underground railway, the City Architect's Department produced detailed plans of its own, which have now been taken further by way of a prize competition. What is at stake here is nothing less than the redevelopment of Alexanderplatz to a standard at which it will rival the finest city squares anywhere in the world. The site is of particular importance because as well as lying at the very center of Berlin it is the intersection point of a whole medley of different transport routes, underground and above ground, radial roads, city, suburban and main-line train routes, all passing through or tangential to Alexanderplatz. In the circumstances it was clear that in the interests of traffic circulation the ideal shape for the intersection would be circular.

Two combined shop-and-office blocks, facing each other across Königstrasse where it emerges into Alexanderplatz, are now being constructed to designs by Professor Peter Behrens. [. . .]

The building that has been completed is a steel skeleton structure of eight stories standing on a two-story-deep basement foundation, and some of it is built out on massive steel supports over the underground rail tunnel structures. Actual construction above ground level began on 28 July 1930. By 25 October the roof—that is to say, the ceiling of the eighth story—was being concreted. In other words, the construction system used enabled one story to be completed in skeleton form every eight working days—apart from the ground-floor ceiling, which took rather longer.

The building's external appearance has been kept simple, its style *sachlich* in the sense of declaring itself without any prevarication to be an office block. The steel frame construction remains recognizable. The framework appearance lent by the vertical supports and crossbeams is enhanced by the cofferlike recessing, which is intended to improve the daylight-gathering qualities of the windows. Thus the emphasis was not on the dynamic grouping of the building volumes, but on the relative proportioning of the different stories, with the help of superior-grade stone. This material was made from the same attractive *Muschelkalk* [shell limestone] of which Naumburg Cathedral is built, and the facing work involving it proceeded almost abreast of the reinforced concrete construction work.

Comprising some 48,700 cubic meters in total volume, the building is to accommodate café-restaurants or exhibition space in the lower stories, and offices or trade display space above. The first floor projects out by one meter, is fully glazed with large plate-glass windows, and so is particularly suitable for merchandise displays. Access to the main staircase and the lifts is by way of a marble-paneled foyer with a number of inset display cabinets. Passenger lift provision consists of two paternoster lifts and two express lifts with an operating speed of 1.75 meters per second [about 5.5 feet per second]. These rise to the flat roof level, which is laid out as a spacious terrace area suitable for a variety of purposes. The individual stories below are offered initially as space available to be divided up variously as incoming tenants may require. On either side of the access corridors, the offices proper are always reached by way of an anteroom. The building is fitted out with steel windows constructed on the Marcus system, which is effective in excluding drafts and permits easy adjustment. The metal frames are the slenderest practicable, letting in maximum daylight, and along with the uncluttered modern approach to office furnishing, this means that the light for working in is extremely good. The building is heated by means of a differential-vacuum system, which combines the advantages of conventional steam heating with those of hot-water heating. Maintenance of a variable vacuum permits the steam temperature to be adjusted in line with the outside temperature, and hence, via a central regulator, to the actual extra heat requirement at any given time. The temperature of the radiator surfaces thus corresponds to that given by a hot-water system, while on the other hand the heating level can be increased rapidly, and the frost hazard associated with hot-water heating does not arise. This type of heating has proved its worth in United States skyscrapers, and is additionally in demand because it is economical. There is also to be a ventilation system designed to provide the same conditions year-round.

157

Irmgard Keun

GILGI—ONE OF US

First published as Keun, *Gilgi—eine von uns* (1931; reprint, Munich: Deutscher Taschenbuch Verlag, 1989), pp. 10–11. Translated by Michael Loughridge.

Gilgi is sitting in the streetcar. She had meant to walk, but it's too late for that now. Beside her, opposite her, in a long row, all the people going to work. Tired faces, discontented faces. They all look alike. All with the same daily routine, all feeling the same way about it, hence mass-produced uniformity. Any more fares—any more fares *please?* Nobody here is enjoying what he is doing. No one likes being who he is. Wan-faced slip of a girl with the nice legs, would you not rather be tucked up in bed getting your beauty sleep? Suntanned girl in the hiking boots, it looks as though it's going to turn out nice today—would you not rather be getting some exercise walking in the city's forest park? Feeding the tame deer with the chestnuts you collected last autumn?

Any more fares please?—Any more fares please? They are on their way to work. Day after day, on their way to work. One day is just like another. Tingalingaling—people getting out, people getting in. They're on their way. Always on their way. Eight-hour day, typewriter, shorthand pad, salary reduction, end of the month—always the same, always the same. Yesterday, today, tomorrow—and ten years ahead, too.

You young ones, not yet thirty—do *you* have no other face but that hope-deferred early-morning face? It's Sunday tomorrow. Will there not be little flights of fancy stirring in your eyes by this afternoon? I'm right, am I not, young man, no one buys such a handsome bright yellow tie unless he secretly believes that one day he'll be the boss, with his own car and a foreign bank account? Respectable young lady from a good family, I'm right, am I not, you wouldn't be wearing that bright-colored necklace if you weren't hoping someone might come along who thinks it looks nice on you? Little redhead, would you have spent those twenty marks on the perm if you had not been dreaming of beauty contests and a film contract? After all, Greta Garbo was a salesgirl once. The journey to work. Day after day. Will anything ever happen to break the uniformity of the days that pass? What could it be? Douglas Fairbanks, the lottery win, the film contract, the fairy-tale rise to fame, pennies from heaven? Will it happen? No. Really, no prospect at all of change or interruption? That's different: there is. What will it be? Ill health, staffing cutbacks, unemployment. But—we're still on our way. Yes, we're on our way. Thank goodness for that.

Gilgi looks out of the window. All those dispirited people there in the streetcar—no, she has nothing in common with them, she is not one of them, does not want to be one of them. They are gray and tired and apathetic. And if they are not apathetic, they are hanging on for a miracle. Gilgi is not apathetic, and she does not believe in miracles. She only believes in what she gets done and what she earns. She is not content, but she is happy. She is earning money.

158

Else Lasker-Schüler

THE SPINNING WORLD FACTORY

First published as "Die kreisende Weltfabrik" in Lasker-Schüler, *Konzert* (Berlin: Rowohlt, 1932; reprint, Munich: Deutscher Taschenbuch Verlag, 1986), pp. 50–52. Translated by Iain Boyd Whyte.

Anyone who has discovered a tree or path within themselves may not have eyes for the real town around them. And this is especially true of those creative spirits who are able, by good fortune, to look out from the lighthouse of their stormy hearts across a capital city, across Berlin, that endless field of houses.

Nevertheless, it is a mark of weakness to ensconce oneself on a green sofa in the hope of unraveling the idyllic spirit of some place or other. "To be able to work in peace." Preferring to flee into the comfortable wasteland of the aesthete in order to compose an ode; the artist-photographers, the chatterers with their smooth, patent-leather skin. Some friend or other owns a little house in the country where they master the premature spring of their literature. Coming from afar, batty ramblers in Greek togas wander past the garden. The strings of their sandals flutter around their legs, and their lips disgorge rich poetry, which they carry in string bags as the fruits of their knowledge. But heavens above, he who dares will give himself up to the mix of people in the city center. We artists are, after all, creators—the material comes from within. Do you really think that the good Lord retreats back to a village? Like the aesthete, does his novelistic soul breathe only on meadows of Worpswede[1] or on the Lüneberg heath? [. . .]

This Berlin, spinning world factory! Tempo: its inhabitants run on wheels, become nerveless and find how to remodel themselves, are able to turn themselves into machines. Nevertheless, they are still more appealing than the small-town residents (present company excepted), who crawl on their bellies. Here in Berlin, there is a passionate welcome for those who have remained human, who can still take the wheels off their shoes—the test set by the metropolis. Those who pass remain vital and affirm their worth. And so, too, with money. The rich man is not necessarily a demon, or a sentimental money box, or a vinous barbarian. But cold Satan will freeze the souls of those who choose not to share their "spiritual wealth." Of course, my love for the city of Berlin, for all great cities, does not stop me from loving the meadows and woods. No one is more thrilled than I by everything that grows out of the earth, as I collect acorns, chestnuts, berries, and all the blossoming delights along the path, and spare the stalks of grass from the brutality of my footstep. Water is my playmate, with its mussels and seaweed. But for writing and drawing, what I need above all is myself. I'm still waiting in vain, however, for myself, for my rich new dawn. What love will shine across my heart and draw out from me the flowering of the word: poetry.

For a long time I have no longer harvested from the vineyards of my life, and yet I breathe the same breath. Have the hard times asphalted my heart or the breeze of reality extinguished its sun? I'm stumbling in the dark.

The great city, any city, the smallest village on earth have nothing at all to do with production, but rather, often a single individual. Our metropolis resounds to the scream, the deafening din of technology; fear of death carries a warning face behind empty, painted masks, while longing rises with the moon. Our Berlin is strong and terrible, and its wings know their course. And that's precisely why the arts return again and again to Berlin: *the dynamo of art is to be found here,* running neither too slow nor too fast. This reality is truly mystical.

The falling away of one's friends is not to be avoided—an operation that brings with it the danger of bleeding to death. My house and his shared the same nervous system. My heart commemorates the burial. Friendship in the metropolis: the artist's consolation. But *love* is his revelation, his *ascension. This* is the only journey the artist needs.

NOTE

1. Worpswede, a village south of Bremen, was home to a celebrated artists' colony, founded in 1889 by the painters Fritz Mackensen, Otto Modersohn, and Hans am Ende. They were subsequently joined by Heinrich Vogeler in 1894 and by Paula Modersohn-Becker, who lived there from 1898 until her death in 1907. The poet Rainer Maria Rilke also lived in Worpswede from 1900 to 1902.

159

Hans Fallada

LITTLE MAN, WHAT NOW?

First published as Fallada, *Kleiner Mann—was nun?* (1933; reprint, Rastatt: Moewig, 1980), pp. 132–33. Translated by Michael Loughridge.

So here he is at the Kleiner Tiergarten again, a place Pinneberg has known since boyhood. It has never had any special charm as a place, no comparison with its big brother on the other bank of the River Spree; in fact it's really just an apologetic strip of grass and greenery. But today, the first day of October, half wet and half dry and half cloudy, half sunny, with the wind coming from all over and lots of brownish-yellow, ugly leaves catching the eye, it looks particularly depressing. Not that it's deserted, though, not remotely so. There are masses of people here, gray in their clothing, their faces wan—unemployed workers waiting, waiting for they know not what—not work, anyway, who bothers waiting around for that nowadays . . . ? They're simply standing about, aimlessly. The rooms they live in are no pleasanter, so why should they not stand about? There's no point thinking about going home; they'll have to go back there anyway in due course, to their so-called homes, and it will still be far too early.

Pinneberg ought to be on his way home. In fact he should be getting a move on, very likely Lämmchen will be waiting for him already. But still he lingers, standing among the unemployed workers; then he walks a few yards, then stops again. To look at him, he's not one of them—far too nattily turned out for that. He is wearing the warm chestnut-colored ulster that Bergmann let him have for thirty-eight marks. And his black homburg hat, that was Bergmann, too, not quite abreast with current fashion, too broad brimmed; let's say twenty-three for the hat, Pinneberg.

FIGURE 35. The unemployed outside the Labor Exchange on Sonnenallee, Neukölln, 1932. Landesarchiv Berlin, 230 747.

Outwardly, then, Pinneberg has nothing in common with those unemployed people. But the way he's thinking . . .

He has just been to see Mr. Lehmann, head of Personnel at Mandel's department store. He had applied for a job there, and he got the job, just one of those straightforward business transactions. Yet somehow, now that he has concluded this transaction—and never mind that it has actually made him a wage earner once more—Pinneberg feels much closer to these folk earning nothing than he does to the big earners. It is these people here he belongs to, because it could happen any time at all: he could find himself standing around here as they do; there is nothing he can do about it. There is nothing to stop that happening to him.

Oh yes, of course he is one of millions; government ministers harangue him in their speeches, exhort him to shoulder the burden, accept the sacrifices, be a patriotic German, put his money in the savings bank, and vote for the pro-state party.

He complies, or doesn't comply, depending—but he doesn't swallow a word of what they say. Not a word. Deep down, he just knows: they're all trying to get something out of me, but do something for me?—Not likely! Whether I live or die, that's neither here nor there to that lot. Can I afford to go to the pictures or not, that's a matter of total indifference, can Lämmchen put some decent food inside her or is she driven up the walls, will our kid have a happy life or go to the wall—who cares a scrap?

And all these folk standing around here in the Kleiner Tiergarten, and a right little zoo it is, too, look at them, no dangerous beasts here, half-starved specimens of the proletariat, hopes extinguished; for them at least things are exactly the same. Three months out of work and it will be good-bye to the chestnut-brown overcoat, good-bye to better times. Who knows, maybe come Wednesday evening Lehmann will get in a tiff with Jachmann, and all of a sudden I'm nobody. Bye-bye!

It's only these characters here that I have something in common with . . . Yes, they have it in for me a bit themselves, to them I'm a swell or a wing-collar proletarian, but that's for now. I know how long that will stick. Today, today still drawing pay—tomorrow on the dole . . .[1]

NOTE

1. The concluding sentence has echoes of the harp girl's song in Theodor Storm's novella *Immensee* (1850):

> Heute, nur heute
> Bin ich so schön;
> Morgen, ach morgen
> Muß alles vergehn!
> Nur diese Stunde
> Bist du noch mein;
> Sterben, ach sterben
> Soll ich allein!

160

Herbert Rimpl and Hermann Mäckler

A GERMAN AIRCRAFT FACTORY

The Heinkel Works in Oranienburg

First published as Rimpl and Mäckler, *Ein deutsches Flugzeugwerk: Die Heinkel-Werke Oranienburg* (Berlin: Wiking, 1938), pp. 139, 5, 6. Translated by Iain Boyd Whyte.

The creations of the celebrated German aircraft builder Professor Ernst Heinkel originated in his factory on the Baltic. A large range of light and heavy planes and seaplanes were developed and first flown here, where the lowland plains and coastal bays offered excellent and diverse conditions for test-flying.

The anniversary year 1932 brought twofold confirmation of the preeminence of this firm, with world records for two of the Heinkel machines, the He 64 and He 70. While the He 64 proved itself against all others to be the fastest machine in Europe, the He 70, which was built to carry mail and passengers, beat the previous fastest machine, the American "Orion," by some fifty kilometers per hour. The superiority of the He 70, confirmed by a series of eight world records, led Deutsche Lufthansa to approach Dr. Heinkel with the commission to develop a fast, two-engine machine.

In response to this commission, the He 111 was developed in 1935. When the machine—which repeatedly had the opportunity to demonstrate its outstanding characteristics—was put into serial production, the output of the Heinkel works rose so rapidly that the existing factory area was in no way near adequate to the task. As the original factory had already expanded dramatically in pace with burgeoning air travel, the time had come to explore ways in which to develop the plant in a more controlled and organic manner. Several times previously, the boundaries of the original, generously conceived site had already been breached. The prospect of further fragmentary expansion, therefore, was not particularly promising, particularly because in aircraft manufacture, as in all serial production, product flow and volume are directly dependent on the clarity of the sequence and the rational relationship of the component workshops, one to the other. The analysis of the problem, which aimed initially only at a partial solution on a larger or smaller scale, led ultimately to the decision to build a completely new factory, whose independence would guarantee its own airfield and its own housing. This decisive solution guaranteed large-scale series production and freed up the old factory for other tasks.

[. . .]

It is a particularly pleasant task to build a blacksmith's shop for the *Luftwaffe* [German air force]. When Professor Dr. Heinkel commissioned me in the late autumn of 1935 to plan and construct a new factory, it was clear to me that a workplace had to be built here that provided the best technical conditions for the serial production of aircraft, that was also well protected from aerial attack, but that would also be a place where the German worker could operate healthily and with good cheer. Meetings and planning sessions with the commissioner, Dr. Ernst Heinkel, followed immediately. As a creative engineer and as a warm-hearted colleague, his role in the construction of the factory was much more than that of a mere client, for even on the architectural planning he worked deep into the night for weeks on end. He finalized every dimension in width and height, and every machine and crane. His particular delight, however, was directed toward the planning of the many buildings that serve the health and well-being of his staff.

[. . .]

The disposition and fitting out of the factory halls was carried out in such a way that they would be equal to all anticipated future demands in aircraft construction. Once the operational sequence and its subdivisions had been established, the architectural design of the plans and elevations followed, together with the planning of the workers' housing.

The architectural solutions were determined in their scale by the machines and the men. In the industrial buildings many of the dimensions arose from the machinery—the presses, cranes, and building cradles, but primarily from the aircraft themselves. With the housing, in contrast, the scale came solely from the inhabitants. The landscape also contributed to the discussion. For the main factory, this is a pine-clad plateau; for the works housing, a quiet, flat landscape, crossed by avenues of birch and oak trees, and terminated at the eastern end by the low-level forestation of the hill on which the factory stands.

The style of the factory is purely industrial, marked by powerful building masses with large glazed areas, brick walls with massive folding doors running to a hundred meters and more in length, towerlike flanking pylons, chimneys, elevators, railway tracks, and loading ramps. Sensibly, this industrial style has been adapted as appropriate for the administration building, the factory school, the health center, the staff buildings, the many subsidiary buildings, and the security accommodations, in order to create an architectural unity. As a result all these buildings, irrespective of the variations derived from the internal functions, display a crisp style that is firmly rooted in the sphere of technology. In the housing estate, in contrast, where the design is derived from human needs, emotion and temperament come into play: in the brickwork of the houses, with their gardens and sheds, and also in the community center, the town hall, the schools, and shops. Even the waterworks, although intended to fulfill a purely technical function, blends in with the atmosphere of the estate—of flowers around the houses, playing children, and smoke hanging above the tiled roofs. For both tasks a form had to be found that resonated with the landscape and allowed the work of the human hand to grow organically out of the soil, without rejecting nature. Given the scale of the task, the solution included the design of complete landscapes. This placed a high responsibility on the planners, for it was necessary to alter the face of a landscape that had formed over the millennia, without failing the expectations of the great today.

[. . .]

May this book be dedicated to the victorious German *Luftwaffe*.

14

COMMODITIES AND DISPLAY

"Capitalism," wrote the economist Werner Sombart in 1911, "means nothing other than the dissolution of the economic process into two constituent elements—technology and commerce—and the primacy of commerce over technology."[1] This preeminence of commerce, which Sombart had already identified before World War I, became a dominant feature of urban life in Germany after the hyperinflation of the early 1920s had been brought under control by the introduction of the *Rentenmark* in November 1923. In the prewar period, private incomes and professorial salaries had nurtured a bourgeois intelligentsia that prevailed across German society as the ultimate arbiter of intellectual value and artistic taste. This social group suffered particularly heavily over the inflation years and found its authority challenged in the stabilization years by the influx of American culture that followed the Dawes Plan, and by the industrial inventiveness and productivity that blossomed in the later 1920s. In the process, high culture was challenged by mass culture, and the *Literat* and the professor were replaced by the entrepreneur, designer, and engineer as the voices shaping German national identity. In the context of the capital city, the prime vehicles for these new voices of commerce were shop windows, billboards, illuminated advertisements, exhibitions, and even loudspeakers in public places. All these devices were brought together in the ultimate shrine to commodity fetishism: the modern department store.

The Americanization of the city, and the skyscraper debate that ignited in Berlin in 1919, have already been addressed in these chapters. At the level of surface rather than structure, the response of the intelligent Berliner to the dramatic new challenges posed by the Americanization of commerce and marketing can be judged from an article written by Adolf Behne in 1924, which merits citing at some length. Behne was responding to a proposal to ban all advertising in Berlin as a means of keeping the street lines clear and the architecture uncompromised by signs and billboards. As a committed modernist, he rejected such controls, and advocated instead the complete opposite:

> As an alternative to this radical solution, which is not a solution, there is another radical solution: to remove all restrictions on advertising . . . The advocates of this solution can claim with some justice that official intervention in matters of economics and aesthetics has seldom proved successful, and that the best prospects of an improvement are that it will happen of its own accord if advertising is allowed to develop its full potential unhindered. These "liberals" concede that we would indeed have to endure a particularly unpleasant phase initially, a phase of no-holds-barred advertising freedom, bordering on vandalism . . . but with the prospect of better things emerging from the experiment: self-limitation, self-discipline, due deliberation and understanding.
>
> [. . .]
>
> Matter-of-fact advertising will not disfigure the streets, especially if the street itself is matter-of-fact in character. I do not claim that such a street will live up to the full Romantic ideals of a Pre-Raphaelite enthusiast. But it will never be a horror to match our artistically conceived streets with artistic advertisements subject to the artistic approval of the official city architects and city art curators. It will not always be tasteful . . . Goodness me, what a dreadful thought! . . . but at the same time it will never rival the tastelessness of our present officially sanctioned good taste. What is certain is that it will always have vitality, while our present streets are—provincialism run riot.

The opposite of provincialism, of course, was Americanization, and for a progressive Berliner the North American example in advertising—as in jazz, the Charleston, scientific management, and rationalized production techniques—was the one to follow. Behne continues:

> The American knows—and he knows it as a businessman, not as a moralist—that old-style European advertising has had its day. Who today still believes what the market-stall barker has to say, no matter whether his attention-catching antics are a rapscallion's improvisations or the brushstrokes of a much-admired academician? In the United States, the customer wants factual information. He is going to buy from the seller who provides him with the promptest, most accurate, and most trustworthy information. Here the image has no merit in its own right. The place for pictures is in the museum. [. . .] With his approach of offering logically conceived and appropriate advertising, the American producer is designing it from the point of view of the customers—not, as the European does, from the point of view of the seller. Advertising based on the seller's viewpoint inevitably leads to excess, and from there, for the higher-minded, to the toxic antidote of art. And the intolerable thing is precisely this mixture: clamor mingled with art.[2]

Before the war, the key issue in advertising and display was one of framing both the window and the goods within in it such a way that they became the objects of the focused desire of the public on the street.[3] The contained world of the display window, in which the facade of the shop was opened up in a measured way to reveal carefully chosen samples of the delights within, was challenged in the 1920s by the massive expansion of advertising billboards on the North American model and by the advent of neon advertising. This was a recent development, patented in 1915 by the French chemist Claude George and introduced to the United States in 1923 by two signs on a Packard automobile dealership in Los Angeles. The combination of large billboards and neon lights opened the prospect of twenty-four-hour advertising, and the scale of these innovations dwarfed the scale at which the traditional decorative elements of the Berlin streets had operated. No longer did the buildings allow glimpses of the goods on sale: rather, the massive commercial advertisements allowed glimpses of the buildings. As the Berlin-based architect Hugo Häring noted in a text cited in this section:

> Advertising is well on the way to supplanting architecture. First, the creation of shops—with all their requirements for window area, display cabinets, name boards, and advertising placards—began to hollow out buildings from underneath, working upward to the first and second floor; and now illuminated advertising is working downward from the roof to continue the destruction of architecture. What remains in the way of architectural interest at third- and fourth-story level is fragmented, bereft of any claim to be regarded as architecture.[4]

Symptomatic of this tendency was Arthur Korn's 1926 remodeling of the Wach- und Schließgesellschaft building in Berlin, which saw the traditional decorative cornices, moldings, and pediments scraped off the facade, which was then turned into a massive advertising billboard by day and an abstract artwork by night. The lighting technology was greatly boosted by the presence in Berlin of a booming film industry, and the lighting effects achieved on cellulose in such films as *Metropolis,* which appeared in 1927, soon found their way onto the city streets in the work of the leading modernist designers. In the same year, for example, the architect brothers Hans and Wassili Luckhardt transformed a conventional apartment-house facade on Tauentzienstrasse into a light box composed of five broad, neon-lit bands, ascending from the street and interspersed with dark bands of shadows. A year later, and in the same year that he had first visited New York City, Erich Mendelsohn designed the showroom and offices for the fur dealers C. A. Herpich and Sons. Replacing the frontages of three existing buildings, reinforced steel frame was clad in bronze and travertine. The strong contrast between dark and light achieved in daylight was reinforced even more at night, when the lighting scheme, as in the Luckhardt design, reduced the facade to a series of dramatic light and dark striations.

The city planner Werner Hegemann had dubbed Berlin "the city of stone" in his celebrated book of the same name, first published in 1930. In its commercial streets, however, Berlin had by that time become a city of light. The new, illuminated Berlin was celebrated in October 1928 in the exhibition "Berlin im Licht," which had a light column sponsored by the Osram lighting company as its symbol. In the following year, four thousand light bulbs were used in one display to illustrate how a dirty shirt could be washed clean in only fifteen minutes using Persil. The major light installations served not only as advertisements, but also as landmarks—none more than the Protos corner on the Kurfürstendamm, where the wonders of Protos electrical appliances were proclaimed on seven illuminated panels.[5]

Lighting was incorporated into the architecture of the street not only to advertise commercial products but also to promote the buildings themselves. The Lichtburg Kino (castle of light cinema), for example, was opened in 1929 in Berlin-Gesundbrunnen, with a two-thousand-seat auditorium and a variety of cafés, bars, and restaurants. The architect, Rudolf Fränkel, incorporated one thousand light bulbs into the facade, which also carried the name Lichtburg in 1.2-meter-high illuminated red letters. To complete the image, three naval searchlights were mounted on the roof, beaming the message of the castle of light into the night sky. Similar effects were also employed at the massive Karstadt department store, built on Hermannplatz, Neukölln, in 1927–29, whose twin towers were topped by massive light columns that soared 70 meters above the street.

Reporting enthusiastically on the Light Week in October 1928, a Berlin journalist announced: "For four days all of Berlin—this rushing, blossoming world city—will show to its inhabitants and guests a performance that, in glamour and color, splendor and beauty, cannot be matched in the centers of the world."[6] The power of light as a means of constructing a glamorous, beguiling, and ultimately fictive world was not lost on the propaganda masters of National Socialism, who put the brilliant lighting technologies developed in late 1920s Berlin to telling use to illuminate such showpiece events as party rallies, the 1936 Olympic Games, and the state visit of Benito Mussolini in 1937, of which the *New York Times* reporter wrote: "Unter den Linden, Berlin's via triumphalis, blazed forth tonight in all the glory of its new lighting effects created for the meeting of Chancellor Adolf Hitler and Premier Benito Mussolini as hundreds of golden Nazi eagles, perched on as many gleaming white pillars along that avenue, seemed to gaze proudly at the spectacle."[7]

NOTES

1. Werner Sombart, *Die Juden und das Wirtschaftsleben* (Leipzig: Duncker & Humblot, 1911), p. 132; quoted in Frederic J. Schwartz, *The Werkbund: Design Theory and Mass Culture before the First World War* (New Haven, Conn.: Yale University Press, 1996), p. 85.

2. Adolf Behne, "Reklame als Bilder-Rätsel," *Das Tage-Buch* 5 (1924); reprinted in Behne, *Das Tagebuch*, ed. Stefan Grossmann (Königstein: Athenäum, 1981), pp. 844–48.

3. See above, text 33: Karl Ernst Osthaus, The Display Window.

4. Hugo Häring, "Lichtreklame und Architektur," *Moderne Bauformen: Monatshefte für Architektur und Raumkunst* 27, no. 3 (March 1928): Mitteilungen aus der Fachwelt, pp. 2–3.

5. On lighting in 1920s Berlin, see Janet Ward, *Weimar Surfaces* (Berkeley: University of California Press, 2001), pp. 92–141.

6. Hans Erasmus Fischer, "Eine Fahrt durch Berlin im Licht," *Berliner Lokal-Anzeiger,* 13 October 1928, quoted in Ward, *Weimar Surfaces,* pp. 109–10.

7. Otto D. Tolischus, "Imperial Symbols Will Greet Il Duce: Berlin Blazes in New Glory in Preparation of Visit of Mussolini to City," *New York Times,* 24 September 1937. (See also below, fig. 49.)

161

Alfred Döblin

BERLIN CHRISTMAS

First published as "Berliner Weihnachten" (1923); republished in Ruth Glatzer, *Berlin zur Weimarer Zeit* (Berlin: Siedler, 2000), p. 131. Translated by Iain Boyd Whyte.

It was an amazing Christmas. A riot of buying. But now without the excitement of the devaluation crisis.[1] The extravagant street trading on the Potsdamer Platz, Leipziger Platz, and Alexanderplatz was a spectacle for both the eyes and ears. Suddenly everything was there, even oranges—which were a real rarity this year, only to be seen behind shop windows. Books became cheap and affordable overnight. You can sit in a café and even eat a piece of cake without destroying the basis of your existence; you can travel by streetcar without second thoughts.[2] The war is over, and the foreign enemy, inflation, has gone. And now something remarkable: previously one read explanations day after day, read hypotheses, profundities, and stupidities about the question: why did the mark fall, sink, plummet? But nobody bothers now about the question (in journalistic German: about the problem): why isn't it plummeting now? Why doesn't it simply go down? Who or what is stopping it? Our politicians are no more intelligent, the parties are sleeping on their programs—a sleep true to their principles. The businesspeople are still there with their earnings, and Herr Clemenceau still makes the same dangerous face at the border.[3] The mark has stabilized without the chancellor traveling abroad, without the League of Nations, without foreign loans or charity. But why? And why not earlier? I admit that this question interests me more than the war debt. It interests me actively. All the world wishes to erect a monument to the Hercules who mastered our German currency snake. But perhaps the snake is only—full, very full. How very understandable, considering the pleasing number of deaths and the political unrest. The wise snake retires from business before its bursts.

NOTES

1. The mark stabilized with the introduction on 15 November 1923 of the Rentenmark. See Bernd Widdig, *Culture and Inflation in Weimar Germany* (Berkeley: California University Press, 2001), pp. 47–48: "Within a few weeks, the hyperinflation had disappeared as quickly as it had arrived a year and half before."

2. See below, text 205: *Berliner Tageblatt,* Cycling in Berlin.

3. Georges Clemenceau (1841–1929) was the premier of France from 1906 to 1909 and again from 1917 to 1920.

162

Alfred Gellhorn

ADVERTISING AND THE CITYSCAPE

First published as "Reklame und Stadtbild," *Die Form,* 1926, pp. 133–35. Translated by Michael Loughridge.

What is once established is not upset without a struggle. But there is a difference between young blood forced to assert itself, rapid development colliding with the inertia of the static mass, and an already fully developed entity having to repulse what is about to be thrust upon it from outside. For that is how the pros and cons of advertising differ from disputes in the art world. And there is a further difference: in relative strengths. Recent art is bound to be the weaker party, but advertising tends to be the stronger party when there is a conflict, because it derives from the same source as the individual citizen's life—namely, the business of earning. And that business is sacred.

So is this going to be an attack on advertising? Nothing of the kind! The present purpose is not to take sides, but to develop concepts. Advertising is here—and is immensely powerful. Faced with such a thing, one does best to come to grips with it and derive positive value from it. Praising one's wares is part of the business. If there was a time when the close intimacy of patriarchal small towns in our grandparents' day still knew the reputation of a given firm as something so firmly established that there was nothing more to be said about it, if there was then a time when the extended family of customers remained constant in size—that time has now gone. Even in the smaller towns, it is never the same people who come in and buy things—because industry has created a homeless proletariat that cannot be linked to the shopkeepers by shared local roots. This, too, had some good consequences, as any development does. Hand in hand with it, along came competition, which raises standards. We know, of course, that often it is the most inferior products that are the most vigorously advertised. But that is by no means a general rule, and in any case it would hardly be acceptable for such phenomena to be prevented. Here the regulatory brake has to be either the needs of the customers or the best interests of the sellers themselves. If one accepts market economics as a fact of life, one must also recognize that the market has to be allowed to determine for itself what forms it is going to take.

There remains the question of how to set limits. A military bandsman, thumping the drum or blowing into the trumpet, must move correctly in relation not only to those on the saluting point but also to those all around him in the parade. Advertising has its by-products of noise and light, and its form and coloring are supposed to be in keeping with the local surroundings. In the mountains of Switzerland or on the Canal Grande, no one is going to appreciate signs and billboards that might be suitable for railway station forecourts.

But there, too, it can be done well or badly, and why should we confine ourselves to the negative side, which is bound to manifest itself in any case? Let us instead try to find where promising potential exists, and try to ensure that it develops. Let us take up the fight on behalf of appropriate advertising of the highest quality, against both the resistance of those who do not understand it and the folly of its own advocates. It matters not what attitude an individual happens to have vis-à-vis economic activity: for this is life and should be accepted and affirmed.

Advertising is not art, but business. Advertising *may* choose to make use of art. But then the art must serve the advertisement. Otherwise it would be behaving like the architects who used to disguise a secular building as a Greek temple. It is a great error to demand of advertising that it should accommodate itself to the particular harmony of a cityscape, or even contribute to such harmony, where the actual architecture has failed to generate it. Harmony is no less one-sided a concept than symmetry or beauty. Our age is much too fast moving to be adequately served by Greek ideals. And advertising is a phenomenon of our age. It must be crass, must shout aloud, shock people. True, it also has to exercise attraction. *But what matters most is that it should have immediate, prominent impact.* Any attempt to inhibit this is wrong. Anyone who believes that advertising is necessarily harmful to the public interest has failed to comprehend the potential that has been opened up. Everyone has seen the views of New York and Paris: by daylight a gray-toned chaos—but in the glitter and splendor of nighttime advertising they become a magical illuminated spectacle. Where this has not yet been achieved in our cities, we need to put it in place as rapidly as possible. Around the Potsdamer Platz there is still too much unplanned darkness, reminding us of the lack of architectural balance. The historical cities are opposing illuminated advertising of all kinds; the city of Halle wants to keep its market square as it is—a place of many towers and sufficient bad buildings to spoil the ensemble, where the dark of night is conducive to a romantic *frisson* as old robber sagas reawaken, accompanied sometimes by their unwelcome modern counterpart. It is true that, once a month, the friendly moon is there in the sky, except when it is obscured by clouds. Otherwise, with the best will in the world one can find no reason why the pretty square, which in this case has continued to be the town's commercial center, should not have illuminations installed. We are a feeble generation, for we sacrifice the necessities of life to our piety. That was not the style of the ancient Romans or of Renaissance popes. Or perhaps rather we are a generation of the unfree, nurse-maided and ruled over by people with no understanding of life.

Moderate voices seek a compromise solution—and confuse advertising with a display of civic prestige. Granted, the latter is indeed a form of advertising, but only one of many. *Advertising is applied psychology.* Any stimulus to purchasing belongs within its ambit. The house, the shop, correspondence, announcements and signs, drumming memory into people at every step they take. And sometimes there have to be special shows laid on to promote stimulus and the remembering. All this needs to be designed, and the more academic the design thinking, the worse the result will be. Which is not to say, however, that a sufficient accumulation of eccentricities will not once in a while turn up a perfectly correct form.

For the crucial thing is that nothing must be permanent. All resources in time lose their currency. The crudest form of change is quantitative increase—because it ends automatically at the limit of human perception, which cannot simply expand indefinitely to match. The appropriate form of change is—just change. Careful determination of an advertisement's valence permits maximum subtlety in handling the sensory responses, and herein lies the secret of effect. Here, if it is true anywhere, the dictum holds good: use any style you like except a dull one. A building's facade, the shop window, temporary and permanent signboards and illuminated signs, rest and motion, fixed and changing elements: all these things are tasks not involving civic prestige, nor art as such, but advertising and its manpower—architects, painters, lighting experts. The more freedom advertising enjoys from restrictive bylaws, the more truly it will develop according to its own internal laws. One hundred and fifty years ago there were ordinances regulating what clothes people might wear; today, that looks after itself. It may be necessary initially to guard against certain excesses, while experience is still limited, and in America it may perhaps never come to pass that a psychologically inept, misconceived advertisement will be rejected by its public. But the people here are not Americans; what we have here is a peaceable and long-suffering people who should not be denied the little touch of life and fun that *unrestricted advertising* would be able to introduce into the grayness of everyday life.

So, am I saying that we do not in fact already have enough to put up with? Yes, indeed I am; we have hardly started. Let us put on circuses as the Roman emperors used to do to enhance their power, festivals as they were celebrated by the community in medieval times and by every natural community, but which are now possible only if created for us by those who have an interest in doing so, and the necessary means. For as long as our cities remain ugly deserts of stone, let us see to taking over the facades of our streets and squares with color and light. And who in our day might have better cause and ampler resources to do this than those for whom no surface is too enormous to be given the treatment? It is not a matter of putting up billboards in front of windows as they do in America, where whole house facades are bought up while behind them work goes on in artificial light, but rather of addressing the facades themselves, recasting them in such a way that they yield the useful space that was not thought of by the original architects. The chaos that currently prevails along such major thoroughfares as, for instance, the elevated railway line from the Zoo to Nollendorfplatz and beyond, the desolate wastes that are city squares: all this is the raw material for enterprising advertisers, whose work—provided their aims are sound and their standards high—will do no damage and can bring only good.

Why should the very nerve of economic life be tucked away and hidden? We all live today by trade and commerce, getting and spending. None of the circulating money is wasted: for it is not the individual transaction that matters, but turnover as a whole. The depression remains all-pervasive, because there is no construction activity. For construction, as the experts tell us, is a key industry—the motor of the entire economy. Everyone knows that this is true, and yet no one acts on it. Well then! If the housing crisis does not spur those into action who already have a roof over their head, let others step in. *Advertising, too, can be a key industry.* It can bring work to the timber, steel, paper, paint, glass, and electricity industries; through these, at second remove, to the construction and textile industries and electricity supply; and finally to the hotel and restaurant trade, transport, and insurance.

It is not true that an impoverished age should go without such things. Our age will remain impoverished as long as it remains stagnant. The things that matter most are: turnover and jobs.

163

Gerta-Elisabeth Thiele

THE SHOP WINDOW

First published as "Das Schaufenster," *Die Form*, 1926, pp. 146–47. Translated by Michael Loughridge.

By the last few years before the war, shop windows had become an established feature of the German cityscape. The movement dedicated to reforming shop-window decoration had its origins in Berlin at about the turn of the century and was not long in making its mark throughout the Reich. It was no less a figure than Alfred Messel who originally propagated the idea, and he used his influence to attract artistic talent to window dressing.

In our day, the shop window is the most effective advertising medium available to the modern retailer. His challenge is to generate maximum impact for the goods on display through a design that combines both logic and artistry.

The applied arts in Germany can look back on years of successful involvement in window dressing. Demand for the latest display types has risen so much that collaboration between artistic and technical talent now seems inevitable. The fast-moving times we live in, like the current zeitgeist, favor the sweeping line and bold use of color. To achieve maximum impact with limited means is the watchword of the day. It takes a high level of artistry to devise the ultimate means of presenting the essentials in the shop's displays while eliminating what is secondary. In modern shop-window arrangement, the aim is not to contrive originality by flouting convention as radically as possible, seeking to succeed through sensation and surprise, but rather to find a solution featuring simplicity and clarity of form, optimum choice of colors, elegant outlines, and technically perfect presentation of the merchandise. To educate ourselves in the use of color is one of the most important and necessary tasks facing us in Germany today, for there is a national shortcoming here that we must overcome if we are to lose our present dependency on neighboring nations whose feeling for color is superior. It would be an extremely welcome advance—and the opportunity is taken here to emphasize this point—if training courses in decoration could be recognized by the state art colleges and crafts-training institutions, taught by artists, architects, and art historians, and offering syllabuses in the history of style and fashion, architecture, and color theory. For color theory, the Ostwald Color Atlas could be a valuable teaching aid,[1] as the course would have to cater to an extremely diverse set of students. However, we should remain mindful of the view of Alfred Lichtwark, who emphasized in his *Die Erziehung des Farbensinnes* [The education of the color sense] that one cannot actually learn colors, but must have them in one's soul, like music.[2]

Fashionable, ready-made garments share pride of place in window decoration with the most exclusive products of the fashion industry. Dresses, coats, hats, and furs, unfailingly stylish in cut and workmanship, require an appropriately artistic setting if they are to appear at their best. The same applies to valuable fabrics in silk and wool, with their wide range of permutations in weave, color, and design, which home and foreign producers are putting on the market in increasingly high quality. The most contentious question in modern window displays of ready-made clothes, and one on which the debating between experts and artists has continued uninterrupted for years, is the use of the wax model. Years ago, the wax mannequin with its saccharine smile became the target of an out-and-out campaign—it was the art trade in particular that launched repeated attacks on the vapidity of the waxworks collections—but, despite all the animosity and various attempts at innovation, the wax figure lives on, still smiling out of the window displays, relishing the victory she has won. Nevertheless, there has been a major advance in the field of manufacturing props for window displays. Several years ago, it fell to

Rudolf Belling to introduce his "fashion sculpture" and thereby initiate a general reform in the field. More recently, working for the Berlin firm of Paul Baschwitz, the sculptor Alexander Gummitsch created a series of figures for window displays that are designed with lines that suggest sophisticated modern women and the grace and elegance of their movements. [. . .] It must be the *product* that catches the eye; for showing off modern fabrics to their best advantage, the new window mannequins clearly serve best.

NOTES

1. Wilhelm Ostwald, a Nobel-laureate chemist, devoted his later years to research into the theory and workings of color harmonies and developed a series of color scales. See *Die Farbenfibel* (Leipzig: Verlag Unesma, 1916) and *Der Farbenatlas* (Leipzig: Verlag Unesma, 1917).

2. Alfred Lichtwark, *Die Erziehung des Farbensinnes* (Berlin: Cassirer, 1901); Lichtwark was an important art educator and the director of the Kunsthalle in Hamburg from 1886 until his death in 1914.

164

Peter Panter (pseud. Kurt Tucholsky)

THE LOUDSPEAKER

First published as "Der Lautsprecher," *Vossische Zeitung*, 13 February 1927. Translated by Iain Boyd Whyte.

A loudspeaker on the street?

If I want a racket, I go home—on the street I want to have my peace. But the noise is a concern.

To enter someone else's property is universally prohibited, and everyone is agreed about trespassing by others. That's not allowed. "What? Here, in my apartment—?" Call the police, the riot squad, the public prosecutor. But no one says anything about trespass committed by noise on the peace and quiet of our ears. Because they don't hear it, and because everyone experiences it, this trespass. So:

The stones of the Berlin houses are eaten away by music. Saturated with sound waves, the poor bricks can barely stand their ground, and we shouldn't be surprised if one day a house suddenly—and in spite of all the building regulations—slowly sinks down, burying the pianos and gramophones under it as it goes. . . . God's mercy is great. For in every house Ingeborg, Edith, or Ruth are howling away because they are "artistic," or pound up and down the scales without pause. No one is more pretentious, one should add, than these amateurs.

That is all for the left ear. The right one is filled up (figuratively speaking) by the bowwow dogs.

These animals that ornament the streets—and from which no ancient sculp-

FIGURE 36. Funkhaus (broadcasting house) (1929–30; Hans Poelzig, architect) seen from the Funkturm (radio tower) (1926; Heinrich Straumer, architect), 1930. Bildarchiv Foto Marburg, 1.194.638.

ture, fountain, or landmark is safe—are there to be called after by their owners. These bay at them: "Fox! Come here! Will you come back here! Come here! *Heeere!*" And then there's a terrible howling, as if a ranch had been attacked by red Indians. In reality, it's only a milk cart going past . . . Dogs don't advance with civilization. Still under the influence of Winnetou,[1] they look for wagon trains, and regard the chief clerk who is pedaling by as a gory murderer.

Even though both ears are well provided for in this way—not to speak of the yelling of the children, which one can hear from miles away, if the dear child either is ill or simply deserved one across the backside—in spite of all this, they have now installed a loudspeaker on the street at the Funkturm.[2] Given the superstructure of the government departments, it is hard to tell who is responsible for this piece of inconsiderateness: the city of Berlin, the broadcasting authorities, or the post office. But it's a shame that the residents, who deserve all our sympathy, have not yet joined together to bring a great big legal action against the rowdies. It's horrid beyond measure. What one does on the street is not entirely clear. Some people read newspapers (once prompting my Aunt Julia to exclaim: "He reads papers on the street like a wild animal!"); some dwell on their thoughts—that's already more difficult—some daydream; some, like my friend Theobold, walk straight past their best friends with an idiotic expression on their face . . . there are so many things that can be perpetrated and tolerated on the street. But not one thing:

Loudspeakers with guttural speeches and loudspeakers with lots of music.

I know: there is already one howling on the boulevards in Paris. And it does. The place where the old Lucien Guitry used to appear is being rebuilt, and one day a black hole appeared on the scaffolding, out of which wailed a trumpet, an operatic bass, a "Vickeline," and a woman who squeaked among the car horns: "*Mon cœur soupire . . .*" Each to her own.

At least that sinks under the general racket, a brightly colored ingredient in the metropolitan orchestra. But here, at the Funkturm—?

In a quiet corner, where an electric streetcar goes by only once each half year, a greasy voice bleats and quacks things that no one understands, as no one has time or inclination to stay long enough to listen to it. Orchestral music rolls by, arty songs are howled, and instruments of unknown origin squeal out. You don't want that sort of thing on the street. It is not only a nuisance for the local residents—for whom one is deeply sorry, since without doubt the value of their property is affected—but also an infantile overestimation of technology, a stupid game. It's as if red Indians were cooking a goat's stomach in a camera they had found. That's not what the machine is for.

And the loudspeaker is not there to break into the peace and calm of one's ears. Whether or not in the process the music is being profaned is something for the musicians to decide; it's probably the case. But it is certain that this menace should not be forced on harmless passersby, who want nothing of it. The technician commissioned to hang it up doubtless thought of himself as very big-city-ish, and stood full of wonder in front of his handiwork. But it is in no way big-city-ish or metropolitan. On the contrary, it's a provincial misunderstanding of the potential of the wireless. If the artistic offerings are bad, then spare us from them. If, however, they are good, then they fall on the ears of the unwilling, the disinterested, the hurrying, those trotting hastily to work. Then it's sad for the art and a trespass on the ears into the bargain. In peaceful moments you don't even want to hear the "latest news" at this spot.

"Attention! Attention! We have just heard . . ." And so it goes hour after hour. We often find the wireless annoying, as it is constantly accompanied by background noise. The aerial for this disturber of the peace should be earthed, and in the interest of general peace dismantled. Here's to never hearing it again!

NOTES

1. Winnetou is a fictional Apache Indian hero in a series of novels written in German by Karl May, who had never experienced the United States at first hand. The novels were enormously successful, are still in print, and inspired several films and an annual Karl May Festival held in the town of Bad Segeberg, Schleswig-Holstein.

2. One of the landmarks of Berlin, the Funkturm (radio tower) was built in 1926 to the design of Heinrich Straumer on the occasion of the Third German Radio Exhibition. It was subsequently incorporated into the Messegelände (exhibition grounds) and dominates the western approaches to the city. See below, text 200: Siegfried Kracauer, Radio Station.

165

Hans Cürlis

NIGHT AND THE MODERN CITY

First published as "Die moderne Stadt und die Nacht," *Wasmuths Monatshefte für Baukunst* 12 (1928), pp. 256–59. Translated by Michael Loughridge.

In the old days buildings were designed, as far as their external appearance was concerned, for the daytime. Moonlight was for atmosphere. The buildings themselves would sleep, like the humans who built them, once darkness had fallen. Sunrise was not yet "an experience." If people were not yet ready for bed, they still withdrew into their houses and secured all the outside doors. *Feierabend,* the end of the working day, still had its literal meaning, *evening to enjoy.* What little lighting they had available was assembled in the parlor. It was not needed outside, and no one would have found a use for it outside.

For reasons unrelated to building practice, humans changed their ways. Night became the chance to sleep. The evening disappeared. The working day ends, but is not followed by the private *Feierabend.* When it gets dark, the artificial daylight is switched on. Light in an abundance as undreamed of earlier as airplanes, films, and gramophone records dominate the city. And this is still only the beginning of lighting technology. A new city has come into being overnight. Of the old city, what remains at night? Nothing. The lighting rips open the ground-floor level of all the great thoroughfares. What a jostle of luridly lit pianos, delicatessens, shoes, radio sets and accessories, off-the-peg clothing, furniture, cinemas, and so on! Every shop owner has made his own contribution through illuminated name boards and other neon advertising. And above all this, like a dirty coat hanging in the dark, rises the building's facade—that no longer is a facade. Light surges out of the buildings and breaks up the continuity of the street. Illuminated anarchy prevails. There is only one law: one and all must illuminate their wares. The signs of the time: the Potsdamer Station announces its position in neon letters; a church in Moabit offers Bible texts. If the modern church really understood the signs of the times, it would have led the field here long ago.

If basic shop-window presentation has never been fully mastered, illuminated shop windows and neon advertising have proved completely beyond the grasp of those who install them. The campaign of enticement to buy on the largest scale possible is not fought out with the artistic means available, as far as building

FIGURE 37. "Berlin im Licht," advertising pillar from the Berlin Light Week exhibition, 1928. Berlinische Galerie, Landesmuseum für Moderne Kunst, Photographie und Architektur—Photographische Sammlung, B6-FS 59/89,86.

facades are concerned. Good architecture used to be subordination, integration, permanence of built structures, but today advertising is a conscious breaking of molds, intentionally demonstrative contrast with the neighbor, forced inconstancy. The assault on the customer's purse cannot be launched frequently enough or variously enough. Impact can be calculated only for the briefest of periods. One can no longer actually build anything; one can only "decorate." As the night is ours and can advertise for us, we bathe our merchandise in light. Where the building itself is part of the goods for sale, we bathe the whole facade in light—this is the first step. We use high masts to direct beams of light onto the facade. However, this light has no ability to differentiate. It washes on to the profiling and flattens it. That does nothing to support the impression that the owner is seeking to create. Here is something strange and new. It may be that one actually does erect a sumptuous facade. But it will fulfill its role only during the day. At night it no longer belongs in the realm of art. It belongs to advertising. And this purpose can be achieved in full, even if the building plan is not fully implemented. This of course does not prevent the architect from seeing the display window as a challenge and integrating the particular solution tactfully and pleasingly into the street's general scheme.

166

Hugo Häring

ILLUMINATED ADVERTISEMENTS AND ARCHITECTURE

First published as "Lichtreklame und Architektur," *Moderne Bauformen* 27, no. 3 (March 1928): Mitteilungen aus der Fachwelt, pp. 2–3. Translated by Iain Boyd Whyte.

Advertising is well on the way to supplanting architecture. First, the creation of shops—with all their requirements for window area, display cabinets, name boards, and advertising placards—began to hollow out buildings from underneath, working upward to the first and second floor; and now illuminated advertising is working downward from the roof to continue the destruction of architecture. What remains in the way of architectural interest at third- and fourth-story level is fragmented, bereft of any claim to be regarded as architecture. This is a continuing process, and irreversible; and there is no prospect of a negotiated agreement. (In this field, even conservation programs and expert assessors will be unable to salvage anything in the longer term.) The fact is that the commercial building no longer has an architectural facade; its exterior has become a framework on which to hang advertisements, slogans, and illuminated advertising. The rest is window area. Thus the current requirement is to start from windows, slogans, and other advertising, and build up from them a composite structure whose ultimate purpose is once again simply—advertising. A structure for which traditional architectural concepts are inadequate: and yet still a structure for which there needs to be orderly planning, regulation of techniques, clear specification of purpose, prevention of free-for-all. The concepts "good" and "bad" still apply.

There is a significant new factor: nighttime effect—that is, the structure's appearance when illuminated. Historically, the effect created by a house with lit up interior was never taken into account at the planning stage. Today that effect is consciously planned, even in residential projects, as the Taut house shows;[1] and in large firms, office blocks, factories, and halls it represents a central feature of the design planning. The building's nighttime facade is as a rule still more impressive, powerful, and substantial than its daytime appearance. If the interior lighting is supplemented by external lighting, with neon signs and spotlights, the nocturnal appearance will be still more decisive. Who recognizes by day the facade of the theater he has been to a hundred times by night? In consequence, the daytime facade has lost some of its importance; that means the role of architecture in the facade is also very much less critical, whereas the nighttime visual appearance now has to be planned. The daytime appearance is secondary.

The designs for daytime and nighttime appearance both have to be applied to the facade, and must coexist there. This gives rise to the highly intricate problem of designing a structure to be unified, complete, and self-sufficient both by day and—in artificial lighting—at night. The problems that had to be faced here are closely related to those that the painter Nikolas Braun had been investigating for years through his illuminated sculpture.

The facades designed by some contemporary architects for commercial buildings no longer set out to create a traditional architectural form with columns, subdivisions, infills, and so on—which was still Messel's aim with the Wertheim building—but merely reiterate the pattern of window bands and advertising text bands that largely make up the outer shell of commercial buildings. Because the wording has to be illuminated at night, these architects place the light sources beneath or above the texts, thus adding installations that recall conventional architectural forms in as far as they resemble lighted cornices. This simple, clear facade structure represents an essentially appropriate solution for both diurnal and nocturnal conditions.

But there are other ways yet in which these insights may be utilized in creating facade design. Arthur Korn uses a different set of principles in his design for the Wachthof building. Kosina, too, in his tourist-services building, goes much the same way as Korn. For the nocturnal image, Korn varies the structure of his daytime facade through effects of light, making use of rows of floodlights, illuminated panels, and transparency effects to create what amounts to a new composition. Furthermore, these facades present different aspects to the passerby according to the angle from which they are seen, while the facades mentioned earlier remain as it were static. In one direction the Wachthof's spotlight installations show a wide, solid band of rather diffuse light, while to those approaching from the opposite direction part of this effect is blocked off, leaving only a narrow band of light. Such devices are a distinct step closer to actual illuminated sculpture or light sculpture, and indicate unmistakably one path for commercial facade design to follow: namely, that of generating an original composition from a variety of illuminated surfaces, from tube lighting, from concealed light sources, from transparencies, texts, company trademarks, and so on. Not to be overlooked also are moving texts, and pennants spotlighted against the night sky. Because the facade itself is not a plane surface but permits the use of depth effects, the potential for light sculpture is considerable, particularly with regard to the effects that may be created using corner sites. Given that for many businesses the effectiveness of the nighttime presentation is more important than what appears by day, it is clear that the emphasis in future will lie on designing the nocturnal facade in its own right, as opposed to the present practice of superimposing nighttime lighting devices on a preexisting architect-designed daytime facade.

The current position is no doubt transitional. The arbitrary and promiscuous coexistence of architectural remnants and advertising installations cannot be prolonged indefinitely. In practice, it has to be accepted; it will continue for quite some time to come. It nevertheless seems important to propose and to reflect on the principles that might in future govern facade design for commercial buildings—more specifically, those that are purpose built or conversions.

Considerations of city planning are prompting today's architects to return to applying an overall design concept to whole streets, and consequently to suppress idiosyncrasy in individual houses. It can be foreseen that in time this trend will be accompanied by calls for a whole-street approach to issues of design for nighttime appearance. At present it is apparent that the nighttime streetscape presents a farrago of the most variegated illuminated advertising, and it is not hard to see that the introduction of some discipline would benefit all concerned. In this field, as in others, the early stage of chaotic activity will be succeeded by one featuring a more concerted approach to illuminated advertising, and more rational organization of this exceedingly expensive activity.

NOTE

1. This is a reference to the radically modern house that the architect Bruno Taut built for himself in 1926–27 in Dahlewitz, a village south of Berlin, employing a quarter-circle plan and striking color contrasts throughout. See Bruno Taut, *Ein Wohnhaus* (Stuttgart: Franckh'sche Verlagsbuchhandlung W. Keller & Co., 1927). See also below, text 173: Bruno Taut, The New Home: Woman as Creative Spirit.

167

Joseph Roth

THE REALLY BIG DEPARTMENT STORE

First published as "Das ganz große Warenhaus," *Münchner Neueste Nachrichten*, 8 September 1929; reprinted in Roth, *Berliner Saisonbericht: Unbekannte Reportagen und journalistische Arbeiten, 1920–39* (Cologne: Kiepenheuer & Witsch, 1984), pp. 320–23. Translated by Michael Loughridge.

Actually, the city already had big department stores. Even so, there were still some people who felt that it could do with a really big one. A few of them were not too happy that the existing department stores had a mere four, five, or six floors, and soon they began to indulge in ambitious dreams of department stores that were ten, twelve, even fifteen floors high. Not that there was any notion of getting up nearer to God in this manner—which would have been a hopeless endeavor in any case. All that we have learned indicates that one does not approach Him more nearly by climbing higher and higher toward the clouds, but rather the contrary: by living in closer proximity to the dust from which we are made. No, it was not that! The people who dreamed of really big department stores were concerned solely with getting themselves above the level of the smaller department stores; in this they resembled modern sprinters, one of whom beats the others with the aim not of reaching his destination earlier, but of arriving anywhere at all before the others do. The department-store dreamers dreamed of a skyscraper. And so, one day, they built the really big department store, and all the people went along to see it for themselves, and so did I . . .

The old, and merely big, department stores are small in comparison, not far removed from ordinary plain shops, although in essentials the really big department store is not really all that different from the merely big ones. It has more stock, more lifts, more customers, stairs, escalators, tills, sales personnel, liveries, display racks, crates, and cardboard boxes. True, the goods do seem to be cheaper. So very many of them are crowded so closely together that they can hardly help regarding themselves as of inferior worth. They are abased in their own eyes, lower their prices, and become more humble; cheapness is the humility of merchandise. And as there are so many customers all together in one place, the goods are not demanding so much of the customers; and they, too, become humble. So while at first sight the really big department store might have seemed like a work of arrogance, a sinful tempting of Providence by humans, one came to realize that in fact it is just a gigantic shell housing human pettiness and human modesty—a huge confession of earthly cheapness.

The escalator seems to me to be a revealing example: it takes people upstairs by doing the climbing for them. In fact, it does not even climb, it scurries. Each of its treads scurries uphill with a customer on top, as if fearing he would turn back. It carries him toward goods that he might never have approached using a conventional staircase. When all is said and done, it does not matter whether the goods are brought on a down escalator to the waiting customer, or the customer taken on an escalator gliding upward to the waiting goods.

To be sure, there are conventional stairs, too, in the really big department store. But they are "freshly polished"; anyone going up them runs the risk of slipping, and if he does, it will be on his own head. It would have been preferable to do without the antiquated things altogether, which beside the lifts and elevators have a positively bucolic look, like ladders. To make them look still more perilous, they were freshly polished. Almost unused, they bear their own excessively smooth-surfaced treads aloft. Relics of that bygone age that knew nothing more recent than castle ruins and merely big department stores—not the really big ones.

They might perhaps have made the really big department store much higher still, had they not taken the view that it should have a roof terrace on which customers could eat, drink, admire the view, and listen to music—without getting cold. But that was in fact the view they took, even though by and large it does not seem to be an inherent trait of human nature that the purchase of linens, kitchenware, and sports equipment should bring on an urgent need to drink coffee, eat cakes, and listen to music. Perhaps these needs were there already, rooted in basic human nature, and with them in mind it was decided to install the roof garden. During the daytime lots of people sit there, eating and drinking, and although I can't be sure they are doing so without real appetite, it still looks as though they are sitting there drinking purely in order to demonstrate that the terrace is necessary. Indeed, it is conceivable that their very appetite is there for demonstrative purposes only. Even when their personal mobility was sharply reduced by the process of hauling them uphill on the escalators, it still sufficed to identify them as customers; but once on the roof, they lapsed into a passivity that renders them indistinguishable from stock. And although they do pay, it is more as if they were being paid . . .

Completely motionless, they are entertained by an excellent orchestra. Their gaze roams over distant spires, gasworks, horizons. The rare delicacies are offered so assiduously and to so many that their rarity suffers. And just as inside the building the stock and the customers became humble, so, too, the delights on the roof become humble. For everyone, all things are attainable. All things are accessible to anyone.

And so the really big department store should not be regarded as a sinful enterprise on the lines of, say, the Tower of Babel. On the contrary, it just proves that it is impossible for the contemporary human spirit to overstretch itself. It can even build skyscrapers: and what follows is not a deluge, but a nice little profit.

168

Alfred Wedemeyer

BERLIN'S LATEST DEPARTMENT STORE

First published as "Berlins neuestes Warenhaus (Karstadt A.G.)" in *Das Neue Berlin,* ed. Martin Wagner (Berlin: Deutsche Bauzeitung, 1929), pp. 166–68. Translated by Michael Loughridge.

With its seven-story, thirty-two-meter-high main building surmounted by two four-story towers adding another twenty four meters (plus aircraft beacons of fifteen meters), Rudolph Karstadt AG's new department store stands at one of the city's busiest junctions, the Hermannplatz in Neukölln. The building itself occupies 8,200 square meters of a site extending to 12,500 square meters. The total usable floor space amounts to 72,000 square meters.

The building's structural frame is of ferro-concrete and was made from eleven thousand tons of cement, forty-eight thousand cubic meters of Elbe gravel aggregate with a 33.5 percent crushed basalt component, and thirty-two hundred tons of steel. For the facings, Franconian *Muschelkalk* [shell limestone] applied over the concrete structure.

COMMODITIES AND DISPLAY   457

FIGURE 38. Karstadt department store, Neukölln (1928–29; Philip Schaefer, architect), 1929. Landesarchiv Berlin, II 2970.

The ground plan of the building reflects the regular spacing of the load-bearing members. The interior is designed around three light wells, one 475 square meters in area, the others 230 square meters each.

Served by two lines of the Berlin urban railway network, the store has its own underground station in the basement, with sales kiosks and access to the Gesundbrunnen–Neukölln and north–south lines. The store above is reached via an escalator, a wide staircase, and three lifts. In all, the building has a further twenty-four passenger lifts, twenty-four escalators, eight freight elevators, thirteen catering lifts, one vehicle hoist, and eleven fire-resistant stairways.

The basement floor comprises the railway station, a bathing establishment with individual tubs, showers, and massage for ladies and gentlemen, a section of the hairdressing salon (the other part is on the second floor), and a basement sales floor. The cafeteria and tearoom on the second floor seat eight hundred and have their own general and fancy bakery with electric ovens. On the third floor there is a restaurant for six hundred people. The kitchens serving it are Berlin's largest electricity-based catering unit to date. The fifth-floor food halls are impressive not only in size but in the standards of hygiene they set. The top floor accommodates offices, workrooms, studios, and the staff canteens.

One highly innovative feature is the 4,000-square-meter roof garden, believed to rank among Europe's largest. Numerous flower beds with limestone edging flaunt a rich variety of blooms grouped by color.

For the safety of customers and staff, all ceilings are linked to the sprinkler system, which has nine thousand outlet nozzles in all. Safety is further enhanced by a drencher system, which in the event of fire would put down curtains of water dividing every level of the building, from roof to ground floor, into separate compartments and preventing the spread of smoke damage.

From a large-scale refrigeration plant, coolant in the form of superchilled brine is supplied to the entire building via a fully duplicated system of pump units and piping. This plant is also responsible for cooling the fresh-air ventilation of the cafeteria, tearoom, and restaurant. The heating plant has thirteen boilers with a total of 700 square meters of heating surface. At all external doorways, warm air is pumped in by electric motors so that drafts are totally eliminated. In winter, prewarmed air is pumped into the ventilation system in the same way, and the stale air is extracted by rotary fans.

Hot water is supplied by boilers with 150 square meters of heating surface and four preheaters. The plant is designed for pump operation and is fully equipped with up-to-the-minute measuring and control systems.

Electricity for lighting and heating is drawn from a transformer station comprising eight transformers of six hundred kilowatts each. In the event of a power failure, the system switches over automatically to emergency supply from batteries. Other technical features are a telephone switchboard with fifteen outside lines and 170 extensions, and electric communication systems.

169

Ludwig Hilberseimer

THE MODERN COMMERCIAL STREET

First published as "Die neue Geschäftsstrasse," *Das neue Frankfurt* 4 (1929). Translated by Michael Loughridge.

The commercial city street is not the wholly modern phenomenon that many today assume it to be. It was there in all the ancient centers of trade. In his English jottings, Heinrich Heine reports how the house fronts along the principal thoroughfares of the City area of London were filled right up to the eaves with long-winded names and numbers, usually gilt and in relief, and that visitors were spellbound by the wonderful array of novel and attractive articles laid out in the shop windows. He tells also of the art of shop-window display, of the contrasting colors and the variety that lent the English shop windows their special allure.—Clearly the problems of one hundred years ago were exactly the same as those of today. The commercial street is made from the same elements now as it was then, even if the scale has become gargantuan. The only new element is the potential afforded by lighting, and this has indeed brought about a radical modification of the street scene. The modern phenomenon of locating centrally has led to the emergence of new types of building: department stores, business premises, and offices. These new types did not suddenly appear: they had in fact developed over some time in response to need. Thus the department store, the most distinctive of these new building types, developed from the residential apartment block: in floor after floor, internal walls were removed and larger windows installed. Once a building could no longer offer sufficient space, a second and then a third were added, until one day the proliferation resulting from this random growth process would make it necessary, in the interests of business efficiency, to construct an entirely new building dedicated exclusively to the purpose in question. In due course the further development and expansion of the business would ensure that this building, too, became a limitation; yet further new construction would become necessary, and these extensions, however skillfully grafted on to the existing buildings, would then suffer from essentially the same disadvantages—notwithstanding a more suitable basic design—as had those first-generation business premises created by running apartment blocks together and converting them for commercial use. The building that most comprehensively illustrates this epoch is the Wertheim department store on Leipziger Platz in Berlin—a complex that has progressively evolved over the years to the point where, today, it occupies almost the whole frontage of a city block of impressive dimensions. A further phase of the process can be seen in the Tietz store at Alexanderplatz, Berlin. Here, a complex of about the same overall dimensions as the Wertheim store came about not through piecemeal extensions, but as a single project, thus benefiting naturally from all the advantages that unified planning can confer for the efficient running of the business.

Like the department store, the commercial building also has passed through this development phase. The Scherl newspaper office complex in Berlin, for example, remains to this day a development of many former separate apartment blocks, multifariously interlinked to create a labyrinth of working spaces and corridors at different levels. The impracticability of running a business in these conditions has now obliged the Scherl group, too, to commission a new headquarters; and work on some aspects of this is already in progress.

Another type of commercial building, one in which office accommodation is taken up by individual businesses, has not yet reached the same stage of refinement in Berlin that it has in, say, Hamburg. Over and above the office blocks erected by large businesses for their own purposes, such accommodation is in strong demand from smaller firms without the resources to erect an office block independently. These office blocks, too, like nonretail premises and department stores, are a development from the apartment block, and in Berlin, even when built specifically for offices, they do not exceed the size of a single apartment block. For a commercial office block to be useful, it must offer tenants not only rooms for their own day-to-day use, but larger meeting rooms for conferences and the like that they would not be able to afford as sole users. Such requirements can be best met if the office block is free of any inheritance from individual buildings, instead taking up whole city blocks and thus acquiring a radically new potential.

The war and the subsequent economic crisis interrupted development, bringing an almost complete stop to the conversion of commercial premises. Fresh building activity here was devoted for the most part to redesign of the facades; interesting though individual examples may be, these are really nothing more than masks concealing an organism quite different from what the exterior suggests. The way this process usually works out is that only the ground- and first-floor accommodation finds takers—because these floors command a high enough price for it to be worth a firm's while to convert or build new. It is very rare for the whole facade to be redesigned, though this was the case with, for example, the conversions involving Mendelsohn, or the brothers Luckhardt and Anker. For the same reasons, new commercial construction is as a rule only two-storied, as in the retail developments at the Zoo by Poelzig, at the Lehniner Platz by Mendelsohn, and at the Hallesches Tor by Hilberseimer.

In recent years, however, and in contrast to this hiatus in building development, the appearance of the city street has been transformed by advertising, particularly in combination with the use of light. However much the individual building may seek to retain its dominance, and to impose itself on the modern street scene by virtue of the individuality and character of its facades, it now finds itself submerged and lost under the slogans and advertisement assemblies, the frameworks of which, particularly at roof level, impose instead a characterless uniformity on the street even by day. At night, architecture of any kind simply disappears, swamped by the unrestrained use of illuminated advertisements.

In the wider context, as Häring has pointed out in an essay in *Moderne Bauformen* on illuminated advertising and architecture, advertising is well on the way to supplanting architecture.[1] First, the creation of shops—with all their requirements for window area, display cabinets, name boards, and advertising placards—began to hollow out buildings from underneath, working upward to the first and second floor; and now illuminated advertising is working downward from the roof to continue the destruction of architecture. What remains in the way of architectural interest at third- and fourth-story level is fragmented, bereft of any claim to be regarded as architecture. The commercial building no longer has an architectural facade; its exterior has become a window-punctuated framework on

COMMODITIES AND DISPLAY 461

which to hang advertisements, slogans, and illuminations. Thus the current requirement is to start from windows, slogans, and other advertising and build up from them a composite structure whose ultimate purpose is once again simply—advertising. Recent facade designs allow for illuminated advertising and incorporate the lettering into the balustrades to form words, so that in streets with extensive runs of new or converted commercial properties there is now what virtually amounts to a standardized approach to advertising. Desirable though this approach might seem, the notion actually conflicts with the very essence of advertising, as the effectiveness of any advertisement naturally depends on the extent to which it stands out from the uniformity of the street background. Where architecture is stable, advertising is labile, always subject to displacement by a new idea.

The idea of illuminated advertising emancipated from horizontal bands has been realized in the latest commercial building designs by Mies van der Rohe. In these, the entire facade consists of a steel-framed matte-glass skin, which gives full scope for the advertising material to be deployed independent of structural divisions.

The development of the commercial street, as seen currently in the transformation of existing buildings into department stores, offices, and other commercial premises, has by no means run its course but is still very much in progress. By contrast, the street itself has so far almost completely escaped this development process. While the volume of traffic has increased immeasurably, actual road space remains exactly what it was in an age when traffic, relative to now, was minimal. Just as buildings used for commercial purposes had to be progressively extended in response to increasing demands, without achieving the position that only a proper planning process could have created, so the response to the huge demands imposed by city traffic has been and remains a series of attempts to satisfy them with palliatives, stopgap remedies that have no lasting effect—instead of accepting that a full-scale remodeling of the city's street layout is essential, for there is no other way to relieve the situation.

Up to the present, European cities have happily avoided the unplanned skyscraper development that has made American cities intolerable, but they have not coped successfully with modern traffic problems. European cities could have their own skyscrapers without repeating the mistakes made in the United States. Quite the contrary, in fact: this type of construction would make it possible to gain the road space needed for today's traffic without depriving buildings of the requisite light and air.

Following on from an outline proposal on the layout of a high-rise city that was drawn up as long ago as 1924, the March issue of *Kunstblatt* reproduces a schematic layout for a city-center development with skyscrapers, one that features all these advantages without increasing the building density, achieving its purpose simply by redisposition of the building masses on the site, concentrating them into high-rise buildings. This allows for the required wide separation, which must be not less than the building height. The space between buildings is sufficient to permit a multilevel system of roads, and in turn the complete separation of pedestrian and vehicular traffic; there would also be sufficient parking space for cars on all roads. The courtyard areas adjacent to the buildings would have the same breadth as the thoroughfare, and in an unrestricted planning situation could serve variously to accommodate exhibition halls, salesrooms, or warehousing.

A proposal of this nature differs from all the partial solutions in that it involves reconstruction of the entire city center—an undertaking of incalculable cost. Nevertheless, any part solution adopted should be assessed in relation to the most comprehensive plan. What makes the present city intolerable is its street layout, and none of the partial improvements make any difference to that.

NOTE

1. See above, text 166: Hugo Häring, Illuminated Advertising and Architecture.

170

Alfons Paquet

CITY AND PROVINCE

First published as "City und Provinz," *Die neue Rundschau: XXXX. Jahrgang der freien Bühne*, vol. 1 (Berlin and Leipzig: Fischer, 1929), pp. 618–28. Translated by Iain Boyd Whyte.

[...]

Beyond its practical functions, every world city has its representative tasks. It has the task of making things visible. Exhibitions, displays, trade fairs are platonic acts, the final step of all production activity. They are indispensable as points of orientation and starting points for commerce. The exhibition system of a society is part of its transportation system; it serves to assert the everyday routines of life with tangible and visible simulacra, be they advertisements, guidebooks, or instruction manuals. The parade and the theater, architecture, garden design, and every sort of decoration are forms of display. Out of their fusion emerges the exhibition as an autonomous undertaking. To make visible that which is representable only in the mind, and to subordinate it to our volition, is the task of the true exhibition. The exhibition is an instrument of the will.

[...]

15

HOUSING

Throughout Europe, the urge for social and political reform that followed World War I found powerful expression in housing. Following the dehumanization and insanity of the war, the safety, security, and privacy offered by one's own roof and front door had boundless appeal. It is not surprising, therefore, that the defeated nations, Germany and Austria, invested considerable resources and high expectations in housing reform as the path to social well-being. In both countries the agenda was set by the capital cities, Berlin and Vienna, although Frankfurt also played a major role in the German housing debate.

In the immediate aftermath of the war, the Expressionist impulse proposed a utopian socialism that would overcome the evils of capitalism through brotherly love and glass architecture. By the mid-1920s, the same idealistic impulse for social improvement still survived, but stripped of its romantic illusions. Whereas the radical architects saw themselves in 1918 as the messianic leaders of a new priesthood of the arts, they now offered themselves as engineers and social scientists, destined to create a better world through calculation rather than faith. Indeed, the same architects who had dreamed of glass temples in 1919 were the most vigorous advocates of rationalist and functionalist design and technology in the later 1920s.

Between the utopian fantasies of Expressionism and the very pragmatic rationalism of the mid-twenties came rampant inflation, which precluded any form of large-scale building. Only after the stabilization of the mark in November 1923 could serious consideration be given to the housing question. The statistics tell a clear story. At the end of the war, the housing shortage in Berlin was variously estimated at 100,000 to 130,000 dwellings. Only 9,000 social housing units were built, however, between 1919 and 1923. In contrast, 135,000 units were completed between 1924 and 1930, at which point the world economic crash brought the program to a premature halt.

The ability to plan large-scale housing developments in Berlin was a direct result of the consolidation in 1920 of eight towns, fifty-nine rural communities, and twenty-seven rural estates into a single administrative entity known as Greater Berlin (Groß-Berlin). For the first time in its history, the city could follow coherent and rational planning principles, and appoint a single director of building to pursue this goal. The post of municipal building director (Stadtbaurat) was filled initially by Ludwig Hoffmann, and from 1926 to 1933 by Martin Wagner. The administrative reorganization was supported in turn by tax reforms that followed the currency reform of 1924, and by the 1925 Reform Building Ordinance, which introduced the zoning of industry and housing, and reduced the potential for building at high densities by banning transverse buildings and side wings. This effectively banished the courtyard format that had dominated Berlin housing since the 1870s.

In Berlin the essential partner for new house-building initiatives was the trade-union movement. In the autumn of 1923, the German Trade-Union Congress (Allgemeiner Deutscher Gewerkschaftsbund), on the initiative of Martin Wagner, set up a central agency for funding cooperative housing. The following March DEWOG (Deutschen Wohnungsfürsorge-AG für Beamte, Angestellte und Arbeiter) was set up, with Wagner as its director and its goal the restructuring of union finances on the model of private trusts. The Berlin arm of DEWOG, which carried the acronym GEHAG (Gemeinnützige Heimstätten-Aktiengesellschaft), was established in April 1924. The prime ambition of GEHAG was to achieve the greatest possible economies in the construction of housing in order to achieve low rents. To achieve this goal, Wagner employed leading modernist architects, most notably Bruno Taut, to design standard housing units that could be repeated in great numbers. To the "artist's socialism" that continued to drive Taut's work, Wagner brought a detailed knowledge of the American building industry and of its financing. As Martin Wagner explained: "If we want to overcome capitalism, we must adopt new and different approaches. We must learn to dominate it intellectually and turn the means of its success into a tool for ourselves."[1]

Martin Wagner's doctoral dissertation, submitted to the Königliche Technische Hochschule Berlin in 1915, addressed the health-giving qualities of gardens and greenery in the city.[2] Five years later, Bruno Taut argued for the dissolution of the city and the establishment on the land of a network of small, self-sufficient communities. The Horseshoe Estate at Britz brought together both of these preoccupations, and replaced the hard, brick-and-stone world of the nineteenth century and the closed, courtyard blocks of the tenement house with generously spaced row housing, set in carefully composed gardens designed by the eminent landscape architect Leberecht Migge. Built between 1925 and 1927, the Britz estate housed over one thousand apartments in four standard types and became a symbol of the social democratic ambition to create housing that was generously provided with light, air, and access to green space. The long facade facing Fritz-Reuter-Allee in the Britz estate was painted bright red, earning it the nickname "the Red Front," and the close relationship between the social democratic city council, the trade unions, and vocal architectural modernism inevitably provoked the wrath of the conservative factions in both architecture and politics.

The Britz initiative was the first of a series of major *Großsiedlungen* designed by leading modernists and located at the edge of Berlin, creating a ring of green housing around Berlin. As the architectural historian Fritz Neumeyer has noted: "During the latter half of the 1920s Berlin was a single great laboratory for public housing. No other city achieved such architectural quality in its housing developments, experimented in such variety, or could match Berlin's figures for housing volume."[3] With finance from the trade-union housing associations and enabled by the 1925 building ordinances, seventeen large-scale social housing schemes were built in Berlin between 1925 and 1931. Among the most significant early developments was the Waldsiedlung "Onkel-Toms-Hütte" in Zehlendorf (1926–31), by the architects Bruno Taut, Hugo Häring, and Otto Rudolf Salvisberg, which housed some five hundred units in three types, set in beautiful parkland on the edge of the Grunewald, but with a direct railway link to the city.

Not all the new building was located at the green perimeter of the city, however, and the modernist architectural elite was also engaged in inserting new housing types into the large city block pattern imposed in the nineteenth century by the Hobrecht plan of 1862. A pioneering scheme was the "Schillerpark" estate, commissioned by the "Berliner Spar- und Bauverein" [Berlin Savings and Building Society] and built in three phases between 1924 and 1930 to the design of Bruno Taut. Although adhering at the perimeter to the existing street lines, Taut's three-story blocks opened through loggias and balconies onto large green spaces, which were landscaped by the eminent garden designer Walter Rossow. Toward the end of the decade, and with direct funding from the city, this model of modernist urban living was further developed at the Carl Legien Estate, designed by Bruno Taut and Franz Hillinger, which could accommodate some twelve hundred residents in a series of five-story, U-shaped blocks, interspersed with greenswards.

The ongoing housing shortage, coupled with the discontinuation of the house interest tax, led the city to invest 15 million reichsmarks in housing and to ease the building regulations that had been imposed earlier in the decade. The results were two major developments: the Weiße Stadt [White City] estate in Reinickendorf, and the *Großsiedlung* Siemensstadt. Both were located in the industrial, northern suburbs of Berlin. The Weiße Stadt comprised some 1,270 apartments plus shops, a kindergarten, and a doctor's practice, designed by three architects: Otto Rudolf Salvisberg, Wilhelm Büning, and Bruno Ahrends. Further plans for schools and communal sports facilities fell victim to the world economic crisis. The Siemensstadt estate, sited directly adjacent to the main factories of the electrical engineers Siemens & Halske, was even larger, with 1,800 apartments. The individual housing blocks, although united by a commitment to high modernism, reflected the very different approaches favored by their illustrious designers: Otto Bartning, Fred Forbat, Walter Gropius, Hugo Häring, Paul R. Henning, and Hans Scharoun. The creative tensions of high modernism can be seen very clearly in this group of buildings. Under the banner of functionalism, Gropius and Bartning created strongly rational and anonymous structures that used repetitive forms to generate a fixed number of options in terms of size and occupancy. This was entirely in accord with the pragmatics of the factory assembly line or the aesthetics of the Tiller Girl, characterized by cultural critic Siegfried Kracauer as "the aesthetic reflex of rationalism pursued by the dominant economic system."[4] In contrast to this rigid adherence to the ideologies of mass production and mass entertainment, Scharoun and Häring produced housing blocks that, although fully committed to modernism, were also willfully allusive and organic in their design. The architectural theorist Manfredo Tafuri once called this confrontation "one of the most serious ruptures within the modern movement,"[5] and his analysis is confirmed by contemporary responses to the functionalist dictates of high rationalist modernism. Adolf Behne, for example, who was by no means hostile to architectural modernism and had even published a book titled *Der moderne Zweckbau* [Modern functional building] in 1926, had doubts about the remorseless application of functionalist criteria to housing design:

> The architect today tends to be more health-minded than the sanitary inspector, more sociologically inclined than the sociologist, more statistical than the statistician, more biological than the biologist. But he is too inclined to forget that hygiene, statistics, biology, and sociology are of real value only if they do not gobble up the space people have for living. "From the biological point of view," Gropius writes, "what the healthy individual most needs at home is fresh air and daylight, whereas limited space will suffice. It is therefore not true that salvation lies in making rooms larger; the imperative is rather: put in bigger windows and economize on living space." The ideal home, then, would be a bench at the Zoo or a tree stump in the Grunewald forest?"[6]

With the gathering pace of the economic crisis in 1930 and the discontinuation of house-building subsidies in Berlin in 1931, the park bench rather than the *Großsiedlung* did indeed become a menacing option for the unemployed.

The backlash against a purely functionalist conception of mass housing, which was already gathering pace by 1930, found a natural support after 1933 in National Socialist ideology that damned modernist architecture and urbanism as Bolshevist, and favored instead housing that reflected the simple life on German soil, drawing heavily for its symbolism on vernacular models. In Berlin, this urge found quintessential expression in the SS-Kameradschaftssiedlung, built in Zehlendorf in 1937–39. Sited, with a certain irony, almost directly across the road from Taut's Onkel-Toms-Hütte development, this housing for the SS came straight from the pages of the Brothers Grimm, with high-pitched roofs, red tiles, and rustic shutters.

Housing for the broader population was not, however, a pressing issue for the National Socialist administration. Comparative statistics make this clear: while some 170,000 new dwellings were constructed in Berlin between 1925 and 1932, only 102,000 were built between 1933 and 1945. The various trade-union-based housing associations were consolidated into one institution, the Gemeinnützige Siedlungs- and Wohnungsbaugesellschaft [GSW]. There were grandiose plans in Albert Speer's scheme to transform Berlin into "Germania" to build large-scale estates on the southern and eastern edges of the city that would house around 650,000 people in total, and a further scheme to construct an estate at Charlottenburg-Nord for 20,000 residents. While foundation stones were actually laid at Charlottenburg, none of these schemes was implemented.

NOTES

1. Martin Wagner, quoted in Jörn Janssen, "Produktion und Konsum von Wohnungen sozialisieren?" in *Martin Wagner, 1885–1957,* exhibition catalogue (Berlin: Akademie der Künste, 1985), p. 27.
2. Martin Wagner, "Das sanitäre Grün der Städte" (doctoral dissertation, Technische Hochschule Berlin, 1915).
3. Fritz Neumeyer, "Nexus of the Modern: The New Architecture in Berlin," in *Berlin, 1900–1933: Architecture and Design,* ed. Tilmann Buddensieg (Berlin: Gebr. Mann, 1987), p. 74.
4. Siegfried Kracauer, *Das Ornament der Masse: Essays* (Frankfurt: Suhrkamp, 1977), p. 54.
5. Manfredo Tafuri, *Architecture and Utopia: Design and Capitalist Development* (Cambridge, Mass.: MIT Press, 1976), p. 117.
6. Adolf Behne, "Dammerstock," *Die Form: Zeitschrift für gestaltende Arbeit* 5 (1930), p. 164.

171

Fritz Schumacher

THE SMALL APARTMENT

First published as Schumacher, *Die Kleinwohnung: Studien zur Wohnungsfrage*, 2nd ed. (Leipzig: Quelle & Meyer, 1919), pp. 3-6. Translated by Michael Loughridge.

FOREWORD TO THE FIRST EDITION, DECEMBER 1916

Of all the cultural changes wrought by the Great War, one of the most profound may lie in the fact that among the broad mass of the people it wakened the idea and the dream of a decently civilized setting for their life at home.

The problem of how to reform the small apartment is one that we architects have been working on, quietly yet passionately, for a long time, for we see it as one of the key issues for the upward progress of our nation over the coming years; and now, at last, it has made the breakthrough to wider public awareness. In the past, concern for small-apartment design was widely regarded as a kind of architectural dilettantism, and aroused the same instinctive antipathy with which a broad swathe of our contemporaries respond to all our supposedly "patronizing" endeavors for the promotion of architectural understanding; but this burden of detraction has now been lifted from us. It is emerging more and more clearly that it is not architectural issues that are at stake here, but *social* issues pure and simple; in fact the focus is on identifying that point where due concern for the good of society must engage. All efforts to influence society for the better by persuasion alone fade into mere prattle when they are confronted by the stark realities of the actual environment that individuals have to live in.

There is no force with greater potency than the home to influence minds for the good or ill of society.

Discussion of housing matters tends to center on practical issues, which for evaluative purposes lend themselves fairly readily to eloquent statistics. Psychological factors, unfortunately, are beyond the reach of statistics, but that does not mean they are less important. Some of them impinge on questions of population; others on social and welfare policy. Considerations relating to the race issue on the one hand and to the whole question of social attitudes on the other become intertwined, so to speak, in the formulation of housing policy. Neither of these can be usefully tackled in isolation from the other: there has to be a broad approach.

Thus, while it seems simple and self-evident that we should call for healthy and civilized dwellings to be provided, fulfillment is a very different matter; just how difficult and complex in practice is known only to relatively few.

May this little publication help give insight into the thought processes of those striving to achieve such fulfillment. Ideas are only lightly sketched in, so that the broad outlines are not lost in the detail. For a deeper understanding, the reader will need to consult the books cited in the discussion below; but much can perhaps be communicated without the use of words, if he will give close attention to the pictorial studies that illustrate the present volume. The book is, after all, simply the reflection of practical work done.

FOREWORD TO THE SECOND EDITION, MAY 1919

At its second edition, this little book remains confronted by the same great tasks to whose solution the first edition attempted to contribute; but the background against which those tasks are seen is now a different one.

The human distress that prompted its call for action has grown. The dark shadow of housing scarcity, a threat appearing on the horizon when it was first written, now fills our entire sky. That does not come as a surprise, certainly; but on the other hand it was not envisaged that the battle against this phenomenon would be fought under remotely as severe a handicap as that which we are in fact experiencing: the lack of materials. It had indeed been anticipated that bricks would be scarce, but no one foresaw, surely, that the coal supply would collapse and thereby cripple the brick-making industry to the present extent.

As a direct result, the chapter dealing with alternative methods of building has assumed much greater importance. Much technical expertise and much enterprise has been invested in these new building methods, and while they will never entirely supplant bricks and mortar, they nevertheless represent a substantial enrichment of the construction options open to us. To the extent that the results of these endeavors can be adequately summarized after the sweeping conspectus afforded by the Berlin Exhibition, this has been achieved by the *Reichswohnungs-kommissar* [Reich Commissioner for Housing] in a clearly laid-out paper.[1]

Though new external circumstances have made the situation more difficult, there has also been a compensating change within: a new resolve. The unquenchable drive of our times toward complete social rebirth has greatly strengthened the resolve to persevere with all the new approaches that have been developed. Hardly any other problem has been as enthusiastically worked on as the housing situation.

The first tangible expression of this effort has taken the form of new legislation, though so far it has only provisional character—the most prominent measures having been the emergency legislation on relief from building-cost inflation and on the special rights of expropriation vested in the office of a "housing commissar." A number of other restrictions still being used recently to oppose building permissions have now likewise been swept away as part of the same process. This provisional legislation can reasonably be seen as the vanguard of a fundamental public-housing reform that will attend with proper seriousness to the imperatives arising from current land reform and will direct the state's financial resources on a planned and orderly basis toward coping with the housing problem. In towns and cities across the country, a practical start has been made, with various specific initiatives under way; many municipalities have committed themselves to housing projects indicative of their preparedness to accept real sacrifice.

One observes all this in the way one watches the thin line of light beginning to grow and gleam from the far horizon of a leaden sky. Hope begins to blossom, and the only thing that dampens the growing optimism is the fact that this long-awaited breakthrough of insight and readiness to act has come just at a time when expenditure of determination and effort is being so sadly frustrated by external circumstances—and the expenditure of money for given purposes increasing so alarmingly.

Notwithstanding all these retarding factors, one thing one can be observed with a certain satisfaction: all the circumstances averse to the building of smaller homes *as a general proposition* have tended to favor the *specific* sector involved with estates of small houses with gardens. The materials shortages constituting an insuperable obstacle to the construction of larger residential blocks can be circumvented in the case of small houses through the application of the new construction methods. In the current acute crisis, the problem of building quickly enough is leading to a concentration of interest on housing types in which the availability of garden ground means that the lengthy business of installing a sewage system can be dispensed with.

It is thus not only from passionate longing, but also as a practical response to the current urgent need, that such strong emphasis has been placed on the building of estates of small houses with their own gardens. The policy change this represents will require reform of current land legislation and changes to regional development planning if it is to establish itself firmly. Only in that way can the abnormal manifestations of an impulsively acting, excited, breathless transitional period develop into the solid achievements of a considered cultural policy. And only then will it become clear where the economic limit lies in individual cases—that is to say, the extent to which an ideal can be turned into reality. What we are witnessing at present in this area is sheer ferment, and cannot be treated as if it were a continuing state.

It can thus be said that the broad outlines of the thinking presented in this book have not so far been materially affected by the events we are living through. Of things that were tentatively envisaged, many have come closer to hand; and much that was still highly controversial even a short time ago is now beginning to appear self-evident; but our objective, taken as a whole, remains where it was.

That means it still lies ahead—and there will be many arduous stages to overcome before we can begin to get near it: reason enough to send this little book out into the world again.

NOTE

1. Reichs- und Preußischer Staatskommissar für das Wohnungswesen, "Druckschrift Nr. 2: Ersatzbauweisen" (Berlin: Wilh. Ernst & Sohn, 1919).

172

Kurt Tucholsky

150 KAISERALLEE

First published as "Kaiserallee 150," *Berliner Tageblatt,* 18 June 1920. Translated by Iain Boyd Whyte.

You're looking for an apartment? Just by chance I know of one—I deal with things like that now and then and make a little money on the side—yes, I know one. It's very well located, not exactly in the town center—one's happy to get anything. . . . But it's not too far out—no. It—the house that has the empty apartment—is on the borders of Wilmersdorf and Friedenau. In the Kaiserallee. Number 150 Kaiserallee.

You can already see the house as you approach from Kaiserplatz and go through the tunnel under the railway bridge. You can see from far off. It's a big, yellow-colored box—I won't make it out to be better than it is. It's completely simple and undecorated, and can't even boast any stuccowork. I hear that they build like this in England. But the English have no taste. I ask you: no stucco! That's why I admire the grand houses on the west side in Berlin. You know what you've got with them.

So the house is very simple, with only a couple of big trees at the front. But they don't spoil the view from the windows or make the rooms inside dark. I wouldn't recommend anything like that. You walk in—fine. It's the second-floor apartment on the right-hand side that's just become available. It will be free on 15 May; and I'll tell you why.

But first you'll want to know what sort of house you'll be moving into. You don't know me, of course, but you should; you should have heard of me and of my good reputation as a property agent. But first the house.

To the left on the ground floor lives the porter. The owner put him in this apartment rather than the damp cellar flat. He's a bookbinder, tinkers all day at his workbench, and looks after the front door. Go and ask him about the other occupants. I've already talked to him, and he's happy to help with details. (His apartment, happily, doesn't smell of lunch.)

Opposite, on the ground floor right, he said, lives a retired senior civil servant; a very progressive man, by all accounts. He would have nothing to do with the Kapp-Putsch, and removed the black-white-red flag that some urchin or other had hung at the window.[1] No, he hasn't got any children. He lives with his wife. They do a lot of good works.

A landed gentleman lives on the first floor. This is his city apartment. He doesn't get any food parcels from his estate—no, he gets his ration cards here in the city and eats only what he is entitled to.

On the other side of the first floor lives a Berlin theater director. He's always giving away free tickets to the others in the house, is always willing to talk to actors, and shares out the roles fairly and correctly. That's what the actors say.

Now, the porter doesn't know any more, but I can help you here. If you want to move in and are not averse to giving me the modest provision of 4 percent. But you don't want to do that, do you?

So: up until now the publisher of a not particularly salubrious weekly lived on the second floor. You can imagine, nakedness . . . and the like. (But don't worry, you won't see any of it in the apartment.) But at a certain point, he saw that it couldn't go on, and that it wasn't very chic to bring out things like that. So he gave it up and now lives in a little fourteen-room bungalow at the seaside . . . He was never suitable for the house.

That would be your empty apartment. A lovely, quiet, five-room flat, with bathroom and central heating. No really. It works. No, of course not now, but in the wintertime. I'll tell you about it when we talk about the house owner. The doors shut, the walls are so thick that you don't hear in one room what is being said in the next; the plumbing for the bath works, the tub is intact. It's that kind of apartment.

The landlord lives on the third floor. Yes, the landlord himself lives in the house. He's a Berlin landlord, or better, a Friedenau landlord, but in spite of that he did not put up the rents again, even though it would be allowed by the regulations. Nobody has ever phoned up the tenants' conciliation board. There's no need to. He happily makes all the necessary repairs, without any legal proceedings or grumbling. And he keeps the place warm, like in the good old days. Every quarter year he goes through the house, visiting the tenants, and asking if they are happy, and if anything is wanting . . .

On the fourth floor left lives a young widow (comfortably furnished). She does not want to marry again and is happy on her own. On the fourth floor right lives a young lady, an unmarried young lady. She's lived here for two years now in this house—but—and the porter can confirm this—she has never had a gentleman visitor. When she goes out at night, she returns alone by midnight at the latest. It's that sort of house.

So that's the tenants. Wait!

NOTE

1. Named after its nominal leader, the nationalist civil servant Wolfgang Kapp, the Kapp-Putsch was an uprising by elements of the German army under the command of General Walter von Lütt-

witz, who marched on Berlin on 13 March 1920 in protest against troop reductions. The putsch found no support among either the general population or the army high command, and it lasted for only a few days.

173

Bruno Taut

THE NEW HOME

Woman as Creative Spirit

First published as Taut, *Die neue Wohnung: Die Frau als Schöpferin* (Leipzig: Klinkhardt & Biermann, 1924), pp. 94–99, 101–2, 103–4. Translated by Michael Loughridge.

VI. THE IDEAL HOME

Pride of place does not go to any single attribute of the home, but to the combination of all its attributes. What has to be achieved is an organism that is the perfectly fitting shell of contemporary human beings (defined by their fruitful attributes) and that is in that sense akin to clothing—an extension of clothing, so to speak. The fruitfulness of human beings, their creativity—not only the creativity of the individual, emphatically that of the collective also—is to be found, as always, in their reshaping of things. In our times, the visible signs of this reshaping are all phenomena that in time past did not exist, or perhaps even quite recently did not exist—in other words, essentially the things created by modern industry. These things have changed the shape of our contemporary life, and they will change the shape of the home, too. This becomes clear when one looks at different means of transport—the motorcar, the airplane, the motorboat, the ocean liners, and the railways—or again when one really experiences the wonder of those inventions that brought a revolution and now belong to us for all time—of telegraph and telephone, radio communication, electricity, of all applications of mechanical power, including now the increased use of water and wind power, of the kitchen range, which uses the principle of the fireless cooker, of modern heating, and so on.

[...]

The ideal home, then, has as little connection with aesthetics as any of the abovementioned things; but also as much as any of these things. The same applies to all that is practical; this, too, either is not present at all or is there in a state of perfection, so that it is simultaneously more than practical—that is, aesthetic and ethical, too. In such an organically functioning system, housekeeping tasks are bound to become a joy instead of a burden. This is possible—because any work can become a joy if only it is capable of being structured coherently, so that its final outcome is implied in each individual subtask completed. How the outer shell acquires its shape from this has been described in the preceding chapters, and it follows that lightness, clarity, orderly layout, absence of clutter, absence of even the slightest museum feel, of stuffiness are prime necessities if the woman is to have joy in her work. Now she can structure her activity just as the man does in his professional work, and now she can become creative in how she goes about it. What eminent tasks lie waiting for her to take on, even in tidying—not just in the practical side of it, but in the mental and emotional sphere—has likewise been discussed.

The practical and the aesthetic as a unity: hence the ideal home flawlessly beautiful. A shell for the human being, his protection, the vessel for his first and last thoughts, words, and actions, his "nest." It has taken on a new shape, the tangible form of this nest, a shape quite different from the bowery fantasies that the last fifty years have been building around the nest metaphor. No sentimentality here, no trace of romantic idyll, no dreamy haze, any more than you find these things in the turbine hall and control room of the power station, but different again, and shaped in combination with the intimacy of utterly private, individual human life; the dream in it as an expansion of inwardly felt, still insufficient clarity, the shell, which is the "four walls," so simple, but at the same time so unbanal, so far removed from the merely schematic in color and material, that it expands the dream, the vision of the future, and by that dream is in return itself expanded.

After all that has been said here, it is superfluous to describe the best and most attractive way to arrange the different rooms and the furniture; how we can do this better than before is something that in essence we know already, and at the real beginning, when the woman starts to become creative, the ideal will take on ever-clearer outlines, and one will be able to select the very best from all homes that have been created, so as to form it into this ideal, combining clarity of form and everyday practicality for living. To portray the ideal itself now, today, would be to preempt this creative process, to tie the woman's hands once more and limit her to doing mere men's work.

[. . .]

For the ideal of the home, however, there is perfect slogan: Woman as Creator.

[. . .]

The woman's contribution will become a constructive one; she gets rid of anything that hampers the assembly process, and with what remains she puts together the brand-new apartment—the reconstructed home.

[. . .]

VII. THE NEW WAY OF HOUSE BUILDING

The man will now be able to build the new type of house only once his path, too, has been cleared for him by the freeing of the woman. His freedom, mobility, and willingness to set off on the new path long since prepared and waiting will be a consequence of the freeing of the woman—for every form of enslavement drags in those who outwardly seem not to be its victims. Once the last mouse finds no hiding place left in the living room, once the musty feel has been cleared out, once people have stopped dressing the windows, the lamps, the tables in little skirts and petticoats, the time will have come when more can be demanded from the house itself.

[...]

One might, for instance, model house-building methods on motorcar manufacture. First of all, top-quality raw materials, scrupulously selected on criteria of durability and lightness, then the experimental assembly of these elements in as rational a manner as possible to make test houses, which are then studied and modified at length until the optimum house in terms of appearance, of practical convenience, and of ease of construction has been achieved. A specified period would have to be reserved for this purpose. It is obvious enough that the drawing-board stage of design would have less importance than hitherto; it would still provide a starting point in various respects, but the real decisions would stem from the practical experiments—that is to say, from experience gained by actually living in specific house types undergoing repeated modification, right up to the point when the individual components, rationalized into a small number of standard parts, can be sent to the factories for mass production. Then the houses are delivered in sections and quickly assembled on-site.

[...]

House building will from now on be home building as well, the two fusing into a unity such as we have not yet experienced; for what the new occupants will bring along with them is reduced now to nothing more than their own life and its movable trappings. It has already been mentioned that the content of these lives of theirs can now become much richer and more individualized; for only where there is freedom from clutter can the personality fully unfold. The concepts of individualism and collectivism are transcended in the higher synthesis, in the natural and real unity of man and woman.

As this book has insisted throughout, the woman will be the prime creator: for she has to *start with herself* and catch up to the point that the man generally has reached, in terms of how he organizes his life, through his work in the office, the factory, in all professions allowing a light and nimble spirit.

And so in the end the woman, creator of the home, can also become the creator of the house, and it can be approvingly and joyfully proclaimed:

Der Architekt denkt
Die Hausfrau lenkt.

[The architect proposes
The housewife directs.]

174

Martin Wagner

VIENNA—BERLIN

Housing Policies Compared

First published as "Wien—Berlin. Ein wohnpolitischer Vergleich," *Wohnungswirtschaft* 2, no. 9 (1 May 1925), pp. 69–71. Translated by Michael Loughridge.

The two capital cities of Vienna and Berlin currently face housing shortages of roughly equal dimensions. In Vienna, a city of about 2 million inhabitants, a count has revealed 105,000 homeless and about 25,000 needing to be placed urgently. In Berlin, a city of 4 million, about 250,000 were registered as homeless. For the number requiring urgent rehousing, a figure of 50,000 would probably not be too low. The question then is: what kind of construction program have the two cities put in place in order to combat this housing crisis?

Let us first consider the case of Vienna. In this city, governed by a Socialist majority, building activity remained negligible after the war, right up to the final days of the Austrian monarchy. In the five years from 1919 to 1923, only about five thousand new homes were built in total. However, at the end of 1923 the Vienna city fathers were galvanized into action: on 21 December that year (almost the precise moment at which our German mark reached its nadir value), they resolved that in the next five years the city would put up five thousand new housing units annually, part in the form of apartment blocks, part in new residential estates, and would earmark the annual sum of 24 million gold marks, for expenditure on this project, in the advance financial planning. This was action of a kind only now being timidly—and quite inadequately—imitated in a number of German cities.

What were the principles on which Vienna undertook to carry through this construction program? Much though we admire the daring and the generous liberality of the Vienna city fathers, we cannot but deplore, on social as well as economic grounds, the fact that Vienna based its entire construction program almost exclusively on the use of tall buildings comprising five or six stories. On the other hand, it has to be conceded that local conditions in Vienna did tend to favor the erection of tall buildings—the city having at its disposal, in comparison with Berlin, very much less expansion land with preexisting transport infrastructure, and hence much less scope for low-rise development. Several further factors were also relevant. The political differences between Vienna and the Austrian state, with its bourgeois regime, had inhibited city expansion; the state was unable to provide capital for any substantial expansion into the wider environs, for which transport links would have been crucial; and transport policy generally in Vienna had been far from exemplary even before the war.

Given, then, that these considerations impose outer limits on the low-rise housing plans that Vienna can entertain, the city has made a virtue of necessity by focusing its program initially on the construction of hygienically designed small and ultrasmall apartments, of floor area ranging from 20 square meters up to an absolute maximum of 70 square meters. The smallest apartments (20 square meters), the so-called Garçon-Stüberl [bachelor lodgings], are aimed at single people, bachelors, and widows, and consist of one room with the requisite adjoining cubbyhole, a small scullery with sink, and so on. Larger flats generally have two or three fair-sized rooms, and these are distributed to the most urgent rehousing cases according to size of family.

The acquisition of the building land was carried out on the amplest scale. The city chose not to build on such individual vacant sites as were available, because these seldom permit new construction that can be regarded as satisfactory either architecturally or from a public health point of view. Instead, it has bought up, to date, 7 million square meters of new building land, so that the public monies can at least be invested in exemplary fashion, in the form of large residential complexes designed in conformity with the very latest design thinking. The purchase very neatly exploited the contemporary slump in property values, securing exceptionally cheap building land for the benefit of the community.

[...]

While we have expressed regret above that the City of Vienna switched from low-rise development to high-rise, thereby increasing the number of tenement blocks, it must also be pointed out that the new blocks are high-rise development of an unusual kind. At ground-floor level the large residential complexes have cooperative stores, even meeting rooms, and in one or two instances a library is provided. At attic level there are spacious work areas. The central courtyard areas surrounded by the blocks have been attractively laid out with lawns and ornamental fountains. There are children's playgrounds, complete with paddling pools. As regards furnishings and equipment, the buildings have some admirable features unknown in the old private-landlord tenement blocks. Here, the larger apartments have parquet floors. On the communal landings, cupboards give access to gas and electricity meters for each flat, so that the meter reader no longer needs to be admitted to the flat (this arrangement is already found in the United States). Drying lofts are generally not provided. Instead, housewives can make use of laundry rooms equipped with washing machines and special drying chambers that require only five minutes to dry washing mechanically. If the weekly wash for a family of five begins at seven in the morning, every item will be back in the apartment, ready for ironing, by two o'clock the same afternoon. Each residential block also has a generous-size set of baths with modern facilities.

As already said, the Vienna policy of preferring multistory buildings is not what we would regard as a good example to follow. Yet it is impossible not to admire the generous scale of the building program itself. What does the city of Berlin have to offer in comparison? In order to bring out the difference in approach as clearly as possible, we have set out individual program items in tabular form as follows:

VIENNA	BERLIN
1. An annual construction program of 5,000 units (exceeded by a margin of 1,000 in year 1 and 5,000 in year 2).	1. Berlin vaunts itself on having financed a 10,000-unit construction program. But this "finance" exists only on paper.
2. Continuity in the construction program, enabling the housing market to adjust accordingly and giving the homeless real prospects.	2. Building program is approved for one year ahead and not counted as having been "drawn up" until the private firms and housing associations have implemented it or are at least in a position to implement it. For 1925, to date (today is 23 April 1925), no program has yet been drawn up.
3. Priority for the most urgent cases, with special provision for the financially needy.	3. Most residential construction financed by the City of Berlin is for those in less urgent need of rehousing, who are able to source 50 percent or more of the funding themselves or through third parties.
4. The residential construction program is financed 100 percent by the city.	4. The problem of financing home building is left by the city to wealthy individuals.
5. City authorities influence the urban-planning and aesthetic aspects of the housing blocks, also the standard of the fitting out of the apartments.	5. Public monies are squandered on a host of separate small and minuscule construction projects; no planning control is exercised, and nothing is done to further the modernization of the home.
6. Rent levels are based strictly on those of older buildings and on tenants' ability to pay.	6. It is left to private developers to fix rents, with the result that in some cases tenants of new buildings are being asked to pay 2 to 3 times the prewar figure.

7. Vienna buys up building land in order to keep it in public ownership and to build up assets for the community.	7. Berlin buys up building land in order to pass it on to private capital to milk the resulting property income in perpetuity.
8. The civic administration has influence on the construction prices charged by developers and building supplies manufacturers.	8. Enlargement of private-capital profits in the construction and building supply trades by policy of total nonintervention though central civic resourcing to the tune of approximately 50 million gold marks per annum could have a decisive bearing on prices even in Berlin.
9. Substantial enhancement of resources by using general taxation to supplement the yield from the residential construction levy.	9. Very modest subsidizing of residential construction aimed at helping the less well off, raised from general taxation.

It cannot be validly objected that the City of Berlin's housing policy is tied to the laws, statutes, and regulations of the German Reich and of the State of Prussia. It is true, certainly, that the City of Berlin is not entitled to put all the money it receives from rent tax into the provision of new housing: it has to pass on half to the state for general purposes, and of the other half a large part has to be handed over to the equalization fund. But similar restrictions were imposed on the City of Vienna by the Austrian state, which can hardly be regarded as well disposed toward a Socialist city corporation. However, for the purposes of our comparison, let us not fall out over details. What matters is the *generous spirit* in which the City of Vienna has tackled the housing problem, and of which in Berlin barely a trace is to be found—even though the City of Berlin likewise had a Socialist majority, retained a Socialist council long after this majority had disappeared, and to this very day, with the council majority gone, too, has a Socialist as director of housing policy. But we have heard nothing to indicate that the Housing Department has made any serous attempt to draw up a long-term program for the provision of new housing, and there is even reason to suppose that this department has not felt it necessary to study the Vienna residential construction program, although over a year has passed since it appeared.

175

Ludwig Hilberseimer

ON STANDARDIZING THE TENEMENT BLOCK

First published as "Über die Typisierung des Mietshauses," *Die Form*, 1926, pp. 338–40. Translated by Michael Loughridge.

The existing city tenement block is a failed hybrid between private home and military barracks. It recalls the private home in its attempt to catch the eye by special emphasis on the facade, and in its attempt to make a "highly individual finish" suggest a semblance of real individual life. It recalls the barracks in its unbendingly schematic layout, especially as regards the ground plan and the articulation of the housing blocks.

Those currently opposing a consistent program of standardization tend to miss the point that the existing tenement block is not standardized, but rigidly schematic in design. Ground plans of comparable tenement flats are as alike as peas in the pod. Why? Because the layout is determined by the unbridled greed of speculative developers sucking the last drop of value from the likewise equal-sized parcels of ground. These ambitions came up against strict boundaries in the form of the building regulations, limits that could not be exceeded, but that were exploited to the full. And so, necessarily, the same circumstances produced the same result. Following changes to the building regulations, a new ground-plan schema for tenements emerged, the result of the same forces—and in fulfillment of the requirements that have to be observed.

Ground plans arrived at in this way are always the result of the speculative impulse of developers, modified by the building regulations. The individuals who will live in the place are in nobody's mind. In any case, given the current housing shortage, they can have no influence whatever on how the apartment is designed. They have to be thankful to get one in the first place. The idea of choice will hardly even occur to them.

Where this purely schematic approach to design ignores the needs of the users, proper standardization must take precisely those needs as its starting point. The endeavor to standardize is not a way of schematizing design but of perfecting it and reducing costs. The apartment itself should offer real comfort and irreproachable hygiene at minimum expense. The number and size of the rooms is determined by the requirements that are genuinely essential. Rooms are needed for living, eating, sleeping, washing, and cooking, and the function of the ground plan is to group and organize these. The smallest apartments demand particular care at the design stage—as, regrettably, this is where financial limitations are most severe. The unstructured nature of the usual minimum-size apartment obliges those living in it to use all the rooms for sleeping in, which means that there is no true living room and dining room. Consequently all meals have to be taken in the kitchen, in spite of the bad air caused by the cooking. However, if the designer organizes the available living space in the light of actual requirements, and restricts room size to what is really needed, an apartment layout can be devised that always fulfills the basic requirements.

The ground-plan system illustrated here represents an attempt to meet the domestic requirements of families of different sizes. The aim is to standardize room sizes while maintaining consistent allocation of space by function. This is because standardization will in future have to extend beyond individual construction details to embrace spatial units. The floor-plan variants for three, four, five, six, and seven occupants are all based on the same spatial elements and satisfy the corresponding functional requirements. The basic constituents are entrance lobby, loggia, kitchen, bathroom, double and single bedrooms, and these recur as standard in all sizes of apartment. Only the largest room, the living-and-dining room, increases in size in relation to the number of occupants.

In the second design illustrated, which has three apartments per staircase, the same standardization of rooms is applied for, respectively, two-, four-, and six-person apartments, and in fact carried further, as in view of the severe limitation of space, the main living room is the same size as a double bedroom, which when partitioned creates two small single bedrooms. Thus, disregarding entrance lobby, kitchen, and bathroom, there are only two standard room sizes, but these offer every kind of permutation of use.

A prerequisite for this economically efficient standardizing of apartments is that all storage for clothing, linen, boxes and trunks, crockery, and so on and all kitchen equipment should also be built in as standard. When space is extremely limited, it can no longer be possible, as it used to be, to leave matters to chance. For the same expenditure that formerly went on creating free space, one can have everything that is necessary built in, so that in the future the only freestanding furniture items that need to be thought about will be beds, tables, chairs, and other seating.

With the elimination of the ornamental furnishing items that currently clutter our apartments, even the smallest units will become much more spacious, so that a modern apartment of limited overall size will actually have much more usable floor space than a larger traditional one. This will result in full attention being focused once more on the few remaining items of movable furniture. Through being few in number, these will gain in significance, and their usefulness and worth will be recognized and appreciated once more.

176

Leo Adler

HOUSING ESTATES IN THE BRITZ DISTRICT OF BERLIN

First published as "Siedlungen in Berlin-Britz," *Wasmuths Monatshefte für Baukunst* 11, no. 10 (1927), pp. 385–90. Translated by Michael Loughridge.

Two of the biggest housing developments in Greater Berlin are the two in progress at Britz, one for the Deutsche Gesellschaft zur Förderung des Wohnungsbaues [German Society for the Promotion of Homebuilding] and the other for the Gemeinnützige Heimstätten A.G. (GEHAG) [Homes for the Community Ltd.]. The former scheme, the earlier of the two, was initiated by the now deceased architect Engelmann and is being completed currently by Fangmeyer; the GEHAG development was begun by Taut and Wagner in 1926, and work is still in progress. The older estate comprises 892 homes, the more recent one 520 in six-family units and 480 in individual dwellings. The two estates are contiguous, the boundary between them being the "Grüner Ring" [Green Ring]. This proximity greatly facilitates comparison.

The heart of the whole complex is the horseshoe-shaped grouping of buildings in the center. Although of spacious dimensions, this horseshoe—it surrounds an artificial lake with sloping banks and three terrace levels going up to the line of houses—is rather marred by an overobtrusive color scheme. On the inside of the circle the color effect (white plaster facades with colored balcony loggia) does not break up the wall areas themselves, but on the outer facades the blue used for the attic wall is extended in vertical strips right down to the (much narrower) entrance doors, and the effect of this whim is to mislead the eye as to the internal structure, the left-hand half of each building appearing to form a unit with the right-hand half of its neighbor, and vice versa.

But Taut's willfulness with color—conspicuous also in the Weißenhof estate in Stuttgart—goes further. Gable elevations in some cases have a color scheme involving dark red for the larger area up to the chimney, white for the smaller area, and pale yellow for the building itself.

[...]

The horizontal slabs, presumably intended to afford some protection from the elements, are hard to justify in practical terms. As they have no guttering and are dead level, snow will lie on them until it thaws and the meltwater runs off—directly onto the "protected" steps, on which one might feel it never rains but it pours. The moisture penetrates the layers of plaster finish in the immediate area and destroys them promptly and completely—as was observed in the very first winter, 1926–27. [...] Certainly, any lingering emotional attachment to tradition has received short shrift. "Unfortunately, despite all the lip service paid to rationaliza-

FIGURE 39. Großsiedlung Britz (Horseshoe Estate) (1925–31; Bruno Taut and Martin Wagner, architects) from the air, c. 1931. Bundesministerium für Arbeit und Soziales.

tion, it has to be acknowledged as a fact that rational judgment still continues in far too many instances to be swayed and overruled by maudlin emotion . . . " Are we to take Bruno Taut's comment as applying only to emotional attachment to tradition—or could "emotion" conceivably also be directed *against* tradition?

[. . .]

In all issues of building engineering proper, however, reason must rule. The design of the dormer structures creates a series of snow traps and is as indefensible as the substandard quality of the plasterwork, in which the grossly excessive roughness of the finish invites destruction by damp and frost [. . .]. To return to the more general issue, however: technology and rational judgment alone do not suffice to create art; we can safely assume the horseshoe with its axial link eastward and the school as focus, when they found their way onto Taut and Wagner's blueprints, were the expression of a (most welcome!) *feeling* for effect in urban design, in exactly the same way that the so-called objectivity tirelessly extolled in spoken and written word is in fact a delusion on the part of those who proclaim it. Or again, the series of little windows, like beads on a string, in the stairwell towers of the blood-red terrace have the air of a stealthy piece of *ornamentation*—introduced for emotional reasons. It would not be easy to make a rational case for introducing

FIGURE 40. Dörchläuchtingstrasse, Großsiedlung Britz (Horseshoe Estate) (1925–31; Bruno Taut and Martin Wagner, architects), 1926. Landesarchiv Berlin, 271 578.

them: there is more glazier and bricklayer labor involved than with ordinary windows, which means higher costs; the apertures are placed at landing level, causing dazzle to people ascending the stairs. Moreover, they evoke the spirit of the gallant Knight von Behne even more than would a diagonally hung carpet.[1] As one walks past, one instinctively flinches at the thought of a hail of missiles hurled from the apertures in the crenellated "keeps" at roof level . . . This development on the periphery does not accord the residential blocks the "modest status" that Taut's own words declared to be "appropriate" for them; rather, it is reminiscent of Behne's characterization of the "tenement block as last surviving medieval castle."

NOTE

1. The Knight von Behne: the critic Adolf Behne.

177

Walter Gropius

LARGE HOUSING ESTATES

First published as "Großsiedlungen," *Zentralblatt der Bauverwaltung* 50, no. 12 (1930), pp. 233–40. Translated by Michael Loughridge.

The *basic requirements* for the general planning of a large residential development are: *daylight, fresh air, sunshine; tranquillity; limited population density; good ac-*

cessibility; rationally designed, convenient apartment interiors; pleasant overall ambience.

Daylight, fresh air, and sunshine: The best of the available block layout patterns with respect to daylight and insulation, taking account also of all economic and other hygienic considerations, is probably linear planning [*Zeilenbau*] aligned north–south, provided that lateral separation of the individual blocks is adequate. Linear planning has several indisputable advantages, compared with perimeter block designs, in that all apartments have equal exposure to sunlight, air flow between the buildings is not impeded by transverse blocks, and ill-ventilated corner apartments are done away with. The design sketches presented here employ north-and-south-aligned exclusively.

Tranquillity: Linear planning makes it possible to take *motor roads* at right angles past the ends of the residential blocks, while the blocks themselves are served only by *access footpaths* reserved for pedestrians—a measure that not only reduces the estate's road-building and access costs, but ensures the all-important quality of tranquillity for the residents by keeping away the dust, noise, and fumes generated by motor vehicles. The estate's own (business) traffic flow is planned strictly on the same principles—that is, on an east–west axis past the block ends. In addition, grassed areas have been provided that separate the roadways from the block ends and function as *noise insulation zones* for the blocks closest to the roads, and are also used to create individual gardens for single-family houses. At no point are the east–west-aligned *estate roads* allowed to feed directly into the public roads system (main routes), which ensures that the estate remains completely undisturbed by through traffic. Instead, the estate roads terminate at one end in a *feeder road* that follows a line along—but not too close to—one periphery of the estate, running parallel to the S-Bahn [urban railway] line and eventually giving direct access to the *regional road network*.

As commercial enterprises and other facilities liable to generate noise have been placed in relatively isolated positions, schools and school playgrounds likewise, there is good reason overall for the residential areas to enjoy exceptional tranquillity. Existing woodland was also largely left intact and will provide further welcome muffling of noise.

Limited population density: The worst slums in the cities have their origin in unscrupulous land development. The *building regulations* of recent decades are evidence that, in parallel with the increase in knowledge, there has been a steady improvement in regulatory control over this most basic of problems in housing. The civic authorities are charged with imposing limitations to commercial exploitation of residential building land to the extent necessary to safeguard public health. The architect setting about designing a large housing estate from scratch has the task of finding the just balance between, on the one hand, the financial demands imposed by the land price and by costs for the requisite road building, services installations, and any local terrain problems—and, on the other, the equally pressing need for space, so that the residential suburb to be created will enjoy healthy and reasonably uncrowded conditions. A crude arithmetical approach to land use, with densities planned to the statutory maximum, can lead to dangerous planning failures that in any case would come home to roost in financial terms once the housing crisis is finally over. The crucial point is the total rental income needed for solvency, calculated from the sum of costs arising from land purchase, development, construction, and financing. Where land in outlying parts is still cheap—that is, will not impose excessive upward pressure on rentals—it is essential to space residential areas out, setting buildings farther apart and reserving green spaces, so as to create salubrious environments that will continue in the long term to be perceived as offering a satisfactory quality of life.

[. . .]

Pleasant overall ambience: In the writer's opinion, consistent adherence to the linear planning system and the resulting orderly alignment and recurrence of the single units and blocks, logical consequences of the policy of ensuring that each resident enjoys equal amenity, also ensure that the estate is impressive architecturally and as an example of urban design. The natural accidents of terrain, the way it is accommodated in the design, the spacing generated by the thoroughfares, the interspersing of trees and other vegetation among the buildings to open and close the sightlines—all these features generate agreeable contrast, relax and enliven the grid plan, mediate between buildings and humans, create dialogue, and lend scale. For architecture emphatically does not begin and end with its functional value, with mere fulfillment of a purpose—unless it be that our psychological need for a harmonious living environment, and for symmetry and proportion in the structures without which our senses could not perceive space, is the manifestation in all of us of function and purpose at a higher level.

178

Werner Hegemann

BERLIN AND WORLD ARCHITECTURE

On the Berlin Building Exhibition

First published as "Berlin und die internationale Baukunst: Zur Berliner Bau-Ausstellung," *Der Querschnitt* 5 (1931), pp. 301ff; reprinted in *Berlin im "Querschnitt,"* ed. Rolf-Peter Baacke (Berlin: Fannei & Walz, 1990), pp. 167–71. Translated by Michael Loughridge.

The impish calumny that architecture is "frozen music" was probably invented by the depressed wife of an architect, her resentment over her hardworking husband's profession made acute by malaise following from overindulgence in ice cream. The lady's "frozen music" can still occasionally bring on queasy feelings.

But many of Berlin's buildings are reminiscent of the works of art that skilled confectioners conjured up out of iced products and sent in to grace the banqueting table. Similarly, the Baroque masterpieces (such as the Zwinger in Dresden) recall extravagant birthday cakes and their icing; and the showpieces of religious Gothic are fantasy versions of those high *Baumkuchen* cakes.[1] But in Berlin today, as was the case 120 years ago, the most sought-after architectural ideal is moving back toward much simpler and smoother outlines than those that still live on among confectioners. Architectural styles go in and out of fashion like clothes. Indeed, some of them are already being created in the capital—Berlin is truly coming on!—whereas earlier they used to be imported almost on a regular basis from Frankfurt, Vienna, or Munich. Frederick the Great imported them from all over the world—Italy, France, Britain, China, and in particular from Dresden and Vienna. Only in the age of Schinkel did Berlin itself for a while lead the field in architectural design.[2]

At the moment, serious thought is being given in Berlin to the idea of—at long last—brushing down the Reichstag building and the cathedral to remove all the "ice sculptures" and curlicues reminiscent of the confectioner's art. The aim is to return these two significant buildings, standing respectively at the western and eastern ends of Unter den Linden, to a state of fitness for daily use. Conservative and Liberal politicians, speaking with one voice or in mutual contradiction, see much promise in this timely metamorphosis. These farsighted individuals realize that once the Reichstag and the St. Pauli church are again available for daily use, both parliamentarism and religion will become modern again, and the threat of dictatorship, along with peril from the godless, will have been vanquished once more. The influence of architecture as mother of the plastic arts and of the unremunerative arts can never be overstated.

Berlin also has conscientious artists, however—artists who are not prepared to switch their artistic convictions year by year as fashions change. It is not only the reactionaries who hold fast to the old conviction that architectural forms derive naturally and inevitably from the material used and the building. The name given to this is still *Neue Sachlichkeit* [new objectivity].

The new protagonists of this age-old and perennially new, true objectivity—for example, the brothers Luckhardt[3]—actually deplore the practice of taking the hammer to the old decorations and wedding-cake confections, as is now being done with so many buildings in Berlin. The effect is to make these old masonry buildings look like modern constructions in steel or concrete. But as the old buildings lose none of their old heaviness, they can never attain the almost airborne lightness and elegance with which the modern steel and concrete buildings bring delight to modern hearts. Conversely, steel-skeleton buildings never quite lose their innate lightness even when perversely subjected to cladding with stone blocks and made over to look like old masonry buildings. For many observers, it in fact took the three-dimensionality of these stone blocks to make the ponderous solidity of the old stone buildings tolerable. And the sculptings with which Gothic architecture, German rococo architecture, and Berlin's Wilhelminian period so lavishly bestrewed their buildings were divinely sanctioned necessities, sacrosanct, not to be touched by impious human hand. That at least is the view of the most devoted adherents of modern architecture. They fear for the future development of steel-frame architecture: that it will suffer by association when people begin, as they soon will, to get bored with the gaunt boxes that can so easily result from reworking massively heavy masonry buildings to simulate light constructions in steel and concrete—never a completely successful operation.

In a building made of stone, the load-bearing piers have to be at least forty centimeters thick, or the whole heap of rock will fall in. By contrast, a modern steel-frame building can have columns a mere twelve centimeters thick. It has better springing than an interior-spring mattress, or a tennis racquet. Its walls are not called on to bear loads; they are simply a lightweight and highly effective barrier excluding wet, cold, and noise. The steel skeleton is mantled around by the heat engineer, just as in times past the old half-timbered houses had their wall infill added once the frame was complete. But the material the modern architect has at his disposal for the purpose is very much more efficient than brick.

For the external finish of a building, too, there are now materials available that are much more durable and much cleaner than plaster or brick. Erich Mendelsohn,[4] in other ways such a modernist, loves to clad his buildings in the good old fashion with travertine slabs, which have holes like cheese and can trap water and dirt. But the Telschow building at Potsdamer Platz—put up only recently by the Luckhardt architects and shortly to be demolished again because of the impending reconstruction of the square—is already clad with cloudy opal glass panels, so smooth that every half-decent thundershower washes them clean.

The Luckhardt brothers are the authors of the authoritative and superbly illustrated volume entitled *Zur neuen Wohnform* [the modern home]. In their elegant new villas in Dahlem and on the Heerstrasse, the Luckhardts are working with such ideas as glazed tiles on window surrounds, and for plinth cladding, huge, easily opened plate-glass windows, the palest of colors, and encaustic wall treatments, which were all the rage in ancient Pompeii. If as a result of our modern technology these new methods catch on and can be made economic, we will at long last see our Romantics' visions of the South taking on tangible form here amid our gray northern gloom. Improved urban planning will put the detached home with garden within the reach of many. House and garden will flow into one another. The dingy appearance of our gray-clad cities will be banished by the new self-cleaning walls and the glowing colors of the new architecture.

Berlin's modern architecture has been accused not only of lacking local pedigree and not being a purely Berlin-bred product, but of being an unpatriotic, international affair. This objection applies to every one of our great eras in architecture. The most purely Germanic period in architecture was probably that of the so-called Romanesque. But Romanesque architecture is not convincingly represented anywhere in Berlin. Even the Romanische Café [Romanesque Café] is only half in a true Wilhelminian and German style; the other half, like its customers, is international in character. Gothic architecture, too, was international. We learned it from France, and perhaps to some small extent from Persia. This is why people are so fond of calling it quintessentially German. But it was in later centuries that our architecture really became an international affair. Schinkel's predilection for flat roofs, too, is derived from southern lands. The architecture that is modern in Berlin today is criticized, then, on the grounds that it was actually invented by Otto Wagner in Vienna, by [Henry] Van der Velde in Holland, and [Auguste] Perret and Le Corbusier in Paris. But such criticisms are myopic. What modern architecture really amounts to is an international concert—albeit without music—in which the Reich Germans have long been playing first violin, and in which the Berliners, too, have no cause to be ashamed of their contribution. For many foreigners, especially those living in Britain, Scandinavia, and the United States, the very concept of modern architecture is currently much more strongly associated with Germany than, for example, with France. The notorious 1925 Exhibition of Arts, Crafts, and Architecture in Paris spawned various pieces of architecture of almost as depressing a standard as the World Exhibition in 1900 in Paris.

The Berlin Building Exhibition is currently on. Although explicitly devoted to "the architecture of the future," and constituting a particularly important step forward for modern international architecture, the exhibition can quite appropriately term itself "Exhibition of German Building," so strongly has the coming style of architecture taken on German identity. No attentive observer of the battles being fought among German architects at present can fail to see that even the more conservative and the most radical of the combatants have a shared vision. Even Schultze-Naumburg,[5] a conservative and the protégé of Frick,[6] the Thuringian ex-minister, has in his time made an important contribution to the contemporary process of cleaning up our architectural styles and our urban design in general; to say nothing of such fine but cautious artists as [Alfred] Messel or [Paul] Bonatz or [Paul] Schmitthenner. If innovation and daring are looked for, many of the leading spirits in the modern movement are currently working in Berlin; apart from the formidable younger grouping—of whom Luckhardt and Erich Mendelsohn were mentioned above—there are also sixty-year-olds such as Peter Behrens, who is collaborating with City Architect Wagner to give Alexanderplatz its astonishing new face, and Hans Poelzig, designer of the new broadcasting building and jointly responsible with Wagner for the new exhibition buildings.

Architecture is not music, whether frozen or thawed. And modern architecture is most emphatically not modern *atonal* music. Goethe once described architecture as "silent music." Today it looks as if music has exhausted the expressive potential of the traditional scales. It will have to fall silent or have recourse to new scales and new laws of harmony. But within the known laws of architecture, in complete contrast, there is still vast potential remaining to be explored. Construction in steel is barely a century old; in concrete, much younger still. We are not nearly at the limits of what can be achieved here. The same applies with regard to urban planning. In Berlin in particular, realization is only now dawning of what the new developments in transport could mean for the urban planning of the future. People are beginning to appreciate just how efficient and how agreeable our modern means of transport can be. At the same time, we must not be so shortsighted as to hide our transport links in ruinously expensive tunnels, bankrupting the city: they must be designed as graceful elevated railways, or—still more cheaply and effectively—as overhead monorails passing clear over the congested traffic of the city streets. Then, at last, vast outlying tracts of the metropolis can be opened up, and land for houses and gardens offered cheaply to all. Accommodating people in vast urban barracks will at last have become a thing of the past.

At the "German Building Exhibition," which from May to August will attract hundreds of thousands of visitors to the area around the Funkturm [radio tower], one of the most important sections is the first one, the "International Exhibition of Urban Planning and Housing." It will be the first major urban-design exhibition to have been held in Berlin since 1910. It will open the eyes of innumerable people to the fact that the Berlin system of housing people in barrackslike tenements has had its day. The current trend to decentralization in city planning means only very limited areas need be assigned to high-rise business use, and fairly modest areas for hotels and luxury apartment blocks. Modern transport facilities and, above all, the dispersal of industry—which is necessary in any case for economic reasons—will enable our cities to become more open in character, and will give hundreds of thousands of ordinary people the chance to live in elegant low-rise houses combining all the modern conveniences of the city with the pleasures of rural life.

NOTES

1. *Baumkuchen*—literally "tree cakes"—are baked on a horizontal spindle, with the dough drip-fed and baked as the cake rotates past a grill. The result is a circular cake with an irregular profile and a hole through its center, which is then covered in chocolate.

2. Karl Friedrich Schinkel (1781–1841), one of the most significant European architects of his generation, was responsible for the remodeling of Berlin in the early nineteenth century and for many of the most important buildings in the city center.

3. The brothers Hans (1890–1954) and Wassili (1889–1972) Luckhardt were leading modernist architects in Berlin, responsible for radical "Neues Bauen" housing in the 1920s and larger housing projects and public buildings into the 1950s. Like many of their modernist contemporaries, Hans and Wassili Luckhardt also designed furniture.

4. Erich Mendelsohn (1887–1953) enjoyed great eminence in Berlin in the 1920s as the architect of the iconic Einstein Tower in Potsdam (1919–1921) and as the designer of dynamic, modernist commercial buildings. Exiled in 1933, he emigrated via England (where he had a group practice with Serge Chermayeff) to Palestine, and from there to the United States, where he both taught and practiced as an architect.

5. Paul Schultze-Naumburg (1869–1949), architect, teacher, and writer, first came to prominence with a series of reforming tracts published between 1902 and 1917 under the general title *Kulturarbeiten*. In the 1920s he published vigorously antimodernist, pro–National Socialist tracts on art and aesthetics. In the Berlin context, his best-known work is the Cecilienhof, built in Potsdam in 1913–17 in the English neo-Tudor style and used for the Potsdam Conference in July and August 1945.

6. In 1930 Wilhelm Frick became the first National Socialist minister in a provincial government when he was appointed Minister of the Interior in Thuringia. In this role he appointed Paul Schultze-Naumburg (see above) as director of the Building School in Weimar and polemicized against the Bauhaus. When the Nazis came to national power in 1933, he was appointed Minister of the Interior and held this post until August 1943, when he was appointed Protector of Bohemia and Moravia until the German defeat in 1945. He was executed at Nuremberg on 16 October 1946.

179
Martin Wagner
ADMINISTRATIVE REFORM

First published as "Verwaltungsreform" in Ausstellungs-, Messe- und Fremdenverkehrsamt der Stadt Berlin, *Deutsche Bauausstellung Berlin 1931: Amtlicher Katalog und Führer* (Berlin: Bauwelt/Ullstein, 1931), pp. 113–14. Translated by Michael Loughridge.

In an age of the remolding and transvaluation of all values, it is only too easy to fall into the error of imagining that the reorganization of a business or an administrative structure can be in itself the source of all subsequent success and riches. Nothing could be further from the truth than this blinkered view, one that cannot be repudiated firmly enough yet is dear to Modernist firebrands. To organize means to create *organic form,* and organic form is not a property only of inanimate things, for it embraces the *executive and creative work of individual human beings and whole groups of human beings.* To organize is therefore not to create something *definitive,* something *in its final form,* which—once it has this form—is set to continue as it is for the next century. The structure of an administration, the way it is organized, cannot be called good unless it can be made, in the very highest degree, *flexible* and *adaptable,* and also *responsive* to contingencies as they occur. Only then is it also economical, only then is it useful, only then does it cease to be an end in itself!

In urban planning, we do not yet have an organization of such caliber. The public, along with some groups among the professionals, still conceive of "urban planning" as the specialized knowledge or specialized technical ability concerned with building lines, urban-expansion plans, or so-called regional planning. But the insight that a new creation consists of more than a concept and a plan, that it involves a process of *execution* as well; the insight that urban planning would be no more than idle chatter and trivial paperwork were not the planning *organically of a piece with the execution, yoked to it under the direction of a single controlling mind*—that is an insight that is only just beginning, albeit too hesitantly, to gain wider currency. City planners are not specialists; they are directors and coordinators of the vast operation of shaping the fabric of the city. They are specialists in *universality*, they are midwives and organizers, they determine the order of importance of things and of deadlines; in short, they are conductors of an orchestra in which the players are technologists and creative artists.

This more comprehensive view of urban planning has been almost entirely pushed aside in our age of developing technology and the continual emergence of new and significant branches of urban planning. Energies are dissipated on minutiae, wasted in clashes of will, hampered by bureaucracy; all this occurs, as one would expect, to a much greater extent where the context is a major city, partly because it is there that technological specialization is further advanced, but also because, given the volume of work devolving on these specialized branches, it was only natural that almost all cities created individual departments relating to them. In a given instance, all these departments will belong to the same city yet be working under totally separate leadership. We find a Surveying Department, a Highways Department, a Drains and Sewers Department, a Ports and Bridges Department, a Department of Mechanical and Heating Engineering, one of Structural Engineering, a "City Planning Department," a Department of Tourism, a Department of Building Conservation—still commonly referred to today as the *Baupolizei*—and various others. "Wanting, though, is Nature's subtle bond,"[1] the organic link that would bind these departments into a unity and force them to work to a common program and toward a common objective.

[. . .]

Were a centralized organization embracing all the technical subbranches of urban planning to be achieved, it might certainly be expected that there would no longer be room for six *separate* conductors of the orchestra, only for one *single* coordinator. The beneficiaries of the current squandering of energies—bureaucracy, petty rivalries, discussions, and frictions—will be deprived of their usual fodder. The fullest possible development of the creative potential of all, from the most junior technician or administrative assistant to the senior architect heading one of the specialized planning subbranches, is the true meaning and the purpose of what we are currently trying to achieve: the reorganization of the system of technical operations involving the fabric of the city.

NOTE

1. "Nature's subtle bond": Goethe, *Faust,* line 1939.

180
Ilse Reicke
WOMEN AND BUILDING

First published as "Frauen beim Bauen," *Dresdner Neueste Nachrichten,* 29 April 1931. Translated by David Frisby.

The forthcoming major Berlin Building Exhibition is of the greatest interest for women of all strata, occupations, and walks of life. Already from its theme, it promises a whole series of special offerings and impressions for the female visitor. The women of Berlin have actively engaged with enthusiasm and interest in this major Berlin event, and as a result the exhibition will display a special building that, under the name *Ring der Frauen* [Women's Circle], is to be dedicated as a focal point for female cultural achievements. Exhibiting in this building are numerous women's associations in Berlin including the *Stadtverband* [city association] and key Catholic and nationalistic organizations. This "Women's Circle" has been designed by Peter Behrens for the Association for German Applied Arts. The connection between Professor Behrens and the city association is represented by Else Oppler-Legband, active in the artistic and technical aspects of the construction, while the business direction of the project also lies with a woman—Paula Samoje, the director of the Association of German Businesswomen.

The Women's Circle, to which I strolled today, is recognizable at the present time by its rudiments. Nonetheless, at the appointed time everything will be beautifully and solidly completed. The whole structure will be erected very speedily within ten days as a *Trockenbau* [dry build], using iron and a mortarless, fast-drying material. This means that its elevation is not so high, for the plans show only a single-story circular construction with four protruding apses. The connection from one apse to the others is made by means of covered walkways with showcases displaying everything that is worthy of the interest and attention of women. However, the fourth apse is conceived as an open terrace on which tea can be drunk and where dancing can take place. Since this terrace will be surrounded by water, the dancers will be concealed from the all too inquisitive public by a poetic cooling and breathing wall of water—namely, by a veil of spraying fountains.

The Women's Circle is designed to serve as the location and framework for a whole series of events that are planned by the various organizations for different afternoons. From among these organizations—and to take merely a few examples—there will be the Gymnastics Association, the women's section of the Association for German Peoples Abroad, the Association of Female Citizens, the Ladies Automobile Club, the "Ladies Club of 1930," founded by Katherina von Kardorff, the German Lyceum Club, the Montessori Society, and also the women's section of

FIGURE 41. Women's Circle, German Building Exhibition, Berlin (Peter Behrens, architect), 1931. Landesarchiv Berlin, 219 196.

the Central Association of White Collar Workers—the white collar workers' union—and the Association of Female Office and Commerce Workers. Alongside the highly diverse special events organized by these associations, there will also be children's festivals, invitations to tea, and the like.

In addition, a quite special female event, one that hopes for countless visitors from all over Germany, will take place on the 8th and 9th of June, not in the Women's Circle but in the Blue Salon of the major exhibition hall. The motto of these two days—As We Build, So We Dwell [*So baut man, so wohnt man*]—from a female perspective represents the high point of the whole exhibition. The speakers will be Dr. Marie-Elisabeth Lüders on "Planned economy in the household"; the architect Ruth Geyer-Raak on "The dwelling of our times"; Dr. Neundoerffer (Offenbach) will speak on "The housing estate and the small dwelling from an educational perspective"; and Professor Poelzig or Professor Mebes have agreed to speak on "Modern architecture." These lectures will take place in the mornings. However, in the afternoons, the female visitors will be directed by female guides—who have been trained especially for this purpose by Dr. Lüders—through all that is of relevance to women in the whole exhibition. This is certainly one of the most praiseworthy installations, and one that has been painfully absent in some of the other major exhibitions.

Since the dawn of human history, the woman has been the defender and administrator of the home. Today, however, as a citizen with equal rights, she has become much more—namely, the home's planner and builder, in both the literal and metaphorical sense. And the fact that she is gaining a new vision, a new power, new knowledge, and new goals in this her most primary sphere of life is the ultimate and most appealing aspect of the major forthcoming exhibition.

181
Siegfried Kracauer
BUILDING EXHIBITION IN THE EAST

First published as "Bauaustellung im Osten," *Frankfurter Zeitung*, 23 June 1931. Translated by Iain Boyd Whyte.

In the Köpenicker Strasse, which runs as straight as an arrow from infinity to infinity, there is a place among the housing complexes that forms one of the most miserable courtyards imaginable. It could have come out of a Dickens novel, so closely is big-city poverty tied here to historic obsolescence. Some courtyards are miserable on account of their modern functionality; but this one is a ruin. It is enclosed by early industrial brick walls, with old cars and motorcycles that have seen better days spilling out of the repair shop on one side. Cheerlessly the courtyard slinks past them, as if withdrawing ever deeper into the past. The sky can hardly follow, but countless windows look down on the courtyard's progress and accompany it to the bitter end.

The building that forms its termination used to house a button factory on the ground floor. All the buttons that were produced here have long since been pulled off. The abandoned rooms, which remind one of workshops from the time of Zola, now come to the assistance of a *proletarian building exhibition*. It is staged by a group of young engineers and architects, who have joined together to form a "Collective for Socialist Building" and see themselves as the counterpart of the exhibition in the Messehallen.[1]

Effectively displayed propaganda material covers the whitewashed walls. It is made up of short texts, statistics, and photographs, and inevitably follows one theme: the responsibility of the present economic order for the current housing misery, and pointers to the better conditions that prevail in Russia. This summary treatment cannot but lead to skewed results, but some less obvious facts are well illuminated. The National Socialist proposal for the solution of the housing question is aptly characterized and dismissed. Understandably, the main focus of the exhibition lies in the depiction and criticism of proletarian living conditions. The enormous number of families living as subtenants confronts the number of empty patrician apartments like an indictment. Pictures of Zille's architectural milieu join together under the title "Everyone ought to visit Berlin once!" which in its usual meaning promises more attractive destinations.[2] Prostitution and crime are portrayed very strikingly, and denounce the international housing shortage as their breeding ground. The despairing unemployed and those who have been evicted from their lodgings sometimes clutch at means of self-help, whose grotesque improvisations are also captured. There is also a photomontage entitled *Beyond the Borders of Berlin,* which is something quite different from the usual idyllic weekend house. It pictures cave dwellings on rubbish dumps; battered autos that serve as garden sheds; shelters made of egg boxes. These are images of the true state of affairs, and form a not inconsequential supplement to the main Building Exhibition.[3]

This depiction of the current situation is followed by a materialist study of city building. It attempts to show—using examples drawn from antiquity, the Middle Ages, and the age of absolutism—that the development of historical cities was conditioned by the prevailing relations of production and the social stratification that reflected them. The link from here to the contemporary city is not difficult to find. The principles on which the association of exhibitors proposes to proceed are in general accord with the guidelines recently developed by Ernst May in his Berlin lecture. Roughly, the basic elements of this program are the development of a systematically expandable minimal housing unit for each family, commercial fabrication of housing types, and the creation of a favorable link between the place of production and the residential area.

Whoever visits the official exhibition in the west of the city should not miss this one in the east. This exhibition has put down its roots in an environment that could itself be a demonstration model. And precisely because of its one-sidedness, it sharpens our eyes for certain planning devices and ambitions whose unstoppable expansion can be sensed in certain halls in the Messehallen.

NOTES

1. The 1931 German Building Exhibition, Berlin, staged from May through August in Berlin's main exhibition halls (Messehallen).

2. Heinrich Zille (1858–1929) was an artist celebrated for his caricatures of life in working-class Berlin. The reference to Zille's milieu points to the book of drawings published in 1913 under the title *Mein Milljöh.*

3. See above, text 178: Werner Hegemann, Berlin and World Architecture: On the Berlin Building Exhibition.

182

Heinz-Willi Jüngst

HOUSING FOR CONTEMPORARIES
[ON THE 1931 GERMAN BUILDING EXHIBITION, BERLIN]

First published as "Wohnbau für Zeitgenossen," *Der Querschnitt* 5 (1932). Translated by Iain Boyd Whyte.

The *Neue Sachlichkeit* [new objectivity] is, in the meantime, a rather aging discovery, all of whose achievements and priorities are aimed at completely uniting the entire world in the most concentrated and practical way. It was invented with the purpose of leading mankind—who has been led astray for centuries—nearer to paradise.

THE EXTERNAL WALL

The nature-seeking tendency of the newly standardized human type demands that the entire external wall be dissolved into glass. By this means the surrounding air, light, and sun will be brought into the house, and modern life will be led out into the broad world beyond. And a little bit of warm air will be lost in the process. The aesthetics of the modern man demands that he live in the open at all times of day and must never shut himself off from the outside world, not even in bad weather. Since the inspired discovery of the glass toilet, lots of air is also necessary at those inconvenient moments in one's life. The man drilled in hygiene takes it as a particular delight when he is able to freeze or roast in his glass box, his eyes having long since become accustomed to the flood of light. He smiles at those backward souls who look to their houses for a sense of privacy and domestic security, and is pleased when he can see his four columns as transparent glass by day and as curtains at night. All of domestic life is now played out on the street. Precisely because savings are being made everywhere, one can best begin with the exterior wall. The "very latest thing" is on display in the "Apartment of tomorrow" (single-story house by Mies van der Rohe), where the entire external wall is dissolved into large plate-glass shop-window panes, which stretch from floor to ceiling. With one touch of the button, the expensive bronze frame silently sinks down by means of an electric motor into a massive vertical slit. You're left sitting in the living room—out in the open. A disappearing window such as this is, of course, too expensive and unpractical for a department store, but will soon become standard in single-family houses. Anyone who is worried about inquisitive looks can always build a wall around his house.

THE INTERIOR WALLS

People have realized that something finally has to be done with the internal dividing walls. On grounds of economy the attempt is made to fit as many walls as possible into the smallest apartments by creating a specific room for every bed, every basin and water closet. In the two-story apartment designed for a tower block (architects Haesler and Völker), the five beds are located in five separate, equal-size bedrooms, and the three basins and two water closets are all in individual cells on the upper floor. As there is still too much room to squeeze the body through, the idea of creating a separate space for each single item of furniture suggests itself, so that every table and chair can make its presence felt. It is different in luxurious houses. Here, and also on grounds of economy, the internal walls are abandoned entirely, in order to achieve an intensified spatial effect. If you don't want to dispense entirely with the dividing walls, the provisional installation of a thin plywood wall suffices. When it divides the living and dining areas—as in the Single Story House by Mies van der Rohe—this plywood wall can be veneered with Makassar ebony. The separation of the individual sleeping, living, working, eating, washing, and so on alcoves with harmonica sliding doors is very practical, and imparts a delightfully lively and provisional tone. Most practically, these doors should be made of white imitation leather. The square-meter price for this has just fallen from 75 to 52 reichsmarks, so that one can manage nicely with around 55 reichsmarks per square meter. In the little "House for a Sportsman" (architect Marcel Breuer), these walls extend up to only 2.13 meters, so that all six walls cost only 2,750 reichsmarks. As these sliding walls cost around only twice as much as wooden doors and six times as much as a completed brick wall, this pioneering invention will doubtless make its way soon particularly into small houses.

SINGLE-ROOM APARTMENT

The claim of the architectural profession that the 45 or 60 square meters specified as the maximum size for small apartments by the 1931 federal law has long since shown itself to be nonsense. Also, the fear that building costs would go higher the more one compressed and subdivided the ground plan is at best unproven. In the One-Room Apartment (architect Fieger), in which all the rooms can be used both day and night in double functions, one can make do with far less ground area (for example, 40 square meters for four beds). During the day: a large, open-plan living room or (with subdividing sliding wall) two rooms for living and eating, children's play, and eating. At night: two bedrooms with folding beds and breakfast corner. These apartments are ideal for the deaf and dumb, and very educational for those of an excitable and nervous disposition.

FUNCTIONS OF THE ROOMS

The new theories of function have not been devised in order to make the rooms more livable, but rather so that the inhabitant, through engagement on practical-philosophical issues, can penetrate the philanthropic-altruistic thought processes of the art of higher dwelling, and, as a result, will long for a better life in the hereafter, and sooner rather than later. The modern, unstable, unified man needs a healthy functionalism that frees him from the "slavery of housework" and forces upon him an exactly thought out set of user's instructions, explaining how he should move between the whitewashed coulisses of his apartment, glittering with glass and metal. Only when the free life of the individual has been given up and all joyful movement expired will we discover the true charm of modern living: only then will we learn, like marionettes, to order our existences as a function of the plan and the furnishings. In the fevered search for new solutions, we find many ways to make the impossible possible. Not only is every room painted a different color, but every wall. Even better: each wall is constructed from a different material. The door openings reach to the ceiling. And when the "functional structural and spatial geometry" does not quite manage either to emphasize or establish the balance of power in Europe, you can always plant a rubber tree or cactus. You can even swap over entire rooms for functional reasons. Indeed, the least likely room combinations are possible if they can be justified by some theory or other. There are also plausible and practical reasons. One needs only to think of the famous oral examination in which the rigorous professor asked the ill-informed student: "How will you prevent the kitchen from steaming up and the WC from smelling?"—"Dead easy, I'll simply swap the functions of these rooms."

STEEL FURNITURE

The *Neue Sachlichkeit* consciously seeks its aesthetic sense through the expression of banality and coarseness: chairs formed of bent chrome-plated steel tubes, or assembled out of several parts in the most clumsy and primitive way; metal tables of a similar construction covered with a glass top. Poverty of form and function, and the lack of expression or spirit, are intentionally stressed. The public has long since weaned itself from its old-fashioned partiality for bad conductors. Following the friendly persuasion of the architects and the advertisements of industry, it is now seen as an advantage that the steel furniture feels so warm in the summer and so cold in the winter.

THE STAIRCASE

It is a welcome sign of a reform-thirsty, bravely progressive age that wood and even concrete, that most modern of materials, are spurned for staircases. The patent steel staircase with perforated treads favored today (boarding house by the architect Vorhoelzer and others; two-story apartment by Haesler and Völker; viewing tower by Walter Gropius) has far greater advantages. It is easily assembled, rapidly installed, playfully delicate to the eye, and sways gently and rather teasingly with every step. The steps are made of lattice steel, which has already proved itself efficient as a boot scraper, with as wide a mesh as possible, so that those high-heeled shoes at last have to go. The risers can be dispensed with entirely, enabling pointed shoes to last longer. The entire stairwell, with all its shaky spirals and convolutions, can be surveyed from top to bottom in one glance. Indeed, as is so popular today, the entire architectural scheme can be seen from below. The fire brigade is absolutely delighted at this innovation, since this steel staircase immediately expands in the heat, and pulls with it all the structural elements attached to it, particularly the steel frame, and the fire is immediately smothered at its source by the collapsing walls.

THE NEW MATERIALS

In addition to the ancient building materials (clay, pumice stone, straw, limestone, plaster, cement, and so on), the new, synthetic materials (slag bricks, wood wool, wood fiber, cork, peat, asbestos, asphalt, among others) have become common. Recently, less valuable materials (straw, seaweed, coconut and sugarcane fibers) have been ennobled by some sort of process and extolled with heroic enthusiasm. Unfortunately, these substitute building materials cost a fortune, although this is explicable in terms of demand, the high price of patenting, transportation, customs charges, and other social costs. The issue today is less about systematically researching the value of the surrogates, . . . but simply about the imperative to do something new. But why has the wonderful Frankfurt discovery (the May system), which casts the entire wall in one piece [. . .], not been developed further?[1] It must be possible to manufacture a stone substance like paint: you then have only to cut windows and doors in a cardboard box of the right size, dunk the whole thing in stone paint, and voilà: the house is finished!

NOTE

1. As the city architect of Frankfurt am Main between 1925 and 1930, Ernst May created a celebrated series of housing estates in which thousands of standardized apartments were built very rapidly using advanced concrete constructional techniques.

183

Gottfried Feder

THE GERMAN HOUSING DEVELOPMENT BOARD

First published as "Das Deutsche Siedlungswerk," speech, May 1934, *Bauwelt,* no. 19 (1934); reprinted in Anna Teut, *Architektur im Dritten Reich, 1933–1945* (Berlin: Ullstein, 1967), pp. 311–14. Translated by Iain Boyd Whyte.

[. . .]

Without mutual support and without unified leadership, the existing agencies could essentially serve only their respective local or personal goals, or the intentions of their patrons or interested parties. Nothing else was to be expected, as they were all the children of the liberal era. There could be no talk of unified leadership and of the planning of the housing program as a postulate of the national economy, which could be linked to the vital relocation of industry.

Here lies the decisive turn of events in the realm of housing development; here lies the transition from the fragmentation and disunity of the previous housing developments, which had petered out in housing estates for the workers and for the unemployed, in small-scale housing initiatives and estates built in the outer suburbs, conceived without organic unity or any sense of connection, to the Deutsches Siedlungswerk [German Housing Development Board], as the chancellor has designated it.[1]

I have accepted with great joy the call of my Führer to solve this enormous task.

In my many public utterances and speeches I have always vigorously stressed the political and demographic importance of the *Siedlung,* but have warned against the romanticism of those housing developments that could not give those who settled in them a guarantee of long-term employment. Housing developments, by which I mean new estates and new towns set in countryside, should be built only at places where the economic preconditions exist for an extended life, for the long-term employment of the settlers on the basis of local raw materials, which are processed on the site, through the creation of new industries, or the relocation of existing ones.

Housing developments at the periphery of the city, often located at an excessive distance from the city center and the places of work, can be approved only insofar as they allow the old and unhealthy housing quarters in the city to be demolished, so that our large cities can gain light and air—fresh lungs, as it were.

By no means everyone is suitable for relocation in a *Siedlung.* One will have to prove that the demands of racial hygiene are satisfied, whether good genotypes and fecundity can be determined in the forefathers. The absence of mental illness and genetic deficiencies is also a precondition for the necessary racial-hygienic qualities of the *Siedlung.*

In its core central area, the planned *Siedlung* should reflect the healthy mixture of various occupations, so that the *Siedlung* can expand on the basis of its own energy.

The question of location needs particularly careful consideration. First, communications should be checked: proximity to the state autobahns, and to lakes, rivers, woods, and so on; suitable climatic and soil conditions; and much more.

From the viewpoint of political demography, the *Siedlung* will become an almost compelling national necessity, which can be confirmed by the following two sets of comparative statistics.

As the largest transportation undertaking in Germany, the Berliner Verkehrs-Aktiengesellschaft (BVG) employs around 24,000 workers and officials, the majority of whom are married.[2] The BVG, thereby, feeds around 40,000 adults. Between them, these 40,000 adults have 14,400 children. Even more worrying is the ratio among the office staff and higher management of the BVG, who with a total of 2,000 paid employees—around 3,500 adults have only 700 children among them.

If the figures cited above for 40,000 are translated to the entire population, this would mean that a nation of 40 million in the present generation would shrink in the next generation to 14.4 million! In other words: the metropolis is the death of the nation.

The dispersion of the large cities, the return of the populace to their roots in the soil and to long-term resettlement on the land, is one of the most important tasks of the Third Reich. The resolution of the misery of the large cities and the creation of healthier living conditions, especially for the rising, are imperative duties for a Reich government that is aware of the needs of the people.

The Deutsches Siedlungswerk will perform this duty!

[. . .]

These new housing developments and small new towns will be model examples of the best German architecture in their insertion into the landscape, their integration into the great rhythm of the newly awakened German economic life, in their creation of healthy social relationships, in comradeship and rootedness with the maternal German soil, and with him who has awakened them and given them new form: Adolf Hitler.

NOTES

1. On the various meanings of *Siedlung*, see the introduction to section 8 "The Green Outdoors."
2. Established in January 1929, the BVG ran the bus, streetcar, and subway networks in Berlin.

184

Herbert Hoffmann

THE RESIDENTIAL ESTATE ON BERLIN'S GROSSE LEEGESTRASSE

First published as "Die Wohnsiedlung an der Großen Leegestrasse in Berlin-Weißensee," *Moderne Bauformen* 35 (1936), pp. 257–59. Translated by Michael Loughridge.

The architects [Paul] Mebes and [Paul] Emmerich were also responsible for the Potsdam residential estate for wounded veterans, those small double houses that seem part and parcel of the countryside, arranged as they are around a village green, and that actually fulfill the old dream of the warrior being provided after the campaign with land of his own to settle down on. Featured in our April issue, the veterans' estate could be said to have taken its place in a long lineage reaching back to land allocations made to veterans of the ancient Roman armies, and represented in Prussia by Frederick the Great's colonies. There is a natural feeling of history repeating itself now with the very recent planned resettlement of families going back to the land.

The large residential estate by the same architects, which we are presenting to our readers today, arose out of entirely different requirements—those of the world metropolis Berlin itself.[1] The objective here on the city outskirts is to create new housing meeting modern public-health standards and sufficient to cater to a very large number of Berlin families—in other words, to set about reducing the housing shortage and the associated squalor in which so many in our capital city have to live. The new houses provided have to be light and airy, easily run, and with good transport links to the city center so that they are conveniently placed for the daily journey to and from work.

As Government Architect [*Baurat*] Binder explains in the article that introduces this issue of the journal, there can be no question, in such cases, of seeking to realize some kind of ultimate residential ideal; the aim, rather, is the best possible use of the circumstances as they are. Not the least important consideration in this respect, at a time of depressed real incomes, is the need to keep rentals at an affordable level. If well-equipped and easily run two- and three-room apartments are to be made available at such rentals, there is no option but to concentrate them in large blocks. If one avoids what used to be the frequent practice of building the blocks tightly around light wells or courtyards, disregarding the need for air circulation and sunshine, and instead arranges them as long narrow blocks, set well apart from each other so as to allow for grassy areas and playgrounds, then one is achieving the aim of "best possible use" in the existing circumstances; and by providing labor-saving communal facilities, one can considerably enhance the attractiveness to the housewife of every apartment as a place to live.

If the project as a whole is entrusted to an architect of real ability, and he does not rest until the very last detail is satisfactorily resolved, one can be confident that the horrors great and small traditionally associated with the *Mietskaserne*, or barracks block, have been banished, and that tenants will live in surroundings of which they can be proud.

Romantic as it would be to offer roof gardens to the tenants as a substitute for small gardens of their own in which to pass their summer evenings, it is of no great consequence, on the other hand, if these large building volumes are capped by pitched roofs of appropriate size. In residential buildings on this scale, the traditional house shape has become irrelevant. In our view they will have to find their optimum design in the same way as other major buildings serving other purposes. That those living there should have the sense of home, and thus an emotional bond to the place, is no less important to this type of living, in a large community, than elsewhere. The sheer size of the metropolis has given rise to a new set of problems demanding a new set of answers. In the estate on the Große Leegestrasse, we may justly feel that we have been presented with one of the necessary solutions by the team who created it for the Gemeinnützige Wohnungsbau A.G., the architects Paul Mebes and Paul Emmerich.

What has been constructed so far is less than half of the project. The decision to build in three long blocks between two existing roads meant that the buildings could be situated thirty-two to thirty-four meters apart. The main facades have a satisfactory alignment, facing either northwest or southeast. So that the middle block does not feel like the old-style back building, and also for easy access from the two flanking roads, an open space was created at the center of the development. The wide passageways under the two outer buildings—giving them an arcaded character—feed directly into this open area. The communal facilities are all located here and are thus easily accessible from every apartment in the complex via the internal paths. They include a play area with a paddling pool, a covered bad-weather area for older children, mechanized and fully equipped laundry rooms, the society's offices, and (on the Leegestrasse side) the estate's six shops. The artwork decorating the covered passages, the animal sculptures by the paddling pool, the lawns nearby, and the flower decorations on the balconies make this central square an attractive communal area for festive occasions. It is shared by the families from all 604 apartments completed so far. A final total of 1,572 apartments is planned.

NOTE

1. The first phase of this large-scale housing project was built in 1932–34, but as the text confirms, it was not complete in 1936 at the time of publication. The estate thus straddled the National Socialist takeover of power in 1933.

185

Anonymous

THE CONSTRUCTION OF COMMUNITIES ON THE BASIS OF THE PEOPLE, THE LAND, AND THE LANDSCAPE

First Planning Manual Issued by the *Reichsheimstättenamt* of the German Labor Front, "Urban Design and Housing Planning" Division, Berlin 1940

First published as *Siedlungsgestaltung aus Volk, Raum und Landschaft: 1. Planungsheft des Reichsheimstättenamtes der DAF* (Berlin: Deutsche Arbeitsfront, Hauptabteilung "Städtebau und

Wohnungsplanung," 1940); reprinted in *Hitlers sozialer Wohnungsbau, 1940–1945*, ed. Tilman Harlander and Gerhard Fehl (Hamburg: Christians, 1986), pp. 114–17. Translated by Michael Loughridge.

1. TOTAL PLANNING AND DESIGN—A POLITICAL MANDATE: POLITICAL AND ADMINISTRATIVE PREREQUISITES FOR TOTAL PLANNING AND DESIGN

The immense energy that drove the repopulation of the German lands in the years after we took power, even as resources were being strained to the utmost to strengthen the economy for national defense, testified vividly to the upsurge in our times of *völkisch* [popular national] vitality, and will redouble once the war forced upon the German nation has been concluded. This phase of rapid growth, short in its overall duration, will have a major impact on individual regions, differing according to the economic and sociological structure of each area concerned. By the time this development commences there must be clarity about the political and technical principles involved and about the modalities of the application to all construction activity, in due administrative form, of laws derived from the people, the territory, and the landscape [*Volk, Raum und Landschaft*].

[...]

If the German *Volk* is to be remembered in honor by its descendants in years to come, it is vital that all construction activity involved in settling rural and urban areas and in the work of expanding villages and towns should express the harmony of the nation's development with the spatial restraints of our land and of the landscape that constitutes the home of our people.

[...]

The relief of the land hunger in the east and the solution of the community's most serious social problem—provision for every German of the type of living accommodation appropriate to his need—are the means for the safeguarding and perpetuation of the German family, and are contingent upon total planning and design of the landscape in which we live [*Landschaftsraum*].

The party, the state, and the economy—the three central pillars supporting the life of the nation—work together in harmony, and in fulfillment of their mission, to ensure the proper laying of the foundations for this historic task. The *party*, as the creative strand in the nation's life, formulates the political mandate and designs the architectural and physical forms to be assumed by community life within our landscape. The *state* provides the legislative framework that ensures that the active will of the party is implemented. The *economy* is responsible, subject to the ideological guidance of the party and direction by the state, for choosing the most appropriate methods of implementation.

In matters of architectural planning and design, the party cannot be limited to compiling and promulgating guidelines; the party represents the will of the nation, and thus it must in all cases be the party, by its creative acts, that determines the shaping of the community.

Just as in the earliest era of German cultural history the character of whole cities and whole tracts of settlement land bore the imprint of a small number of responsible leaders, so now, within our meticulously organized national life, the task of shaping the landscapes of Greater Germany and their future settlement profile must be the responsibility of the party (as the guiding spirit that shapes the whole of our national life) and of the creative energies bundled with it.

In light of the above, the sequence of procedures in addressing the far-reaching tasks that lie before us will be as follows.

In the course of ongoing collaboration between the party forward planning department concerned with these issues and the appropriate subdepartments within the Reich Department of Regional Planning [*Reichsstelle für Raumordnung*], the location and the expansion limits of settlement areas within the overall land-use pattern will be determined. The forward planning department of the party, working in consultation with the State Building Authority [*Staatsbauverwaltung*] and the local authorities, will design the layout and form of future residential centers, will determine the provision of accommodation on the basis of the social structure of the community, and will specify the detailed building program. The State Building Authority will be responsible for ensuring that these guiding principles are rigorously observed by the local authority, the independent architect, and the contractor. These last three are responsible for carrying out the work, in constant close consultation with the relevant party forward-planning office.

Within a very short time, this clearly prescribed collaborative structure will of itself suffice to ensure that the huge construction program moves forward smoothly, and will furthermore create the basis, in the form of a rigorous and unified system of control, on which truly comprehensive land-use planning for the German territory can be undertaken.

[. . .]

The design character of our cityscapes in this modern era must be consonant with the fundamentals of the National Socialist Weltanschauung [philosophy of life]. The laws derived from the people, the territory, and the landscape [*Gesetze aus Volk, Raum, und Landschaft*] are the foundations on which the political and physical structure of the new city must be built. The cityscape and each individual structure within it must be integrated into the great overarching landscape context, just as they in turn have derived their form from the vital concerns of the community. The development and building of a new city must be guided by overriding political principles. Landscape-related, economic, and cultural imperatives must also be observed.

Specifically, this means:

Suitable integration of urban development into the surrounding area, limits to be imposed in accordance with particularities of local landforms.

Design of an organically functioning urban structure with due account taken of the community's characteristic way of life, social structure, and cultural needs. Structural subdivision of the overall planning area into residential communities, these to be made identifiable as distinct political units by appropriate architectural design means. Drawing together of the residential communities by linking all to a central cultural institution that generates a strong centripetal focus within the city and is at the same time the city's supreme symbol. The overall urban design must reflect the character of the national community as molded by National Socialism; this means showing due regard for the mutually distinct functions of private home life and of public life:

1. Home living as the central and defining characteristic of the built city: to be designed for maximum closeness to the soil and neighborhood cohesiveness.
2. Positioning and landscaping of the city's prestige buildings (party offices, administrative centers, community facilities).
3. Provision of economic infrastructure in the form of sufficient and properly planned distribution facilities.

[...]

DESIGN FOR DOMESTIC LIVING

All planning procedures relating to housing will be subject to new requirements reflecting the National Socialist understanding of nation [*Volk*], of life, and of homeland [*Heimat*]. The overall process of developing our society [*sozialer Volksaufbau*] will involve many individual priorities that the various accommodation types must serve, adapting where necessary. Foremost among these priorities, along with the obvious hygienic requirements that living accommodation must meet, is that of developing a culture of living fully worthy of the living standard of the German people. The objective must be to enable every German to fulfill his healthy aspiration to a home of his own in which his family can live, if possible in close touch with the land beneath and around them. To the extent that this culturally and demographically important objective cannot be achieved in the cities, it is important that the urban dwelling should reflect the ideal as closely as possible.

16

MASS AND LEISURE

The radical architects and city planners of 1920s Berlin saw the future of their professions in the repetition of standardized cells or units, which would form the basis of the mass housing blocks, which in turn would shape the new cityscape. Among the immediate results were the great housing estates planned and built in the late 1920s, around standard dwelling units, that defined the new Berlin. The pragmatic, nonsentimental nature of this housing, perfectly captured in the German word *Sachlichkeit,* reflected and reinforced work patterns, social structures, and a leisure industry that, although not unique to Berlin in the Weimar period, were to be found there in a particularly high state of development.

The great commentator of this new Berlin, which was not to be found in the Baedeker travel guide, was Siegfried Kracauer. Kracauer, who had trained as an architect in the immediate prewar period, emerged in the 1920s as one of the most perceptive cultural commentators of his generation, and found words and categories to describe the aesthetic response to industrial and social rationalization and to the disintegrative tendencies of post-1918 Germany. In absolute contrast to the previous, Expressionist generation, which had focused on the profundities of human existence, on the essential and the spiritual, Kracauer looked at the surface phenomena and the superficial concerns and distractions of urban life in order to comprehend the postwar age. As he argues in a celebrated sentence that opens his essay "The Mass Ornament," first published in 1927: "The position that an epoch occupies in the historical process can be determined more strikingly from an analysis of its inconspicuous surface-level expressions than from that epoch's judgments about itself."[1] To locate the superficial phenomena that would ultimately explain the core values of Weimar Berlin, Kracauer turned to the marginal and ephemeral spaces of the city: the dance hall, the cinema, the hotel lobby . . . the "pleasure barracks," regimented spaces in which the rationalized workers were conditioned to spend their leisure time. However feeble these entertainments were, he argued, they revealed more of the current realities than any number of noble artistic sentiments expressed in obsolete forms.

Kracauer's anthropological gaze was directed in particular at a social class that had burgeoned in post–World War I Germany: the white-collar worker. As David Frisby has explained: "The substantive context for Kracauer's analysis of this 'unknown area' lies in the rationalization of production and distribution after the instigation of the Dawes Plan in 1924 in Germany, with its attendant dramatic increase in large scale organization, the sharp increase in the number of white collar workers in commerce, banking, transport and industry, and the increasing proportion of women in the white collar sector."[2] This was the class most exposed by the social ruptures of the war and its aftereffects, which saw the church and the military diminished to the point of extinction, the historical German states reduced to political impotence, and the Kaiser exiled. In aesthetic terms, the particularity and the power of these institutions had been asserted through decoration—the decoration of Baroque palaces and neo-Baroque cathedrals, of coats of arms and civic ritual, of military uniforms. These visual decorations were matched, in turn, by the appropriate linguistic embellishments. For centuries, precisely these decorative schemes had endowed ritual and political significance on the prosaic and practical, turning the shelter into a church or the humble hat into a cuirassier's helmet or a royal crown.[3]

By the 1920s, the institutions that had empowered this traditional system of decorative signs and symbols were either moribund or entirely redundant. New sign systems and references were needed for the army of white-collar workers that had emerged from the wreckage, under the tutelage of their North American counterparts. Reflecting the mechanics of the factory and the conveyor belt, the visual languages of these systems shunned the curvaceous, the sensuous, and the organic in favor of geometric forms, grid relations, and polished surfaces, which could be repeated endlessly in their mathematical perfection. The ordered lines of the Tiller Girl dance troupes provided Kracauer with the perfect metaphor: "When they formed an undulating snake, they radiantly illustrated the virtues of the conveyor belt; when they tapped their feet in fast tempo, it sounded like business; when they kicked their legs high with mathematical precision, they joyously affirmed the progress of rationalization; and when they kept repeating the same movements without ever interrupting their routine, one envisaged an uninterrupted chain of motorcars gliding from the factories into the world, and believed that the blessing of prosperity had no end."[4] Under the dictates of mass ornament the individual body is transformed into a carefully controlled but anonymous element within a larger formation. Team games and mass sport conformed to the same pattern, bringing agreed rules and goals to the otherwise unstructured leisure time of the white-collar workers. The contrast between these salaried employees and the artisan and proletarian workers was addressed by Kracauer in an essay entitled "Refuge for the Homeless," in which *home* refers not merely to shelter, but to a coherent existence with well-defined roles and values. As a refuge from this disturbing state of cultural homelessness, argued Kracauer, gigantic new cinemas, sports stadia, and pleasure palaces like the Haus Vaterland were established in Berlin, where "glamour becomes substance, distraction stupor."[5] The power of distraction is fragile, however, and when the waiter switches off the glamour, the gray light of the eight-hour day shines through once again.

Berlin was the undisputed center of mass cultural production in 1920s Germany and its most eager consumer. Public radio broadcasting was launched in Berlin in 1923 with a regional service, followed in 1926 by the nationwide station, Deutsche Welle, also based in Berlin. Popular journalism flourished, led by titles like the *BZ am Mittag* and the *Berliner Illustrirte Zeitung*, with a circulation that peaked at 1.8 million copies in July 1929. The most powerful press baron of the period, Dr. Alfred Hugenberg, owned not only the *Berliner Lokal-Anzeiger, Der Tag*, and the *Deutsche Allgemeine Zeitung* (the official organ of the German Foreign Office), but also Ufa (Universum Film Aktiengesellschaft), which had enormous studios at Neubabelsberg and at Staaken, on the western edges of Berlin. As *Time* magazine reported in September 1928: "Dominating Neubabelsberg, as no producer is able to dominate Hollywood, are the studios of the mighty Ufa, chief among European cinema companies. Here were filmed such popular and artistic successes as *Variety, The Last Laugh, The Cabinet of Dr. Caligari*."[6] Symptomatic of the power of the new medium was the presence of Reich Chancellor Gustave Stresemen at the premiere of Fritz Lang's film *Die Nibelungen—Siegfrieds Tod* in February 1924. Lang went on to make the most celebrated of all the Ufa films from this period, *Metropolis*, which received its world premiere on 10 January 1927 in the Ufa-Palast am Zoo, the most prestigious of the 130 cinemas owned by Ufa at that time.

In a radio talk first broadcast on 24 January 1926, Siegfried Kracauer addressed the papier-mâché world of the Ufa studios in Neubabelsberg, noting that "the things that rendezvous here do not belong to reality. They are copies and distortions that have been ripped out of time and jumbled together. They stand motionless, full of meaning from the front, while from the rear they are just empty nothingness."[7] The beguiling surfaces of the film, however, were marketed in the products of the Berlin fashion industry, which was concentrated in the city center, around the Hausvogteiplatz. In this way, film, the press, and fashion were mutually reinforcing: "The different branches of cultural production in Berlin fed off each other: stars of stage and cinema had their images reproduced and amplified by the illustrated press; women could study the designs of Berlin fashion houses as worn by an actress in a Pabst film, by a revue singer or a model in the *Berliner*

Illustrirte—even if their budget only ran to buying cheaper imitations in the nearest department store."⁸

Sport was also brought into this self-referential nexus. The American boxer Jack Dempsey, for example, was taken to Ufa's Staaken studios in June 1925 to see the sets for *Metropolis* and doubtless to be photographed in the process. Under such headings as *Leibesübungen* (literally, "body exercises") and *Turnen,* gymnastics and physical education had a long history in nineteenth-century Germany, often associated with broader communal and military goals. The word *sport* was reserved around the turn of the century for competitive disciplines like athletics, rowing, and boxing, and team games like soccer, which were highly developed in Britain and the United States, and were predicated on winning, on individual performances, and on the breaking of records. These were the sports that flourished in Germany in the 1920s, and were reported not only in the popular press, but in the feuilleton pages of the broadsheets and in upmarket journals like *Der Querschnitt, Die Weltbühne,* and *Die neue Rundschau.* Nowhere was the fusion of mechanization, rationalization, personal performance, and tangible results more cleverly exploited than in the six-day cycle races. The event first appeared in Madison Square Garden in 1896, and was introduced to Europe in Berlin in 1909. From 1911 it became an annual event at the Sportpalast on Potsdamer Strasse, falling out only during the war years. This was the epitome of Taylorized sport, as high-performance, professional athletes rotated around a geometrically determined track with the mechanical regularity of machines for days and nights on end, to the delight and distraction of the public and the profit of the organizers. Just as Kracauer found the white-collar workers emotionally and intellectually homeless, so the journalist Egon Erwin Kisch contrasted the baseless spectacle of the six-day race with the healthy state both of the workers' sports associations and of the noble sports clubs dedicated to motoring, tennis, golf, or polo.⁹

The linkage of national pride, industrial modernity, and sporting excellence on one hand, and the subjugation of individual expression in favor of mass ornament on the other, were forces easily exploited by the National Socialist regime. In the words of Karsten Witte, "The fascists were able to mobilize those energies that lay devoid of meaning, substance and interpretation, so that the masses could actually claim to see their own triumph of the will in that megalomaniacally contrived and hypertrophically staged spectacle in Nuremberg."¹⁰

NOTES

1. Siegfried Kracauer, "The Mass Ornament," in Kracauer, *The Mass Ornament: Weimar Essays,* trans. and with an introduction by Thomas Y. Levin (Cambridge, Mass.: Harvard University Press, 1995), p. 75.

2. David Frisby, *Fragments of Modernity* (Cambridge: Polity, 1985), p. 165.

3. Significantly, Kracauer's architectural dissertation, submitted in 1914 to the Technische Hochschule in Munich, was on the decorative art of the blacksmith in Berlin and Potsdam from the seventeenth to the early nineteenth century.

4. Siegfried Kracauer, "Girls and Crisis"; quoted in Frisby, *Fragments of Modernity,* p. 149.

5. Siegfried Kracauer, "Shelter for the Homeless," in Kracauer, *The Salaried Masses,* trans. Quintin Hoare (London: Verso, 1998), p. 93.

6. Anonymous, "In Neubabelsberg," *Time,* 10 September 1928.

7. Siegfried Kracauer, "Calico-World: The UFA City in Neubabelsberg," in Kracauer, *Mass Ornament,* p. 281.

8. Elizabeth Harvey, "Culture and Society in Weimar Germany," in *Twentieth-Century Germany,* ed. Mary Fulbrook (London: Hodder Arnold, 2001), p. 62.

9. See Egon Erwin Kisch, "Ein Sportsmann als Schiedsrichter seiner selbst," in *Der Sport am Scheideweg,* ed. Willy Meisl (Heidelberg: Iris, 1928), p. 11.

10. Karsten Witte, "Introduction to Siegfried Kracauer's 'The Mass Ornament,'" *New German Critique* 2 (1975), p. 66.

186

Bruno Taut

ON NEW THEATERS

First published as "Zum neuen Theaterbau," *Das hohe Ufer* 1, no. 8 (August 1919), pp. 204–8.[1] Translated by Fiona Elliot.

Let us turn our backs on that abhorrent institution that we call theater nowadays!

Capitalist department stores for art connoisseurs. Expensive ticket prices. War profiteers or at least well-to-do citizens, there they sit, ogling and sniffing at each other; the safety curtain still conceals the department store for art connoisseurs, and when it goes up, pitch darkness descends and the audience has to peer toward the stage as though at a peep show—whether they so desire or not—to where the art wares are on sale. And whether these are good value for money or not may be decided by those who regard art as something enjoyed by connoisseurs—moreover, as something with a price tag.

But we will turn away in disgust from this horrendous "play." All productive, forward-looking spirits should boycott these establishments and swear a solemn oath in each other's presence never to set foot again in any such temple of the Muses.

To hell with them all, even if they are already there! We will turn our thoughts to the future instead.

. . .

The first, greatest, and hardest action needed to liberate dramatic art will be undertaken not by the artist, but by the statesman. The theater business must be rescued from the capitalist mire in which it threatens to suffocate and entirely rot away; it must be given a place in the fresh air of the wider public, an independent existence of its own. There it will elevate the united masses and perhaps one day become a cult. All art comes from the same source after all: mystery plays in the medieval cathedral, merriment outside the cathedral, boisterous romps and the annual fair around it.

However, external liberation from capitalism is of course of no effect without the necessary mental and artistic preparation. The "free people's stage"—the Volksbühne in Berlin—has on its facade the patronizing, bourgeois maxim: "Die Kunst dem Volke" [Art for the People]. And so it is inside: everything is exactly as in the commercial theater with its shareholders—an auditorium in genuine pyramid mahogany with superior sculptures by Metzner. Here is your very own front room, you proletarians, your own cold splendor, *your own* court theater! Anyone looking into the auditorium from the stage could easily imagine he was looking into polished coffin. At the Volksoper at Charlottenburg, a rather simpler solution was found: they just built a shed. And the music of Mozart, Weber, and Verdi certainly does sound there as though it is coming from "another" world.

. . .

Everything in theater design hinges on *one* spot in the building, on the exhaustive attention of the architect to one thin line on the floor plan—that spot where an expanse of fabric rises upward and reveals a new glittering world to the assembled masses, where the space is not merely expanded in purely physical terms, but where expansion is also mental and intellectual, or at least should be, as our minds draw breath and our lungs burst; in short, we are talking of the curtain. There is no modern theater where this spot does not mark an absolute division between two worlds: audience on one side, actors on the other. As long as the curtain is closed you can chatter and eye each other, but once it goes up you are to hold your tongues and gaze at me alone! Perfectly clear instructions—what for? Well, I would say, for a festive occasion. No, no, heaven forfend—you will have your wares, paid for with your hard-earned money, delivered in nice, neat packages.

This division of a vast building at a spot where there is no natural division in the space, but where only a curtain hangs—this subjugation of the architect to a bit of cloth (for what else is the safety curtain?) could almost be described as madness. There is only *one* way that the theater builder could, by his design, influence what happens onstage for the better. The architect need not simply behave like a craftsman engaged to complete a task, merely fulfilling a certain function; he can also reshape that function anew. And he will do this if he manages to unite the stage and the auditorium, creating an undivided theatrical space that equally embraces those giving and those receiving, so that there is in fact neither giving nor receiving—a space where all present, actors and public alike, come together as one enraptured whole.

[...]

I believe that an awareness of this merger between stage and auditorium will also lead the architect along quite new paths in his approach to the rest of the theater. Divisions between the classes, the ludicrous grandeur of the foyer, the undignified "dignity" of the external design will thus disappear and it will also be possible to deal more straightforwardly with the technical apparatus that is usually a stumbling block for the theater architect today. At present the technical element of theater is too obtrusive: it has to be simplified, albeit in an artistic sense; it must not become simplistic. Today it is not the designers who build theaters, but with very few exceptions it is the "experienced theater man," who describes himself as an architect and has all the technical tricks up his sleeve. In reality he is an engineer, although unfortunately he is not entirely that, either, for if he were, he would admit that the theater is in every sense an artistic matter, and he would bow to the demands of the day. Nowadays theaters have become manufacturing companies, mass-producing goods for cash.

At which point I find myself back where I started: the deliverance of the theater in a social sense. And here the architect can do no more than propose an ideal for the future.

One day the spacious, generously built town—albeit not so much a "town" in the old sense as more properly a "*Siedlung*"[2]—should be topped by a group of different buildings that truly draw people together.

NOTES

1. *Das hohe Ufer* was a short-lived avant-garde journal published in Hanover in 1919/1920. In addition to Bruno Taut, its contributors included the architects Walter Gropius, Hans Poelzig, and Heinrich Tessenow. Writers like Klabund, Georg Trakl, and Franz Werfel also contributed, and illustrations were commissioned from Lyonel Feininger, Arnold Topp, and Kurt Schwitters.

2. On the various meanings of *Siedlung*, see the introduction to section 8, "The Green Outdoors."

187

Egon Erwin Kisch

ELLIPTICAL TREADMILL

First published as "Elliptische Tretmühle," 1919; reprinted in Kisch, *Der rasende Reporter*, (Berlin and Weimar: Aufbau, 1990), pp. 269–74. Translated by Iain Boyd Whyte.

For the tenth time—so it's a birthday—the Six-Day Race is raging in the Sportpalast on Potsdamer Strasse. Thirteen cyclists, each one belonging to a pair, began on Friday at nine o'clock in the evening to push on the pedals. Seven thousand people took their expensively bought seats, and since then the crazy carousel has

FIGURE 42. The winners of the twenty-ninth Berlin Six-Day Race: Buysee (left) and Deneef (right), in the Sportpalast, Berlin, 1 January 1933. Ullstein Bild, 69090698.

been going day and night. The cyclists cover around 700 kilometers in twenty-four hours, and there are hopes that they will threaten the world record, the historic word record set when in 1914, over six nightless Berlin days, the trifling distance of 4,260,920 kilometers was covered, at which point the World War broke out.

For six days and six nights the thirteen cyclists look neither to the right nor to the left, but straight ahead. They drive themselves forward but are always on the same spot, always on the oval of the racetrack, on the long straights or on the curves that rise up almost vertically. Uncannily bunched, sometimes at the head of the pack, sometimes at the back, and sometimes—and then the public yell, "Hip, hip!"—a couple of meters ahead of the pack. But when one of them has been ahead for a couple of laps, he ends back where he was before, sticking with the bunch of thirteen.

They stay on the same spot as they charge forward, traveling at fantastic speeds over distances that are as long as the diagonals of Europe, like Constantinople to London or Madrid to Moscow. But they don't get to see either the Bosporus or Lloyd George; no Escorial and no Lenin; not a hint of a harem or of a lady riding along Hyde Park's Rotten Row; no Carmen bewitching Don José, and no socialists with short, dark hair and Marx's *Theories of Surplus Value* in their overcoat. They stay on the same spot in the same loop with the same people—a deadly earnest, murderous merry-go-round. And when it is all over and the 144th hour has rung out, the winner—approaching delirium tremens—sinks mumbling from his bike in victory, a model of physical hardening.

For six days and nights, thirteen pairs of legs press on the pedals, the right leg on the right pedal, the left leg on the left pedal; thirteen backs are bent downward while the head nods incessantly, once to the right, once to the left, according to which foot is pushing at that particular moment; and thirteen pairs of hands do nothing but hold the handlebars. In the meantime, their thirteen partners lie exhausted in underground boxes and are massaged. Six days and six nights.

Outside, the newspaper girls carry the morning papers from dispatch, the first streetcars leave the garage, workers go into the factories, a husband gives his young wife a morning kiss, a policeman relieves another at the street corner, customers come into the café, someone considers whether he should wear the gray-and-black striped tie today or the knitted brown one, the dollar gains, a criminal finally decides to confess, a mother spanks her sons, typewriters clatter, factory sirens hoot the lunch break, the Deutsches Theater stages a play by Georg Kaiser that takes place during the Six-Day Race,[1] the waiter fails to bring the steak, the boss sacks an employee who has four children, one hundred people push and shove at the cinema ticket office, an aged playboy seduces a girl, a lady has her hair dyed, a schoolboy does his mathematical problems, in parliament there are stormy scenes, and an Indian feast in the rooms of Philharmonic Hall, people sit on the toilet in their houses and read the paper, someone has a dream of appearing in a ballroom dressed only in an undershirt and pants, a high school boy can't sleep since he won't be able to explain Pythagoras's theorem, a surgeon amputates a leg, people are born and people die, a bud blossoms and a blossom withers, a star fades and a scaffolder climbs up the front of a house, the sun sparkles, and recruits learn to shoot, thunder rumbles, and bank directors hold office, beasts of prey are fed at the zoo, and a marriage takes place, the moon shines, and the conference of ambassadors frames resolutions, a millwheel rattles, and innocent folk sit in jail, people are good and people are bad—while all the time the thirteen, with their rears on a spherical triangle formed from leather, travel around and around endlessly and incessantly, with shaven heads and hairy legs.

At the same time, the earth rotates to get light from the sun, the moon rotates to bring nocturnal light to the earth, and the wheels rotate to create wealth. Only we humans spin around and around senselessly and about nothing in our arbitrary ellipse for six days and nights. The author of the sun, the earth, the moon, and mankind looks down from his celestial atelier onto the masterpiece of his creation, onto his intentional self-portrait, and observes that man—for as long as it took to form the world—strides along his own path, right, left, right, left—*Gott denkt, aber der Mensch lenkt* [literally, "God thinks, but man steers"].

Poe could not have thought this one up: that at the edge of his terrible maelstrom a cheerily excited crowd of spectators would be standing and cheering on the devastating rotation with hip-hips and hurrahs. It happens here, and the two times thirteen victims generate themselves the maelstrom in which they descend into the depths of hell. If an inquisitor had dug up such a torture, called something like the "elliptical treadmill," he would have been bound to the wheel himself, even in the darkest Middle Ages. But in the twentieth century we have to have six-day races.

A pistol shot rings out: the battle within the battle. Go! Go! Thirteen visibly pounding hearts pound even more visibly, legs pump even faster, right, left, right, left, the roaring of the public becomes hypertrophic. "Hipp, hipp!" You might be in an asylum for the ravingly insane, or even in parliament. Is it an accident when the Dutchman, Vermeer, shoots off his bike in a steep arc and lands in the middle of the crowd? Does it change anything that Tietz stays down? No, it doesn't change a thing when the ball bounces out of the roulette wheel. You simply take another one. If a rider breaks a record, you scream applause, but if he breaks his neck—what is it to you? The race goes on; the living roulette balls roll on.

It is well known in Berlin sporting circles that even unhappy marriages are soothed by the Six Days. The henpecked husband can stay out for six days and nights, completely without control and without fear of a wigging. Even the jealous husband leaves his wife unwatched and without mistrust to go wherever she wants—right, left, right, left—to eat, drink, or sleep with her friends, since hubby is immersed body and soul in the Six-Day Race. Once there, the spectators don't budge, regardless of whether they have been given time off by the boss or have called in sick, whether they have closed the shop or left the completion of their business to their employees, whether they neglect to visit their clients, whether they are striking or unemployed. To break off prematurely from this entertainment is an exception—as, for example, in the case of Herr Wilhelm Hanke, of Schönhauser Strasse number 139. On the third day of racing, the announcer shouted left, right, left through his megaphone to the seven thousand spectators: "Herr Wilhelm Hanke, Schönhauser Strasse 139, should return home immediately. His wife has died!"

NOTE

1. In Georg Kaiser's stage play *Von Morgen bis Mitternacht* (From morning to midnight; 1920), the six-day cycle race and the frenzy of the audience stand for the rampant and meaningless pursuit of money.

188
Adolf Behne
GROSSES SCHAUSPIELHAUS, SCALAPALAST

First published as "Großes Schauspielhaus, Scalapalast," *Sozialistische Monatshefte* 27, no. 56 (14 February 1921), pp. 164–65, 166. Translated by Ishbel Flett.

Hans Poelzig converted the Zirkus Schumann in Berlin into the Großes Schauspielhaus for [Max] Reinhardt. The circumstances that place such restrictions on creativity must be taken into account. *Neues Theater* could not have been created here, since it is hardly what Reinhardt would have wanted, and even if he had, he would certainly not have achieved it. There is little to indicate "new" theater in the performances. *Lysistrata,* for instance, was staged in exactly the same way as any *Kammerspiel* could have staged it, possibly even better. Evidently, Reinhardt was primarily concerned with acquiring the much-cited "broader framework" for his predominantly picturesque approach to directing. Of course, Reinhardt's conservative, retrospective tendencies are reflected in the architecture of Poelzig, who would undoubtedly have been better served by building something essentially new, as he himself would surely have preferred. In the end, only the outward appearance of the building is convincing. But that in itself is a major achievement, enriching Berlin with a beautiful work of architecture. The overall effect of this impressive building with its closed and minimally perforated walls, with its stringent verticality strongly underlined by slender pilaster strips, is quite striking in its remarkable situation between narrow streets—and, as befits a theater, singularly exciting. The clear interaction of the angular volumes is full of inner tension, and the simple yet distinctive cornices are executed with an energetic line that generates an extraordinarily expressive sense of movement. The outward appearance raises enormous expectations with regard to the interior. The building seems almost like a huge tent on a magnificent fairground—an impression further heightened by the rough-plastered rendering and the rusty hues of red, yellow, and brown. It is delightful in the unaccustomed freshness of its almost provisional appearance. Here, at last, is a work that is neither ponderous nor pompous, without empty gestures of prestige or gravity, a heartfelt and nonchalant work. The fact that the interior is a disappointment rather than an extension of this is hardly the fault of the architect. It was surely impossible to find a convincing form for the internally ambiguous program. However beautiful Poelzig's stalactite dome may be when the spotlights cast their rays through its twilight, its purpose is unclear. It does not bring together the massed audience, nor does it accentuate the setting. It hovers somewhere between the two. In spite of these shortcomings, however, the interior is one of the most precious architectural achievements of our day. Only the foyers with their pillars of light, admittedly the most famous feature, are remarkable for the spectacular *presentation* with which they call our bluff. It is regrettable that, here, Poelzig's architecture *acts* theatrically instead of *being* theater. These, however, are minor flaws. On the whole, this is an impressive achievement, and a pleasing one at that. One senses an individual at work here who is unencumbered by the ballast of aesthetic erudition and who does not consider it the most important task of architecture to be solemn and grand. There is a subtle hint of early medieval, even Roman, functional buildings, just as there is in the factory building at Lubahn, but without a trace of historicist revivalism.

[. . .]

The collaboration between architects Walter Würzbach and Alfred Gellhorn, the sculptor Rudolf Belling, and the painter Hans Brass is also a team effort. They created thoroughly eccentric interior designs for some of the rooms in the Scalapalast, the most interesting of which are undoubtedly the two rooms designed by Belling. Those involved maintain that, in this project, they found that a free, comradely, direct, and improvised approach motivated the craftsmen enormously, and this is perfectly plausible. Nevertheless, I would hesitate to ascribe any artistic significance to these rooms. They are witty and clever, but entirely void of substance and typically fashionable. Today, they are worth advertising, but tomorrow nobody will be interested in them. Such rooms are just what we need least: Expressionism in architecture seems to have been dreamed up for no other reason than to secure a place in art history as the *first Expressionist architects.* And the funny thing is that art has long since moved on from this kind of Expressionism; even in painting. It cannot be denied that the task of designing a casino or a dance hall (and an appealing and lovely task it is, too) can involve choosing the most free, the most unexpected, and the most mobile forms that can be developed on the basis of its designation, audience, and movement. But precisely this development of form on the basis of material and function seems to me to have been neglected here. When the rooms were still empty, they had the look of some strange cinematic architecture. The *Kunstblatt* has now published photographs of the furnished rooms, and it is quite disconcerting to see how unfitting the tables and chairs seem in these rooms; not because they are not Expressionist as well, but because the rooms themselves are artificial constructs. This whole thing is ten years too late. When the Marmorkino was built, they would have been *interesting.* Today, we have the impression that some smart decorators, eager to be the *first* in Europe, have lost their way and are now straggling behind. Any work so clearly aimed at creating an effect is, ultimately, fruitless, and this particular work is all too clearly aimed at an all too fancy effect. Such catchphrases as sculptural handling of space are not the thing here; nor is it movement at any price.

189
Siegfried Kracauer
ROLLERCOASTER RIDE

First published as "Berg- und Talbahn," *Frankfurter Zeitung*, 14 July 1928; republished in Kracauer, *Schriften*, vol. 5, fasc. 2, *Aufsätze, 1927–1931* (Frankfurt am Main: Suhrkamp 1990), pp. 117–18. Translated by Ishbel Flett.

In the Lunapark fairground at Halensee, a painted backdrop of New York rises between the swimming pool and the racecourse. The lurid skyscraper facades jut vertiginously into the night sky. In reality, these backdrops cover only a small area. They serve as props on a stretch of track that meanders through them in all directions.

On Saturday evening—the morning of workers, ordinary folks, and employees—a crowd escaping the city gathers at the gates of this urban illusion. From within, a constant shrieking clamor can be heard. Sometimes, at the least expected place, a fairground car comes into sight, only to disappear again just as suddenly. Actually, it is not the car itself that can be seen, but the flying streak of human figures. As soon as they stop, the cars fill up again. They are long and narrow, and each row of seating is just big enough for a couple.

The ride starts slowly. Its gradual ascent to the level of the upper-floor windows is not, in itself, an unfamiliar sensation. After all, metro trains also emerge from the underground, and, as they climb upward, the many shorthand typists can glimpse into the offices in which they normally write. Yet here, amazingly, the car presses on higher than any elevated train—up to the height of, say, the thirteenth floor. The workers, the ordinary folks, the employees, oppressed on weekdays by the city, now conquer New York in the air above Berlin. They are victors, with the magically painted palaces spread at their feet.

The car has arrived at a Moorish dome. Since when have skyscrapers been crowned with domes? One sharp curve and the dome is out of sight; gone is the splendor of the palaces. The facades were mere facades, simple sets fronting a huge wooden support frame. Posts and beams and struts: scaffolding forms the core of these magnificent fronts. Only a moment ago, the city flaunted its wonders, and now it bares its skeletal bones. So that's New York—a painted board with nothing behind it? The little couples are mesmerized and disillusioned at the same time. Not that they simply dismiss the overblown urban imagery as humbug, but they do see through the illusion, at which their conquest of the facades no longer means a great deal to them. They are in a place where things show themselves from two sides, holding the shrunken skyscrapers in the palm of their empty hand, liberated from the world whose splendors they know.

The car accelerates. It hurtles down into the abyss at immeasurable speed. The passengers scream as one. Everybody has to scream. Even if they clenched their teeth, they would be screaming now.

Primitive instincts force the scream out. Those routinely suffocated by the rigid structure of things are set free by the outward confusion, by the jumble of facades and wooden frames. Galvanized by the crazy speed, they lapse into uproar. The passengers yell in fear of being dashed to pieces, trembling at the edge of the world, terrified by the vision of danger. Their screaming is elemental.

It is also something else besides. It is also the scream of bliss at racing through a New York whose very substance is sublated and no longer poses a threat. It is almost as though they were all screaming because they feel they are free at last. A cry of triumph: here we are, immersed in happiness, hurtling ever onward. Hurtling at a breakneck speed that might mean death; at the same time, it also means fulfillment.

The scream continues unabated. In a never-ending frenzy, the game comes to an end. The secrets of gloomy tunnels are probed in a flash; blurred facades rush past. The world has become a frenetic scribble. Before the tumbling barriers, swishing lines, and rushing fragments, these are no longer workers, ordinary folks, and employees, but people stretching from pole to pole like flying streaks: from crest to trough, from the heights to the depths and back again.

Arrival. Finished. The ride took only a few minutes and traversed the world. The exhausted body is still trembling. In the fairground that was the cosmos, New York towers aloof. A shadowy figure sits in a pavilion set before the backdrop, keeping an eye on things. He is a tired man. He does not see the skyscrapers, the Moorish domes, or the tiny red light shimmering in the darkness.

190

Berliner Börsen-Courier
[CINEMA]

First published in *Berliner Börsen-Courier*, 2 November 1923. Translated by Iain Boyd Whyte.

When I went to the cinema the day before yesterday and was already standing at the ticket office, I was appalled at the high entry prices, and my hand pulled back at the last moment. But it was too late. I had already asked for a seat. "Two, please," said the cashier. In today's language that means 200 billion. I tried to convince myself with the (hopeless) thought that I would have money tomorrow, and passed over a 500-billion note. This provoked a small incident. The lady at the cash desk, inevitably, had just taken a billion note and didn't have a penny change left (as it is still so sensibly expressed) . . . I could actually have done without the ticket, as the price was too high in any case. My (highly developed) instinct for business, however, saved me from this folly. After a long hesitation, the cashier gave me 3 billion back in the form of four gold marks [*Goldanleihestücken*]. I took them with deep distrust and with the certain feeling that I'd been duped, which one constantly has these days when receiving money from someone else.

Today the gold marks stand at over 500 billion. I've sold the four coins, seen the film for nothing, and earned over 1.5 billion. I'll now go to this cinema more often; but I'm not going to give its name. In these times you should keep your business contacts to yourself.

191

Alfred Flechtheim

GLADIATORS

First published as "Gladiatoren," *Der Querschnitt* 1 (1926), pp. 48ff; reprinted in *Berlin im "Querschnitt,"* ed. Rolf-Peter Baacke (Berlin: Fannei & Walz, 1990), pp. 84–85. Translated by Ishbel Flett.

"More light!"[1]

Although every Berlin premiere fills the columns of the daily newspapers to capacity, the theaters are empty.

Only the cabarets and Mr. Max Reinhardt's fur-coated orgies at the Komödie play to full houses, thanks to the critics. Georg Kaiser's *Jewish Widow* had to close. The critics failed it utterly. Kaiser should have written his play in French and had it translated into German by Julius Elias.

For Hans Breitensträter's fight against Pablo Uzcudun, the fifteen thousand seats in the Sportpalast were completely sold out eight days in advance.

Because the audience increasingly senses that the theater is all about cronyism. Just as the fight between van der Veer and Breitensträter is said to have been. For the Sportpalast audiences are not made up just of brewers' draymen and chauffeurs; all of bourgeois society is there: princes and princesses, painters and sculptors, literati and high finance, and all the actors who are not performing this evening. How come?

Because the audience senses that what is happening in the boxing ring is real drama and not just some misinterpreted Joan of Arc story. What happens within the space of half an hour in the ring surrounded by fifteen thousand excited people is real drama that bears no comparison with any theater performance.

A major boxing match cannot be a put-up job, because boxing, by its very nature, is of an intensity that brooks no prearranged deals. Boxing is energy at its utmost potency. Great boxers give their all. It takes them months to prepare for a fight, and the tension in the ring is transmitted to the audience, transmitted to Max Slevogt and to the brewer's drayman, to Tilla Durieux and to the mannequin from Gerson's department store.[2]

The fight between the German and the Spaniard was an unprecedented event. Their work was comparable to that of general staff officers. There was no shame in Breitensträter losing; his was an honorable defeat. He fought like Hector after taking leave of Andromache, he fought against Paolino and against Carpentier, one against two. Paolino had called upon the European king of boxing as his training partner, and Breitensträter had seconded him in the fight. He seconded like a general in charge of his troops, like an electric boat remote-controlled from the shore. His manager Descamps (who recalls Poiret and Vollard) had got this Basque bull to train in a way no German boxer has yet achieved. Paolino, strong as one of Widow Miura's *toros bravos*, weighed in at ten kilos more than Breitensträter. The weight difference gave him an added advantage right from the start. Added to this was the notion that he had everything to lose in this fight. If Breitenstäter were to win, Paolino's chances of becoming European champion would be soured. Because nobody doubted that he would beat Spalla. The German had nothing to lose. Had he won, he would have met the Italian in the ring and Germany would have had one more man of great caliber. And that would have been of enormously value to Germany, for in Germany we have very few figures of major international rank, and could well have done with another alongside Bode, alongside the Einsteins, alongside Richard Strauss.[3]

To dwell on the details of the fight here would be carrying coals to Newcastle. The average person knows what a boxing match is, and has pored over every phase of this major event in the *Berliner Zeitung* and the *Acht-Uhr-Abendblatt.*

But the fact that this fight—in which strength, spirit, and experience prevailed as one—was an artistic issue, more artistic than any Berlin theater performance, is evident to all who had the good fortune to attend this tremendous show.

I congratulate Breitensträter on this fight. The effort was Kokoschkaesque.[4] This time around, he failed. But next time—!

NOTES

1. "More light!" ("*Mehr Licht!*") are reputedly the last works spoken by Goethe before his death in Weimar on 23 March 1832.

2. Max Slevogt (1868–1932) was a German Impressionist painter; Tilla Durieux (1880–1971) was an actress.

3. Wilhelm von Bode (1849–1925) was an art historian and director general of all Prussian museums from 1906 to 1920.

4. Kokoschkaesque: in the manner of the painter Oscar Kokoschka (1886–1980).

192

Gerhard Krause

THE GERMAN STADIUM AND SPORTS FORUM

First published as *Das Deutsche Stadion und Sportforum* (Berlin: Weidmannsche Buchhandlung, 1926), pp. 7–8. Translated by Iain Boyd Whyte.

German Stadium [Deutsches Stadion]—a series of vivid images suggest themselves to our imagination: pine trees in the March of Brandenburg sand, the lofty grandstands of a horse-race track, a well-lit tunnel under the playing field, an expansive concrete basin nestling into the ground. The lush green oval of the greensward makes a charming contrast with the black and white ring of the running and cycling track that surrounds it. The balustrade that runs around the center of the seating area glows pale yellow, and is interrupted only along one of its long sides by the glittering mirror of the swimming pool. A smiling sun above—and laughing youth within. A joyful bustle, with suntanned figures everywhere; the most cheerful and animated activity—and yet there is seriousness in this play.

[. . .]

In the eyes of the world the Stadium was an expression of the powerful unity of sport; for the sportsmen themselves a constant admonition to strive toward this goal. But it was not simply as a monument to unity that the Stadium made a deep impression on the visitor; for one also perceives in the Stadium a distinctive mark of sporting culture and recognizes in astonishment that sport also declares here its will to culture [*Kulturwille*]. Until now, we had to make do with ugly sandlots set between wooden fences and high, black firewalls. If there were viewing stands, they were knocked together from wood, as were the huts that served as changing rooms. But precisely those sportsmen who used the facilities most enthusiastically were also the most aware of the inadequacy of this state of affairs. For where there is light and joy, life and movement, there must also be beauty. This longing for an artistically perfect shrine for sport was first realized in the German Stadium. In its simple form, its clear, taut lines, its inspired boldness of scale, and its scheme of decorative sculpture, the architect [Otto] March has created a work of classical beauty. Artistic laws have been employed for the first time in a sporting structure; and for the first time a special place has been created for those who have incorporated sport into their philosophy of life. Both in its overall conception and in its immaculate order and upkeep it satisfies their hearts' desires and accommodates their need for sophisticated and refined form. The cultural significance that thereby found expression both worked to promote sport across the entire nation, and also had an educative function for sport itself: it was simultaneously an emblem of and a testimonial to sporting culture.

And a third quality has given the Stadium its own fascination over the years:

it became a temple of memory and of national consecration. How many recollections of festive celebrations and ennobling contests are tied to this arena? Celebrations in which our entire people were involved, and in which the history of our suffering and joy in recent decades has been reflected.

[. . .]

It would, of course, make no sense to portray the Stadium as a symbol of power, of unity, of the will to culture through sport, and as a witness and mirror of German history, if the general public did not also recognize these characteristics and had not drawn the consequences for its own conduct. But this is just the case: the building of the German Stadium was a great deed, and has generated further achievements. It has stimulated new developments in Germany in the construction of playing fields and sports arenas. [. . .] The Berlin model emboldens others to similar buildings: the stadia in Cologne, Frankfurt, Kassel, Dortmund, Breslau, Liegnitz, Neise, Hamburg, Bremen, Nuremberg, and in other cities are, in a certain way, the children of the mother building in Grunewald.[1]

NOTE

1. The Kaiser-Wilhelm-Stadion was designed by Otto March and opened in 1913 in Berlin-Grunewald. It was intended to house the summer Olympic Games planned for 1916. Renamed the Deutsches Stadion after World War I, it was replaced by the 1936 Olympic Stadium, built to the design of Otto March's architect son, Werner March.

193

Matheo Quinz

THE ROMANISCHE CAFÉ

First published as "Das Romanische Café," *Der Querschnitt* 8 (1926), pp. 608ff; reprinted in *Berlin im "Querschnitt,"* ed. Rolf-Peter Baacke (Berlin: Fannei & Walz, 1990), pp. 59–62. Translated by Ishbel Flett.

The Romanische Café has the feel of a huge public bath, divided into a large pool for swimmers and a smaller pool for nonswimmers. Visitors to these two sections have little in common with one another. Where the revolving doors divide the two pools, which are worlds apart, stands Nietz, the doorman, who is the most important person here after Höxter. He directs the traffic magisterially, having adopted the sober and discreetly energetic tone of a keeper in a mental asylum. Only guests known personally to Mr. Nietz, whose names he knows so that he can call them to the telephone without paging them loudly throughout the café, are regarded as accepted guests, artists or otherwise. Most of them are advertising salesmen. Artists that Nietz does not know simply do not exist.

The nonswimmers' pool is populated mainly by Egon Erwin Kisch, who has the astonishing ability to conduct scintillating conversations at all tables simultaneously while reading all the newspapers, and without missing any chance of casting a fascinating glance at all the women who pass by the pool. When Kisch is not in Berlin, the pool becomes noticeably emptier.[1]

There are two corners of the nonswimmers' pool where the Communist section of the Romanische Café meets; one table is occupied daily by the good old Talmud readers, and a real existing god was once even invented at this very table. The Flechtheim table is also in the nonswimmers' section,[2] and, overseeing everything, at the far end of the café, the psychiatrist Dr. Emanuel observes his dear patients and seeks out potential patients. Surgeons and the like do not frequent this café; the specialist field of the resident doctors Dr. Benn and Dr. Döhmann is not to be mentioned for reasons of discretion, but is noted in the address book.[3]

The circle around the nonswimmers' pool is remarkable. There are journalists representing the political spectrum all the way from the *Rote Fahne* to the *Kreuzzeitung*.

Public prosecutor Caspary sits beside [legal theorist] Gumbel of *Zwei Jahre Mord* fame, while Bronnen and Leonhard Frank rub shoulders with Arthur Rebner as they drink their coffee.[4] The art dealers are there, from Flechtheim to the world's leading female art dealer. Valeska Gert and Celly de Rheidt, Jessner and the director of the Liebhabertheater in Groß-Salze; and just about every artist from Otto Dix to Mopp, Krauskopf and Lederer.[5] One painter even goes by the name of Feigel. Incidentally, all the painters have been suffering for some time from chronic Dolbinitis. They draw portraits of one another at incredible speed.

In the nonswimmers' pool there are also some guests who never sit down—apart from Höxter, who has to go around all the tables on business. There's a mathematician who also has such talents as swallowing worms and throwing a boomerang, and who wears white trousers and a monocle with which he gazes around the pool once an hour on average. Stefan Grossmann[6] also strolls through the hall, but only in the evening, before he goes to bed.

Between the pools, at the Cap des Arrivés, is the Grandees' Table, geographically situated quite clearly in the swimmers' section. Here, Slevogt and Bruno Cassirer[7] throne in dignity. Only a chosen few may take a seat here, but those few have made the table their raison d'être. Here, the art instructor Scheffler[8] speaks one thousand words a day to Cassirer's stable of artists (Cassirer's own trainers don't frequent *this* café). Here, Orlik demonstrates—between two tea parties and four suppers—that it is possible to draw with the right and left hand simultaneously without being a Menzel.[9] It was here that Grossmann invented the sport of drawing without looking at the paper—a skill long since surpassed by Orlik,[10] who draws on a piece of paper in his trouser pocket. The grandees hold audience daily until nine o'clock. Then, Slevogt has to leave the table whether he wants to or not, because this is when the landlord eats his schnitzel here. Not even Orlik can do anything about it.

The swimming pool is occupied by those who have money, or at least pretend to, which is to say, film people, has-been stage directors, advertising salesmen, cigarette salesmen, and the poet Oskar Kanehl.[11] The guests in this section are treated with great respect by the waiters; they tend to drink mocha, especially the film people. This is where the money sits, but also some who dodge their bills or go out wearing the wrong overcoat. (It should be noted that these gentlemen are among the swimmers; the nonswimmers preferring to borrow openly, which is the only thing likely to persuade an enraged visitor to change over from the small pool to the large pool). It is here, in the sunshine of capital, that the young girls bask. They have lovely names: Joa, the Infantin of the Romanische Café; Bibiana, who was trained by Peter Altenberg; Anja, whom the painter Meidner was determined to teach how to pray; Mottchen, of whom it is said that she once ruined a man completely (the man did not frequent the Romanische).[12] They all make every effort to appear as fine ladies. Some of them might even achieve that status, as Takka-Takka did, and above all Nadja, the oft-painted and much loved Nadja, who is now seen only rarely between trips to Cairo or Biarritz. It is impossible to tell which of the young ladies is currently romantically involved with whom; let alone who is currently married to or divorced from whom. Only the café's lawyer, with his classical features, is party to such inside knowledge, and on such things he remains silent, just as he has done for twenty years. Yet there is only a handful of regulars Hans Braun has not guided with tact and success through their divorce proceedings, and hardly any of the young girls here has not provided the grounds for at least one divorce.

Life in the Romanische Café goes on from five in the afternoon to one in the morning. At other times it is a lonely place, with only a few of the finest people, such as the former dadaist Huelsenbeck,[13] eating their schnitzel here, or a few poor devils on the lookout for a patron who will save them. Only on Sunday at lunchtime is all hell let loose: what is spread out over a ten-hour period during the week descends upon the café for a bourgeois Sunday afternoon stroll through the Romanische.

In the early morning, between eight and ten, the air is infernal: cold smoke, rancid powder, floor polish, and dust. It is around this time that the gamblers drop in from the countless little dens in the west of the city, and the loving couples, or at least one half of them, arrive from the seedy little hotels of ill repute around the Zoo. They are weary, hung-over breakfasters, but the waiters welcome them: they do not linger over their cup of coffee for eight or ten hours, as is otherwise the custom at the Romanische Café, but go meekly on their tired way home, or off to work. Whereas the others are boisterous when they leave, annoyed at having to break off their important discourse on Picasso, Sarotti, Mussolini, and their weighty discussions on business, art and enterprise. They all feel so important, almost as important as Mr Meier, who thinks the world will come to a standstill if he misses his drink with the regulars at the corner bar.

NOTES

1. Egon Erwin Kisch (1885–1948) was a journalist, dubbed "the Racing Reporter" (*Der rasende Reporter*); see above, text 187: Egon Erwin Kisch, Elliptical Treadmill.
2. Alfred Flechtheim (1878–1937) was a collector, art dealer, and publisher; see above, text 191: Alfred Flechtheim, Gladiators.
3. Alfred Benn (1886–1956) was a doctor (venereologist), poet, and prose writer. Benn and Kisch (*see above*) had a highly publicized argument in 1932 on the relationship between politics and art.
4. Arnolt Bronnen (1895–1959) was a writer and radio dramaturge. Leonhard Frank (1882–1961), although trained as a painter, gained fame as a novelist and playwright. He also wrote movie scripts in Hollywood in the early 1940s. Arthur Rebner (1890–1949) was a film songwriter and composer.
5. Valeska Gert (1892–1978), was an actress, dancer, and writer. Celly de Rheidt, was a dancer who ran a nude ballet company. Leopold Jessner (1878–1945), theatrical producer and director, was closely associated with Expressionist drama. Otto Dix (1891–1969) was a painter. Max Oppenheimer, called "Mopp" (1885–1954), was a painter and writer. Bruno Krauskopf (1892–1960) was a painter. Hugo Lederer (1871–1940) was a sculptor.
6. Stefan Grossmann (1875–1935), a leading left-liberal journalist, was the sometime feuilleton editor of the *Vossische Zeitung* and the editor, between 1920 and 1927, of the weekly *Das Tage-Buch*.
7. Max Slevogt (1868–1932) was an Impressionist painter. Bruno Cassirer (1872–1941) was an art dealer and publisher.
8. Karl Scheffler (1869–1961),was a journalist and publicist.
9. Adolf Menzel (1815–1905) was one of the greatest German painters of the nineteenth century.
10. Emil Orlik (1870–1932) was a painter and illustrator.
11. Oskar Kanehl (1888–1929) was a left-wing poet linked to the KPD (German Communist Party).
12. Peter Altenberg (1859–1919) was a pseudonym of the Viennese writer Richard Engländer. Ludwig Meidner (1884–1966), an Expressionist painter, was best known for his apocalyptic cityscapes, painted shortly before the outbreak of World War I.
13. Richard Huelsenbeck (1892–1974), painter and poet, founded the Berlin Dada group and in later life worked as a psychoanalyst in New York, under the name Charles R. Hulbeck.

194

Hans Poelzig

THE CAPITOL CINEMA

First published as "Das Capitol," *Der Querschnitt* 10 (1926), pp. 750ff; reprinted in *Berlin im "Querschnitt,"* ed. Rolf-Peter Baacke (Berlin: Fannei & Walz, 1990), pp. 165–66. Translated by David Britt.

Today's movie theaters tend to cloak themselves in a diluted form of Baroque or rococo, as a sop to tradition, despite the entirely modern purpose for which they are built. In this there is certainly an element of pretension, of pandering to the instincts of the masses, as well as cowardice and an inability to contribute to the authentic evolution of architectural form. For a modern movie auditorium is clearly not at all the same thing as an eighteenth-century theater.

Clearly, too, every client who wants a cinema built will have to insist on having the actual *organism* of his building designed in a modern way. By this I mean that the architect—doing battle with public building codes—must make full use of all the available space while employing a minimum of materials: the screen or stage must be fully visible from every part of the house, and the acoustics for music or speech must be as good as they can be. The purely formal aspects of the commission concern the client only to the extent that a good solution will receive a good press and improve the reputation of his building. Not that this latter point counts for a great deal, since with a movie house the proprietor has ample opportunity to praise the beauties of his own theater at length in press advertisements.

There is neither motive nor compulsion to make the building logical and modern in the details of its design. Quite the contrary: the proprietor runs the risk—as he sees it—that some overly audacious artistic experiment will drive the average audience away. Hence all the hesitancy; hence, also, the prevalence of compromise solutions that respect modernity in the organization of the building and ornamental tradition in its decor.

However, there is one area above all that must afford the starting point for consistently modern visual design. This is *lighting*. The proper exploitation of the potential of electric lighting, whether direct or indirect, demands interiors that will show off this form of illumination to its best advantage: spaces configured in terms of its potential. The architect must therefore devise spatial forms that not only favor the full use of modern technology but are actually created with its possibilities in mind. Since our movie theaters more or less dispense with daylight altogether, and since no form can be seen in the absence of light, artificial light must enter into the architect's calculations as a *space-creating* factor.

195

J-S

REVIEW OF WALTHER RUTTMANN'S FILM *BERLIN: THE SYMPHONY OF A GREAT CITY* (1927)

First published as "Berlin: Die Sinfonie der Großstadt," *Die Filmwoche*, no. 40 (5 October 1927), p. 949. Translated by Iain Boyd Whyte.

A film that [...] runs aground on a catchword of our times: on "rhythm." This "rhythm" is a totally fateful catchword. A big city, a world city, a "present-day life" must have rhythm, and one must understand this rhythm, live within it, "swing" within it—in fact, I don't know what else one must do with this unfortunate rhythm. [...] And yet—this catchword is actually here, and therefore the film, poor thing, must also serve it. [...]

As the program so correctly remarks, the film is an experiment—a bold, worthy experiment; a thankful and, above all, technical experiment. And one that has not been successful. One that could not be successful! For Berlin is much too little surface, much too little external form. Berlin is a colossal entity, a diversity that is incapable of being grasped comprehensively by a single film, a profound soul, a great happiness, and a huge impoverishment. Berlin is an immense soul, it is a great affliction and destruction, it is ascent and hope. Berlin is the deepest inner sentiment, it is the immeasurable fate of the heart. And it has very little to do with cats and dance bars and elevated railways. The film *Die letzte Droschke von Berlin* [The last hansom cab of Berlin] could have been titled "Berlin"—the old resisted the new, social perspectives came into conflict with technical innovations, a family was destroyed, a new one was built up and developed . . . this is an experience of the concept of Berlin. [...] And yet, Mr. Ruttmann could quite rightly reply that that is not the point; he wishes to display the face of Berlin. All to the good. But even that, too, must fail. The face of Berlin, as he has interpreted it and as he has revealed it, is not a Berlin face but simply a metropolitan face as such. The tower of the Berlin Town Hall doesn't change this one bit. Ruttmann reveals how human beings in any metropolis go about their work, how they enjoy themselves. How they live on the surface. A symphony? No, not on any account. We will have to judge this film as a document—a document of the fact that one cannot accomplish the impossible. Technically—now here something quite outstanding has been achieved.

196

Leo Hirsch

CINEMAS

First published as "Kinos," *Berliner Tageblatt,* 15 November 1927; reprinted in *Glänzender Asphalt: Berlin im Feuilleton der Weimarer Republik,* ed. Christian Jäger and Erhard Schütz (Berlin: Fannei & Walz, 1994), pp. 209–11. Translated by Ishbel Flett.

There are two species of cinema in Berlin—the *tame* and the *wild*. Another mutation, the home cinema, would be added to the list only by the theoretical pedant, to whose bespectacled eyes lions, white mice, and Eva the Whale all march together as mammals. The tame cinemas, for the most part, pride themselves on screening premieres. The wild cinemas merely have new releases and play all the films that the dictates of their owners or distributors oblige them to show. The tame cinemas tend to be situated between Halensee and Potsdamer Platz, and go by the name of *Lichtspielhaus* [literally, "light-playhouse"]—and indeed, they do have lots of light, both inside and out. The wild ones simply call themselves *Kino* [literally, "cinema"], put great store in the scope of their program, and bask in the lurid colors of their posters rather than in bright lights. No matter how they present themselves and their films, they are a species we can no longer imagine lacking in the urban fabric or in the cities as such, and if there were a modern-day equivalent of *panem et circences,* it would surely be *bread and cinema.*

How delightfully young cinema still is; how delightfully fast it has grown; and how delightful it is, as well, to be a contemporary, witnessing at first hand how *decadent* it is already becoming in that sumptuous overrefinement that heralds the fall of all civilizations. It is a truly young genre, with only the third generation now at the helm. Even as recently as 1900, there was no permanent cinema in Berlin. Films were shown in fairground booths and occasionally in cabaret theaters. Some of the "showmen" of these early days are still alive, fossils now cast in the new and more dignified role of "movie-theater directors," having started out with one-and-one-third-meter-long strips of celluloid and an "announcer" singing some strange folk song by way of accompaniment. As the "business" began to mushroom, custom-built movie theaters emerged. Strictly speaking, they were not really built at all, but created by gutting shops or ground-floor apartments, which explains why the earliest cinemas tended to be long, narrow corridors.

The craters from which films still erupt in the *center,* the *north,* and the *southeast* of the city are among the wild variety of the species. There is nothing aristocratic about them, and whereas the thoroughly democratic price of twenty *pfennigs* for any seat prevailed before the war, the same seat is now available for half a *mark,* with "children and the unemployed" paying half that price—though the latter were previously acceptable only in His Majesty's uniform, and the former banned completely. For many, the attraction of the *Lichtspielhaus* is its very lack of light. "Come in, come on in!" the man in green livery would call out to us. "I have the darkest cinema in Berlin!" And, in the bliss of youth, we were willingly persuaded. We enter these long, gloomy, stuffy dark rooms no less willingly today, but, in our eyes, their romanticism has taken on a new form.

In these little suburban and inner-city cinemas, the program, the audience, even the films themselves are different from those in the premier cinemas. The "preview" consists, in about half these cinemas, of cabaret acts rather than cultural presentations or cinematic grotesques: there may be a fine performance by Mr. Nadragé the ventriloquist, or a man from Vienna lecturing on Konnersreuth,[1] or three old hags dancing à la rococo. And when the film about the Rhine finally begins, from the stuffy background come the strains of the overcultivated Widetzky Quartet singing *"Ein rheinisches Mädchen."* The audience participation is extraordinary. Ribald banter about the plot and the actors—"What a mess they've made of you!"—tears that are certainly not made of glycerin, or a frenzy of whistling—for example, at the Hindenburg film by the "Deutsch-Vaterländische Film-Gesellschaft." Here, Chaplin is regarded primarily as a comic, and here, Liane Haid is a star. The more *Potemkin*-esque films trigger even more impassioned reactions. But on the whole, there are no hard and fast rules; there are some 350 cinemas in Berlin, and they do not all attract the same audiences.

The newer movie theaters in the west and also the palatial cinemas in the working-class neighborhoods (the Mercedes-Palast seating three thousand), are not long and narrow, but have a square ground plan like theaters. As it happens, many of the seats in the early cinemas offered a distorted view, if at all. In Berlin's most beautiful cinema, the Beba-Palast Atrium, for instance, there is not a single pillar blocking the view. Its decor and facilities not only are pompously magnificent, but actually surpass the theaters themselves, providing thirty-two en suite dressing rooms for the personnel.

Whereas the small cinemas often have just one piano player, or at best a fiddler, and some a Pianola that plays "Nun ade, du mein lieb Heimatland" at the death of the little blond hero, two years ago Ernö Rappée conducted a seventy-strong orchestra at the Ufa-Palast am Zoo, and Ludwig Klopfer, whose management of the Tauentzien-Palast is exemplary, recently installed the biggest organ on the continent, with twenty-eight-meter pipes. Here, as in the Ufa-Palast, ventilation is provided by an electric zeppelin that sweeps through the building during the interval, spraying eau de cologne. Many such supposedly secondary matters lend the mass auditorium of the cinema a kind of culture and style.

This would not be possible without a circumspect film-theater manager, and so such names as Ludwig Klopfer, Hans Brodnitz (Capitol, formerly Mozart-Saal), and Polke (Beba-Palast) deserve to be mentioned here. Finally, the flag should be hoisted for a cinema that fell in the battle of film: the "Fox im Palmenhaus." This cinema, which now houses the comic cabaret on Kurfürstendamm, is sorely missed. It was, so to speak, a German-American institution. Its use of illuminations and loudspeakers to advertise the cinema was unheard of at the time (1924). The first cinematic grotesques by Fox were all but undermined by saxophone and percussion, and it was only in the most spectacular play of light and dark that the lions in the office and Snooky the chimp could hold their own alongside the blues and the Charleston in the film with Jackie Coogan [*Circus Days*, 1923]. But best of all was a film version of Dante's *Divine Comedy*, so dire that it was truly magnificent. As the audience streamed in for the premiere, ice-cold blocks were pressed into their hands; it was Berlin's first Eskimo ice cream, and in the middle of the film, the white screen suddenly rose, and there on the stage were Anita Berber and Henri [Chatin-Hofmann], dancing completely naked—Dante.

NOTE

1. Theresa Neumann, born in Konnersreuth in 1898, was blinded and paralyzed in a fire in 1918. Her sight and walking were restored in 1925 by a series of miraculous cures, and stigmata appeared on her body on Good Friday 1926, accompanied by the ability to speak in Aramaic, Hebrew, and Latin.

197

Billy Wilder

BERLIN RENDEZVOUS

First published as "Berliner Rendezvous," *Berliner Börsen-Courier*, 13 November 1927; reprinted in Wilder, *Der Prinz von Wales geht auf Urlaub: Berliner Reportagen, Feuilletons und Kritiken der zwanziger Jahre* (Berlin: Fannei & Walz, 1996), pp. 55–56. Translated by Ishbel Flett.

Rendezvous (French; pronounced *rongdayvoo;* "present yourselves"): a date, a meeting, an appointment at a certain place, the appointed place itself.

That is the definition given in *Meyers Konversationslexikon*, sixth edition, vol. 16, P–R.

Adam, for instance, was wont to meet Eve by a certain apple tree. As for Ramses, he patiently waited for his favorite evening after evening at the third corner of the twelfth pyramid. Caesar, on the other hand, arranged to meet Vercingetorix in the rain under the bridge over the Rhine. And Casanova, whose goings-on cannot even begin to be described in the space available here, is said to have noted his rendezvous in a morocco-bound folio as thick as a Berlin telephone directory.

There are rendezvous for business, for pleasure, for love, and for friendship, and consequently, those we go to gladly and those we go to reluctantly.

Naturally enough, rendezvous at apple trees, by pyramids, and under the bridges of the Rhine have gone right out of fashion. These days, people tend to prefer a café or a restaurant. They meet outdoors, in busy squares, by statues and clocks, at tram stops, or in front of theaters and cinemas.

In Berlin, three places play the leading role: the Kranzlerecke, the Berolina on Alexanderplatz, and the Normaluhr clock at the Zoo.

As far as the *Kranzlerecke* goes, it is distinctly reminiscent of one of the world's classic meeting points: the Sirkecke in Vienna. It is the rendezvous of international society, meeting point of the beau monde who stay at the hotels on the boulevard of Unter den Linden. Madame wears chinchilla fur and does not hang around for long, her pinscher keeps a lookout for monsieur and barks. Moustaches smelling of Parisian pomade, sharply pressed trouser creases, car horns sounding like a well-rehearsed saxophone concert. Of course, Berliners meet there, too, albeit seldom—generally to go to the theater together or take a stroll through the evening museum that is Berlin city center.

Alexanderplatz is where young girls have their rendezvous. From every street and every corner there is a constant flow of secretaries and saleswomen gravitating toward Alexanderplatz, crowding around the bus stops and at the metro stations. Waiting. Sullenly. Surely he'll arrive. Just three more minutes, and if he hasn't arrived by then ... he doesn't arrive. The girl decides to count to one hundred. She counts to nine hundred. No sign of him. The quarter hour's allowance is long overstepped. I'll throttle him, she says. And then he arrives. And they flutter away arm in arm.

The most popular summer rendezvous is the *Normaluhr* at the Zoo. Nature's gate. Swamped by families on Sundays. Kith and kin. Weekend day-trippers. Young adults. Boy Scouts. People up from the country with buttonholes. A lady companion for the Wannsee lake. Or for the cinema on Kurfürstendamm. Or for five o'clock tea. For the Lunapark.[1] Or for the Zoo. All gawking up at the clock. Which sometimes goes so fast, and sometimes goes so slow. But there are also rendezvous that are not kept.

What possessed me to choose that bench in the Tiergarten park as a meeting place, where I waited in vain for her? And it didn't hail and it didn't rain.

NOTE

1. On the Lunapark, see above, text 189: Siegfried Kracauer, Rollercoaster Ride.

198

Siegfried Kracauer

UNDER PALM TREES

First published as "Unter Palmen," *Frankfurter Zeitung,* 19 October 1930. Translated by Ishbel Flett.

The palm tree is an important part of the mirage that appears time and again on the horizon in the desert of everyday Berlin. It is a plant that has become fashionable even in the smaller bars, restaurants, and cafés of every neighborhood. Innumerable people burdened with a hard life want, at the very least, to be able to relax under palm trees with impunity.

In most cases, the palm trees serve as a sign of distant climes. Since what is bad is close at hand, what is good is sought in those exotic regions where coconuts grow, where cannibals live peacefully side by side, and where nobody has ever heard of unemployment or National Socialism. The growth of the palm trees is, as it were, in direct proportion to the growth of misery.

I recall a new café opening in the west of Berlin; it was crowded from day one. And for good reason, too: it is a little oasis. Painted palm groves fill the walls with quiet green, real bamboo stalks and canes flourish in the middle of the room, and real palm fronds adorn the tree bark that decorates every nook and cranny. The illusion of foreign parts, for which the palm tree is a metaphor, is further heightened by a special trick. Instead of being immersed immediately in an exotic atmosphere, the visitor arrives in it. The main rooms have been given the appearance of ship's decks by design, so that guests become travelers voyaging from their

FIGURE 43. Kurfürstendamm, c. 1930. Bildarchiv Foto Marburg, 1.061.972.

gray homeland toward sunnier climes, as on the posters of a shipping line. They recline on comfortable deck chairs, awaiting the arrival of the painted natives who approach the cruise liner in a boat. The tenting suspended above them gives an impression of tropical heat and shelter from an imaginary sun. And, as they sip their mocha, it is as though the pleasure of lingering in the landscapes of childhood dreams portrayed on postage stamps is mingled with the sense of dissipation triggered by their foray into utopia. It almost seems as though they had reached it. The gentle sounds of the gramophone reach their ears, while pale green palm fronds on the walls sway above their heads.

The people who escape to these unreal continents are, for the most part, young: they are artists and writers, or those who aspire to be, and young professionals who appreciate what they consider to be higher things. The air they breathe here is heavy and oppressive. Yet its oppressiveness is not just a product of the tropical climate imbued by the painted palms, but is generated by the guests themselves. Many of them obviously confuse the blue skies above the tents with the blue haze of their own imaginings—those who consider themselves a cut above the rest because they are reclining in armchairs on a ship's deck, and those who indulge in the fantasy of the fairy-tale island to avoid facing up to their own inner emptiness. They mistake the hot air of the conversation for the glow of the sun, and the fata morgana for a sheltering refuge. Sometimes the undercurrent of mutterings swells to a wave that sweeps through the rooms. When this happens, the palm groves fade back into the walls, the natives gnash their teeth, and the entire ship runs aground on a coral reef.

That is what almost all the palm-treed establishments are like. There is really only one exception, located in the centre of Berlin, between streetcar tracks and the rush of city traffic. Entering it is like entering a living room that expands into a wonderful interior world. Here, the palms are no pale reflection of distant places, no mere fata morgana intended to console those with a miserable home life, but real plants adorning a *home* that continues to exist in spite of the misery. They have put down roots in tall, slender wooden pillars and dominate the upper realms of the room. There is much to discover in their green fronds. Monkeys and snakes frolic there, and sometimes the reddish peel of oranges can be glimpsed. It is a cheerful jungle vegetation, echoed in the murmuring of many little fountains, its colors fused in a spangle; the boundless spangle of the corrugated metal that panels the walls to conceal them. Beneath this scintillating ceiling, the room is divided into many tiny booths in which lovers can settle just as the snakes and monkeys settle in the palm trees. These are not places to flee to, but places to withdraw into. And instead of drifting farther and farther into foreign parts, one merely penetrates ever deeper into familiar territory, which then takes on a sparkling sheen like the metal on the walls.

Office workers, entrepreneurs, and students frequent this café. They are by no means seeking escape from the everyday in the confines of a pleasant parlor, but are, if anything, exploring what they already possess and developing capacities they never thought of before. The palm tree is their pointer toward happiness. Their cheeks flushed, they dance, or embrace tenderly in the booths. The dim light camouflages the shabbiness of their jackets and blouses. It changes over from red to green with the same fluidity as the feelings of the dancing couples. And, as in the *Paradis bleu* in Paris, they are surrounded by that air of melancholy reserved for those who are happy.

199
Curt Moreck (pseud. Konrad Haemmerling)
A GUIDE TO "LICENTIOUS" BERLIN

First published as Moreck, *Führer durch das "lasterhafte" Berlin* (Leipzig: Verlag moderner Stadtführer, 1931), pp. 11–12, 20, 28–30, 142–46, 156–58, 160–62. Translated by Iain Boyd Whyte.

In Wilhelmine Berlin, big-city life pulsed through Friedrichstrasse. It was here that one felt the pulse of the metropolis, that one sensed its driving energies, inhaled its particular atmosphere, exhausted its very essence. For the man from the provinces, the bustling street between Friedrichstrasse Station and Leipziger Strasse, cut in two by the self-consciously noble promenade of Unter den Linden, was the quintessence of a fairy-tale world full of light, women, and eroticism. This was the height of his desires, agitating him back at home with longing for its alluring secrets, and filling him, when he dared to plunge into the vortex, with the exciting thrill of anticipation. At that time Friedrichstrasse embodied and made tangible the cosmopolitan life of Berlin. It was a clarion call to the bourgeois instincts that had established the entertainment industry in the section of the city dedicated to monarchical representation. In the short era of the [Weimar] republic, however, the previously dominant mind-set became a fossil, and with it the former amusement quarter of Berlin, in spite of repeated attempts to reanimate it.

[. . .]

Those kilometer-long streets in the west of the city between Wittenbergplatz and Halensee—Tauentzienstrasse and Kurfürstendamm—present a completely different world: absolutely modern and completely contemporary.

[. . .]

Tauentzienstrasse is a decidedly afternoon street. It lives most strongly and intensively in the time between five-o'clock tea and dinner, and is at its most stimulating when, behind the Romanesque silhouette of the Gedächtniskirche, the sky is shimmering in the chalky white colors of a blue-green sunset, and white light shoots across the arc lamps. Then the meaningless and sober side streets sink into a furtive darkness that obliterates the painful stucco of the miserable gable ends. It also blurs the inviting signs for various pensions and hotels, at some of which the guests drop by only for a short stay, and the posters in murky-windowed vestibules, in which even murkier souls offer their "services to clients." Sites of joyless pleasure . . .

There is a certain dubiousness about these side streets, with their ponderous town houses, behind whose demure facades diverse forms of unbourgeois immorality are concealed and where new-age libertinage seeks refuge, even though the most sedate uprightness resides next door. This dubiousness is determined by those apparitions that present on Tauentzienstrasse the totality of eroticism, perversity, and debauchment. For this is the realm of violent Venus, the promenade of the noble female knights of the Order of the Marquis de Sade. Under the spreading shop lights of "KaDeWe,"[1] whose range of goods fulfils all the needs of the modern age, pass those professionals who have cultivated a particular erotic need in modern man. They put normality under pressure around here, even though normality has defended its positions along the entire front. But the professionals already dominate through the energy that their occupation demands of them. Anyone free of the fetishist inclination who is attacked by these high-heeled women with boots reaching up to their knees will hardly be able to extract himself from the humor, the bizarreness, and the scurrility of these peacocklike posturers as they make their entrance in full war paint. For cash (at inflated prices!), these visions enact for the desirous male the comedy of a perversity that through its very commerciality avoids the tragic fate of degeneration.

[. . .]

The real big-city dweller senses it in his veins and nerves when the electric current shoots into the millions of light bulbs and sets them ablaze, so that the streets are suddenly framed in a fireworks display. At that point he can no longer endure his desk. He craves the sea of light as hints of the electric power glint across onto his limbs. Even a stroll under the neon advertising signs is like an invigorating shower, which gives him a lift, bringing vitality, expectation, and hopes of new experience and adventure. At least something sensational.

For sensationalism is an imperative for modern man. He needs it like a whip for his nerves, or like an addict needs his needle. He needs it in varying dosages: some more, others less. He needs it and looks for it—when he feels he must buy it—in a diluted form offered by the cinema. This is the seductive power of cinema, with which it has conquered the masses. This the reason why countless cinemas compete with other places of amusement. It is so comfortable to enjoy life there in its most concentrated form, below the silky rays of the studio lamps. Furthermore, most of the Berlin cinemas are imposing buildings with a comfortable atmosphere. The cinema palaces of the major film companies are clustered around the Gedächtniskirche, announcing above their doors in flaming letters what is currently running on the screen . . .

[. . .]

Change of scene. Kommandantenstrasse. The club is called "Magic Flute." In the generous doorway the guests are welcomed by a dignified-looking man in a dark suit. One level up, gentlemen, to the Florida Room. In the stairwell the secretive sign "BfM." The ignorant read this as "Bund für Männer" [Association for Men]. Insiders know that this is the sign of the Association for Men's Rights, which fights against the disenfranchisement of same-sex relations, against discrimination, outlawing, and persecution. One is obliged to leave coats in the cloakroom, and a modest entrance fee is charged. It is immediately clear that orderliness is important here. Female guests, even in male company, are politely turned away. Even the suggestion that there are already women in the room is of little avail, and it is explained with a smile that this might be a misapprehension. It is perfectly fine for two evening dresses to sit together at the same small table. The room is spacious but fairly full: only a few of the little round tables are free. The guests sit at them in twos, threes, and fours in the dim light. The room itself is decorated in the oriental style. A *Magic Flute* ambience. Palm trees, Chinese lanterns . . . The dance floor is full. How calmly, rhythmically, and elegantly these people dance. All around twenty years old. Blond, brunette, and dark, well groomed and well dressed, with smooth partings, expressionless eyes, and fresh faces. Conversation is conducted in hushed tones, and shrillness appears to be intentionally avoided. Very striking how little alcohol is indulged in. On most of the tables there are only tall glasses with lemonade and a straw. A sympathetic picture, these slender dancing figures. Only here and there a rather too feminine wiggle of the hips, a waistline trimmed too tightly and emphasized by the cut of the jacket. The Chinese lanterns are dimmed. Red spotlights illuminate the dance floor. The violinist announces "Gesellschafts-Tyrolienne!" The couples organize themselves and perambulate around the dance floor, come to a halt and form two circles, face to face, embrace each other, and dance three steps sideways followed by one back and one forward again. Then the outer circle moves one place to the right, changing partners to dance with the neighbor of the first dancer, and so on until the end. The tone is one of calm devotion to the music, to the dance, and to the partner. There is a strange sense of bliss, of a fantastical world, of bizarre beings. The young ladies, who are not ladies at all, but who move so naturally and gracefully in their long evening dresses, dance from time to time with each other or with other young men. They are given away only by their hands, which are a little too sturdy, and by their naked arms, which lack the soft, feminine line.

[. . .]

No fewer in number in Berlin than the men-only establishments are the subsidiaries of Lesbos. They, too, are simpler and more *bürgerlich*, tending more toward coziness and intimacy than the luxury and pomp of their Parisian equivalents, where the *grand monde* rendezvous. The sophisticated lesbians, who in Paris openly display the stations of their divergence from the normal path, prefer here intimacy, and meet their fellow spirits in clubs dedicated to a particular sort of conviviality in which they are shielded from the inquisitiveness of the public, or they meet in places that are not recognized as gathering points for those of differing persuasions. This does not reflect a Philistine morality or any sort of feeling of shame, but merely a desire to avoid being rubber-stamped.

And other women, too, who are entirely normal, but from time to time play with the idea of a foray into the abnormal, fondly seek out the ambience of the woman's bar, which is strange and thus appealing for them. Usually in the company of a man, since this is not universally frowned upon. Indeed, there is great tolerance toward the other sex, and here and in the men's clubs, both men and women claim the right of entry and hospitality. Indeed, many women enjoy dancing with men who are sexually disinterested in them, but who because of their inclinations have more dance in their limbs; for the secret of femininity is rhythm.

It's different with the lesbians. They don't dance with men, and at best tolerate them as guests. The unspoken rule is: "Men must do what they are told here!" And sometimes it is an entirely exceptional privilege even to allow men admission to the club at all.

[. . .]

Bülowstrasse and its neighborhood is the quarter for lesbian love. The Violetta ladies' club is located in the Nationalhof. Entrance for the opposite sex is difficult. The penetrating curiosity of men is shunned. For many lesbian women, Violetta is the home that they would otherwise not have. Working girls spend their free evenings here, looking for distraction, amusement, sociability, and love. We need love as much as we do heat in the winter or water when we are thirsty. What is life without love? The day for them means nothing but work, and life has many worries. So they look for love, that love for which they yearn and for which nature has shaped them. If it is not the correct love, what can they do about it? One must make nature responsible—she must have known what she intended. For nature does not make mistakes, she is wiser than we are . . . The young women who must remain patient and friendly behind their counters in the face of the incomprehensible wishes of the customers rediscover here the real laughter that they have had to imitate all day; here they find sympathetic fellow sufferers of daily life, and here they can forget their loneliness. When they dance, all the heaviness is lifted from them, and they sense the joy for life that had been buried all day.

NOTE

1. KaDeWe: Kaufhaus des Westens, one of the great department stores in Berlin. Sited on Tauentzienstrasse at Wittenbergplatz, it was designed by the architect Emil Schaudt and opened in 1907.

200

Siegfried Kracauer

RADIO STATION

First published as "Sendestation," *Abendblatt*, 23 January 1931. Translated by David Britt.

Anyone who looks the new Berlin Broadcasting House straight in the eye—it stands on Masurenallee, close to the Funkturm [radio tower] and the Exhibition

Halls—is almost inevitably compelled to reflect on the astonishingly rapid success of the German radio industry. From inconspicuous, private-enterprise beginnings, it has rapidly evolved into a universally recognized institution, and now public life without it is unimaginable. Having started in makeshift accommodation, it is now migrating into gigantic and would-be prestigious buildings. Important though it might be to explain and interpret this unprecedented triumph, I have no intention of doing so on the occasion of the inauguration of [Hans] Poelzig's building. That would take us far beyond the matter in hand and lead us into a discussion of our social and intellectual climate in general. There will be time enough for that. Meanwhile, a look at the Masurenallee building may afford some insights that go beyond the merely architectural.

The large, symmetrical complex that contains the head offices of the Reichs-Rundfunk-Gesellschaft [Reich Broadcasting Company], Deutsche Welle [German (Short) Wave], and Berliner Funk-Stunde [Berlin Radio Hour] is extraordinarily functional and clear in its layout—as is indicated by the fact that its ground plan, like that of any good spatial arrangement, has the charm of a beautiful ornament. The form is roughly triangular, with the longest side forming the main facade. The other two sides are slightly curved. Fanning out from the internal patio, the three Funk-Stunde studios, complete with rehearsal rooms, and the studio of Deutsche Welle extend into the curved wings—an arrangement that not only serves to cut the studios off from traffic noise but also ensures convenient access from all the administrative offices. The outer parts of the triangular building contain, among other things, a lecture hall, the Reichs-Rundfunk-Gesellschaft boardroom, the offices of the Broadcasting Commissariat, and a room for the future Broadcasting Museum. It is also planned to have a basement bar for the artists and—above the central studio space—a roof garden with adjoining lunchroom. Forethought extends to the provision of four hotel rooms, in which studio guests in transit will be able to spend the night.

I pass over the long-range ventilation shafts, the ingenuity with which cabling is incorporated in the corridors, and other technical refinements. Of more general interest is the decor of the three studios. Around them, on each floor, run soundproof corridors; for acoustic reasons, they are constructed in a gently conical form. Of the main studio hall, nothing need be said except that it is immensely large. It will be completed and fitted out only at such time as more knowledge of acoustics has been obtained. One of the two flanking studios has plastered walls; the other is lined with wood throughout. This means that its movable wall panels need only be reversed to produce, as if by magic, walls of whitish Celotex that can be used to create any desired acoustic. All three studios have galleries running around them, and keyboard organs to raise the tone.

The decor is sparse and austere. The facade is 150 meters long, in somber, blue engineering brick, with dark brown strips of ceramic tiling that ascend from ground level with obsessive regularity, so close together that one expects to be able to riffle though them like the pages of a book. Happily, the side elevations are less fanatical and content themselves with ornamental stringcourses in light-colored engineering brick. The internal patio, also lined with ceramic tiles, is no laughing matter; and the colors in the hallways are serious and businesslike. The studios have a purely functional look, silently proclaiming that they are technically perfect and will promptly transmit everything that ever can, may, or will be heard within them. The portentous sense of mission that prevails throughout the triangular block is relieved only by the graceful light fittings on the staircases that face the inner courts.

All in all, an edifice that is forbidding rather than cheering; and decidedly more reminiscent of a corporate business headquarters than of a place of intellectual and artistic achievement. I am almost afraid that there is a mismatch between its bureaucratic weightiness and the broadcasts that come from it. Looking at it, I am involuntarily reminded of the big department store on Hermannplatz, a massive citadel that looks as if it bristles with hidden cannon rather than with salesgirls and merchandise.[1] What do the broadcasts say? They undoubtedly include such momentous topics as public housing, heart sounds, winter sports, the unemployment problem, and the pioneers of the *Heilstunde* [Health Hour]; but they also, and equally, offer pure entertainment: concert parties, revues, radio dramas, and concerts. Well might the artistes feel qualms of unease on entering these studios. The Muses themselves might catch a chill in the administrative corridors.

One thing, at all events, is certain: this building does not perfectly represent the kind of work for which it was built. On the other hand, it clearly sets out to represent something. What does it actually stand for? I don't really know. All I know is that—like many other buildings designed to give visible form to a specific content—it purveys a high-flown rhetoric that does not coincide with the content in question: an autonomous rhetoric, as it were, that swaggers through the world on its own hook. Why such majestic isolation, one is tempted to ask.

In the case of the broadcasting house, whose magnificent layout betrays the master hand of Poelzig, I can only think that the reason for the surfeit of dignity and the furrowed brow is that the idea of the building is not powerful enough to make an appropriate form possible. The neutrality of broadcasting is a compromise that reflects no higher unity; it is an enforced consequence of power relationships among the political parties. And so, by necessity, the abundance of the programs on offer all too often stands for nothing but padding to fill endless hours of time, and their diversity is the reflection of incoherent public demands. The architect thus finds himself faced with the task of giving three-dimensional expression to the content of an institution that—for all its laudable attempts to achieve quality—has, for the moment, no prospect of achieving much in the way of positive content. He has no alternative but to dispense with the inadequate support that he is given and create the sacerdotal garment out of whole cloth, as he sees fit. Architects in general are all too often let down by their content: not that this is any excuse for the pompous facades that one so constantly encounters, in Berlin more than anywhere.

Not only does Poelzig's building indirectly convey the understandable vagueness of the broadcasting idea: it also betrays an essential characteristic of radio itself. It is no accident that it has the forbidding look of an industrial corporate headquarters. Its whole stylistic posture indicates that the mental output achieved here is a commodity. In the three studios, like any manufactured product, that output is produced, packaged, and delivered by wireless means to consumers' homes. This dual significance—as creative work and commodity—gives that output the uneasy quality that is also the most prominent characteristic of the new building. Perhaps it involuntarily betrays the true, hidden nature of broadcasting, as a large-scale business that converts the production of scholars, writers, and artists into ready-to-use products.

NOTE

1. The Karstadt store on Hermannplatz in Neukölln; see above, text 168: Alfred Wedemeyer, Berlin's Latest Department Store.

201

Hermann Sinsheimer

BOXING RING

First published as "Box-Arena," *Berliner Tageblatt*, 3 September 1931. Translated by Ishbel Flett.

The Poststadion at Lehrter Station, with thirty thousand people scattered into it, looks like a supremely overpopulated island. Outside, the ocean of the city roars only in the sound of the urban railway. The people on the island swarm like locusts in a mass covering what little greenery there is, pressing toward the center of the oval where the little temple of the boxing ring stands. It is a cultic spectacle. The individual is a mere drop upon the earth, but the mass seems like a paean to the Creator; it is elemental—a flood of heads, an excess of looks, a murmur of voices. To be in the midst of it, next to a little woman who wears profound silence as she wears her horn-rimmed spectacles, and next to her husband, who devours his urge to comment along with the first ice-cream wafer; being in the midst of it, before anything stirs in the little temple, is a radical escape from life, a new insular existence.

Thirty thousand people and ten boxing men—it is a world apart, a balcony on everyday life, and when a late summer sky arches gently, almost aristocratically, over it all, with a few innocent white clouds shyly meandering through the sunlight, it makes for an excellent Sunday. Loveliest of all, however, is the solitude among all these people. The few one might know are anonymous even in their fame. What remains is the self and a few neighbors and the mass. The mass, its opinion and emotion, speaks through the mouth of the neighbors. There is a direct path from all to each. It is a sociability that gains it final greetings through the sweeping arch of the sky and the gentle breeze. Boxing, like any sport, is just one of the occasions, one of the reasons, to seek out the lovely, exciting solitude of the mass. One could sit like this for hours, even without the spectacle of the boxing match, enjoying the multifarious miracle of humanity.

But people want to see a role model and find themselves reflected in it. The role model here is strength, courage, and stamina. You settle down comfortably on the bench, collapsing under your own weight—and up there in the ring, the muscles and sinews, the senses and the nerves of the lightweights and heavyweights are tensing. They are part of the thirty thousand bodies, a select extract of the mass. The mass fights, too, punching and taking punches. Their breath surrounds the ring like a vast reservoir on which the figures up there draw, and their opinions and hopes hang over the ring like light and shadow.

The little woman with the horn-rimmed glasses hammers her silence into the fight. One can see victory and defeat already mirrored in the lenses of her spectacles. Her silence is suspicious; it screams inwardly, a sign of the utmost emotion. Her husband, by contrast, finds his participation in the fight thwarted by dialectics. He ought to be right up in the front row, at the ring, where the steeled and sparring connoisseurs are seated, criticizing every movement of leg and arm, counting the boxers' every breath, calculating the force of each punch in terms of horsepower. This man says, "Pathetic," and says it with such vehemence that it seems the boxer he is speaking about should wince at the very sound of such chastising words. Or he says, "Gotcha," and one is astonished that the boxer on the receiving end of the punch does not fall to the ground like a sack. The silent woman is thinking only of the end result, in eager anticipation, while the eloquent man casts his thoughts and words from round to round throughout the fight. By the time it is over, he is as exhausted as all the boxers put together. But no wreath adorns his shoulders, though he has come here to gain a victory in spectating. The woman is released on leaving the match, but the man will fight each fight again in his dreams. He is the martyr among the spectators.

Seen from the ring, there is something uncanny about the huge, dense mass covering the gentle slope and the edge of the arena. The clearest view and the loudest cries come from here—an exchange of fire. Across the farthest distance, the most fervent passion sparks into the ring. What discipline keeps this mass, this overwhelmingly outnumbering crowd, on the edges and on the periphery! They could surge toward the ring, tens of thousands of them, and who could stop them? But they stay in their seats, or where they are standing—merely a metaphor for the danger that threatens the center of the island. And their remoteness, like a kind of exile, is expressed in self-made mass entertainment. The mass becomes satirical. "Krücke," especially, that hero of the six-day cycle race, wittily and mercilessly says out loud what the mass is thinking. Nature and training have given "Krücke," a robust and stocky invalid, a voice like a megaphone with which he can yell over any distance and shout down any rival. The crowd hangs on his every word—a second Thersites. They want to hear him say what they themselves are thinking. Krücke admonishes the boxers before the fight and declares the verdict to them when it is over—he is umpire and spokesman of this immense sporting tribunal of ostracism: woe betide the accused!

The fights began at three and went on until eight in the evening. Daylight did not last as long. As the last fight was under way, twilight filtered in, turning the huge circle of the arena into a vast cloud. The mass at its fringes rebelled against the fading, gloomy day. The two boxers up there were fighting in unwelcome shadow, their faces swallowed up by the twilight; the match became ghostly.

The fight in question, between Charles the Belgian and Hein Müller of Cologne, was for the European heavyweight title. It was a fight between a man and a boy. Hein Müller has a crumpled, childlike face with a big mouth and white teeth, unruly hair, and angular bones. What could this lad possibly pit against the big Belgian, ten kilos heavier? Charles is a perfect specimen of a man. With the dark, slightly twisted features of a prelate: black hair; dark, melancholy eyes; a crooked nose; and a firm, determined mouth. A mountain of a man, but finely formed. One is inclined to think he must have brought the decisive blow for the kid from Cologne all the way from Brussels in his fist. But in the close-of-day air, he fought like a close-of-day man. While his opponent flitted through the twilight like the dawn itself. It was exciting, the way he hit the Belgian, and how he took everything his rival served up like some minor castigation. It was so exciting that the little woman took off her horn-rimmed spectacles, which were of little use in the dark, and barely watched at all. She knew what was coming. Her husband no longer spoke; he just gurgled. And even before the victory of the lad from Cologne was announced, programs and cushions and other light objects went flying into the ring—instead of flowers and wreaths for the victor, Hein Müller. His broad, jovial mouth radiating from the little temple. And when his victory was finally announced, he leaped into the mass, into the midst of its jubilation—into the vast, seething tangle over which night broke like a huge wave riding in from the ocean of the city.

And now tens of thousands of legs crept through the gates—an army, a nation, an incalculable crowd, itself as dark as night. The edges emptied, and the middle, and both were now one. As they jostled, they relived the fights again, astonished at the Belgian who had been defeated and was now no longer a champion, and his image stayed with them, for it was as melancholy as the night into which they went.

202

Siegfried Kracauer

BERLIN AS A SUMMER RESORT

First published as "Kurort Berlin," *Frankfurter Zeitung*, 19 July 1932. Translated by David Britt.

Berlin today wears people out more than ever; it also redoubles its efforts to refresh them, the better to wear them out in future. Such is its solicitude that there is now no need to head out to Wannsee in search of relief; for it can be found in the city itself, just where the strain is greatest. To this end, a number of small and serviceable oases have appeared over the past few months. These are conveniently located for the economic crisis and the election campaign, and within easy walking distance of the nearest street battles.

For instance, across from the Anhalter Station the rooftop of a high-rise has been set aside entirely for rest and recuperation. You wing your way upward in the elevator, past ten stories in which commercial life—if it does not exactly flourish—at least vegetates, and reach a platform that has some claim to be called a high-altitude resort. For this is no mere asphalt rectangle; it is a kind of artificial alpine pasture. An expanse of lush, green lawn extends atop the stifling offices, and from an underlying terrain of cashbooks and files a luxuriant flora springs up in countless tubs. Here the sunlight seems brighter than down below; here the wind blows as if across a mountain peak. The special enchantment of this sky-high landscape consists, however, in the presence of a number of deck chairs, which are available for use without charge. In these, anyone who so wishes may pass the time—if he has it to spare—from early morning until late at night, and may make believe that he is on the terrace of a castle in the air. True, nothing is to be seen from this terrace but Berlin, which he knows already; but this is not the familiar Berlin from which he has just escaped. The city shimmers in the sun, as alien as a blue painted plate. Its poverty, its unemployment, and its political turmoil are all concealed beneath the rooftops that stretch away to every point of the compass, shrouded in a light veil of mist from which only domes, towers, and high-rise buildings emerge. Is this still Berlin? What presents itself to those in the deck chairs is not the city itself but its unreal glitter—a glitter that has detached itself from the streets and squares and conveys a pure, summer-vacation tranquillity. The visitors to this resort are refreshed by the peace, acquire a suntan, and enjoy the panorama from which they themselves have come, for all the world as if it were an inaccessible mountain range. To complete the illusion, they are provided with a telescope, which serves not so much to bring objects closer as to relegate them to a distant, other world.

There has recently been an attempt to achieve the same refreshing sense of remoteness at ground level. Of course, the longing is harder to satisfy amid the din of the streets than high above the rooftops, and special precautions are re-

FIGURE 44. Strandbad Wannsee (1929–30; Richard Ermisch and Martin Wagner, architects), c. 1930. Berlinische Galerie, BG-FS 20/80, 4, © Phyllis Umbehr/Galerie Kicken Berlin/DACS 2011.

quired. One recently opened café, close to a main traffic junction, affords its customers the desired sense of relaxation by transporting them to an *undersea nature reserve*. Between the tables are illuminated glass tanks, in which the most extraordinary fish swim in a carefree fashion. They make their entrances in swirling garments, glitter in many colors, and bear difficult Latin names, which are thoughtfully displayed on little brass plates. Fortunately, however, there is no need to learn all the names by heart: just follow the movements that these underwater creatures make. And, as you watch them constantly and aimlessly swimming past pale growths and wafting ferns, you begin to recover from the effects of the world above the waterline. These illuminated aquaria set an example that captures all hearts—filling them, as it were, with the mute wisdom of the fish. It may be that the patrons here relax all the more readily because the activity beneath the rippling waters blocks their view of the adjoining tables. The faces glimpsed through the glass walls never become too alarmingly distinct, and their words remain inaudible. And so one is left alone, with only these silent beings for company, and is obliged to follow their example.

Both sky and seabed are in downtown Berlin. I do not know which seems more miraculous: that there is no need to travel anywhere in order to find relief in these heights and depths, as if in a summer resort; or that one can return so abruptly from so remote a voyage.

203

Werner March

THE BUILDINGS OF THE NATIONAL SPORT ARENA

First published as "Die Bauten des Reichssportfeldes," *Rundschau Technischer Arbeit* 16, no. 31 (29 July 1936), pp. 1–3. Translated by Iain Boyd Whyte.

THE PLAN OF THE FÜHRER

With this provisional project [to remodel an existing stadium, the Deutsche Stadion, for the 1936 Olympic Games], we came before the Führer on 5 October 1933. He listened to a two-hour lecture explaining the existing installation and then concluded by putting the plan on a completely new basis with a few broad guidelines: "The Grunewald-Rennbahn must disappear. This solves the problem of the stadium, which needs to be completely reworked; a linked stadium and racetrack will only ever produce a half answer; either we build a whole solution or we don't build anything at all!"

After he had fully recognized the need for a new stadium concept with a smaller arena, he demanded that a dedicated parade ground be installed beside the stadium. He also insisted that the athletics stadium and the parade ground should be linked together as a unity, with both elements in close harmony with each other. He then approved the Dietrich-Eckhart-Freilichtbühne [Dietrich Eckhart open-air stage], for whose dimensions the landscape seemed to be preordained.

Finally he required that the State Sports Academy should be enlarged in a monumental style. In essence, this made it possible to take up again the basic outlines of an old plan that my brother Walter and I had already produced for a competition in 1926.

THE GENERAL VIEW OF THE BUILDINGS

The German mind created a group of buildings, which—very similar to those of ancient Olympia—united the spiritual, the educational, the competitive, and the patriotic. Beside the athletics stadium we built a swimming pool, hockey fields, a horse-riding stadium, tennis courts, and, based upon these facilities, an academy of sport linked to an administrative facility, the Reichssportverwaltung [State Sport Administration]. In addition, we have a forum, large-scale grounds for

patriotic rallies, and a theater—a shrine to the arts—all of which seem to be predetermined by their natural surroundings. The site of the National Stadium is a plateau set high above Berlin, with no building development around it, far removed from industrial pollution and bad air, surrounded to the east by the deep cutting of the Hamburg main line, by the suburban railway to the south and west, and to the north by the Murellenschlucht, the army exercise ground. The site is also surrounded, as it were, by a deep valley, making it possible for the architect to design a strongly resolved, clearly delineated urban ensemble, visible to the viewer from all angles. Seen from whatever viewpoint, the overall impression is not of some sort of aesthetic or formalistic tricks, but of simple, natural, and attractive building groups that emerge from the organic composition of the whole complex.
[. . .]

THE SIGNIFICANCE OF THE PARADE GROUND FOR FUTURE RALLIES

Following the instructions of the Führer, the parade ground was designed to have the closest relationship to the stadium. In a subsequent discussion in the Reich Chancellery, the Führer developed further the principal ideas. For the staging of great national rallies—future May Day rallies, for example—the layout of the National Stadium should allow the communal masses to be structured in a way that allows a close relationship to the Führer or to the individual speakers. The individual formations would then assemble separately—the Arbeitsfront [German Workers' Front], for example, on the running track; the SS on the parade ground; and the Hitler Youth in the open-air amphitheater. There they receive the Führer's welcome. When this is finished, the Führer proceeds through the Olympic Stadium to his speaker's dais. The great speech of the Führer is then transmitted by loudspeaker, audible in all of the locations.

In order to realize the harmonic relationship of stadium and parade ground that had been demanded by the Führer, a portal-like opening into the stadium was necessary. We chose here a radical incision, with two powerful blocks that terminate the enormous motion of the viewing terraces and from which a monumental staircase leads down into the arena. The tunnel [a survivor from the old stadium] also emerged here, so that the upper opening with the Olympic flame, the monumental staircase, and the tunnel joined together to create a unique, ceremonial portal, the Marathontor [Marathon Gate]. The parade ground is closed off on the west side by a high wall, a sort of *limes* [Latin: "boundary wall (sometimes fortified)"], with a gently curved contour that picks up the curve of the running track. At the center of this wall is the monumental Langemarck Hall and bell tower. Above and beyond the Olympic Games, this structure is intended to give the whole complex a deeply symbolic content. The most appropriate solution here, we felt, would be to honor the young volunteers of Langemarck,[1] who went to their death in the World War with a song on their lips. Later, when the bell no longer rings for the Olympic Games, it will remind us of this fellowship, which should be our symbol and example.

NOTE

1. Langemarck, Belgium, was the scene of heavy fighting throughout October and November 1914, in which the German volunteer army was decimated. It has special significance as a site of memorial, as the location of the only German cemetery in the Ypres Salient.

17

TECHNOLOGY AND MOBILITY

The British diplomat Harold Nicolson was posted to Berlin in 1928; a year later he sought to understand its attraction. "What on earth," he wondered, "gives this city its charm!" The answer: "Movement in the first place. There is no city in the world so restless as Berlin. Everything moves. The traffic lights change restlessly from red to gold and then to green."[1] In the immediate postwar years in Berlin, the traffic—like everything else—was constrained by the hyperinflation. Between the end of the inflation in 1923 and the global economic downturn that began in 1929, however, motor-vehicle ownership in Germany increased by some 45 percent. Thanks to their accessibility to the less affluent, motorcycles accounted for a considerable element of this expansion; cars also became cheaper over the decade, thanks to the example of Henry Ford in the United States and the introduction of rationalized production techniques. By 1925, 171,000 vehicles were registered—twice the 1921 total—161,000 of which were motorbikes. They were joined the following year by a further 30,000 cars and 100,000 motorbikes.[2]

The effect of these increases on the Berlin traffic was dramatic: so much so that a census was taken on 25 July 1928 to measure one day's traffic on Potsdamer Platz, the junction of five main arteries, the busiest intersection in Europe at the time, and the site of the first traffic lights in Germany, installed in 1924. The results are remarkable: 33,037 vehicles in total crossed the Potsdamer Platz, of which 18,678 were cars, buses, and vans; 3,361 were motor bikes; and 960, horse-drawn carts. Although challenged by buses and private cars, streetcars still played a major role in Berlin at this time, with 900 million individual journeys on ninety-two routes accounting in 1928 for half the public transportation in Berlin. On 25 July that year, no less than 3,361 streetcars trundled across Potsdamer Platz. Similar congestion prevailed at all the major intersections, prompting the city planning authorities, led by Martin Wagner, to initiate radical remodeling schemes. As the semiofficial journal of city planning, *Das neue Berlin,* assured its readers in 1929: "The city of Berlin is confronted by the enormous task of giving new form to its most important intersections. Over the next three to ten years, *Plätze* such as Alexanderplatz, Potsdamer Platz, Hallesches Tor, Das "Knie" [now Ernst-Reuter-Platz], Auguste-Viktoria-Platz [now Breitscheidplatz], Spittelmarkt, Molkenmarkt, and others will be given an entirely new look. This new configuration of the *Plätze* will be contingent upon the reordering of the traffic and the building of underground railways."[3] The underground railway was seen at the time as the mass-transport system of the future, with a renovated streetcar system and the bus network providing the necessary feeders.

The boom in car ownership provoked new thinking on road design not only in the city center but also in the approach roads. Berlin took a leading role with the AVUS (Automobil-Verkehrs- und Übungsstrasse), a motor-racing and test track that ran through the Grunewald toward Potsdam on the southwest side of the city. Initially planned in 1907, it was completed only in September 1921 and comprised two six-mile-long straights, with turning loops at each end. The first race on the new track was won by Fritz von Opel, who reached speeds of over ninety miles per hour on the straights. This was good advertising for the Germany car industry, and not least for the Opel car company, which had been founded by Fritz von Opel's grandfather, Adam Opel. One of the most popular small cars built in Germany in the 1920s was the Opel 4PS, affectionately known as the *Laubfrosch* (tree frog), because it was generally painted green. Introduced in 1924, it was aimed at the lower end of the market, and 120,000 were produced by 1931, using the mass-production techniques developed in the United States by Henry Ford. The proud owners of the little green car could roar up and down the AVUS for five reichsmarks per circuit, in emulation of their motor-racing heroes. Opened in this way to the public, the AVUS served not only as a racetrack but as the model for subsequent express highways—most directly, the German autobahn network that was to follow a decade later, and to which the AVUS itself was connected in 1940. Sweeping unhindered through the Grunewald and avoiding the congestion of the old city, the AVUS established the model for the autobahn network. In the words of Paul Bonatz, the architect and autobahn bridge builder who was closely involved with the autobahn program in the later 1930s: "The autobahn does not follow the old settlement pattern of the overcrowded valleys. In connecting large cities, the autobahn looks for free spaces; it travels over high plateaus and along mountain ridges, vaults over valleys; finding in the process a new, rhythmic law of motion, an undulating motion that comes nearest to flying."[4]

The metaphor of flight as a meeting place of romantic sensibility and technological progress also informed the relationship between Berlin and the rail network in the 1920s and '30s. The legendary "Schienenzeppelin" (Zeppelin on rails), which first appeared in the 1930s, not only looked like an airship but also went almost as fast. On 21 June 1931 it covered the 170-mile stretch from Bergedorf near Hamburg to Berlin-Spandau in 98 minutes, reaching speeds in excess of 140 miles per hour in the process. Parked for some days afterward at the Grunewald Station, it became an object of pilgrimage for the Berlin populace. While the "Schienenzeppelin" was too light and too fast to go into normal service, it spawned a streamlined, diesel-powered service dubbed the "Fliegender Hamburger" (Flying Hamburger), which by 1935 could link the central stations in Hamburg and Berlin in 142 minutes. The propaganda value of these achievements was not lost on the National Socialist regime, which lost no time in hailing the new service as the fastest in the world, beating the British in the process.[5]

The images of flight that embellished both road and rail travel were underpinned by the commercial aviation industry that flourished in Germany in the 1920s, with Berlin as its undisputed epicenter. A new airport was opened in 1924 on the site of the former Tempelhof parade ground. In January 1926, the two main airlines that flew out of Tempelhof—Aero Lloyd and Junkers Luftverkehr—were consolidated into one company, Deutsche Luft Hansa (renamed Lufthansa in 1933), and in the same year, as a mark of the ambition of German aviation, two of the new company's aircraft flew to Beijing. Beginning with a Berlin–Zürich service launched in April 1926, the domestic and European network expanded very rapidly, with the result that Berlin had flight connections with all the European capitals within a few years. Indeed, Luft Hansa's Berlin-to-Madrid service, a distance of thirteen hundred miles, was the longest service flight in Europe when it was initiated in January 1928. As the director of the British Civil Aviation Authority, Sir Sefton Brancker, noted at the time, Berlin was the hub not only of German aviation in the late 1920s, but of European civil aviation.

NOTES

1. Harold Nicolson, "The Charm of Berlin" [original in English], *Berlin im "Querschnitt,"* May 1929; reprinted in *Berlin im "Querschnitt,"* ed. Rolf-Peter Baacke (Berlin: Fannei & Walz, 1990). pp. 174–75.

2. Statistics from Gideon Heimann, "Von der Avus zur Reichsautobahn," in *Die Reise nach Berlin,* exhibition catalogue (Berlin: Siedler, 1987), p. 120.

3. Martin Wagner, "Das Formproblem eines Weltstadtplatzes: Wettbewerb der Verkehrs-A.G. für die Umbauung des Alexanderplatzes," in *Das Neue Berlin,* ed. Martin Wagner (Berlin: Deutsche Bauzeitung, 1929), p. 33. For more on Wagner's plans to remodel Berlin and more of this text, see above, text 123: Martin Wagner, The Design Problem of a City Square for a Metropolis.

4. Paul Bonatz, "Dr. Todt und seine Reichsautobahn," *Die Kunst im Dritten Reich,* no. 3 (1942); quoted in Anna Teut, *Architektur im Dritten Reich* (Berlin: Ullstein, 1967), pp. 301–7.

5. The Flying Hamburger's top speed of 102 miles per hour easily beat the previous record, which was the 76 miles per hour reached on the Swindon–Paddington line in England.

204

Friedrich Krause and Fritz Hedde
SWINEMÜNDER BRIDGE

First published as "Swinemünder Brücke" in Krause and Hedde, *Die Brückenbauten der Stadt Berlin von 1897 bis Ende 1920* (Berlin: Zirkel, 1922), p. 43. Translated by Iain Boyd Whyte.

Only after repeated attempts was the final form of the ornament arrived at, whose application arose initially from the attempt to eliminate the hardness of the connections between the diagonal elements and the lower chord, and further from the fact that the lights on the ends of the beams needed a mediating connection with bare ironwork. From this artistic decision it was only a small step further to accentuate individual structural members through architectural elements. The pylons, for example, are crowned with pointed columns, and the play of forces in the main elements of the bridge is represented by the bandlike decorations on the connecting points of the suspension flange. The railings follow their functional form, as do the supporting arms for the lights over the walkways, which, like the arc lamps on the crossbars, are effortlessly incorporated into the whole design. Unfortunately, the skewed layout, the low elevation over the site, the lateral position of the crown of the bridge, and the close proximity of ugly tenement blocks were intrusive circumstances that the bridge design was unable to eliminate.

NOTE

The Swinemünder Brücke was a road bridge over the railroad tracks at Gesundbrunnen, built in 1902–05 to the design of the architect Bruno Möhring, using an iron construction and a reinforced concrete deck.

205

Berliner Tageblatt
[CYCLING IN BERLIN]

First published in *Berliner Tageblatt*, 2 September 1923, 1st supplement. Translated by Iain Boyd Whyte.

From being a means of mass transport, the streetcar has already changed into a transportation facility for the few.... The excessive price rises of the Berlin streetcar lines have led to the widespread use of the bicycle. This device, which was already condemned as unmodern, has suddenly become truly timely again. Bicycles have been pulled out the junk room and the attic and set free in the service of transportation.

Berlin is now the city of bicycles. It has taken the place of Copenhagen, whose pedaling army was world famous. If you stand in the morning and afternoon rush hours on the main suburban arteries, endless rows of cycling Berliners glide by. The bicycle is now the cheapest means of transport for the civil servant, for business people, and for trippers. It is obedient to your own will, and is independent of price and strike chicaneries.

206

Joseph Roth

DECLARATION TO THE GLEISDREIECK

First published as "Bekenntnis zum Gleisdreieck," *Frankfurter Zeitung*, 16 July 1924. Translated by David Britt.

I honor the Gleisdreieck.[1] It is a symbol, the source and focus of a life cycle; it is the fabulous product of a force that enshrines a promise for the future.

It is a *center*. All the vital energies of its environment begin and end here—just as the heart is both start and finish of the bloodstream that courses through the veins of the body. Such is the heart of a world whose life resides in throbbing drive belts and striking clocks, in the unremitting rhythm of levers, and in the siren's wail. Such is the heart of the earth, spinning a thousand times faster than the alternation of day and night would suggest, with an incessant rotation that appears to be insanity but is the result of mathematical foresight. To sentimental and backward-looking persons, its headlong speed seems to shatter inner strength and healing balance; but, in reality, it engenders life-giving heat and the blessing of motion.

At triangular or rather polygonal junctions the great, glistening iron veins converge, gather power, and fill themselves with energy for the long haul and the wide world: triangles and polygons of veins, formed from the paths of life: *all honor to them!* They are stronger than the weakling who despises and fears them; they will not only outlast him but crush him. He who is not stirred, elated, and proud to see them does not deserve the death that the Deity of the Machine has in store for him. Landscape! (What does the word imply? Woods and pastures, stalk and grain.) "Iron landscape" is possibly the term that best does justice to the playgrounds of machines. Iron landscape: a magnificent temple of technology beneath the open sky, to which the mile-high factory chimneys burn clouds of living, potent, fertile, mobilizing incense. The machines worship without end, amid the wide expanses of this landscape of iron and steel, which extends farther than the human eye can see and is ringed by the gray horizon.

Such is the realm of the new life. Its laws are immune to happenstance and momentary impulse, its motion is implacable regularity, and among its wheels the

FIGURE 45. Gleisdreieck Station and junction, 1927. Stadtmuseum Berlin, Nachlass Max Missmann, GE 2006/695 V.

brain operates, sober but not cold: reason, firm but not inflexible. Only stasis creates cold; motion, intensified to precisely calculated performance limits, always creates heat. The weakness of the living, yielding to the slackening flesh, is not in itself proof of life; and the unbending strength of iron construction, in a material that never slackens, is no proof of lifelessness. On the contrary, this is the highest form of life: living substance that is unyielding, immune to whim, nerveless. In the realm of my Triangular Junction the will of the logical brain prevails, because it has implanted itself not in an unreliable body but in the body of unconditional certainty: the body of the machine.

For which reason, in this metallic realm—just as in the abstract world of philosophy and astronomy, the world of clear and great truths—humanity is small and feeble and forlorn, relegated to the status of a modest means to a proud end. There goes a man in uniform, amid all the dizzying complexities of the tracks. The man is tiny, and in this context he has no significance except as a mechanism. He counts for no more than a lever; his effectiveness extends no further than that of a switch. In this world, any form of human expression counts for less than a mechanical signal from an instrument. Here a lever matters more than an arm, a signal more than a gesture; here it is not the eye but the lamp that counts, not a shout but the piercing whistle of an opened steam valve; here not passion but prescription—*law*—is all-powerful.

The cabin that belongs to the trackwalker, the human being, looks like a tiny toy box. And this reflects the insignificance of all that goes on there, whether through him or to him: the fact that he begets children, that they fall sick, that he digs potatoes and feeds a dog, that his wife scrubs floors and dries laundry. Even the great tragedies that unfold within his soul vanish here, along with the minutiae of his daily life. The man's eternal humanity is a bothersome adjunct to the importance of his job.

What right have little heartbeats to be heard when we are stunned by the thunderous heartbeat of a world? Look at the clear, straight lines of the Triangular Junction, a valley silvered with myriad lamps: this is as solemn a sight as the star-filled sky. Like the crystalline firmament, this holds longing and fulfillment within its compass. This is a staging point and a beginning: the audible opening strains of a symphony of the future. The tracks glide and shimmer: elongated dashes, joining one country to another. In their molecules is the throb of distant, rolling wheels; trackwalkers spring up along the way; signals blossom, green and luminous. Steam escapes from opened valves; rods move of their own accord, and miracles come true, thanks to a mathematical system that remains concealed.

Such is the vastness of the new life. That the new art—which must give form to that life—can find no way to express it is all too evident. This is a reality *too big* to be appropriately represented. No "faithful" depiction is adequate. First, we must feel the ideal, intensified reality of this world: the Platonic *eidolon* [idea] of the Triangular Junction. We must honor its cruelty, recognize the *ananke* [necessity] that resides in its deadly effects, and choose to perish by its laws rather than live happily by the "humane" laws of the sentimental world.

The world of the future will be one vast Triangular Junction. The earth has undergone a number of metamorphoses in accordance with natural laws. It is now passing through another, in accordance with constructive, conscious, but no less elemental laws. Sorrow for the loss of the old forms that are passing away is like the grief of some antediluvian creature at the loss of the prehistoric world.

Shy and dusty, the grasses of the future will blossom between metal railroad ties. "Landscape" is now donning an iron mask.

NOTE

1. In its heyday, the Gleisdreieck was a triangular site in central Berlin, bounded by the railroad tracks that serviced the Anhalter Station, the Anhalter freight station, locomotive sheds, and other neighboring stations. See above, text 35: The Concourse of the Anhalter Station.

207

Ignaz Wrobel (pseud. Kurt Tucholsky)
BERLIN TRAFFIC

First published as "Berliner Verkehr," *Berliner Tageblatt*, 9 November 1926. Translated by Iain Boyd Whyte.

The Berlin press is trying to drum a new idée fixe into the Berliners: traffic. And the police are supporting the press in the most telling way. The measures that are being taken in this town to organize the traffic, measure it statistically, put up signs, divert ... are downright ridiculous. Is it that heavy? No.

When you come to Berlin, people ask you with almost imploring looks: "The Berlin traffic is absolutely colossal, isn't it?" Now, in my experience, at its peak the Berlin traffic corresponds to that in a medium-size Paris street at six in the morning. A very average Paris street, nothing more. And to counter this infantile frenzy, I have to say that I don't understand the desire to be impressed by the sheer volume of traffic. A certain times of day, six lanes of traffic are jammed together on the Place de l'Opéra. So? Does that enhance Paris? Does Paris become more valuable as a result? It proves nothing more than the fact that when the Paris city center was built, there was no idea of traffic like this. It proves that the concentration of office areas and dense residential occupation is unhealthy—a difficulty that in all probability will never be resolved but will at some point lead to the decentralization of the big cities. This six-abreast line of automobiles is proof of all sorts of things, none of them pleasant. You should hear the old Parisians talking about the boulevards, saying that whenever they went out they made a little diversion on the boulevard since it was so nice to walk there. And today it is a motley hell, a chaotic spectacle. The Parisian is happy when he's back down the side street. There's nothing at all impressive about this.

Now, Berlin doesn't have this traffic but fancies that it does, and the police regulate this imaginary traffic in a way that no one in Paris ever has regulated or ever would. I can confirm that there is not one sensible Berlin driver who would deny that the police with all their hand signals and rotations are simply a nuisance to the traffic, and that everything would work much better if they weren't there. The times one waits for a barricade of cars to cross on the Kurfürstendamm are as long as those on the Champs-Elysées—but it makes sense there to have such long pauses in the traffic flow. In Berlin, in contrast, the pause simply serves to cause a jam that was not there before.

What is so characteristic about this alarming nonsense of overorganization and howlings in the press is that it is driven by purely by the self-interest of offi-

FIGURE 46. Auguste-Viktoria-Platz (now Breitscheidplatz), c. 1930. Landesarchiv Berlin, 23274.

cialdom to create work for itself. You should see the way in which the civil servants, who are paid for doing their jobs, have recently presented themselves in the press with prima donna performances as "leading public authorities." This ridiculous overestimation of perfectly simple functions appears even more grotesque as the reality bears no relation to the fuss. I've often asked myself where Paris would get to if it made such a hullabaloo about such straightforward matters—and it would certainly have grounds enough. But no Parisian cares a straw about such boundlessly important questions as whether the streetcar tracks on the rue Réaumur should be taken up or not. . . . It hardly features in the newspaper. Everything else more or less sorts itself out; the police make mistakes or achieve sensible ordinances, and, besides, most people have other things to worry about.

The puffing up of German officialdom, however, with the benign support of the press, is gradually taking on forms that start one wondering if these harmless departments might not represent in some way the theater of the Metternich era—namely, distraction from the essentials. Papa state holds up a colorful doll for the childish subjects, something like a policeman with white armbands, so that they sit still while their pockets are picked.

"The Green Wave in the Friedrichstrasse" is a headline on the first page of the newspaper. There is less talk about the red wave that's pouring through the prisons; about the unparalleled obscenities in East Prussian prisons; about the disgraceful and unjust treatment handed out to imprisoned Communists.

It is not just the overpopulation—the urge to create at any cost a justification for existence by means of superfluous activity—that helps inflate the utterly trivial activity of the traffic police. That would be harmless enough . . .

But the ballyhoo also reflects a deep urge among new Germans to see themselves as the Americans of their imaginations. He can do without being a fine chap [*Kerl*]—but to live in a town with a "Ssiti" and a "Brodweh" enhances his prestige.

Do you think our traffic is no "problem"? Ach! We're so problematical.

A friend recently announced his visit to Paris. "I'm coming to study the French solution to the problem of the metropolis . . ." Where else? But he will assuredly not even notice that there is neither a problem nor a solution here, but only Paris.

It seems to me that the constant supervision of the administration is much more important than the artificially inflated bureaucracy. It is all fine and dandy when the "president of sentence implementation" gives a speech at the Hedwig Wangel Foundation,[1] but it would be more important if the man were to pay attention for once to what is happening in his own department, and whether the most basic dictates of humanity are not being violated there.

[. . .]

But the traffic plague is encroaching across the country, and what is good in Berlin is cut-rate in Bückeburg.[2] Not a single car far and wide—but two traffic policemen; one car on the horizon and a wild series of wavings, blowings, and whistlings begin. Yet for all that, the Germans drive less well than the Parisians; for all that, lumbering pedestrians and brutal car drivers are unable to come to terms with each other; for all that, nothing works out.

Because it is not a matter of the organization, but of something quite different, and because real life begins where German imagination ends.

NOTES

1. Hedwig Wangel (1875–1961; born Amalie Pauline Hedwig Simon) was a German film actress. At the time of writing, her most famous film was *Die letzte Droschke von Berlin* (1925).

2. Bückeburg, a small town in Lower Saxony, was once the capital of the tiny principality of Schaumburg-Lippe.

208
Billy Wilder
NIGHTTIME JOYRIDE OVER BERLIN

First published as "Nächtliche Spazierfahrt über Berlin," *Berliner Börsen-Courier* (6 December 1927); republished in Wilder, *Der Prinz von Wales geht auf Urlaub: Berliner Reportagen, Feuilletons und Kritiken der zwanziger Jahre* (Berlin: Fannei & Walz, 1996), pp. 57–59. Translated by Iain Boyd Whyte.

NIGHT FLYING IN GERMANY AND HOW IT IS ORGANIZED

"Oh, I do wonder . . ."—it was the lady on my left speaking; she was pressing her nose against the icy-cold glass of the cabin window and peering downward (we were just passing over Schöneberg)—" . . . I do wonder whether my husband has got home by now." A mere quarter of an hour before, she had been a pitiable bundle of nerves, shivering with fear or cold, teeth chattering. But she had pretended she wasn't frightened at all, did her best to keep up the bluff in front of the whole group, despite the three thundering engines, and applied lipstick till her mouth was ringed as redly as Tempelhofer Feld with all its neon lights.

But now, as we circled and banked repeatedly over nighttime Berlin at our cruising height of two thousand feet, none of the nine passengers doubted her sang-froid, or indeed even the wholehearted concern that she was displaying (in the darkness) for her husband down there in Schöneberg.

Same for all of us, after all. Ice cool.

And what lay below us? Berlin, a sea of lights.

How did the engines sound? Purring like sewing machines. What lay behind us? The doubts of a skeptical generation. And somewhere ahead of us, quite near now, a *bal paré* [dress ball] on a giant airplane, with a billiards tournament to follow. That is how fast things are advancing.

And now nighttime, too, is being used for air travel.

In 1924, when we heard that United States airships had begun regular day and night services between New York and San Francisco, we shook our heads dubiously. We were still not quite persuaded that even daytime flying was safe, and here were these technological futurists planning to harness the night—the dark, dangerous, frightening night; taking to the air whatever the time of day, flying regardless of whether the ground was to be seen below or not.

Night flying is not done for sport; what lies behind the introduction of nighttime air services is that great distances can be covered. The changing seasons—not winter alone, even autumn and spring—make it necessary to keep flying after darkness falls. And we may not want to lose a day over the journey; daytime is for working.

Among the European nations, Germany led the way in night flying. The Berlin–Warnemünde–Stockholm route became an overnight mail service in 1924, and

Berlin–Copenhagen and Berlin–Hamburg soon followed. In 1926, for the first time, the Berlin–Königsberg route was flown by night and with paying passengers on board, as the middle leg of the London-to-Moscow air service. In recent years, a start has been made on equipping landing grounds, routes, and the airplanes themselves for night services. Signaling by means of lights was introduced, wind-direction indicators and landing strips were outlined with powerful lights, green and white and red. Indeed, it was not thought unrealistic to attempt to eliminate the visibility deficit relative to daytime almost completely by constructing a pathway of lights to follow, and so at intervals of thirty kilometers a powerful revolving light was erected. Between these again, there are conspicuous neon lights spaced five kilometers apart. These light beacons are manned every night; each one marks an emergency landing ground. But there is no need to dwell on that thought, for a carefully devised system of signals, the use of wireless telegraphy, landing lights, and magnesium lights installed in the wings of the airplanes all add up to guaranteeing the same safety level by night as by day. As for the pilots, they are all seasoned aviators with long experience, and it is considered a mark of distinction to be employed as a pilot on night flights.

Director Milch explained all this yesterday while introducing the Tempelhof Airfield's nighttime illumination, and concluded by declaring that one of the foremost priorities for international air navigation is the general introduction of air services on all routes, by night as well as by day. At a point not very far into the future, we shall be able to fly all routes with great ease and regardless of the time of day and of the weather conditions.

On the Berlin–Hanover and Berlin–Königsberg routes, work is already complete. Berlin–Cologne, Berlin–Halle–Munich, and Berlin–Breslau are in the course of preparation, and only next spring new Junkers airplanes will help ensure that all German air routes will have day and night Luft Hansa services.

Like a giant bat, our plane flitted over Berlin; we could distinguish the individual streets and squares of the city below, and were amazed that it was possible to have the whole huge distance from the Funkturm [radio tower] to the Rummelsburg power station in our field of view.[1] We were still hoping to fly along the length of the Kurfürstendamm when the plane banked once and then suddenly we were down, trundling over the Tempelhof Airfield turf. Seconds ago, millions of lights had blazed up at us from below; now we were surrounded by darkness and night, and now the air station, which had resembled a matchstick from the air, loomed above us like a skyscraper.

NOTE

1. On the Rummelsburg Power Station, see above, text 153: Fritz Stahl, The Klingenberg Power Station at Berlin-Rummelsburg.

209
Bernard von Brentano
THE PLEASURE OF MOTORING

First published as "Das Vergnügen zu fahren" in Brentano, *Wo in Europa ist Berlin?* (Frankfurt: Insel, 1993), pp. 76–79. Translated by Iain Boyd Whyte.

Work it out: if I go by foot I never leave the spot. In Berlin you can't even walk from Kurfürstendamm to Friedrichstrasse. No one has that much time. But to go out, into freedom, into the green, into nature—to go, in short, to where I want to go—I can never walk that far, as I would need my annual leave just to get there. We all have to motor. Perhaps the constant compulsion to travel has compromised it a little, at least the idea of motoring for pleasure. You see comparatively few happy faces on the upper decks of buses, although this elevated seat offers for only twenty pfennigs the air of a health resort and the panorama of a good film. Perhaps the pleasure in motoring first really comes when you drive yourself. Like every process, you have to understand it to enjoy it. The discrepancy between those who could enjoy it and those who actually do is immense. There is clearly a misunderstanding here by the generation that, forced to motor, still extols the foot traveler. For many thousands of years, the delight of travelling on foot—of making a route march—was unknown to man, until it was discovered in the eighteenth century by the brothers Stolberg, if I'm informed correctly. This happened, I think, when horses became more expensive. But now, as automobiles are becoming cheaper, distances are increasing, and the world becomes a continent, there is no longer any reason to walk. We should mount the horses that drink petrol. They offer something that everyone loves, the businessmen or civil servant, even the writer—namely, the pleasure of getting away.

Driven by a salty lunch, I took a sharp right-hand curve across the square toward the café. In front of it, the red automobile, 6/30 horsepower with the shiny black roof, was parking alongside the other cars. I could assume, therefore, that I wouldn't have to drink my coffee on my own. Chance is always happy: a third person who joined us both needed and wanted to go to Wannsee, and was moaning about the distant railway station. So we drive to Wannsee. The weather is wonderful. A few light-gray clouds scare off nervous drivers; but the light-blue sky that we know shines behind them gives us and the others courage. As far as the AVUS the city is very Sunday-like, neither boring nor amusing.[1] We're glad that we shall soon be escaping from it. Once on the AVUS, speed is the main thing. All the pent-up frustration caused by streetcars, carriages, buses, traffic, and traffic lights—this compressed yet effortless desire for speed—is discharged here. Afterward you feel better for it. There is also an element of sport when you overtake the first car in front. We don't speak about this, of course, and pretend that nothing has happened, looking straight ahead. The man in front was a total———but let's not talk about that.

At the end of the AVUS lies the Wannsee. The third person was dropped off, the rumble seat folded down. We're alone and in Wannsee. We don't turn back now, but carry straight on, and the joy of driving begins. Distances are no distances. Everything is near. The hills aren't high, but pretty and afford us views. Their surroundings surround us, and whatever I discover in the distance I can soon see nearby. The heart beats against the chest, and an old and useful sense of place and home is reawakened. The countryside lies there as silently as a farmer at sunset; as beautiful as a girl at the beach. The farmer answers if you ask him; and the girl—who knows when you'll meet her? You just have to go there.

That's what the car likes to do. In Teltow we're already at the River Havel; in Werder in the middle of the broad waterscape, which although so close to Berlin is still very distant from the city. The grass is green, as if dyed, spick-and-span as a row of vegetables. The trees are still bare. The woods are as transparent as display windows, offering their first buds to the sun and to whoever discovers them. You can motor slow and fast. You can also stop, climb out, and look at something. This waterscape, for instance, that lies here flat and free, very large, very broad, not at all like lakes, but more like contemporary creations. Things that one can swim in, row, sail, and motor on. We always keep the tempo of the age. That demands receptivity. Few realize how important this resonance is, which must prevail between the tempo of the age and the human tempo. Many illnesses can have no other cause than the failure to achieve this resonance. In this little car we have the speed of the little man—but *the* little man who is a cogwheel in the gearbox of the global corporation. We have the pace of the great man who telephones with New York. The car annuls false differences in that it produces true ones. Alexander the Great rode on a white horse among his mounted soldiers; but there were many white horses in his army. The World War generals could not march with their soldiers. For that reason they were so far removed from the individual soldier that they could no longer understand each other. The generals—at least externally—had the tempo of technology, the soldiers the tempo of the Napoleonic army, marching a century earlier.

One car is like another. The vehicles that come from the world's factories resemble each other like—people or horses. But their drivers already share the language of the brake and the steering wheel. We discover the diversity of the world in the unified motion of the foot brake. Only by their heads can one differentiate the occupants of one car from those of the others.

Since it is Sunday, the girls are standing at the ferry. A man is nice if he is sitting in a car, even nicer in a good-looking car. No one can deny the girls this wisdom. Nor would it do any good, as only their eyes do the talking.

[...]

Cars approach us; drive past. The fact that one has no grounds for envy is attributable entirely to the machine. And if one has no grounds for envy, then one has a profound reason for joy. The road to Potsdam is really splendid. The red car goes like a hunting dog. Evening is coming, and we with it. We are catching it up, and we'll make good use of it. Why should we dismiss it when it can be so pretty?

At the end of the AVUS this time is Berlin. Lots of little lights sparkle in the towering houses. Way below, close to the dark ground, we drive into the city streets.

NOTE

1. Built by a private company as both public road and test track, the AVUS (Automobil-Verkehrs- und Übungsstrasse) runs from the western suburbs of Berlin to Potsdam and was the first autobahn-style road in Germany. Work began in 1909, but the war intervened and the AVUS was completed only in 1921. Motor races were held on the AVUS from the very beginning, and the first AVUS race, in 1921, was won by Fritz von Opel. The AVUS was incorporated into the national autobahn network in 1939.

210

Vicki Baum

GRAND HOTEL

First published as Baum, *Menschen im Hotel* (Berlin: Ullstein, 1929); published in English as *Grand Hotel*, trans. Basil Creighton (London: Michael Joseph, 1972), pp. 197–98.

The next thing was that Otto Kringelein sat strapped in the little cockpit in a comfortable leather seat and "pushed off" into the grey-blue of the March sky. Next him sat Gaigern whistling softly and that was some consolation in a moment of utter prostration.

At first it was no more than a bumpy ride in a car and then the machine began to make a furious and appalling racket. Suddenly it shook off the earth beneath it and climbed. It did not by any means soar. It was not such a simple business as Kringelein's dream flights on his tenor notes. It sprang up into the air as though up steps—sprang and sank, sprang and sank. This time the sense of uneasiness was not in his legs as during the motor run at 120 kilometres an hour, but in his head. Kringelein's skull hummed. It became thin. It became quite glassy, and he had to shut his eyes for a moment.

"Air-sick?" asked Gaigern [. . .] "Do you feel bad? Have you had enough?" he added kindly.

Kringelein pulled himself together manfully and courageously and replied with a cheery "No." He opened his eyes in his humming glassy head and fixed them first on the floor of the machine, which at least had its relative stability, and then raised them to the little oval of glass in front. Through this he saw again the figures and the trembling pointer. The pilot turned his keen profile and gave Kringelein a friendly smile. Kringelein was much relieved and highly honoured by this glance.

"Three hundred metres up at a hundred and eighty an hour," Gaigern shouted in his humming and deafened ears. Then all at once everything became gentle, light and smooth. The machine climbed no higher. It banked to the tune of its metallic engine voice and swept on above the city lying dwarfed beneath. Kringelein ventured to look out.

The first thing he saw was the sunlit, ribbed metal sheets of the wings, and they seemed to quiver with life; then—far below—Berlin chequered in tiny squares, with green cupolas and a ridiculous toy railway station. A patch of green was the Tiergarten, a patch of blue-grey with four white specks of sails was the Wannsee. The edge of the little planet lay far beyond, arched in a gentle curve. Over there were mountains and forests and brown plow land. Kringelein relaxed his cramped lips and smiled like a child. He was flying. He had stuck it out. He felt fine. He had a new and vigorous sense of his own being. For the third time that day his fear left him and gave place to happiness.

He tapped Gaigern on the shoulder and in response to a questioning look said something that was swallowed up unheard in the noise of the engine.

"It is not so bad after all," Kringelein said. "There's nothing to be afraid of. It isn't so bad."

And with Kringelein included not only the monstrous tailor's bill and not only the run on the AVUS, and not only the flight in the aeroplane, but everything else as well, and in particular the fact that he had soon to die, to die right out of this little world, leaving all its terrors behind and climbing perhaps even higher than aeroplanes can fly.

211

Siegfried Kracauer

PROLETARIAN RAPID TRANSIT

First published as "Proletarische Schnellbahn," *Frankfurter Zeitung*, 25 April 1930. Translated by David Britt.

A few days ago, the main section of the Neukölln–Gesundbrunnen subway line was inaugurated. This forms part of the northern and eastern rapid-transit network, which had previously been neglected in favor of the western suburbs. In the fall, the line through Frankfurter Allee will probably be added, which would leave the east, at any rate, reasonably well catered for. The ambitious construction program also envisages other new lines; but, in urban transportation, dreams do not always come true. Times are hard, and even the line just built has met with opposition over its financing.

It runs right across the downtown area, from proletarian districts to proletarian districts, from factories to factories. It tunnels beneath an immense world of workers and businesses. The stations are as technological and as functional as modern hospitals, with simple iron supports, shiny tiled walls, plain lettering, and every imaginable light signal: all well organized, practical, and entirely hygienic. In places, the iron structure is encased in column shafts that actually boast a capital: nice, round columns that one cannot help loving, just because they are such an anachronism, a greeting from another world above. Rosenthaler Strasse Station, with its pink-tinged wall panels, even seeks to create the illusion that the place really is a "Rosy Dell."

However, the traveling public on this route does not look very susceptible to illusions. Times are hard, and even the neat cars and the clean stations cannot remedy that. Men with tool bags, youths in leather jackets, office clerks, workingmen, and women with shopping bags and children fill the benches and passageways. They have either been shopping or are on their way to work. On other routes, things are more cheerful than they are down here in the lower depths of the economy. Many weary faces; chatter about clothes is noticeably absent. It is a relief to hear a baby crowing somewhere. All the same, this subway will make life a little easier for the hundreds of thousands who live close to it.

If you leave the train at some point and emerge into the daylight, you find yourself not—as in the Arabian Nights—among glittering palaces but among shattered, rocky landscapes. And yet the malaise that hangs over these is better than the bogus peace of the palaces. Halfway along the route is Alexanderplatz: still currently a gigantic lumber room, stacked with hoardings and half buildings. The wind blows through the gaps into bottomless depths. Then there is Gesundbrunnen: a vast expanse of railroad tracks and fragmentary blocks of houses, all open on every side and random in their distribution: no sign of any perspectival structure, or of any conclusion to satisfy the contemplative eye. In between are long streets, gray streets, streets with balconies that imprison summer greenery, brick facades, churches, funeral parlors, courtyards, and children. But life in these wildernesses is irrepressible, and at the two ends of the line it raucously proclaims its refusal to knuckle under. On Hermannplatz, down in Neukölln, is the massive citadel of the Karstadt department store: a monumental edifice that invites the world in with a menacing gesture.[1] Behind Gesundbrunnen Station rises, like a billboard, the white facade of the Lichtburg, which consists entirely of horizontal curves and is totally a product of the newest *Neue Sachlichkeit*.[2]

From here, a little over thirty minutes on the bus brings you to Kurfürstendamm. Admission reserved for persons of quality; luxury bodywork; well-dressed people. (Though times are hard here, too.) The two parts of the city merge imperceptibly, and yet seem infinitely remote from each other. Time and again, we find to our dismay that no rapid transit can lessen the distance between them.

NOTES

1. See above, text 168: Alfred Wedemeyer, Berlin's Latest Department Store.
2. The Lichtburg (literally, "castle of light") was a cinema at Gesundbrunnen in the north of Berlin, built to the design of Rudolf Fränkel and opened in 1929. Its facade was dominated by a forty-meter-high neon-lit drum and a glazed roof pavilion from which searchlights shone out across the city. Regarded as one of the grandest cinemas in Berlin, it was damaged during the war but reopened in 1948 first as a theater for opera and then once again as a cinema—the Corso Cinema. It closed in 1962 and was demolished in 1970.

212

Peter Panter (pseud. Kurt Tucholsky)

TRAFFIC PASSING OVER THE HOUSE

First published as "Verkehr über dem Haus," *Vossische Zeitung*, 30 July 1931. Translated by Iain Boyd Whyte.

When I took the house, I asked the gardener: "Look, is it really quiet here?" I've got a thing about that. I've got to have it quiet, so quiet you can hear the misprints rustling in all the books. The gardener looked up at me, quite cool. He had been in the act of securing a dispatched magpie on the shrubbery branches next to a dispatched crow, something he did to deter other birds from devouring his beans and his strawberries. And there it all was now, growing away, vegetables and meat, and fruit salad, all together. "Is it quiet here?" he repeated. "—Dead quiet. So quiet you'd go mad. Except . . . No, that's of no consequence."—If there is one thing that really puts the wind up me it is something that exists but is of no consequence. I've been through it before. "Just what exactly is of no consequence—?" I asked. The landlady had come up and now intervened. "He means the airplanes," she said. "The place here is directly underneath the air route to the Continent."

So that was it. As a stage direction, noises off, it was certainly up-to-date. We had had the lot—barking dogs, lady pianists, lady singers, people always coming to the door . . . But airmen? Airmen flying over our house? This was something quite new. So we took the lease. The airmen did their flying so nice and quietly, the landlady had said.

So, here I am, out sitting in the garden, and as I write every now and then one of these things comes by, plowing its way along through the air with that well-known throb, and I'll look up and watch it a bit on its way. There it goes.

FIGURE 47. The "Graf Zeppelin" flying above Wilhelmstrasse, Berlin, 15 August 1929. 1929 Landesarchiv Berlin, II 6060.

Sometimes, when it is overcast and rainy, like today, these gentlemen fly really low, so low that you can read the crate's registration as it passes. They come along of a morning, they come of a noontide and an evening, and one of them comes very late at night, but that one is not a passenger airplane, I've been told, it is a mail flight, and I find that very comforting. Letters don't make so much din. There they fly . . .

What their system is, I haven't worked out yet. The pilots, those tenor voices of the air, zoom around in a fairly casual manner; at least that is what it looks like from below. No white-gauntleted bobby floats across to confront them with upraised arm; it looks as though anarchy reigns. But no doubt things will settle down. For the time being, anyway, they sometimes fly on the left, that's what's expected in Britain, and sometimes on the right, which makes you think you are on the Continent, but that's just an illusion, we are not on the Continent here. And just tell me, where do you think we would we be if, say, all vehicles everywhere were driven in accordance with the same traffic regulations? Anyway this lot are not driving at all. Tractors and things are for driving. This lot fly.

There they fly... An eighteenth-century French engraving, now, let's say Fragonard, would do you something a bit saucy in that line—you have your airplane watcher down here with an enormous telescope, your airplanes flying over, and he is busy studying the ladies', er, dainty little feet. But that's a nonstarter here; the best I can do is get an eyeful of the round windows in the passenger cabin. And there's another thing: who should be living just down the road here but your man [Edgar] Wallace himself[1]—but do you think they have ever chucked anyone out of these airplanes, even just one single time? Not likely. And I've got the whole thing beautifully worked out: there you are, you've got this unfortunate chap on the way down, he's bound and gagged, of course, but he cuts all that off in a jiffy with a Tauchnitz edition [*Tauchnitzband*],[2] lands on my lawn here, says "How do you do?" of course, and "Isn't this weather just perfect?" and off he goes to the police station, and when the other lot get to London the cops are waiting and that's that. It's not really a lot to ask for your money. But nothing doing.

Sometimes, when they roar their way over, they are above the clouds; then you hear them but you don't see them. Sometimes they fly high—ever so high; those times they are like little glittering points of light up there in the sky. In the evenings sometimes you see them with their cabin lights on. That is really pretty—like old stagecoaches trundling across the sky.

There they fly. I really like watching them as they disappear, and if there is a greenhorn sitting in the cabin up there, I can be pleased about that, too, because I know something that he doesn't. He doesn't know what will be waiting for him at the airfield when they arrive in London—but I do. He's going to be asked what his business is here, and whether he really is who he says he is, and whether he has the means to prove his identity, and all that sort of stuff. But just now this greenhorn has no idea that's coming. For now he is just getting hauled along through the air, and he's just sitting there and every so often checking he's still got his little white bag. And looking down.

He can see my cottage here. Like a matchbox.... Listen! There's another one; hear the droning noise? The wind's straight toward the house, from the sea—and it does sound grim, that droning. Like a tooth being drilled up there in the sky. Amazing, when you think of it—a great heavy thing like that, and it flies! No, we haven't had a forced landing as yet, though we do have these emergency landing strips round here. But no action so far. A little while back there, there was one came trundling along, it had enormous propellers, looked really weird, like a flying paddle wheeler—that sort of thing. All in all, there really is so much traffic passing over the house here, it's not safe to let the children fly the nest.... Well, maybe it's not quite that bad yet. But not long now, and that's how it will be.

NOTES

1. Edgar Wallace (1875–1932), British novelist, playwright, and journalist, was a prolific author of detective fiction. He published 175 novels and was wildly successful, with some titles selling as many as 5 million copies.

2. Christian Bernhard Tauchnitz (1816–1895) was a Leipzig publisher who specialized in the works of English-language authors. "The Collection of British and American Authors" survived his death, and nearly fifty-eight hundred titles by eight hundred authors had been published by the time the series was concluded in 1943.

213

Siegfried Kracauer

THE CULT OF THE AUTOMOBILE

First published as, "Autokult," *Abendblatt*, 24 February 1931. Translated by Iain Boyd Whyte.

Had I not known it perfectly well already, I would be finally convinced of the fact now that I have been to the International Auto Show on the Kaiserdamm: the automobile is one of the very few things nowadays to enjoy universal respect. Virtually no other object I can think of ranks so high in popular esteem. Taxi drivers and gentleman motorists, youths of proletarian appearance and off-duty policemen, elegant young bloods and men saving up for motorbikes—in short, all sorts who ordinarily cannot stand the sight of each other—are here on a common pilgrimage through the exhibition halls, pausing for devotions as they pass radiators, ignition systems, car-body parts. It is as if in the presence of the finished product all social distinctions are swept aside, however significant a role they may have played—to go by Ilya Ehrenburg's impressive account—during the manufacturing process.[1] A pilgrimage it is indeed, making its slow way as at Lourdes from station to station, and at each of them experiencing a new revelation. No doubt many will leave feeling that they have seen the light. Most visitors have certainly come well prepared mentally. I have never before found myself caught up in a crowd so knowledgeable about the things that it has come to cluster around. Take a large body of people at a public meeting and you may be able to persuade them of all sorts of implausible things; but here the crowd is nobody's fool: they can see deep into the engines that are being displayed. This is a crowd composed wholly of experts, and I am probably the only one among them unable to penetrate beyond the surface of things, unable to tell what is essence and what is mere appearance, aesthetic semblance. The essence of front wheels, crankshafts, heavy trucks—all the others are probing deep into it, subjecting it to informed scrutiny, criticizing. From the man in the windproof jacket to the top-brass army officer, all of them, they are dedicated to the same object of study; it is a new Scholasticism, practiced by all with equal fervor. The army general wears a brilliantly polished star on his uniform and is followed around by a number of adjutants, who to some extent play the role of intermediaries in his viewing of the car exhibits.

The crowds are at their densest around the popular cheap cars. These inspire covetousness and are gazed at with emotions that, however pleasurable, are not of the disinterested aesthetic kind. Various features of the cars are explained to anyone who will listen; people squeeze into them and wax as enthusiastic about their comfort as if they had just become the owners. Should the economic crisis be over by Christmastime, one would not be surprised to see some of these vehicles gift-wrapped under the tree. Cheek by jowl with these Lilliputian creatures, some veritable monsters of cars have set up their abode, ensuring that the wealthy, too, are well catered for; but it all makes for a motley assortment. The displays are at least arranged so as to satisfy the thirst for knowledge. In many cases the body shell or engine housing has been removed, and the technological part that remains is seen poised above a mirror surface and revolving gently on its own axis, like a horizontal mannequin. On another stand, an entire car has been split vertically along its length, so that it looks like a demonstration model from a school of anatomy. With the exception of balance sheets and trade secrets, all that is intimate and inward to the automobile appears here revealed to the public eye, and the humblest little rivet is eager to present itself in as popular a light as possible.

Of this inner world beyond the appearances of things, much remained incomprehensible to me. I did, however, note some special features that will have meaning for the layman. One that deserves mention is a car whose four seats can be fitted together to provide beds for two. A friend was telling me only the other day about a night excursion into the *bois* by automobile, how they had seen a deer suddenly appear in the headlights, and what a romantic experience it was to be out there alone in the forest. Now all romantic spirits can have real home comfort as well and combine the delights of the sylvan setting with those of the night's repose. And then there was the mobile weekend cottage, which can be attached to any car, if one has a car. In this most minuscule of homes there is in fact room not only for a single happy pair, for at a pinch, if the situation requires it, a second couple can be accommodated as well. It would take a Sinclair Lewis to do justice in words to the ingenuity that has gone into fitting out the interior: the retractable canvas awning, the camping stove, the mechanism for raising and lowering the floor, and the whole array of household equipment contained in this simple box, though really it can't possibly all fit in. It must be wonderful to pass the night ensconced in such Procrustean precision, measured off by the centimeter, and then to sleep the next night in a proper hotel room.

Coming out of a cinema after the show, one has the momentary illusion that the film is still running and that all the street life one sees is staged. Something similar may befall some of us as we leave the auto show. The streets outside the exhibition hall are packed solid with parked cars, and all these utilitarian devices now convey the impression that they are there purely for exhibition purposes, parked in a line so that those passing can study them. I scarcely dare to take a taxi. Who knows if it might not suddenly bare all its ball bearings or spontaneously split into two identical halves.

NOTE

1. Ilya Ehrenburg (1891–1967) was a Russian writer and journalist.

214

Siegfried Kracauer

ON BOARD THE "HAMBURG FLIER"

Special Press Trip, Berlin to Hamburg

First published as "Im 'fliegenden Hamburger': Pressefahrt Berlin-Hamburg," *Morgenblatt*, 1 January 1933; reprinted in Kracauer, *Berliner Nebeneinander: Ausgewählte Feuilletons, 1930–33* (Zürich: Epoca, 1996), pp. 302–5. Translated by Iain Boyd Whyte.

DEPARTURE

It's about half past ten. Waiting at the platform in the Lehrter Station is the *Reichsbahn*'s [German Imperial Railways'] new high-speed railcar, ready to receive the press representatives invited along on a demonstration run. With its white-and-purple color scheme, the car stands out brightly against the dark station background. Exceptionally slender in outline, it has a lightness that makes it seem to float just above the rails. The elegance of its styling has a good scientific basis. Wind resistance increases as the square of the speed, so to keep it as low as possible both ends of the vehicle are sharply tapered, the interior ceilings are low, and the sides are enclosed at bogie level with metal panels. All this contributes to the railcar's very compact appearance. We board, though not before the scene has abruptly been flooded by a brief blaze of light—from several Jupiter arc lamps—in which the train gleamed so brightly as to redouble the feeling of unreality. Departure 10:35. Punctual running will be vital on this trip, as we are due to overtake three stopping trains and any number of freight trains.

THE INTERIOR

The railcar accelerates quickly, but through the suburbs it maintains a slow enough tempo to allow us to form our impressions of the interior. It is divided into two halves of equal length, open parlor cars, separated by the centrally placed toilets and refreshments servery, which is fitted out like a bar. Second class only;

overall capacity one hundred passengers. In order to save space in the passenger parlor car, the only luggage space is in nets fixed along the walls, but there are luggage stowage areas at both ends. The red carpeting tones in harmoniously with the other interior fittings, and further improves the already good soundproofing. The hum of the engines is never loud enough to drown out conversation, and in fact makes a pleasant background. Anyone needing to stretch his legs can walk up and down to his heart's content in the aisle between the seats—three together on one side, and one on the other. The appointed halfway haven on this little local journey is the bar, where everyone goes to meet everyone else.

SPEED

After Spandau, the railcar begins to work up to its full speed. At the front of the passenger compartments, and placed so as to be visible from every seat, two large dials register the speed that has been attained in kilometers per hour. Turned by an expert hand, they move swiftly up from the 100 figure to 150 and then yet higher. Over 150 kilometers [90 miles] per hour—are the human senses capable of comprehending such velocity? We sense it through our hearing, our tactile nerves, our eyes. The humming grows in volume and develops into a sustained, wonderful tone that one soon ceases to hear consciously. (When it fades away at slower speeds, one hungers for its return.) The car sways very slightly right and left, and now one must push harder to open the central door. All these sensations are complemented by images of the passing landscape. True, the plain in the distance does not move with us, it just stretches mute and static to the horizon; but all the nearer objects around us are caught up in the frenzy of speed. Faster than ever before, the telegraph poles whip past, and the stations are turned into stretched-out blurred surfaces, their windows continuous ribbons and their name boards illegible. To savor such speed to the full is one of the supreme delights. Initially, perhaps, the sensation it brings is an invigorating, bracing one, but in a while, to the body that has grown accustomed to it, it brings an almost unearthly state of calm. It is as though one were entering strange precincts, in which silence reigns, and from where one no longer has any wish to return and set foot on earth again.

IN THE DRIVER'S CAB

The driver's cab, which we are allowed to visit during this journey, has a functional yet surreal quality reminiscent of those utopian technological projects portrayed in certain contemporary films as casually as if they were already reality. And yet this is no dream world knocked together out of stage flats, but tangible, dependable reality. The memory of the film set is doubtless caused by the peculiar shape of the driver's compartment, dictated in fact solely by technical reasons. At the front, it tapers to a cone, and its low side walls are entirely of glass. At the control panel, the driver is accompanied at present by an observer, and this arrangement will continue for the time being. The driver himself has only one hand control to operate: a crank handle by means of which he regulates the speed; his task is thus considerably simpler than that of the driver of a locomotive. What a prospect! As machinery becomes more complicated, operating it becomes simpler. All that remains is a crank handle and a hand to grasp it. This apart, the whole of the intellectual effort needed to propel the railcar forwards at ninety miles per hour has been invested in its twin Maybach diesel engines. But no, not all of it: the driver still remains responsible for observing signals, although a whole range of safety measures to back him up have been incorporated. He turns his crank handle from time to time and concentrates fully on the track stretching arrow-straight in front of him. It zips from sight beneath us, and is gobbled up on either side by the cab windows.

SOME PARTICULARS

Gradually, the train's velocity begins to have a soporific effect, and some of the passengers have even nodded off. With nothing new happening just now, this is a suitable moment to interject some enlightening facts provided by the gentlemen from the *Reichsbahn* management—though I shall refrain from listing purely technical data, which will interest only the expert. As regards the train's speed, first of all, this is being held somewhat below the maximum that could already be reached, as the railcar has to fit into the pattern of existing traffic. It would be feasible to make up trains out of several such cars rather than run them singly, but for the moment it has been decided to use short train units, operating them more frequently where this is justified. An important point made was that the introduction of these modern engines by no means makes steam power redundant. Quite the contrary, in fact: the hope is that, as with the introduction of gas, competition from the new type of engine will lead to improvements in the old system of steam propulsion. In a few months' time, once a bend outside Wittenberge has been straightened out, the journey time to Hamburg should be reduced to two hours. (The ordinary express takes three hours.)

ARRIVAL

Our speed slackens; houses become houses again. Out in the open country, we saw repeatedly how groups of people would stop to stare in fascination at the train and then wave as if to a bringer of good tidings, or to a friend; but now, from Bergedorf on, the groups of people have become crowds. Amazing: house balconies, road intersections, suburban station platforms are now full of people eager to watch the shiny new train pass by. They follow it with their eyes as if it were the fulfillment of a cherished private dream. At 12:55 we pull into Hamburg Central Station. Here, too, hundreds have been waiting, and stare at the railcar in silent homage. Sparklingly new, physically present and yet almost beyond belief, it comes to rest, a dazzling hero fresh from the triumph, amid the gloom of the great station.

Leaving the station in the thick of the crowd, I hear a workman say: "If you could get a ride on that, you'd be laughing, all right." Yet it is not envy talking; there is no trace of envy in his words. They do, however, speak of a longing for a time when we are allowed to laugh.

215

E. Neumann

OBJECT—SUBJECT

First published as "Objekt—Subjekt," opening speech at the First German Road Construction Day, Munich: Nation, Motor Traffic, and Road Construction, *Die Bauzeitung*, no. 17 (1934). Translated by Iain Boyd Whyte.

[...]

For with the motorcar, technology has once again given us an individual means of transport, after turning us into members of the herd with railways and streetcars, rental apartment house, and factory hall. [...] To regard the use of motor vehicles only from the standpoint of economic returns is entirely one-sided. For other influences of a psychological nature have long had a say in the matter. For the man who is very stretched in the work process is no longer master of himself, along with thousands of others; he must travel back and forward to his place of work on public transport, along preordained routes and at specified times. In his work, every step, each hand movement is determined. The subordination that has resulted from the rationalization of labor can be found not only in manual workers, but also deep in the realms of the civil servants and white-collar workers, and even the self-employed. It is quite natural and explicable that people whose right of self-determination has been limited in this way look for ways to free themselves in some way or other, and to impose their will for a change on some entity. The motorcar offers a most suitable vehicle for this; the man who is normally only an object can see himself just for once as the subject, and assert his own will on the gas pedal.

It is the irrational in mankind. The motor industry should promote these concerns, which cannot be considered only from an economic standpoint, but as things that make our lives more worth living. And this also explains the passionate desire that people have to own a motorcar and their interest in the road-building program. May the Reich chancellor, Adolf Hitler, awaken this vital sense in the German people and give it new impetus.

216
Anonymous
THE INTERCONTINENTAL AIRPORT AT TEMPELHOF

First published as "Der Weltflughafen Tempelhof," *Monatshefte für Baukunst und Städtebau* 22, no. 3 (March 1938), pp. 81–95. Translated by Iain Boyd Whyte.

Granted, it is the finished job that really counts. The architectural form and the impact that that form will make, both from outside and within, will of course be discernible to the practiced eye in advance, on the basis of the drawings and the completed shell alone. But it is not until the architect finally steps back, not until he personally takes a walk around the site perimeter, no longer as a participant but in the role of a mere observer, and the building project has cast him off, become autonomous, become a thing with a life of its own: not until then has the moment come to speak about the project as a whole. And yet, often it can be uncommonly instructive to be allowed to glimpse something of the process of realization to see a project under construction. Such insights are all the more valuable in the case of very large projects involving many different kinds of input. The complexity of the assignment, so formidable for the architect, so prone to be glossed over and underrated when at last everything has been brought together successfully in the finished structure, can be best appreciated during these earlier stages. The sight of a great work while it is still in the making, still being worked on, shows the architect particularly vividly as the creative spirit. It shows him in his workshop and gives an idea of the many registers he must be able to draw on if he is to deploy them fluently in the desired harmony. The various requirements—the project brief and its innumerable demands, the effective use of technology, the visual impact of the new structure, both on its immediate urban setting and in terms of its own architecture—all these considerations emerge clearly if one has the chance to follow a planning process from its beginnings right through to a moment such as the one pinpointed by the present publication by Tempelhof Airport. We believe that, as in the case of Ernst Sagebiel's first large-scale project in Berlin, the Air Ministry building, a similar account here of the architect's work in connection with the Tempelhof Airport project will be useful and will become an important record.

This project, conceived on the grand scale both technically and in terms of its public importance, owes its inception to the rapid and accelerating growth of air transport. So significant has been the increase, indeed, that progressive enlargement of existing facilities has generally not been possible. Instead, the new imperatives call for a radically new design response. To put the situation in perspective: since 1932, the passenger and freight volume carried by air has approximately tripled. The European air-route network is steadily expanding, and has external links in the shape of new routes to North and South America and of regular time-tabled flights to South Africa and the Far East. The growth statistics of aviation have been paralleled by the expansion of technological support and the rise in aircraft cruising speeds.

The consequence of all this for the capital city of the Reich was an urgent need for expansion of its air-transport support facilities. This in turn dictated that it would not suffice to supplement what was already in place by adding further buildings—a palliative measure that would have had only a limited period of usefulness: what was needed now was a radically new concept. At existing airports, constant extensions and additional construction work have increasingly left the original design unrecognizable, obscured behind a motley array of prefabricated hangars, showy passenger terminals and administrative blocks, and wooden huts and staff housing. Now, Professor Sagebiel has solved the design problem with a unified overall concept on a scale adequate to the demands that can be expected in the future. Over and above its primary function, however, the intercontinental airport at Tempelhof will be a very distinctive and prominent feature of the cityscape of the *Reichshauptstadt* [capital city of the Reich], and acts as a resounding affirmation of the importance of modern aviation. For the architect, mindful of the various fields of activity that have relevance for aviation as such, has drawn these ancillary domains into his overall design: the central purpose is to serve air transport, but airport administration has been properly catered for, and allowance has also been made for a new public passion—the fascination with human flight, unmistakably demonstrated by the huge attendances at the Aviation Open Days held at Tempelhof to date.

The Central Berlin airport at Berlin-Tempelhof is also the center of the European air-route network. It has the unusual feature of being located almost in the center of the *Reichshauptstadt* (2.5 kilometers [1.5 miles] from the city center), an advantage described by Field Marshal Göring in his address at the topping-out ceremony as unique and exceptionally valuable. If there were other considerations that might favor transferring the airport to an outlying district such as Staaken, they paled into insignificance in comparison. And in relation to other European capitals, the advantage is patent: London's airport at Croydon is 14 kilometers [9 miles] from the center; Le Bourget, 12 kilometers [7 miles] from Paris; Aspern, 10 kilometers [6 miles] from Vienna.

Two years ago the Reich's minister for aviation, Hermann Göring, gave the order for planning to begin for a new Tempelhof that would match up to the Führer's ideas for an airport on the grand scale. As some broad stretches of ground adjacent to the existing airfield had still not been built over, it proved possible to extend it very substantially. [. . .] The new Berlin Airport will be the world's biggest airport. It has passenger reception halls, restaurants, vehicle garaging, and aircraft hangars of unprecedented dimensions. Here, for the first time anywhere in the world, passengers will be able to board their airplane in a covered boarding and disembarkation area measuring almost 400 meters [440 yards] from end to end. The roof of this boarding area extends for almost 400 meters in width and 50 meters [55 yards] in depth, entirely without support pillars. The aircraft hangars adjoin it on both sides.

Particular attention has been given to designing the restaurants and catering facilities. High above the aircraft boarding area, and almost 40 meters [44 yards] above the flying field, the principal restaurant has seating for two thousand people. The planners have had the foresight to provide for the possibility of airport events attracting mass audiences. Apart from the open spaces along the perimeter of the flying field, which are capable of accommodating hundreds of thousands of people, the roofs of the hangars and the aircraft boarding area have been designed in the form of grandstands, and have room to seat eighty thousand spectators.

217

Jakob Werlin / Albert Speer
ON THE AUTOBAHNS OF THE REICH

First published as two untitled texts in Fritz Todt, ed., *Die Strasse* 5, no. 1 (1938), n.p. Translated by Iain Boyd Whyte.

DIRECTOR JAKOB WERLIN

More than two thousand kilometers of this gigantic road network have now been completed, in five years of resolute hard work. The vehicle user today—and there can hardly be one remaining in Germany who has never driven on these roads—can no longer imagine the landscape devoid of these silver-gray ribbons of concrete, the stone-built bridges and flyovers. He has as good as forgotten that alongside the completed stretches of autobahn the old national road is still there, with its restricted width and its bends. Who now does not heave a sigh of relief when the link road brings him to the autobahn, on whose level surface he will find his "progress" incomparably more rapid, where there are no obstacles to avoid and no dangerous intersections, where nothing forces him to stop moving and he can thus reduce wear and tear on his brakes and on the vehicle itself to a minimum. Clutch mechanism and gearbox have a holiday, being virtually never needed on the autobahn. This means there are very substantial cost savings relative to the old national roads. Average speeds are 65 percent higher and journey times reduced by 48 percent on average, while fuel consumption is approximately 50 percent lower; tire wear will obviously also be notably low. On this straight road, driving becomes flying. The vehicle is reassuringly safe while moving at speeds that would be the height of recklessness on the old roads. No one, as far as can be humanly foreseen, needs fear an accident while driving sensibly. And it is in this respect in particular that the autobahns of the Reich represent nothing less than the achievement of the ultimate, unsurpassable ideal form for a traffic route—a triumph we owe to our Führer's inspired creative vision.

Closely geared to the progress of the construction work, the process of making Germany a fully motorized nation has continued with unshakable momentum. Indeed, in a sense it may be said that only the autobahn can create the space that this process demands. [. . .]

PROFESSOR ALBERT SPEER, *GENERALBAUINSPEKTOR* [CHIEF GOVERNMENT ARCHITECT] FOR THE REICH CAPITAL BERLIN

At the laying of the foundation stone in the Runder Platz in Berlin on 14 June, the Führer made it absolutely clear that our immense new building projects are conceived not so much for the present day as for the decades and the centuries to come. It is common knowledge that the new east–west and north–south axes do not terminate at the existing city boundaries, but are being extended to link up with the Greater Berlin Autobahn Ring. Within the area enclosed by the Autobahn Ring, further orbital roads are being planned—these, too, with the object of completely solving the traffic problem. The radial roads—that is, the present main roads entering and leaving the capital—are being improved to meet modern traffic requirements and provide efficient feeder routes from and to the autobahns. The AVUS is being upgraded as an autobahn feeder route.[1] All these facts demonstrate how closely Berlin's construction projects and those of the Reich autobahn are interlinked. In both, looking, as always, squarely toward the future, the will of the National Socialist Reich is unmistakable. The architectural expression it will find in the new Berlin now being born will be complemented and completed in the grand design of the Reich autobahn network. The current rapid increase in vehicle numbers, which will be further accelerated by the launch of the *Volkswagen* [People's Car], shows in particular, in Berlin as elsewhere, how closely city planners and Reich autobahn planners must collaborate if they are to do justice to the tasks set them by the present age and the future. The expressed will of the Führer is that Berlin must be made truly the capital of the Greater German Reich; it is therefore essential that Berlin be tightly linked to all parts of the Reich by way of the Reich autobahn.

NOTE

1. See note to text 209: Bernard von Brentano, The Pleasure of Motoring.

218

Hans Stephan

THE AUTOBAHN

In Stephan, *Die Baukunst im Dritten Reich, insbesondere die Umgestaltung der Reichshauptstadt* (Berlin: Junker und Dünnhaupt, 1939), p. 8. Translated by Iain Boyd Whyte.

The first constructional feat of National Socialism, the state autobahn network, while serving its intended purpose as a means of transportation, is consciously integrated, in contrast to the nineteenth-century railway network, into the German landscape. For all its functionality it is firmly grounded in the rules of aesthetic design at both large and small scale, and expands beyond its practical task to become a work of art of lasting value. Even more significant is its idealistic meaning. For there is nothing that portrays so directly before our eyes as the autobahn network the new spirit of unity of the German nation and of the German *Lebensraum* [literally, "living space"].[1]

NOTE

1. *Lebensraum*—living space—is a term coined by the geographer Friedrich Ratzel (1844–1904) to argue that prosperous species and races need to expand geographically to maintain their vigor and vitality. The term and the argument were adopted by Hitler in the 1920s to justify German expansionism and colonization in the east, and specifically in Poland and the Soviet Union.

18

FROM BERLIN TO GERMANIA

Had he not been preoccupied with world domination, Adolf Hitler would happily have worked as an architect and city planner. Before the First World War he sought to establish himself as a topographical painter, producing amateurish watercolors of Vienna and Munich. As he subsequently recalled, the city's monumental architecture made an enormously powerful impression on him: "For hours and hours I could stand in wonderment before the Opera and the Parliament. The whole Ringstrasse had a magic effect on me, as if it were a scene from the Thousand and One Nights."[1] Thwarted in his attempts to study architecture, Hitler turned to politics. Following the unsuccessful Munich Beer Hall putsch of November 1923, he was locked up in Landsberg prison for nine months. During his incarceration, he made drawings of monumental structures—domed halls and triumphal arches—and also began work on his manifesto, *Mein Kampf,* in which he specifically attacked the commercial forces that were shaping the contemporary city: "If a similar fate should befall Berlin as befell Rome, future generations might gaze upon the ruins of some Jewish department stores or joint-stock hotels and think that these were the characteristic expressions of the culture of our time."[2] Joseph Goebbels's diaries confirm that Hitler was already working on plans for the rebuilding of Berlin in February 1932, almost a year before he became Reich chancellor in January 1933—plans grounded on a monumental architecture that would give, in Hitler's view, expression to the spiritual and emotional values of the German people.

Architecture and city planning were key elements in Hitler's geopolitical landscape. Indeed, the propaganda machine subsequently insisted that the great vision for the reordering of Berlin had come from Hitler himself: "The essence of the plan is that a National Socialist Berlin will not be attached superficially to the urban confusion of the liberal city, but rather that the inner structure of the giant city will be altered with revolutionary force and given new form with the greatest constructional clarity. With inspired vision the ordering hand of the Führer has drawn [. . .] the intersecting axes of the two monumental routes and the four magnificent radials."[3] The task of implementing this massive rebuilding program was entrusted in January 1937 to a young and very inexperienced architect, Albert Speer. Far from confirming the revolutionary genius of Adolf Hitler, Speer's plan for Berlin was very simple in its basic strategy, and merely combined the principal elements of the earlier proposals of Mächler and Wagner—namely, two axes, running north–south and east–west.

At their extremities, the axes were planned to link with the outer autobahn ring and with a further four inner ring roads providing concentric circulation. The central section of the north–south axis was conceived as a vast parade ground, designed to house the principal public buildings, ministries, and commercial offices of the new Reich on a boulevard 7 kilometers long and 120 meters wide. It was anchored at each end by new railway stations, and housed the two iconic monuments first sketched by Hitler in Landsberg prison: a monumental victory arch, and an even more monumental domed hall intended as the hall of the people and conceived, in Speer's own words, as "essentially a place of worship."[4]

A contemporary newspaper article captures well the megalomanic dreams nurtured by the National Socialists for Germania, as Berlin was to be renamed: "In his definitive statement of the 28 January 1938 on the redevelopment of the capital city of the Reich, the General Building Inspector for the Capital City of the Reich [Albert Speer] announced, among other things, that 'In future, anyone who emerges from the main hall of the new Southern Station will see, soaring upward at the other end of the monumental new main street of Berlin, 5.5 kilometers away and right at the center of the city on the site of the present Alsenstrasse, an assembly hall that in its dimensions is appropriate to the scale and the significance of Berlin as capital of the Reich. In front of this monumental building, the Königsplatz, with an area of over 220,000 square meters, allows the staging of large-scale rallies of around 1 million participants.'"[5] In designing such giant spaces to house the party faithful, Speer was responding to the mobilization of the masses that had characterized German political life as the Weimar Republic moved toward its demise. On the local scale, street fighting between left- and right-wing gangs was a daily occurrence in Berlin. In the broader context, political rallies attracted enormous audiences, mobilized to listen to the demagogues. According to the journalist William Shirer, Adolf Hitler spoke in the course of only one day to 60,000 people in Brandenburg, to nearly the same number in Potsdam, and to 120,00 that evening in the Grunewald Stadium in Berlin, with a further 100,000 listening to his speech outside the stadium via loudspeaker.[6] Speer's Great Hall was designed to hold over 150,000 people—fewer than those who attended Hitler's speeches on the day in question, 27 July 1932.

The Great Hall was to be sited on the northern edge of a vast parade ground, flanked on the remaining three sides by the existing Reichstag building, by a massive "Führer-Palais," and by an equally large building for the Army High Command. The theme of state and civic control was amplified by the three major blocks to the north of the Great Hall, flanking the water basin, and intended for the German Navy, the City Council, and the Berlin Police. This politicization of urban space was further developed on the east–west axis, whose central core was to be anchored in the historic city center by a vast Museum of Ethnography, described by Alfred Rosenberg—a minister charged at that time by Hitler to oversee the ideological education of the party—as "a new and revolutionary museum, proceeding from the great racial ideas, and taking into consideration our German tasks for the future."[7] Farther west, in the Tiergarten, the nineteenth-century Siegessäule (Victory column) was moved in 1938 from its original location in front of the Reichstag to a new site on the east–west axis, to mark Hitler's fiftieth birthday. Had Speer's plan been full implemented, the figure of Victory atop the column, celebrating the Prussian triumphs over Denmark (1864), Austria (1866), and France (1870–71), would have looked westward, up the hill to the "Mussoliniplatz" (now Theodor-Heuss-Platz), where her gaze would have alighted on a giant figure—*Preparedness,* by the sculptor Arno Breker—set upon a columnar plinth designed by Speer. This giant warrior, unsheathing his sword, would have faced toward the west and toward France, challenging the old enemy to raise arms against the new Germany. Moving westward again, the belligerent and racially tainted program for the axis found further expression in the stadium and surrounding facilities built for the 1936 Olympics, and in a University City, planned for the banks of the Havelsee at Pichelswerder. Focused around a new Faculty of Defense Studies, only fragments of the new university were built, and were subsequently buried under the rubble of the Teufelsberg after 1945.

Supporting the omnipresent themes of race and war, Speer and his architects studded the plans for Germania with shrines to death and sacrifice redolent of the ecstasy of the *Götterdämmerung*—the twilight of the gods. These included a Museum to the Great War right in the city center, a Hall for the Unknown Soldier on the north–south axis in the Tiergarten, and two Langemarck halls, one behind the Olympic Stadium and the other in the University City. Langemarck is a village in Belgium where, according to the myth nurtured by the National Socialists, the German volunteer regiments had stormed the positions of the enemy in November 1914, singing the national anthem, "Deutschland, Deutschland über alles," as they went to their deaths. These vast, empty halls, burdened with false pathos, had no purpose beyond spurring German youth to further and greater sacrifices for country and party.

While the National Socialist plans for Berlin represent an extreme example of the aestheticization of power, the means employed to realize these plans reveal the brutality that underpinned this power. The architectural plans drawn up by Speer's all-powerful agency, the Generalbauinspektion (General Building Inspectorate, or GBI), were used as a mechanism by which to transform the German political economy into a mechanism that could impose the National Socialist objectives on the nation, not least the architectural objectives. In Berlin, this meant that the increasingly draconian laws enacted to appropriate Jewish-owned property were implemented to clear the sites in readiness for the construction of Germania. The houses and apartments forcibly seized from their legal, Jewish owners were put at the disposal of the GBI to rehouse non-Jewish residents displaced by site clearance and demolition. An explicit relationship existed, in consequence, between the rebuilding program for Berlin and the expulsion of the Jews from the city.[8]

With a gruesome irony, many of the displaced Berlin Jews were forced to work in the concentration camps as slave laborers, producing the building materials for Germania. In March 1938 a cover organization named DEST (Deutsche Erd- und Steinwerke) was set up to serve the mutual interests of Speer's GBI, and Himmler's SS. The outcome was an expansion and a refocusing of the concentration-camp system to supply the vast quantities of building materials needed for the Germania project. Under the management of DEST and the control of the SS, brickworks were established in the concentration camps at Sachsenhausen, north of Berlin; at Neugamme, near Hamburg; and at Buchenwald. Sand and gravel were sourced from the banks of the Vistula at Auschwitz, and stone quarries were opened at Flossenbürg, Mauthausen, Groß-Rosen, and Natzweiler. The magnitude of these undertakings was matched only by the brutality of their implementation. With Germania in mind, DEST was contracted in August 1938 to produce 120 million bricks a year in the largest brickworks in the world, which was to be located at the Sachsenhausen camp. At the scale of a single project, the architect Wilhelm Kreis estimated in May 1939 that the construction of the Soldiers' Hall to his design would necessitate over one and a half million cubic meters of white granite of the type that could be sourced at the concentration camps at Flossenbürg and Mauthausen. Through the use of slave labor in the camps, the National Socialist regime not only sourced stone for Germania, but also destroyed in the process those considered to be enemies of the state.[9]

Only fragments of this monstrous scheme were actually built before the demands of the war economy took precedence over the construction of Germania. Allied air raids on the city began as early in the war as 25 August 1940 and culminated in the daylight raid of 3 February 1945, in which almost a thousand bombers took part. The consequences, in terms of both loss of life and the destruction of the urban fabric, were appalling. In 1941, Hitler had boasted that Berlin would one day be capital of the world. By the time of the unconditional surrender, signed on 8 May 1945, Berlin was the scene of apocalyptic destruction. Of the major elements planned for the two axes, only the central airport at Tempelhof and the Olympic Stadium survived the war and the immediate postwar demolitions.

NOTES

1. Adolf Hitler, *Mein Kampf* (London: Hutchinson, 1940), p. 28.
2. Ibid., p. 230.
3. Gerdy Troost, *Das Bauen im neuen Reich* (Bayreuth: Gauverlag Bayerischer Ostmark, 1938), p. 56.
4. Albert Speer, *Inside the Third Reich* (London: Weidenfeld and Nicolson, 1970), p. 153.
5. "Das neue Berliner Stadtbild," *Frankfurter Zeitung,* Reichsausgabe, 12 April 1938.
6. See William Shirer, *The Rise and Fall of the Third Reich,* vol. 1 (London: Folio Society, 1995), p. 180.
7. Alfred Rosenberg, quoted in Hans J. Reichhardt and Wolfgang Schäche, *Von Berlin nach Germania* (Berlin: Transit, 1998), p. 78. On the politicization of space in the context of Speer's extension to the existing Reich chancellery, see Iain Boyd Whyte, "Reflections on a Polished Floor: Ben Willikens and the Reichskanzlei of Albert Speer," *Harvard Design Magazine,* Fall 1998, pp. 56–63.
8. For details, see Reichhardt and Schäche, *Von Berlin nach Germania,* pp. 159–179; and Paul B. Jaskot, "Anti-Semitic Policy in Albert Speer's Plans for the Rebuilding of Berlin," *Art Bulletin* 78, no. 4 (December 1996), pp. 622–32.
9. For an account of the slave-labor program, see Paul B. Jaskot, *The Architecture of Oppression: The SS, Forced Labour and Nazi Monumental Building Economy* (London: Routledge, 2000).

219

Siegfried Kracauer

SCREAMS ON THE STREET

First published as "Schreie auf der Strasse," *Frankfurter Zeitung,* 19 July 1930. Translated by David Britt.

The streets in the west of Berlin are clean and inviting; they are decently wide, and often there are rows of neat little trees in front of the houses. But, despite the pleasant—not to say patrician—impression that they convey, one is often seized, in walking along them, by an unprovoked sense of panic. Why? I do not know. I know only that sometimes, as I cross familiar streets, I am overtaken by the fear that there will be a riot, and that something bad is going to happen. Perhaps my fear stems from the way these streets have of seeming to vanish into infinity; because the buses that clatter along them have passengers who, as they proceed to their remote destinations, gaze out across a landscape of sidewalks, shop windows, and balconies as indifferently as at a river valley or city where they mean

FIGURE 48. German Communist Party demonstration, 1 May 1929, Landesarchiv Berlin, II 8 090.

never to alight; because on those streets an innumerable host of humanity is on the move, a constant flow of new individuals heading for unknown places, their paths intersecting like the maze of lines on a dressmaking pattern. However that may be, I sometimes have the feeling that every possible hiding place conceals an explosive that may go off at any moment.

With undiminished clarity, I remember an evening in the neighborhood of the Kaiser-Wilhelm-Gedächtniskirche. A small party of us were sitting together when suddenly I realized that some kind of crisis was brewing across the vast expanse of the square. Nothing happened, no glass was broken, and the automobiles kept to their usual trajectories. But the afternoon atmosphere that hangs over weary masses of humanity and shabby house fronts was charged with an intolerable tension. After a brief pause, a commotion did break out. A troop of National Socialists—still in uniform in those days—accused the café customers of mocking them, clambered over the parapet, and went on the rampage. Finally the police showed up and restored peace.

I had not been expecting this particular upheaval but another, which would probably have had no specific cause—and which did not happen, probably because the National Socialist shindig cleared the air.

In Berlin there are whole neighborhoods where the penetrating scent of political violence hangs in the air: Neukölln, for instance, or Wedding. There, the streets are ipso facto marching streets. There, even amid the monotony of daily life, it takes no special gift of intuition to surmise that demonstrations are a common sight; that at times the windows fill with wives and children who gaze down at the surging throng beneath; that the houses are regularly shaken by the steady tread of many thousands; and that banner proclamations and red flags constantly surge past these gray walls. Such scenes have a tangible, an almost objective feel to them, which conveys itself to the streets where they take place. Those western streets inspire a fear of a different kind; it has no specific object. There are no proletarians on those streets; nor do they ever witness riots. The people who live there do not belong together, and the climate is not one in which collective action can ever be taken. There, no one expects anything of anyone. The streets stretch away into a vague distance, inconsequential and empty.

Is it this emptiness that makes them momentarily seem so sinister? Once more, I do not know. I can only say that Tauentzienstrasse glitters evilly in the sunlight like an inhuman foe, and that on all those streets of which I speak there collects from time to time an excitement that, were it made visible, would resemble the raging forest of zigzag lines on a paper pattern. And I also know that on the streets close to Kurfürstendamm—where children work inside open ground-floor windows, and a veterinarian walks his canine patient in the front yard—weird screams are heard from time to time. It is characteristic of these that one never finds out their cause. The first time I heard one, I went to investigate and found a drunk, who stumbled off in silence as soon as I approached. The second time, the scream—a girl's shrill scream—hung in the air above the heads of a young couple who seemed to have just made up a quarrel and were now sauntering arm in arm in the moonlight. The third time, the scream undoubtedly meant murder. I dashed around the corner at once, redoubling my efforts when I saw other people running alongside me. We crossed the roadway and turned into the street from which the scream had come. There, the few passersby turned to watch us in astonishment before slowly strolling on their way. A door slammed and locked in our faces.

I now suspect that on those streets it is not the people that scream but the streets themselves. When they can bear their own emptiness no longer, they scream it all out of themselves. But I really do not know.

220

Irmgard Keun

THE ARTIFICIAL SILK GIRL

First published as *Das kunstseidene Mädchen* (1932; reprint, Stuttgart: Ernst Klett, 1981), pp. 42–43, 45–46; published in English as *The Artificial Silk Girl*, trans. Katharina von Ankum (New York: Other Press, 2002), pp. 55–56, 60–61.

I'm in Berlin. Since a few days ago. After an all-night train ride with 90 marks left. That's what I have to live on until I come into some money. What I have since experienced is just incredible. Berlin descended on me like a comforter with a flaming floral design. The Westside is very elegant with bright lights—like fabulous stones, really expensive and in an ornate setting. We have enormous neon advertising around here. Sparkling lights surround me. And then there's me and my fur coat. And elegant men like white-slave traders, without exactly trafficking in women at the moment, those no longer exist—but they look like it, because they would be doing it if there was money in it. A lot of shining black hair and deep-set night eyes. Exciting. There are many women on the Kurfürstendamm. They simply walk. They have the same faces and lots of moleskin fur—not exactly first class, in other words, but still chic—with arrogant legs and a great waft of perfume about them. There is a subway; it's like an illuminated coffin on skis—under the ground and musty, and one is squashed. That is what I ride on. It's interesting and it travels fast.

So I'm staying with Tilli Scherer in Münzstrasse, that's near Alexanderplatz. There are unemployed people here who don't even own a shirt, and so many of them. But we have two rooms and Tilli's hair is dyed golden and her husband is away, putting down tram tracks near Essen. And she films. But she's not getting any parts, and the agency is handling things unfairly. Tilli is soft and round like a down pillow and her eyes are like polished blue marbles. Sometimes she cries, because she likes to be comforted. So do I. Without her, I wouldn't have a roof over my head. I'm grateful to her and we're on the same wavelength and don't give each other any trouble. When I see her face when she's asleep, I have good thoughts about her. And that's what's important: how your react to someone while they're sleeping and not exerting any influence over you. There are buses, too, very high ones like observation towers that are moving. Sometimes I go on them. At home, we had lots of streets, too, but they were familiar with each other. Here, there are so many more streets that they can't possibly all know each other. It's a fabulous city.

[. . .]

So I arrived at Friedrichstrasse Station, where's there's an incredible hustle-bustle. And I found out that some great Frenchmen had arrived just before I did, and Berlin's masses were out there to greet them. They're called Laval and Briand—and being a woman who frequently spends time waiting in restaurants, I've seen their picture in magazines.[1] I was swept along Friedrichstrasse in a crowd of people, which was full of life and colorful and somehow it had a checkered feeling. There was so much excitement! So I immediately realized that this was an exception, because even the nerves of an enormous city like Berlin can't stand such incredible tension every day. But I was swooning and I continued to be swept along—the air was full of excitement. And some people pulled me along, and so we came to stand in front of an elegant hotel that is called Adlon—and everything was covered with people and cops that were pushing and shoving. And then the politicians arrived on the balcony like soft black spots. And everything turned into a scream and the masses swept me over the cops onto the sidewalk and they wanted those politicians to throw peace down to them from the balcony. And I was shouting with them, because so many voices pierced through my body that they came back out of my mouth. And I had this idiotic crying fit, because I was so moved. And so I immediately belonged to Berlin, being right in the middle of it—that pleased me enormously. And the politicians lowered their heads in a statesmanly fashion, and so, in a way, they were greeting me, too.

And we were all shouting for peace—I thought to myself that that was good and you have to do it, because otherwise there's going to be a war—and Arthur Grönland once explained to me that the next war would be fought with stinky gas which makes you turn green and all puffed up. And I certainly don't want that. So I too was shouting to the politicians up there.

NOTE

1. The French prime minister, Pierre Laval, accompanied by the foreign minister, Aristide Briand, made an official visit to Berlin on 26 and 27 September 1931 for talks with Chancellor Heinrich Bruning. Laval was very impressed by Bruning, enthusing to the German press: "What a man! I wish there were more such men in France!"

221

Heinrich Hauser

THE FLOOD OF HUMANITY AT TEMPELHOF

First published as "Das Menschenmeer von Tempelhof," *Neue Rundschau,* 1933, no. 1; reprinted in *Glänzender Asphalt: Berlin im Feuilleton der Weimarer Republik,* ed. Christian Jäger and Erhard Schütz (Berlin: Fannei & Walz, 1994), pp. 326–31. Translated by Iain Boyd Whyte.

On 1 May, the Tempelhofer Feld was the most powerful magnetic force field in the world. The nearer you approached it, the stronger its power of attraction became. It was impossible to break free from it. Tens of thousands who actually wanted to keep away were sucked into the stream of the marching procession—not by force, but following an inner instinct: man's herd instinct.

Above the masses that were streaming from all sides toward the meeting place—almost bursting the streets apart—lay a peculiar numbness. The thunder of their marching, the roar of their voices, their urgent pressing forward in one direction overcame them like an intoxication. A strange, tentative animation like that of the blind marked their faces, while in their movements lay the peculiar impulse of a colony of ants before the nuptial flight. Those observers of the march who sat on every available balcony or wall, and at every window, seemed to belong to a quite different race.

The squadron of planes circled over the masses, guiding them again and again in the direction of Tempelhof. When the throbbing of their motors broke thunderously into the street canyons, casting menacing shadows, they created such excitement, as though they were harbingers of some great, primeval event—like the restlessness of birds before an earthquake or a solar eclipse.

The light of the sinking sun transfigured Berlin. It gilded the sappy new greenery, lit up the gray house facades, colored the hair of young girls blonder, lent a glow to the human face. The whole day long, starting in the morning, the masses were on the march. Half a million people had been encamped on the field since midday, straining to hear the loudspeaker, looking at the aerobatics of the pilots, eating the sandwiches and coffee they had brought with them, stretching out on the patchy grass and waiting. All the while the space around them steadily contracted as ever more people streamed in. The whole thing was like a monstrous ship in a dock that was filling with water, and that would soon float.

At around seven o'clock the advancing columns came to a standstill. The throng of people had become too dense for the streets to hold them. And the stream of people behaved just like a stream of water: the flow was strongest at the center and moved more and more slowly toward the edges. Right at the side little eddies broke away. These were the ones who had given up hope, who wanted to abandon the race and find new strength in the pub.

At the perimeter of the field the masses ran into the first weirs and dams of the control squads. Mounted police towered like islands above the surging heads. SA storm troopers bound themselves together with their shoulder straps to form a brown wall. In this way they brought the surge to a halt. What then happened was exactly like a watering system. You have to imagine the Tempelhofer Feld as a great big meadow that had to be watered—using people. The weirs and dams formed an enclosing dyke around the whole area, past which pushed the floods of people. At certain points they were channeled through the dams: the brown wall opened up when the SA people lifted their strap-linked arms above shoulder height, and the human streams poured into the field. Once inside, the mass of people was guided via fences and barbed wire in something like a giant cattle pen, divided according to a system of numbers. There they were split up into groups and finally stood still.

Wherever the blockages were becoming dangerous, when the laughter and the cheerful pressing of the human stream started to compress too tightly, wherever the women started to shriek and the men to curse, the whistles of the SA lookouts, who stood elevated on poles or on lampposts, would sound. Then brown walls would push into the stream and steer it back into calmer waters.

People were hanging like bunches of grapes from every tree, lamppost, fence post, or signpost. Every window opening, balcony, and roof on the streets bordering the field was black with people. How strange that the impression of great masses of people is always one of darkness, almost blackness, in spite of all the light-colored spring clothing.

The field was transformed into a completely different landscape. High above the sea of heads rose gigantic floodlighting gantries, which look like ancient war machines, like the movable towers used to assault cities. The most enormous flags that one had ever seen fluttered in the gentle breeze, looking like sails billowing on the sea of the masses. Between the floodlighting and loudspeaker towers a net of wires was hung. Along the edges of the sea and lit by burning torches stretched rows of booths and tents—enough for a whole Munich *Bierfest*—which served as the food store for the millions, as first-aid posts, and as the military camp of the SA. The ground on which one was walking was so deep in paper—the most typical attribute of today's man—that the marching steps of the masses rustled, as if they were going through dried leaves. Fine brown dust started to rise in ever thicker clouds and settled over the sea of people like a gray cloud. Within six hours the grass was completed trodden and destroyed. Aircraft subsequently reported that the roar of the people drowned out the engine noise several hundred feet up.

Toward eight o'clock, in the uncanny twilight of dusk, the searchlights began their game. Their massive carbon rods hissed as their blue-white arms of light played across the sea of heads. Millions of shadows began a ghostly dance as every person and every thing threw an array of shadows in the crossing beams of the searchlight. This battle of the shadows, fought out by the competing searchlight towers, was like something out of a fantasy, like the battle of the ghosts in the Thousand and One Nights. The great gaping mouths of the loudspeakers opened up, and massive voices burst forth—the voices of giants, whose echoes resounded in such a way that it was hard to understand the words. The German national anthem rose above the ocean like a wave. Millions of hands rose slowly above the heads and slipped like the foam of the surf over the oncoming waves. The batteries of water bottles that were stacked up at the edge of the camp sparkled. Ten thousand banners in an unstoppable parade shook like a forest during a storm, and the fluttering flags glowed like flowing blood.

At the far end of the field the grandstand appeared. I saw it from about one and a half kilometer's distance. It looked like the cloud bank of a tropical sunset, glowing in red, black, and white. The banners were red, the new wood white, the masses black. But whereas the cloud bank rises slowly and imperceptibly, an unrelenting sparkling and shimmering lay above this scene, which seemed to be made of entirely of swaying mirrors and colored crystals. No details could be made out from this distance, but the very idea that this cloud bank was made up of human masses was dreamily monstrous.

A new voice boomed out from the loudspeakers, fractured against the street fronts, onto the ocean of people, and collided with its own echoes: Hitler was holding his grand speech.

A strange rapture and elevation settled across the ocean. It was as if every single atom of the mass had joined to create a feeling of infinity—the same feeling produced by the sea when you see it for the first time. And then came the fireworks. They began with red rockets, which cut spiraling paths into the heavens and then exploded with loud, thunderous blasts. That was the first proclamation. What followed simply cannot be described in words. The whole of the eastern sky was transformed into a fata morgana of colored fire, a manmade vision such as no theatrical effect of nature could create. Palm forests of colored flame shot up and sank together again in showers of shooting stars. Batteries of giant canons rose into the air and shot fireballs, which detonated and then fell into the ocean of people in long, arching claws of fire. The heavens glowed with white-hot embers that streamed downward in misty waves, as if the city was about to be buried under an avalanche. The whizzing sound of the ascending rockets was like shellfire, and the thunder of the explosions like an artillery barrage. The impact of the light and color was hard on the limit of what the human eye can bear. It was an experience for which all comparisons are lacking. Even in the dying red glow in which the fireworks expired one saw streams of shadows chasing after each other beneath waving banners: the last waves of the great roaring and stamping deluge of humanity, which was as fearsome as the sight of a enormous herd of animals fleeing from a prairie fire.

Simultaneously the ebb tide set in: the march home began.

[...]

A thousand meters away from the Tempelhofer Feld the flood began to break up into drops, and each drop of humanity became once again an individual. We were exhausted. We had been in the roaring surf and had surrendered ourselves to it entirely. Now we had returned once again to the shore of our own selves.

No one who was there will ever forget that day.

222

Joseph Goebbels

BERLIN AWAKES

First published as Goebbels, *Das erwachende Berlin* (Munich: Fritz Eher, 1934), pp. 12, 15–16, 21–22. Translated by Iain Boyd Whyte.

As absurd as it might sound, Berlin is a city of soldiers and will always remain that. The Prussian kings made it into this, and what was implanted in this population by way of law and order, discipline, and mass resolve has, so to speak, become flesh and blood in the Berliner. In the worst moments of the Spartacist madness a snappily played military march could make the wildest Bolshevist falter.[1] Nothing is so convincing here as the calm and firm march step of soldiers, individuals serving one purpose, whatever it might be. Even in the tenement housing blocks of Wedding and Neukölln,[2] you see tattered photographs hanging, showing father or uncle as a fusilier guard.

An incomparable sobriety makes the atmosphere of the capital clear and transparent, like glass. There are no vague outlines here that give color rather than contour; the contours here are sharp and clearly drawn and mercilessly separate those things that do no belong together. Nothing is further from this city than shallow sentimentality. Its life has created its own style, which in turn has transferred itself to all those who breathe, work, and earn their daily bread here.

[. . .]

In August 1914 this gray mass of the people one again found its true voice. In the red bars out in the suburbs, the readers of *Vorwärts* raised their glasses to the Kaiser or ran singing through the streets.[3] The war had brought them back to their senses again. Ignoring the cowardly rabble-rousers, who made a party-political issue out of their own difficulties, the masses declared themselves as a people and a nation, and submitted themselves in silence and full, inner fervor to the eternal law that stood over them.

Those in power did not see the signs of the time. They did not reach out to the sympathetic masses who were moving toward them in order to sacrifice themselves for the state. Instead, they gave their hand to those who seduced the masses. They no longer wanted to recognize political parties, only Germans, even among those who were already preparing to sharpen the dagger in order to thrust it at the time of greatest need into the back of the battling army.

From that point on, Berlin was the open wound of the Reich. Secret sabotage fomented there, first in hidden insinuations, in disguised hints, and then less disguised, and ultimately audaciously and cynically. It broke the will of the people to resist, stopped the supply of munitions, dragged the ideal of manly heroism into the dirt, trod on truth and belief, and undermined and ate away at the fabric of the state from the inside out, until it finally collapsed in November 1918. Berlin was estranged from the rest of the nation. It had distanced itself from the roots of the soil and fallen into the hands of nomadic destroyers who refused to believe in the people [*Volk*], in the past, and in history. They were anxious only to do away with the values of the Prussian-German state in order to save themselves from having their own worthlessness measured against them. The gates of the city opened, and through them poured the dirty, viscous stream of immigration from the east. First they came in the thousands, and then in the tens and hundreds of thousands. They started in the Scheunenviertel as fur dealers and petty crooks,[4] and in a few years were established in the city center, from where they spread into the noble villas of the west end. By now they were journalists, clothing manufacturers, respected financiers. They formed public opinion; they supplied the city with what it needed for its existence and gave credit from the millions that they had previously cheated out of the people.

Berlin was lost to the Reich. It lived its own frivolous existence. As if with magnetic power, it pulled people from the land onto the glowing surface of its asphalt, until they were consumed by the heat. A coffin of stone, a crematorium, in which fertility was reduced to a laughable farce, the subject of jokes and mockery, as if it was degrading and the cowardly hedonism that had replaced it was the last word in wisdom. The monarchy had already abandoned this city. The bourgeoisie could not hold it, and Marxism triumphed across the board. Then, out of gray of the fog and rain arose November 1918.

The revolution began. Red marauders, dressed in sailors' uniforms, took control of the city. Where law and discipline, order and firmness had once prevailed, the mob took over. The basest instincts were mobilized. Criminality brazenly stretched up its head, laid its hands cynically on Bismarck's Reich. The Soldiers Councils lounged around in the parliament. The scum of the people vaulted onto the abandoned throne of power. Spartacus ruled the hour.

From that point on Berlin found no peace. In an eternal conflict of positions Berlin was torn back and forth between two extremes. The battle for the city was rejoined once again, and would not find an end until it had been conquered once again for German national values. At that point, only a few thought it possible. These few were rarely to be found in the educated and affluent classes; they belonged mainly to the anonymous masses. They were the sons of the *Vorwärts* readers, who had become aware, and in whom the eternal blood of the soldier had once again begun to flow and pulse.

[. . .]

Meanwhile we went into the lion's den. Perhaps we were not entirely clear at the start what was waiting for us. We began the fight regardless of how and when it would lead to victory. We gave this struggle its impulse, its hot breath, its wild tempo, its thrilling slogans, and its frantic activity. We drove and forced our

FIGURE 49. Unter den Linden decorated for the state visit of Benito Mussolini, September 1937. Berlinische Galerie, Landesmuseum für Moderne Kunst, Photographie und Architektur—Photographische Sammlung, BG-FS 58/85,7.

names and ideas into this city. It became a battle for Berlin, which lasted some eight years and cost streams of blood and tears. But for all of that it was begun by a disillusioned minority who swept this million-strong city unstoppably along with itself and ultimately destroyed it. For years we waded through dirt and filth. There was not a vice that was not ascribed to us, and no virtue that was not denied us. But we risked all!

[. . .]

On the streets of this fantastic, scintillating city with all its secrets and underground layers, with the young men of this city, who in the last sense of their essence are soldiers, the battle for Berlin was fought. It was seen through to the end for the sake of the Reich. It took its toll in blood and lives, but it achieved its goal: Berlin no longer belongs to Marxism. The young, reawakening Germany has once again embraced this city.

The fight for Berlin began as a hopeless enterprise, but was nevertheless risked by a band of audacious men. Pursued by derision and mockery, they followed their chosen path. They buried their dead on the vast cemeteries of this city, took their wounded to the hospitals and brought them out again, stood beside the white gravestones of their dead in order to lay at the feet of their fallen comrades in bitter silence the solemn pledge to hold out to very end. Out of blood and tears a new, German Berlin has arisen. With fanaticism and faith, the brown columns have marched forward over the graves and have planted the flag of the new Reich on the pinnacles of power. We give our thanks to the brave soldiers of the old guard who at no point wavered or gave up hope; our salute to the dead comrades who in the cemeteries of Berlin once again slumber in German soil.

Under the command of their *Sturmführer*, Horst Wessel, they march in the ranks of those who have passed on, which we shall all join when our work has been done.

NOTES

1. The Spartacist League (*Spartakusbund*) was a left-wing Marxist revolutionary movement that enjoyed a brief but vigorous life in Germany in the aftermath of World War I. During the German Revolution of 1918 and 1919, it sought to incite a revolution in Germany on the model of the Bolshevik Revolution in Russia. The newly formed Weimar government reacted vigorously, and brutally put down the uprising with the aid of the Freikorps—a paramilitary army composed of former servicemen. In the process the leaders of the Spartacists, Rosa Luxemburg and Karl Liebknecht, were murdered while in police custody. After the revolution, the Spartacist League was reconstituted as the German Communist Party (KPD). See also above, note to text 129: Käthe Kollwitz, Diary entry, 25 January 1919.

2. Wedding and Neukölln were working-class boroughs of Berlin, both strongholds of Socialism and Communism in the 1920s and early 1930s.

3. *Vorwärts* was the official newspaper of the German Socialist Party (SPD). Its first edition was published in October 1876.

4. The Scheunenviertel, to the east of the Rosenthaler Strasse and Hackescher Markt, was a favored destination for poor Eastern European Jews fleeing from the pogroms in Russia and Poland at the end of the nineteenth century. It was adjacent to Spandauer Vorstadt, the focus of Jewish cultural and commercial life in Berlin, and near the New Synagogue in Oranienburger Strasse, the largest in Berlin, which opened in 1866.

223

Herbert Hoffmann

THE AIR MINISTRY BUILDING

First published as "Das Reichs-Luftfahrt-Ministerium," *Moderne Bauformen* 35 (1936), pp. 425–26. Translated by Iain Boyd Whyte.

The Air Ministry Building is the first major building of the new state in Berlin, the capital of the Reich. Furthermore, it is simply the largest governmental building project to be completed and was realized in a very short time. If one further takes into consideration that this massive building is located in the center of the capital, near Potsdamer Platz and the ministerial quarter, one has reason enough to consider it closely right from the outset. With pleasure we can now establish that the Air Ministry is entirely worthy of this close scrutiny when approached from the position of architectural design. [. . .] The state leadership has not overlooked any contemporary technical means that is appropriate for advancing the project and for heightening the functional impact of the building. Yet the commission is not to be considered achieved simply through the deployment of technical and organizational skills. Both merely establish the self-evident basis on which the building will achieve beauty and dignity. In the case of an airship hangar, a dam, or an industrial building, these aesthetic values can be drawn directly from the technical realm. But when the state puts up a building in the center of the capital city that represents not only itself but also the nation, it should continue the tradition of the great works of architecture produced during the great periods of building. What then counts are the eternal laws of good proportion, of the expressiveness of cut stone, and of the joy in decoration. And these laws can have an impact amid the bustle of the metropolis only when they are informed at both large and small scale with the power of a new formal vocabulary and with self-belief.

With its main front on the Wilhelmstrasse measuring over 200 meters, the Air Ministry Building extends its side wings into the Leipziger Strasse as far as the Preußenhaus[1] and into the Prinz-Albrecht-Strasse as far as the Haus der Flieger [aviation house]. The more often you let the building work on you as you pass, the more clear it becomes that a building on this scale no longer fits into the cityscape as we had formerly known it. It creates its own laws and demands a shift of attitude, to which future developments will have to adjust. The important corner on the Leipziger Strasse is accentuated by the increased height of the corner block and by the powerful recession of the side wing that leads to the Preußenhaus. The true focus, however, lies at the centre of the long facade on the Wilhelmstrasse, where the center of the three courtyards is designed as a *cour d'honneur*. Architecturally, this is emphasized by the high windows with powerfully projecting frames adjacent to the cenotaph monument, and by the striking railings on the street front, with two pylons decorated by eagles.

[. . .]

The Air Ministry contains around two thousand working rooms. Its frame is of reinforced concrete, with steel used only for the raised corner facing Leipziger Strasse. A silver-gray shell limestone was chosen for all the outward-facing facades, and the same material but in a warmer color was used in the courtyards. While it is true that it masks the load-bearing skeleton, the powerful outer skin remains honest in that it is clearly recognizable as cladding. The resulting flat surfaces make an effective counterpart to the window frames, most of which, in well-judged contrast, thrust out vigorously and on the principal fronts carry cornice decorations and eagle-bearing balcony rails.

The painterly decoration of the building and the conscious use of good German stone and wood in the internal decoration also find expression on the exterior. We would commend the frieze by Professor Douglas Hill on the Leipziger Strasse, portraying busts of field marshals and military decorations. Working together with the sculptor W. E. Lemcke, the architect designed the bronze gates below the arcades and the reliefs incised into the stone of the columns at the entry to the inner courtyards. Also the eagles on the pylons of the railing on Richthofenplatz and the national emblem on the Prinz-Albrecht-Strasse are the work of Lemcke.

With this building, designed by Ernst Sagebiel, the young German *Luftwaffe* [air force] has been given a ministry that will also be admired abroad as testimony not only to the military preparedness of the Reich but also to its cultural volition. To this work the architect has added the not inconsiderable project of the large-scale replanning of Tempelhof Airport.[2]

NOTES

1. The Preußenhaus was the National Socialist name for the Herrenhaus, originally completed in 1904 to the design of Friedrich Schulze-Kolbitz. Damaged in World War II, it housed the Academy of Sciences, the State Planning Commission, and the National Economic Council during the years of the German Democratic Republic. After reunification, the architects Schweger & Partners were commissioned to refurbish the Herrenhaus to house the Bundesrat, a function it assumed in August 2000.

2. See above, text 216: The Intercontinental Airport at Tempelhof.

224

Adolf Hitler

THE BUILDINGS OF THE THIRD REICH

First published as "Die Bauten des dritten Reiches" (extract from a speech given to the Reichsparteitag in 1937), *Baugilde der Fachgruppe Architekten in der Reichskammer der bildenden Künste* 19, no. 26 (15 September 1937); republished in Anna Teut, *Architektur im Dritten Reich* (Berlin: Ullstein, 1967), pp. 188–90. Translated by Iain Boyd Whyte.

Never in German history have greater and more noble buildings been planned, begun, and constructed than in our time. And this is the most important thing of all. For architecture also determines sculpture and painting. Besides music, it is the most elementally powerful of the arts that man has invented. It, too, has been betrayed for decades. Its degradation to artistic nonsense and, indeed, to fraud has taken place under the motto of *Sachlichkeit*. During the creative poverty of a liberal, bourgeois era, the construction of buildings serving the community dwindled in contrast to those representing the interests of bourgeois capital and interest groups: industrial structures, banks, stock exchanges, department stores, hotels, and so on. Just as National Socialism sets the greater community of the nation, of the "Volk," above these interests, so it will give this community priority over private interests in the representation of the nation. This is decisive. The greater the demands that today's state makes of its citizens, the more powerful must the state appear to these citizens.

When so often the talk is of "economic necessity," one should bear in mind that most of these necessities make great demands on the willingness of the people to make sacrifices, without this community learning either to see or to understand why a higher goal should be given precedence over its own interests.

There is no epoch in the life of the nations in which the attempt has not been made to express the transcendent interests of the community through the visible imprint of great works of architecture.

But precisely the achievements and results of this endeavor have communicated to the people the true spirit of community, thereby securing the preconditions for the creation and preservation of human culture rather than the zealous pursuit of mere economic interests such as profit, dividends, and the like. This monumental emphasis of the community has helped to establish an authority, without which there can be neither a lasting society nor a social economy. It makes no difference if this authority has its roots in religious institutions or in secular ideas. In any case, the authority that has rescued the German people in the twentieth century from collapse and saved it from the chaos of Bolshevism is not the authority of an economic interest group but that of the National Socialist movement, of the National Socialist Party, and the National Socialist State! The opposition will sense it, but above all the supporters must know it: our buildings are created to reinforce this authority! The structures that you see rising up in this city [the party rally buildings in Nuremberg], those being planned for Berlin and Munich, for Hamburg and other cities, and which in part are ready to be built, or which already stand completed in front of you, are intended for the benefit of this authority!

This is the purpose that lies behind these building works! And because we believe in the eternal survival of this Reich—as far as we can count in human measures—these works should also be eternal. This means that they should satisfy the demands of eternity not only in the grandeur of their conception, but also in the clarity of their ground plans and in the harmony of their proportions.

The small, day-to-day demands have changed over the millennia and will change further in all eternity. But the great cultural documents of humanity, hewn from granite and marble, have also stood for millennia. And they alone are the one truly tranquil and constant factor offering escape from all the other things. At all times in periods of decline, humanity has looked to them to find anew the eternal, magical power, and has always found there the strength to master confusion and create a new order out of chaos. For this reason, these buildings should not be conceived for the year 1940 and not for the year 2000, but—like the cathedrals of our past—should project their existences into the millennia of the future.

And when God today allows the poets and singers to be warriors, he has also added to the combatants the architects, who will ensure that the success of this struggle will find its indestructible hardening and confirmation in the documents of a once great art!

Petty spirits may not understand this; but they have failed to comprehend our entire struggle. It may also make our opponents bitter, but their hate alone has not been able to hinder our successes so far. At some future point people will understand with the utmost clarity how great the blessing is that radiates across the centuries from these mighty buildings. For it is precisely these buildings that will help—politically, to unite and strengthen our nation; communally, to create a sense of proud togetherness; socially, to expose the foolishness of our worldly differences when contrasted with these stupendous and gigantic witnesses of our community; and psychologically, to fill our citizens with an endless self-confidence: the self-confidence that springs from being German!

At the same time, however, these mighty works will present the most sublime justification for the political strengths of the German nation. This state should not be a power without culture or a strength without beauty. For even the arming of a nation is morally justified only when it represents the shield and sword of a higher mission. We are striving, therefore, not for the raw violence of a Genghis Khan, but for a realm where power serves the creation of a strong and well-defended community that is the bearer and guardian of a higher culture!

225

Anonymous

THE NEW BERLIN CITYSCAPE

First published as "Das neue Berliner Stadtbild," *Frankfurter Zeitung,* Reichsausgabe, 12 April 1938. Translated by Iain Boyd Whyte.

In his definitive statement of 28 January 1938 on the redevelopment of the capital city of the Reich, the General Building Inspector for the Capital City of the Reich [Albert Speer] announced, among other things, that "in future, anyone who emerges from the main hall of the new Southern Station will see soaring upward at the other end of the monumental new main street of Berlin, 5.5 kilometers away and right at the center of the city on the site of the present Alsenstrasse, an assembly hall, which in its dimensions is appropriate to the scale and the significance of Berlin as capital of the Reich. In front of this monumental building the Königsplatz, with an area of over 220,000 square meters, will allow the staging of large-scale rallies of around 1 million participants."

226

Adolf Hitler

SPEECH AT THE TOPPING-OUT CEREMONY FOR THE NEW REICH CHANCELLERY, GIVEN IN THE DEUTSCHLANDHALLE, AUGUST 2, 1938

Reprinted in Angela Schönberger, *Die neue Reichskanzlei von Albert Speer* (Berlin: Gebr. Mann, 1981), pp. 177–82. Translated by Iain Boyd Whyte.

[...]

I know that there are certainly people today who are asking if so much has to be built: wherever one looks there is construction or demolition in order to build again. If people have not been somewhere for three or four months, they don't even know if it will still be there when they return, or what they will find in its place! I find this understandable, especially among all those people who in the past were also politically lazy. For I arrived at a time in which a scandalous amount of work had to be tackled immediately in every possible area. In doing this, I could not authorize the time that had been available to my predecessors to consider and investigate everything in detail. We had to seize the initiative straightaway. When I came to power, there were nearly 7 million unemployed in Germany. There had already been enough talking, scrutinizing, and debating; the time had come for vigorous action—to avoid the situation that we now see, for example, in America, where the number of unemployed has risen to 13 million. At that time I was convinced that the first and most important industry to be revived should be the building industry. It is a key industry, and has an immense importance that had not been recognized by my predecessors, which is perhaps our fortune and their misfortune. But I saw this and began, therefore, to build immediately. The planning for this construction followed two directions: on one hand, in the direction of pure utility, with the objective of satisfying practical needs such as house building, road building, the construction of canals, and so on; on the other hand, in the direction of beauty, of noble and monumental building works.

Perhaps I can begin with the utilitarian buildings. We find so often that although the purpose of the building appears to be clearly determined, the people responsible have not been able to build in a way that is appropriate to this function; in other words, they build something that proves yet again on completion to be too small or inadequate to the task. This applies above all to the old buildings designed to meet our transport needs. If you travel now through Berlin, you will see that everywhere the streets are being excavated and dug up, but believe you me, this appears as excessive only to those who can't think beyond today. I can see in front of me the development of traffic and know that in ten years' time, the volume of motor traffic will be immense. The others have no idea how enormous this will be. And if we do not build the streets now for this traffic, we certainly will not be able to build them once the traffic is there, because it will be too late. When a street is closed now for three months, the people grumble that once again they have to go the long way around, and then they scream that it is faster in any event on foot than in a car. How will this be when the car has become the people's means of transportation; when instead of 2 million cars in Germany there are perhaps 7, 8, or 9 million? And it is for this time that I am building, not for 1938 or '39, not even for 1940 and not for 1950, but for the year 2000, and 2200, and 2400! Three hundred years ago in a city of thirty-seven thousand inhabitants, the Berliners had the courage to construct Unter den Linden; and we shall also have the courage to lay out now the streets appropriate to the future. Traffic alone is one of the many things that were neglected in Germany. Uniquely, we have become a country or a Reich in the course of recent decades, and our former states all had their own roads, which must now be cast in the same mold. This is now happening. Then there are canals to build, and countless other things like utility buildings, factories in particular for our four-year plan—in short, an enormous profusion of tasks and constructional works. I want to construct all these buildings—and I must stress this—for the future: not for us, but for the future. But above all, I also want to give to this new state that we have created, which is and should be the state of the German people—to this state I want also to give those buildings that are necessary for the representation of another image. When I erect these buildings, it is not for me. I do not know how long I shall live. The first of these buildings will be finished, perhaps, when I no longer exist. But this is quite independent of a single individual. I am not only the Reich chancellor, but also a citizen. And as a citizen I still live in the same apartment that I had before I came into power. As Reich chancellor and leader of the German nation, I wish for Germany to be represented not only in the same way as every other state, but better than the others. And, you will understand that I am too proud to occupy former palaces. I do not do that. The new Reich will construct its own rooms and buildings itself: I don't go into palaces. In other states the leaders are always somewhere in a palace: in the Kremlin in Moscow, the Belvedere in Warsaw, in the Royal Palace in Budapest, or the Hradschin in Prague. I now have the ambition to raise buildings for the new German people's state that will bear comparison, without any hint of shame, with these formerly royal edifices.

[...]

We are all transient beings. As capital of the German Reich, however, the city must live on and must really endure for the future. I do not know who will occupy these buildings. God willing, they will also be the best sons of our people, regardless of the social class from which they come. But I do know that no one will be able to look down on this son because he comes from the lowest social class. From the moment in which he is called to represent Germany, he is the equal in rank and birth of any foreign king or emperor. I have trust and faith in the future of the German people's state, and intend that it should be a worthy representative of the German people. To this end, I intend to erect a beautiful, mighty, and proud capital city for the German Reich. Some people, perhaps, will not fully understand this, but I have done many things in my life that were not understood at the outset. This I willingly endure. Only the future will be able to judge what it means that we considered not only the eternal, simply material interests, but also gave thought to the truly beautiful, representative tasks of our *Volksgemeinschaft* [German national community]. And compared with the general building program, the Reich Chancellery does not represent that much. You may already have heard that of the 400 million bricks that are laid in Berlin each year, this building has taken 20 million—a relatively small amount, just a small fraction. But the building on which you are working will survive for many centuries, even if it at some later point will have a different function that we don't yet know. It will serve its present function only for around ten to twelve years, and will then serve some noble state and national purpose. But this year in particular I have found it necessary to erect this building, because a magnificent, powerful, and rich city has joined the German Reich,[1] a beautiful, wealthy city with a great and ancient culture and wonderful buildings. Just for this reason, it is necessary for Berlin to change its face and adapt to its great, new, German mission. For this reason I decided this year, in the knowledge that this still-open problem would be resolved,[2] to give my architect Speer the commission to complete the planned extension of the Reich Chancellery by 10 January . . . 10 January 1939. For the reception of the diplomats was planned for this day, and I wanted to receive them in the new building that had been constructed especially for the Reich, in the house of the Greater German Reich. This, of course, was an impossible demand in the eyes of the experts. Only my party comrade Speer did not hesitate for a moment, and asked merely for six hours working. After six hours he came up with the plan, and assured me that the old structures would be pulled down by 15 March, that the topping-out ceremony would take place on 1 August, and that the building would be completed by 10 January. That, *Volksgenossen* [patriotic comrades], is no longer the American tempo; that is already the German tempo.

[. . .]

[The Reich Chancellery] will not simply be the creation of the man who commissioned it, but just as much of the master architect who worked out the plan, and of his assistant architects and engineers. But it will also be the creation of every foreman, of every worker, of every laborer, all of whom are setting down their individual monuments. It is a monument to our national community and to our working community. And this is perhaps the proudest satisfaction that anyone can have. There are, of course, difficult and disagreeable weeks at the beginning, but when a work like this is finished, it is truly a monument to a magnificent mutual effort, which will be admired over the centuries, just as we admire the great works of the past. We know very well that if there had not been building in the past, we would probably still be housed like savages. So above all, as I am standing among you, I would like to thank my workers, men and women, for your diligent work and for your devotion to the building. Even though I could not visit you that often, I have seen everything. And when a building project of this size begins in January with the demolition of the old structures and already celebrates its topping-out ceremony on 1 August, that itself says enough about the work that has been done here. I would also like to thank those who are not here today, but who have been called away to another building project. I can speak to you quite openly. This year, warned and made wise by experience with foreign powers, I have made the decision to enclose the German state to the west with steel and concrete, so that no power in the world can penetrate it. This will spoil the fun of anyone who wants to start a fight with us. It, too, is a gigantic enterprise, the greatest that the world has ever seen, and a number of your colleagues have been called to go there.

NOTES

1. Vienna: On the morning of 12 March 1938, German troops crossed the German–Austrian border. One day later, Hitler announced the *Anschluss* (annexation) of Austria into the German Reich.
2. The "problem" of the annexation of Austria.

227

Hans Stephan

BERLIN

In Stephan, *Die Baukunst im Dritten Reich, insbesondere die Umgestaltung der Reichshauptstadt* (Berlin: Junker und Dünnhaupt, 1939), pp. 11–20. Translated by Iain Boyd Whyte.

The remodeling of Berlin is entrusted to the hands of the architect Albert Speer, who was appointed General Inspector for the Capital City of the Reich [Generalbauinspektor für die Reichshauptstadt] by the Führer and Reich chancellor on 30 January 1937. The Führer's proposal read: "A General Inspector will be employed to supervise the ordered urban planning of the Capital City of the Reich. […] The General Inspector will draw up a master plan for the Capital City Berlin. With this he must ensure that all open spaces, streets, and buildings that influence the cityscape are worthily executed according to unified principles. The General Inspector is authorized to take the measures and make arrangements necessary for the attainment of this goal. […]"

For the realization of his commission, all the official agencies of the German Reich, of the province of Prussia, and of the capital city of the Reich are at his [Speer's] disposal. He himself is directly accountable to the Führer and Reich chancellor.

[…]

In future, the backbone of Berlin's built configuration will be formed by an extended cross axis: the north–south axis and the east–west axis, whose four terminations will be connected to the Reichsautobahnring.

[…]

In its middle section the north–south street will stretch between the Nordbahnhof and the Südbahnhof—gigantic new stations, set seven kilometers apart, which will be linked underground by six express rail tracks. The public and social life of the world city will be concentrated on the north–south street. A continuous chain of elegant shops will be housed at street level in the commercial and administrative buildings that will be developed here according to carefully considered plans. Theaters and premiere cinemas, coffee shops, and a generous scheme of neon lighting will fill this street with colorful life. Public buildings and buildings for cultural institutions will enrich the cityscape. The foundation stone for the tourist office was laid on 14 June 1938 on Runden Platz as one element in a unified reconstruction of the *Platz*.

As the city crown, however, and visual focus of the seven-kilometer-long north–south street, the mighty building of the Hall of the People [Volkshalle] will soar up at the rear of the enormous parade ground that will take up the site of the present Königsplatz. Deriving from the new spirit of our time, it will act as symbol and crown for the city and the Reich, just as once the Acropolis and the medieval cathedral, grounded on spiritual convictions, were the crowning symbols of their epochs.

In its scale and in the planning of its large-scale buildings, the project reaches far beyond the limits of the city. It also extends very consciously beyond the present, with the intention of determining the overall character of the capital city and of bearing testimony for a distant future to the powerful will of our age. In the process, it issues a set of long-term goals similar to those of the Prussian princes, who created, in a small city in the March of Brandenburg with fifty thousand inhabitants, the buildings that to this day determine the face of a city with a population of millions.

Out of the capital of Prussia is emerging today the capital city of the greater German Reich.

228
Albert Speer
REPLANNING THE CAPITAL OF THE REICH

First published as "Neuplanung der Reichshauptstadt," *Der Deutsche Baumeister* 1, no. 1 (1939), pp. 3–4; republished in Anna Teut, *Architektur im Dritten Reich, 1933–1945* (Berlin: Ullstein, 1967) pp. 196–200. Translated by Iain Boyd Whyte.

When we survey the results of the urge to build in our age, we see the new buildings in the German cities and countryside joining together into an ever more complete picture. It is a picture of the strong and self-confident epoch that we are living through and forming through our own willpower.

The words the Führer already penned in his book in 1924, his thoughts on architecture and city building, have, today, already become to a great extent reality.

The massive autobahn network that already traverses the Reich for three thousand kilometers, joining the regions together, is a lasting symbol of our age, which has brought about a total revision of the thoughts and emotions of a nation that is becoming ever greater. With the construction of the autobahn net and with the general reordering of the whole county, the beginnings of a new practice of city building are emerging in cities both large and small.

Here, too, the Führer himself has seized the initiative and made the decision to pursue a systematic city-planning policy in some of the larger cities in the Reich. On 30 January 1937, the Führer declared to the parliament that the development of Berlin into a genuine and real capital for the German Reich will represent the pinnacle of urban design in our age.

Following the ideas of the Führer, which he had already developed many years ago, I have drawn up a plan for the new capital of the Reich whose skeleton is the cross formed by two large-scale axes that traverse Berlin from east to west and north to south, connecting the city center with the peripheral autobahn ring. Whereas the east–west axis is already in part in place and simply needs significant widening and extending as far as the autobahn to the east and west, the north–south axis—the truly representative core of the new capital of the Reich—marks a complete restructuring in the heart of the city.

This enormous new thoroughfare, which measures 38.5 kilometers from autobahn to autobahn, has its center of gravity a middle section of around 7 kilometers, on which the largest and most representative buildings of the German Reich will be relocated. The ends of this inner-city north–south axis will be marked by two great new railway stations, constructed in the north and south of the city, which will replace no less than ten of the present, antiquated terminals. In the process, the entire railway network will undergo a thorough renovation, and at the same time the enormous freight yards and sidings of the state railways will disappear from the city center. One of the largest these railway areas, the tract south of the Potsdamer and Anhalter stations, will be claimed by the new axis and by its subsidiary sites.

Near the point at the heart of the city where the two axes intersect will arise the largest building in Berlin, the Great Hall of the German People.

With the two axes, which bring the traffic flow from the four cardinal points into the heart of the city, and above all the new north–south axis, the entire building plan of Berlin will be given a new orientation. For not only will the major public buildings line the great thoroughfares, but sites will also be given to private developers, whose new, large-scale structures will further enhance the dominating impression of the new urban design of central Berlin. In this way, both private and public monumental architectures will no longer be randomly located, as they were previously, somewhere in the municipal area, but thanks to their planned location will form an element in the new city crown [*Stadtkrone*], which will dominate the entire urban area.

The building zones, however, will be oriented not in rings around the center, but along the axes. This means that, in contrast to previous practice, the building heights will not decrease in concentric bands moving away from the city center. Instead, the entire cruciform formed by the axes will be the center, with the buildings on each side diminishing in size to lower, more open structures, and then giving way to broad open spaces for recreation. Some of the largest of the already existing arterial roads that lead from the outskirts into the city center will contribute to this system, and will have the same functions in the zonal plan as the major axes. In this way, large wedges of linked green space will ultimately be pushed as deeply as possible into the inner city. For this purpose, extant areas of greenery will be tied together, in the course of time, by prohibiting building development on the link sections.

At the same time, the existing high-speed railway network will be corrected and, together with future buildings, oriented to the radial-development plan. I see housing as one of the most important elements in the remodeling of Berlin. Large, linked estates of new housing must be constructed before work can begin on clearing the old housing stock. Through the development of the major axes, in particular in the south, extensive new building land will be opened up, in close proximity to the city center, which will make possible the construction of several hundred thousand new apartments.

Today, two years after the Führer's directive, not only is the structure planning already completed. Beyond that, new building projects are going ahead at full speed on many sites in the capital of the Reich. The first monumental building, the new Reich Chancellery in the Voßstrasse, has already been inaugurated. The east–west axis has been doubled in width and in a few months will be already completed and given over to traffic from the Brandenburg Gate to Adolf-Hitler-Platz—a distance of around seven kilometers.[1] With the building of the Faculty of Defense Studies,[2] a beginning has been made in the construction of the new University City. On 14 July last year, with the simultaneous commencement of work on sixteen major building projects, the mobilization of labor and the tempo of construction have been increased even more.

NOTES

1. The large square and traffic intersection at the highest point of the east–west axis in Berlin's Westend was originally called Reichskanzlerplatz and was renamed Adolf-Hitler-Platz in 1939. A plan to call it Mussoliniplatz was never implemented. After the end of World War II it reverted to Reichskanzlerplatz before acquiring its current designation as Theodor-Heuss-Platz, named after the journalist, editor, and politician Theodor Heuss, who was appointed the first president of West Germany in September 1949.

2. See above, text 128: Adolf Hitler, Speech at Foundation-Stone Ceremony of the Faculty of Defense Studies.

229

Adolf Hitler

TABLE TALK, 21–22 OCTOBER 1941

First published in English as *Hitler's Table Talk, 1941–1944*, trans. Norman Cameron and R. H. Stevens (London: Weidenfeld & Nicolson, 1953), pp. 81–83.

What is ugly in Berlin we shall suppress. Nothing will be too good for the beautification of Berlin. When one enters the Reich Chancellery, one should have the feeling that one is visiting the master of the world. One will arrive there along wide avenues containing the Triumphal Arch, the Pantheon of the Army, the Square of the People—things to take your breath away! It's only thus that we shall succeed in eclipsing our only great rival in the world, Rome. Let it be built on such a scale that St. Peter's and its Square will seem like toys in comparison!

For material we'll use granite. The vestiges of the German past, which are found on the plains to the North, are scarcely time-worn. Granite will ensure that our monuments last for ever. In ten thousand years they'll be standing, just as they are, unless meanwhile the sea has again covered our plains.

[. . .]

FIGURE 50. Rebuilding plan for Berlin (Albert Speer and GBI, architects): Great Hall, 1939. Private collection, London.

My acts are always based upon a political mode of thinking. If Vienna expressed the desire to build a monument two hundred meters tall, it would find no support from me. Vienna is beautiful, but I have no reason to go on adding to its beauties. In any case, it's certain that my successors won't give any city the grants necessary for such works.

Berlin will one day be the capital of the world.

ACKNOWLEDGMENTS

5. From Alfred Kerr, *Wo liegt Berlin? Briefe aus der Reichshauptstadt 1985–1900*. © Aufbau Verlagsgruppe GmbH, Berlin 1997. **6.** From Alfred Kerr, *Mein Berlin. Schauplätze einer Metropole*. © Aufbau Verlagsgruppe GmbH, Berlin 1999. **8.** From *Début eines Jahrhunderts: Essays zur Wiener Moderne*, edited by Wolfgang Pircher (Vienna: Falter, 1986). Copyright © by Dr. Nicolaus Sombart. Reprinted with Permission of Dr. Nicolaus Sombart. **9.** From *Neue Rundschau* (May 1907). Copyright © by Suhrkamp Verlag. Reprinted with permission of Suhrkamp Verlag. **10.** From August Endell, *Die Schönheit der großen Stadt* (1908, reprint, Berlin: Archibook, 1984). Copyright © by Dr. Joachim Endell. **12.** From *Neue Rundschau* (August 1909). Copyright © by Suhrkamp Verlag. Reprinted with permission of Suhrkamp Verlag. **15.** From *Zeit-Echo*, no. 15 (1915–1916). Copyright © by Suhrkamp Verlag. Reprinted with permission of Suhrkamp Verlag. **21.** From *Berliner Architekturwelt*, 13 (1911). © Ernst Wasmuth Verlag Tübingen-Berlin. **23.** From *Berliner Architekturwelt*, 14, no. 10 (October 1912). Copyright © by Technische Universität Dresden Universitätsarchiv. Reprinted with permission of Technische Universität Dresden Universitätsarchiv. **25.** From *Town Planning Review* (January 1914). Copyright © by Robin Bloxsidge Publisher, Liverpool University Press. Reprinted with permission of the publisher. **26.** From David Frisby and Mike Featherstone, *Simmel on Culture* (London: SAGE Publications, 1997). Copyright © by SAGE Publications Ltd. Reprinted with permission of SAGE Publications. **27.** From *Deutsche Bauzeitung*, 32, no. 35 (30 April 1898). Copyright © by Konradin Mediengruppe. **28.** From *Neue Rundschau* (December 1907). Copyright © by Suhrkamp Verlag. Reprinted with permission of Suhrkamp Verlag. **29.** From Karl Scheffler, *Moderne Baukunst* (Berlin: Bard, 1907). Copyright © by Dody Scheffler-Platz. Reprinted with permission of Dody Scheffler-Platz. **32.** From Karl Scheffler, *Die Architektur der Großstadt* (Berlin: Cassirer, 1913). Copyright © Dody Scheffler-Platz. Reprinted with permission of Dody Scheffler-Platz. **34.** From *Die Kunst: Monatshefte für freie und angewandte Kunst*, 18, no. 32 (1915). Copyright © by Nachlass Paul Westheim. **36.** From

Alfred Kerr, *Mein Berlin. Schauplätze einer Metropole.* © Aufbau Verlagsgruppe GmbH, Berlin 1999. **38.** From *Deutsche Bauhütte* (3 April 1902). Copyright © by Dody Scheffler-Platz. Reprinted with permission of Dody Scheffler-Platz. **39.** From August Endell, *Die Schönheit der großen Stadt* (1908, reprint, Berlin: Archibook, 1984). Copyright © by Dr. Joachim Endell. **43.** From *Deutsche Bauzeitung*, 24 (1890). Copyright © by Konradin Mediengruppe. **47.** From Werner Sombart, *Das Proletariat* (Frankfurt a.M.: Rütten & Loening, 1906). Copyright © by Dr. Nicolaus Sombart. Reprinted by Permission of Dr. Nicolaus Sombart. **50.** From Karl Scheffler, *Die Architektur der Großstadt* (Berlin: Cassirer, 1913). Copyright © by Dody Scheffler-Platz. Reprinted by permission of Dody Scheffler-Platz. **51.** From Käthe Kollwitz, *Ich sah die Welt mit liebevollen Blicken: Ein Leben in Selbstzeugnissen*, edited by Hans Kollwitz (Wiesbaden: Fourier, 1971). Copyright © by Erbengemeinschaft Käthe Kollwitz, Berlin. Reprinted with permission of Erbengemeinschaft Käthe Kollwitz. **52.** From *Deutsche Bauhütte*, 14, no.16 (4 April 1912). Copyright © by Vincentz Network, Hanover. Reprinted by permission of Vincentz Network. **56.** From Alfred Kerr, *Mein Berlin. Schauplätze einer Metropole.* © Aufbau Verlagsgruppe GmbH, Berlin 1999. **59.** From *Berliner Kaffeehäuser* (Großstadt-Dokumente, no. 7. Berlin: Seemann Nachfolger, n.d. ca. 1905). Copyright © by Christina Müller and Lena Unger. Reprinted with permission of Christina Müller and Lena Unger. **64.** From *Die Bauwelt*, no. 21 (1911). Copyright © by Nachlass Paul Westheim. **66.** From *Berliner Architekturwelt*, 14, no. 9 (Sept. 1912). © Ernst Wasmuth Verlag Tübingen-Berlin. **67.** From Else Lasker-Schüler, *Gesichte: Essays und andere Geschichten* (Leipzig: Wolff, 1913). Copyright © by Suhrkamp Verlag. **68.** From *Sozialistische Monatshefte*, 20, no. 1 (1914). Copyright © by Emmy Lorenz, Christine Schily, Susanne Kiefer-Taut and Le Than Thuy Taut. Reprinted with permission of the copyright holders. **71, 72, 74.** From Alfred Kerr, *Mein Berlin. Schauplätze einer Metropole.* © Aufbau Verlagsgruppe GmbH, Berlin 1999. **77.** From *Berliner Architekturwelt*, 8 (1906). © Ernst Wasmuth Verlag Tübingen-Berlin. **78.** From *Berliner Architekturwelt*, 9 (1907). © Ernst Wasmuth Verlag Tübingen-Berlin. **80.** From *Neue Rundschau* (October 1910). Copyright © by Suhrkamp Verlag. Reprinted with permission of Suhrkamp Verlag. **81.** From Robert Walser, *Das Gesamtwerk*, vol. 1, edited by Jochen Greven (Geneva: Kossodo, 1966). Copyright © by Suhrkamp Verlag. Reprinted with permission of Suhrkamp Verlag. **82.** From *Berliner Architekturwelt*, 14 (1912). © Ernst Wasmuth Verlag Tübingen-Berlin. **84.** From *Sozialistische Monatshefte*, 23, no. 2 (1917). Copyright © by Nachlass Paul Westheim. **85.** From Wilhelm Bölsche, *Hinter der Weltstadt: Friedrichshagener Gedanken zur ästhetischen Kultur* (Leipzig, 1901). Copyright © by Jürgen Bölsche. Reprinted with permission of Jürgen Bölsche. **93.** From *Sozialistische Monatshefte*, 21, no. 2 (1915). Copyright © by Nachlass Paul Westheim. **94.** From Martin Wagner, *Städtische Freiflächenpolitik* (Berlin: Carl Heymanns, 1915). Copyright © by Harvard Design School. Reprinted by permission of Harvard Design School. **95.** From *Wasmuths Monatshefte für Baukunst*, 4, no. 5/6. Copyright © by Emmy Lorenz, Christine Schily, Susanne Kiefer-Taut and Le Than Thuy Taut. Reprinted with permission of the copyright holders. **96.** From *Der Sturm*, 4, no. 196/7 (February 1914). Copyright © by Emmy Lorenz, Christine Schily, Susanne Kiefer-Taut and Le Than Thuy Taut. Reprinted with permission of the copyright holders. **106.** From Paul Wolf, *Städtebau: Das Formenproblem der Stadt in Vergangenheit* *und Zukunft* (Leipzig, 1919). Copyright © by Dr. Sabine Wolf. Reprinted with permission of Dr. Sabine Wolf. **107.** From Bruno Taut, *Die Stadtkrone* (Jena: Diederichs, 1919). Copyright © by Emmy Lorenz, Christine Schily, Susanne Kiefer-Taut and Le Than Thuy Taut. Reprinted with permission of the copyright holders. **108.** From Otto Bartning, *Vom neuen Kirchbau* (Berlin: Cassirer, 1919). Copyright © by Otto-Bartning-Archiv der Technischen Universität Darmstadt. Reprinted by permission of Otto-Bartning-Archiv der Technischen Universität Darmstadt. **109.** From Peter Behrens and Heinrich de Fries, *Vom sparsamen Bauen* (Berlin, 1919). Copyright © by Bauverlag BV GmbH. Reprinted by permission of Bauverlag BV GmbH. **110.** From Käthe Kollwitz, *Ich sah die Welt mit liebevollen Blicken: Ein Leben in Selbstzeugnissen*, edited by Hans Kollwitz (Wiesbaden: Fourier, 1971). Copyright © by Erbengemeinschaft Käthe Kollwitz, Berlin. Reprinted with permission of Erbengemeinschaft Käthe Kollwitz. **111.** From Bruno Taut, *Die Auflösung der Städte* (Hagen, 1920). Copyright © by Emmy Lorenz, Christine Schily, Susanne Kiefer-Taut and Le Than Thuy Taut. Reprinted with permission of the copyright holders. **112.** From *Martin Mächler—Weltstadt Berlin*, edited by Ilse Balg (Berlin: Galerie Wannsee Verlag, 1986). Copyright © by Ilse-Balg-Stiftung. Reprinted with permission of Ilse-Balg-Stiftung. **113.** From *Frankfurter Zeitung*, 2 March, 1921. English language copyright © by New York Association for New Americans, Inc. **115.** From *Wasmuths Monatshefte für Baukunst*, 5 (1920/21). © Ernst Wasmuth Verlag Tübingen-Berlin. **116.** From Joseph Roth, *Berliner Saisonbericht: Unbekannte Reportagen und journalistische Arbeiten 1920–39*, edited and foreword by Klaus Westermann (Cologne: Kiepenheuer & Witsch, 1984). English translation copyright © by Granta Books. **117.** From *Wasmuths Monatshefte für Baukunst*, 7 (1922/23). © Ernst Wasmuth Verlag Tübingen-Berlin. **118.** From Egon Erwin Kisch, *Gesammelte Werke in Einzelausgaben, Band 10: Mein Leben für die Zeitung 1926–1947*. © Aufbau Verlagsgruppe GmbH, Berlin 1983. **119.** From *Probleme der neuen Stadt Berlin: Darstellungen der Zukunftsaufgaben einer Millionenstadt*, edited by Hans Brennert and Erwin Stein (Berlin: Deutscher-Kommunal-Verlag, 1926). Used with permission of Landesarchiv Berlin. **120.** From *Uhu: Das Monatsmagazin*, edited by Christian Ferber (Berlin: Ullstein, 1979). Copyright © by Dody Scheffler-Platz. Reprinted with permission of Dody Scheffler-Platz. **121.** From *Wasmuths Monatshefte für Baukunst*, 12 (1928). © Ernst Wasmuth Verlag Tübingen-Berlin. **122, 123.** From *Das Neue Berlin*, edited by Martin Wagner (Berlin: Deutsche Bauzeitung, 1929). Copyright © by Harvard Design School, Alexandra Otto and Eva Gießler-Wirsig. Reprinted with permission of Harvard Design School, Alexandra Otto and Eva Gießler-Wirsig. **124.** From *Zentralblatt der Bauverwaltung*, 50, no. 9 (5 March 1930). Copyright © by Nachlass Max Berg. **126.** From Walter Benjamin, *Gesammelte Schriften III, Kritiken und Rezensionen*, edited by Hella Tiedemann-Bartels (Frankfurt a.M.: Suhrkamp, 1980). Copyright © by Suhrkamp Verlag. Reprinted with permission of the publisher. **127.** From *Berlin im "Querschnitt"*, edited by Rolf-Peter Baacke (Berlin: Fannei & Walz, 1990). Used with permission of Fannei & Walz Verlag, Berlin. **128.** From *Hitler: Reden und Proklamationen 1932–1945*, edited by Max Domarus (Neustadt a. d. Aisch: Schmidt, 1962). English translation copyright © by Bolchazy-Carducci Publishers, Inc. **129, 132.** From Käthe Kollwitz, *Ich sah die Welt mit liebevollen Blicken: Ein Leben in Selbstzeugnissen*, edited by Hans Kollwitz (Wiesbaden: Fourier, 1971). Copyright © by

Erbengemeinschaft Käthe Kollwitz, Berlin. Reprinted with permission of Erbengemeinschaft Käthe Kollwitz. **133.** From Hans Ostwald, *Sittengeschichte der Inflation* (Berlin: Neufeld & Henius). Copyright © by Christina Müller and Lena Unger. Reprinted with permission of Christina Müller and Lena Unger. **134.** Excerpt from *Mein Kampf* by Adolf Hitler. German text copyright © by Bayrisches Staatsministerium der Finanzen. UK copyright © by The Random House Group Ltd, published by Pimlico. US copyright © 1943, renewed 1971 by Houghton Mifflin Company, translated by Ralph Manheim. Used by permission of Bayrisches Staatsministerium der Finanzen, The Random House Group Ltd. and Houghton Mifflin Harcourt Publishing Company. **135.** From Joseph Roth, *The Wandering Jews* (London: Granta Books, 2001). English translation by Michael Hofmann. Translation copyright © by Granta Books. **136.** From *Die Weltbühne*, vol. 24 (1928). Copyright © by Suhrkamp Verlag. Reprinted by permission of Suhrkamp Verlag. **137.** From Alfred Döblin, *Berlin* (Berlin: Albertus, 1928). Copyright © by Etienne Doblin. Reprinted with permission of Etienne Doblin. **138.** From Franz Hessel, *Ein Flaneur in Berlin* (Berlin: Arsenal, 1984). Copyright © by Bernd Witte. Reprinted with permission of Bernd Witte. **140.** From Moritz Goldstein, *Berliner Jahre: Erinnerungen 1880–1933* (Munich: Verlag Dokumentation, 1977). Copyright © by Walter de Gruyter GmbH & Co. KG. Reprinted with permission of Walter de Gruyter GmbH & Co. KG. **141.** From Karl Scheffler, *Berlin: Wandlungen einer Stadt* (Berlin: Cassirer, 1931). Copyright © by Dody Scheffler-Platz. Reprinted with permission of Dody Scheffler-Platz. **142.** From Siegfried Kracauer, *Schriften*, vol. 5.3, edited by Inka Mülder-Bach (Frankfurt a.M.: Suhrkamp, 1990). English language copyright © by New York Association for New Americans, Inc. **143.** From *Strassen in Berlin und anderswo* (Berlin: Arsenal, 1987). English translation by David Britt. English language copyright © by New York Association for New Americans, Inc. **144.** From *Berlin im "Querschnitt"*, edited by Rolf-Peter Baacke (Berlin: Fannei & Walz, 1990). Used with permission of Fannei & Walz Verlag, Berlin. **145.** From Ernst Erich Noth, *Die Mietskaserne* (1931, reprint, Frankfurt a.M.: glotzi Verlag, 2003), with an afterword by Lothar Glotzbach. Copyright © by glotzi Verlag. Reprinted with permission of the publisher. **146.** From Siegfried Kracauer, *Schriften*, vol. 5.3, edited by Inka Mülder-Bach (Frankfurt a.M.: Suhrkamp, 1990). English language copyright © by New York Association for New Americans, Inc. **147.** From *Gabriele Tergit: Atem einer anderen Welt, Berliner Reportagen*, edited by Jens Brüning (Frankfurt a.M.: Suhrkamp, 1994). Copyright © by Jens Brüning. Reprinted with permission of Jens Brüning. **148.** By Christopher Isherwood, from *The Berlin Stories*, copyright © 1935 by Christopher Isherwood. Reprinted by permission of New Directions Publishing Corp. UK and commonwealth copyright © 1954, Christopher Isherwood Estate, used by permission of The Wylie Agency (UK) Limited. **149.** From *Prager Tagblatt*, 14 November, 1922. Copyright © by Etienne Doblin. Reprinted by permission with Etienne Doblin. **150.** From Ludwig Hilberseimer, *Großstadtbauten* (Hanover: 1925). Ludwig Hilberseimer Papers, Ryerson and Burnham Archives, The Art Institute of Chicago. Reproduction © The Art Institute of Chicago. **151.** From Franz Hessel, *Ein Flaneur in Berlin* (Berlin: Arsenal, 1984). Copyright © by Bernd Witte. Reprinted with permission of Bernd Witte. **153.** From Fritz Stahl, *Das Großkraftwerk Klingenberg* (Berlin: Wasmuth, 1928). © Ernst Wasmuth Verlag Tübingen-Berlin. **154.** From Hans Hertlein, *Siemensbauten* (Berlin: Wasmuth, 1928). © Ernst Wasmuth Verlag Tübingen-Berlin. **155.** From Egon Erwin Kisch,

Gesammelte Werke in Einzelausgaben, Band 10: Mein Leben für die Zeitung 1926–1947. © Aufbau Verlagsgruppe GmbH, Berlin 1983. **157.** From Irmgard Keun, *Gigli-eine von uns.* © 1979 Claassen Verlag in der Ullstein Buchverlage GmbH, Berlin. **158.** From Else Lasker-Schüler, *Konzert* (Frankfurt a.M.: Suhrkamp, 1996). Copyright © by Suhrkamp Verlag. Reprinted with permission of the publisher. **159.** From Hans Fallada, *Ausgewählte Werke in Einzelausgaben, Band 2.* © Aufbau Verlagsgruppe GmbH, Berlin 1962. **161.** From Ruth Glatzer, *Berlin zur Weimarer Zeit* (Berlin: Siedler, 2000). Copyright © by Etienne Doblin. Reprinted with permission of Etienne Doblin. **165.** From *Wasmuths Monatshefte für Baukunst*, 12 (1928). © Ernst Wasmuth Verlag Tübingen-Berlin. **166.** Copyright © by Baukunstarchiv, Akademie der Künste, Berlin. **167.** From Joseph Roth, *Berliner Saisonbericht: Unbekannte Reportagen und journalistische Arbeiten 1920–39*, edited and foreword by Klaus Westermann (Cologne: Kiepenheuer & Witsch, 1984). English translation copyright © by Granta Books. **168.** From *Das Neue Berlin*, edited by Martin Wagner (Berlin: Deutsche Bauzeitung, 1929). Copyright © by Konradin Mediengruppe. **169.** From *Das neue Frankfurt*, 4 (Dresden: Verlag der Kunst, 1929). Ludwig Hilberseimer Papers, Ryerson and Burnham Archives, The Art Institute of Chicago. Reproduction © The Art Institute of Chicago. **170.** From *Neue Rundschau, XXXX. Jahrgang der freien Bühne*, vol. 1 (Berlin and Leipzig: Fischer, 1929). Copyright © by Paquet-Archiv. Reprinted by permission of Paquet-Archiv. **171.** From Fritz Schumacher, *Die Kleinwohnung: Studien zur Wohnungsfrage*, second edition (Leipzig: Quelle & Meyer, 1919). Used with permission of Martin Heisenberg and siblings. **173.** From Bruno Taut, *Die neue Wohnung: Die Frau als Schöpferin* (Leipzig: Klinkhardt & Biermann, 1924). Copyright © by Emmy Lorenz, Christine Schily, Susanne Kiefer-Taut and Le Than Thuy Taut. Reprinted with permission of the copyright holders. **174.** From *Wohnungswirtschaft* 2, no. 9 (1 May 1925). Copyright © by Harvard Design School. Reprinted with permission of Harvard Design School. **175.** From *Die Form* (1926). Ludwig Hilberseimer Papers, Ryerson and Burnham Archives, The Art Institute of Chicago. Reproduction © The Art Institute of Chicago. **176.** From *Wasmuths Monatshefte für Baukunst*, 11, no. 10 (1927). © Ernst Wasmuth Verlag Tübingen-Berlin. **178.** From *Berlin im "Querschnitt"*, edited by Rolf-Peter Baacke (Berlin: Fannei & Walz, 1990). Used with permission of Fannei & Walz Verlag, Berlin. **179.** From *Ausstellungs-, Messe- und Fremdenverkehrs-Amt der Stadt Berlin, Deutsche Bauausstellung Berlin 1931: Amtlicher Katalog und Führer* (Berlin: Bauwelt/Ullstein, 1931). Copyright © by Harvard Design School. Reprinted with permission of Harvard Design School. **181.** From *Frankfurter Zeitung*, 23 June, 1931. English language copyright © by New York Association for New Americans, Inc. **182.** From *Berlin im "Querschnitt"*, edited by Rolf-Peter Baacke (Berlin: Fannei & Walz, 1990). Used with permission of Fannei & Walz Verlag Berlin. **186.** From *Das hohe Ufer*, 1, no. 8 (1919). Copyright © by Emmy Lorenz, Christine Schily, Susanne Kiefer-Taut and Le Than Thuy Taut. Reprinted with permission of the copyright holders. **187.** From Egon Erwin Kisch, *Gesammelte Werke in Einzelausgaben, Band 6: Der Rasende Reporter, Hetzjagd durch die Zeit, Wagnisse in aller Welt, Kriminalistisches Reisebuch.* © Aufbau Verlagsgruppe GmbH, Berlin 1972. **188.** From *Sozialistische Monatshefte*, 27, no. 56 (14 February 1921). Copyright © by Eva Gießler-Wirsig and Alexandra Otto. Reprinted with permission of Eva Gießler-Wirsig and Alexandra Otto. **189.** From Siegfried Kracauer, *Schriften*, vol. 5.2, edited by Inka Mülder-Bach (Frankfurt a.M.: Suhrkamp, 1990). English language copyright © by New York Association for New Americans, Inc. **191, 193.** From *Berlin im "Querschnitt"*, edited by Rolf-Peter Baacke (Berlin: Fannei & Walz, 1990). Used with permission of Fannei & Walz Verlag, Berlin. **196.** From *Glänzender Asphalt: Berlin im Feuilleton der Weimarer Republik,* edited by Christian Jäger and Erhard Schütz (Berlin: Fannei & Walz, 1994). Used with permission of Fannei & Walz Verlag, Berlin. **197.** From Billy Wilder, *Der Prinz von Wales geht auf Urlaub: Berliner Reportagen, Feuilletons und Kritiken der zwanziger Jahre* (Berlin: Fannei & Walz, 1996). Used with permission of Fannei & Walz Verlag, Berlin. **198.** From *Frankfurter Zeitung,* 19 October, 1930. English language copyright © by New York Association for New Americans, Inc. **199.** TK. **200.** From *Frankfurter Zeitung—Abendblatt,* 23 January 1931. English language copyright © by New York Association for New Americans, Inc. **201.** From *Glänzender Asphalt: Berlin im Feuilleton der Weimarer Republik,* edited by Christian Jäger and Erhard Schütz (Berlin: Fannei & Walz, 1994). Used with permission of Fannei & Walz Verlag Berlin. **202.** From *Frankfurter Zeitung,* 19 July, 1932. English language copyright © by New York Association for New Americans, Inc. **206.** From Joseph Roth, *Berliner Saisonbericht: Unbekannte Reportagen und journalistische Arbeiten 1920–39,* edited and foreword by Klaus Westermann (Cologne: Kiepenheuer & Witsch, 1984). English translation copyright © by Granta Books. **208.** From Billy Wilder, *Der Prinz von Wales geht auf Urlaub: Berliner Reportagen, Feuilletons und Kritiken der zwanziger Jahre* (Berlin: Fannei & Walz, 1996). Used with permission of Fannei & Walz Verlag Berlin. **209.** From Bernard von Brentano, *Wo in Europa ist Berlin?* (Frankfurt a.M.: Insel, 1993). Copyright © by Suhrkamp Verlag. Reprinted by permission of Suhrkamp Verlag. **210.** From Vicki Baum, *Grand Hotel* (London: Michael Joseph, 1972). English translation by Basil Ceighton. Copyright © David Higham Associates Limited. Reprinted with permission of the David Higham Associates Limited. **211.** From Siegfried Kracauer, *Schriften,* vol. 5.2, edited by Inka Mülder-Bach (Frankfurt a.M.: Suhrkamp, 1990). English language copyright © by New York Association for New Americans, Inc. **213.** From *Frankfurter Zeitung—Abendblatt,* 24 February 1931. English language copyright © by New York Association for New Americans, Inc. **214.** From Siegfried Kracauer, *Berlin Nebeneinander: Ausgewählte Feuilletons 1930–33* (Zurich: Epoca, 1996). English language copyright © by New York Association for New Americans, Inc. **215.** From *Deutsche Bauzeitung,* no. 17 (1934). Copyright © by Konradin Mediengruppe. **219.** From Siegfried Kracauer, *Schriften,* vol. 5.2, edited by Inka Mülder-Bach (Frankfurt a.M.: Suhrkamp, 1990). English language copyright © by New York Association for New Americans, Inc. **220.** From Irmgard Keun, *Das kunstseidene Mädchen* © 1979 Claassen Verlag bei den Ullstein Buchverlagen GmbH, Berlin. English translation copyright © The Other Press, New York. **221.** From *Glänzender Asphalt: Berlin im Feuilleton der Weimarer Republik,* edited by Christian Jäger and Erhard Schütz (Berlin: Fannei & Walz, 1994). Used with permission of Fannei & Walz Verlag, Berlin. **222.** German text copyright © Bayrisches Staatsministerium der Finanzen. Used with permission of Bayrisches Staatsministerium der Finanzen. **224.** From Anna Teut, *Architektur im Dritten Reich* (Berlin: Ullstein, 1967). German text copyright © by Das Bundesarchiv, Koblenz. **226.** From Angela Schönberger, *Die neue Reichskanzlei von Albert Speer* (Berlin: Gebr. Mann, 1981). German text Copyright © by Das Bundesarchiv, Koblenz. **228.** From Anna Teut, *Architektur im Dritten Reich*

(Berlin: Ullstein, 1967). Copyright © by Nachlass Albert Speer. **229.** Adolf Hitler, *Table Talk* (London: Weidenfeld & Nicolson, 1953). Used with permission of Orion Publishing Group Ltd.

The editor and publisher are most grateful to the copyright holders listed above for permissions granted to translate, reproduce, and publish material in this book. Although every attempt has been made in all instances to identify rights holders and to obtain the appropriate authorization, the editor and publisher apologize in advance for any unintended errors or omissions, which they will seek to rectify in further printings. Please address inquiries to: University of California Press, 2120 Berkeley Way, Berkeley, California 94704–1012.

PHOTO CREDITS

Architekturmuseum der Technischen Universität Berlin: 28
Art Institute of Chicago: 29
Berlinische Galerie: 1, 15, 21, 37, 44, 49
Bildarchiv Photo Marburg: 10, 12, 36, 43
Bpk / Kunstbibliothek, SMB, Phototek Willy Römer, 19
Bruno Taut, *Die Auflösung der Städte* (Hagen: Folkwang, 1920): 27
Bundesministerium für Arbeit und Soziales: 39
Großer Verkehrs-Plan von Berlin (Berlin: Verlag der Liebelschen Buchhandlung, 1902): 7
Landesarchiv Berlin: Front cover, 5, 11, 16, 18, 20, 22, 23, 24, 25, 26, 30, 33, 34, 35, 38, 40, 41, 46, 47, 48, back cover
Pracht-Album der Berliner Gewerbe-Ausstellung (Berlin: Werner, 1896): 9
Private Collection, London: 50
Stadtmuseum Berlin, Nachlass Max Missmann: 2, 3, 4, 6, 14, 31, 32, 45
Town Planning Conference, London, 1910 (London: RIBA, 1910): 8
Ullstein Bild: 17, 42

INDEX

Abercrombie, Patrick: *Berlin: its Growth and Present State*, 73–75
ABOAG (Allgemeine Berliner Omnibus AG), 407–8, 409n1
Academy of Sciences, 599n1
Ackerstrasse, 135; Meyers Hof, 154*fig*18, 155*fig*19
Adenauer, Konrad, 412, 413n2
Adickes, Rudolf: *The Need for Spacious Building Programs*, 55–57
Adler, Joseph (?): *The Opening of the Tauentzien Palace Café*, 204–5
Adler, Leo: *Housing Estates in the Britz District of Berlin*, 343n2, 482–84
Admiralspalast, 196–99
advertising, 437–40, 442–45, 462. See also Litfaßsäulen; lighting, 452–54, 460–61
AEG, 2, 77–78, 80n3, 98, 101n2, 209; tram electrification, 109
AEG factories, 78, 98–101, 100*fig*12, 421, 422, 424n1; strikes, 283; turbine factory, Huttenstrasse, 416–18
Aero Lloyd, 553
Ahrends, Bruno, 466
aircraft, 568–71; manufacture, 434–36
Air Ministry building, 597–99
airports. *See* Templehof Airport
air travel, 553, 561–62, 565–66, 577–78
Albrecht, Heinrich: *Working Class Tenements of the Berlin Savings and Building Society*, 145–47

Albrechtshof villa colony, Tiergarten, 206
Aldershof, 392
Alexanderhaus, 350*fig*30
Alexanderplatz, 19, 397–400; rebuilding, 350*fig*30; U-Bahnhof, 398
Alexanderplatz Competition, 318, 319n7, 349–52, 428–29
Alexandra-Stiftung, 138–39
Allgemeine Elektricitäts-Gesellschaft. *See* AEG
Allgemeiner Deutscher Gewerkschaftsbund (German Trade Union Congress), 464
Allgemeine Städtebau-Ausstellung zu Berlin (Universal Urban Planning Exhibition), 62–64
allotments, 126, 245–46, 260–61, 267, 309–10, 326; Gartenfeld Jungfernheide, 246
Altenberg, Peter (pseud. Richard Engländer), 527, 528n12
Altgelt, Martin, 84
Alt-Glienicke, 268
Alt-Kölln, 59
American building industry, 464
Americanization, 11, 316–17, 437–38
Anhalter Station, 62, 67, 68, 98, 107, 111–12, 346n1, 352, 557n1
Anker, Alfons, 460
anti-Semitism, 206, 207, 246, 585, 586n8
Archipenko, Alexander, 278
Architekten-Verein zu Berlin (Association of Berlin Architects), 50

Architektonische Rundschau, 50
Armour and Company, 332, 332n2
Arnhold, Eduard, 207
Aschinger's Restaurant, 88–91, 89*fig*11
Ashworth, Philip A: *Berlin*, 59–62
Association for German Applied Arts (Verein für deutsches Kunstgewerbe), 493
Association of Berlin Architects (Vereinigung Berliner Architekten), 50, 146
Asylum for the Homeless, 126
Auguste-Viktoria-Platz, (now Breitscheidplatz), 552, 559*fig*46
Auschwitz concentration camp, 585
Ausschuss Groß-Berlin (Committee for Greater Berlin), 50
Autobahn, 552, 565n1, 579–80, 581, 606, 607
aviation industry, 553, 577–79
AVUS (Automobil-Verkehrs- und Übungsstrasse), 427, 427n1, 552, 563, 564, 565n1, 580

Baacke, Rolf-Peter, 553n1
Balcke, Alfred J, 226
Baluschek, Hans, 114
Barg, Ilse, 319n6
Barnay, Ludwig, 212, 212n4
Bartning, Otto: *Church Architecture Today*, 302–3; Siemensstadt, 466
Baschwitz, Paul, 447
Bauer, Leopold: *The Economic Unsustainability of the Large City*, 288–90
Bauermeister, Friedrich: *On the Great City*, 284–86
Bauhaus, 4, 173, 491
Baum, Vicki, 209; *Grand Hotel*, 565–66
Beba-Palast cinema, 532
Beckman, Max, 368
Begas, Reinhold, 215, 217n1
Behne, Adolf, 78, 80n2, 437–38, 441n2, 466, 467n6, 483, 483n1; *The Competition of the Skyscraper Society*, 334–35; *Großes Schauspielhaus, Scalapalast*, 518–19; *The New Berlin—World City*, 347–49
Behrens, Peter, 78, 98–101, 292, 403. *See also* AEG factories; Alexanderhaus, 350*fig*30; Alexanderplatz Competition, 428–29; government buildings competition, 318, 319n7; *The Influence of Time and Space*, 127–29; *On Low-Cost Housing*, 303–7; on New York skyscrapers, 344; Platz der Republik, proposal for redesigning, 353; Ring der Frauen pavilion, 493–95

Belling, Rudolf, 519
Benjamin, Walter, 4, 5n2, 107, 110n1, 209, 245, 248n2; *A Jacobin for Our Time*, 358–62
Benn, Alfred, 526, 528n3
Berber, Anita, 532
Berg, Max, 317, 319n3; *The Platz der Republik in Berlin*, 352–53
Berlin: as capital city, 1, 3, 49, 60–61, 172, 315, 347, 365–66, 368; cityscape, 13–16, 16–17, 17–18, 19–24, 35–41, 601–2, 605–7; compared to Chicago, 17–18; compared to London, 25–26; compared to New York, 31–32; compared to Paris, 402–3, 558–60; compared to Vienna, 31–33, 476–79; in film, 3, 529–30; life expectancy in, 3; map, 60*fig*7; population statistics, 382; redevelopment, 386–89
Berlin Alexanderplatz (Alfred Döblin), 368
Berlin Asylum Association, 126
Berlin Broadcasting House (Berliner Rundfunkhaus), 540
Berlin Building Exhibition, 1931. *See* Deutsche Bauausstellung, Berlin
Berlin Cathedral (Berliner Dom), 45*fig*5, 173
Berlin City Hall (Rathaus): strikes, 283
Berlin Commission for Workers' Health (Berliner Arbeiter-Sanitäts-Kommission), 136
Berlin Dada Group, 528n13
Berliner Arbeiter-Sanitäts-Kommission (Berlin Commission for Workers' Health), 136
Berliner Architekturwelt, 64n2
Berliner Bodengesellschaft (Berlin Land Company), 237
Berliner Börsen-Courier, 521–22
Berliner Dom (Berlin Cathedral), 45*fig*5, 173
Berliner Funk-Stunde (Berlin Radio Hour), 541
Berliner Gewerbe-Ausstellung (Berlin Trade Exhibition), 80–84, 108, 174, 212n2
Berliner Illustrirte Zeitung, 12n8, 174, 510, 511
Berliner Kunstausstellung 1927, 353, 353n3
Berliner Lokal-Anzeiger, 510
Berliner Morgenpost, 411
Berliner Rundfunkhaus (Berlin Broadcasting House), 540
Berliner Schloss, 20, 21, 24n3, 377
Berliner Sechstagerennen (Six-Day bicycle race), 515*fig*42, 516, 517n1
Berliner Spar- und Bauverein (Berlin Savings and Building Society), 136, 145–47, 268, 465
Berliner Tageblatt: Sunday in Berlin, 182–83
Berliner Verkehrs-Aktiengesellschaft (BVG), 409n1, 502, 502n2

Berliner Zimmer, 147
Berlin im Licht Exhibition, 440, 451*fig*37
Berlinische Bodengesellschaft (Berlin Land Company), 237
Berlin Land Company (Berlinische Bodengesellschaft), 237
Berlin-Mitte: redevelopment proposal, 1928, 317, 319n4
Berlin North, 16–17, 246
Berlin Potato Shortage, 281–82
Berlin Prater, 140, 143n2
Berlin Radio Hour (Berliner Funk-Stunde), 541
Berlin Savings and Building Society (Berliner Spar- und Bauverein), 136, 145–47, 268, 465
Berlin Six-Day Race (bicycle race) (Berliner Sechstagerennen), 515*fig*42, 516, 517n1
Berlin Structure Plan, 49, 65, 67, 339, 354, 355
Berlin Trade Exhibition (Berliner Gewerbeausstellung), 80–84, 81*fig*9
Berlin West, 221–23, 230–32; urban development, 95–97
Bernhard, Karl, 241n3
Berolina, 19, 533–34
Bestelmeyer, German, 318
Beusselstrasse Station, 125
bicycle races, 511, 514–17
Bie, Oscar: *Life Story of a Street*, 41
Bielenberg and Moser: Europahaus, 347n3
Bismarck, Otto von, 49, 207, 354
Bleichröder, Julius, 207, 213
Bloch, Ernst: *Berlin, Southern City*, 46–48; *Berlin After Two Years*, 379–81
Blücherplatz and Hallesches Tor, 1907, 47*fig*6
Bluhm, Detlef, 370n1, n4
Blum, Otto, 67, 71, 315
Bochum, 73
Bode, Wilhelm: *Alfred Messel's Plans for . . . Royal Museums*, 192
Bodemuseum, Museum Island, 190–91, 191n1, 192
Bodt, Jean de: Parochialkirche, 250n1
Bölsche, Wilhelm, 236, 248n2; *Beyond the Metropolis*, 248–50
Bolshevik Central Committee, 371n1
Bolshevik Revolution, 597n1
Bonatz, Paul, 489, 552, 553n4
Borchard, Wilhelm: *The Picnic Season*, 239–41
Borsig engineering company, 2, 77, 413
Botanical Gardens, 157, 158n1
Boxer Rebellion: return of German troops, 181–82

boxing, 522–23, 543–45
Brancker, Sefton, 553
Brandenburg Gate (Branderburger Tor), 21–22, 30, 39, 40*fig*3, 191, 386
Brass, Hans, 519
Braunschweig, Riddagshausen, 261n1
Breidbach, Olaf, 229n2
Breitensträter, Hans, 522
Breker, Arno: *Preparedness*, 584
Brentano, Bernard von, 427n1; *The Pleasure of Motoring*, 563–65
Breuer, Marcel: House for a Sportsman, 498
Briand, Aristide, 590, 590n1
bridge design, 554
Briggs, Asa, 172, 176n1
British Civil Aviation Authority, 553
Britz, 389, 389n3; Hufeisensiedlung, 341, 343n2, 347, 383, 464–65, 482–85
Brix, Joseph, 67, 71
Broadcasting Commissariat, 431
Broadcasting Museum, 431
Brodnitz, Hans, 532
Bronnen, Arnolt, 526, 528n4
Brüstlein: *The Rudolf Virchow Hospital in Berlin*, 187–89
Bruning, Heinrich, Chancellor, 590n1
Buchenwald, 585
Buddensieg, Tilmann, 101n2, 467n3
Bücher, Karl, 251
Bückeburg, 560n2
Bülowstrasse, 112–14, 540; Station, 64n2, 109, 113
Büning, Wilhelm: Weiße Stadt, 466
building boom, 172, 242–44
building materials, shortage, 469, 470
building regulations, 49–50, 159–60, 465, 469
Building School, Weimar, 491n6
Bund Deutscher Architekten, 334, 335n1
Bundesrat, 599n1
buses, 108, 110, 406–9
BVG, (Berliner Verkehrs-Aktiengesellschaft), 502, 502n2
BZ am Mittag, 510

Cabinet of Dr Caligari, 510
Café Bauer, Unter den Linden, 177–79, 184–85
Café Dalles, Neue Schönhauser Strasse, 375
Café Gärtner, Potsdamer Strasse, 28
Café Grunewald, 212–13
Café Josty, Potsdamer Platz, 27, 29n1, 184, 186, 217
Café Kranzler, Unter den Linden, 177, 184

cafés, 177–79, 183–87, 204–5, 534–36, 535*fig*43.
   See also names of cafés; Viennese, 183–87
Café Schiller, Gendarmenmarkt, 185
capitalism, 316–17
Carl Legien estate, Prenzlauer Berg, 465.
   See also housing, social housing
car ownership, 551–52, 553n2
cars, 571–73; psychological aspects, 576–77
Carsten, Wilhelm von, 355–56
Cartarius, Ulrich, 276n6, 276n7
Cassirer, Bruno, 526, 528n7
Cecilienhof, Potsdam, 491n5
cemeteries, 63
Central Association of White Collar Workers
   (Gewerkschaftsbund der Angestellten), 494
Chancellery (Reichskanzlei), 602–5, 609
Charlottenburg, 2, 49, 50, 51, 57, 74, 75, 75n2,
   136, 207, 211, 222, 223, 246, 260, 274, 352, 418,
   467, 513; Town Hall, 223–25, *fig*.24
Chatin-Hofmann, Henri, 532
Chermayeff, Serge, 491n4
Chicago: compared to Berlin, 17–18
child health, 307
church architecture, 302–3
cinemas, 326, 521–22, 528–29, 530–32. *See also*
   names of cinemas
Circus Days, 532
city: definition of, 2
city crown (Stadtkrone), 292, 295–301, 316, 325,
   606, 608
City Hall (Stadthaus), 199–200
civic unrest, 283–84, 292, 371n1, 375, 583, 586–
   88, 587*fig*48; Charlottenburg Town Hall,
   274–75; Lustgarten, 375
Clemenceau, Georges, 440, 441n3
club for working women, 148–50
coffeehouses. *See* cafés
Collective for Socialist Building, 495
color in architecture, 269–70, 297, 422, 465, 482
Colze, Leo: *The Department Stores of Berlin*,
   94–97
commercial buildings, 458–62
Committee for Greater Berlin (Ausschuss
   Groß-Berlin), 50
Coogan, Jackie, 532
Corso Cinema, 568n2
cost of living, 294
Courths-Mahler, Hedwig, 359, 362n2
Cremer & Wolfenstein: U-bahn, 109
Creutz, Max, 276n7; *Charlottenburg Town Hall*,
   223–25; *The New Kempinski Building*, 225–29

crime, 167–71
Cubism, 278
Cürlis, Hans: *Night and the Modern City*,
   450–52
cycling, 554–55. *See also* Berlin Six Day race

Dahlem, 488
Dante, 532
Dawes Plan, 3, 411, 437, 509
Deforestation Around Berlin, 57
Delaunay, Robert, 278
Delbrück, Hans, 209
Delphi-Palast Cinema, Kantstrasse, 212n2
Dempsey, Jack, 511
department stores, 94–97, 97–98, 437, 454–56,
   456–58. *See also* Wertheim Department
   Store
Dernburg, Heinrich, 35n1
DEST (Deutsche Erd- und Steinwerke), 585
Deutsche Allgemeine Zeitung, 510
Deutsche Arbeitsfront (German Workers'
   Front), 413, 549
Deutsche Bauausstellung, Berlin (German
   Building Exhibition), 486–91, 493, 496,
   496n1, 496n3, 497–500
Deutsche Edison Gesellschaft. *See* AEG
Deutsche Erd- und Steinwerke, (DEST), 585
Deutsche Gartenstadtgesellschaft, 246–47,
   250–51, 268, 291, 292
Deutsche Gesellschaft für Förderung des
   Wohnungsbaues, 482
Deutsche Luft Hansa, 553
Deutschen Wohnungsfürsorge-AG für Beamte,
   Angestellte und Arbeiter (DEWOG), 464
Deutscher Werkbund, 104n1
Deutsches Siedlungswerk (German Housing
   Development Board), 500–504
Deutsches Stadion (German Stadium), 524–25,
   548
Deutsche Welle, 510, 541
Deutsche Werkstätten für Handwerkskunst,
   223n1, 229n1
DEWOG, 464
Diepenbrock, Alexander: Admiralspalast, 199n1
Diesbach, Heinrich, 211n1
Dietrich-Eckart-Freilichtbühne, 548
Dilthey, Wilhelm, 174
diphtheria, 326. *See also* public health
Divakara, 297
Divine Comedy, 532
Dix, Otto, 3, 526, 528n5

Döblin, Alfred, 368; *Berlin*, 381–85; *Berlin Alexanderplatz*, 368; *Berlin Christmas*, 441–42; *General Strike in Berlin*, 414–15
Dresden railway station, 114
Duisberg, 73
Duncan, Isadora, 209
Durieux, Tilla, 522, 523n2

east-west axis, 318, 332, 583, 584, 606, 607, 609, 609n1
Eberstadt, Rudolf, 71, 134, 137n1
economic collapse, 413
economic crisis: effect on housing, 466
Edel, Edmund: *Berlin W.*, 221–23
Eesteren, Cornelius van: Unter den Linden proposals, 1925, 317
Ehrenburg, Ilya, 571, 573n1
Einstein Tower, Potsdam, 491n4
elevated railway. *See* railways, elevated and underground railway
Elias, Julius, 522
Emmerich, Paul, 502–4; *Nordstern Administration Building, Schöneberg*, 104–6
Emperor's Gallery (Kaisergalerie), 9, 12n3, 15
Endell, August, 12, 102–4; *The Beauty of the Great City*, 35–41, 122–24
Engländer, Richard, 528n12
Equitable Palace, Friedrichstrasse, 22–23, 24n7, 91, 98, 101n1
Ermisch, Richard: Strandbad, Wannsee, 547*fig*44
Ethnologisches Museum (Museum of Ethnography), 583
Europahaus, 345, 347n3
exhibition buildings, 82–84
Expressionism, 292, 293, 316, 463, 508, 519, 528n5

Faculty of Defense Studies (Wehrtechnische Fakultät), 365–66, 609, 609n2
Falk, Adalbert, 174
Falkenberg garden city, 247, 268–70, 292
Fallada, Hans: *Little Man, What Now?*, 432–34
Fangmeyer, Emil, 482
Faucher, Julius, 354, 357n1
Fechner, Gustav Theodor, 296, 301n2
Feder, Gottfried: *The German Housing Development Board*, 500–502
Feininger, Lionel, 514n1
female workforce, 148–50, 369–70
Ferris, Hugo, 344

Feuchtwanger, Lion, 209
Finckh, Ludwig, 292
Fischer, Hans Erasmus, 441n6
Fischer, Samuel (publisher), 368
Fischer, Theodor, 63
Flaischen, Cäsar, 363, 365n11
flânerie, 9, 13
Flechtheim, Alfred, 526, 528n2; *Gladiators*, 522–23
Fliegender Hamburger (Hamburg Flier), 553, 553n5, 573–76
Flossenbürg, 585
Fontane, Theodor, 12n2; on *flânerie*, 9; *The Treibel Villa*, 210–11
food production, 293–94, 309
food shortages, 274, 281–82, 291, 293–94, 375–76
Forbat, Fred: Siemensstadt, 466
forced labor, 585, 586n9
fountains, 261–63
Fox im Palmenhaus, 532
Fraenkel, Joseph, 226
Fränkel, Rudolf, 568n2; Lichtburg Cinema, 440
Frankfurt, 463
Französische Strasse, 63
Frederick II (the Great), 21, 232n1
Freikorps, 597n1
Freisinnige Zeitung: Military Parade, 181–82
Freybrücke, 241n3
Frick, Wilhelm, 489, 491n6
Friedenau, 75, 166n1, 471
Friedländer-Fuld, Fritz, 207
Friedrichshagen, 249
Friedrichshagener Dichterkreis (Friedrichshagen Poets' Circle), 246
Friedrichshain, 261–63, 370–71
Friedrichstadt, 370, 370n5; project for the rebuilding, 342*fig*29
Friedrichstrasse, 22, 41–43, 42*fig*4, 62, 185–86, 400–402, 404–6, 537; redevelopment proposals, 317
Friedrichstrasse Competition, 1920, 316, 334–35
Friedrichstrasse Station, 123, 131*fig*16
Fries, Heinrich de: *On Low-Cost Housing*, 303–7
Frisby, David, 11, 13n10, 370n3, 509, 511n2, 512n4
Frister & Rossmann, 77
Fritsch, Theodor, 246
Fritzsche, Peter, 10, 12n4–5; on advertising pillars, 10
Frohnau, 207, 323
Führer-Palais, 584

Fürstenberg, Carl, 208
Fürtwangler, Wilhelm, 368
Fulbrook, Mary, 521n8
functionalism, 266, 415–16, 424–25, 428–29, 463, 466, 467
Funkturm (Radio Tower), 448, 448*fig*36, 450n2, 490

garden cities, 75, 246–47, 258–60, 295, 295n1
Gartenfeld Jungfernheide, 246
Gartenstadt Falkenberg, 247, 268–70, 292
Gartenstadt Staaken, 264–66, 265*fig*25
GBI (Generalbauinspektion), 585
Gedächtniskirche (Kaiser-Wilhelm-Gedächtniskirche), 96, 173, 216, 381, 391, 537, 538, 587
GEHAG, 464, 482
Geist, Jonas, 12n3
Geldner, Paul: housing, Goethepark, Charlottenburg, 136
Gellhorn, Alfred, 519; *Advertising and the Cityscape*, 442–45
Gelsenkirchen, 73
Gemeinnützige Gesellschaft, 138–39
Gemeinnützige Heimstätten-Aktiengesellschaft (GEHAG), 464, 482
Gemeinnützige Siedlungs- und Wohnungsbaugesellschaft, 467
Gemeinnützige Wohnungsbaugesellschaft A.G., 504
Gendarmenmarkt, 21, 24n6
Generalbauinspektion (GBI), 585
General Building Inspectorate, (Generalbauinspektion), 585
Genzmer, Felix, 67, 71
George, Claude, 439
German Building Exhibition (Deutsche Bauausstellung, Berlin), 486–91, 493, 496, 496n1, 496n3, 497–500
German Communist Party, 371n1, 587*fig*48, 597n1
German Garden City Association (Deutsche Gartenstadtgesellschaft), 246–47, 250–51, 268, 291, 292
Germania, 5, 318, 467, 583
German middle class, 46–48
German Revolution, 1918, 371n1, 597n1
German Socialist Party (SPD), 597n3
Germany, cities: population growth, 72–75
Gert, Valeska, 526, 528n5
Gesellschaft für elektrische Hoch- und Untergrundbahnen, 109, 409n1

Gessner, Albert: housing, 136, 165, 166n1
Gesundbrunnen, 108, 418, 440, 566, 568n2; Gesundbrunnen Station, 126, 567; Swinemünder Bridge, 64n2, 121*fig*15, 554
Gewerkschaftsbund der Angestellten (Central Association of White Collar Workers), 494
Geyer-Raak, Ruth, 494
Giesecke, Wilhelm, 86
Giraudoux, Jean: *Berlin, Not Paris!*, 402–3
Gläser, Helga, 210n5
glass architecture, 463
Gleisdreieck, 110, 123, 555–57, 557n1; station and junction, 556*fig*45
Gmindersdorf, 265
Goebbels, Joseph, 357n5, 582; *Berlin Awakes*, 594–97
Goecke, Theodor: *Traffic Thoroughfares and Residential Streets*, 52; *The Working Class Tenement Block in Berlin*, 137–43
Göring, Hermann, 578
Görlitzer Station, 352
Goethe, Johann Wolfgang von, 213, 361, 362n9, 492n1
Goethepark, Charlottenburg, 136
Goldstein, Moritz: *The Metropolis of Little People*, 391–92
Gontard, Carl von, 24n6, 211, 211n2, 362n4
government buildings competition, 318
Graf Zeppelin flying above Wilhelmstrasse, 569*fig*47
Grässel, Hans: cemetery design, 63
Great Berlin Art Exhibition, 1927 (Große Berliner Kunstausstellung), 316, 353, 353n3
Greater Berlin Administrative Union (Zweckverband Groß-Berlin), 51, 74, 75n2
Greater Berlin Competition, 1910 (Wettbewerb Groß-Berlin 1910), 11, 51, 51n4, 62–64, 64–69, 69–71, 315
Greater Berlin Competition 1910, 64–68
Great Hall of the People (Große Halle), 583–84, 610*fig*50
green spaces, 57, 464, 608
Grenander, Alfred: U-bahn, 109; Wittenbergplatz U-Bahnhof, 110
Gropius, Walter, 368, 499, 514n1; *Large Housing Estates*, 484–86; *The New Architectural Idea*, 286–87; Siemensstadt, 466
Großbeeren, 355
GroßBerlin, 2; as administrative unit, 50, 76n2, 464; competition for a plan for the development of, 50; expansion, 256–58, 340–43, 347–

49; formation of, 340n1, 367–68; urban planning, 256–58, 319–24, 347–49
Große Berliner Kunstausstellung, 1927 (Great Berlin Art Exhibition), 316
Große Leegestrasse estate, 502–4
Großer Verkehrs-Plan von Berlin, 1902, 60*fig7*
Grossmann, Stefan, 526, 528n6
Groß-Rosen concentration camp, 585
Großsiedlungen, 465, 466
Großstadt, 251, 284–86, 288; definition of, 2
Grosz, Georg, 3, 368
Grünberg, Martin: Parochialkirche, 250n1
Gründerjahre, 354, 356, 357n1
Grüner Ring, 482
Grunewald, 51, 75, 207, 256–57, 355; sports stadium, 525, 583; villa colony, 208–9
Grunewaldturm, 88n1
GSW (Gemeinnützigen Siedlungs- und Wohnungsbaugesellschaft), 467
Guimard, Hector, 109
Gummitsch, Alexander, 447
Gurlitt, Cornelius, 64n2; *Review of Greater Berlin and the Greater Berlin Competition 1910*, 69, 71

Haeckel, Ernst, 227, 228, 229n2
Häring, Hugo, 439, 441n4, 460; Friedrichstrasse Competition, 316; *Illuminated Advertisements and Architecture*, 452–54; Onkel-Tom's-Hütte, 465; Platz der Republik, proposal for redesigning, 353; Siemensstadt, 466
Haesler & Völker: apartment house design, 498, 499
Hahn, Elisabeth von, 103
Hake, Ernst & Ahrends, Franz: Reichspostamt, Leipziger Strasse, 174
Hallesches Tor, 47*fig6*
Hall for the Unknown Soldier (Soldatenhalle), 584
Hall of the People (Volkshalle), 606, 608
Hamborn, 72, 73
Hamburg, 2, 10, 600
Hamburger Station, 107
Hamburg Flier (Fliegender Hamburger), 553, 553n5, 573–76
Hansaviertel, 54
Harden, Maximilian, 209
Harnack, Adolf von, 209
Hart, Heinrich: *Statutes of the German Garden City Association*, 250–51

Harvey, Elizabeth, 512n8
Hasenheide, 140, 143n2
Hauptmann, Gerhart, 209, 248, 250n2, 380, 381n1
Haus der Flieger (Aviation House), 598
Hausenstein, Wilhelm, 367, 370, 370n2
Hauser, Heinrich: *The Flood of Humanity at Tempelhof*, 590–93
Haussmann, Georges-Eugène, Baron, 11, 73, 75n1
Haus Vaterland, 373*fig31*, 413, 510
Havestadt & Contag, 67, 71, 315
Haxthausen, Charles W, 12n8, 13n9
Hegemann, Werner, 134, 163n1, 440; *Berlin, City of Stone*, 353–58; *Berlin and World Architecture*, 486–91; critique by Walter Benjamin, 358–62; *Should Berlin Build Skyscrapers?*, 345, 346n1
Heimann, Gideon, 553n2
Heine, Heinrich, 301n1
Heinkel, Ernst, 434–36
Heinkel factory, Oranienburg, 434–36
Hellerau, Dresden, 223n1, 229n1, 265
Henning, Paul R: Siemensstadt, 466
Henrici, Karl, 50–51, 51n3
Herrenhaus, 599n1
Hertlein, Hans: Siemens building, 412, 425
Hessel, Franz: *I Learn: Via Neukölln to Britz*, 386–89; *On Work*, 416–18
Heuss, Theodor, 609n1
Hieronimus, Marc, 276n8
Hilbebrandt, Werner, 414n5
Hilberseimer, Ludwig: Berlin-Mitte redevelopment, 317, 319n4; *Buildings for the Metropolis*, 415–16; *The Modern Commercial Street*, 458–62; *On Standardizing the Tenement Block*, 480–81; Project for the rebuilding of Friedrichstadt, 342*fig29*
Hill, Douglas, 599
Hillinger, Franz: Carl Legien estate, 465
Hirsch, Leo: *Cinemas*, 530–32
Hirtenstrasse, 378–79
Hitler, Adolf, 51, 353n3, 440, 441n7, 502, 548–50, 580, 582–83, 586nn1–2, 605, 607, 608; *Buildings of the Third Reich*, 599–601; *My Struggle (Mein Kampf)*, 376–77; *Speech at Foundation Stone Ceremony*, 365–66; speech at Tempelhofer Feld, 593; *Speech at Topping-out Ceremony for New Reich Chancellery*, 602–5; *Table Talk, 21–22 October, 1941*, 609–10

Hitler Youth, 549
Hitzig, Friedrich: Albrechtshof villa colony, Tiergarten, 206–7
Hobrecht, James, 359
Hobrecht Plan for Berlin, 1862, 49, 50, 465
Höch, Hannah, 368
Hoffmann, Albert: *The Wertheim Department Store in Leipziger Strasse*, 84–88
Hoffmann, Herbert: *The Air Ministry Building*, 597–99; *The Residential Estate on Berlin's Große Leegestrasse*, 502–4
Hoffmann, Ludwig: architectural styles, 175; Friedrichshain Fountain, 262; Pergamon Museum, 175; school buildings, 175, 193–95; as Stadtbaurat (municipal building director), 464; Stadthaus (City Hall), 175, 199–200
Hohenstaufen dynasty, 173
hohe Ufer, Das, 514n1
Homann, Klaus, 319n5
homosexual clubs, 538–40
Horace, 371, 373n1
Horseshoe Estate, Britz. *See* Hufeisensiedlung, Britz
horse trams, 108
hospitals, 187–89
hostel for working women, Brückenstrasse, 149
hotels, 209, 229–30
housing, 2, 58–59, 137–43, 303–7, 353–58, 463–67. *See also* garden cities; Mietskaserne; apartment houses, 164–66, 208, 218–21, 465–66, 468–71, 471–72; bourgeois, 75, 206–10, 210–11, 218–21, 221–23, 245, 354–55; building costs, 142, 144, 303–7, 307–8; building design, 135–37, 141–42, 143–44, 145–47, 151, 161–62, 308, 465–67, 480–81, 497–500; building regulations, 55–57, 146, 159, 253, 464–65, 469; building statistics, 467; cost of land, 159; crime, 167–71; density, 74, 134–37; development planning, 2–3, 464, 465, 484–86, 500–502, 503–4, 504–7; health aspects, 136, 153–57, 160, 163, 245, 253–55, 310 (*See also* public health); interior, 140*fig*17, 141–42, 147; living conditions, 135–36, 139–42, 140*fig* 17, 150–52, 153–57, 163, 404, 495–96; overcrowding, 55, 151–52, 154, 160, 167–71, 253–54, 293–94, 356–57; planning, 52–55; policy, 476–79; rents, 135, 161, 252–53, 303–4, 503; shortage, 217–18, 357, 463, 465, 469, 476–79, 496, 503; social aspects, 167–71, 471–72, 473–75; social housing, 137, 173, 463–67, 484–86 (*See also* Carl Legien estate, Prenzlauer Berg; Hufeisensiedlung, Britz; Onkel-Toms-Hütte, Zehlendorf; Schillerpark, Wedding; Siemensstadt; Weiße Stadt, Reinickendorf); speculative building, 74, 134, 159, 172; subletting, 135–36, 152, 167–71
Howard, Ebenezer, 246, 248n5, 295n1
Huber, Anton, 354, 357n1
Huelsenbeck, Richard, 527, 528n13
Hufeisensiedlung, Britz, 343n2, 383, 389, 389n3, 464–65, 482–85. *See also* housing, social housing
Hugenberg, Alfred, 510
Hulbeck, Charles R., 528n13
Humboldthain, 246
Hunte, Otto, 424n2
Huret, Jules, 176, 176n10; *Bruno Schmitz's "Rheingold" for Aschinger*, 189–90
hyperinflation, 316, 369, 437, 442n1, 551. *See also* inflation

ideal home, 473–75
Ihne, Ernst von, 190–92, 208
Imperial Housing Support Fund (Reichswohnungsfürsorgefonds), 264
Imperial Naval Ministry (Reichsmarineamt), 284
industrial areas, 44–46
industrial buildings, 78, 384, 411, 412, 424–25, 434–36
industrial unrest, 275, 283–84, 414–15
inflation, 3, 375–76, 437, 441, 463, 464, 551. *See also* hyperinflation
Invalidenstrasse, 68
Isherwood, Christopher: *A Berlin Diary (Winter 1932–33)*, 409–10
Issel, Werner: Klingenberg Power Station, 420–24

Jacob, Max: *From Apartment House to Mass Apartment House*, 164–66
Jahn, Friedrich Ludwig (Turnvater): Hasenheide, 143n2
Jandorf Department Store, 94–9
Jansen, Hermann: Greater Berlin Competition, 64–67, 71
Janssen, Jörn, 467n1
Jarotzki, J, 227
Jaskot, Paul B, 586n9
Jenkins, Jennifer, 12n6
Jessner, Leopold, 526, 528n5

INDEX

Jews, 206–10, 246, 378–79, 585, 586n8; immigration to Berlin, 595, 597n4
Jüngst, Heinz-Willi: *Housing for Contemporaries*, 497–500
Jugendstil, 222, 229n1
Jungfernheide, 57, 68, 246
Junkers Luftverkehr, 553, 562

KaDeWe (Kaufhaus des Westens), 94–96, 538, 540n1
Kaeber, Ernst: *The Metropolis as Home*, 337–40
Kaes, Anton: *The Weimar Republic Sourcebook*, 5n4
Kaiser, Georg, 516, 517n1, 522
Kaiser, Sepp: Gleisdreieck U-bahn station, 110
Kaiser-Friedrich-Museum, 190
Kaisergalerie, Friedrichstrasse, 9, 15
Kaiserlicher Aero-Club, 209
Kaiserlicher Automobil-Club, 209
Kaiser-Wilhelm-Akademie für das Militärärztliche Bildungswesen (Pépinière), 198, 199n2
Kaiser-Wilhelm-Gedächtniskirche, 96, 173, 216, 381, 391, 537, 538, 587
Kaiser Wilhelm I, 112, 355
Kaiser Wilhelm II, 3, 114n2, 173, 182, 207, 230, 250, 281, 353, 368, 371n1
Kaiser Wilhelm Monument, Porta Westfalica, 190
Kaiser-Wilhelm-Stadion, 525n1
Kaiser Wilhelm Tower, Grunewald, 88n1
Kampffmeyer, Hans: *The Garden City and its Cultural Significance*, 251–56
Kandinsky, Wassily, 277, 278
Kapp, Wolfgang, 472n1
Kapp-Putsch, 471, 472n1
Kardoff, Katherina von, 493
Karlsruhe, 73
Karstadt, Rudolph, 456–58
Karstadt department store, 440, 456–58, 457 *fig* 38, 543n1, 567, 568n1
Kaufhaus des Westens department store, 94–96, 538, 540n1
Kempinski, Berthold, 365n2
Kempinski, M, & Co, 225–29
Kempinski building, 225–29
Kerr, Alfred, 209, 210, 210n7; *Berlin and London*, 25–26; *Herr Sehring Builds a Theater Dream*, 211–12; *In the New Reichstag*, 180–81; *New and Beautiful—Bülowstrasse?*, 112–14; *New Luxury, Old Squalor*, 217–18; on Berlin and London, 11, 25–26; *The Transformation of Potsdamer Strasse*, 27–29; *Up and Down the Avenues*, 212–14
Kessel, Gustav von: *Berlin in a State of War*, 279–80
Kettelhut, Erich, 424n2
Keun, Irmgard: *The Artficial Silk Girl*, 589–90; *Gilgi—One of Us*, 429–30
Kieren, Martin, 319n5
Killen, Andreas: *Berlin Electropolis*, 13n9
Kisch, Egon Erwin, 110, 110n5, 511, 512n9, 525–26, 528n1; *Berlin at Work*, 425–27; *Elliptical Treadmill*, 514–17; *The Impoverishment and Enrichment of the Berlin Streets*, 336–37
Klabund (pseud. Alfred Henschke), 514n1
Kladow, 343
Kleiner Tiergarten, 432–34
Klemperer, Otto, 368
Klingenberg, Walter: Klingenberg Power Station, 420–24
Klopfer, Ludwig, 532
Knobelsdorff, Georg Wenzeslaus von, 211, 211n3, 232n1
Köhrer, Erich: *Berlin Department Store*, 97–98
Königgrätzer Strasse, 63
Königsplatz, 63, 71, 353n1
Königstrasse, 385*fig* 32, 395, 397, 428
Kohler, Karl, 63
Kohn Brothers, 228
Kohtz, Otto, 317, 318, 319n2
Kollwitz, Käthe: *Diary Entry, 1 May, 1922*, 375; *Diary Entry, 11 September 1919*, 307; *Diary entry, 16 April, 1912*, 163; *Diary entry, 25 January, 1919*, 370–71
Konditoreien. See cafés
Korn, Arthur, 439, 453
KPD (German Communist Party), 371n1, 528, 597
Kracauer, Siegfried, 4, 5n3, 413, 414n3, 414n4, 466, 467n4, 508–12, 511n1, 511n7, 511n10, 511nn3–5; *Berlin as a Summer Resort*, 546–48; *The Cult of the Automobile*, 571–73; *The New Alexanderplatz*, 397–400; *On Board the "Hamburg Flier,"* 573–76; *On Skyscrapers*, 326–29; on spatial images, 4, 5n3; on the Charlottenburg underpass, 369, 370n3; *Under Palm Trees*, 534–36; *Proletarian Rapid Transport*, 566–68; *Radio Station*, 540–43; *Rollercoaster Ride*, 520–21; *Screams on the Street*, 586–88; *A Section of Friedrichstrasse*, 404–6
Kranzler-Ecke, 533

Krause, Friedrich: Swinemünder Bridge, 121*fig*15; *Swinemünder Bridge*, 554
Krause, Gerhard: *The German Stadium and Sports Forum*, 524–25
Krauskopf, Bruno, 526, 528n5
Kreis, Wilhelm, 585; government buildings competition, 318
Kreuzberg, 119, 134–36, 140, 162, 162*fig*20
Kreuzzeitung, 526
Kriegerheimstättenbewegung (Veterans' Housing Movement), 308
Kroner, Friedrich: *Overstretched Nerves*, 375–76
Künstlerhaus St Lukas, 212n2
Küpper, Hannes: *The "Provinces" and Berlin*, 363–65
Kunstblatt, 461, 519
Kurella, Hans, 151, 152n1
Kurfürstendamm, 75, 125, 200–201, 208, 214, 217–18, 222, 343, 396, 535*fig*43

labor shortage, 274
Laforgue, Jules, 9; *Berlin: the Court and the City*, 12n1, 13–16
Lagarde, Paul de, 274
Lamprecht, Karl, 80
Landberger Allee Station, 126
land values, 74, 159, 252–53
Landwehr Canal, Kreuzberg: railway bridge, 119*fig*14
Lang, Fritz, 510; *Metropolis*, 3, 421, 422n2, 439
Langbehn, Julius, 274, 276n3
Langemarck, 550, 550n1
Langemarck Hall, 549, 584
Langhans, Karl Gotthard, Brandenburg Gate: as prototype for Pergamon Musuem, 191
Lasker-Schüler, Else: *The Spinning World Factory*, 430–32; *The Two White Benches on the Kurfürstendamm*, 200–201
Last Laugh, The, 510
Latt, Hans, 228
Laval, Pierre, 590, 590n1
Leach, Neil, 414n4
Lechter, Melchior, 86
Le Corbusier, 489
Lederer, Hugo, 526, 528n5
Legel, Carl, 229
Léger, Fernand, 277
Lehrter Freight Station, 68, 71
Lehrter Station, 352
Lehwess, Walter: *The Design Competition for Rüdesheimer Platz*, 237–39

Leipziger Platz, 62, 71, 216
Leixner, Otto von: *Letter Eight: a suburban street in New Moabit*, 143–45
Lemburg, Peter, 414n5
Lemcke, W. E., 599
Lenman, Robin, 210n4
Lenné, Peter Joseph: Hasenheide, 143n2
Leporello picture book, 361, 362n8
lesbian clubs, 539–40
Letchworth, 295, 295n1
Lewitz, Walter: *Architectural Notes on the Universal Urban Planning Exhibition*, 62–64
Lichtburg cinema, 440, 567, 568n2
Lichtenberg, 2, 75n2, 389, 407
Lichtenrade, 57
Lichterfelde, 109, 207, 355, 356
Lichtwark, Alfred, 446, 447n2
Liebknecht, Karl, 370–71, 371n1, 597n1
Lietzensee-Park in Charlottenburg, 260
lighting, 101–4, 439–41
Lindau, Paul, 337n3; *Unter den Linden*, 176–79
Lipps, Theodor, 174
Litfaßsäulen (advertising pillars), 10, 280, 360, 451*fig*37
local government structure, 50
Loesche, Wilhelm: *Berlin North*, 16–17
London: compared to Berlin, 25–26
Luckenwalder Strasse, 162*fig*20
Luckhardt, Hans. See Luckhardt brothers
Luckhardt, Wassili. See Luckhardt brothers
Luckhardt brothers, 293, 369, 439, 460, 487, 488, 489, 490n3; Dahlem villas, 488; Friedrichstrasse Competition, 316; Heerstrasse villas, 488; Telschow building, 488; *Zur neuen Wohnform*, 488
Ludendorff, Erich, 275
Lübeck, 72
Lüders, Marie-Elisabeth, 494
Lüneberg, 431
Lüttwitz, Walter von, 472n1
Luft Hansa, 562
Luftwaffe, 435
Lunapark, 390, 390n2, 520–21
Lutherstrasse, 41
Luxemburg, Rosa, 371n1, 597n1

Mackensen, Fritz, 432n1
Mächler, Martin, 4, 315–16, 318, 329n3, 353, 353n2, 583; *Major Population Center and its Global Importance*, 319–24; *On the Sky-*

scraper Problem, 329–32; Plan for Berlin, 320*fig*28
Mächter, Wilhelm, 329, 329n3
Mäckler, Hermann: *A German Aircraft Factory*, 434–36
Manchesterism, 252, 256n11
Mann, Thomas, 273, 276n1
Mannheimer, Franz, 78, 80n7
Manzel, Ludwig, 86, 88n1
Map of Berlin, 1902, 60*fig*7
Marathontor (Marathon Gate), 549
Marc, Franz, 278
March, Otto, 69; Kaiser-Wilhelm-Stadion, 524, 525n1
March, Werner: *The Buildings of the National Sport Arena*, 548–50; Kaiser-Wilhelm-Stadion, 525n1
Marcuse, Herbert, 254
Margarethenhöhe, Essen, 265
Mariendorf, 283, 392
Marienkirche, 19–20
Mark, stabilisation of, 463
Marmorkino, 519
Marxism, 595, 596, 597n1
Mauthausen concentration camp, 585
May, Ernst, 496, 500, 500n1
May, Karl, 449n1
May Day demonstration, 375
May Day rallies, 549
Mayer & Weber, 227, 228
Mebes, Paul, 494, 502–4; Einküchenhaüser, 166n1; housing, 136, 165–66; Nordstern administration building, Schöneberg, 104–6
Mehring, Walter, 356, 357n5
Meidner, Ludwig, 527, 528n12
Mein Kampf, 582, 586nn1–2
Meisl, Willy, 512n9
Mendelsohn, Erich, 403, 439, 460, 488, 489; Einstein Tower, Potsdam, 491n4; Herpich showrooms, 439
Mendelsohn, Ernst von, 207
Mendelsohn, Robert von, 207
Mendelssohn, Heinrich: *Should Berlin Build Skyscrapers?*, 346, 346n1
Menzel, Adolf, 526, 528n9
Mercedes-Palast cinema, 532
Mercier, Sebastien, 336–37, 337n2
Messegelände, 450n2
Messehallen, 495, 496n1
Messel, Alfred, 91, 92, 98, 445, 489. *See also* Wertheim Department Store; architectural styles, 175, 176n5; banks, 175; housing, 136, 146; Museumsinsel, 190–92; U-Bahn, 109
metropolis: definition of, 2
Metropolis (Fritz Lang), 510, 511
metropolis and technology, 44
Mies van der Rohe, Ludwig, 4, 368, 461; Friedrichstrasse Competition, 316; single story house, 497, 498
Mietskaserne, 2, 58, 126, 137–43, 153–57, 158–63, 245, 308, 353–58, 404, 464, 480, 495, 503. *See also* housing
Migge, Leberecht: Hufeisensiedlung, 465
Millionenstadt: definition of, 2
Mittellandkanal, 387
Moabit, 2, 62, 68, 100, 125, 134, 143–45, 207, 283, 315, 418
modernism in architecture, 172–76, 412–13, 415–16, 422–24, 465–67, 489, 490n3
Modersohn, Otto, 432n1
Modersohn-Becker, Paula, 432n1
Möhring, Bruno, 63, 64n2, 71, 316, 327–28; *On the Advantages of Tower Blocks*, 324–26; Swinemünder Bridge, 121*fig*15, 554; U-Bahnhof, Bülowstrasse, 109, 113*fig*12
Montandon, Marcel, 11
Montessori Society, 493
monuments as national symbols, 377
Mopp (Max Oppenheimer), 526, 528n5
Moreck, Curt (pseud. Konrad Haemmerling): *A Guide to "Licentious" Berlin*, 537–40
Mosse (publisher), 368
motor cycles, 551
motoring, 563–65
Müller, Lothar, 13n9
Müller, William, 63
Müllerfeld, Hannes: *Down with the Garden City!*, 260–61
Mütz, Hermann, 227
Müllerstrasse, 75, 76n3, 245
Münchner Werkstätten für Wohnungseinrichtung (Munich Workshops for House Furnishing), 223n1
Munich, 10, 600
Munich Beer Hall putsch, 582
Munich Workshops for House Furnishing (Münchner Werkstätten für Wohnungseinrichtung), 223n1
Murnau, Friedrich, 209
Museum of Ethnography (Ethnologisches Museum), 583
Museumsinsel, 45*fig*5, 190–91, 191n1, 192

Museum to the Great War (Weltkriegsmuseum), 584
Mussolini, Benito, 440, 441n7; state visit to Berlin, 596*fig*49
Muthesius, Hermann, 209, 269, 292; Deutscher Werkbund, 104n1; *The Modern Country Home*, 218–21; *Small House and Small-Scale Housing Development*, 307–11

National Economic Council, 599n1
National Gallery, Berlin, 207
National Socialism, 4, 5, 6, 353n1, 413, 440, 441n7, 467, 491n5, 504–7, 553, 581, 584, 585, 587–88, 600
National Sport Arena (Reichssportfeld), 548–50
Natzweiler concentration camp, 585
Naumberg Cathedral, 428
neon advertising, 439, 450–52
Nering, Johann Arnold: Parochialkirche, 250n1
Neubabelsberg, 510, 512n6
Neue Gemeinschaft, (New Community) Schlachtensee, 246
Neue Rundschau, 511
Neue Sachlichkeit, 380, 394, 487, 497, 499, 508, 567, 599
Neugamme concentration camp, 585
Neukölln, 134, 143n1, 388–89, 392, 392n1, 440, 456–57, 566, 588, 594, 597n2. *See also* Rixdorf
Neukölln to Gesundbrunnen U-Bahn, 566–68
Neumann, E: *Object—Subject*, 576–77
Neumann, Theresa, 532n1
Neumeyer, Fritz, 465, 467n3
New Synagogue, Oranienburger Strasse, 597n4
New York: compared to Berlin, 31–32; Zoning Resolution, 328, 329n2
Nibelungen—Siegfrieds Tod, Die, 510
Nicholson, Harold, 551, 553n1
Niederbarnim, 75n2
Nielsen, Asta, 273, 276n2
Nikolassee, 183, 207
Nitsche, Rainer, 370n1, 370n4
Noack, Victor: *Housing and Morality*, 167–71
noise pollution, 447–50
Nordbahnhof, 606
Nordstern administration building, Schöneberg, 104–6, 242
north-south axis, 353n3, 583, 606, 607
north-south railway connection, 70

Nosferatu, 209
Noth, Ernst Erich: *The Tenement Barracks*, 404
Nuremberg, 511, 600

Oberschöneweide, 384
Odorico, Isidore, 227
office buildings, 79, 104–6, 398, 459–60
Olbrich, Joseph Maria, 103
Olympic Games, 549
Olympic Stadium, 525n1, 584, 586
Onkel-Toms-Hütte, Zehlendorf, 465, 467. *See also* housing, social housing
Opel, Fritz von, 552, 565n1
Opel car company, 552
opera house, 21, 201–4
Oppenheimer, Max (Mopp), 526, 528n5
Oppler-Legband, Else, 493
Oranienburg, 434
Orlik, Emil, 526, 528n10
Osborn, Max, 80, 80n7, 173, 176n3, 412, 413n1; *The Destruction of Berlin*, 30; *The Fairy-Tale Fountain in the Friedrichshain, Berlin*, 261–63
Osram, 440
Ossietsky, Carl von, 368
Ostbahnhof (formerly Stettiner Station), 107
Osthaus, Karl Ernst: *The Display Window*, 101–4; *The Garden City and City Planning*, 258–60; *The Railway Station*, 129–33
Ostwald, Hans: *Berlin Coffeehouses*, 183–87
Ostwald, Wilhelm, 447n1

Packhof, 68, 68n1
Palais Redern, 230
Pankow, 109
panopticon, 9
Panter, Peter (pseud. Kurt Tucholsky): "*Hang on a Moment!*", 418–20; *The Loudspeaker*, 447–50; *Traffic Passing Over the House*, 568–71
Paquet, Alfons: *City and Province*, 462
parade ground, 549
Paris: compared to Berlin, 381, 402–3, 558–60
Pariser Platz, 30, 40, 62, 230, 317
parks, 246, 256–58, 260, 261–63, 267
Parochialkirche, 248, 250n1
Pépinière, 198, 199n2
Pergamonmuseum, Museumsinsel, 175, 190–91, 191n1, 192
Perret, Auguste, 489

Petersen, Richard: *The Traffic Problems Inherent in Large Cities,* 115–18
Philippi, Felix, 79, 80n6
Pichelsberg, 241n3
Pichelswerder, 584
Pick, Frank, 109
Piscator, Erwin, 368
Piscator-Bühne, 356, 367n5
Planck, Max, 209
Platz der Republik, 318, 352–53
Plauen, 73
playgrounds, 267
Poelzig, Hans, 202, 204n2, 326, 403, 448, 489, 494, 514n1, 541–43, *fig*36; *The Capitol Cinema,* 528–29; Friedrichstrasse Competition, 316; government buildings competition, 318; Großes Schauspielhaus, 329n1, 518–19; *Großes Schauspielhaus, Scalapalast,* 518–19; Platz der Republik, proposal for redesigning, 353
Polgar, Alfred, 369–70, 370n4
population expansion, 1–2, 59, 347, 502
Post Office building, Leipziger Strasse, 174
post WW1 industry/economy, 411–13
Potsdam, 183, 211n2, 211n3, 266, 323, 343, 348, 355, 491n4, 491n5, 502, 565, 583
Potsdamer Bridge, 28–29, 122
Potsdamer Platz, 27–28, 39, 67, 185*fig*22, 216, 386, 395, 396, 441, 551–52
Potsdamer Station, 62, 67, 107, 216, 315, 342, 352, 450, 608
Potsdamer Strasse, 27–29, 39, 185, 216
power stations, 420–24, 420 562, 562n1
Prenzlauer Berg, 143n2, 246; Carl Legien housing, 465
Preuss, Hugo, 360
Preußenhaus, 598, 599n1
Preußische Landesversammlung (Prussian Legislative Assembly), 340n1
prices, 521–22; increase in, 374, 375–76
prisons, 179–80, 254
Prussian Building Land Act, 1875, 74
Prussian Legislative Assembly (Preußische Landesversammlung), 340n1
public health, 75, 136, 137n4, 153–57, 245–47, 326, 503
public lavatories, 336–37
public transit. *See* buses; railways; trams
Pudor, Heinrich: *The People's Park in Greater Berlin,* 256–58
Pulitzstrasse Station, 126

Querschnitt, Der, 511
Quinz, Matheo: *The Romanische Café,* 525–28
Quistorp, Heinrich, 356

Radicke, Dieter, 110n2
radio broadcasting, 510, 540–43
rail travel, 573–76
railways, 107–8, 116, 192, 414, 552–53, 556–58; aesthetic aspects, 118–22, 123–24, 190; elevated and underground railway, 108, 109–10, 113, 115–17, 382, 397, 398, 409n1, 566–68; network, 68, 115–17, 382, 490, 552, 608; north-south connection, 70; planning, 115–17, 115–18, 342, 490, 552; Ringbahn, 107–8, 125–26; S-Bahn, 68, 68n2, 108, 115, 192, 485; stations, 107, 129–30, 342, 607–8 (*See also* names of stations)
Rappée, Ernö, 532
Rapsilber, Maximilian: *Hotel Adlon,* 229–30
Raschdorff, Julius: Berlin Cathedral, 173
Rathausstrasse, 385*fig*32
Rathenau, Emil, 77, 101n2
Rathenau, Walter, 11, 207, 209, 210n3; *The Most Beautiful City in the World,* 214–17
Rathenau House, Grunewald, 219*fig*23
rationalism, 463, 466
Ratzel, Friedrich, 581n1
Rauch, Josef: Friedrichshain Fountain, 263
Rebner, Arthur, 526, 528n4
recreation buildings, 196–99
Reform Building Ordinance, 1925, 464, 465
regional planning, 504–7
Rehberge, 246
Reich Broadcasting Company (Reichs-Rundfunk-Gesellschaft), 541
Reich Chancellery (Reichskanzlei), 602–5, 609
Reich Commissar for Housing (Reichswohnungskommissar), 469, 471n1
Reich Department of Regional Planning (Reichsstelle für Raumordnung), 506
Reichhardt, Hans J, 586nn7–8
Reichsarbeiterstadt (Workers' township), 266
Reichsheimstättenamt (German Labour Front), 504
Reichskanzlei (Chancellery), 602–5
Reichskanzlerplatz (now Theodor-Heuss-Platz), 318, 609n1
Reichsmarineamt (Imperial Naval Ministry), 284
Reichspostamt, Leipziger Strasse, 174

Reichs-Rundfunk-Gesellschaft (Reich Broadcasting Company), 541
Reichssportfeld (National Sport Arena), 548–50
Reichssportverwaltung (State Sport Administration), 548
Reichsstelle für Raumordnung (Reich Department of Regional Planning), 506
Reichstag, 180–81, 352, 377
Reichswohnungsfürsorgefonds (Imperial Housing Support Fund), 264
Reichswohnungskommissar (Reich Commissar for Housing), 469, 471n1
Reicke, Ilse: *Women and Building*, 493–95
Reihenhaus, 266n1
Reinhardt, Heinrich, 224*fig*24, 225
Reinhardt, Max, 209, 329n1, 368, 518, 522
Reinickendorf, 392, 465–66
religious buildings, 325
rental barracks. *See* Mietskaserne
Rentenmark, 437, 441n1. *See also* hyperinflation
restaurants, 88–91, 89*fig*11, 189–90. *See also* cafés and names of cafés
Rheidt, Celly de, 526, 528n5
Rheingold Restaurant, 189–90
Riemerschmid, Richard, 225, 229n1
Riezler, Kurt, 276n8
Rilke, Rainer Maria, 432n1
Rimpl, Herbert: *A German Aircraft Factory*, 434–36
Ringbahn. *See* railways
Ring der Frauen, 493–95
Rixdorf, 2, 73, 139, 143n1, 388
road building, 579–80
Röntgen, Wilhelm, 29
Rogoff, Irit, 414n3
Romanische Café, Das, 489, 525–28
Rosenberg, Alfred, 583, 586n7
Rosenthaler Strasse Station, 567
Rosenthaler Tor, 108
Rossow, Walter, 465
Rote Fahne, 526
Roth, Joseph: *The Declaration to the Gleisdreieck*, 555–57; *If Berlin Were To Build Skyscrapers*, 332–33; *The Really Big Department Store*, 454–56; *The Wandering Jew*, 378–79
Rudolf Virchow Hospital, 187–89
Rüdesheimer Platz, Design Competition, 237–39
Rürup, Reinhard, 210n2
Rummelsburg, 420–24

Ruttmann, Walter, 529–30; *Berlin: Die Sinfonie einer Großstadt*, 3

Saalburger Marble Works, 227
Saarbrücken, 73
Sachsenhausen concentration camp, 585
Sagebiel, Ernst, 577, 599
Salomon, Alice: *A Club for Young Working Women in Berlin*, 148–50
Salvisberg, Otto Rudolf: Onkel-Tom's-Hütte, 465; Weiße Stadt, 466
Sanssouci, 231, 232n1
S-Bahn. *See* railways, S-Bahn
Scarpa, Ludovica, 319n5
Schackow, Heinrich: *BerolIna*, 19–24
Schäche, Wolfgang, 586nn7–8
Schaefer, Philip. *See* Karstadt department store
Schäfer, Carl, 24n7, 98, 101
Scharoun, Hans, 293; Friedrichstrasse Competition, 316, 335; Siemensstadt, 466
Schaudt, Emil: Kaufhaus des Westens, 540n1
Schaumburg-Lippe, 560n2
Scheffler, Karl, 49, 51n1, 78–9, 173, 176n2, 274, 276n5, 526, 528n8; *Berlin: a City Transformed*, 392–97; *Berlin Fifty Years From Now*, 340–43; *The Elevated Railway and Aesthetics*, 118–22; on bourgeoisie, 206, 210n2; on Hoffmann, 175, 176n8; on modern building, 176, 176n9; *Peter Behrens*, 98–101; *The Retail Establishment*, 91–94; *The Tenement Block*, 158–63; workers' housing, 137, 137n5
Scherl office buildings, 459
Scheunenviertel, 386, 595, 597n4
Schienenzeppelin, 553
Schillerpark, Wedding, 465. *See also* housing, social housing
Schinkel, Karl Friedrich, 24n5, 78, 92, 110, 195, 215, 217n1, 229, 230, 244, 301n1, 487, 489, 490n2; Altes Museum, Museum Island, 190–91, 191n1, 192; proposal for cathedral, Leipziger Platz, 71; urban design, 360
Schirmer, Robert, 229
Schlesischer Station, 123, 352
Schloss Bellevue, 55
Schloss Charlottenburg, 24n2
Schlüter, Andreas, 20, 24n2, 215, 217n1
Schmidt, E, 227
Schmidt, Karl, 223n1
Schmitthenner, Paul, 489; Carlowitz, Breslau, 266; Gartenstadt Staaken, 264–66, 265*fig*25,

266n2; government buildings competition, 318
Schmitz, Bruno, 51, 62, 64n1, 67–68; Greater Berlin Competition, 1910, 315; Rheingold Restaurant, 189–90
Schmitz, Hermann: *Introduction to Siemens Buildings*, 424–25
Schmitz, Walter, 12n7
Schmohl, Eugen, 412
Schönberg, Arnold, 368
Schöneberg, 2, 75, 75n2, 354; development, 104, 105; food shortage, World War 1, 281–82; Rüdesheimer Platz, 237–39; Stadtpark, 260
Schönhauser Allee Station, 126
Schönholzer Heide, 246
school buildings, 193–95
Schott, Sigmund: *The Agglomeration of Cities in the German Empire*, 72–73
Schultze-Kolbitz, Friedrich, 599n1
Schultze-Naumburg, Paul, 236, 248n2, 489, 491n5, 491n6; Cecilienhof, Potsdam, 491n5
Schumacher, Fritz, 10, 63; *The Small Apartment*, 468–71
Schwartz, Frederic J, 440, n1
Schwartz, Karl, 319n6
Schwartz, Rudolf, 64n1
Schwarz, Leopold, 368
Schwechten, Franz Heinrich: Anhalter Station, 98, 111–12; Haus Vaterland, Potsdamer Platz, 373*fig*31; Kaiser-Wilhelm-Gedächtniskirche, 173
Schweger & Partners, 599n1
Schwietzer, Heinrich, 199n1
Schwitters, Kurt, 514n1
Sehring, Bernhard, 212, 212n2
Selle & Voderberg, 229
Sennett, Richard, 293n1
Shirer, William, 583, 586n6
shops. *See also* department stores; Karstadt department store; Tietz department store; Wertheim department store: suburban, 144–45
shop windows, 439, 445–47
Siedl, Gabriel, 219*fig*23
Siedlung, 500–502; definition of, 247, 251, 514, 514n2
Siegessäule (Victory Column), 362n5, 584
Siemens, Werner von, 77, 108
Siemens buildings, 412, 424–25
Siemens & Halske, 2, 77, 109, 121, 283, 466

Siemensstadt, 392, 412, 418, 466. *See also* housing, social housing
Simmel, Georg, 12, 13n10, 13n11, 79, 80n5, 207, 246, 291, 293n1; *The Berlin Trade Exhibition*, 80–84
Simon, Amalie Pauline Hedwig, 560n1
Sinsheimer, Hermann: *Boxing Ring*, 543–45
Sitte, Camillo, 50
Skalitzer Strasse, Kreuzberg, 135
skyscrapers, 316–17, 324–26, 326–29, 329–32, 332–33, 334–35, 341, 343, 344–47, 428–29, 454–56, 461; to alleviate housing problem, 329–30, 332–33
Slevogt, Max, 522, 523n2, 526, 528n7
"Sling" (pseud. Paul Schlesinger): *The Telephone*, 374
Socialist Democratic Party, 371n1, 375
social problems, 167–71
Society for the Promotion of the Common Good (Gemeinnützige Gesellschaft), 138–39
Soldatenhalle (Hall for the Unknown Soldier), 584
Soldatenräte (Soldiers' Councils), 595
Sombart, Nikolaus, 209, 210n6
Sombart, Walter, 437, 440n1
Sombart, Werner, 11, 209; *Domesticity*, 150–52; *Vienna*, 31–33
Sonne, Wolfgang, 51n4, 71n1
Spandau, 75n2, 207, 241n3, 264–66, 265*fig* 25, 597n4
Spanish influenza, 275
Spartacus League (Spartakusbund), 275, 292, 371n1, 594, 595, 597n1
Spartakusbund (Spartacus League), 275, 292, 371n1, 594, 595, 597n1
Spar- und Bauverein. *See* Berliner Spar- und Bauverein
SPD (German Socialist Party), 597n3
Speculation in Tempelhof, 57–59
Speer, Albert, 51, 319, 353n3, 583–86, 586n4, 601, 604, 605–6, 610*fig*50; *On the Autobahns of the Reich*, 580; plans for Germania, 467; *Replanning the Capital of the Reich*, 607–9; Siegessäule, 362n5
Spengler, Oswald, 275, 276n10
Spinn & Sohn, 86
Spittelkolonnaden, 360, 362n4
sport, 511, 512n9, 522–23
Sportpalast, 511, 522–23
sports stadia, 524–25
Spree, River: exploitation for recreation, 258

636 INDEX

squares: urban design, 349–52
SS-Kameradschsftssiedlung, Zehlendorf, 467
Staaken garden city, 264–66, 265*fig*25
Staatsbauverwaltung, (State Building Authority), 506
Stadt: definition of, 2
Stadtbahn. *See* railways, S-Bahn
Stadtbaukunst, 64n2
Stadterweiterung: definition of, 2
Stadthaus, 199–200
Stadtkrone, 292, 295–301, 316, 325, 608
Stadtverband (city association), 493
Städtebau: definition of, 2
Stahl, Fritz (pseud. Siegfried Lilienthal), 175, 176n6; *The Berlin City Hall*, 199–200; *The Klingenberg Power Station*, 420–24
State Building Authority (Staatsbauverwaltung), 506
State Planning Commission, 599n1
State Sport Administration (Reichssportverwaltung), 548
State Sports Academy, 548
Staufferreich, 173
Steglitz, 75, 380, 381n3, 392
Stephan, Hans: *The Autobahn*, 581; *Berlin*, 605–7
Stephan, Heinrich von, 16n2, 131, 133n2
Stern, Fritz, 206, 210n1, 274, 276n4
Stettiner railway bridge, 123
Stettiner Station, 68, 107
Storm, Theodor, 434n1
Strandbad Wannsee, 547*fig*44
Strasbourg Cathedral, 331
Straumer, Heinrich, 319n7, 448, *fig*36
Strauss, Richard, 207
streets, 74; lighting, 23, 37–40, 450–52; planning, 49–50, 52–55; regulations for, 53–54; suburban, 143–45
strikes, 275, 283–84, 414–15
Strousberg, Bethel Henry, 355–56, 357n4
structure plans, 65–66
Stübben, Joseph, 50–51
Stüler, Friedrich August: Alte Nationalgalerie, Museumsinsel, 190–91, 191n1, 192; Neues Museum, Museumsinsel, 190–91, 191n1, 192
Stuttgart, 482
Sudermann, Hermann, 380, 381n1
Südbahnhof, 606
Südekum, Albert: *Impoverished Berlin Dwellings—Wedding*, 153–57
Süssenguth, Georg, 224, 225, *fig*24

Suhr, Heidren: *Berlin*, 13n9
swimming pools, 196–97
Swinemünder Bridge, 64n2, 121*fig*15, 554

Tafuri, Manfred, 466, 467n5
Tag, Der, 510
Taschner, Ignatz: Friedrichshain Fountain, 263
Tauchnitz, Christian Bernard, 570, 571n2
Tauentzien-Palast Café, Berlin West, 204–5
Tauentzien-Palast cinema, 532
Tauentzienstrasse, 95–97, 125, 395, 439, 537–38
Taut, Bruno, 64n2, 247, 293, 368, 452, 454n1, 482–84. *See also* Carl Legien, Prenzlauer Berg; Falkenberg, Gartenstadt; Hufeisensiedlung, Britz; Onkel-Toms-Hütte, Zehlendorf; Schillerpark, Wedding; *Alpine Architektur*, 326, 329n1; *Auflösung der Städte*, 292, 293n2, 309*fig*27; *The City Crown*, 295–301; *The Falkenberg Garden Suburb near Berlin*, 268–70; *A Necessity*, 276–78; *The New Home: Woman as Creative Spirit*, 473–75; on architectural style, 203–4; *On New Theaters*, 512–14; *The Problem of Building an Opera House*, 201–4; *Stadtkrone*, 292, 295–301, 301n3; standardized housing designs, 464
Taut, Max, 293, 403
Taylor, Frederick Winslow, 78, 331, 332n1
Tegel, 179–80, 341, 384
Telschow building, Potsdamer Platz, 488
Teltow, 58, 75n2, 382; Canal, 58
Tempelhof: development, 57–59
Tempelhof Airport, 553, 562, 577–79, 586, 599, 599n2
Tempelhofer Feld, 58–59, 242, 257–58, 590–93
tenements. *See* Mietskaserne
Tergit, Gabriele (pseud. Elise Reifenberg): *Home is the 75 (or the 78)*, 406–9
Tessenow, Heinrich, 268, 514n1
Teut, Anna, 553n4
theaters, 174, 211–12, 212n2, 516, 518–19, 522, 526; design, 512–14, 518–19
Theodor-Heuss-Platz (Reichskanzlerplatz), 207, 584, 609n1
Thiele, Gerta-Elisabeth: *The Shop Window*, 445–47
Third German Radio Exhibition, 450n2
Tiergarten, 28, 206–8, 315, 360, 362n5, 369, 410, 584
Tietz Department Store, 94–96, 459
Tiller Girls, 466, 509
Tönnies, Ferdinand, 247

INDEX 637

Tolischus, Otto D, 441n7
Toller, Ernst, 380, 381n1
Topp, Arnold, 514n1
tower blocks. *See* skyscrapers
Town Hall Tower Panorama, 44–46
trades union movement, 464
traffic: Berlin compared to Paris, 558–60; increase in, 551–53
traffic planning, 52–55, 62, 65, 67, 71, 75n2, 115–18, 317–18, 349–52, 461–62, 490, 602
Trakl, Georg, 514n1
trams, 13, 108–10, 114, 157, 207–8, 229, 414
Treibel Villa, 210–11
Treitschke, Heinrich von, 273–74, 359
Treptow: tram network, 109
Treptower Park, 242
Troost, Gerdy, 586n3
Tucholsky, Kurt, 368, 370n1. *See also* Panter, Peter (pseud. Kurt Tucholsky); Wrobel, Ignaz (pseud. Kurt Tucholsky); *150 Kaiserallee*, 471–73; *Berlin! Berlin!*, 371–73
Twain, Mark: *The German Chicago*, 11, 17–18
typhus, 50, 136, 245, 326. *See also* public health

U-Bahn. *See* railways, elevated and underground railway
Ufa (Universum Film Aktiengesellschaft), 510, 511
Ufa-Palast am Zoo cinema, 510, 532
Ullstein (publisher), 368
Ullstein building, Tempelhof, 412
Ullstein family, 207
underground railway. *See* elevated and underground railway
unemployment, 413, 432–34, 433*fig*35, 602
Universal Urban Planning Exhibition (Allgemeine Städtebau-Ausstellung zu Berlin), 62–64
University City, Pichelswerder, 584, 609
Universum Film Aktiengesellschaft, (Ufa), 510
Unter den Linden, 18, 30, 39, 42*fig*4, 61, 176–79, 216, 273, 280, 281, 284, 317, 323, 345, 410, 440, 487, 596*fig*49
Unwin, Raymond, 247, 248n6
urban design competitions, 237–39, 316, 318, 319n7, 349–52, 428–29
urban forests, 57
urban planning: administration of, 491–92

Van den Bruck, Moeller, 274
Van de Velde, Henry, 222, 223n1, 489

Variety, 510
Verband Groß-Berlin, 268
Verein für deutsches Kunstgewerbe (Association for German Applied Arts), 493
Vereinigung Berliner Architekten (Association of Berlin Architects), 50, 146
vernacular architecture, 467
Veterans' Housing Movement (Kriegerheimstättenbewegung), 308
Victory Column, (Siegessäule), 362n5, 584
Viebig, Clara: *Our Daily Bread*, 157–58
Vienna, 326, 605n1; compared to Berlin, 31–33, 476–79
villa colonies, 75, 207–10, 245
Villenkolonien, 75, 207–10, 245
Virchow, Rudolf, 59, 136, 137n4
Virgil, 24n1
Vögele, Jörg, 247n1
Vogeler, Heinrich, 432n1
Voigt, Andreas, Goethepark, Charlottenburg: housing, 136
Voigt, Paul, 208, 210n5
Volksgemeinschaft (German National Community), 604
Volkshalle (Hall of the People), 606, 608, 610*fig*50
Volksoper, Charlottenburg, 513
Volkspark Friedrichshain, 246
Volkswagen, 580
Vollbrecht, Karl, 424n2
Vorhoelzer, Robert: boarding house design, 499
Vorwärts, 594, 595, 597n3

Wachthof building, 453
Wach- und Schließgesellschaft building, 439
Wagenführ, Max: *The Admiral's Palace and its Bathing Pools*, 196–99
Wagner, Martin, 2, 246, 248n4, 316, 317–18, 319n1, 319n5–n7, 357, 368, 464, 467n1, 482–84, 489, 547*fig*44, 583; *Administrative Reform*, 491–92; *The Design Problem of a City Square for a Metropolis*, 349–52; Hufeisensiedlung, Britz, 343n2, 389, 389n3; *The New Berlin—World City*, 347–49; *Should Berlin Build Skyscrapers?* 344–45, 346n1; as Stadtbaurat (municipal building director), 464; traffic planning, 552, 553n3; *Urban Open-Space Policy*, 267–68; *Vienna—Berlin*, 476–79
Wagner, Otto, 489
Wallace, Edgar, 570, 571n1

Wallé, Peter, 174, 176n4
Wallot, Paul, 377n2
Walser, Robert, 33, 207; *Aschinger's*, 88–91; *Berlin W.*, 230–32; *Friedrichstrasse*, 41–43; *Good MornIng, Giantess!*, 33–35; *The Little Berlin Girl*, 232–37
Walter, Bruno, 368
Walter Ruttmann's Film, Berlin: Symphony of a Great City, 529–30
Wangel, Hedwig, 560n1
Wannsee, 113, 546, 563, 564; Strandbad, 547*fig*44
Ward, Janet, 441n5
Wasmuths Monatshefte für Baukunst und Städtebau, 329, 346, 358, 362n1
Wassmann, Hans, 89, 91n2
Weber, Max: *Speech for a Discussion*, 44
Wedding, 2, 75n3, 76, 76n3, 109, 126, 134, 144, 153–57, 245, 408, 588, 594, 597n2
Wedding Station, 126
Wedemeyer, Alfred: *Berlin's Latest Department Store*, 456–58
Wehrtechnische Fakultät (Faculty of Defense Studies), 365–66, 609
Weill, Kurt, 368
Weimar Building School, 491n6
Weimar Republic, 3, 5n4, 266n2, 293, 316, 360, 368, 491n6, 508, 537, 583, 597
Weißenhof, Stuttgart, 482
Weißensee Station, 126
Weiße Stadt, Reinickendorf, 465–66. *See also* housing, social housing
Weltbühne, Die, 511
Weltkriegsmuseum (Museum to the Great War), 584
Weltstadt: definition of, 2
Werfel, Franz, 514n1
Werlin, Jakob: *On the Autobahns of the Reich*, 579–80
Wermuth, Adolph, 360, 362n6
Wertheim department store, 79–80, 84–88, 87*fig*10, 91–94, 98, 215, 217n1, 324n1, 453, 459
Westend villa colony, 207, 354, 356
Westend villa colony, Charlottenburg, 207, 354
Westheim, Paul, 3, 5n1; *Building Boom*, 242–44; *Ludwig Hoffmann's School Buildings in Berlin*, 193–95; *Nordstern: the New Administration Building*, 104–6; *Workers' Housing Estate at Staaken*, 264–66
Wettbewerb Groß-Berlin 1910. *See* Greater Berlin Competition

Wewel-Blake, Jörg, 414n5
White City (Weiße Stadt), 465–66
white collar workers, 494, 509, 511, 576
Whitman, Walt, 203
Whyte, Iain Boyd, 414n3, 586n7
Widdig, Bernd, 441n1
Widetzky Quartet, 531
Wilamowitz-Moellendorf, Ulrich von, 207
Wilder, Billy: *Berlin Rendezvous*, 533–34; *Nighttime Joyride over Berlin*, 561–62
Wilmersdorf, 2, 50, 51, 75n2, 223, 260, 355, 471
Wilson, Woodrow, 275
window dressing, 439, 445–47
Witte, Karsten, 511, 512n19
Witte-Wild, Fritz, 211, 212n1
Wittig, Paul, 110n3, 110n4
Witzleben, 318
Wolf, Paul: *The Basic Layout of the New City*, 293–95
Women's Circle (Ring der Frauen), 493–95; Pavilion, German Building Exhibition, 494*fig*41
Woolworth Building, New York, 331
Workers' and Soldiers' Council, 284
World Exhibition, Paris, 1900, 489
World War 1, 273–311, 278–79, 280–81
World War 2 air raids, 585
Worpswede, 431, 432n1
Wrba, Georg, 63; Friedrichshain Fountain, 263
Wrobel, Ignaz (pseud. Kurt Tucholsky): *Berlin Traffic*, 558–660
Würzbach, Walter, 519
Wuhlheide: heroes' grove competition, 282–83
Wunderwald, Gustav, 3
Wywiorski, Michal, 229

Zehlendorf, 75, 207, 223, 347, 355, 389, 465, 467
Zeitschrift für Bauwesen, 138
Zentralbahnhof, 315
Zetzsche, Carl, 50, 51n2
Zeughaus, 21, 22, 24n4
Zille, Heinrich, 362n10, 375, 496, 496n2
Zille-Berliners, 361
Zirkus Schumann, 329n1, 518
Zola, Émile, 114n1
zoning: Berlin, 464; New York, 328, 329n2
Zuckmayer, Carl: *The Berlin Woman*, 390
Zukunft, Die, 215, 217n2
Zweckverband Groß-Berlin (Greater Berlin Administrative Union), 51, 74, 75n2

WEIMAR AND NOW: GERMAN CULTURAL CRITICISM
Edward Dimendberg, Martin Jay, and Anton Kaes, General Editors

1. *Heritage of Our Times,* by Ernst Bloch
2. *The Nietzsche Legacy in Germany, 1890–1990,* by Steven E. Aschheim
3. *The Weimar Republic Sourcebook,* edited by Anton Kaes, Martin Jay, and Edward Dimendberg
4. *Batteries of Life: On the History of Things and Their Perception in Modernity,* by Christoph Asendorf
5. *Profane Illumination: Walter Benjamin and the Paris of Surrealist Revolution,* by Margaret Cohen
6. *Hollywood in Berlin: American Cinema and Weimar Germany,* by Thomas J. Saunders
7. *Walter Benjamin: An Aesthetic of Redemption,* by Richard Wolin
8. *The New Typography,* by Jan Tschichold, translated by Ruari McLean
9. *The Rule of Law under Siege: Selected Essays of Franz L. Neumann and Otto Kirchheimer,* edited by William E. Scheuerman
10. *The Dialectical Imagination: A History of the Frankfurt School and the Institute of Social Research, 1923–1950,* by Martin Jay
11. *Women in the Metropolis: Gender and Modernity in Weimar Culture,* edited by Katharina von Ankum
12. *Letters of Heinrich and Thomas Mann, 1900–1949,* edited by Hans Wysling, translated by Don Reneau
13. *Empire of Ecstasy: Nudity and Movement in German Body Culture, 1910–1935,* by Karl Toepfer
14. *In the Shadow of Catastrophe: German Intellectuals between Apocalypse and Enlightenment,* by Anson Rabinbach
15. *Walter Benjamin's Other History: Of Stones, Animals, Human Beings, and Angels,* by Beatrice Hanssen
16. *Exiled in Paradise: German Refugee Artists and Intellectuals in America from the 1930s to the Present,* by Anthony Heilbut
17. *Cool Conduct: The Culture of Distance in Weimar Germany,* by Helmut Lethen, translated by Don Reneau
18. *In a Cold Crater: Cultural and Intellectual Life in Berlin, 1945–1948,* by Wolfgang Schivelbusch, translated by Kelly Barry
19. *A Dubious Past: Ernst Jünger and the Politics of Literature after Nazism,* by Elliot Y. Neaman
20. *Beyond the Conceivable: Studies on Germany, Nazism, and the Holocaust,* by Dan Diner
21. *Prague Territories: National Conflict and Cultural Innovation in Franz Kafka's Fin de Siècle,* by Scott Spector

22. *Munich and Memory: Architecture, Monuments, and the Legacy of the Third Reich*, by Gavriel D. Rosenfeld

23. *The Ufa Story: A History of Germany's Greatest Film Company, 1918–1945*, by Klaus Kreimeier, translated by Robert and Rita Kimber

24. *From Monuments to Traces: Artifacts of German Memory, 1870–1990*, by Rudy Koshar

25. *We Weren't Modern Enough: Women Artists and the Limits of German Modernism*, by Marsha Meskimmon

26. *Culture and Inflation in Weimar Germany*, by Bernd Widdig

27. *Weimar Surfaces: Urban Visual Culture in 1920s Germany*, by Janet Ward

28. *Graphic Design in Germany: 1890–1945*, by Jeremy Aynsley

29. *Expressionist Utopias: Paradise, Metropolis, Architectural Fantasy*, by Timothy O. Benson, with contributions by Edward Dimendberg, David Frisby, Reinhold Heller, Anton Kaes, and Iain Boyd Whyte

30. *The Red Count: The Life and Times of Harry Kessler*, by Laird M. Easton

32. *The Dark Mirror: German Cinema between Hitler and Hollywood*, by Lutz Koepnick

33. *Rosenzweig and Heidegger: Between Judaism and German Philosophy*, by Peter Eli Gordon

34. *The Authority of Everyday Objects: A Cultural History of West German Industrial Design*, by Paul Betts

35. *The Face of East European Jewry*, by Arnold Zweig, with fifty-two drawings by Hermann Struck. Edited, translated, and with an introduction by Noah Isenberg

36. *No Place Like Home: Locations of Heimat in German Cinema*, by Johannes von Moltke

37. *Berlin Alexanderplatz: Radio, Film, and the Death of Weimar Culture*, by Peter Jelavich

38. *Berlin Electropolis: Shock, Nerves, and German Modernity*, by Andreas Killen

39. *A Concise History of the Third Reich*, by Wolfgang Benz, translated by Thomas Dunlap

40. *Germany in Transit: Nation and Migration, 1955–2005*, edited by Deniz Göktürk, David Gramling, and Anton Kaes

41. *Weimar on the Pacific: German Exile Culture in Los Angeles and the Crisis of Modernism*, by Ehrhard Bahr

42. *The 1972 Munich Olympics and the Making of Modern Germany*, by Kay Schiller and ChristopherYoung

43. *Berlin Psychoanalytic: Psychoanalysis and Culture in Weimar Republic Germany and Beyond*, by Veronika Fuechtner

44. *Cinema and Experience: Siegfried Kracauer, Walter Benjamin, and Theodor W. Adorno*, by Miriam Bratu Hansen

45. *Siegfried Kracauer's American Writings: Essays on Film and Popular Culture*, edited by Johannes von Moltke and Kristy Rawson

46. *Metropolis Berlin, 1880–1940*, edited by Iain Boyd Whyte and David Frisby

47. *The Third Reich Sourcebook*, edited by Anson Rabinbach and Sander L. Gilman